STREET ATLAS
Lancashire

Contents

PHILIP'S

First edition published 1997
Reprinted in 1997, 1998, 1999, 2000 by

George Philip Ltd, a division of
Octopus Publishing Group Ltd
2-4 Heron Quays, London E14 4JP

ISBN 0-540-06440-8 (hardback)
ISBN 0-540-06441-6 (spiral)

To the best of the Publishers' knowledge, the information in this atlas was
correct at the time of going to press. No responsibility can be accepted
for any errors or their consequences.

The representation in this atlas of a road, track or path is no evidence
of the existence of a right of way.

**The mapping between pages 1 and 238 (inclusive) in this atlas is
derived from Ordnance Survey® OSCAR® and Land-Line® data,
and Landranger® mapping.**

Ordnance Survey, OSCAR, Land-Line and Landranger are registered trade
marks of Ordnance Survey, the national mapping agency of Great Britain.

Printed and bound in Spain by Cayfosa

Digital Data

The exceptionally high-quality mapping
found in this book is available as digital
data in TIFF format, which is easily
convertible to other bit-mapped (raster)
image formats.

The index is also available in digital form
as a standard database table. It contains
all the details found in the printed index
together with the National Grid reference
for the map square in which each entry
is named and feature codes for places
of interest in eight categories such as
education and health.

For further information and to discuss
your requirements, please contact
Philip's on 020 7531 8440 or
george.philip@philips-maps.co.uk

Key to map symbols

(22a)	**Motorway** (with junction number)
	Primary routes (dual carriageway and single)
	A roads (dual carriageway and single)
	B roads (dual carriageway and single)
	Minor through road (dual carriageway and single)
	Minor roads
	Roads under construction
	Railways
	Tramway, miniature railway
	Rural track, private road or narrow road in urban area
	Gate or obstruction to traffic (restrictions may not apply at all times or to all vehicles)
	All paths, bridleways, byway open to all traffic, road used as a public path
	The representation in this atlas of a road, track or path is no evidence of the existence of a right of way
226	**Adjoining page indicators** (The colour of the arrow indicates the scale of the adjoining page – see scales below.)
85	
204 / 199	**Adjoining page indicator** showing the pages adjoining the top and bottom halves of the current page

Acad	**Academy**	Mon	**Monument**
Cemy	**Cemetery**	Mus	**Museum**
C Ctr	**Civic Centre**	Obsy	**Observatory**
CH	**Club House**	Pal	**Royal Palace**
Coll	**College**	PH	**Public House**
Ex H	**Exhibition Hall**	Resr	**Reservoir**
Ind Est	**Industrial Estate**	Ret Pk	**Retail Park**
Inst	**Institute**	Sch	**School**
Ct	**Law Court**	Sh Ctr	**Shopping Centre**
L Ctr	**Leisure Centre**	Sta	**Station**
LC	**Level Crossing**	TH	**Town Hall/House**
Liby	**Library**	Trad Est	**Trading Estate**
Mkt	**Market**	Univ	**University**
Meml	**Memorial**	YH	**Youth Hostel**

	British Rail station
	Private railway station
	Bus, coach station
	Ambulance station
	Coastguard station
	Fire station
	Police station
	Casualty entrance to hospital
	Church, place of worship
H	**Hospital**
i	**Information centre**
P	**Parking**
PO	**Post Office**
Queen Elizabeth's Gram Sch	**Important buildings, schools, colleges, universities and hospitals**
	County boundaries
River Lune	**Water name**
	Stream
	River or canal (minor and major)
	Water
	Tidal water
	Woods
	Houses

■ The dark grey border on the inside edge of some pages indicates that the mapping does not continue onto the adjacent page

■ The small numbers around the edges of the maps identify the 1 kilometre National Grid lines

---

The scale of the maps on pages numbered in blue is 5.52 cm to 1 km (3½ inches to 1 mile)

0	¼	½	¾	1 mile
0	250m	500m	750m	1 Kilometre

The scale of the maps on pages numbered in green is 2.78 cm to 1 km (1¾ inches to 1 mile)

0	¼	½	¾	1 mile
0	250m	500m	750m	1Kilometre

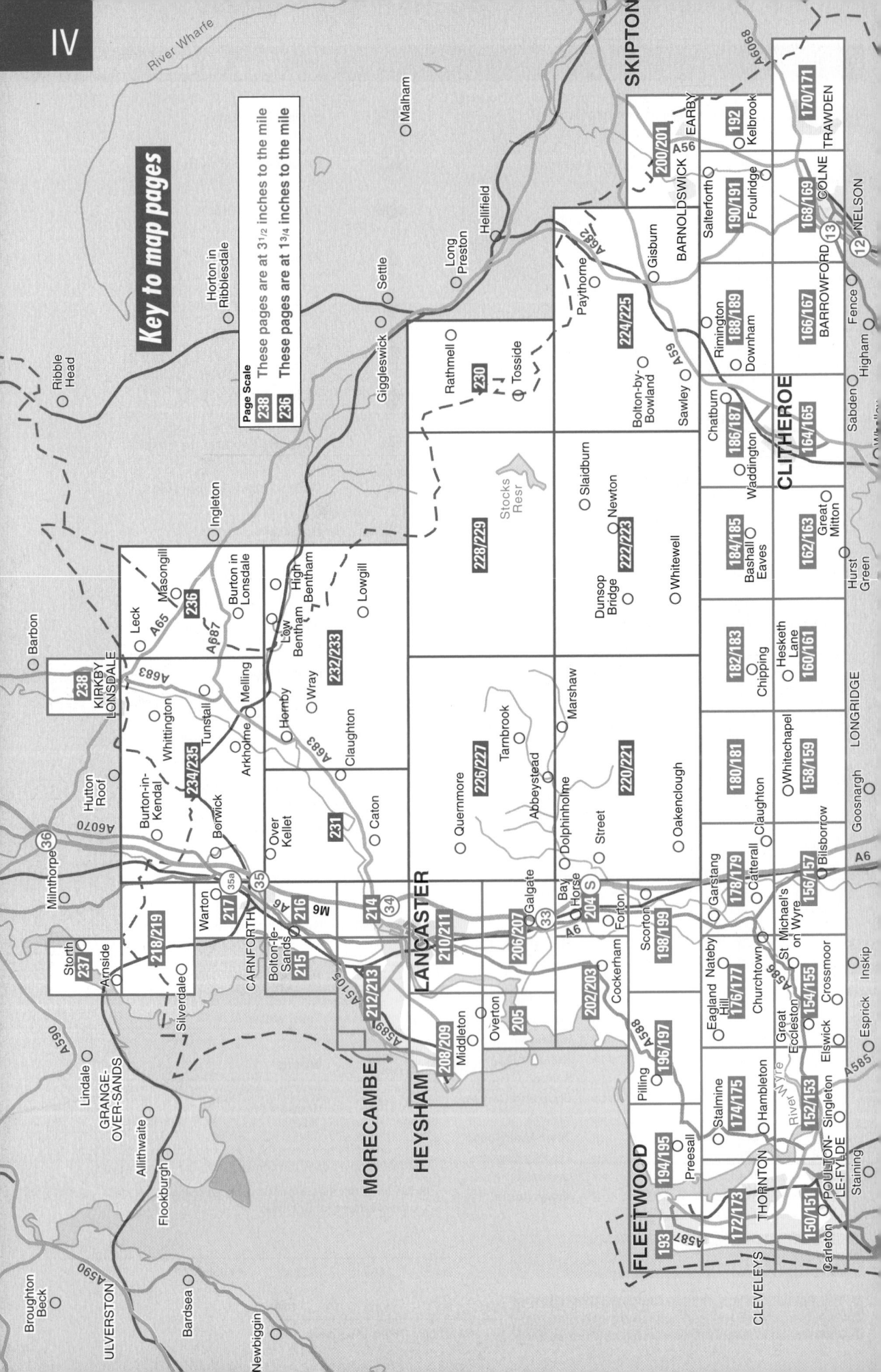

IV

Key to map pages

Page Scale
238 These pages are at 3½ inches to the mile
236 These pages are at 1¾ inches to the mile

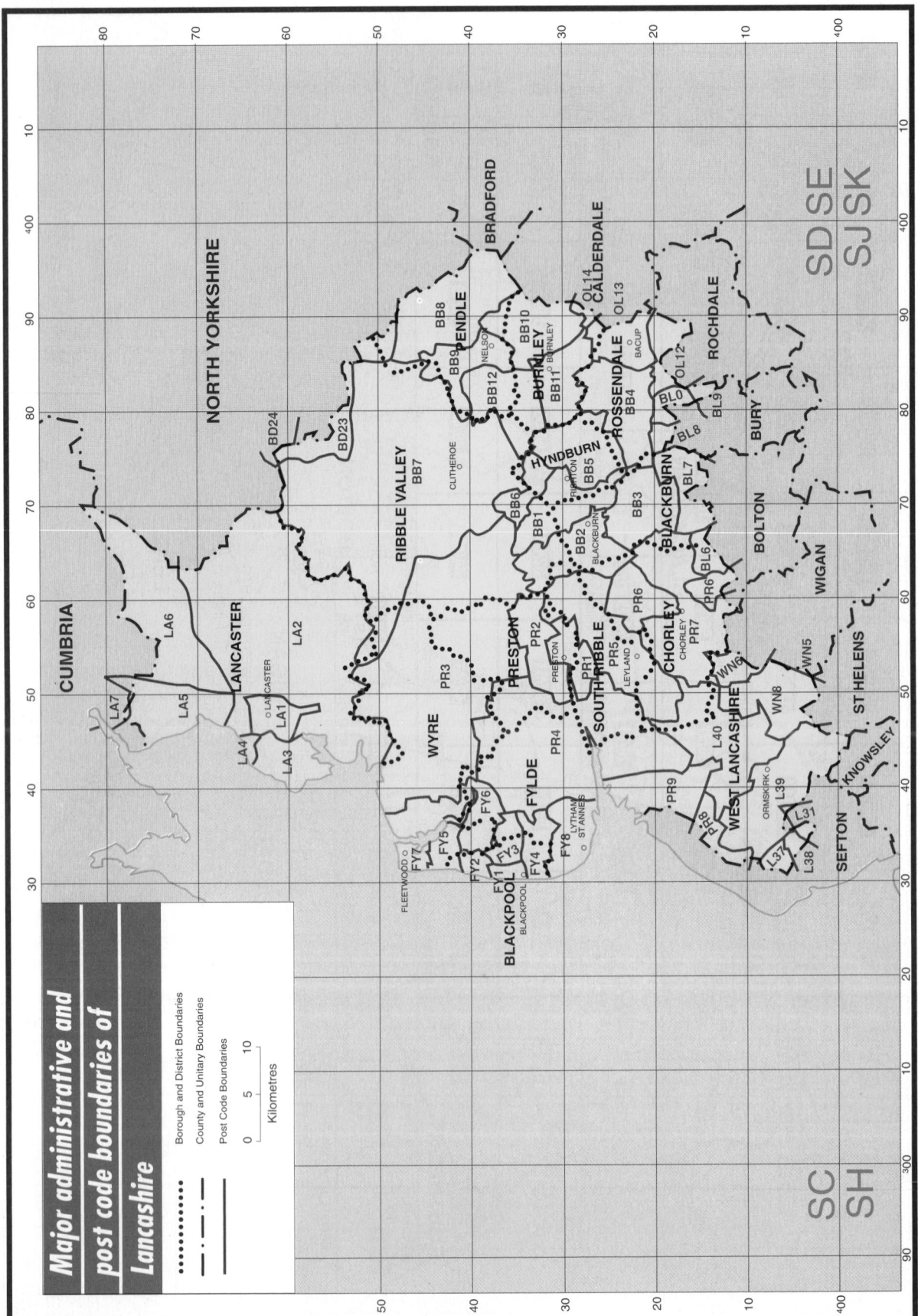

Major administrative and post code boundaries of Lancashire

.... Borough and District Boundaries

—··—··— County and Unitary Boundaries

———— Post Code Boundaries

Kilometres

0   5   10

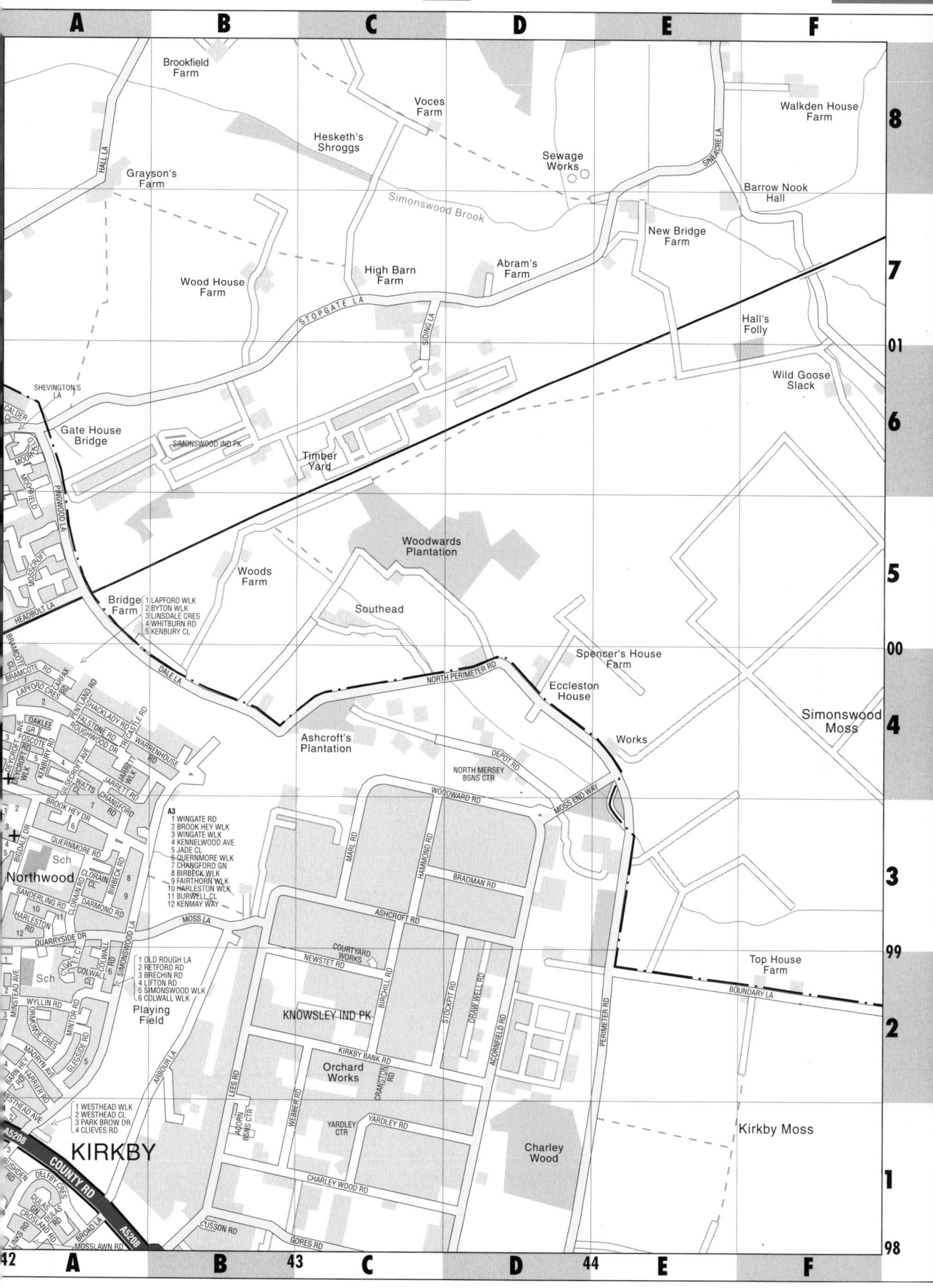

Brookfield Farm

Voces Farm

Walkden House Farm

Hesketh's Shroggs

Sewage Works

Grayson's Farm

Barrow Nook Hall

8

New Bridge Farm

Simonswood Brook

High Barn Farm

Abram's Farm

7

Wood House Farm

STOPGATE LA

Hall's Folly

01

SIDING LA

SHEVINGTON'S LA

Wild Goose Slack

Gate House Bridge

6

CALDER CL

MOOR CL

SIMONSWOOD IND PK

Timber Yard

MOSSCROFT

PROSPWOOD LA

Woodwards Plantation

Woods Farm

5

HEADBOLT LA

Bridge Farm

1 LAPFORD WLK
2 BYTON WLK
3 LINSDALE CRES
4 WHITBURN RD
5 KENBURY CL

Southead

Spencer's House Farm

00

BRAMCOTE RD

DALE LA

NORTH PERIMETER RD

Eccleston House

Simonswood Moss

BRAMCOTE RD

LAPFORD CRES

PENTLAND AVE
SHACKLADY RD
FALSTONE RD
ROSTLE RD
WARRENHOUSE RD

Works

4

OAKLEE GR

FOSCOTE RD

ROUGHWOOD DR

Ashcroft's Plantation

DEPOT RD

CLARAX

BEECHCROFT RD

KENBURY RD

GILSSCROFT AVE

WATT'S RD

CHANGFORD RD

JARRETT RD

NORTH MERSEY BSNS CTR

WOODWARD RD

MOSS END WAY

BROOK HEY DR

A3
1 WINGATE RD
2 BROOK HEY WLK
3 WINGATE WLK
4 KENNELWOOD AVE
5 JADE CL
6 QUERNMORE WLK
7 CHANGFORD GN
8 BIRBECK WLK
9 FAIRTHORN WLK
10 HARLESTON WLK
11 BURWELL CL
12 KENMAY WAY

BIDDALE DR

QUERNMORE RD

MARL RD

HAMMOND RD

BRADMAN RD

3

Northwood

CLORAIN CL

BIRBECK RD

SANDERLING RD

CLORAIN RD

DARMOND RD

HARLESTON

QUARRYSIDE DR

MOSS LA

SIMONSWOOD LA

ASHCROFT RD

1 OLD ROUGH LA
2 RETFORD RD
3 BRECHIN RD
4 LIFTON RD
5 SIMONSWOOD WLK
6 COLWALL WLK

MINSTEAD AVE

Sch

CYGNET CT

COLWALL CL

COLWALL RD

COURTYARD

NEWSTET RD

BIRCHILL RD

STOCKPIT RD

DRAKWELL RD

ACORNFIELD RD

Top House Farm

99

PERIMETER RD

BOUNDARY LA

WYLLIN RD

MINTOR RD

GLESSIDE RD

Playing Field

KNOWSLEY IND PK

2

MADRYN AVE

ORMSKIRK CRES

ARBOUR LA

Orchard Works

KIRKBY BANK RD

CRANSTON RD

WEBBER RD

LEES RD

1 WESTHEAD WLK
2 WESTHEAD CL
3 PARK BROW DR
4 CLIEVES RD

BSNS CTR

YARDLEY CTR

YARDLEY RD

Charley Wood

Kirkby Moss

1

WESTHEAD AVE

A520B

KIRKBY

COUNTY RD

RUSHDEN RD

DELBY CRES

DULAS RD

BROAD LA

CROSLAND RD

A520B

CUSSON RD

MOSSLAWN RD

GORES RD

CHARLEY WOOD RD

98

42
A
B
43
C
D
44
E
F

A B C D E F

8

7

05

6

5

04

4

3

03

2

1

02

27 A B 28 C D 29 E F

Mount
Pleasant

Alexandra Rd
Albert Rd

ELSWORTH CL
STAPLETON RD

Marsh
Farm

HIGGS HILL
LA
PARK CL

Sewage
Works

Range
High Sch

Works

Raven Meols Hills

ST LUKE'S CHURCH RD

Nature
Reserve

Sefton Coastal Path

Cambrai
Cottage

Grange
Farm

Altcar Training
Camp

GRANGE RD

LC

DANGER AREA

River Alt

Sefton Coastal Path

Battery
Cottage

DANGER AREA

Altcar Rifle Range

DANGER AREA

ST GEORGE'S RD

MARK RD

ST STEPHEN'S RD

HESTER CL

KERSLAKE WAY

LOWER ALT RD

PO

ALT RD

SCHOOL RD

NORTHOLME

RATHBONE
RD

VILLAGE WAY

RIVERSIDE

WEST VA

THE ROUND

SANDILANDS
GR

BLUNDELL
AVE

DANGER AREA

Formby
Bank

WIGNALLS
MEADOW

PARKSIDE

SANDILANDS

MOORHOUSES

BRIARY CROFT

HORNBY RD

BLUNDELL AVE

LARKHILL
LA

WITHINS FIELD

BLUNDELL RD

Liverpool Bay

ALTON CL

BRENTWOOD CL

WHITE FI

MAYFIELD CL

LANGLEY CL

RICHMOND CL

BLUNDELL RD

MAYFAIR CL

Sefton Coastal Path

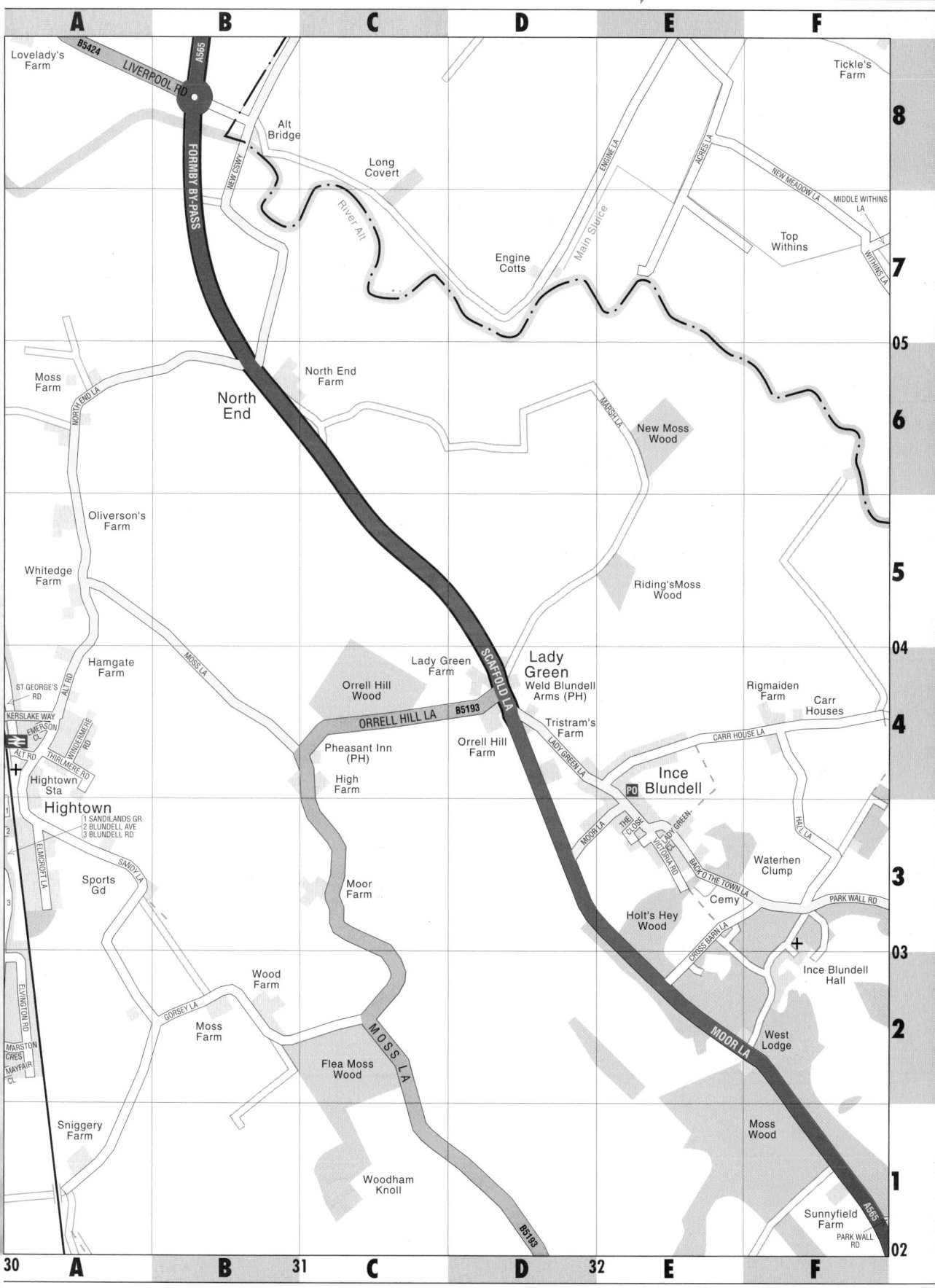

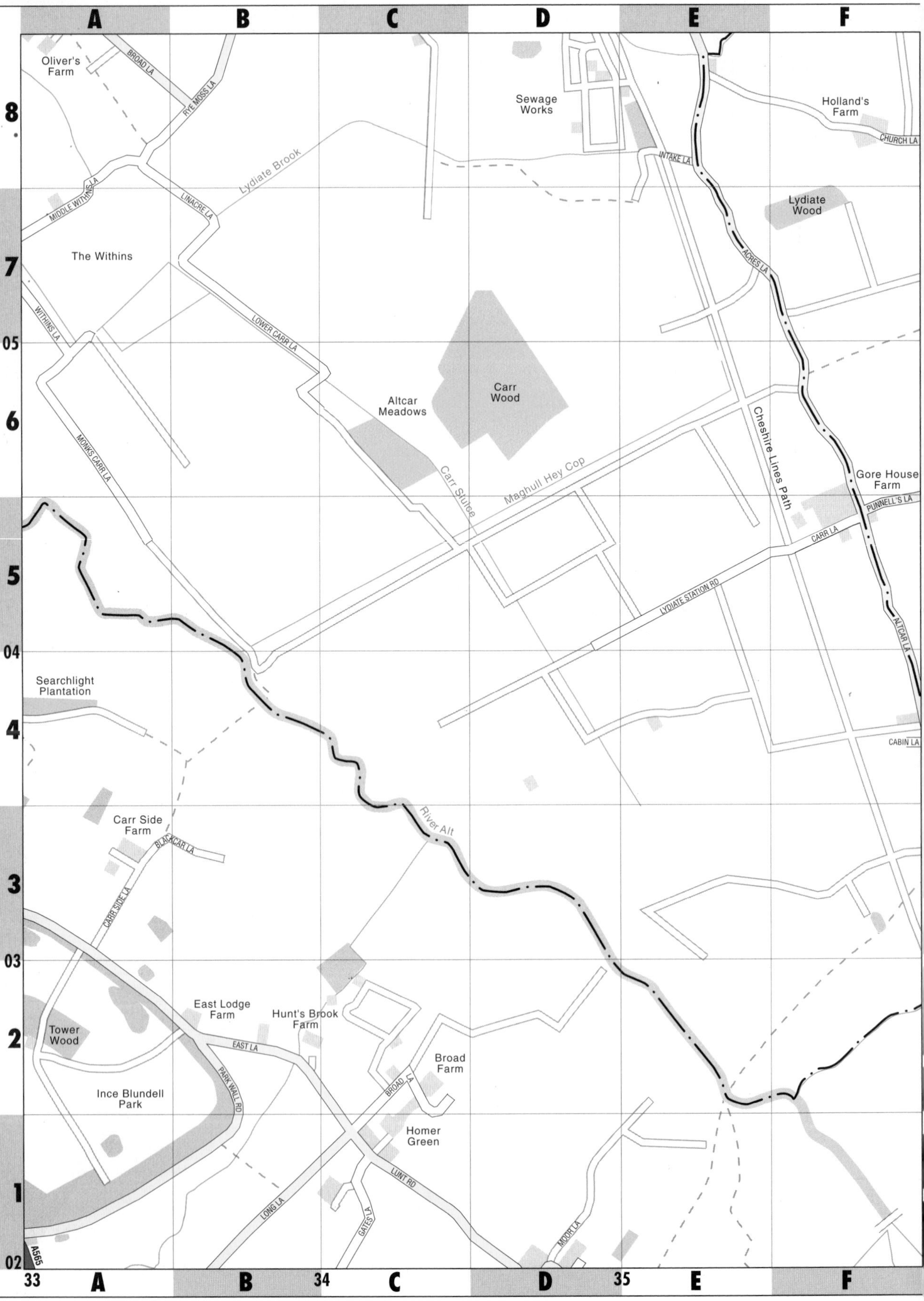

A   B   C   D   E   F

Oliver's Farm

BROAD LA

RYE MOSS LA

Sewage Works

Holland's Farm

CHURCH LA

8

Lydiate Brook

MIDDLE WITHINS LA

LINACRE LA

INTAKE LA

Lydiate Wood

The Withins

7

LOWER CARR LA

ACRES LA

WITHINS LA

05

Carr Wood

6

MONKS CARR LA

Altcar Meadows

Cheshire Lines Path

Gore House Farm

Carr Sluice

Maghull Hey Cop

PUNNELL'S LA

CARR LA

5

LYDIATE STATION RD

ALTCAR LA

04

Searchlight Plantation

4

CABIN LA

Carr Side Farm

BLACKCAR LA

River Alt

3

CARR SIDE LA

03

East Lodge Farm

Hunt's Brook Farm

Tower Wood

2

EAST LA

PARK WALL RD

Broad Farm

BROAD LA

Ince Blundell Park

Homer Green

1

LONG LA

LUNT RD

GATES LA

MOOR LA

02

A565

33   A   B   34   C   D   35   E   F

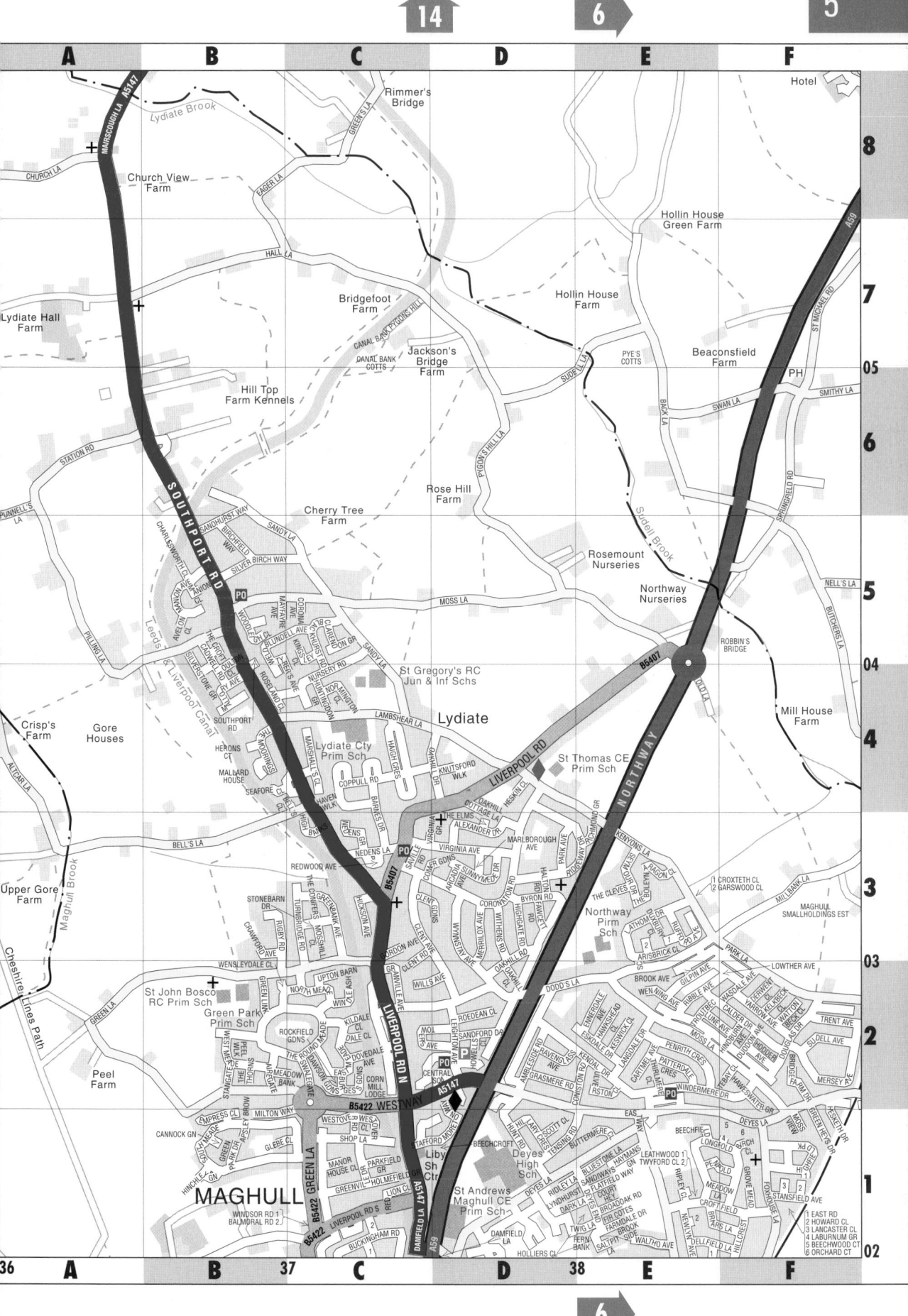

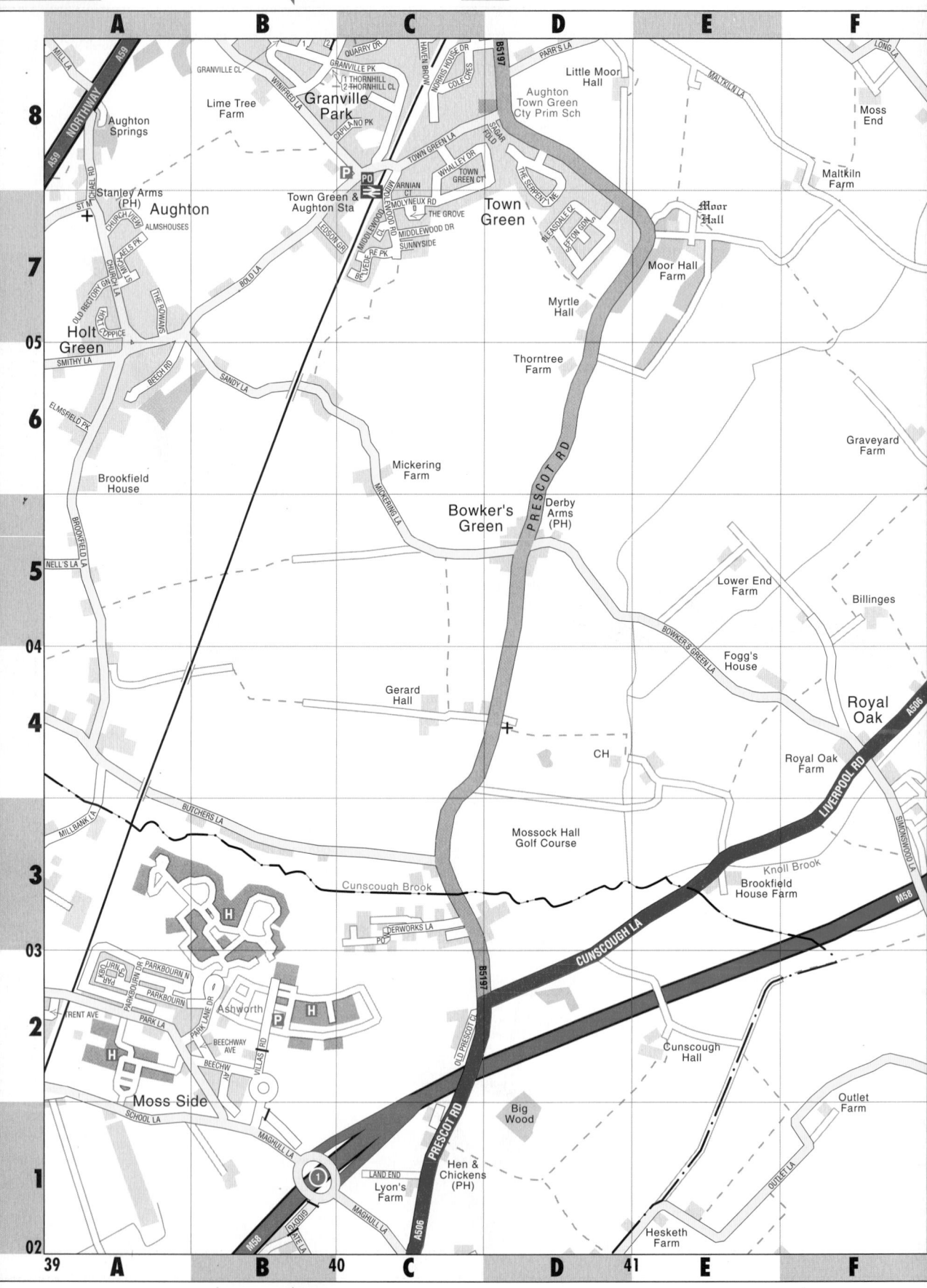

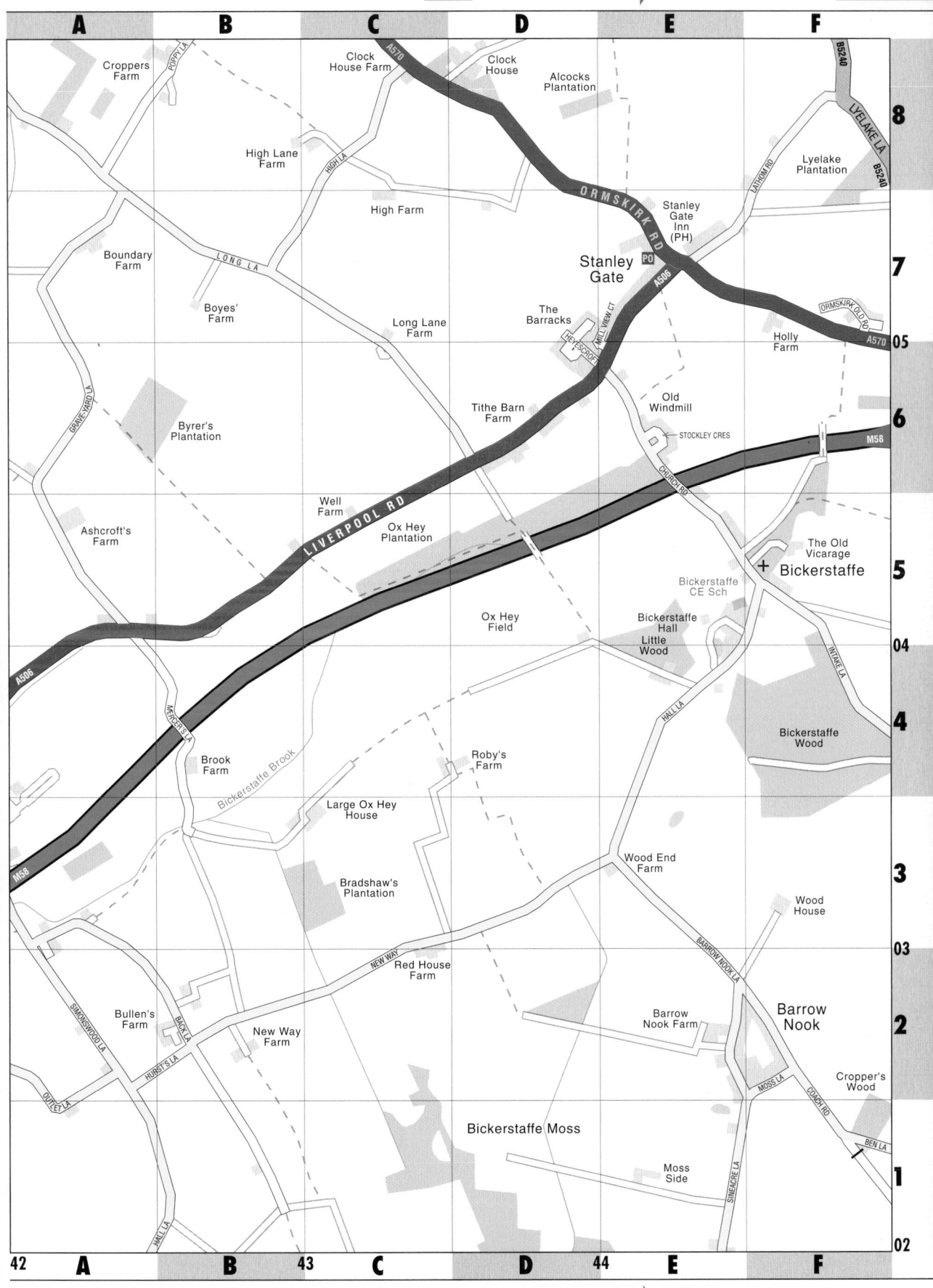

7
17

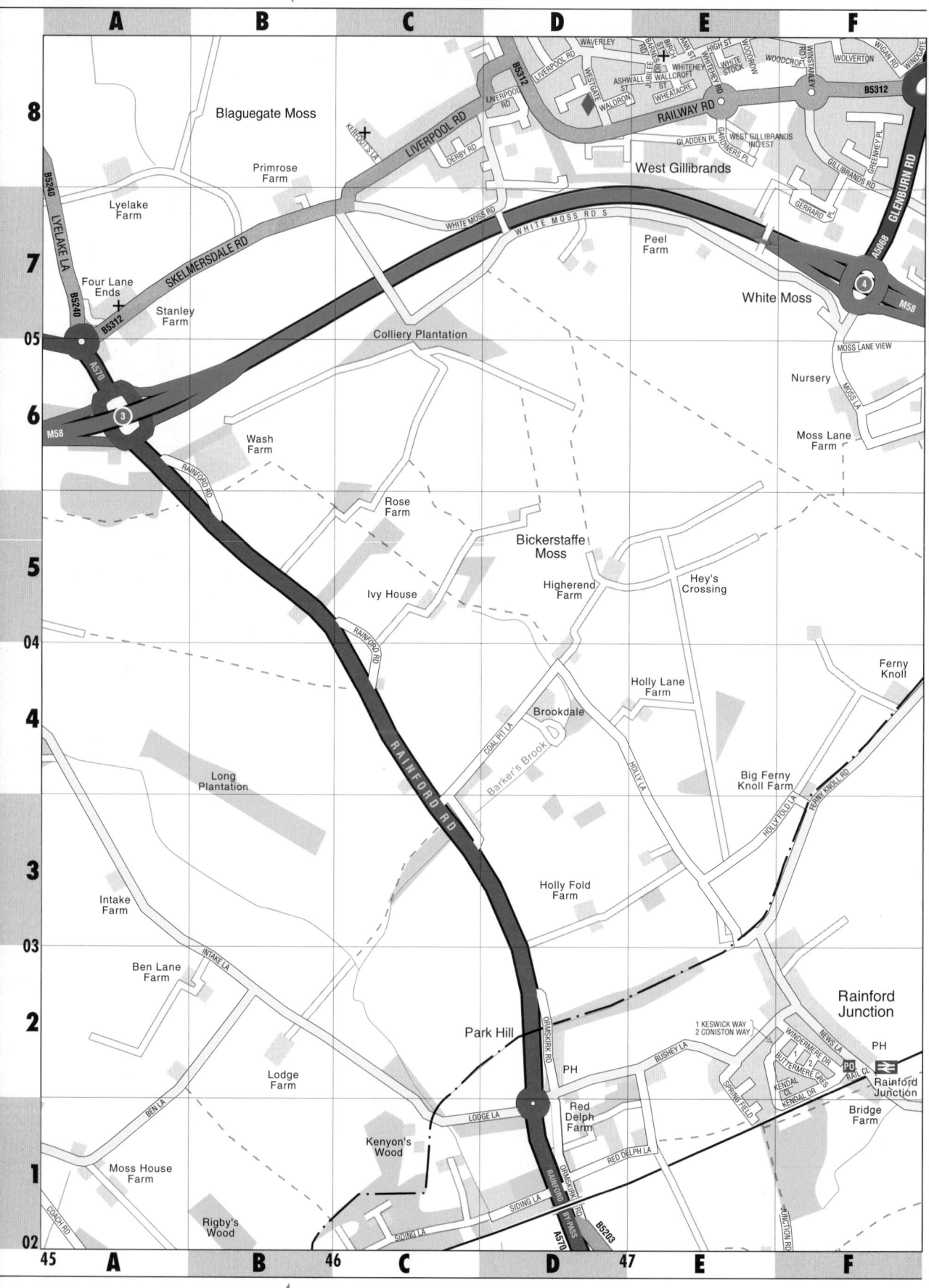

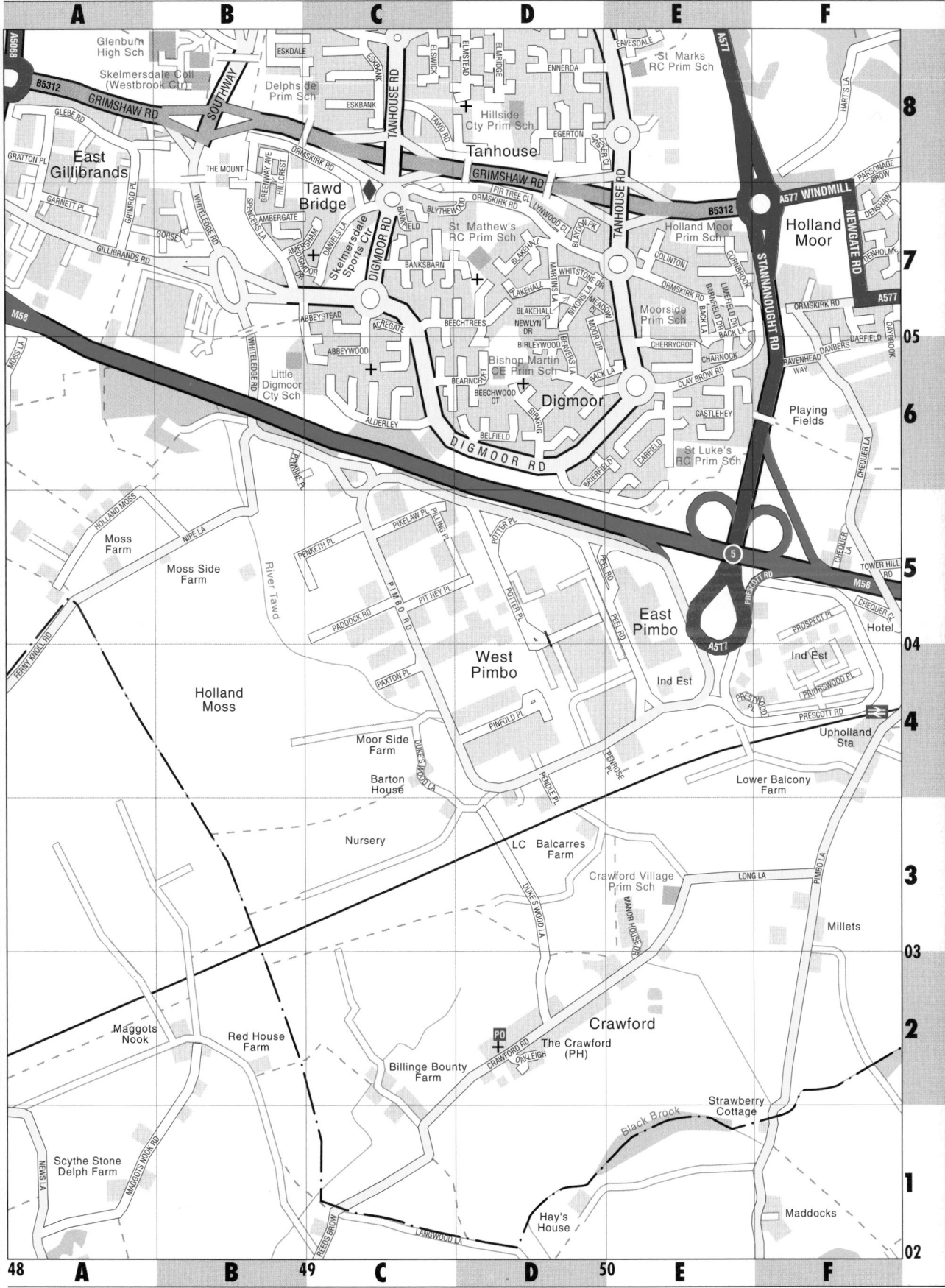

A B C D E F

8 Cloven-le-Dale
LC
Woodvale Airfield

Fisherman's Path
LC
7

09
LITTLE BREWERY LA
Clarence House Sch
BREWERY LA
6 Formby Hills
WEST LA
ST ANNE'S AVE
ST ANNE'S
KENTON CL
PARADISE LA
YORK CL
FISHERMANS CL
ARGARMEOLS RD
RIMMER AVE
STANLEY RD
ST ANNE'S PATH
CANTERBURY LA
Golf Links
STANLAWE RD
MERSEY AVE
GREGSON'S AVE
RED BARNES
WRIGLEYS
MONTAGU RD
ARGARMEOLS GR
CUMMINS AVE
MASSAM'S LA
MANTEL CT
Freshfield Caravan Pk
CH
QUEENS AVE
TIMMS LA
GREEN LA
CRICKET PATH

Picnic Area
P
BADGERS RAKE
FAIRWAYS CT
SHIREBURN RD
VICTORIA WAY
GOLF RD
P
Freshfield Sta
LC
LOWSWOOD
TIMMS CL
5
TOWER END
VICTORIA RD
GRANGE LA
Freshfield
DEANS CT
BORROWDALE
Sandfield Farm
FIRS AVE FIRS CL
COLLEGE PATH
DERBY RD
PIERCEFIELD RD
08
SQUIRREL GN
BIRCH LA
ST PETER'S LINK
HOLMWOOD DR
VICARAGE RD
FRESHFIELD CT
OLD TOWN LA
BYRON CL
GRABURN RD
GORSE WAY
PROCTOR RD
LARCH WAY
COLLEGE RD
VAUGHAN CL
BRECON
OLD TOWN'RS
MANOR LODGE
WILLOW GR
OLD MILL LA
4
Sefton Coastal Path
DUNES DR
HARINGTON RD
ST PETER'S CL
BARKFIELD LA
LENTON AVE
ST GEORGE'S RD
Formby High Sch
FRESHFIELD RD
FORMBY GDNS
ALDERSON CRES
DAVENHAM
Blundell Ave
LARKHILL
P
WICKS CRES
BEECH RD
HOLWOOD GDNS
LONG LA
LONSDALE RD
GREEN CL
WARREN LN
NICE ELMS
HARINGTON GN
HARINGTON CL
HOLMWOOD CL
COPPICE LEYS
FORMBY
CLIFDEN
HALL LA
PAGE CT
SCHOOL AVE
3
St Jerome's RC Prim Sch
DELPH
WICKS LA
WICKS GDNS
BUTTERMERE
WICKS CL
Holy Trinity CE Prim Sch
THE GALLERY
FURNESS AVE
THE CLOISTERS
P
SCHOOL CL
CHAPEL LA
THREE TUNS LA
GREENLOON'S DR
FOXHILL CL
Woodlands Prim Sch
GRASMERE
TARN RD
ENNERDALE
ROSEMARY LA
HEYWOOD
MICHAELS CL
SUMNER RD
CROPTON RD
07
SPRUCE WAY
DENHURST RD
GREENLOON'S LN
CHEWGAT
WOODLANDS CL
RYDAL AVE
EMMANUEL RD
CORSEDALE RD
GRANTON CL
BROWS LN
LEVEL CL
BROWS
ASHURST
DUKES WAY
KIRKLAKE BANK
HAZLEHURST CL
EDENHURST CL
SPRINGFIELD
ELMDALE
CONISTON RD
LANGDALE AVE
MERE RD
ESKDALE CL
ESKDALE RD
MARSH BROWS
P
DUKE ST
2
KIRKLAKE RD
LIME TREE WAY
FIRS
ST LUKE'S DR
BUSHBY'S PK
SPIKEHILL
WARD AVE
CHINDIT CL
BROOKS RD
SEFTON RD
Formby Bridge
Formby Sta
Liby
PHILLIP'S LA
DICKINSON RD
MEADOW CROFT
NORBURN CRES
P
ST LUKE'S CHURCH RD
CHURCH GN
CHURCH WAY
BUSHBY'S LA
PINEWOOD CL
Queen's Rd
FOSTER'S CROFT
SEALAND CL
SEALAND AVE
Eccles Crossing
RAVEN MEOLS LA
KINGS RD
WALKER
GLENDALE
DICKINSON WAY
BIRKEY LA
RAVENSCROFT
BIII'S LA
Shorrocks Hill
MAPLE CL
ELM DR
PINEWOOD CL
St Luke's CE Sch
ELSON RD
GEORGIAN PL
PO
ST ANDREWS
VIEW PORT
BUCKINGHAM RD
KENSINGTON RD
WINDSOR RD
PARK AVE
PARK WAY
NURSERY DR
HARPERL LA
1
Formby Point Caravan Pk
BEECHWOOD DR
ASH GR
CEDAR GR
CHESTNUT WAY
SYCAMORE
JUBILEE GR
CARR'S CRES W
FUNCHAL AVE
CARR'S CRES
CRESCENT
ROSTRON CRES
SANDRINGHAM RD
HAMPTON RD
BALMORAL RD
EDINBURGH RD
LANCASTER
OSBORNE
CASTLE DR
ASHCROFT RD
KENT RD
MARINA RD
ALEXANDRA RD
ASPEN GR
CAMBRIDGE RD
MAYFIELD AVE
SANDHURST
HEYDON RD
BURWELL AVE
STAPLETON RD
BARTON HEYS RD
KEW RD
SUTTON RD
ANDREW'S CL
PARK RD
HOGG'S HILL LA
ALTCAR LA
BELVEDERE DR
Sewage Works
06

ELSWORTH CL
MEDLOW
MELDRETH
ORWELL CL

27 A 28 B C 29 D E F

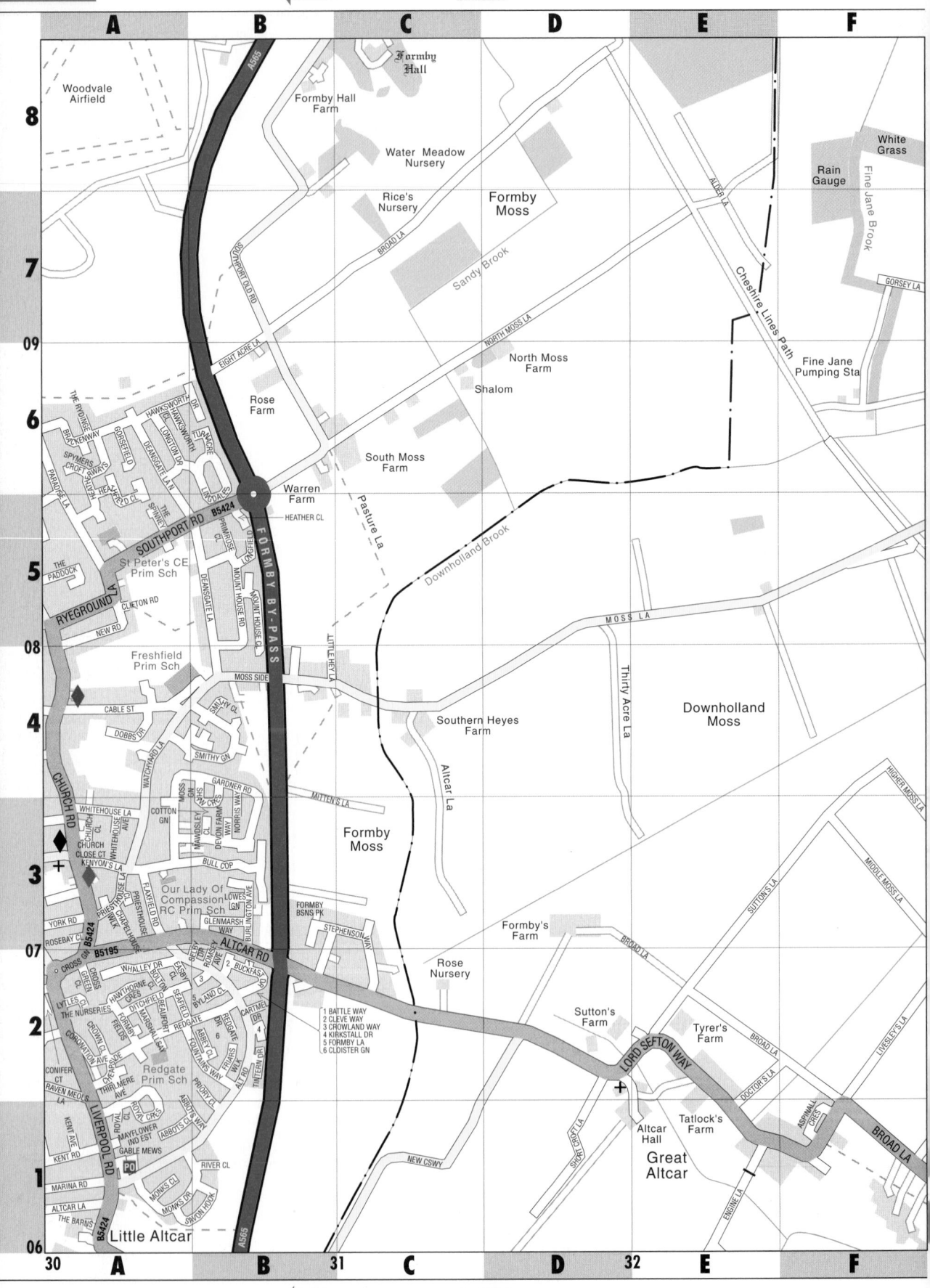

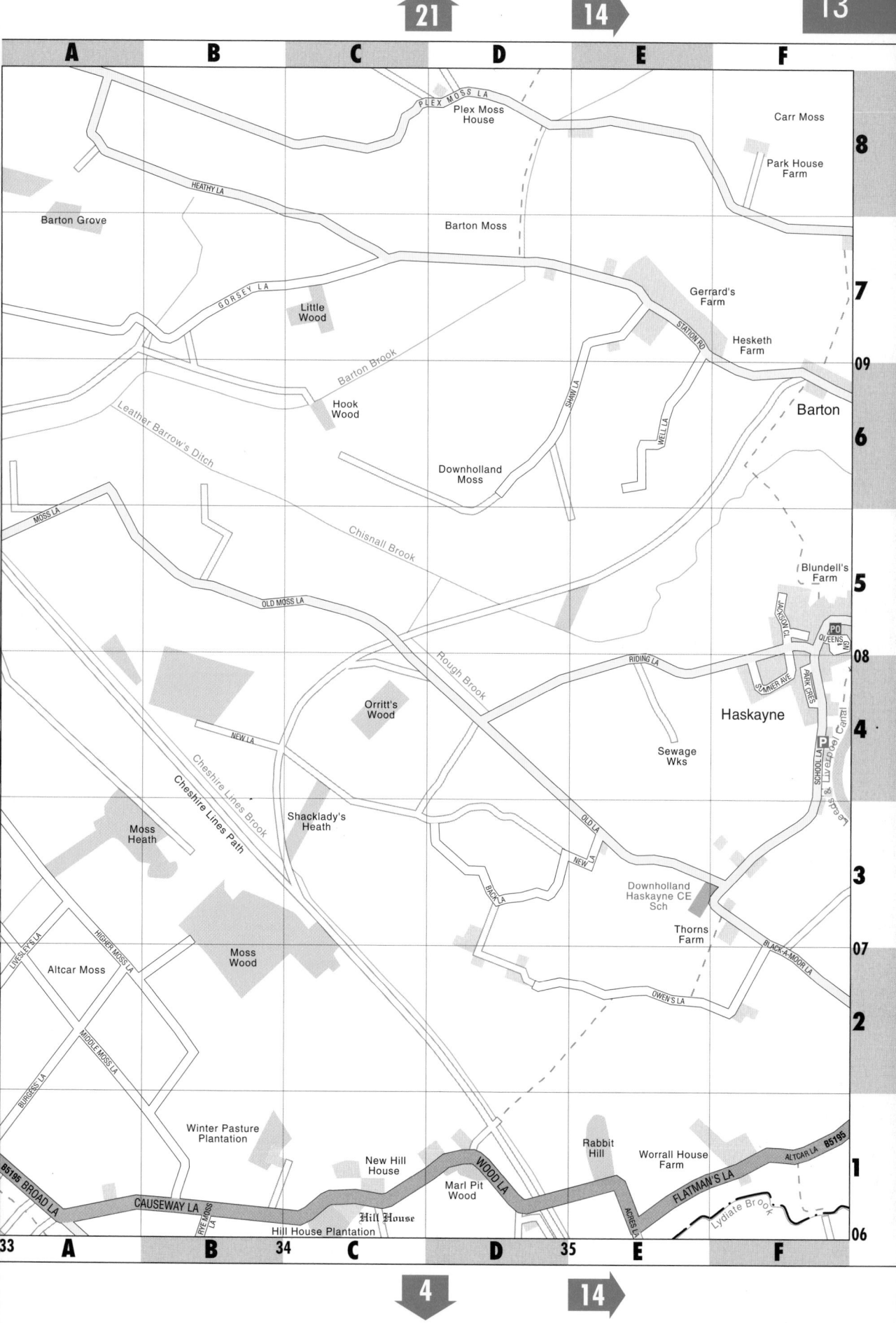

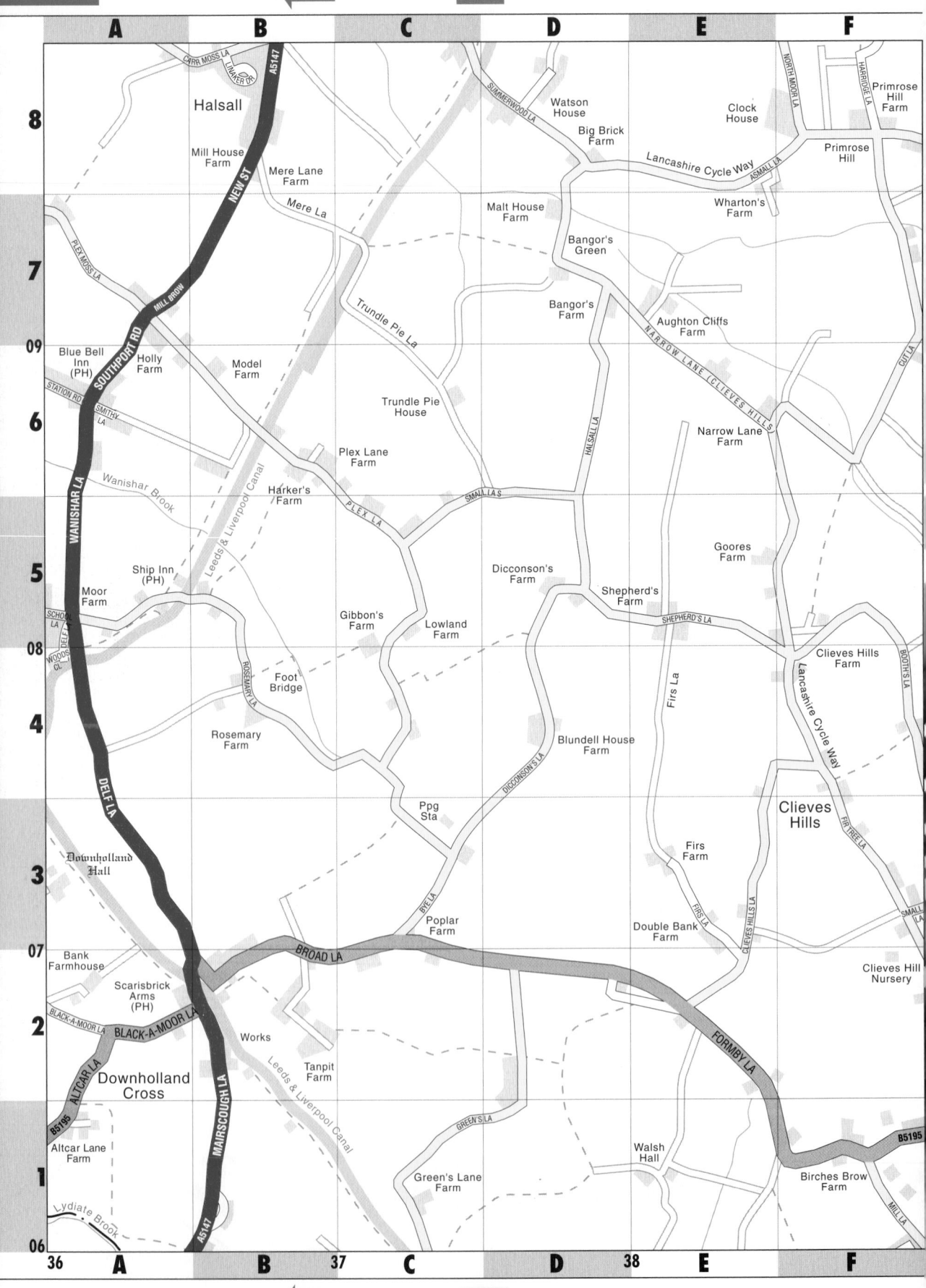

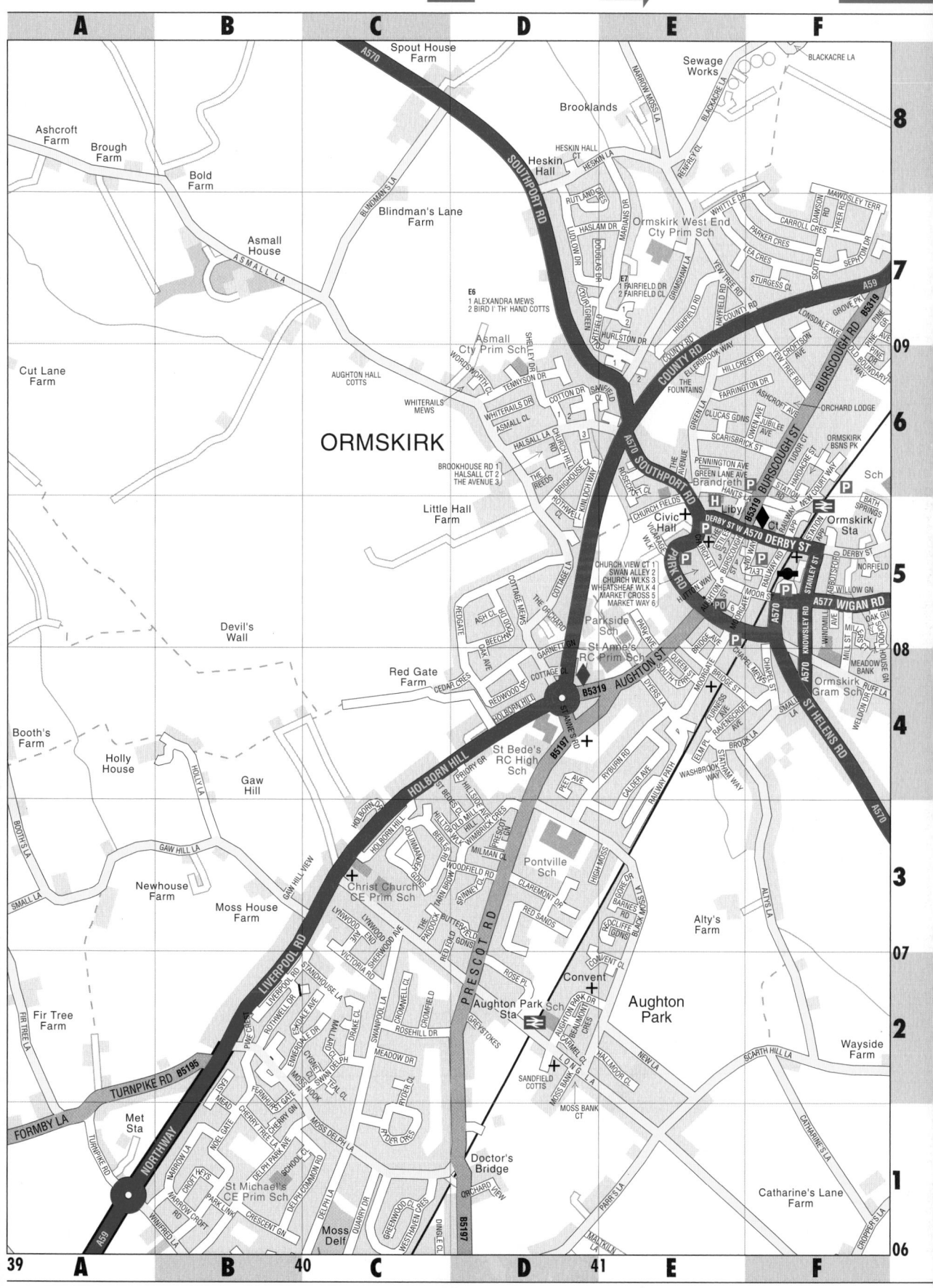

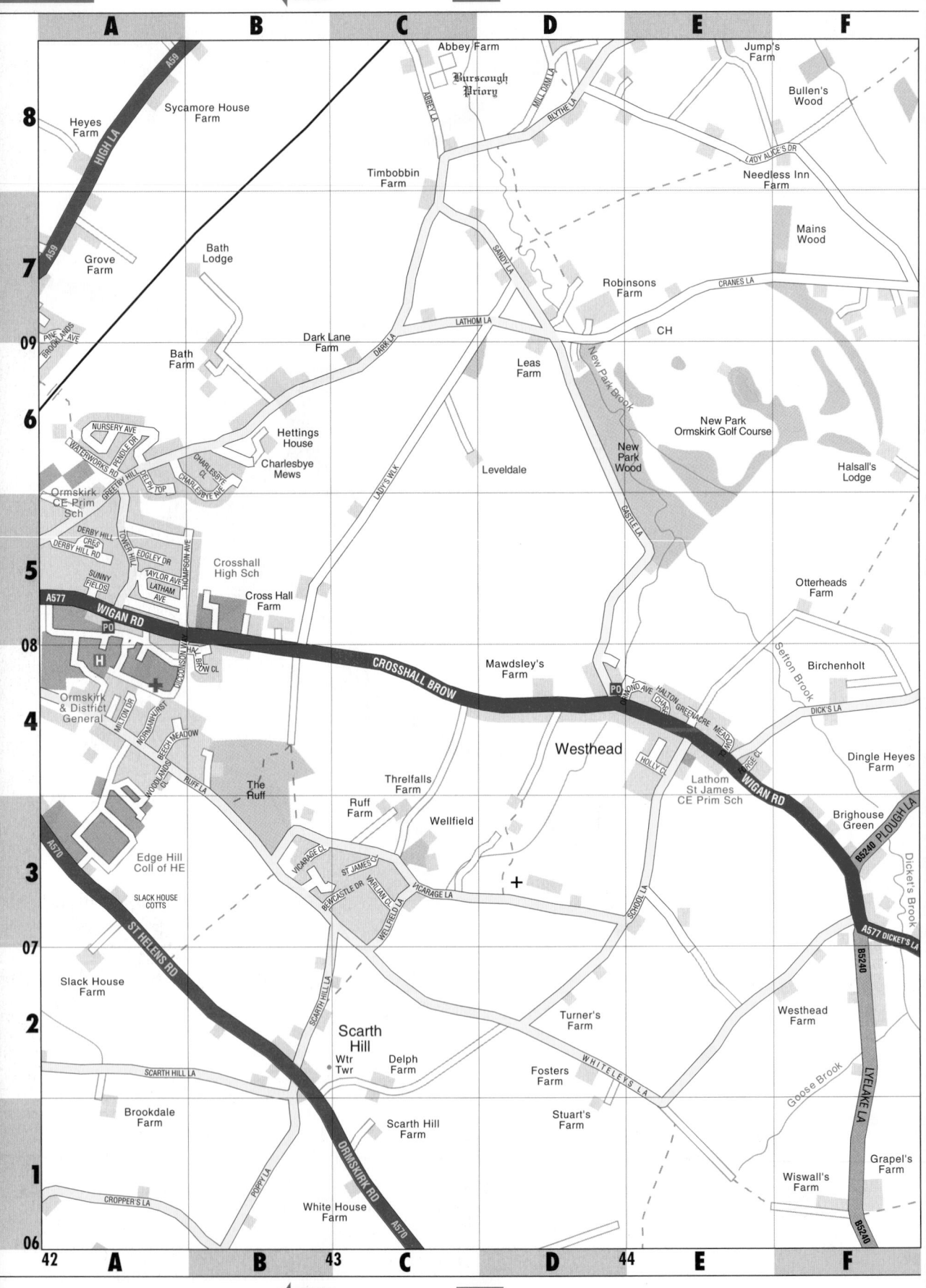

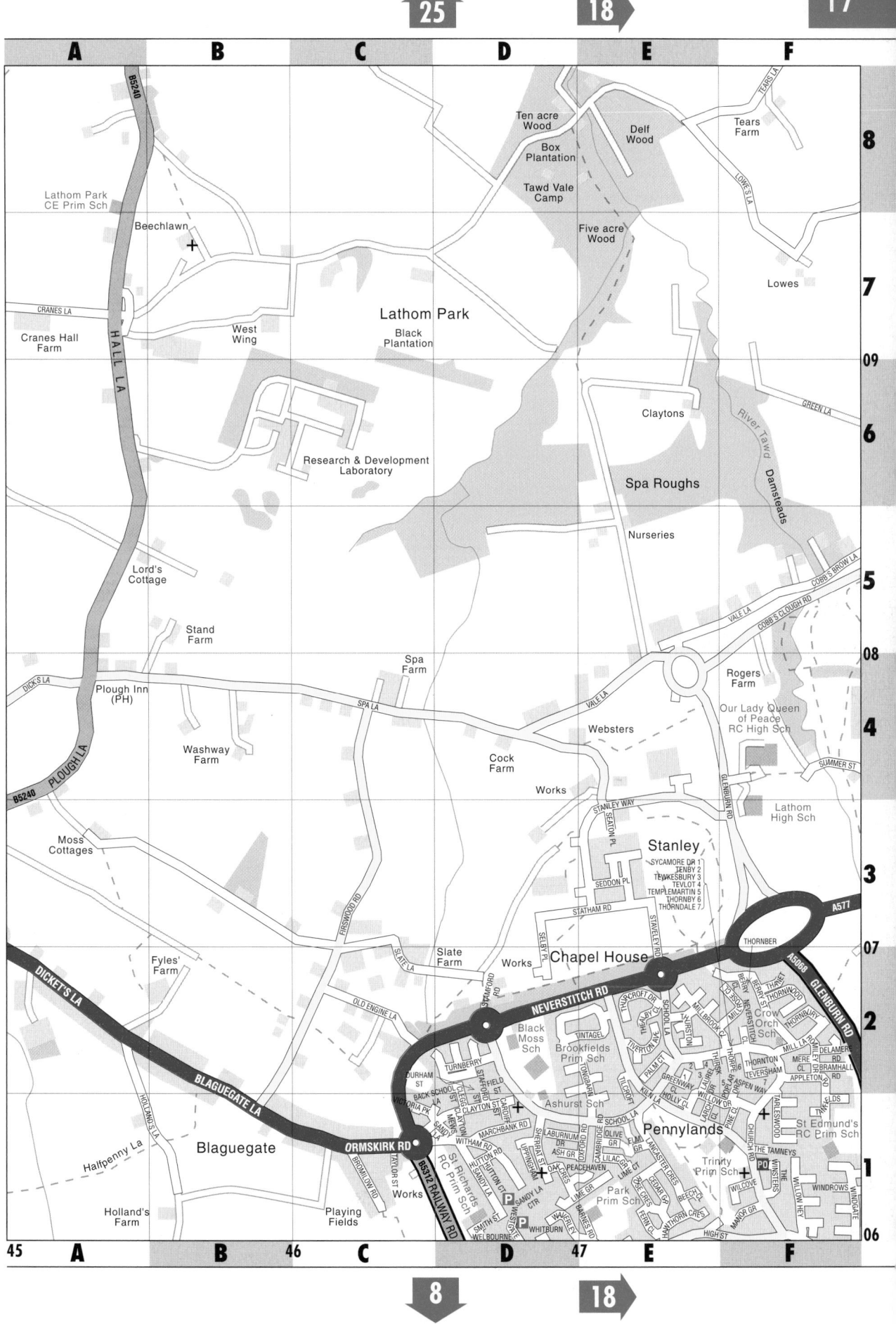

A B C D E F

8
Ten acre Wood
Delf Wood
Tears Farm
Box Plantation
Tawd Vale Camp
Lowes La
Tears La

Lathom Park CE Prim Sch
Beechlawn
Five acre Wood

7
Cranes La
West Wing
Lathom Park
Black Plantation
Lowes

09
Cranes Hall Farm
Hall La
B5240

6
Research & Development Laboratory
Claytons
Spa Roughs
Green La
River Tawd
Damsteads

Lord's Cottage
Nurseries

5
Stand Farm
Cobb's Brow La
Vale La
Cobb's Clough Rd

08
Dick's La
Plough Inn (PH)
Spa Farm
Rogers Farm
Our Lady Queen of Peace RC High Sch

4
Plough La
Washway Farm
Spa La
Vale La
Websters
Summer St
Lathom High Sch

B5240
Cock Farm
Works
Glenburn Rd

Moss Cottages
Stanley Way
Stanley
SYCAMORE DR 1
SENBY 2
TEWKESBURY 3
TEVLOT 4
TEMPLEMARTIN 5
THORNBY 6
THORNDALE 7

3
Seaton Pl
Seddon Pl
Statham Rd

Fyles' Farm
Slate Farm
Selby Pl
Works
Chapel House
Staveley Rd
Thornber
A577
A5069

07
Dicket's La
Old Engine La
Slate La
Friswood Rd
Neverstitch Rd
Glenburn Rd

2
Blaguegate La
Black Moss Sch
Brookfields Prim Sch
Crow Orch Sch
Thiscroft Dr
School La

Durham St
Turnberry
Stafford St
Clegg St
Vintage
Thornton
Teversham
Mere Cl
Delamere Rd
Bramhall

Halfpenny La
Holland's La
Ormskirk Rd
B5312 RAILWAY RD
Ashurst Sch
Pennylands
St Edmund's RC Prim Sch

1
Blaguegate
Brownlow Rd
Taylor St
Works
St Richards RC Prim Sch
Park Prim Sch
Trinity Prim Sch
Windrows

Holland's Farm
Playing Fields
Whitburn
High St

06
45 A 46 B C 47 D 47 E F

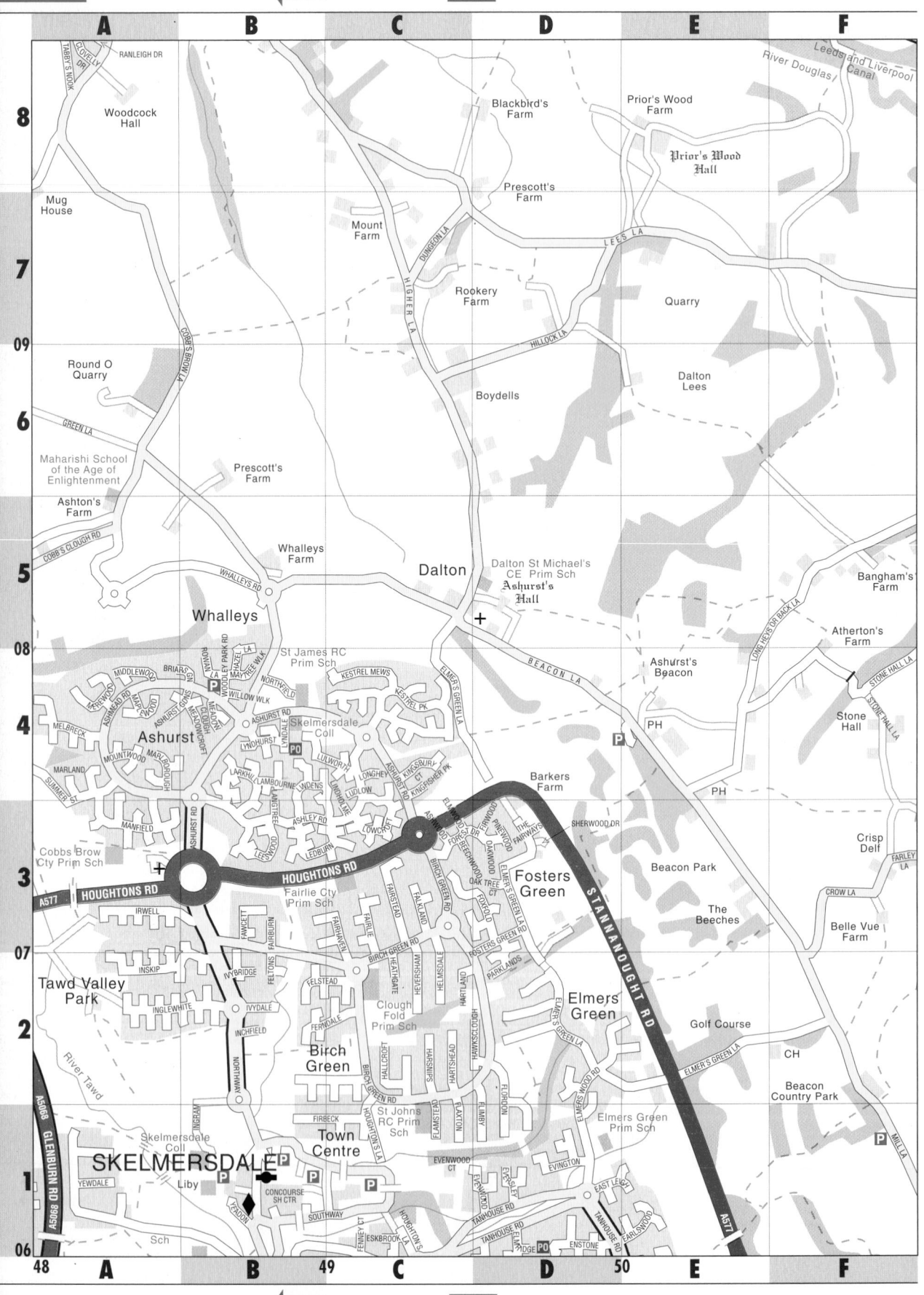

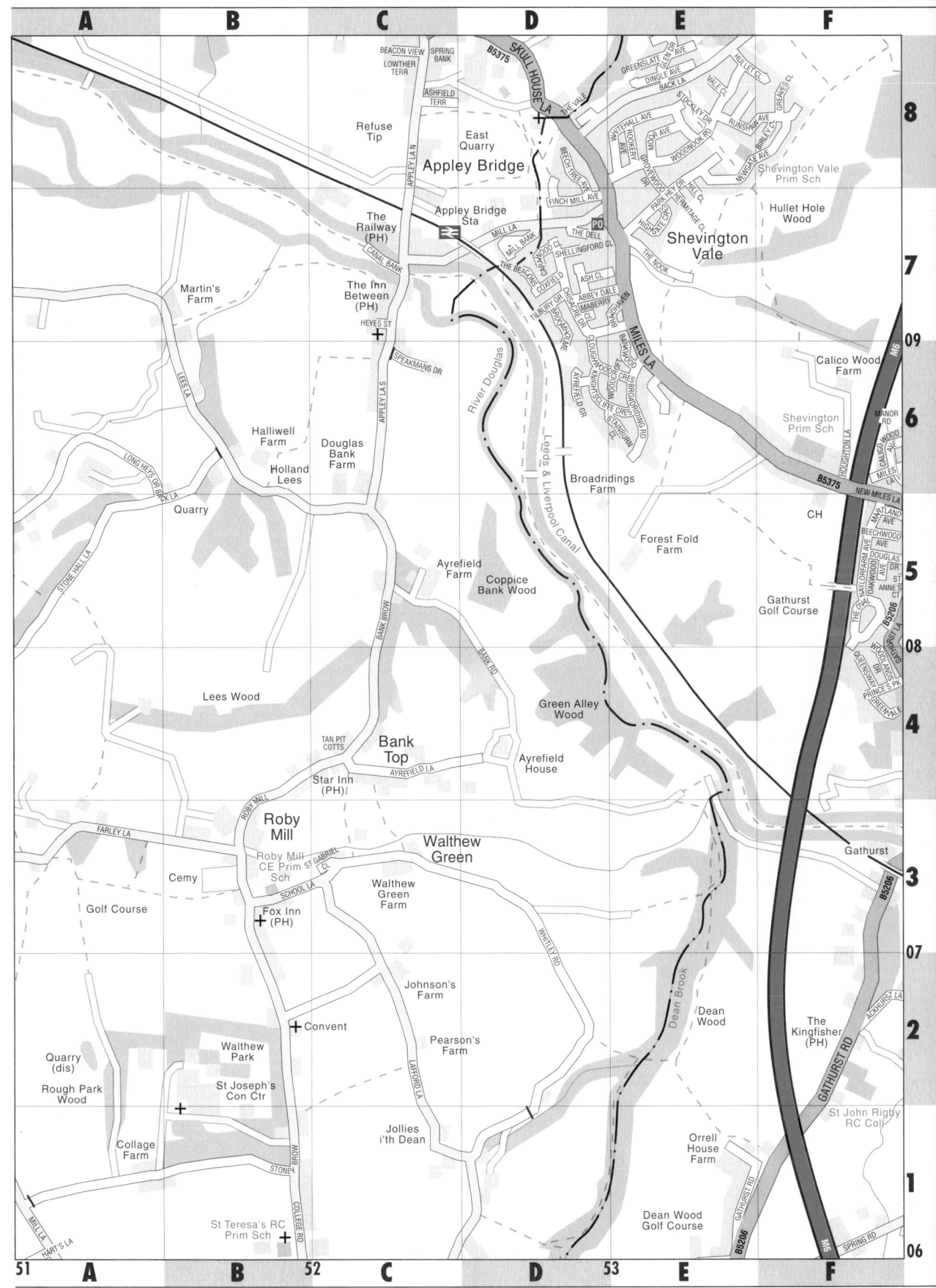

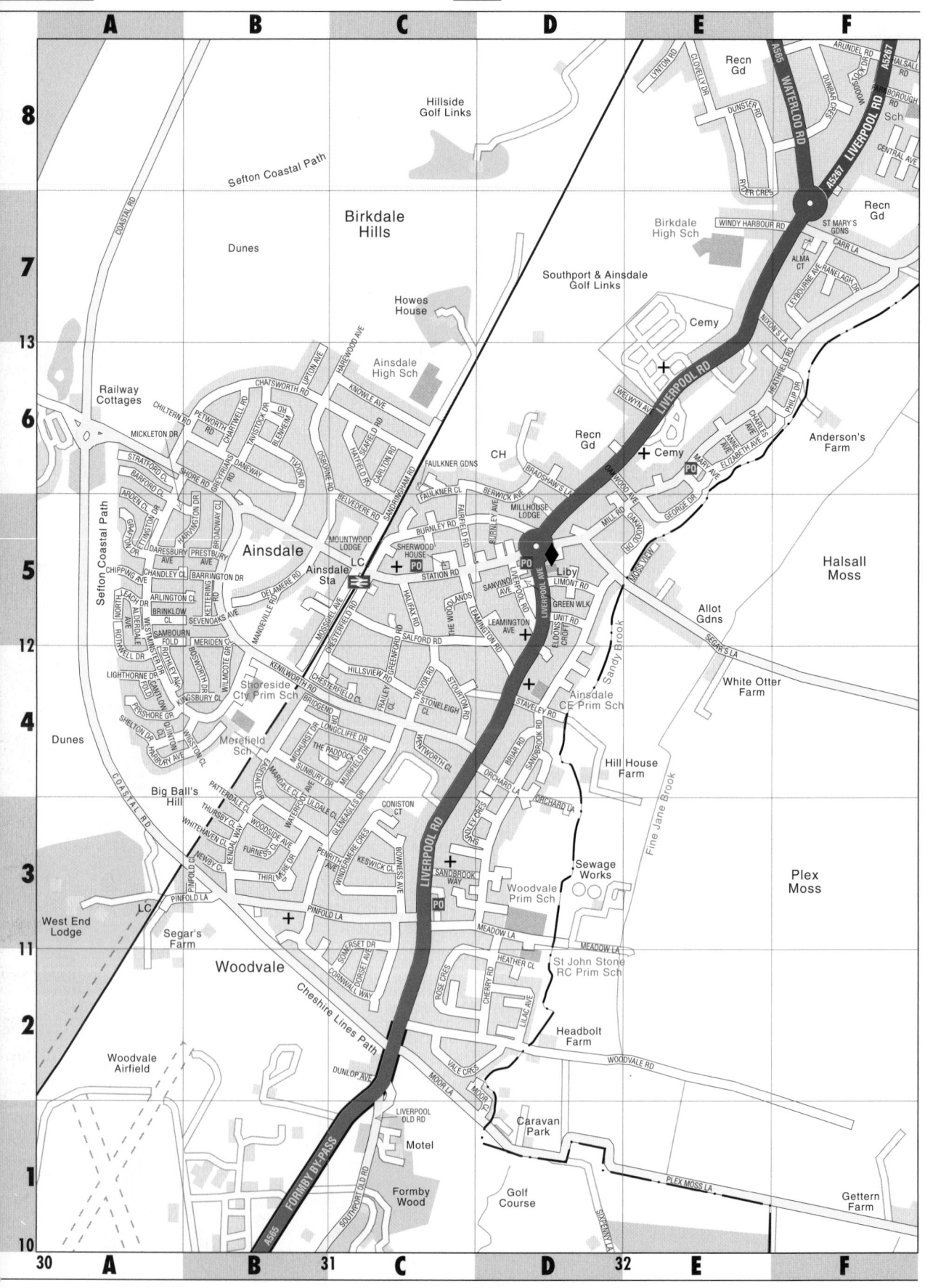

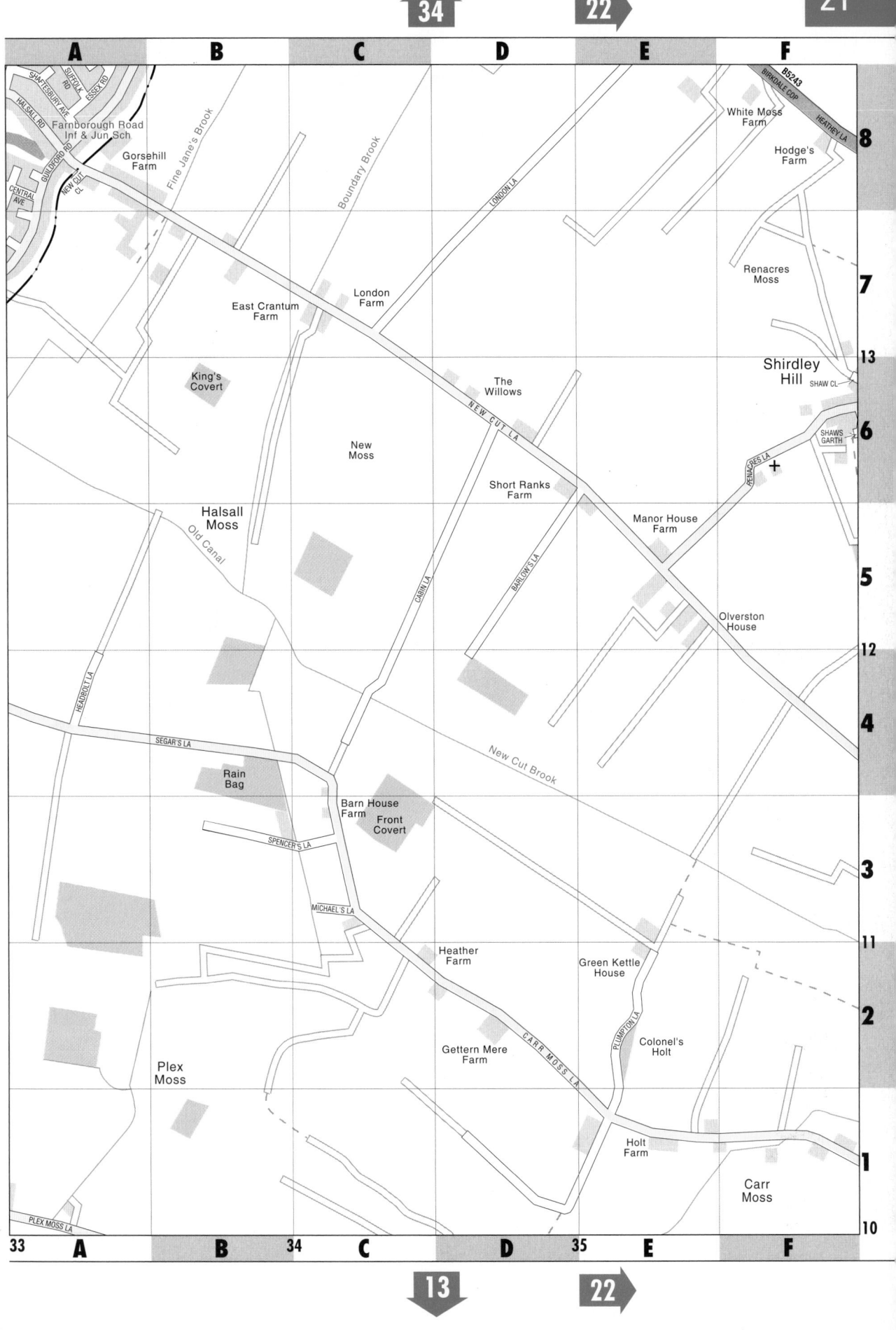

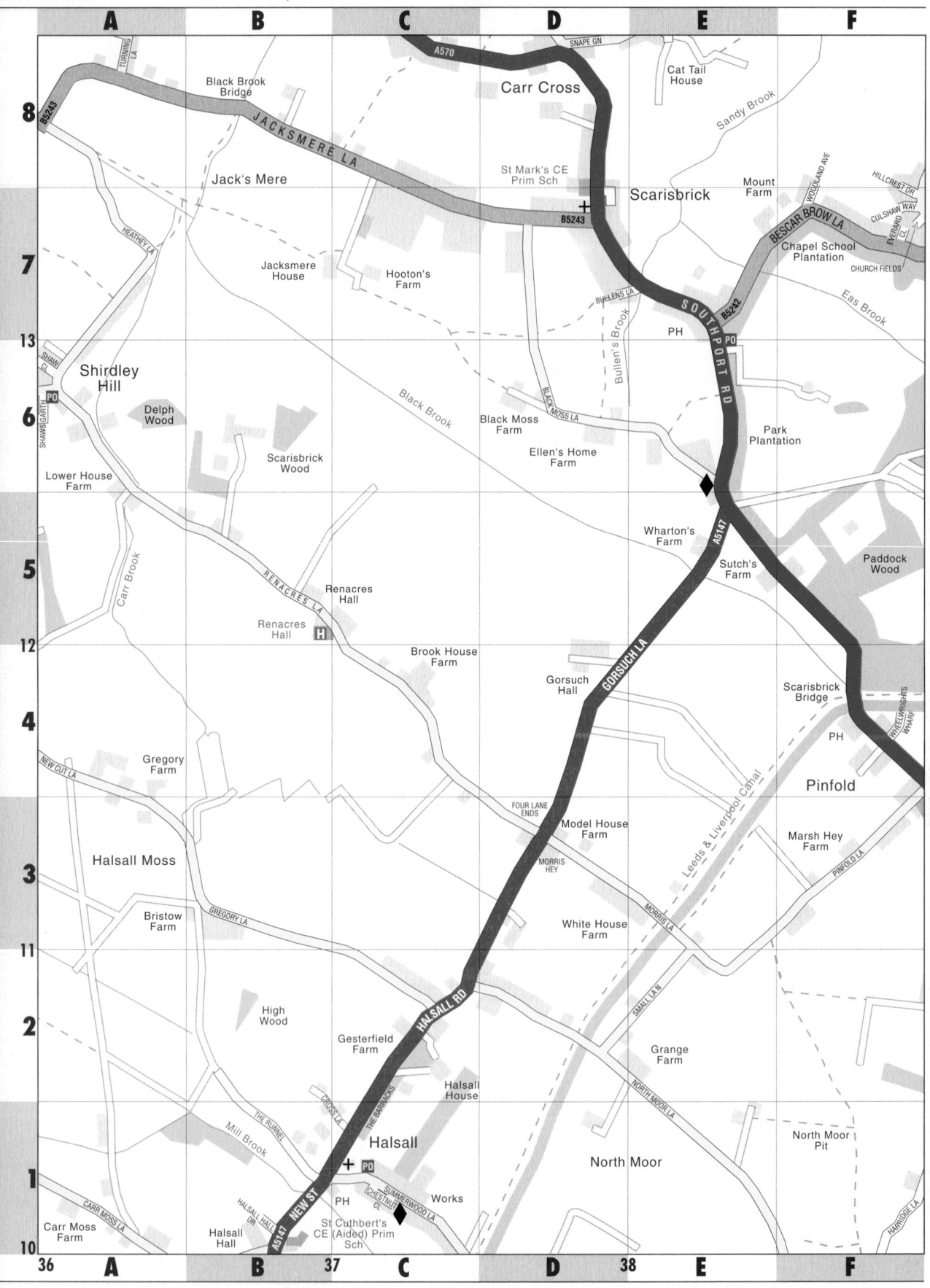

36
24

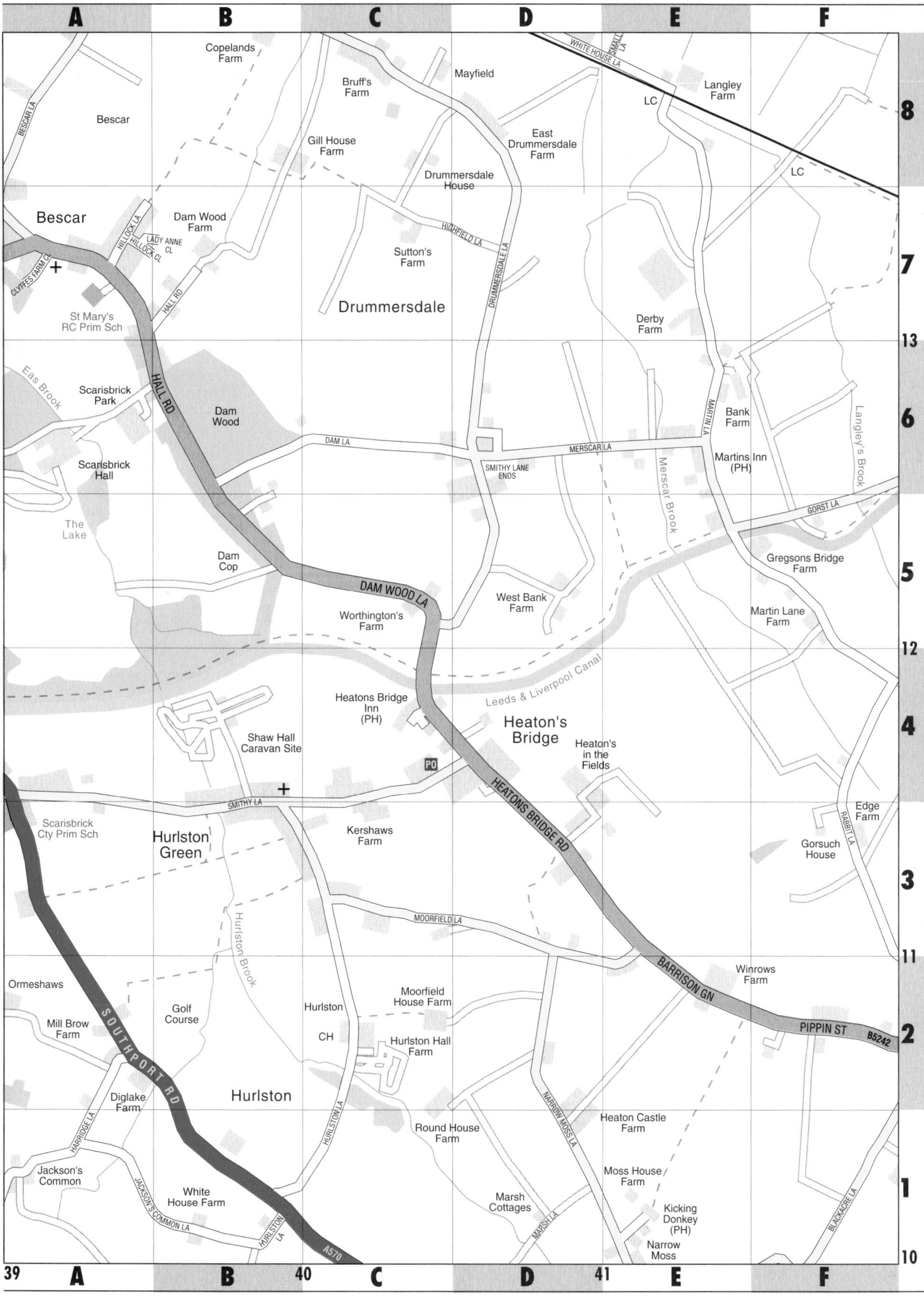
A
B
C
D
E
F
8
7
13
6
5
12
4
3
11
2
1
10
39
40
41
Copelands Farm
Bescar
BESCAR LA
Bruff's Farm
Mayfield
WHITE HOUSE LA
SMALL LA
Langley Farm
LC
Gill House Farm
East Drummersdale Farm
Drummersdale House
LC
Bescar
Dam Wood Farm
HILLOCK LA
LADY ANNE CL
HILLOCK CL
HIGHFIELD LA
Sutton's Farm
DRUMMERSDALE LA
CLYFFES FARM CL
HALL RD
St Mary's RC Prim Sch
Drummersdale
Derby Farm
Eas Brook
Scarisbrick Park
HALL RD
Dam Wood
Bank Farm
MARTIN LA
Langley's Brook
DAM LA
MERSCAR LA
Scarisbrick Hall
SMITHY LANE ENDS
Martins Inn (PH)
Merscar Brook
The Lake
GORST LA
Dam Cop
Gregsons Bridge Farm
DAM WOOD LA
West Bank Farm
Worthington's Farm
Martin Lane Farm
Leeds & Liverpool Canal
Heatons Bridge Inn (PH)
Heaton's Bridge
Shaw Hall Caravan Site
Heaton's in the Fields
PO
SMITHY LA
HEATONS BRIDGE RD
Scarisbrick Cty Prim Sch
Hurlston Green
Kershaws Farm
Edge Farm
RABBIT LA
Gorsuch House
Hurlston Brook
MOORFIELD LA
Ormeshaws
BARRISON GN
Winrows Farm
Moorfield House Farm
Hurlston
SOUTHPORT RD
Golf Course
Mill Brow Farm
CH
Hurlston Hall Farm
PIPPIN ST
B5242
Hurlston
Diglake Farm
HARRIDGE LA
HURLSTON LA
Round House Farm
NARROW MOSS LA
Heaton Castle Farm
Jackson's Common
JACKSON'S COMMON LA
White House Farm
Moss House Farm
Marsh Cottages
Kicking Donkey (PH)
MARSH LA
HURLSTON LA
BLACKACRE LA
Narrow Moss
A570

15
24

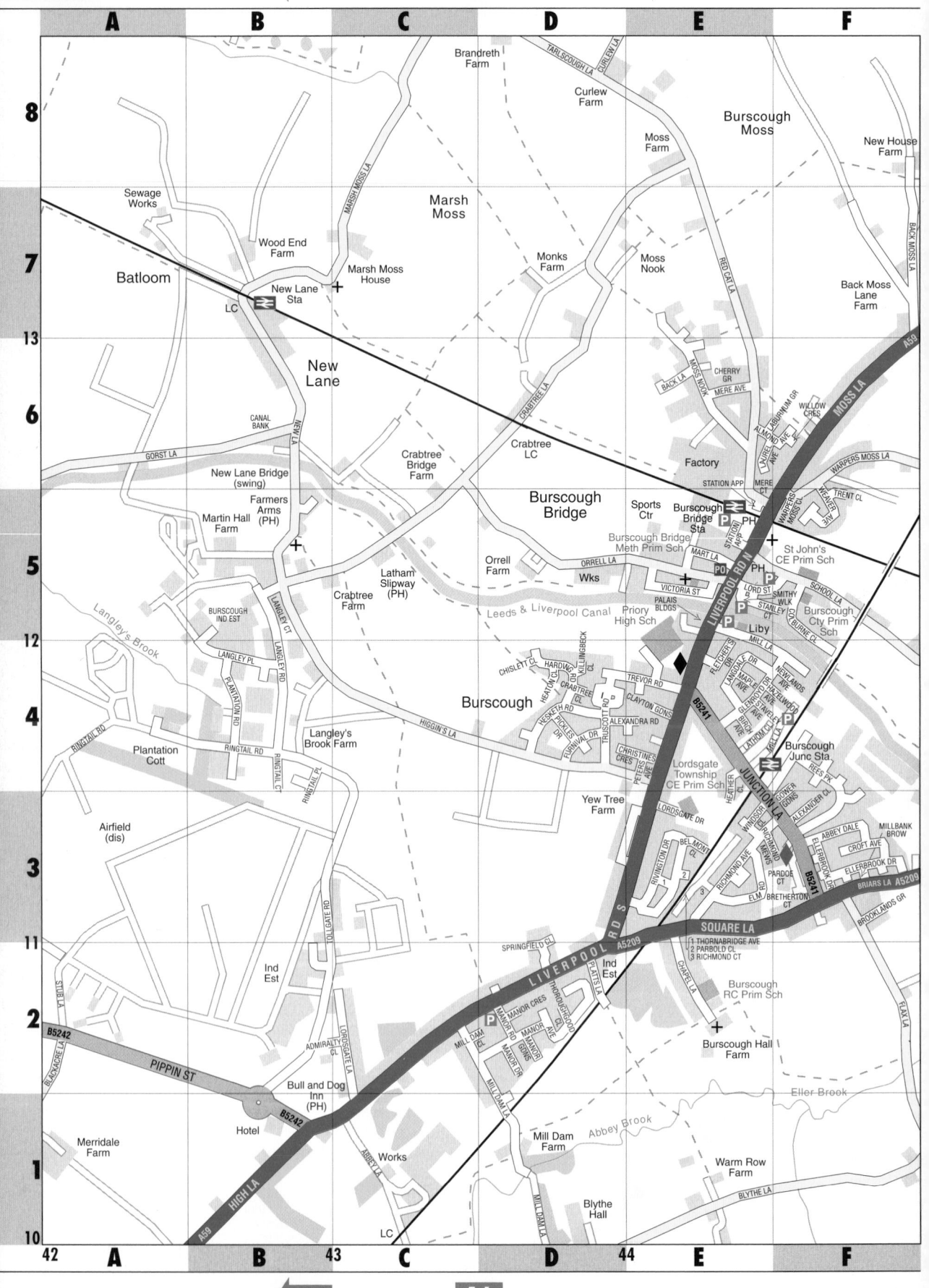
A   B   C   D   E   F

8

Brandreth
Farm

Tarlscough La   Curley La

Curlew
Farm

Burscough
Moss

New House
Farm

Sewage
Works

Wood End
Farm

Marsh Moss La

Marsh
Moss

Moss
Farm

Batloom

Marsh Moss
House

New Lane
Sta

LC

7

Monks
Farm

Moss
Nook

Moss La

Moss Nook

Red Cat La

Back Moss
Lane
Farm

Back Moss La

13

New
Lane

New La

Crabtree La

Back La

Cherry
Gr

Mere Ave

Laburnum Gr

Willow
Cres

Warpers Moss La

6

Canal
Bank

Gorst La

New Lane Bridge
(swing)

Crabtree
Bridge
Farm

Crabtree
LC

Factory

Station App

Laurel Ave

Almond Gr

Mere
Ct

Warpers
Moss Cl

Weaver Ave

Trent Cl

5

Martin Hall
Farm

Farmers
Arms
(PH)

Crabtree
Farm

Latham
Slipway
(PH)

Orrell
Farm

Orrell La   Wks

Burscough
Bridge

Sports
Ctr

Burscough
Bridge
Sta

P   PH

Burscough Bridge
Meth Prim Sch

Mart La

Victoria St

Station Ave

Lord St

P   PH

Smithy
Wlk

Stanley St

School Rd

St John's
CE Prim Sch

Burscough
City Prim
Sch

Liverpool Rd N

12

Burscough
Ind Est

Langley Ct

Langley Rd

Langley's Brook

Leeds & Liverpool Canal

Palais
Bldgs

Priory
High Sch

P   Libby

Mill La

P   Stanley Ct

Fletcher Dr

Lansdale Dr

Maple Ave

Glenroy Ave

Newlands
Ave

Kenilworth Dr

Burne Cl

4

Langley Pl

Plantation Rd

Ringtail Rd

Higgin's La

Langley's
Brook Farm

Burscough

Chislett Cl

Hardwick

Willingbeck

Heaton Cl

Crabtree
Cl

Trevor Rd

Clayton Gdns

Alexandra Rd

Hesketh Rd   Pickles Dr

Furnival Dr

Truscott Rd

B5241

Langdale Dr

Lathom Cl

P

Burscough
Junc Sta.

Plantation
Cott

Ringtail Ct

Ringtail Pl

Christines
Cres

Peters Ave

Yew Tree
Farm

Lordsgate
Township
CE Prim Sch

Heather

Junction La

Rees Pk

Gorner
Gdns

Alexander Cl

Abbey Dale

Millbank
Brow

3

Airfield
(dis)

Toll Gate Rd

Bel Mont
Cl

Rivington Dr

Richmond Ave

2   Mews

3   Richmond Cl

Windsor Rd

Pardoe
Cl

Elm Cl

Bretherton
Ct

B5241

Ellerbrook Dr

Croft Ave

Ellerbrook Dr

Briars La   A5209

Brooklands Gr

11

B5242

Lordsgate La

Admiralty Cl

Ind
Est

Springfield Cl

Liverpool Rd S   A5209

Thorougood

Platts La

Ind
Est

Square La

Chapel La

1   Thornabridge Ave

2   Parbold Cl

3   Richmond Ct

Burscough
RC Prim Sch

2

Bleakacre La

Pippin St

Mill Dam
Cl

Manor Rd

Manor Cres

Manor
Gdns

Manor
Ave

Manor Dr

Burscough
Hall
Farm

Flax La

Eller Brook

1

Merridale
Farm

Bull and Dog
Inn
(PH)

Hotel

B5242

Abbey La

Works

High La

Mill Dam La

Mill Dam
Farm

Abbey Brook

Blythe
Hall

Warm Row
Farm

Blythe La

10

LC

A59

A59

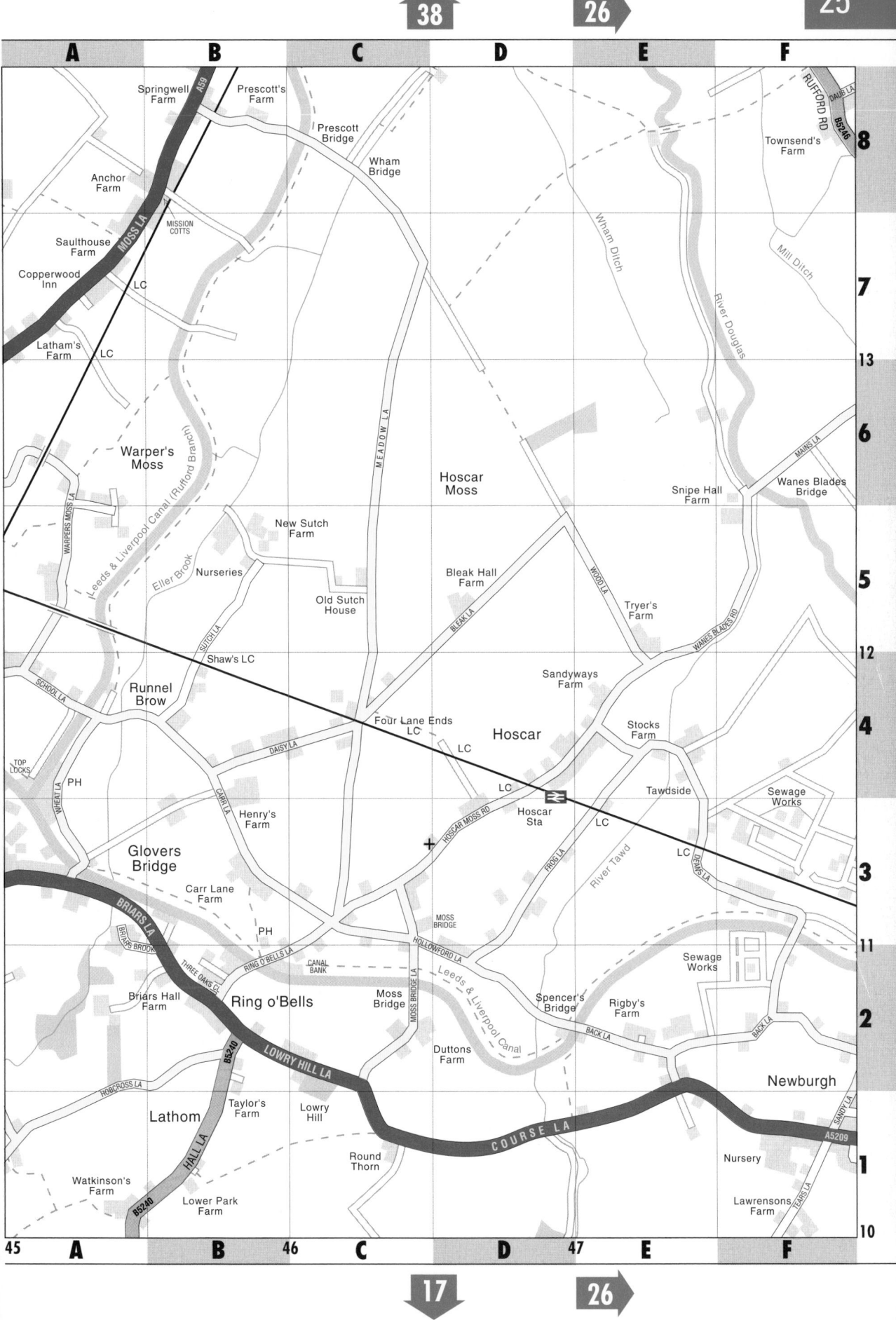

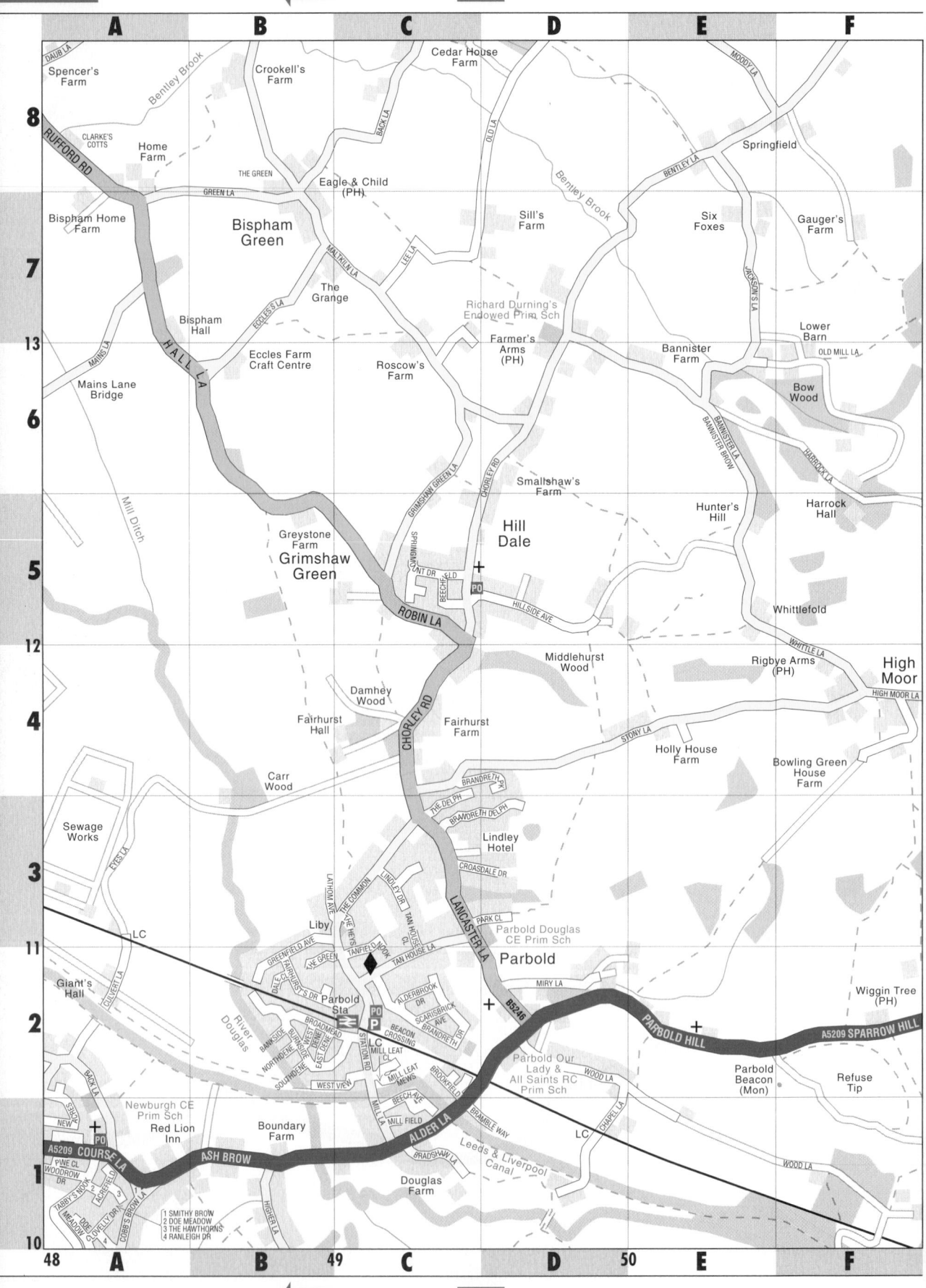

A B C D E F

8
13
7
6
5
12
4
3
11
2
10
1

Spencer's Farm
DAUB LA
Clarke's Cotts
RUFFORD RD
Home Farm
THE GREEN
GREEN LA
Bentley Brook
Crookell's Farm
Cedar House Farm
BACK LA
Eagle & Child (PH)
Sill's Farm
Bentley Brook
OLD LA
MOODY LA
Springfield
BENTLEY LA
Six Foxes
Gauger's Farm
Bispham Home Farm
Bispham Green
HALL LA
MAINS LA
Bispham Hall
ECCLES LA
MILL KILN LA
LEE LA
The Grange
Richard Durning's Endowed Prim Sch
JACKSON'S LA
Lower Barn
OLD MILL LA
Mains Lane Bridge
Eccles Farm Craft Centre
Roscow's Farm
Farmer's Arms (PH)
Bannister Farm
BANNISTER BROW
Bow Wood
HARROCK LA
Mill Ditch
Greystone Farm
Grimshaw Green
GRIMSHAW GREEN LA
SPRINGWOOD
CHORLEY RD
Smallshaw's Farm
Hill Dale
PO
Hunter's Hill
Harrock Hall
ROBIN LA
BEECH
MOUNT DR
HILLSIDE AVE
Whittlefold
Fairhurst Hall
Damhey Wood
Middlehurst Wood
WHITTLE LA
Rigbye Arms (PH)
High Moor
HIGH MOOR LA
Fairhurst Farm
STONY LA
Holly House Farm
Bowling Green House Farm
Carr Wood
CHORLEY RD
THE DELPH
BRANDRETH
BRANDRETH DELPH
Lindley Hotel
CROASDALE DR
LATHOM AVE
THE HEYS
LINDLEY DR
TAN HOUSE LA
PARK CL
Parbold Douglas CE Prim Sch
Sewage Works
EYES LA
LC
Liby
THE COMMON
TANFIELD
TAN HOUSE LA
LANCASTER LA
Parbold
Giant's Hall
COLVERT LA
GREENFIELD AVE
THE GREEN
FAIRHURST'S DR
THE
ALDERBROOK DR
SCARISBRICK AVE
BRANDRETH
MIRY LA
B5246
Wiggin Tree (PH)
River Douglas
BANKSIDE
DERBY
EAST DENE
NORTHDENE
Parbold Sta
PO
P
BEACON CROSSING
LC
PARBOLD HILL
A5209 SPARROW HILL
Parbold Beacon (Mon)
Refuse Tip
SOUTHDENE
STATION RD
MILL LEAT
BROOKFIELD
WEST VIEW
MILL LEAT MEWS
BEECH AVE
Parbold Our Lady & All Saints RC Prim Sch
WOOD LA
Newburgh CE Prim Sch
Red Lion Inn
Boundary Farm
MILL
MILL FIELD
ALDER LA
BRAMBLE WAY
Leeds & Liverpool Canal
CHAPEL LA
LC
WOOD LA
BACK LA
NEW
STACK
A5209 COURSE LA
ASH BROW
Douglas Farm
BRADSHAW LA
PO
PWE CL
WOODROW DR
TABBY'S NOOK
DOE MEADOW
ACREFIELD
O'VELLY DR
COBB'S BROW LA
HIGHER LA
WOOD LA
1 SMITHY BROW
2 DOE MEADOW
3 THE HAWTHORNS
4 RANLEIGH DR

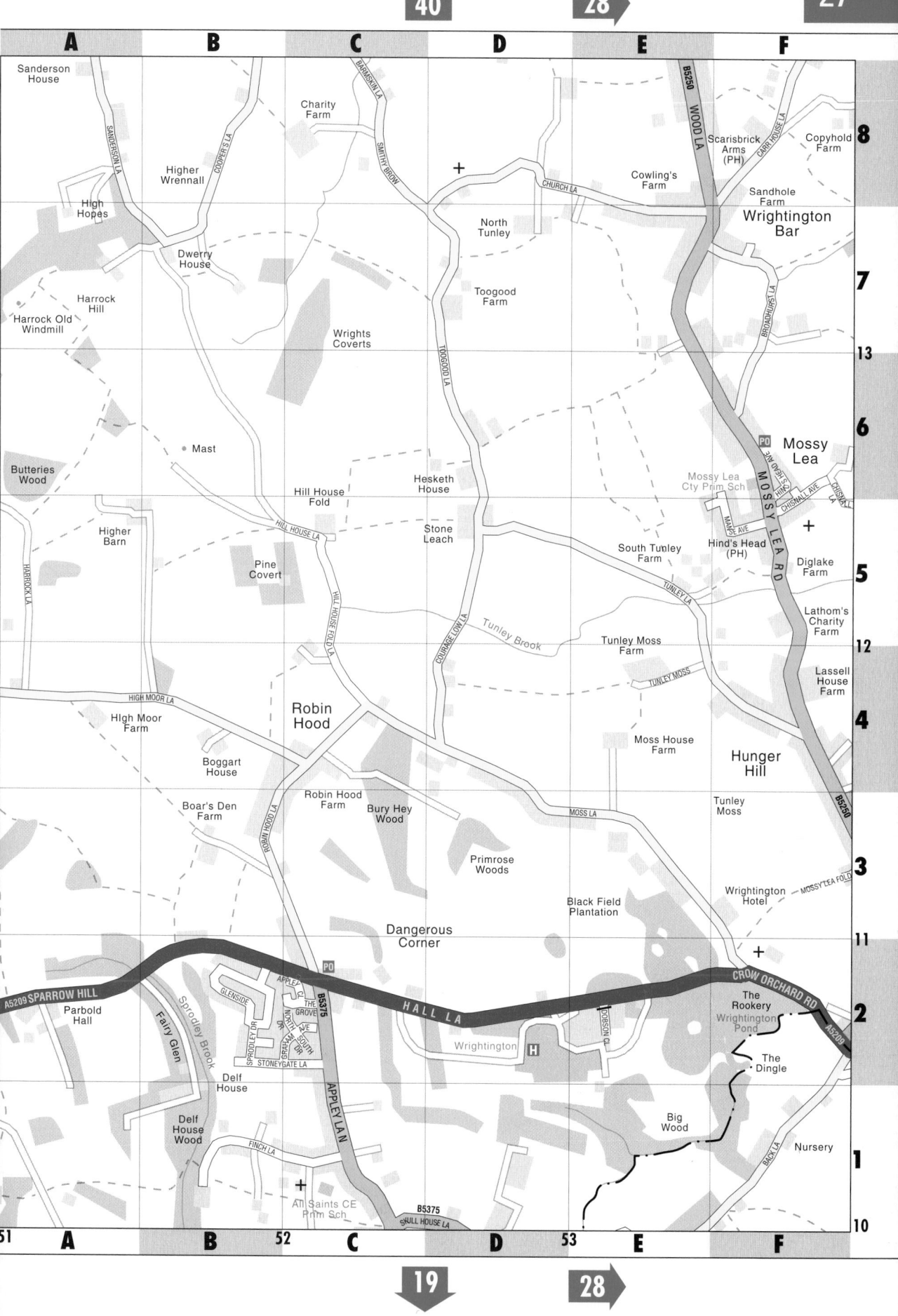

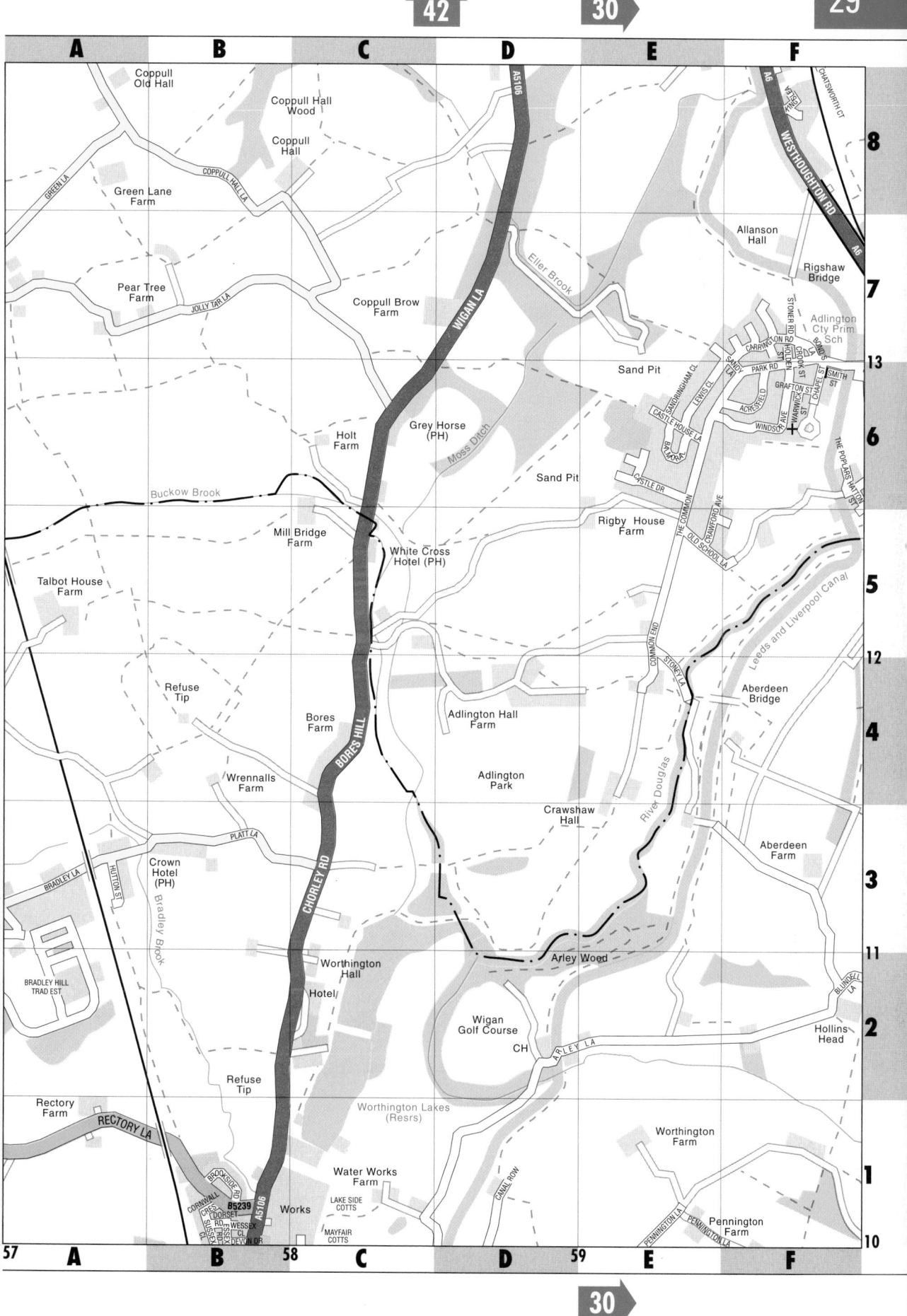

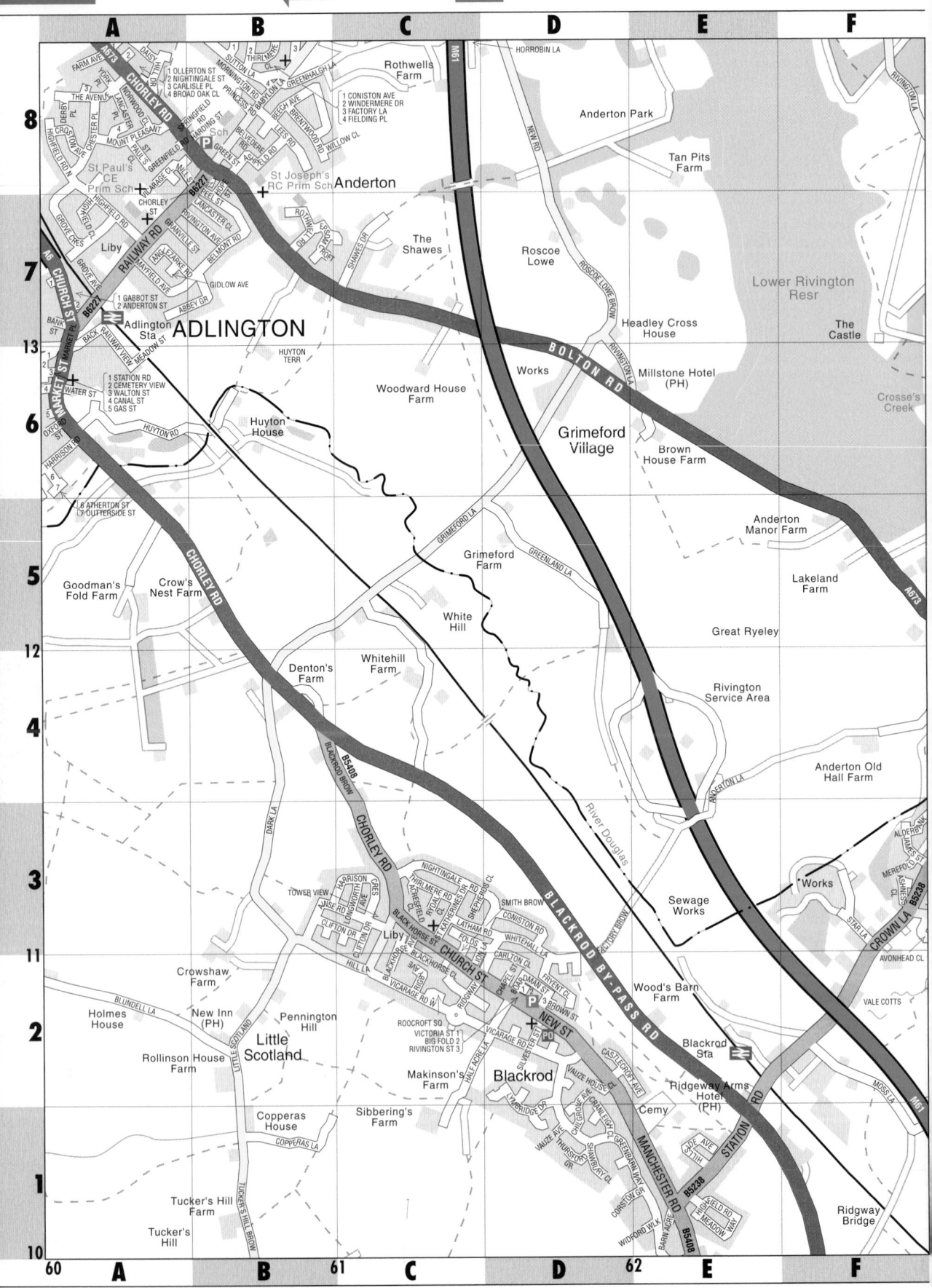

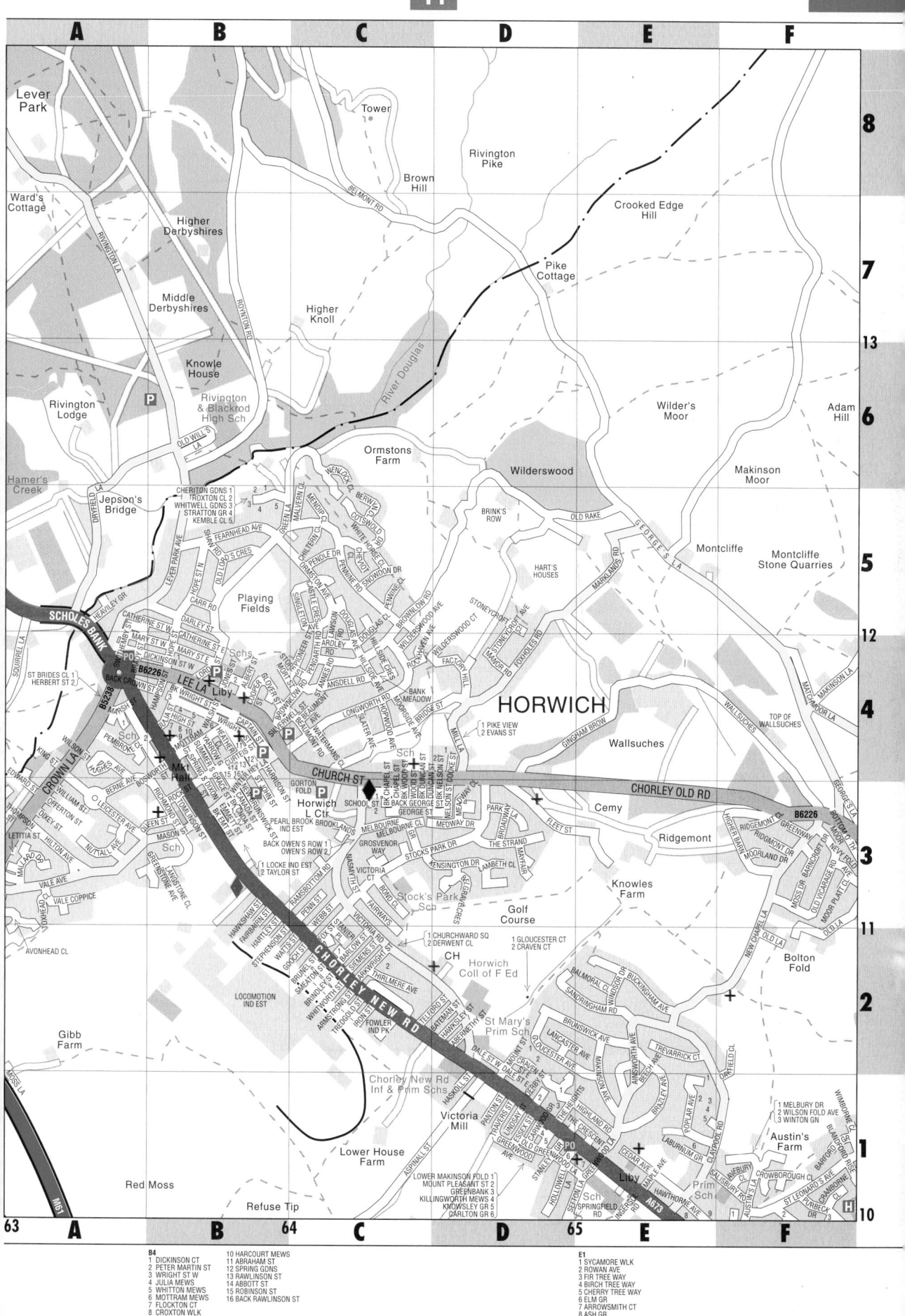

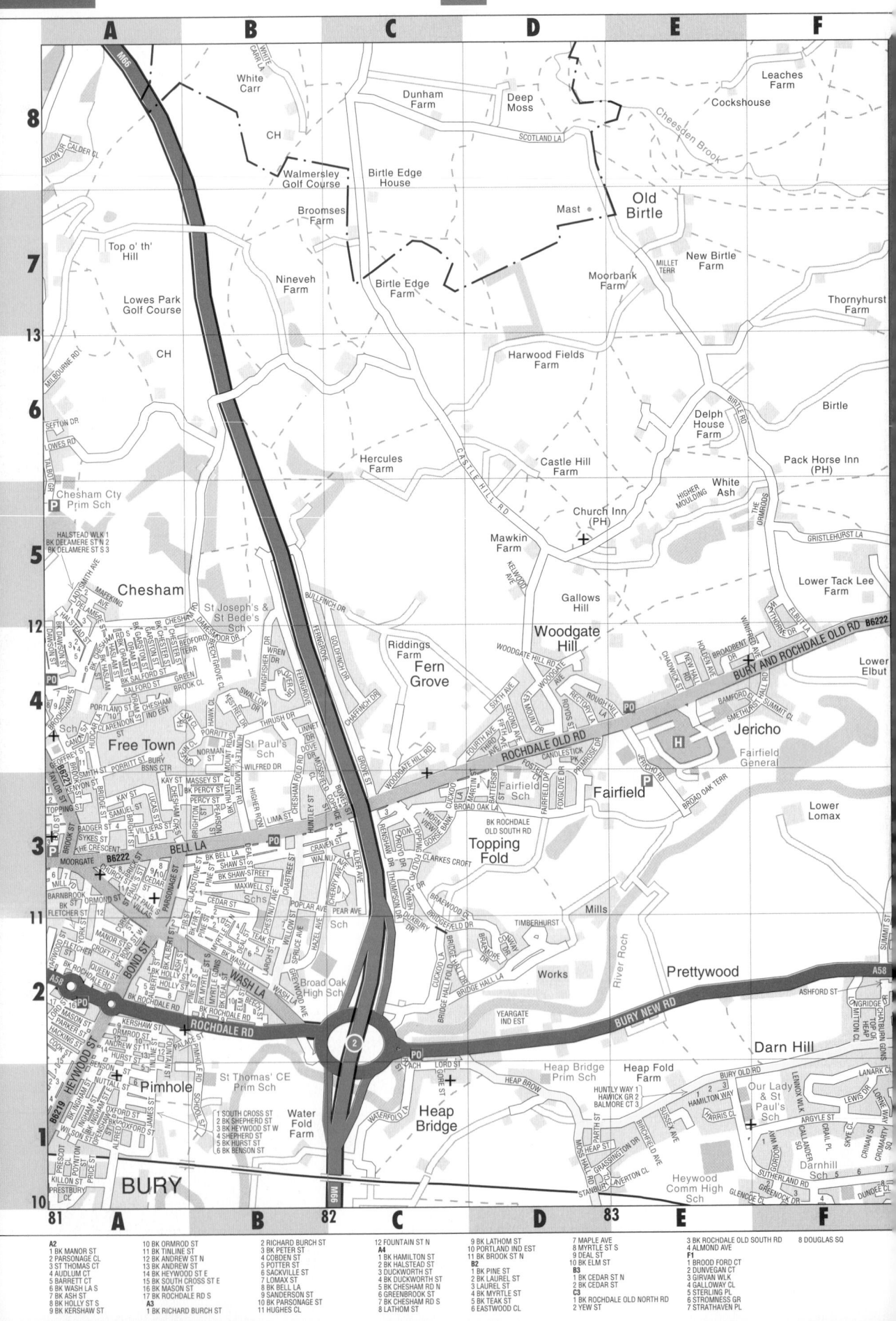

A2
1 BK MANOR ST
2 PARSONAGE CL
3 ST THOMAS CT
4 AUDLUM CT
5 BARRETT CT
6 BK WASH LA S
7 BK ASH ST
8 BK HOLLY ST S
9 BK KERSHAW ST

10 BK ORMROD ST
11 BK TINLINE ST
12 BK ANDREW ST N
13 BK ANDREW ST
14 BK HEYWOOD ST E
15 BK SOUTH CROSS ST E
16 BK MASON ST
17 BK ROCHDALE RD S
A3
1 BK RICHARD BURCH ST

2 RICHARD BURCH ST
3 BK PETER ST
4 COBDEN ST
5 POTTER ST
6 SACKVILLE ST
7 LOMAX ST
8 BK BELL LA
9 SANDERSON ST
10 BK PARSONAGE ST
11 HUGHES CL

12 FOUNTAIN ST N
A4
1 BK HAMILTON ST
2 BK HALSTEAD ST
3 BK DUCKWORTH ST
4 BK DUCKWORTH ST
5 BK CHESHAM RD N
6 GREENBROOK ST
7 BK CHESHAM RD S
8 LATHOM ST

9 BK LATHOM ST
10 PORTLAND IND EST
11 BK BROOK ST N
B2
1 BK PINE ST
2 BK LAUREL ST
3 LAUREL ST
4 BK MYRTLE ST
5 BK TEAK ST
6 EASTWOOD ST

7 MAPLE AVE
8 MYRTLE ST S
9 DEAL ST
10 BK ELM ST
B3
1 BK CEDAR ST N
2 BK CEDAR ST
C3
1 BK ROCHDALE OLD NORTH RD
2 YEW ST

3 BK ROCHDALE OLD SOUTH RD
4 ALMOND AVE
F1
1 BROOD FORD CT
2 DUNVEGAN CT
3 GIRVAN WLK
4 GALLOWAY CL
5 STERLING PL
6 STROMNESS GR
7 STRATHAVEN PL

8 DOUGLAS SQ

A   B   C   D   E   F

8

Princes
Park

Southport
Zoo

Pleasureland

7

VICTORIA WAY

17

PRIORY MEWS 1
THE ELMS 2
THE HOLLIES 3
THE WILLOWS 4
DONNINGTON LODGE 5
TUDOR MANSIONS 6

Victoria
Park

MARINE DR

ESPLANADE

BEACH

PRIORY GDNS

6

BEECHFIELD GDNS

Sunnymede
Sch

A565

B5208

ROTTEN ROW

BEACH RD

BEACH MEWS

Kingswood
Schs

TWISTFIELD CT

Birkdale Sands

BLANDFORD

WESTCLIFFE RD

PALATINE RD

LULWORTH RD

GLOUCESTER RD

CLAIRVILLE RD

5

WARREN CT

CAMBERLEY CL

ASCOT CL

WELD RD

SAXON RD

SAXENHOLME

PALACE RD

PRINCE CHARLES GDNS

16

Dunes

WINDSOR CT

OXFORD GDNS

OXFORD RD

GROVEWOOD

ST VINCENT'S WAY 1
CORNEGHIE CT 2
WELD PAR 3
HOMECHASE HSE 4

SILVERDALE

WESTBOURNE RD

THE HEYS

WESTBOURNE GDNS

LANCASTER RD

LANCASTER CL

KARBURY CL

YORK CHASE

4

LANCASTER GDNS

OXFORD CT

BICKERTON RD

Birkdale
Sta

REGENT

TREESOR

WALMER

GRANVILLE RD

GROSVENOR RD

REGENT RD

GROSVENOR

BELGRAVE RD

SUNNYSIDE

Birkdale Sch
for Hearing
Impaired

BROADLANDS

BELGRAVE PL

WORTHING RD

CROSBY RD

SULBY CL

3

SELWORTHY RD

SANDRINGHAM RD

GAINSBOROUGH RD

CHURCHFIELD

CRICKET PATH

GROSVENOR RD

CLC

CRESCENT RD

CAVENDISH

Royal Birkdale
Golf Links

SELWORTHY RD

TRAFALGAR RD

HARROD DR

CLOVER RD

CONYERS AVE

BURLINGTON RD

STANLEY AVE

15

BREEZE CL

SHERRINGHAM RD

CROKER RD

GREENBANK DR

DUNMARK RD

BLUNDELL AVE

BLUNDELL DR

HARTLEY RD

HARTLEY CRES

Birkdale

2

Greenbank
High Sch

BLUNDELL CRES

KIRKSTALL RD

GRINSTEAD CL

CLIVE RD

RICHMOND RD

CLIVE LODGE

CH

Hillside
Sta

HASTINGS RD

KIRKLEES RD

HILLSIDE RD

CARIGAN RD

ST JOHN'S RD

LANGDALE GDNS

CARNARVON RD

Liby

1

Dunes

LYNTON GR

DUNBAR RD

SANDON RD

Hillside

Birkdale
Hills

CH

Hillside
Golf Links

LYNTON RD

ASHTON RD

PO

A565

LIVERPOOL RD

A565

NORFOLK GR

THE BRIARS

NORFOLK RD

14

COASTAL RD

Sefton Coastal Path

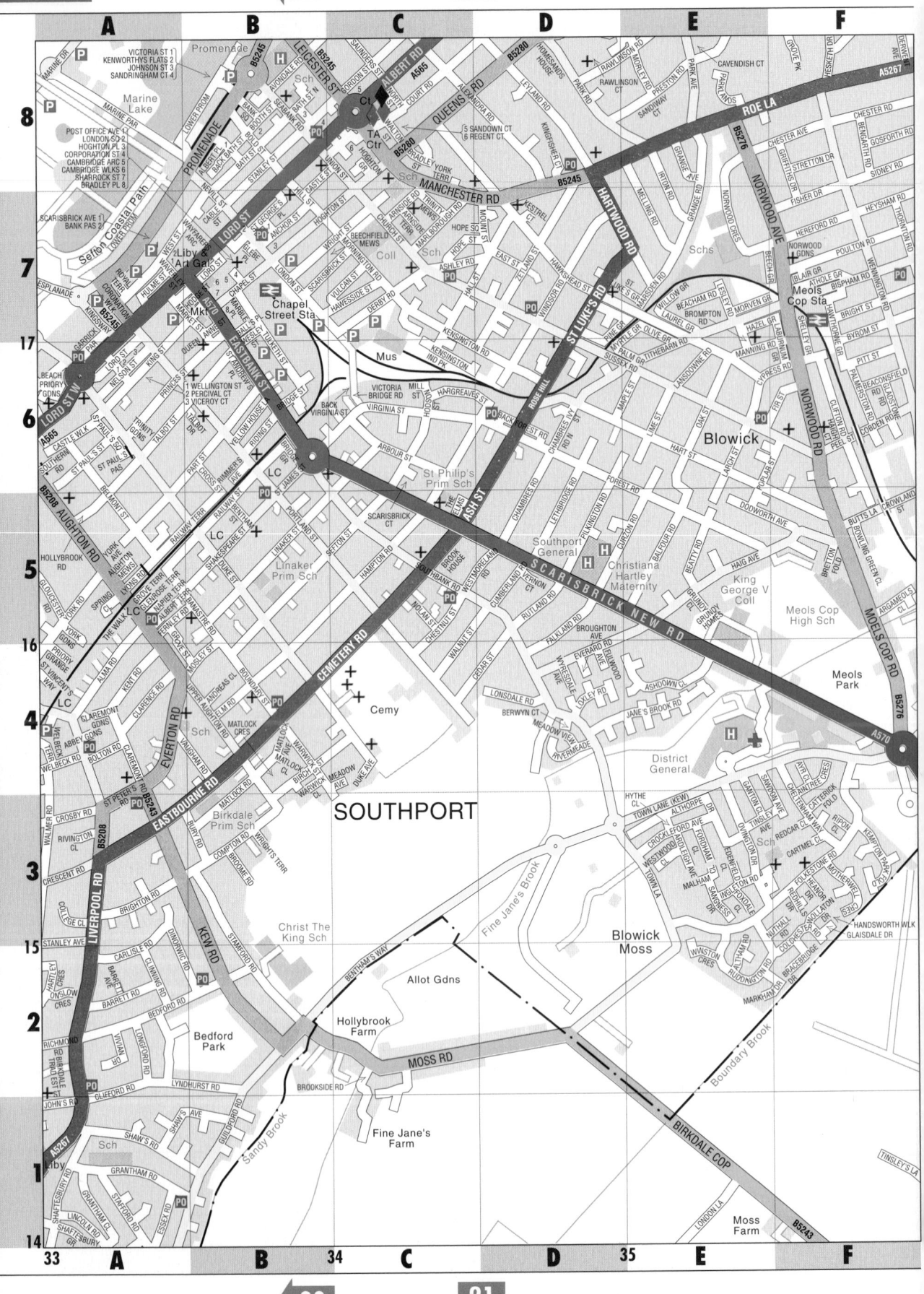

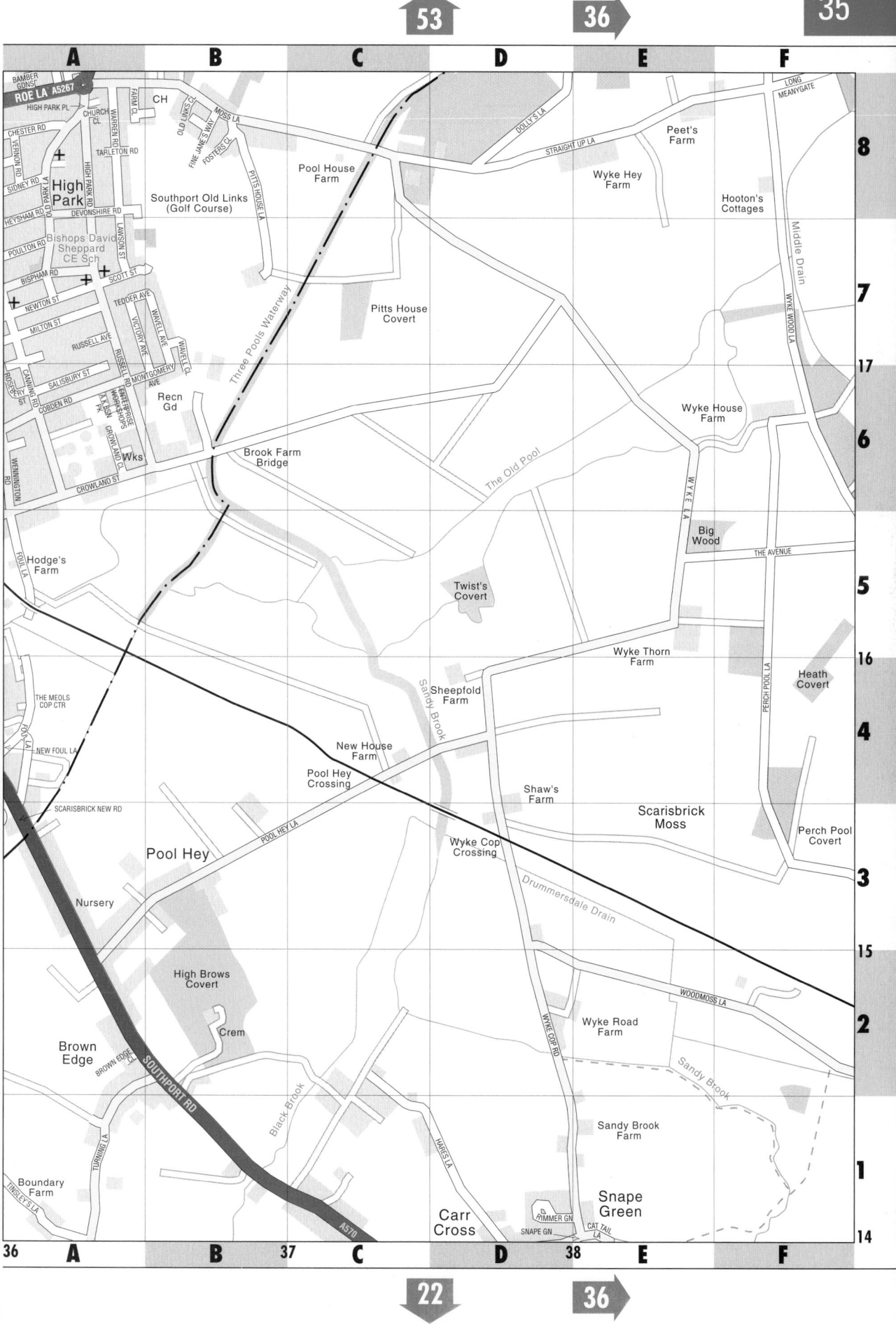

A B C D E F

BAMBER GDNS
ROE LA A5267
HIGH PARK PL
CHESTER RD
VERNON RD
SIDNEY RD
HEYSHAM RD
POULTON RD
BISPHAM RD
NEWTON ST
MILTON ST
RUSSELL AVE
SALISBURY ST
COBDEN RD
WENNINGTON RD
ROSEBERY RD
CANNING RD
CHURCH CL
WARREN RD
HIGH PARK RD
OLD PARK LA
FARM CL
TARLETON RD
SCOTT ST
LAWSON ST
TEDDER AVE
VICTORY AVE
WAVELL AVE
MONTGOMERY AVE
WAVELL CL
AJC DSN
CROWLAND CL
WORKSHOPS
ENTERPRISE PK
CROWLAND ST

High Park
Bishops David Sheppard CE Sch
Recn Gd
Wks

CH
OLD LINKS CL
MOSS LA
FINE JANE'S WAY
FOSTERS CL
PITTS HOUSE LA
Southport Old Links (Golf Course)

Pool House Farm
Pitts House Covert

Three Pools Waterway
Brook Farm Bridge

The Old Pool

DOLLY'S LA
STRAIGHT UP LA
Peet's Farm
LONG MEANYGATE
Wyke Hey Farm
Hooton's Cottages
MIDDLE DRAIN
WYKE WOOD LA
Wyke House Farm
WYKE LA
Big Wood
THE AVENUE

Twist's Covert

Hodge's Farm
FOUL LA

Sheepfold Farm
Sandy Brook

Wyke Thorn Farm
Heath Covert
PERCH POOL LA

THE MEOLS COP CTR
FOUL LA
NEW FOUL LA

New House Farm
Pool Hey Crossing
POOL HEY LA

Shaw's Farm
Scarisbrick Moss
Perch Pool Covert

SCARISBRICK NEW RD
Pool Hey
Nursery

Wyke Cop Crossing
Drummersdale Drain

WOODMOSS LA

High Brows Covert
Crem

Brown Edge
BROWN EDGE CL
SOUTHPORT RD

WYKE COP RD
Wyke Road Farm

Sandy Brook

Black Brook
HARES LA

Sandy Brook Farm

TURNING LA
Boundary Farm
TINSLEY'S LA
A570

Carr Cross

MIMMER GN
SNAPE GN
CAT TAIL LA
Snape Green

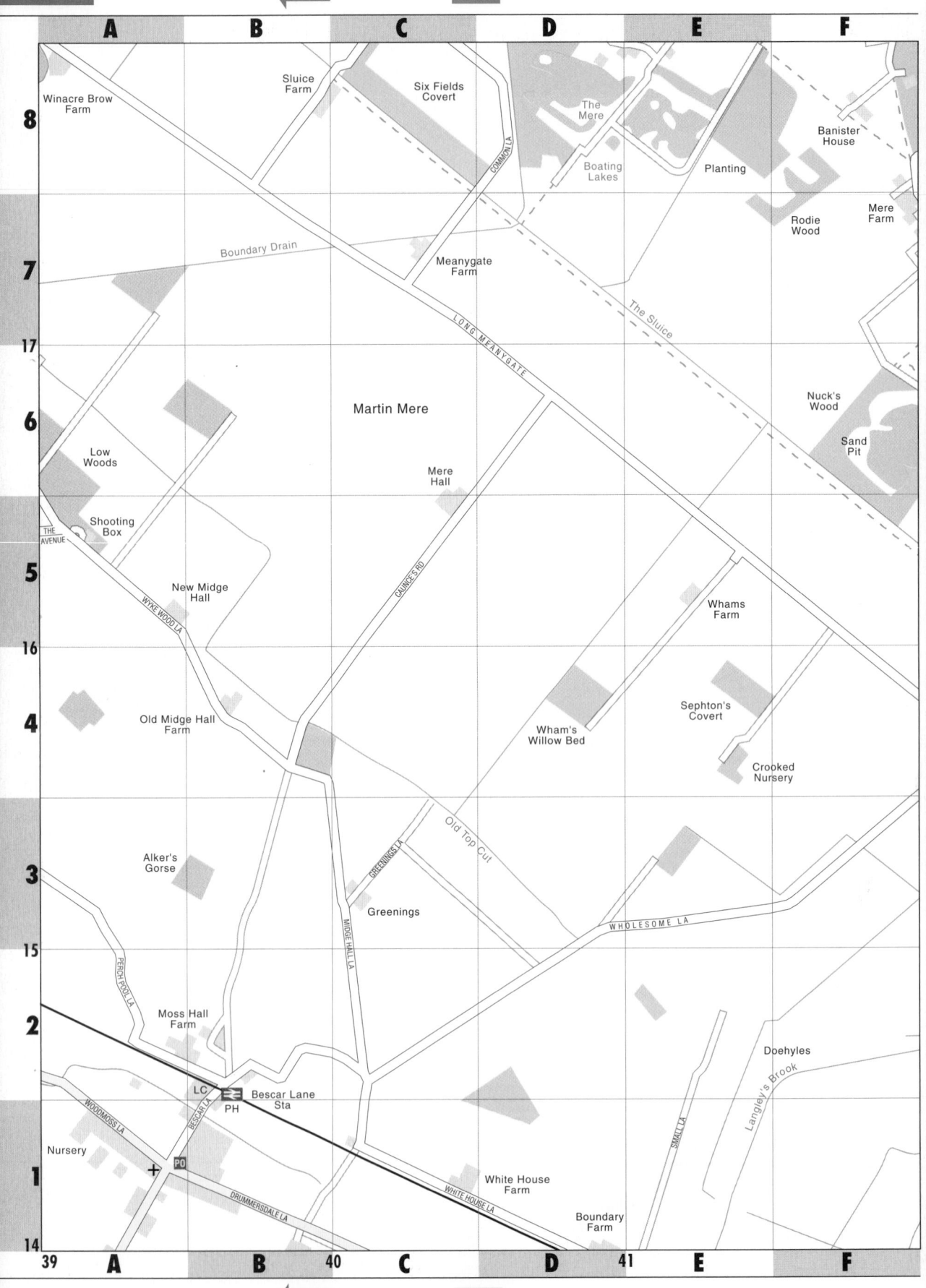

A B C D E F

8 Winacre Brow Farm

Sluice Farm

Six Fields Covert

The Mere

Boating Lakes

Planting

Banister House

Rodie Wood

Mere Farm

7 Boundary Drain

Meanygate Farm

LONG MEANYGATE

The Sluice

COMMON LA

17

6 Martin Mere

Nuck's Wood

Low Woods

Mere Hall

Sand Pit

THE AVENUE

Shooting Box

5 New Midge Hall

CAUNCE'S RD

Whams Farm

WYKE WOOD LA

16

4 Old Midge Hall Farm

Wham's Willow Bed

Sephton's Covert

Crooked Nursery

Old Top Cut

3 Alker's Gorse

GREENINGS LA

Greenings

WHOLESOME LA

MIDGE HALL LA

15

PERCH POOL LA

2 Moss Hall Farm

Doehyles

Langley's Brook

LC

Bescar Lane Sta

BESCAR LA

PH

WOODMOSS LA

SMALL LA

1 Nursery

PO

White House Farm

WHITE HOUSE LA

DRUMMERSDALE LA

Boundary Farm

14

39 A B 40 C D 41 E F

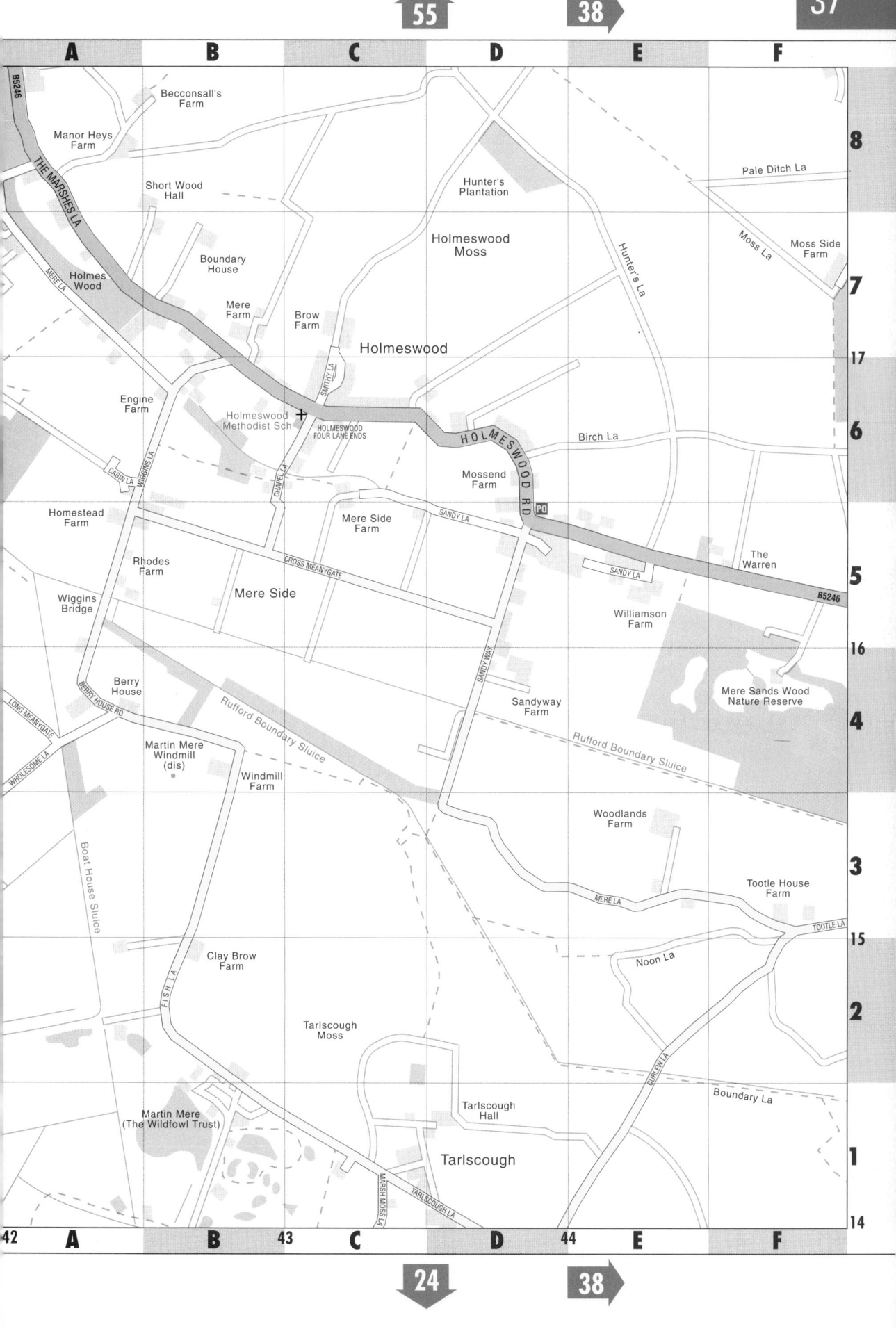

A   B   C   D   E   F

B5246

Becconsall's Farm

Manor Heys Farm

THE MARSHES LA

Short Wood Hall

Holmeswood Moss

Hunter's Plantation

Pale Ditch La

Moss La

Moss Side Farm

MERE LA

Holmes Wood

Boundary House

Mere Farm

Brow Farm

Holmeswood

Hunter's La

8

7

SMITHY LA

17

Engine Farm

Holmeswood Methodist Sch

HOLMESWOOD FOUR LANE ENDS

HOLMESWOOD RD

Birch La

6

WIGGINS LA

CABIN LA

Mossend Farm

PO

CHAPEL LA

Homestead Farm

Mere Side Farm

SANDY LA

SANDY LA

The Warren

Rhodes Farm

CROSS MEANYGATE

Mere Side

B5246

5

Wiggins Bridge

Williamson Farm

16

BERRY HOUSE RD

Berry House

Rufford Boundary Sluice

SANDY WAY

Sandyway Farm

Mere Sands Wood Nature Reserve

4

LONG MEANYGATE

WHOLESOME LA

Martin Mere Windmill (dis)

Windmill Farm

Rufford Boundary Sluice

Woodlands Farm

Boat House Sluice

Tootle House Farm

MERE LA

3

TOOTLE LA

15

FISH LA

Clay Brow Farm

Noon La

2

Tarlscough Moss

CURLEW LA

Boundary La

Martin Mere (The Wildfowl Trust)

Tarlscough Hall

1

MARSH MOSS LA

TARLSCOUGH LA

Tarlscough

14

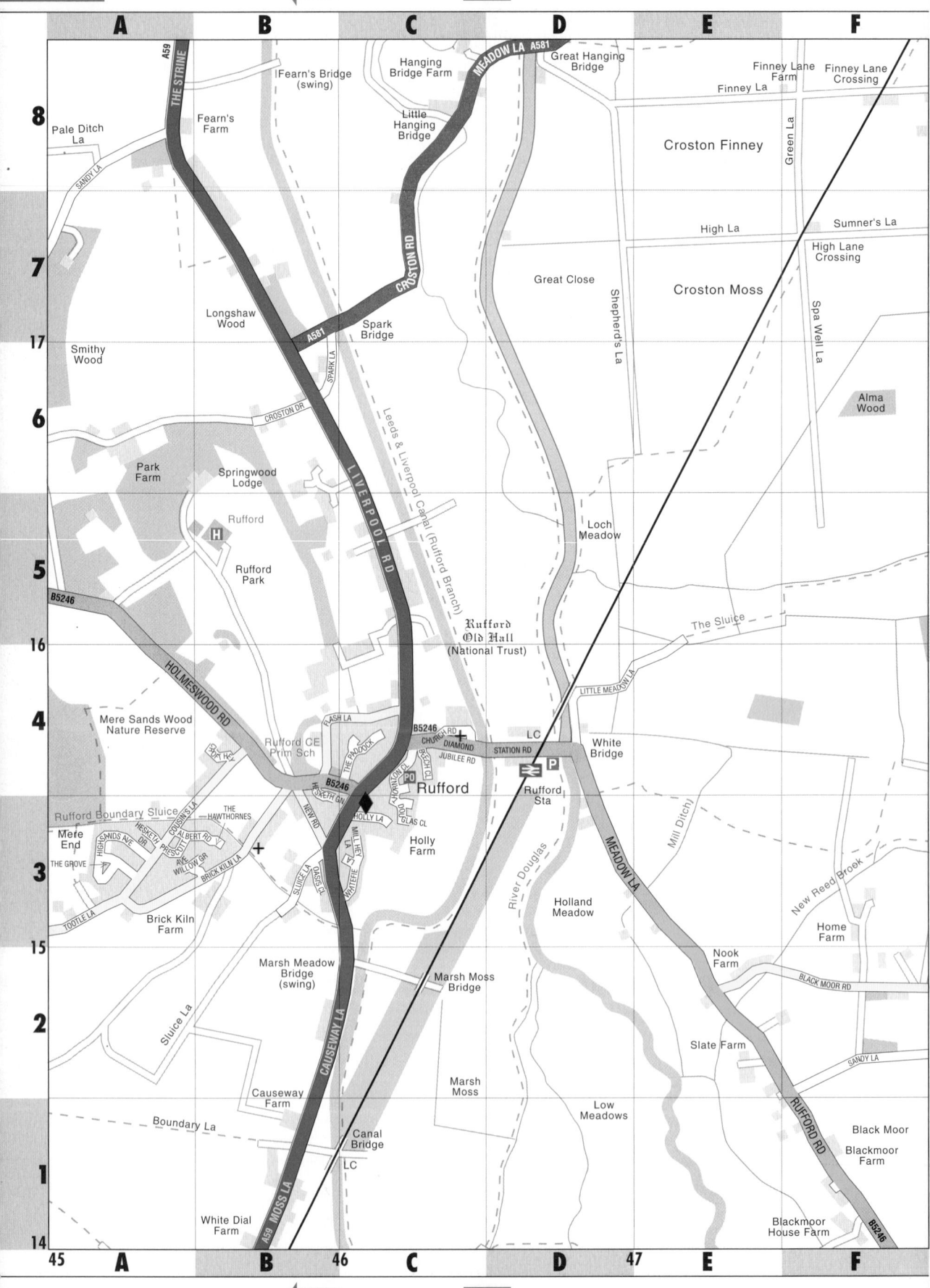

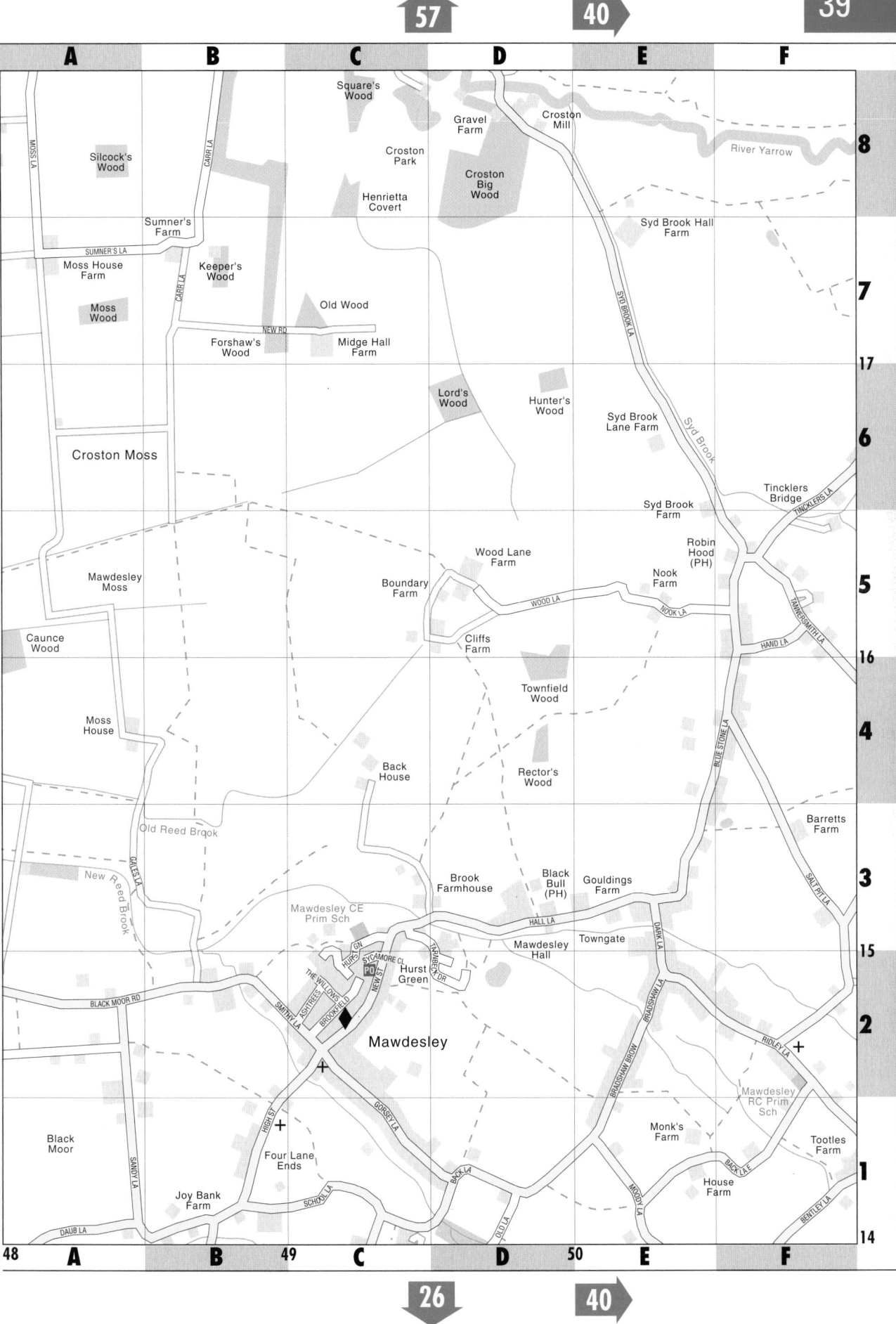

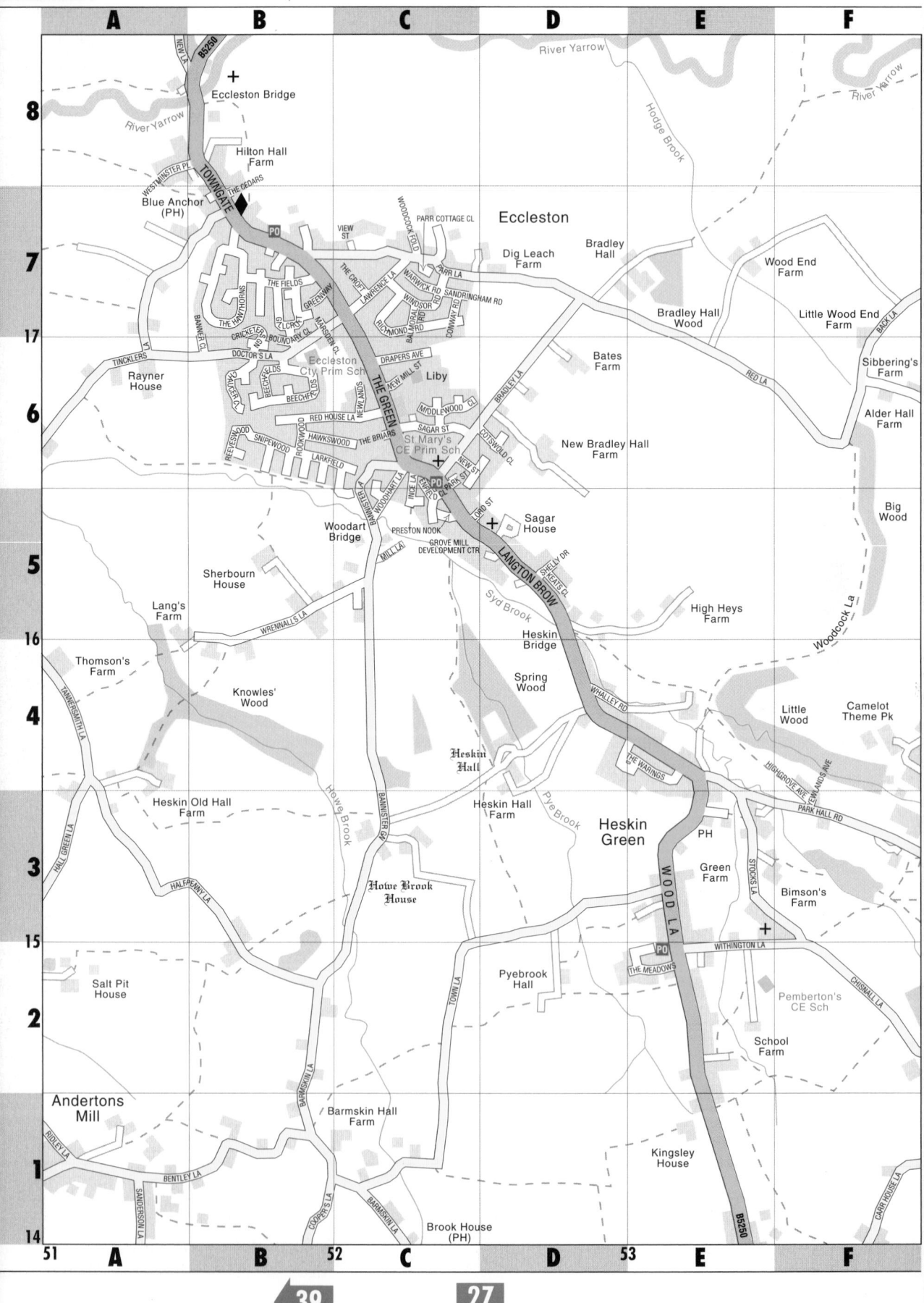

8

Eccleston Bridge

River Yarrow

River Yarrow

River Yarrow

Hodge Brook

Hilton Hall Farm

TOWNGATE

7

Blue Anchor (PH)

WESTMINSTER PL

THE CEDARS

PO

VIEW ST

WOODCOCK FOLD

PARR COTTAGE CL

Eccleston

Dig Leach Farm

Bradley Hall

Wood End Farm

Little Wood End Farm

BACK LA

17

BANNER CL

THE HAYTHORNS

CRICKETER

THE CROFT

GREENWAY

MOSSOM CL

LAWRENCE LA

WARWICK RD

WINDSOR

SANDRINGHAM RD

CONWAY RD

Bradley Hall Wood

Sibbering's Farm

RED LA

TINCKLERS

DOCTOR'S LA

BOUNDARY CL

G'L'CROT

BEECHFIELDS

DRAPERS AVE

NEW MILL ST

RICHMOND

Eccleston Cty Prim Sch

Liby

Bates Farm

BRADLEY LA

Alder Hall Farm

Rayner House

CALDERS

6

REEDSWOOD

SNIPEWOOD

ROADWOOD

HAWKSWOOD

BEECHFK

LARKFIELD

RED HOUSE LA

THE BRIARS

THE GREEN

MIDDLEWOOD CL

SAGAR ST

St Mary's CE Prim Sch

COTSWOLD CL

New Bradley Hall Farm

Big Wood

Woodcock La

NELSTROP

WOODART LA

WICK LA

PARK ST

LORD ST

NEW ST

Sagar House

Woodart Bridge

Preston Nook

Grove Mill Development Ctr

LANGTON BROW

SHELLY DR

SHEATS CL

5

Sherbourn House

MILL LA

Syd Brook

Heskin Bridge

High Heys Farm

16

Lang's Farm

WRENNALLS LA

Spring Wood

Thomson's Farm

Knowles' Wood

Heskin Hall

WHALLEY RD

Little Wood

Camelot Theme Pk

4

TANNERSMITH LA

Howe Brook

BANNISTER GN

Pye Brook

THE WARINGS

HIGHGROVE AVE

NEWLANDS AVE

PARK HALL RD

Heskin Old Hall Farm

Heskin Hall Farm

Heskin Green

PH

Green Farm

STOCKS LA

Bimson's Farm

3

HILL GREEN LA

HALFPENNY LA

Howe Brook House

WOOD LA

WITHINGTON LA

CHISNALL LA

15

BARMSKIN LA

Pyebrook Hall

PO

THE MEADOWS

Pemberton's CE Sch

Salt Pit House

TOWN LA

School Farm

2

Andertons Mill

Barmskin Hall Farm

Kingsley House

1

RIDLEY LA

BENTLEY LA

SANDERSON LA

COOPER'S LA

BARMSKIN LA

Brook House (PH)

B5250

14

A B C D E F

River Yarrow

MILL LA

PINCOCK ST

CROSS BROW WIGAN RD A49

Pincock Bridge

Pincock

Charnock's Farm

Old House Farm

Hypermarket

PH

SOUTHPORT RD A581

FOXHOLE RD

8

Bolton Green

BACK LA

Calderbank Farm

SIBBERING BROW

CHARNOCK BROW

LUCAS AVE

GERMAN LA

Fox Hole Wood

Sewage Works

CHORLEY WEST BSNS PK

OLD WIGAN RD

Sewage Works

Valley Farm

Common Bank

COMMON BANK LA

COPPERWOOD WAY

7

Ratho Park Farm

Charnock Brow Farm

Golf Course

COMMON BANK EMPLOYMENT AREA

Wallets Wood

Worsley Farm

Bowling Green (PH)

Tan House Farm

Yarrow Farm

River Yarrow

17

New Park Hall

Charnock Old Hall

OLD HALL LA

DELPH LA

Charnock Green

Roscoe House

Willow Tree Farm

6

Motel

Parker's i' th' Fields

5

Hotel

Charnock House

DELPH LA

Fisher's Farm

Parker's Wood

Dam Wood

BROOK LA

FOUR LANE ENDS

Charnock House Farm

Charnock Richard

Iddon House Farm

DOB BROW

16

P

PRESTON RD

PO

CHURCH LA

MEADOWLANDS

LICHEN CL

ALMA DR

CHURCH FOLD

Sharrocks Farm

B5251

COPPULL RD

BIRKACRE RD

4

Park Hall L Ctr

P

Yew Tree Farm

CHARTER LA

Charnock Richard CE Prim Sch

LEESON AVE

ALDER DR

WILLOW DR

ROBIN CL

NURSERY CL

PH

FREEMAN'S LA

WHITE GATE FOLD

SHARRATS PATH

15

P

i

Service Area

PARK HALL RD

CHORLEY LA

SOUTHGATES

NEARGATES

WEIRE FOLD

HOLLY CRES

BIRCHWOOD DR

PEAR TREE AVE

THE LAURELS

CLAUDITTA CL

NEW RD

BIRKACRE BROW

3

Welch Farm

Motel

MILL LA

Golf Course

Haydocks Farm

Row High Wood

LONGFIELD AVE

HOLT AVE

OAKWOOD RD

PLEASANT VIEW

LONGWORTH AVE

2

Chisnall House

CROSTON LA

Guest's Farm

Hind's Head (PH)

Coppull

NORTHENDEN RD

MOSS BANK

MAVIS DR

MILL LA

STATION RD

THE HAZELS

ASCOT RD

THE KEYS

THE CHESTNUTS

RVE HEY DR

CLAYTONGATE

THE BRAMBLES

LANCASTER ST

Sch

CHAPEL LA

MILLSTONE CL

BROOK

GOOSE GREEN AVE

CARR HOUSE LA

Knob Farm

M6

THE FOXWOODS

TOWN LA

WHITTLE BROW

Haydock Farm

Whittle Bridge Farm

TANYARD CL

HEWLETT

WESTEND AVE

TANSLEY AVE

A49

B5251

PARK RD

DARLINGTON ST

KIMBERLEY ST

REGENT ST

BENTHAM RD

SPRINGFIELD RD

SOUTH RD

SPENDMORE LA

MILTON CT

ALDER GR

HURST RD

BIRCH RD

RAILWAY COTTS

Liby

1

14

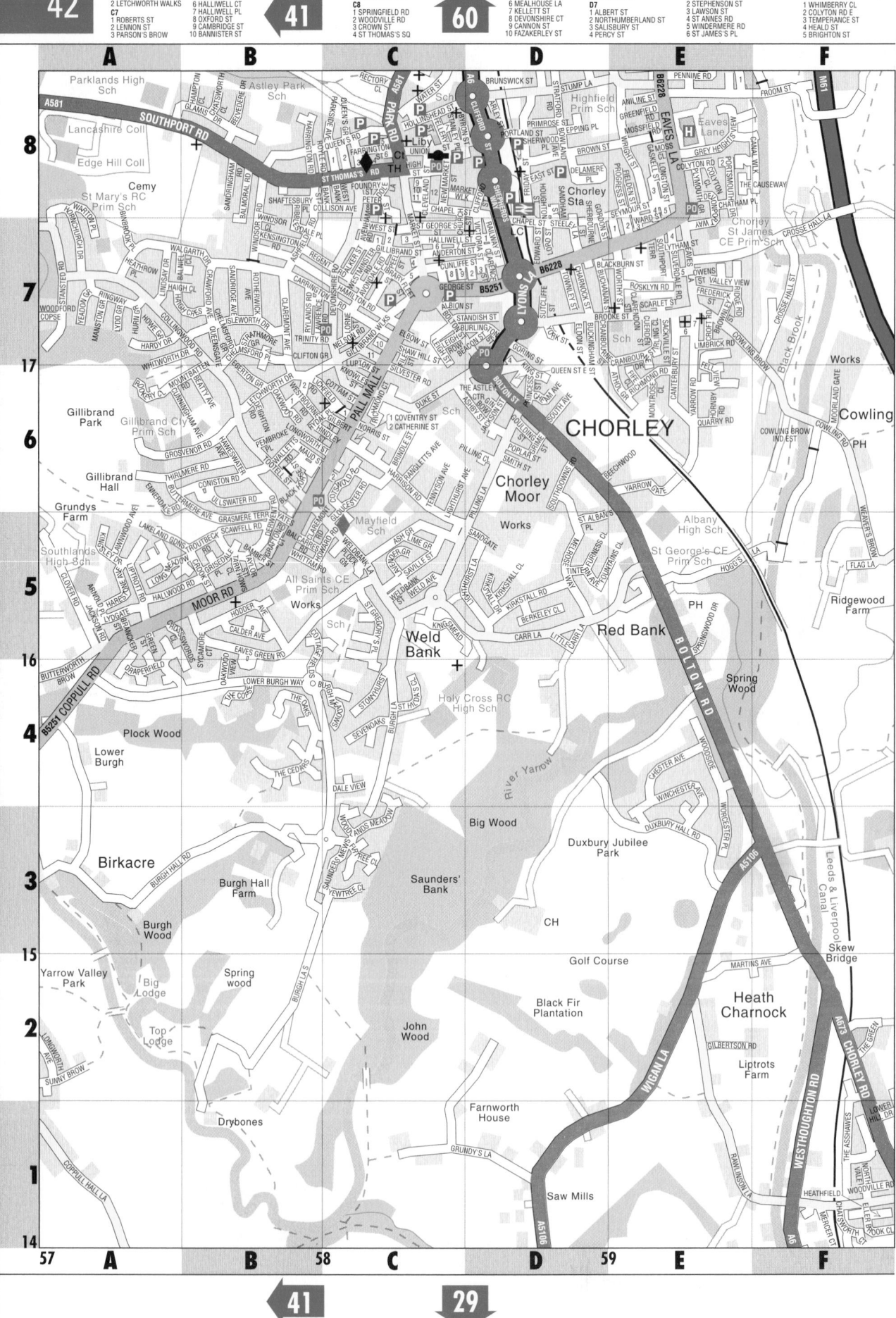

B6
1 VENTNOR RD
2 LETCHWORTH WALKS
C7
1 ROBERTS ST
2 LENNON ST
3 PARSON'S BROW

4 WHALLEY ST
5 CHEAPSIDE
6 HALLIWELL CT
7 HALLIWELL PL
8 OXFORD ST
9 CAMBRIDGE ST
10 BANNISTER ST

C7
11 RAWCLIFFE RD
C8
1 SPRINGFIELD RD
2 WOODVILLE RD
3 CROWN ST
4 ST THOMAS'S SQ

C8
5 BACK MOUNT
6 MEALHOUSE LA
7 KELLETT ST
8 DEVONSHIRE CT
9 CANNON ST
10 FAZAKERLEY ST

11 BACK FAZAKERLEY ST
12 MARKET PL
D7
1 ALBERT ST
2 NORTHUMBERLAND ST
3 SALISBURY ST
4 PERCY ST

E7
1 CAVENDISH ST
2 STEPHENSON ST
3 LAWSON ST
4 ST ANNES RD
5 WINDERMERE RD
6 ST JAMES'S PL

7 ST JAMES'S ST
E8
1 WHIMBERRY CL
2 COLYTON RD E
3 TEMPERANCE ST
4 HEALD ST
5 BRIGHTON ST

41
60
41
29

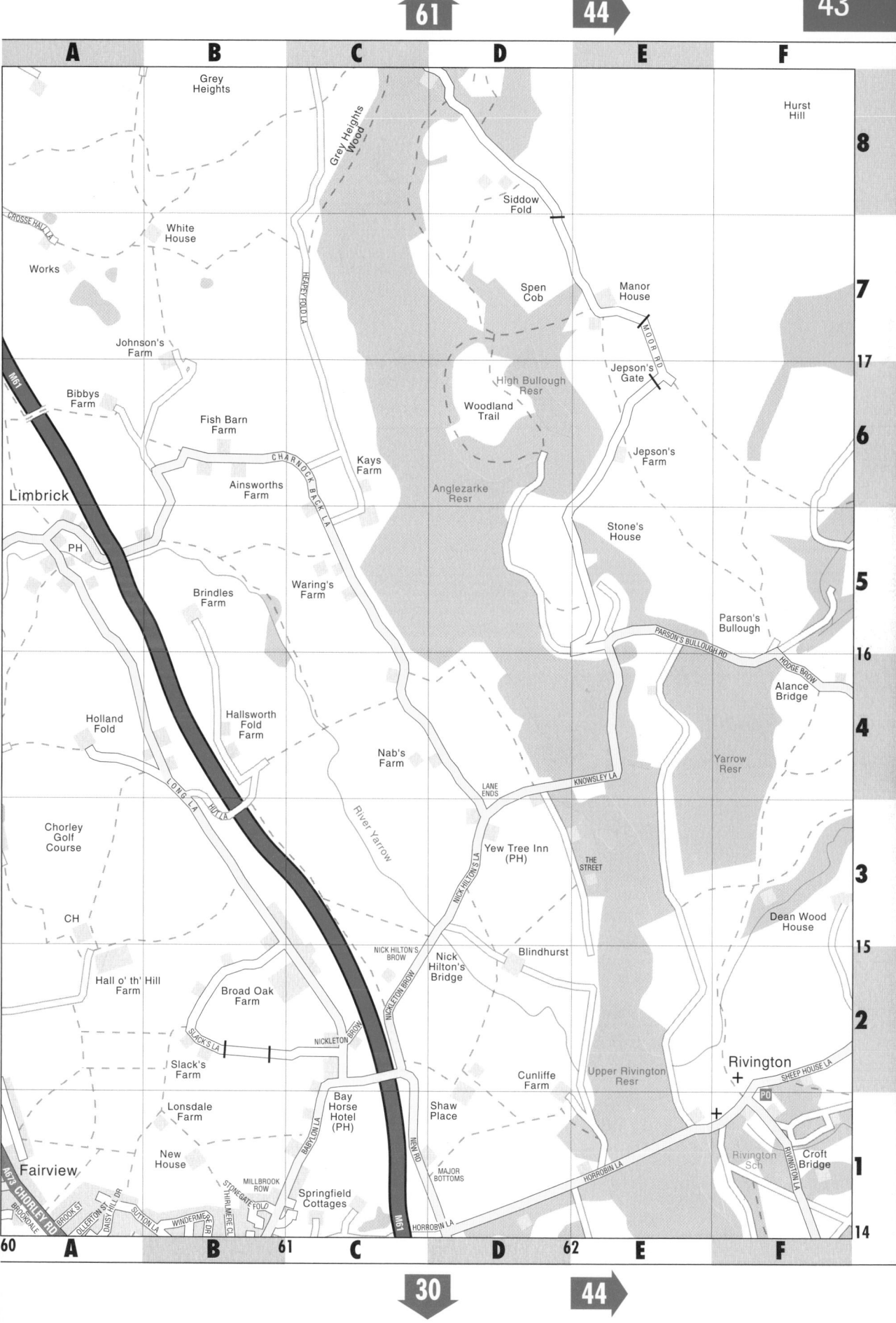

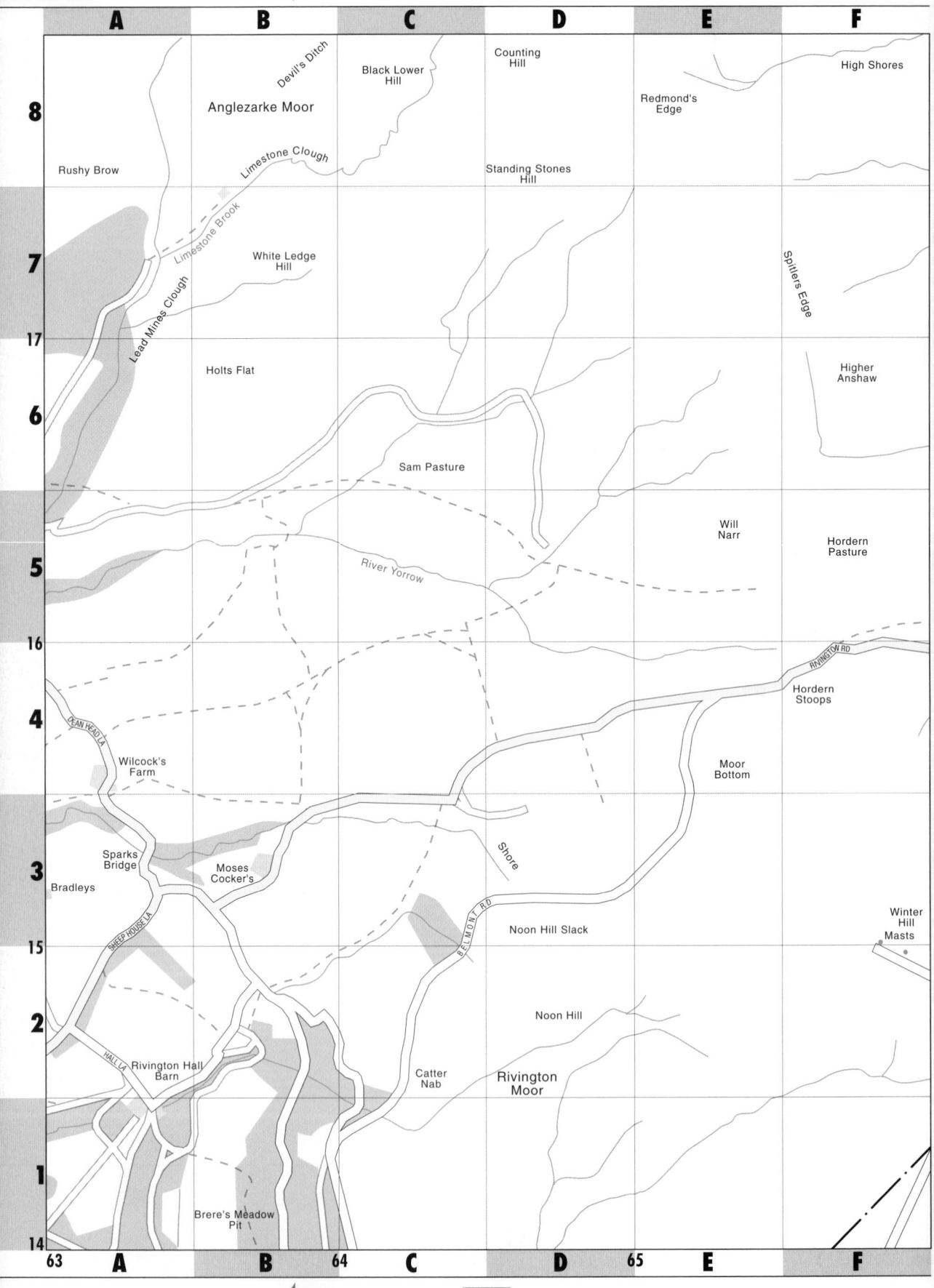

	A	B	C	D	E	F

8

High Shores

Counting
Hill

Devil's Ditch

Black Lower
Hill

Redmond's
Edge

Anglezarke Moor

Rushy Brow

Limestone Clough

Standing Stones
Hill

Limestone Brook

7

White Ledge
Hill

Spitlers Edge

Lead Mines Clough

17

Holts Flat

Higher
Anshaw

6

Sam Pasture

Will
Narr

Hordern
Pasture

5

River Yorrow

16

RIVINGTON RD

Hordern
Stoops

4

DEAN HEAD LA

Wilcock's
Farm

Moor
Bottom

Shore

3

Sparks
Bridge

Moses
Cocker's

Bradleys

SHEEP HOUSE LA

BELMONT RD

Noon Hill Slack

Winter
Hill
Masts

15

2

Noon Hill

HALL LA

Rivington Hall
Barn

Catter
Nab

Rivington
Moor

1

Brere's Meadow
Pit

14

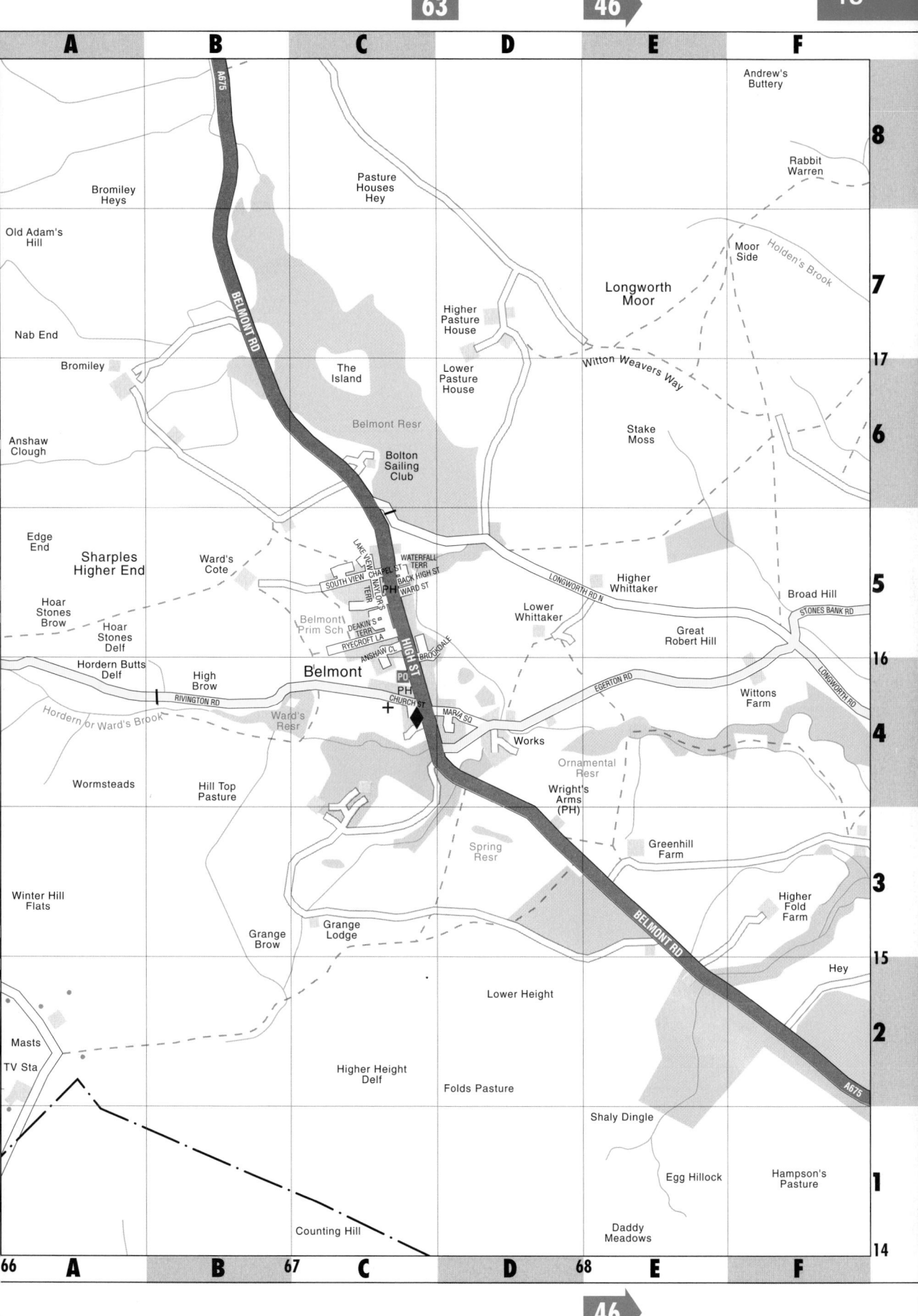

A B C D E F

Andrew's Buttery

Rabbit Warren

Bromiley Heys

Old Adam's Hill

Pasture Houses Hey

Moor Side

Longworth Moor

Holden's Brook

Nab End

Bromiley

Higher Pasture House

Witton Weavers Way

Anshaw Clough

The Island

Lower Pasture House

Stake Moss

Belmont Resr

Bolton Sailing Club

Edge End

Sharples Higher End

Ward's Cote

WATERFALL TERR

Longworth Rd N

Higher Whittaker

Broad Hill

STONES BANK RD

Hoar Stones Brow

Hoar Stones Delf

LAKE VIEW
SOUTH VIEW
CHAPEL ST
NAYLOR'S TERR
BACK HIGH ST
WARD ST
PH

Lower Whittaker

Great Robert Hill

Hordern Butts Delf

High Brow

Belmont Prim Sch

DEAKIN'S TERR
RYECROFT LA
ANSHAW CL

HIGH ST
BROOKDALE

Belmont

Wittons Farm

Longworth Rd

RIVINGTON RD

PO
PH
CHURCH ST
MARIA SQ

Egerton Rd

Hordern or Ward's Brook

Ward's Resr

Works

Wormsteads

Hill Top Pasture

Ornamental Resr

Wright's Arms (PH)

Greenhill Farm

Higher Fold Farm

Winter Hill Flats

Grange Brow

Grange Lodge

Spring Resr

BELMONT RD

Hey

Lower Height

Masts
TV Sta

Higher Height Delf

Folds Pasture

A675

Shaly Dingle

Hampson's Pasture

Egg Hillock

Counting Hill

Daddy Meadows

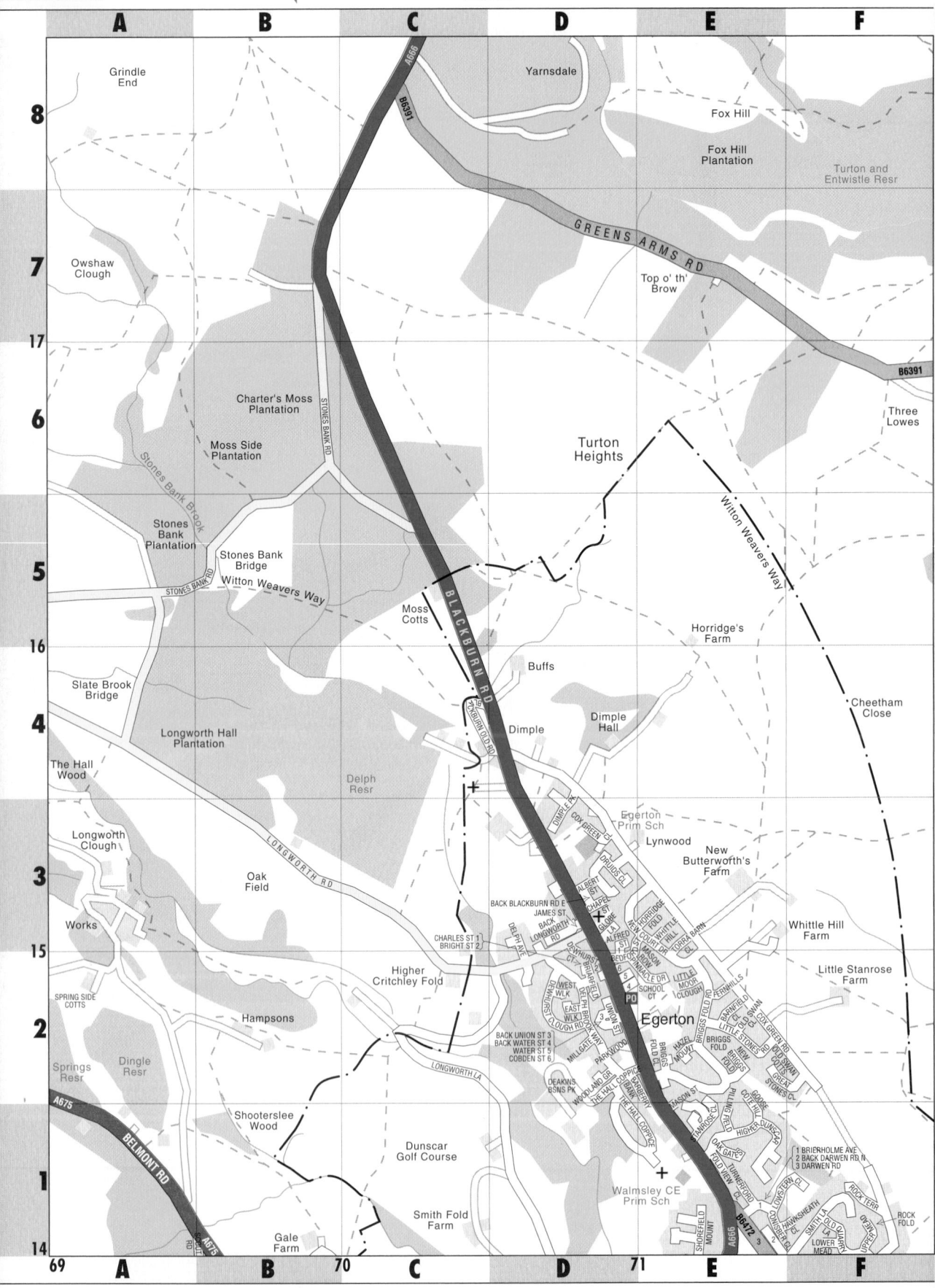

A B C D E F

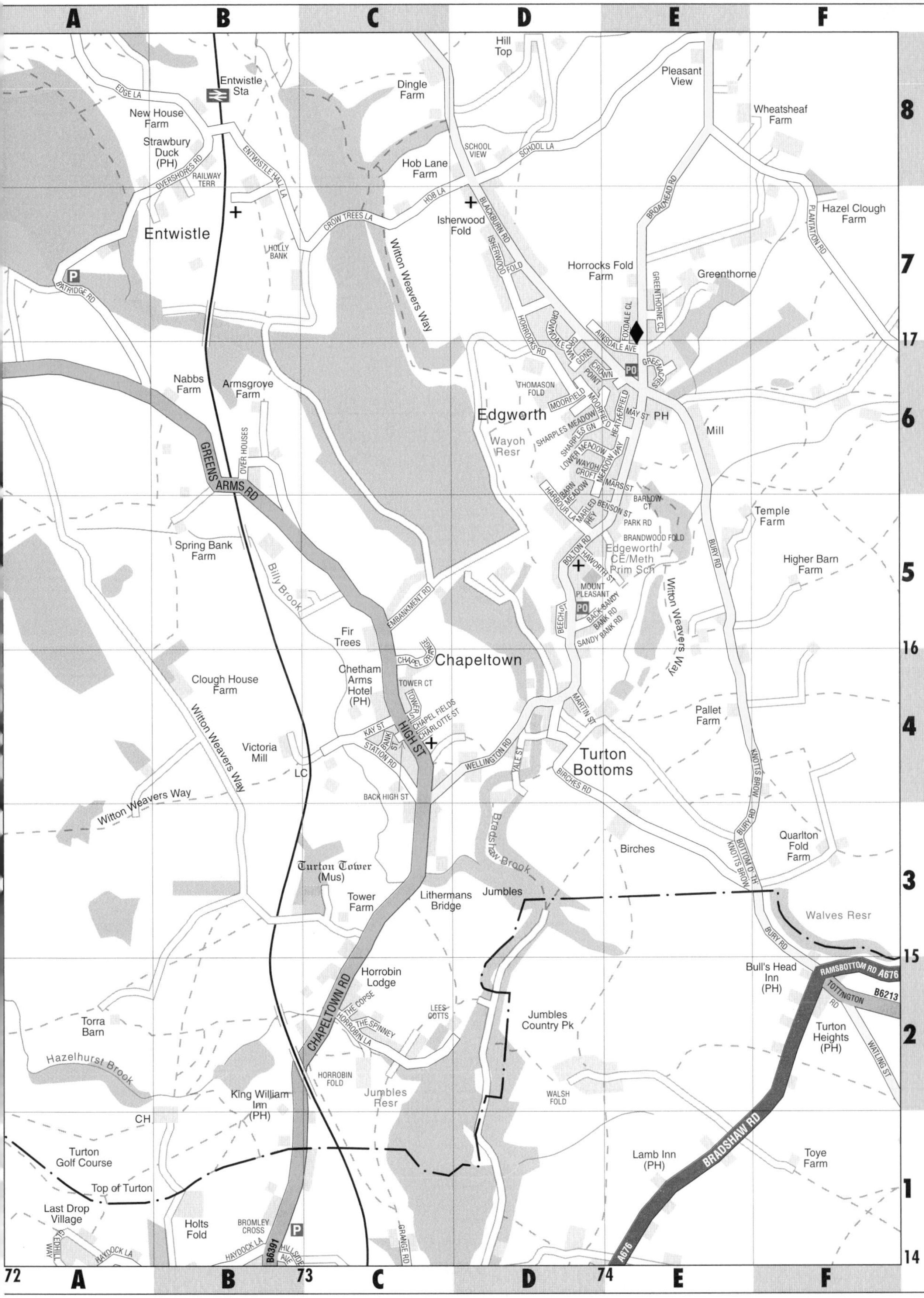

8

New House Farm
Entwistle Sta
FUDGE LA
Strawbury Duck (PH)
OVERSHORES RD
RAILWAY TERR
ENTWISTLE HALL LA
Dingle Farm
Hill Top
Pleasant View
Wheatsheaf Farm
Hazel Clough Farm
BROADHEAD RD
PLANTATION RD

Entwistle
HOLLY BANK
CROW TREES LA
Hob Lane Farm
HOB LA
SCHOOL VIEW
SCHOOL LA
BLACKBURN RD
ISHERWOOD FOLD
Isherwood Fold
Horrocks Fold Farm
Greenthorne
GREENTHORNE RD

7

P
BATRIDGE RD
Nabbs Farm
Armsgrove Farm
Witton Weavers Way
WITTON WEAVERS WAY
HORROCKS FOLD
RAYDALE WY
OXENWOOD
CROWN
AINSDALE AVE
FOXDALE CL
GREY CL
PO
17

OVER HOUSES
Thomason Fold
Edgworth
MOORFIELD
WAYOH WY
MAY ST PH
Mill

GREENS ARMS RD
Wayoh Resr
SHARPLES MEADOW
SHARPLES GN
LOW MEADOW
WAYOH MEADOW
MARS ST
Temple Farm

6

Spring Bank Farm
Billy Brook
HARBOUR LA
MARLED HEY
BARN MEADOW
CROFT
BENSON ST
BARLOW CT
PARK RD
Higher Barn Farm

EMBANKMENT RD
Fir Trees
BOLTON RD
HAWORTH ST
Edgworth CE/Meth Prim Sch
BRANDWOOD FOLD
BURY RD

5

Clough House Farm
Witton Weavers Way
Chetham Arms Hotel (PH)
Chapeltown
MOUNT PLEASANT
BEECH ST
PO
BACK SANDY BANK RD
SANDY BANK RD
Witton Weavers Way

16

Victoria Mill
CHAPEL LA
TOWER CT
CHAPEL FIELDS
CHARLOTTE ST
KAY ST
BANK ST
TOWER ST
HIGH ST
WELLINGTON RD
YALE ST
MARTIN ST
BIRCHES RD
Turton Bottoms
Pallet Farm
KNOTTS BROW

4

Witton Weavers Way
STATION RD
LC
BACK HIGH ST
Bradshaw Brook
Birches
KNOTTS BROW
BURY RD
BOTTOM O' TH' KNOTTS BROW
Quarlton Fold Farm

3

Turton Tower (Mus)
Tower Farm
Lithermans Bridge
Jumbles
Walves Resr
BURY RD

CHAPELTOWN RD
Horrobin Lodge
THE COPSE
HORROBIN LA
THE SPINNEY
LEES COTTS
Jumbles Country Pk
Bull's Head Inn (PH)
RAMSBOTTOM RD A676
TOTTINGTON RD
B6213
15

Torra Barn
Hazelhurst Brook
HORROBIN FOLD
Jumbles Resr
Turton Heights (PH)
WATLING ST

2

King William Inn (PH)
WALSH FOLD
Lamb Inn (PH)
BRADSHAW RD
Toye Farm

1

Turton Golf Course
CH
Top of Turton
Last Drop Village
Holts Fold
BROMLEY CROSS
P
HAYDOCK LA
HILLSIDE AVE
B6391
GRANGE RD
A676

14

REDHILL WAY

72 A B 73 C D 74 E F

47
66

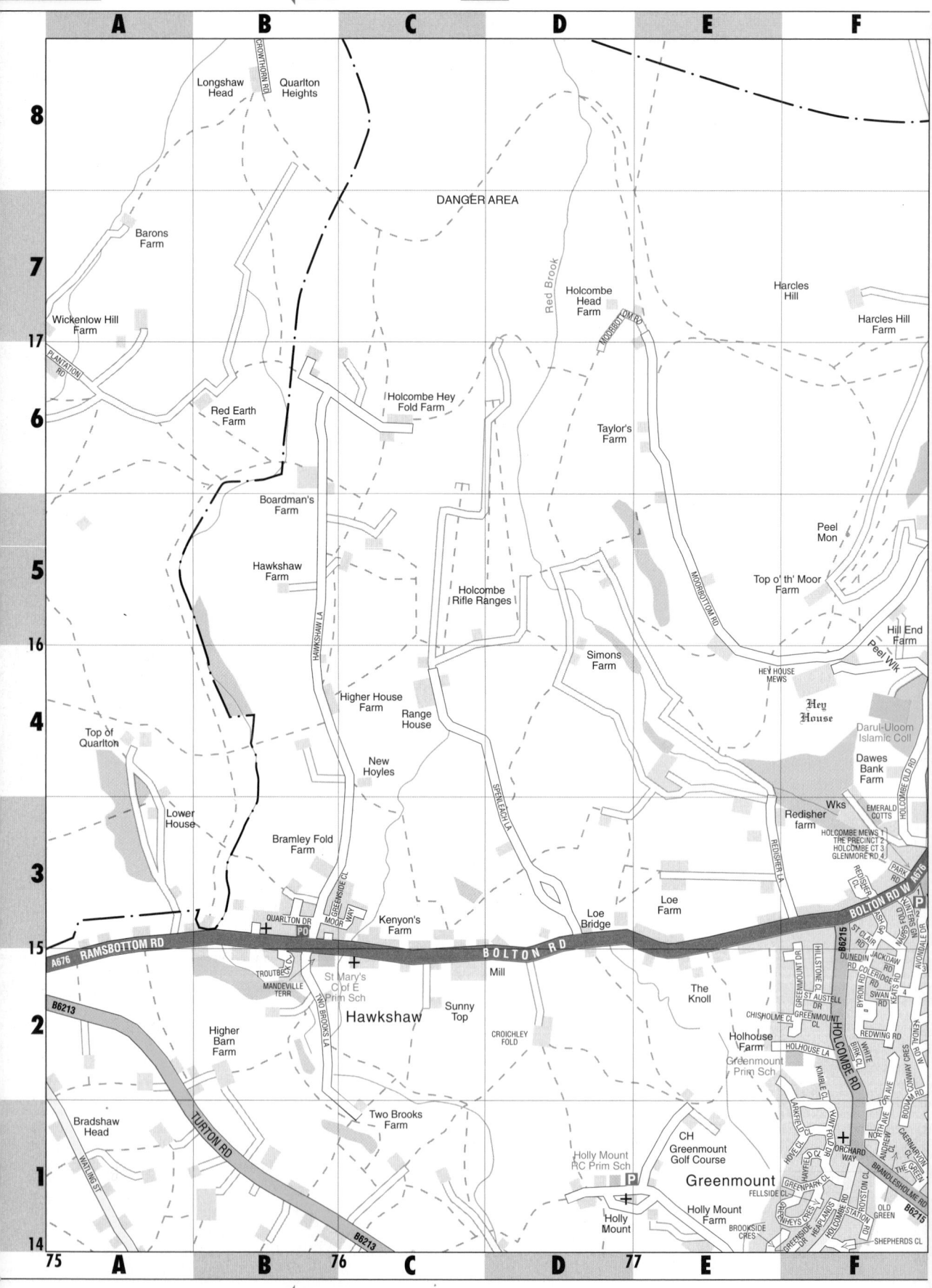

47

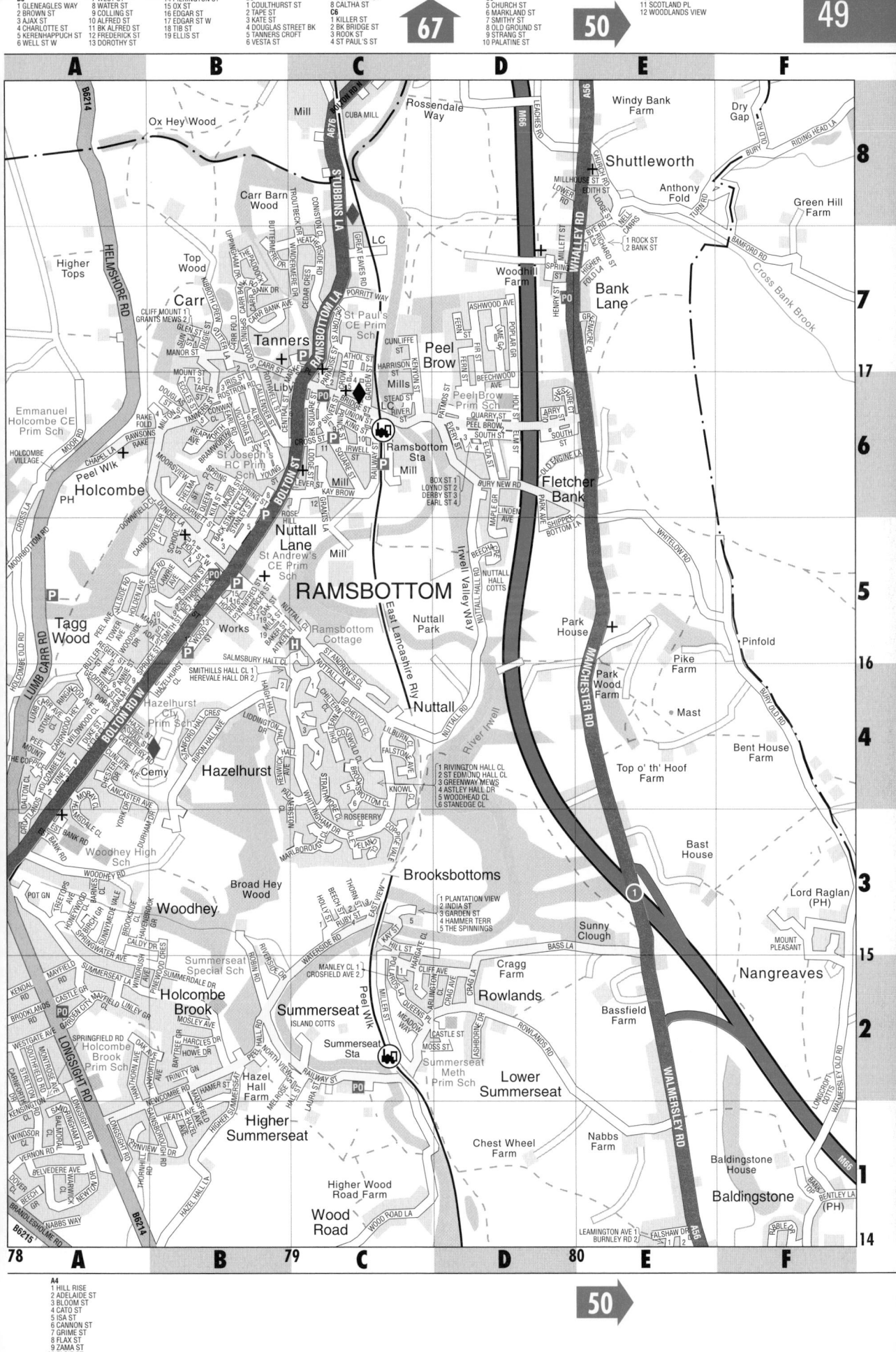

A B C D E F

8

7

17

6

5

16

4

3

15

2

1

14

A B C D E F

RIDING HEAD LA

A680

Mill

Smithy Carr
Farm

Kay Close
Farm

Rossendale Way

COAL RD

Fecit
Farm

FECIT LA

FECIT LA

Turf Moor

Cheesden
Pasture

Man Road Ditch

ROCHDALE RD

Moor Side
Farm

Rossendale
Sch

BLACK LA

Close Nooks
Farm

MOOR SIDE LA

Cheesden Brook

BAMFORD RD

Gate
House

Harden Brook

Cheesden
Bridge

Cheesden

Tom
Hill

Wham
Hill

Harden Moor

Wham Hill
Farm

Lumb
Bridge

New Inn
(PH)

Owd Betts
(PH)

EDENFIELD RD

Ashworth
Moor

Throstle
Hill

Croston
Close

Croston
Close
Bottoms

Ashworth
Moor
Resr

A680

Mam Hill

Ridshaw
Farm

Far Buckhurst
Brow

Kirkby's

CROSTON CLOSE RD

Rough
Lee

Far Croft
Head

Buckhurst
Brow

BUCKHURST RD

Snape
Hill

Buckhurst
Farm

Closes

SALES LA

Top o' th' Hill
Farm

ASHWORTH RD

Sales's
Farm

Whitewall
Farm

Lark
Mount

DEEPLY VALE LA

Deeply
Vale

Deeply
Hill

Wind Hill

Bird
Fields

Copped Hill
Farm

Stand
Lees
Farm

Wind Hill
Farm

Cob House
Nab

Gindles
Farm

BENTLEY LA

M66

Cob House
Farm

Copped
Hill

WHITE CARR LA

Shepherd
Hey

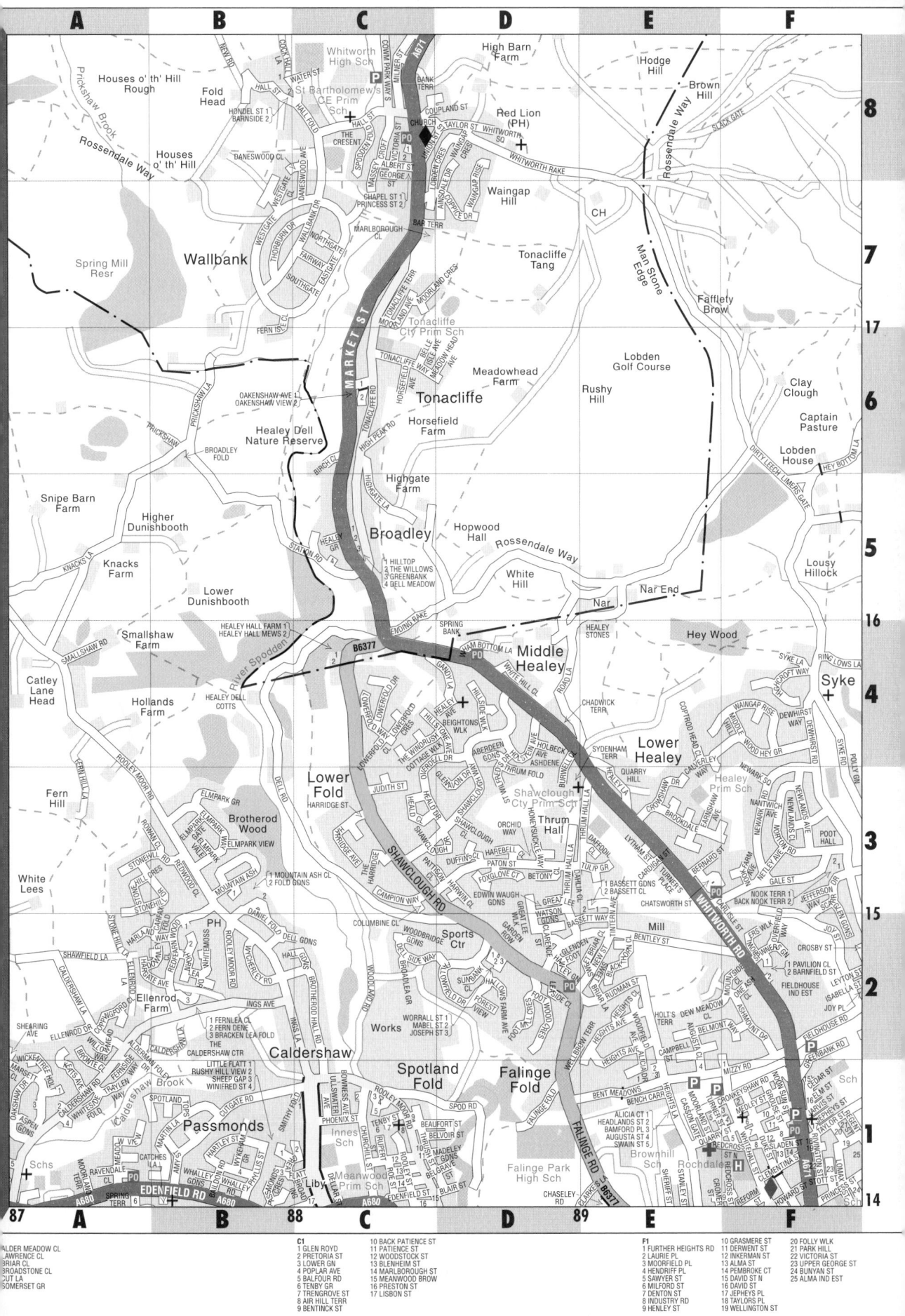

C1
1 GLEN ROYD
2 PRETORIA ST
3 LOWER GN
4 POPLAR AVE
5 BALFOUR RD
6 TENBY GR
7 TRENGROVE ST
8 AIR HILL TERR
9 BENTINCK ST

10 BACK PATIENCE ST
11 PATIENCE ST
12 WOODSTOCK ST
13 BLENHEIM ST
14 MARLBOROUGH ST
15 MEANWOOD BROW
16 PRESTON ST
17 LISBON ST

F1
1 FURTHER HEIGHTS RD
2 LAURIE PL
3 MOORFIELD PL
4 HENDRIFF PL
5 SAWYER ST
6 MILFORD ST
7 DENTON ST
8 INDUSTRY RD
9 HENLEY ST

10 GRASMERE ST
11 DERWENT ST
12 INKERMAN ST
13 ALMA ST
14 PEMBROKE CT
15 DAVID ST N
16 DAVID ST
17 JEPHEYS PL
18 TAYLORS PL
19 WELLINGTON ST

20 FOLLY WLK
21 PARK HILL
22 VICTORIA ST
23 UPPER GEORGE ST
24 BUNYAN ST
25 ALMA IND EST

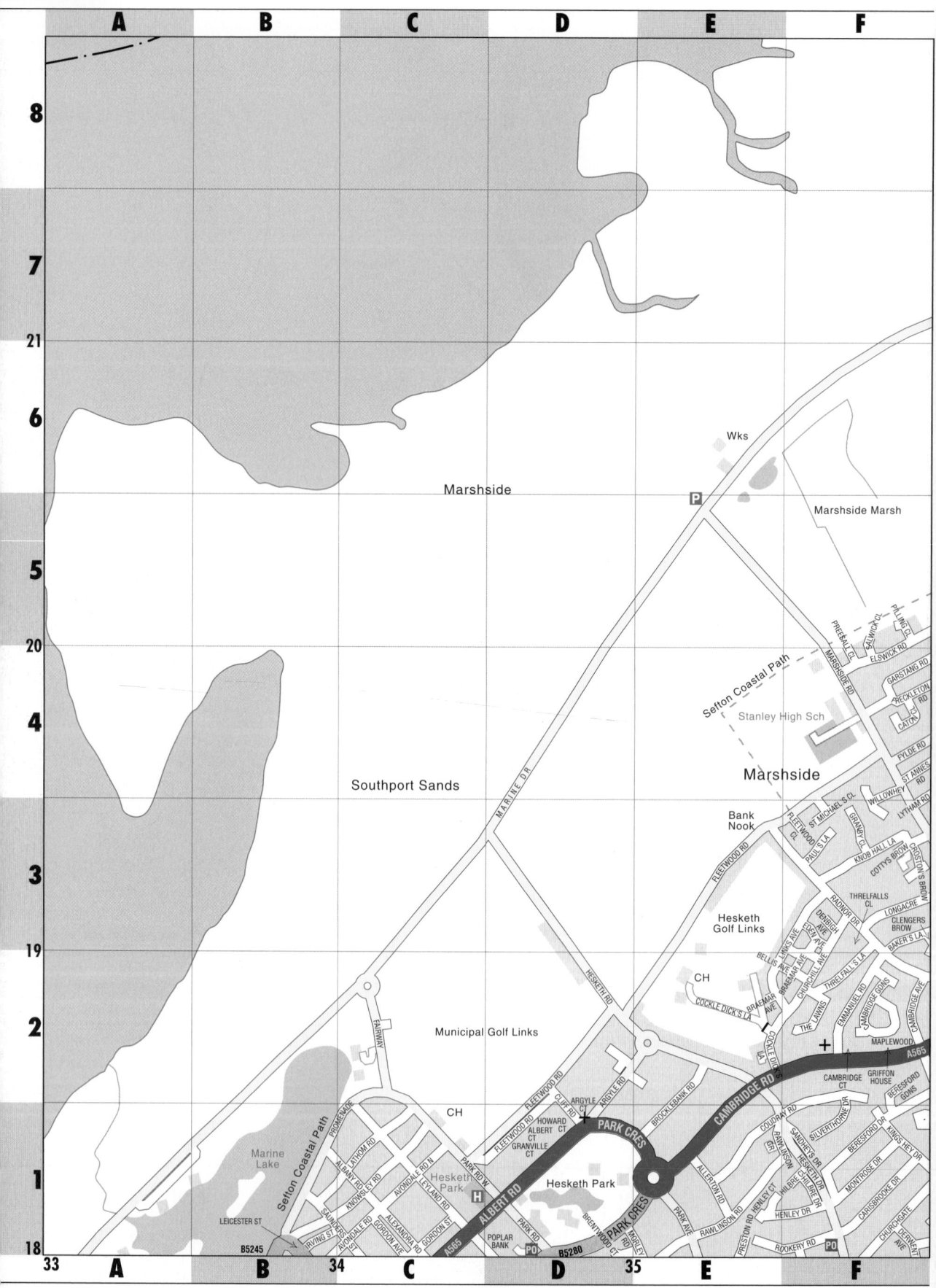

A B C D E F

8
21
7
6
5
20
4
3
19
2
1
18

Wks

Marshside

Marshside Marsh

P

Sefton Coastal Path

PREBALL

PILLING CL
ELSWICK CT
ELSWICK RD
GARSTANG RD
HECKLETON RD
CATON

MARSHSIDE RD

Stanley High Sch

FYLDE RD
ST ANNES RD

Marshside

Bank
Nook

ST MICHAEL'S CL
GRANBY CL
PAUL'S LA
WILLOWHEY
KNOB HALL LA
COTTY'S BROW
PRESTON'S BROW

FLEETWOOD RD

FLEETWOOD CL

Hesketh
Golf Links

THRELFALLS
CL

RADNOR DR
DEDRICH
AVE
LONGACRE
GLENGERS
BROW
BAKER'S LA

CH

COCKLE DICK'S LA
BRAEMAR AVE

BELLIS LINKS AVE
BRAEMAR AVE
THRELFALL S LA
CHURCHILL AVE
THE LAWNS
EMMANUEL RD
CAMBRIDGE GDNS
CAMBRIDGE AVE

MAPLEWOOD

COCKLE DR

MARINE DR

HESKETH RD

Southport Sands

+
A565

Municipal Golf Links

CH

FLEETWOOD RD
CLIFF RD
ARGYLE CT
ARGYLE RD

BROCKLEBANK RD

CAMBRIDGE RD

CAMBRIDGE
CT

GRIFFON
HOUSE
BERESFORD
GDNS

COUDRAY RD
SILVERTHORNE RD
BERESFORD DR
KINGS HEY DR

FAIRWAY

PROMENADE

Marine
Lake

Sefton Coastal Path

Hesketh
Park

H

PROMENADE
ALBANY RD
LATHOM RD
KNOWSLEY RD
SAUNDERS
AVONDALE RD N
AVONDALE RD
LELAND RD
GORDON ST
PARK RD W

CH

HOWARD
ALBERT CT
GRANVILLE
CT

PARK CRES

Hesketh Park

PARK CRES

ALLERTON RD
PARK AVE
RAWLINSON RD

RAWLINSON RD
HENLEY CT
HENLEY DR
WILBRE CHILDREN CT
MONTROSE DR
CARISBROOKE DR

MONTROSE DR
CHURCHGATE

LEICESTER ST

B5245

IRVING ST
AVONDALE RD
GORDON ST
ALEXANDRA RD

ALBERT RD
A565
POPLAR
BANK

PO

PARK RD

B5280

BRENTWOOD CT
MORLEY

PRESTON RD
HENLEY RD

ROOKERY RD

PO

OVERNENT
DERWENT

33 A B 34 C D 35 E F

54

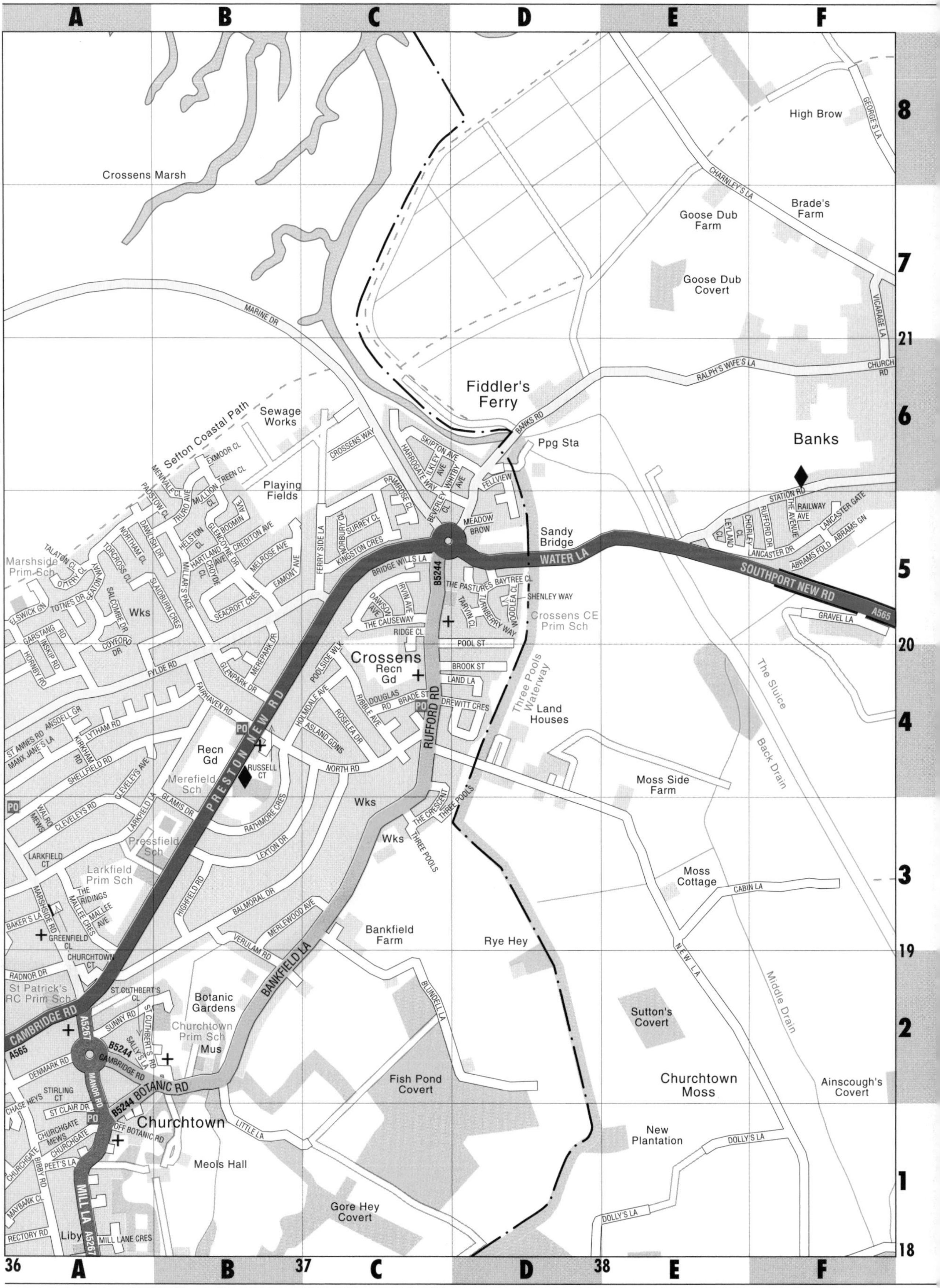

A
B
C
D
E
F
8
7
21
6
5
20
4
3
19
2
1
18
36
37
38
Crossens Marsh
High Brow
GEORGE'S LA
CHARNLEY'S LA
Brade's Farm
Goose Dub Farm
Goose Dub Covert
VICARAGE LA
MARINE DR
RALPH'S WIFE'S LA
CHURCH RD
Fiddler's Ferry
Banks
Sefton Coastal Path
Sewage Works
BANKS RD
Ppg Sta
CROSSENS WAY
SKIPTON AVE
HARROGATE WAY
ILKLEY AVE
WHITBY AVE
FELLVIEW
Playing Fields
PRIMROSE CL
BEVERLEY CL
MEADOW BROW
Sandy Bridge
STATION RD
RAILWAY AVE
LANCASTER GATE
ABRAMS GN
ABRAMS FOLD
LANCASTER DR
THE AVENUE
RUFFORD DR
CHORLEY CL
LEYLAND CL
WATER LA
SOUTHPORT NEW RD
A565
GRAVEL LA
EXMOOR CL
MENDALE CL
TREEN CL
MULLION CL
PADSTOW CL
TRURO AVE
BODMIN AVE
HELSTON CL
GLENCOYNE DR
HARTLAND AVE
CREDITON AVE
NORTHAM CL
DAWLISH DR
MELROSE AVE
EAMONT AVE
FERRY SIDE LA
NORBURY CL
SURREY CL
KINGSTON CRES
TALATON CL
Marshside Prim Sch
OTTERY CL
SEATON WAY
TORCROSS CL
CROYDE CL
MILLAR'S PACE
SEACROFT CRES
SLAIDBURN CRES
BRIDGE WILLS LA
B5244
THE PASTURES
BAYTREE CL
SHENLEY WAY
ELSWICK GN
TOTNES DR
SALCOMBE DR
Wks
DAWSON AVE
IRVIN AVE
TARVIN CL
TURNBERRY WAY
WOODLEA CL
Crossens CE Prim Sch
GARSTANG RD
INSKIP RD
HORNBY RD
COYFORD DR
THE CAUSEWAY
RIDGE CL
POOL ST
FYLDE RD
GLENPARK DR
MEREPARK DR
POOLSIDE WLK
Crossens
Recn Gd
BROOK ST
LAND LA
The Sluice
Three Pools Waterway
DOUGLAS RD
BRADE ST
DREWITT CRES
Land Houses
ANSDELL GR
ST ANNES RD
MANX JANE'S LA
LYTHAM RD
FAIRHAVEN RD
PRESTON NEW RD
HOLMDALE AVE
ASLAND GDNS
ROSELEA DR
RIBBLE AVE
RUFFORD RD
PO
Back Drain
KIRKHAM RD
SHELLFIELD RD
CLEVELEYS AVE
Recn Gd
RUSSELL CT
NORTH RD
Merefield Sch
Moss Side Farm
WALRO MEWS
CLEVELEYS RD
LARKFIELD LA
GLAMIS DR
RATHMORE CRES
THE CRESCENT
THREE POOLS
Pressfield Sch
LEXTON DR
LARKFIELD CT
Larkfield Prim Sch
HIGHFIELD RD
Moss Cottage
CABIN LA
MARSHSIDE RD
THE RIDINGS
MALLEE CRES
MALLEE AVE
BALMORAL DR
MERLEWOOD AVE
BAKER'S LA
GREENFIELD CL
Bankfield Farm
Rye Hey
VERULAM RD
BANKFIELD LA
CHURCHTOWN CT
NEW LA
Middle Drain
RADNOR DR
St Patrick's RC Prim Sch
ST CUTHBERT'S CL
Botanic Gardens
BLUNDELL LA
Sutton's Covert
CAMBRIDGE RD
A5267
SUNNY RD
ST CUTHBERT'S RD
Churchtown Prim Sch
Mus
SALLY'S LA
B5244
DENMARK RD
CAMBRIDGE RD
MANOR RD
Fish Pond Covert
Churchtown Moss
Ainscough's Covert
CHASE HEYS
STIRLING CT
ST CLAIR DR
BOTANIC RD
Churchtown
CHURCHGATE MEWS
CHURCHGATE
OFF BOTANIC RD
LITTLE LA
New Plantation
DOLLY'S LA
PEET'S LA
BIBBY RD
Meols Hall
MILL LA
MAYBANK CL
Gore Hey Covert
DOLLY'S LA
RECTORY RD
Liby
MILL LANE CRES

35

54

53
71
53
36

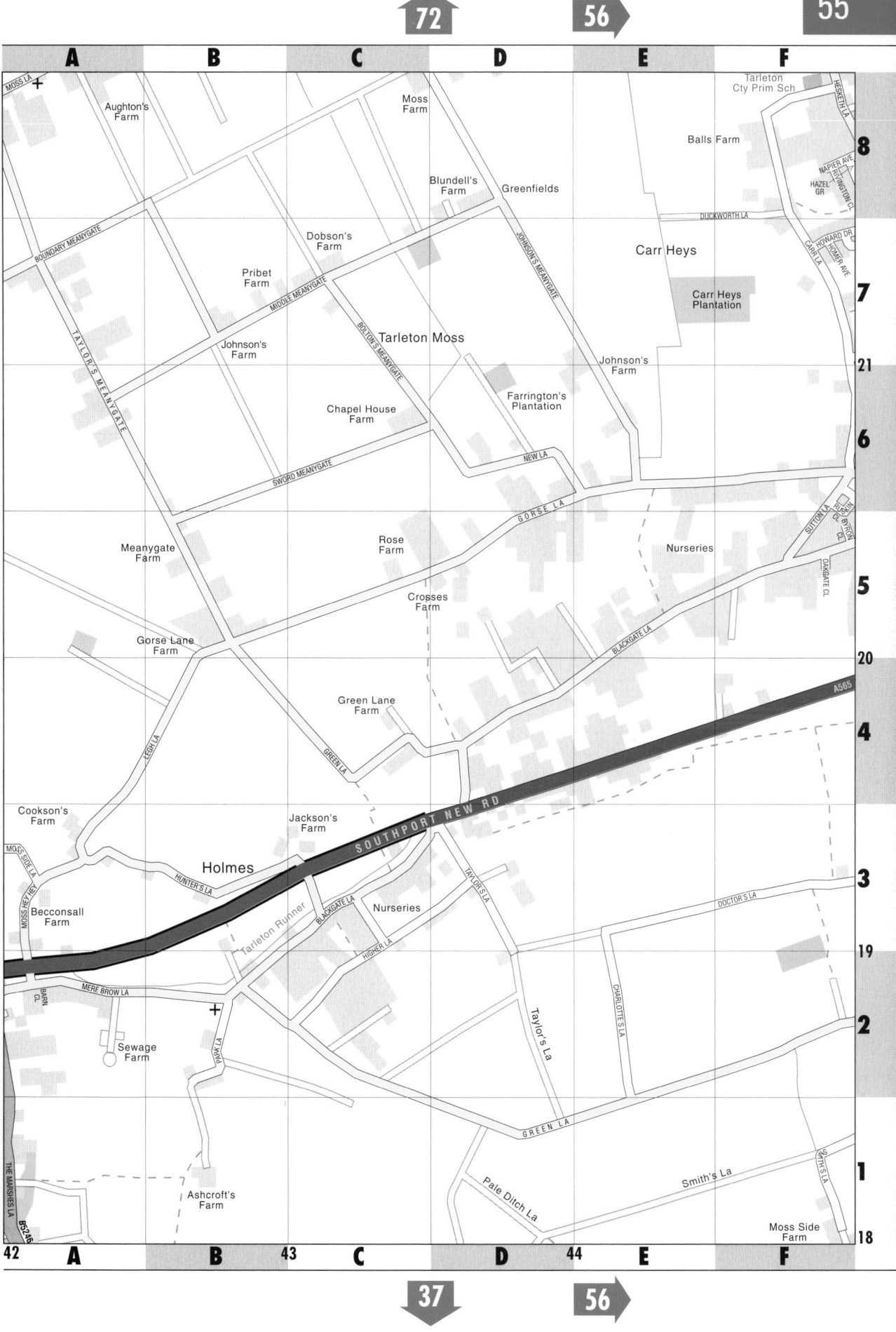

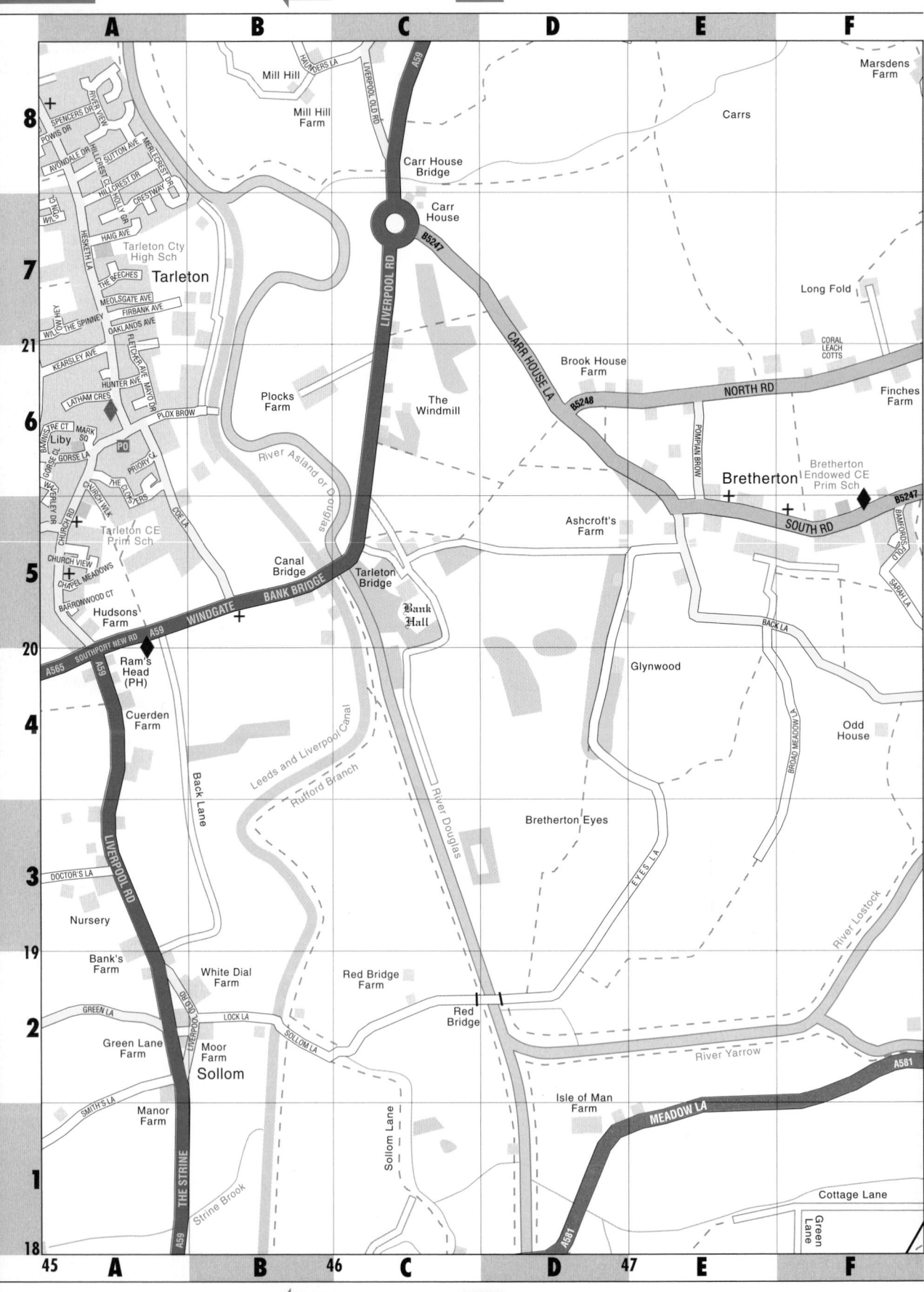

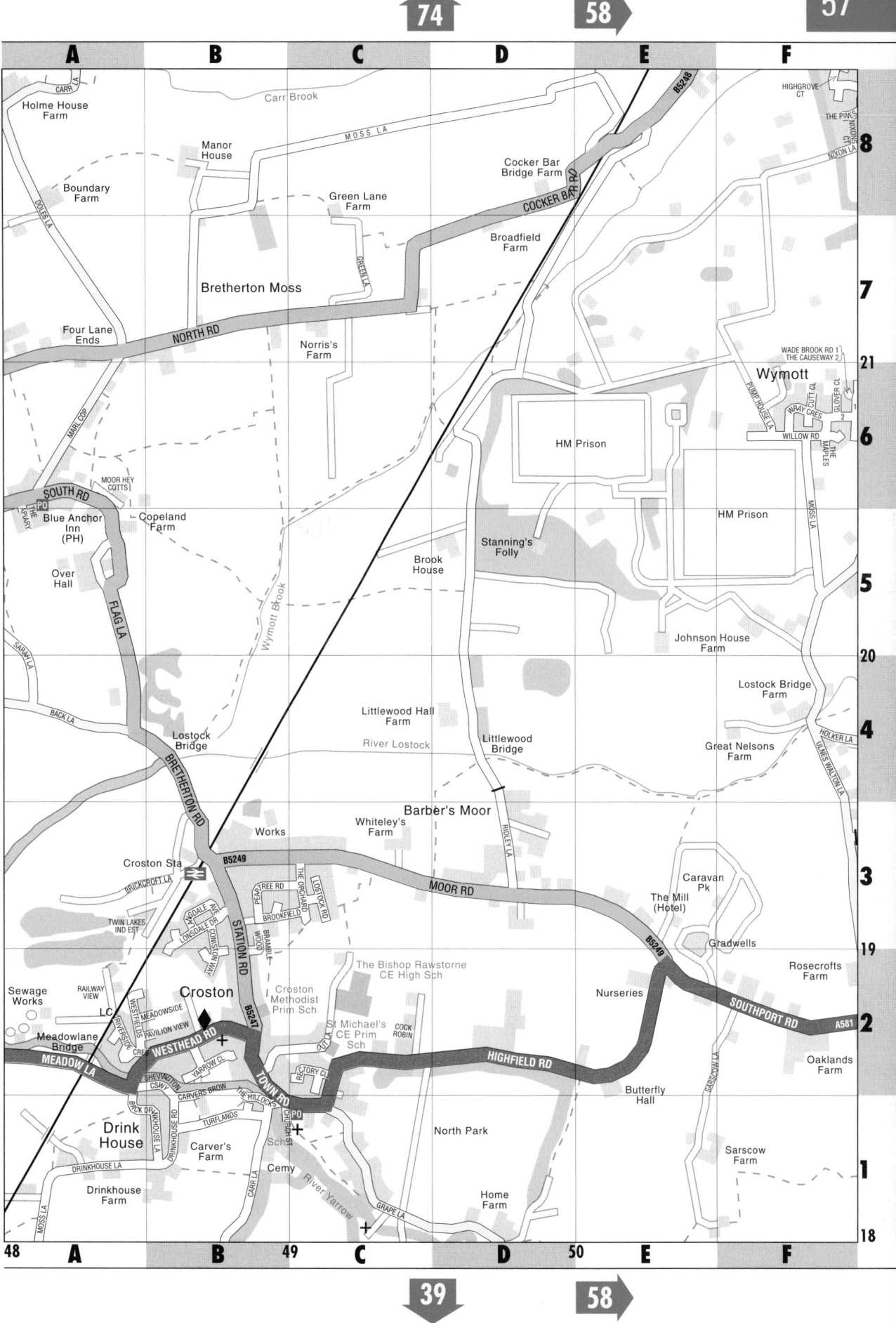

A   B   C   D   E   F

8

CARR
Holme House
Farm
Carr Brook
MOSS LA
Manor
House
Cocker Bar
Bridge Farm
B5248
HIGHGROVE
CT
THE PINS
NIXON LA

Boundary
Farm
Green Lane
Farm
Broadfield
Farm
COCKER BAR RD

DOLES LA

7

Bretherton Moss
GREEN LA
21   WADE BROOK RD 1
THE CAUSEWAY 2
Wymott

Four Lane
Ends
NORTH RD
Norris's
Farm
PUMP HOUSE LA
CUTT CL
WRAY CRES
GLOVER CL
WILLOW RD
THE MAPLES

MARL COP

6   HM Prison

MOOR HEY
COTTS
SOUTH RD
PO
THE VICARAGE
Blue Anchor
Inn
(PH)
Copeland
Farm
HM Prison
MOSS LA

FLAG LA
Over
Hall
Brook
House
Stanning's
Folly

5

SARAH LA
Wymott Brook
Johnson House
Farm
20

BACK LA
Lostock
Bridge
Littlewood Hall
Farm
Lostock Bridge
Farm

4

River Lostock
Littlewood
Bridge
Great Nelsons
Farm
HOLKER LA
ULNES WALTON LA

BRETHERTON RD
Barber's Moor
RIDLEY LA

Works
Whiteley's
Farm
Caravan
Pk

Croston Sta
B5249
PEAR TREE RD
THE ORCHARD
LOSTOCK RD
MOOR RD
The Mill
(Hotel)
B5249

3

BRICKCROFT LA
LONSDALE AV
BROOKFIELD
BRAMBLE WOOD
Gradwells

TWIN LAKES
IND EST
LONSDALE DR
CONISLOW WAY
STATION RD
19   Rosecrofts
Farm

Sewage
Works
RAILWAY
VIEW
The Bishop Rawstorne
CE High Sch
Nurseries
SOUTHPORT RD
A581

LC
MEADOWSIDE
Croston
Croston
Methodist
Prim Sch
St Michael's
CE Prim
Sch
COCK
ROBIN

2

Meadowlane
Bridge
WESTFIELDS
RIVERSIDE
PAVILION VIEW
WESTHEAD RD
VICTORY CL
HIGHFIELD RD
Oaklands
Farm

MEADOW LA
B5247
TOWN RD
CHURCH ST
PO
Butterfly
Hall
SARSCOW LA

SHEVINGTON
CSWY
YARROW CL
CARVERS BROW
THE HILLOCKS
SCH ST
North Park
Sarscow
Farm

Drink
House
BACK DR
DRINKHOUSE LA
TURFLANDS
Carver's
Farm
Cemy

1

DRINKHOUSE LA
Drinkhouse
Farm
CARR LA
River Yarrow
GRAPE LA
Home
Farm

MOSS LA

18

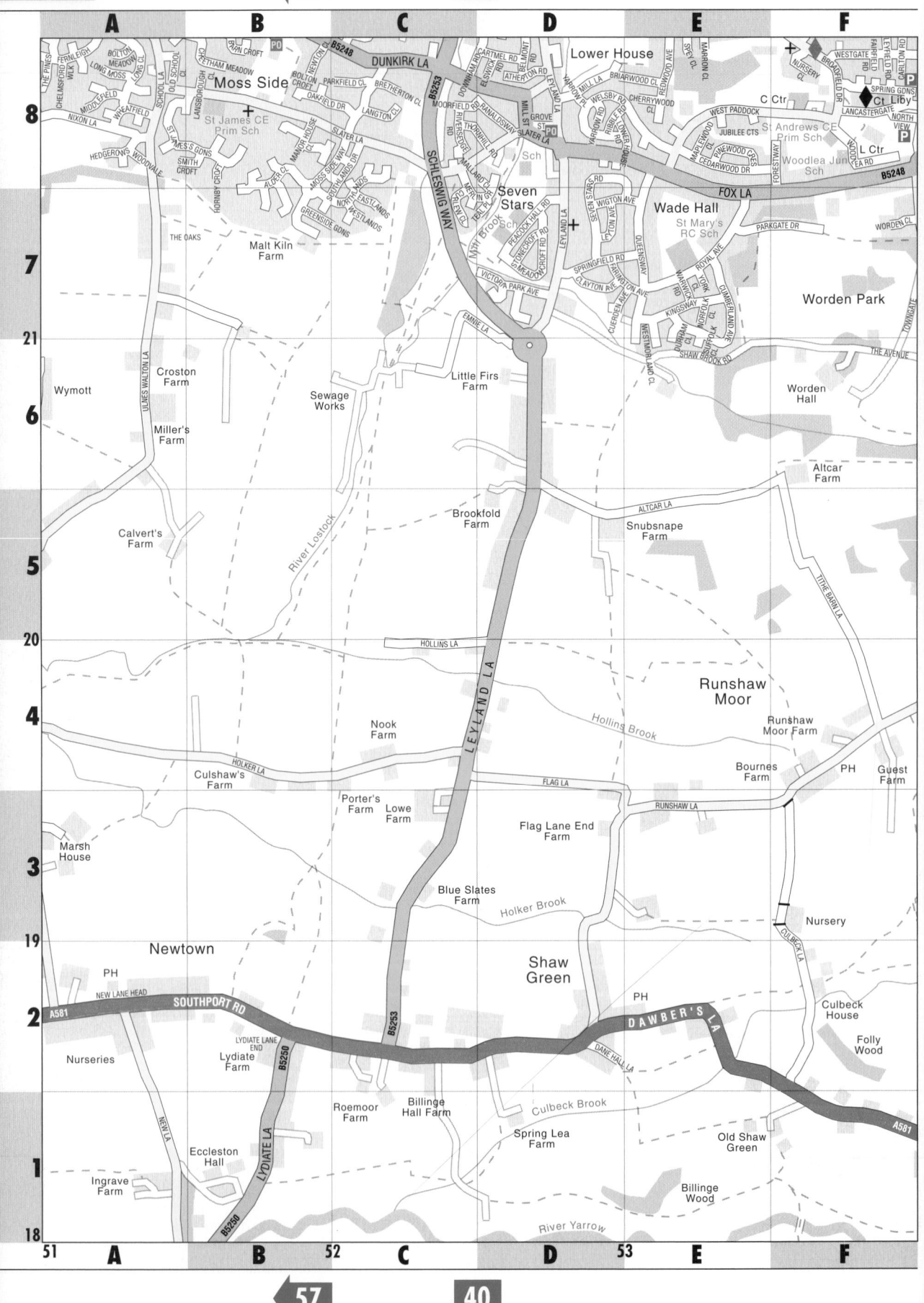

A B C D E F

8

7

21

6

5

20

4

19

3

2

1

18

Moss Side

St James CE
Prim Sch

Dunkirk La

Lower House

Seven
Stars

Wade Hall

St Mary's
RC Sch

Worden Park

Malt Kiln
Farm

Wymott

Croston
Farm

Miller's
Farm

Calvert's
Farm

Little Firs
Farm

Sewage
Works

Worden
Hall

Altcar
Farm

Brookfold
Farm

Snubsnape
Farm

Runshaw
Moor

Hollins La

Leyland La

Nook
Farm

Runshaw
Moor Farm

Culshaw's
Farm

Bournes
Farm

PH

Guest
Farm

Flag La

Porter's
Farm

Lowe
Farm

Flag Lane End
Farm

Runshaw La

Marsh
House

Blue Slates
Farm

Holker Brook

Nursery

Newtown

Shaw
Green

PH

Culbeck
House

New Lane Head

Southport Rd

B5253

PH

Dawber's La

Folly
Wood

A581

Nurseries

Lydiate
Farm

Lydiate Lane
End

B5250

Roemoor
Farm

Billinge
Hall Farm

Spring Lea
Farm

Dane Hall La

Old Shaw
Green

Eccleston
Hall

Lydiate La

Billinge
Wood

Ingrave
Farm

New La

B5250

River Yarrow

Culbeck Brook

A581

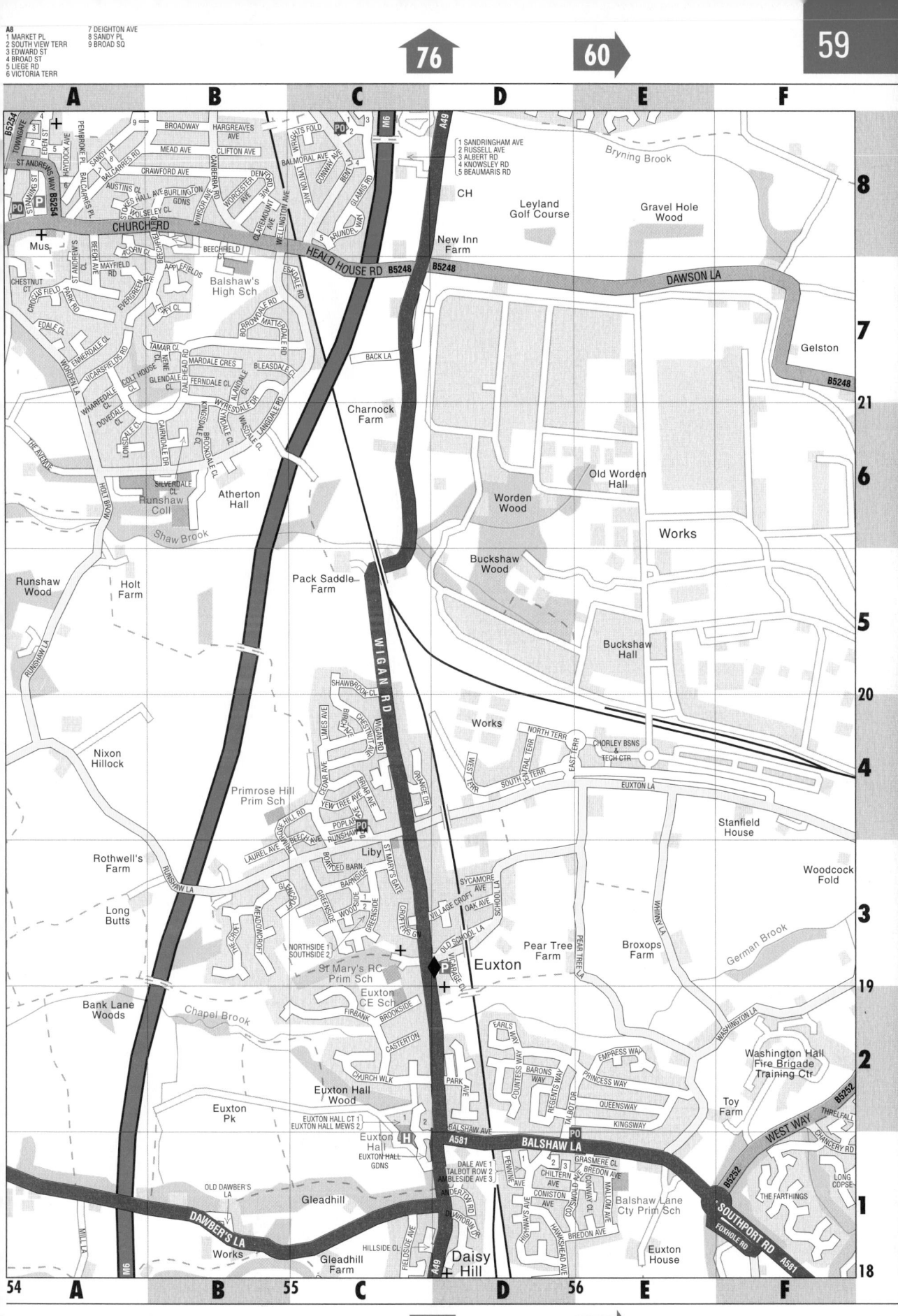

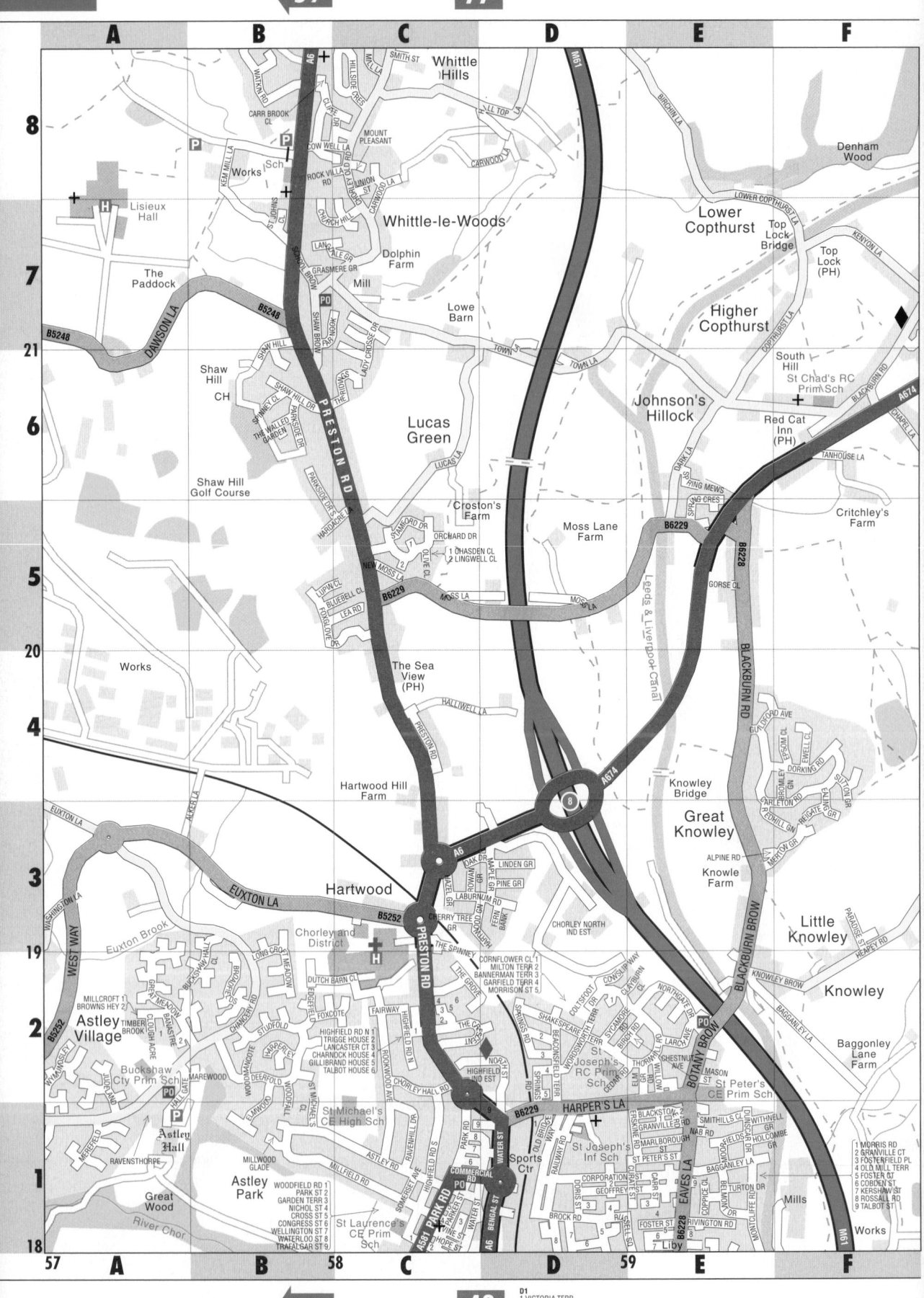

D1
1 VICTORIA TERR
2 VICARAGE ST
3 WESTWELL RD
4 INGLE MEWS
5 RUSSELL SQ W
6 WHINFIELD AVE
7 MAYFIELD AVE
8 BRIERCLIFFE RD
9 PRESTON ST

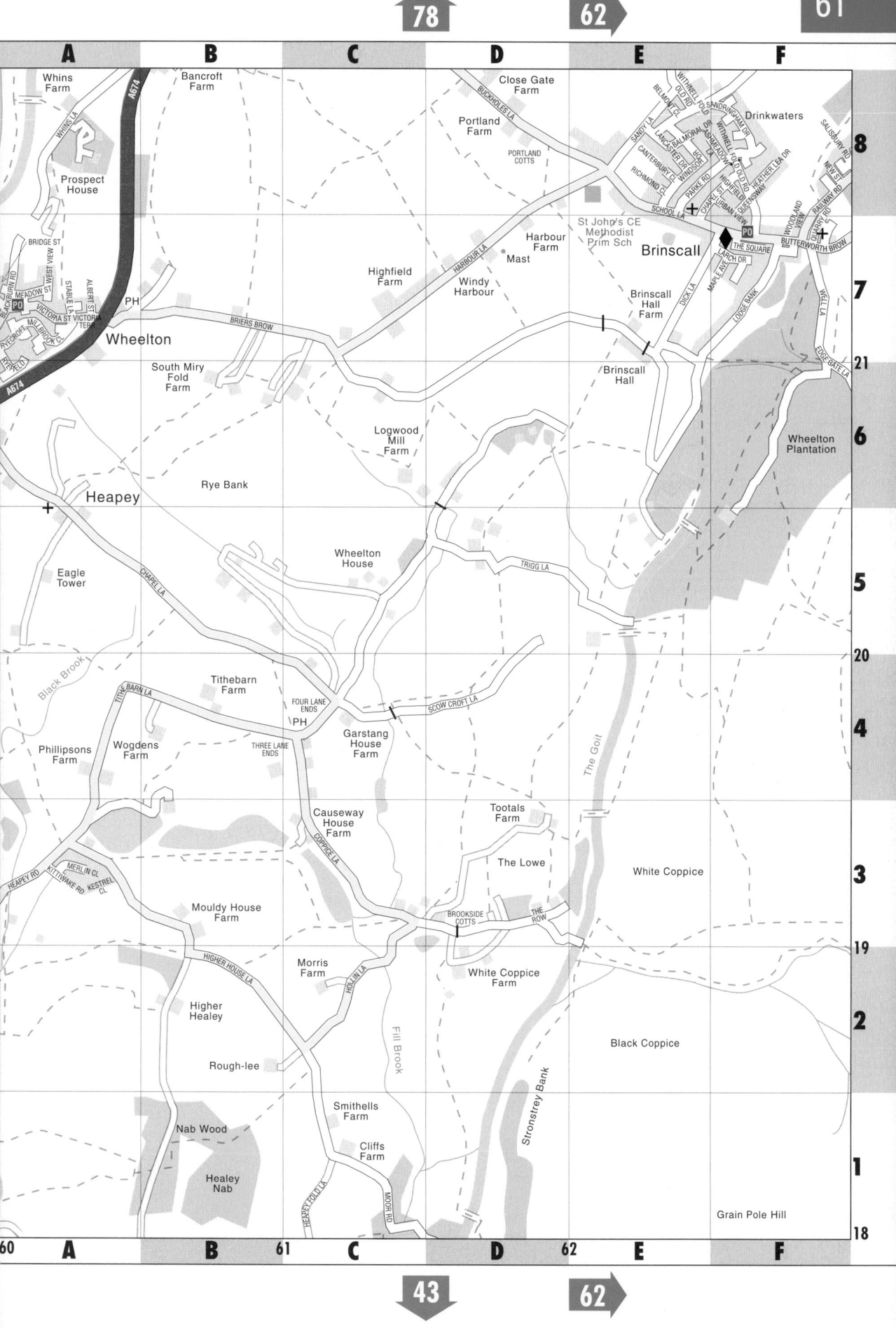

A B C D E F

Whins Farm

Prospect House

A674

Whins La

Bancroft Farm

Close Gate Farm

Portland Farm

BUCKHOLES LA

PORTLAND COTTS

WITHNELL FOLD
OLD RD
BELMONT CL
SANDRINGHAM DR
WITHNELL FOLD OLD RD
Drinkwaters

SANDY LA
LANCASTER DR
BALMORAL DR
ASKHAM DR
WINDSOR DR

CANTERBURY CL

RICHMOND CL
PARKE RD
HIGHFIELD
HEATHER LEA DR

SCHOOL LA

SALISBURY RD

NEWS L

St John's CE Methodist Prim Sch
Brinscall

WOODLAND DR
QUARRY RD
RAILWAY RD

8

BRIDGE ST
MEADOW ST
PARK ST VIEW
PO
STABLE LA
ALBERT ST
VICTORIA ST VICTORIA TERR
PH
Wheelton

BLACKBURN RD
RYECROFT
MALBROOK CL
MILLBROOK CL
PARK FIELD

A674

Highfield Farm

Harbour Farm
Mast

HARBOUR LA

Windy Harbour

Brinscall Hall Farm

PO
THE SQUARE
LARCH DR
URBAN VIEW
CHAPEL ST
LOOSE BANK
BUTTERWORTH BROW

7

BRIERS BROW

South Miry Fold Farm

DICK LA

MAPLE LA

WELL LA

EDGE GATE LA

Brinscall Hall

21

Logwood Mill Farm

Wheelton Plantation

6

Rye Bank

Heapey

Eagle Tower

CHAPEL LA

Wheelton House

TRIGG LA

5

Black Brook

TITHE BARN LA

Tithebarn Farm

FOUR LANE ENDS
PH

SCOW CROFT LA

The Goit

20

Phillipsons Farm

Wogdens Farm

THREE LANE ENDS

Garstang House Farm

4

Causeway House Farm

COPPAGE LA

Tootals Farm

The Lowe

White Coppice

HEAPEY RD
MERLIN CL
KITTIWAKE RD
KESTREL CL

Mouldy House Farm

HIGHER HOUSE LA

BROOKSIDE COTTS

THE ROW

White Coppice Farm

3

Morris Farm

HOLDIN LA

19

Higher Healey

Fill Brook

Stronstrey Bank

Black Coppice

2

Rough-lee

Smithells Farm

Nab Wood

Cliffs Farm

Healey Nab

HEAPEY FOLD LA

MOOR RD

Grain Pole Hill

1

18

A B C D E F

8

Mount Pleasant
Norcross Farm
Dole La
A675
Derby St
Railway Rd
Prospect Terr
Norcross Brow
Twist Moor La
Churchill Rd
Butterworth Brow
Hartington Rd

Roddlesworth La

7

Bolton Rd

Roddlesworth

21

Watsons

6

Edge Gate La

Solomon's Temple

Roddlesworth Moor

Mill La

Hatch Brook

Withnell Moor

Green Hill

5

River Roddlesworth

Cold Within Hill

Calf Hey Bridge

20

Wet Meadows

Belmont Rd A675

4

Ferney Slacks

Brown Hill

Heapey Moor

Wheelton Moor

Brown Hill

3

Drinkwaters

Great Hill

19

Black Brook

2

Adam's Delf

1

Black Hill Upper

Bromiley Pastures

18

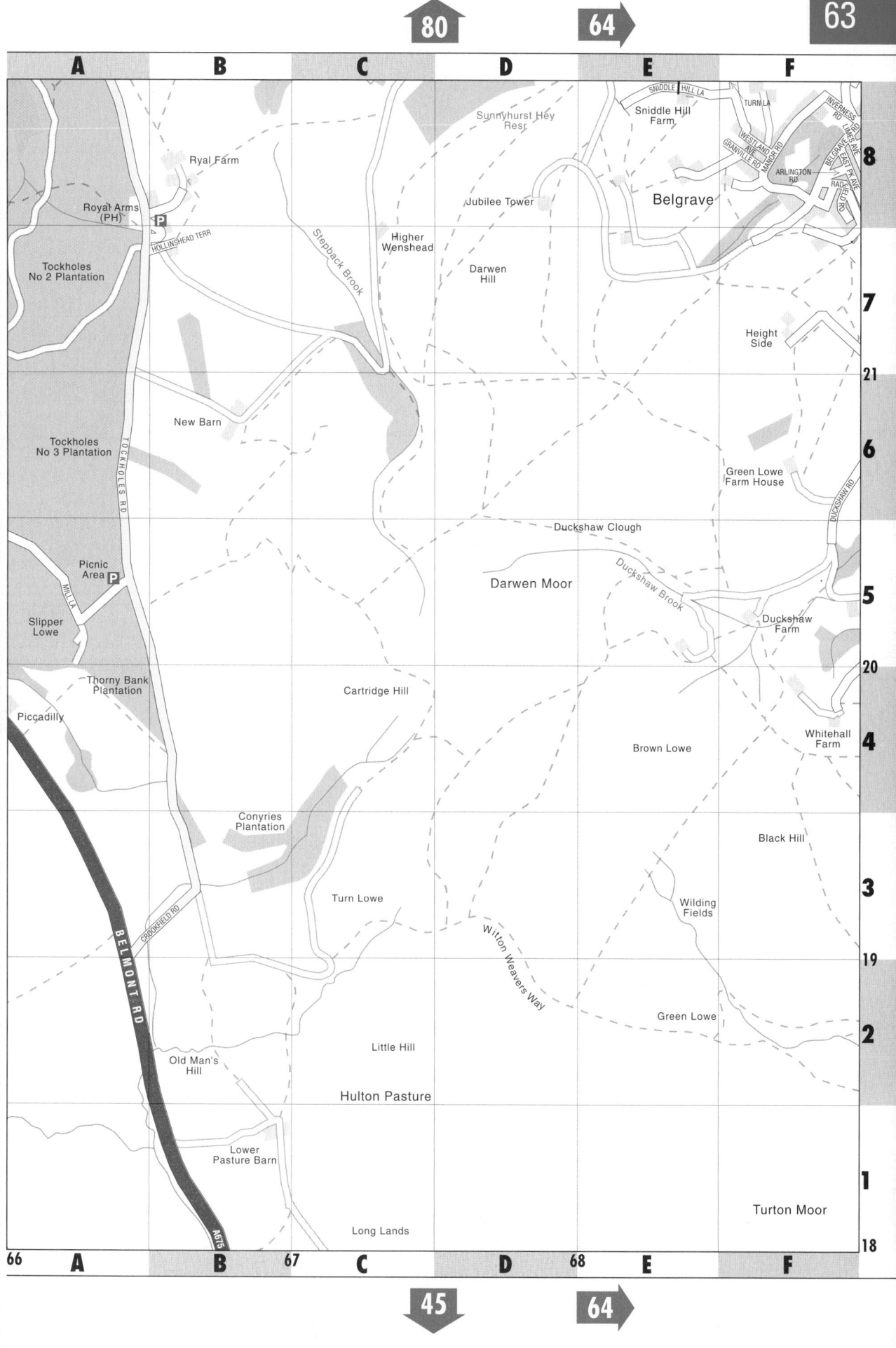

80
64
45
64

A B C D E F

8 7 21 6 5 20 4 3 19 2 1 18

66 A B 67 C D 68 E F

Sniddle Hill La
Turn La
Sniddle Hill Farm
Inverness Rd
Westland Ave
Granville Rd
Major Rd
Belgrave East Pk Ave
Arlington Rd
Radcliffe Rd
Likes Ave

Sunnyhurst Hey Rest
Ryal Farm
Royal Arms (PH)
Hollinshead Terr
Stepback Brook
Higher Wenshead
Jubilee Tower
Darwen Hill
Belgrave
Height Side

Tockholes No 2 Plantation
Tockholes Rd
New Barn
Tockholes No 3 Plantation
Green Lowe Farm House
Duckshaw Rd
Duckshaw Clough
Duckshaw Brook
Darwen Moor
Picnic Area
Mill La
Slipper Lowe
Duckshaw Farm

Thorny Bank Plantation
Cartridge Hill
Brown Lowe
Whitehall Farm
Piccadilly

Belmont Rd
Crookfield Rd
Conyries Plantation
Turn Lowe
Witton Weavers Way
Wilding Fields
Black Hill

Green Lowe

Old Man's Hill
Little Hill
Hulton Pasture

A675
Lower Pasture Barn
Turton Moor

Long Lands

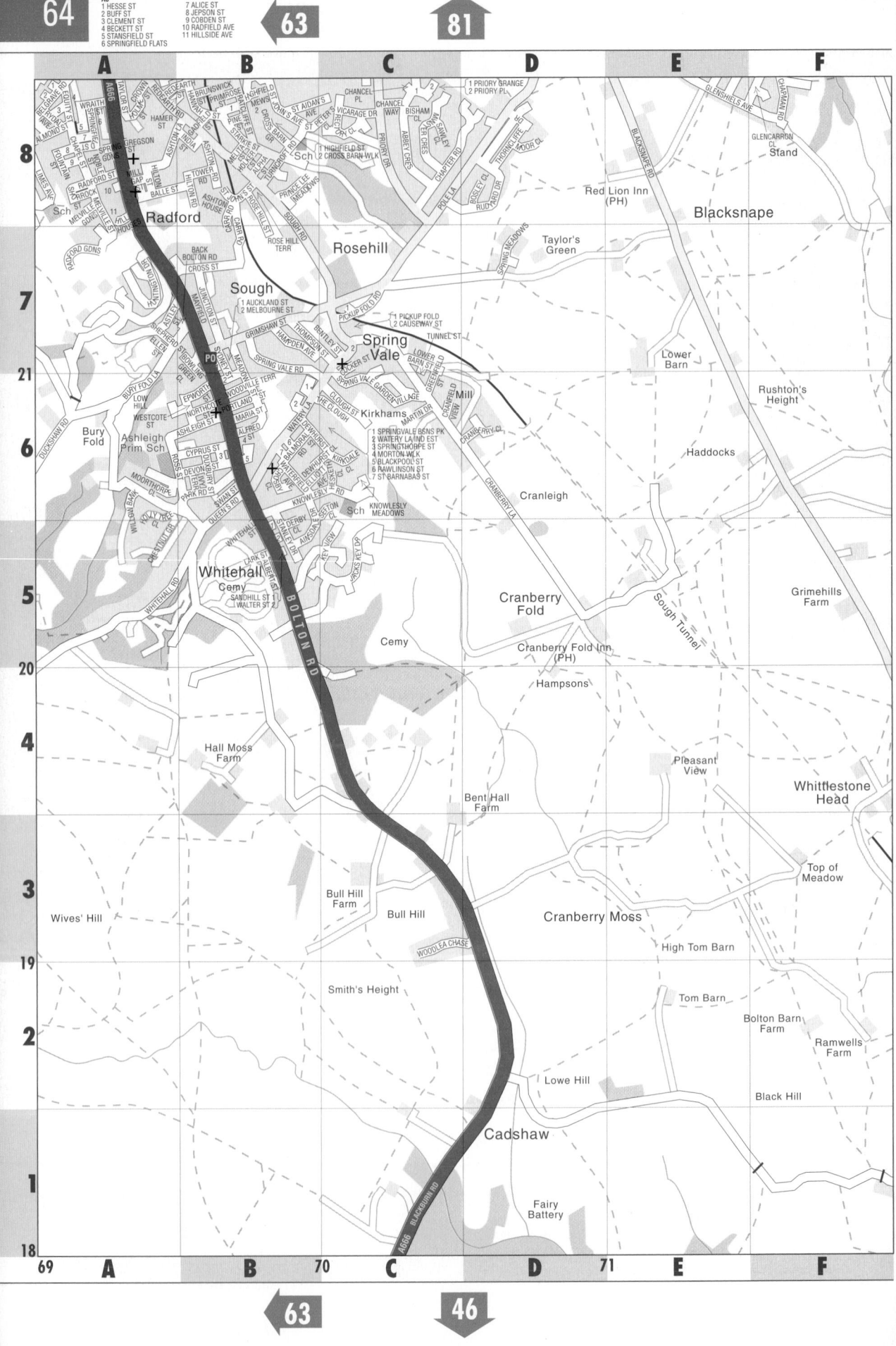

64

A8
1 HESSE ST
2 BUFF ST
3 CLEMENT ST
4 BECKETT ST
5 STANSFIELD ST
6 SPRINGFIELD FLATS
7 ALICE ST
8 JEPSON ST
9 COBDEN ST
10 RADFIELD AVE
11 HILLSIDE AVE

← 63

↑ 81

Radford
Rosehill
Sough
1 AUCKLAND ST
2 MELBOURNE ST
Spring Vale
1 PICKUP FOLD
2 CAUSEWAY ST
TUNNEL ST
Kirkhams
1 SPRINGVALE BSNS PK
2 WATERY LAND EST
3 SPRINGTHORPE ST
4 MORTON WLK
5 BLACKPOOL ST
6 RAWLINSON ST
7 ST BARNABAS ST
KNOWLESLEY MEADOWS
Whitehall
Cemy
SANDHILL ST 1
WALTER ST 2
Cemy
Bury Fold
Low Hill
Westcote St
Ashleigh Prim Sch
Mill

1 PRIORY GRANGE
2 PRIORY PL
Red Lion Inn (PH)
Taylor's Green
Blacksnape
Glencarron Cl
Sfand
Lower Barn
Rushton's Height
Haddocks
Cranleigh
Cranberry Fold
Sough Tunnel
Grimehills Farm
Cranberry Fold Inn (PH)
Hampsons
Pleasant View
Whittlestone Head
Hall Moss Farm
Bent Hall Farm
Top of Meadow
Cranberry Moss
Bull Hill Farm
Bull Hill
WOODLEA CHASE
Wives' Hill
Smith's Height
High Tom Barn
Tom Barn
Bolton Barn Farm
Ramwells Farm
Lowe Hill
Black Hill
Cadshaw
A666 BLACKBURN RD
Fairy Battery

BOLTON RD
A666

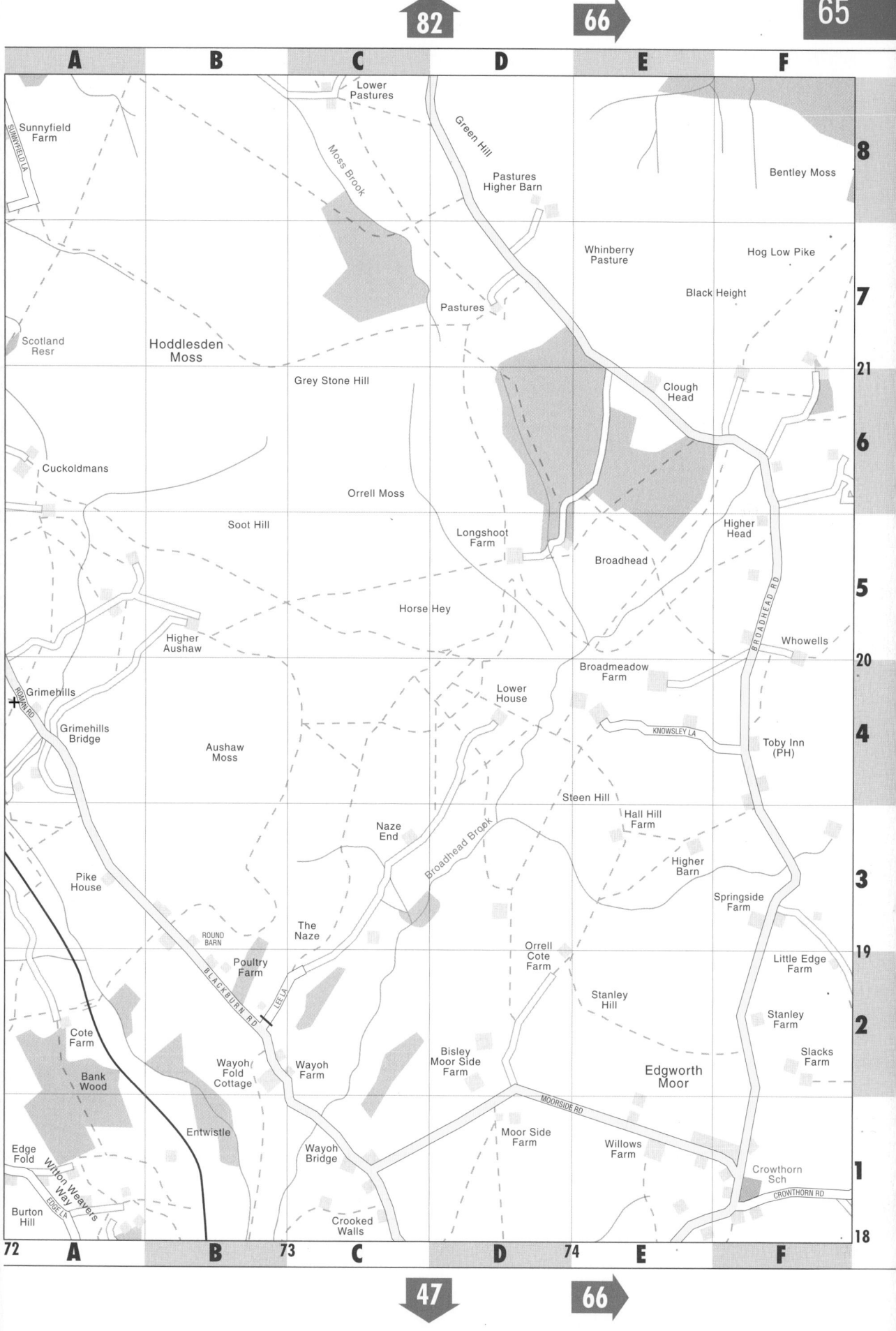

A B C D E F

8
7
21
6
5
20
4
3
19
2
1
18

Sunnyfield Farm
SUNNYFIELD LA
Scotland Resr
Hoddlesden Moss
Cuckoldmans
Soot Hill
Higher Aushaw
Grimehills
ROMAN RD
Grimehills Bridge
Aushaw Moss
Pike House
Cote Farm
Bank Wood
Edge Fold
WITTON WEAVERS WAY
EDGE LA
Burton Hill
Entwistle

Lower Pastures
Moss Brook
Grey Stone Hill
Orrell Moss
Horse Hey
ROUND BARN
The Naze
Poultry Farm
BLACKBURN RD
LEE LA
Wayoh Fold Cottage
Wayoh Farm
Wayoh Bridge
Crooked Walls

Green Hill
Pastures Higher Barn
Pastures
Longshoot Farm
Lower House
Naze End
Broadhead Brook
Steen Hill
Orrell Cote Farm
Bisley Moor Side Farm
MOORSIDE RD
Moor Side Farm

Bentley Moss
Whinberry Pasture
Hog Low Pike
Black Height
Clough Head
Broadhead
Higher Head
Whowells
Broadmeadow Farm
KNOWSLEY LA
Toby Inn (PH)
BROADHEAD RD
Hall Hill Farm
Higher Barn
Springside Farm
Little Edge Farm
Stanley Hill
Stanley Farm
Slacks Farm
Edgworth Moor
Willows Farm
Crowthorn Sch
CROWTHORN RD

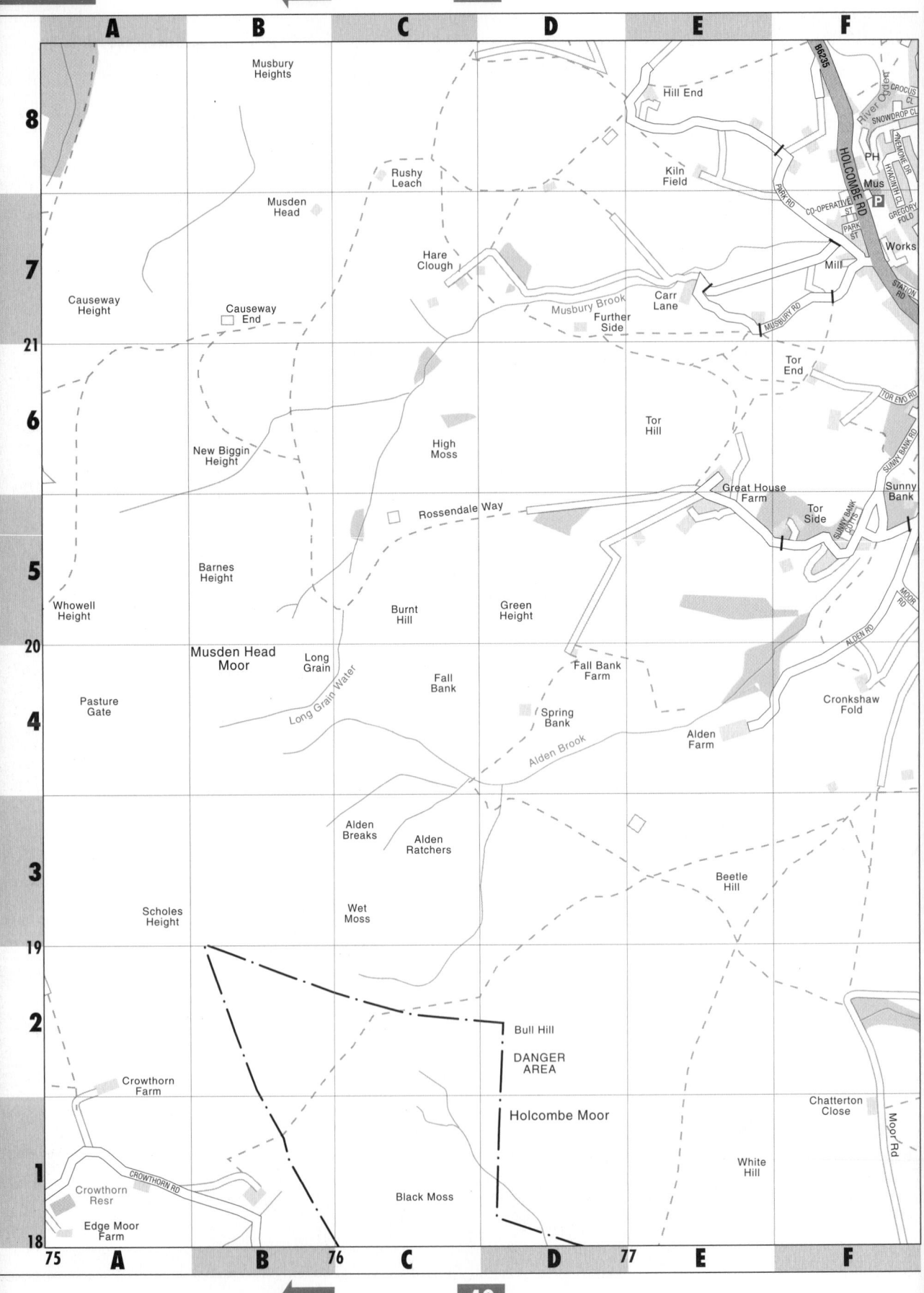

	A	B	C	D	E	F

8

Musbury
Heights

Hill End

River Cr... CROCUS CL
SNOWDROP CL
...MEADOW DR
HYACINTH CL

Rushy
Leach

Kiln
Field

PH

HOLCOMBE RD

Mus

7

Musden
Head

Hare
Clough

Carr
Lane

Mill

PARK RD
CO-OPERATIVE ST
PARK ST
GREGORY FOLD

P

Works

Causeway
Height

Causeway
End

Musbury Brook

Further
Side

MUSBURY RD

STATION RD

21

Tor
End

TOR END RD

SUNNY BANK RD

6

New Biggin
Height

High
Moss

Tor
Hill

Great House
Farm

Sunny
Bank

SUNNY BANK COTTS

Tor
Side

Rossendale Way

5

Barnes
Height

Burnt
Hill

Green
Height

MOOR RD

Whowell
Height

ALDEN RD

20

Musden Head
Moor

Long
Grain

Fall
Bank

Fall Bank
Farm

Cronkshaw
Fold

4

Pasture
Gate

Long Grain Water

Spring
Bank

Alden
Farm

Alden Brook

3

Alden
Breaks

Alden
Ratchers

Beetle
Hill

Scholes
Height

Wet
Moss

19

Bull Hill

DANGER
AREA

2

Crowthorn
Farm

Holcombe Moor

Chatterton
Close

Moor Rd

1

Crowthorn
Resr

CROWTHORN RD

Black Moss

White
Hill

18

Edge Moor
Farm

75	A	B	76	C	D	77	E	F

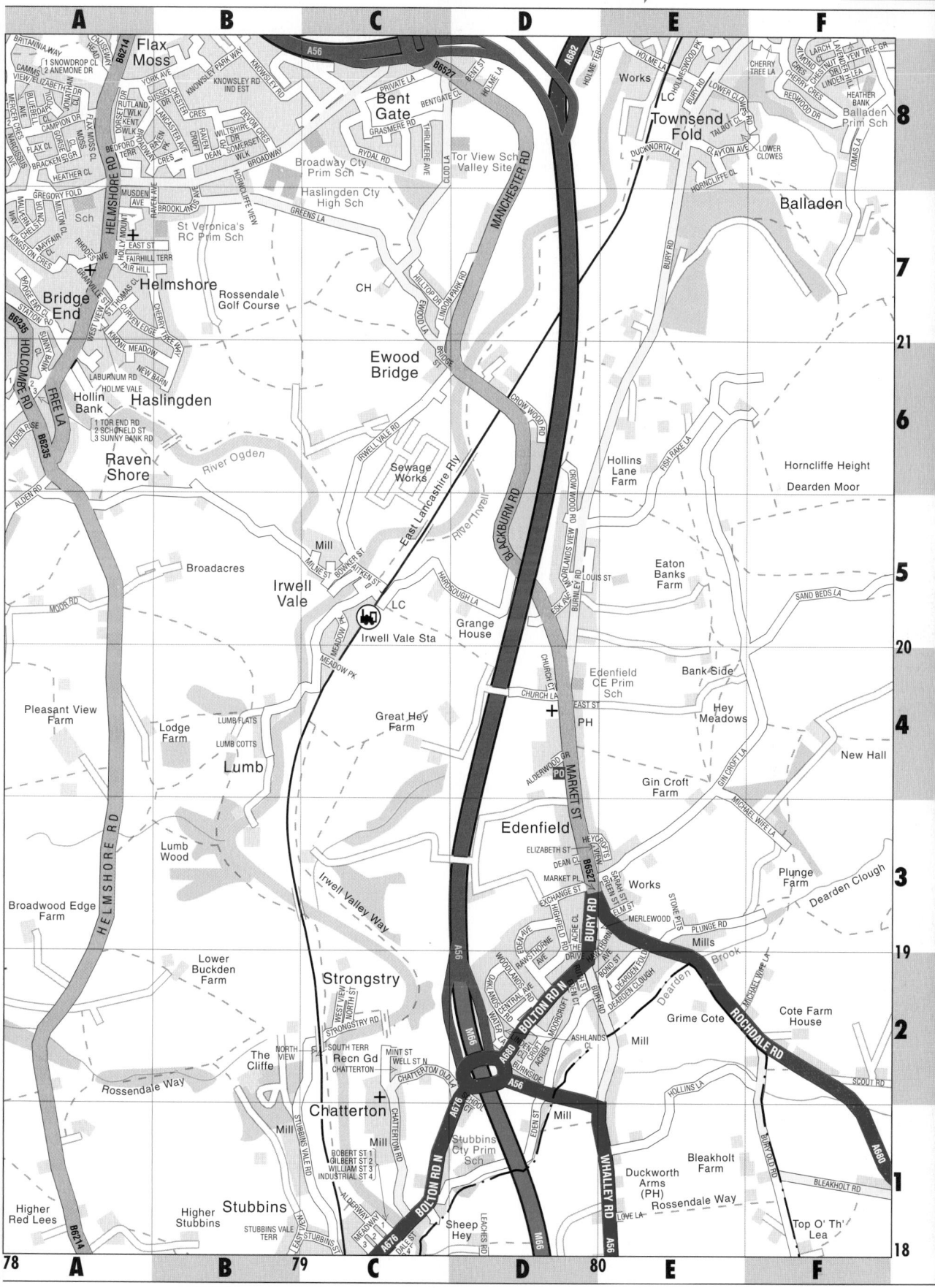

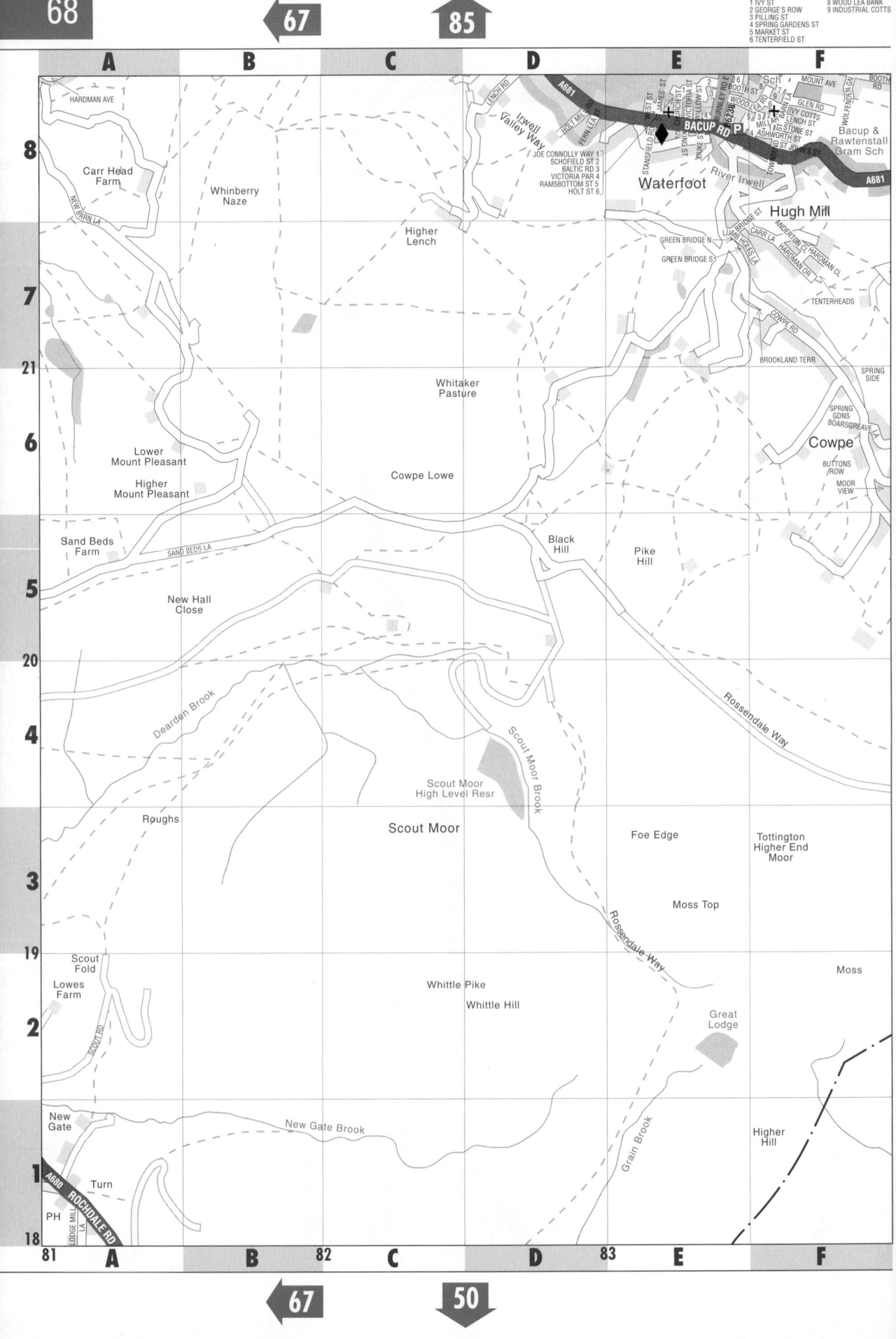

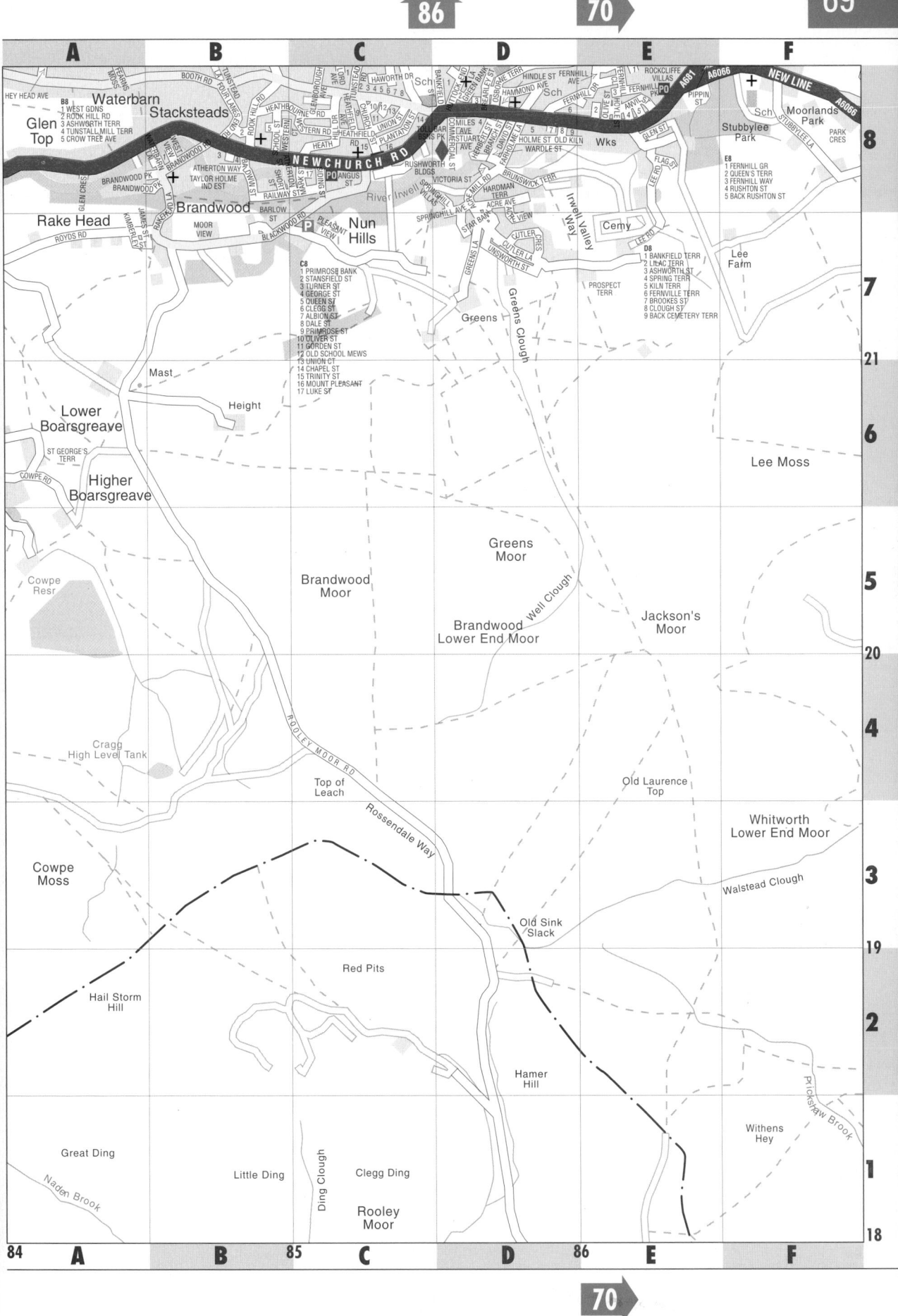

Hey Head Ave

Waterbarn
Stacksteads

Glen Top
B8
1 WEST GDNS
2 ROOK HILL RD
3 ASHWORTH TERR
4 TUNSTALL MILL TERR
5 CROW TREE AVE

Rake Head
ROYDS RD

Brandwood
Brandwood Pk
Brandwood
TAYLOR HOLME
IND EST

NEWCHURCH RD
River Irwell

Nun Hills
P

MOOR VIEW

C8
1 PRIMROSE BANK
2 STANSFIELD ST
3 TURNER ST
4 GEORGE ST
5 QUEEN ST
6 CLEGG ST
7 ALBION ST
8 DALE ST
9 PRIMROSE ST
10 OLIVER ST
11 GORDEN ST
12 OLD SCHOOL MEWS
13 UNION CT
14 CHAPEL ST
15 TRINITY ST
16 MOUNT PLEASANT
17 LUKE ST

Mast

Lower Boarsgreave
ST GEORGE'S TERR
COWPE RD

Higher Boarsgreave

Height

Greens

Greens Clough

PROSPECT TERR

NEW LINE
A681 A6066
A6066

Rockcliffe Villas
Sch
Moorlands Park
Stubbylee Park
PARK CRES

E8
1 FERNHILL GR
2 QUEEN'S TERR
3 FERNHILL WAY
4 RUSHTON ST
5 BACK RUSHTON ST

Cemy
Lee Farm

D8
1 BANKFIELD TERR
2 LILAC TERR
3 ASHWORTH ST
4 SPRING TERR
5 KILN TERR
6 FERNVILLE TERR
7 BROOKES ST
8 CLOUGH ST
9 BACK CEMETERY TERR

Lee Moss

Greens Moor

Brandwood Moor

Brandwood
Lower End Moor

Well Clough

Jackson's Moor

Cowpe Resr

Cragg
High Level Tank

RODLEY MOOR RD

Top of Leach

Rossendale Way

Old Laurence Top

Whitworth
Lower End Moor

Walstead Clough

Cowpe Moss

Old Sink Slack

Hail Storm Hill

Red Pits

Hamer Hill

Prickshaw Brook

Withens Hey

Great Ding

Little Ding

Ding Clough

Clegg Ding

Rooley Moor

Naden Brook

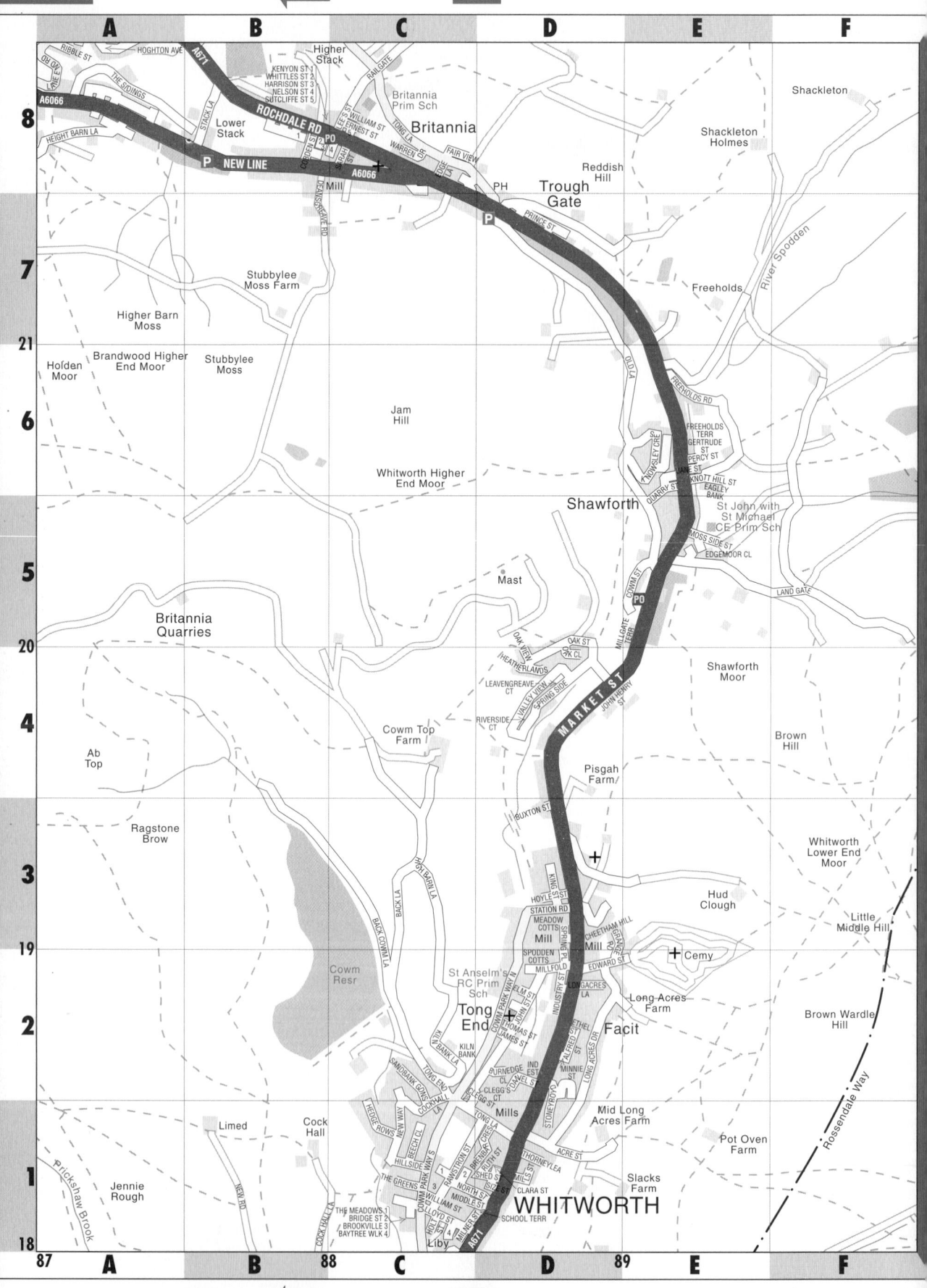

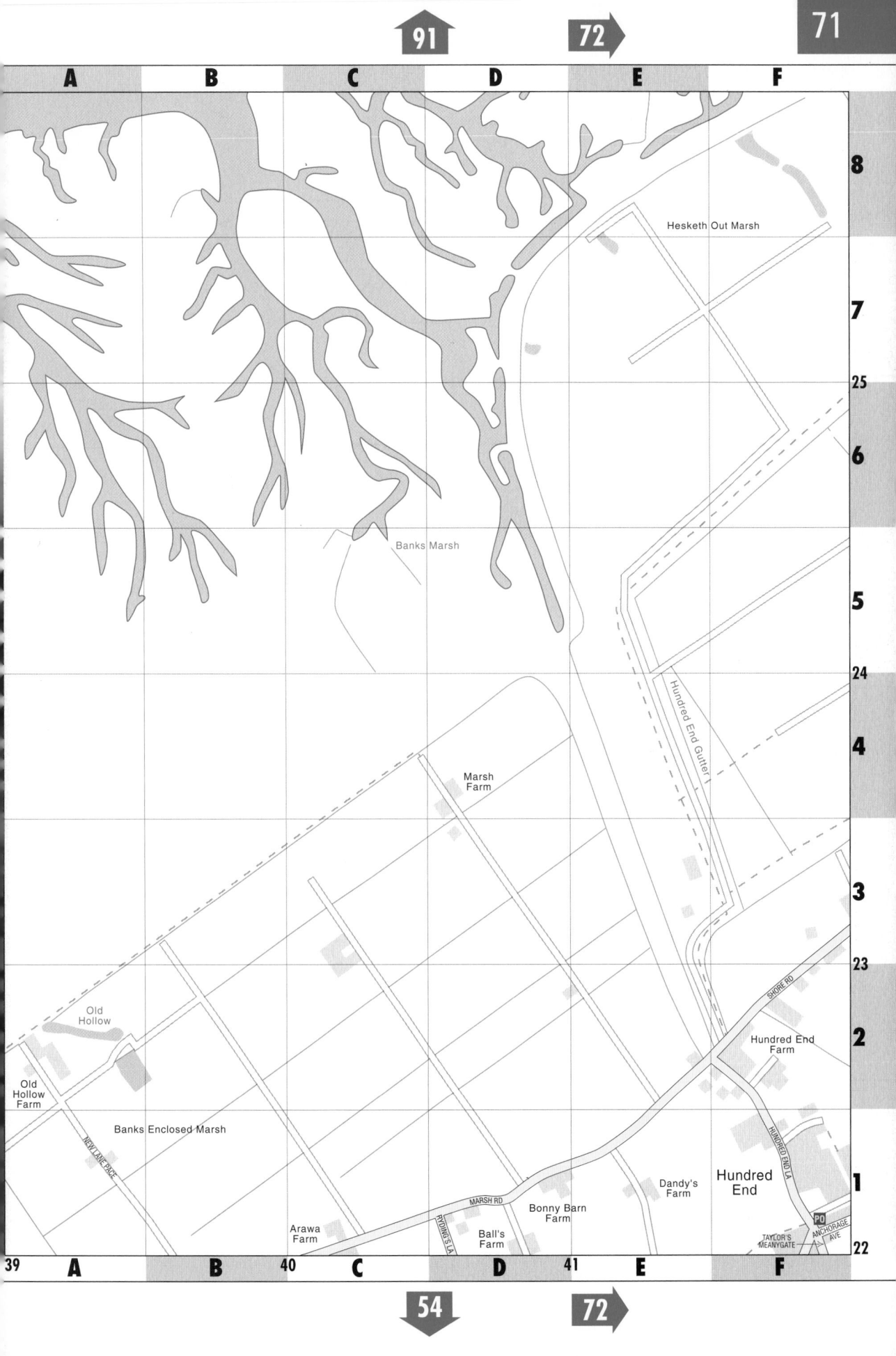

91
72

A   B   C   D   E   F

8

7

25

6

Hesketh Out Marsh

5

Hundred End Gutter

24

Banks Marsh

4

Marsh
Farm

3

23

Old
Hollow

Shore Rd

2

Hundred End
Farm

Old
Hollow
Farm

Hundred End La

Banks Enclosed Marsh

New Lane Pace

1

Dandy's
Farm

Hundred
End

Arawa
Farm

Marsh Rd

Rydings La

Ball's
Farm

Bonny Barn
Farm

PO
Taylor's
Meanygate

Anchorage
Ave

22

39   A   B   40   C   D   41   E   F

54
72

A B C D E F

8

Hesketh Out Marsh

Ribble Bank
Farm

7

Westgate
Farm

25

6 Hesketh New Marsh

GUIDE RD

Anchorage
Farm

Carr Heys Watercourse

5

DIB RD

Hesketh Old
Marsh

24

Hesketh-with-
Becconsall All Saints
CE Sch

MARSH RD

THE BROW

ROSE
GDNS

MEADOW LA

New
Farm

4

GREENFIELD

GLEN PARK DR

LANGDALE
AVE

FAIRWINDS
AVE

SCHOOLFOLD

BELLS FIELD
DR

RIBBLE
DR

DELTA PARK
DR

DELTA PARK
AVE

Hesketh
Bank

SHORE RD

THE WALK

HAZELWOOD
DR

CHAPEL
GDNS

CHAPEL RD

CHANDLERS CROFT

THE GRO

Bank
Farm

CROPPER
GDNS

Wright's
Farm

PARODE CL

CHARLES CL

STATION RD

RIDALE GDNS

BECCONSALL LA

3

New Manor
Farm

NEWARTH LA

ORCHARD
CL

23

Ribble View
Farm

SIDNEY AVE

NORWOOD AVE

PH

Hesketh

SIDNEY AVE

CHERRY
VALE

2

GRANVILLE AVE

WOODLEE RD

MEADWAY

PO

MILL LA

ASTLAND GDNS

MOSS LA

Kingsfold
Christian Sch

Becconsall

SMITH AVE

GREENWAYS

BOUNDARY LA

FULWOOD AVE

Nurseries

Millers
Farm

JOHNSON'S MEANYGATE

Nurseries

HESKETH LA

DOUGLAS
AVE

1

FERMOR RD

Hesketh
Moss

BOUNDARY MEANYGATE

ANCHORAGE
AVE

Pear Tree
Farm

NURSERY
DR

22

42 A 43 B C 44 D E F

River Asland or Douglas

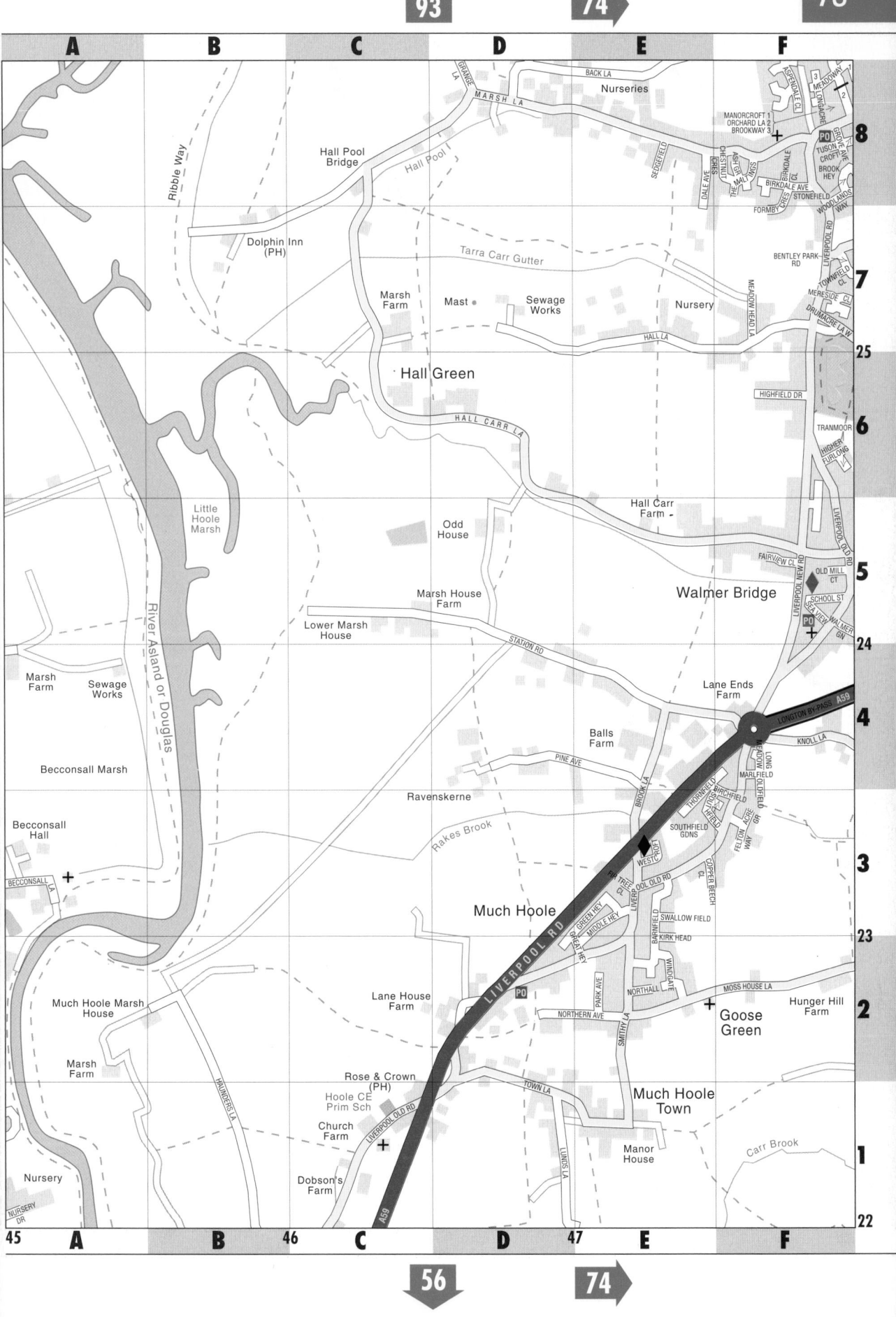

Nurseries

MANORCROFT 1
ORCHARD LA 2
BROOKWAY 3

TUSON
CROFT
BROOK
HEY

PO

MEADOWAY

ASCENDALE CL

MEADOW

GROVE AVE

WOODLANDS WAY

LIVERPOOL OLD RD

8

Hall Pool
Bridge

Hall Pool

SEDGEFIELD

DALE AVE

CHRISTINE

THE MALTINGS

FORMBY CRES

BIRKDALE AVE

STONEFIELD

Dolphin Inn
(PH)

Tarra Carr Gutter

BENTLEY PARK-
RD

TOWNEND

MESERIDE

MEADOW HEAD LA

DRUMACRE LA W

7

Marsh
Farm

Mast

Sewage
Works

Nursery

Hall LA

HIGHFIELD DR

25

Hall Green

TRANMOOR

HALL CARR LA

HIGHER
FURLONG

6

Little
Hoole
Marsh

Odd
House

Hall Carr
Farm

FAIRVIEW CL

LIVERPOOL NEW RD

LIVERPOOL OLD RD

OLD MILL
CT

Walmer Bridge

SCHOOL ST

SEAVIEW

WALMER
GR

5

Marsh House
Farm

PO

24

Lower Marsh
House

STATION RD

Ribble Way

River Asland or Douglas

Marsh
Farm

Sewage
Works

Becconsall Marsh

Becconsall
Hall

BECCONSALL LA

Lane Ends
Farm

LONGTON BY-PASS A59

KNOLL LA

4

Balls
Farm

PINE AVE

BROOK LA

THORNFIELD

LOTUS HEAD

BIRCHFIELD

LONG MEADOW

OLDFIELD

MARLFIELD

Ravenskerne

Rakes Brook

SOUTHFIELD
GDNS

FELTON ACRE WAY

COPPER BEECH

WESTCROFT

FIR TREE CL

GREEN HEY

GREAT HEY

LIVERPOOL OLD RD

BARNFIELD

WINDGATE

Swallow Field

KIRK HEAD

3

Much Hoole

LIVERPOOL RD

MIDDLE HEY

23

Lane House
Farm

PO

PARK AVE

SMITH LA

NORTHALL

MOSS HOUSE LA

Hunger Hill
Farm

Much Hoole Marsh
House

NORTHERN AVE

Goose
Green

2

Marsh
Farm

Rose & Crown
(PH)

TOWN LA

LUNDS LA

Much Hoole
Town

Carr Brook

Hoole CE
Prim Sch

Church
Farm

Manor
House

1

Nursery

NURSERY
DR

Dobson's
Farm

LIVERPOOL OLD RD

A59

22

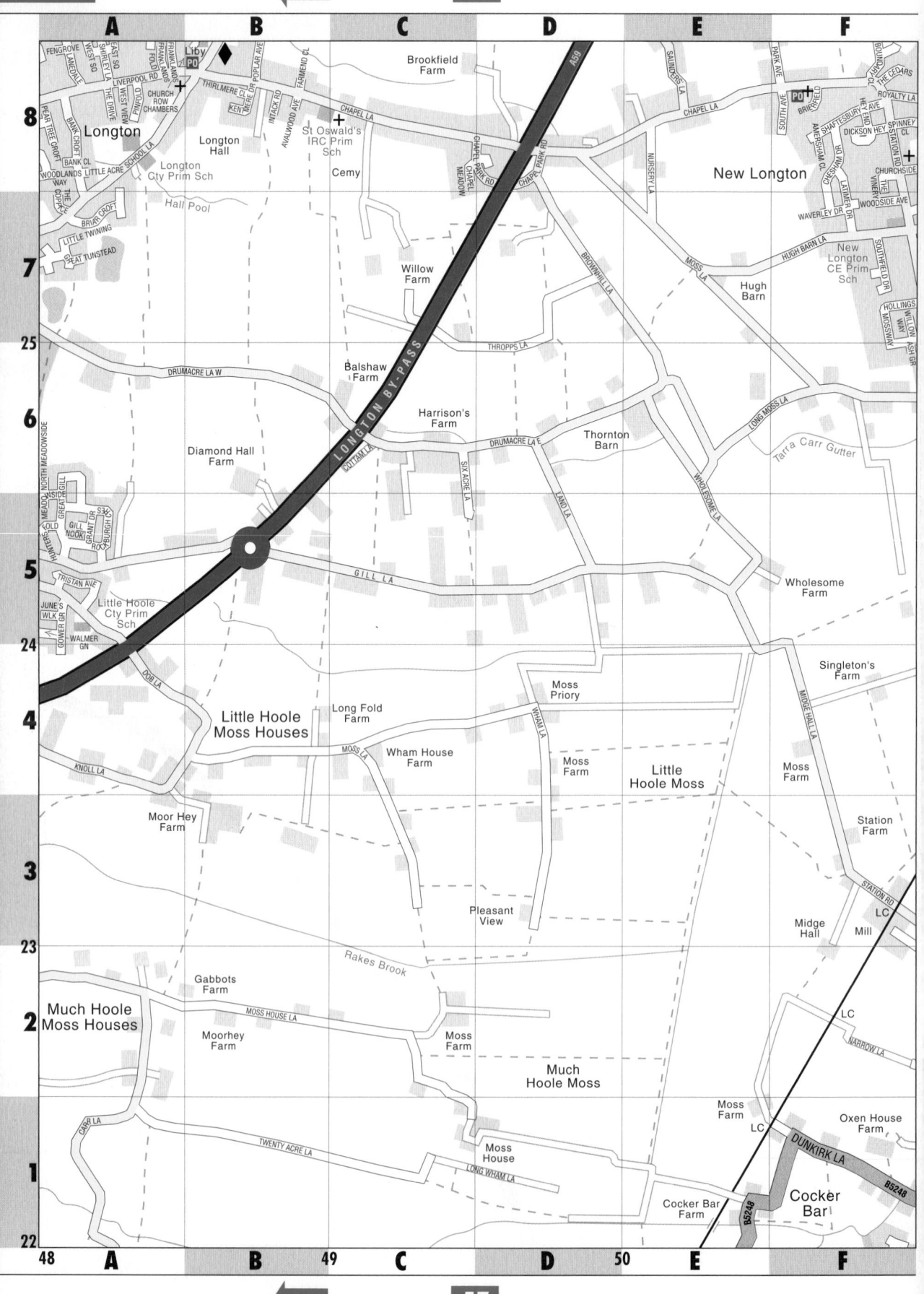

73
94

Longton

Brookfield Farm

New Longton

Longton Hall

Longton Cty Prim Sch

St Oswald's IRC Prim Sch

Cemy

Hall Pool

Willow Farm

Hugh Barn

New Longton CE Prim Sch

Balshaw Farm

Harrison's Farm

Thornton Barn

Tarra Carr Gutter

Diamond Hall Farm

Wholesome Farm

Little Hoole Cty Prim Sch

Singleton's Farm

Little Hoole Moss Houses

Long Fold Farm

Wham House Farm

Moss Priory

Moss Farm

Little Hoole Moss

Moss Farm

Station Farm

Moor Hey Farm

Pleasant View

Midge Hall

Mill

Rakes Brook

Gabbots Farm

Much Hoole Moss Houses

Moorhey Farm

Moss House La

Moss Farm

Much Hoole Moss

Moss Farm

Oxen House Farm

Moss House

Cocker Bar Farm

Cocker Bar

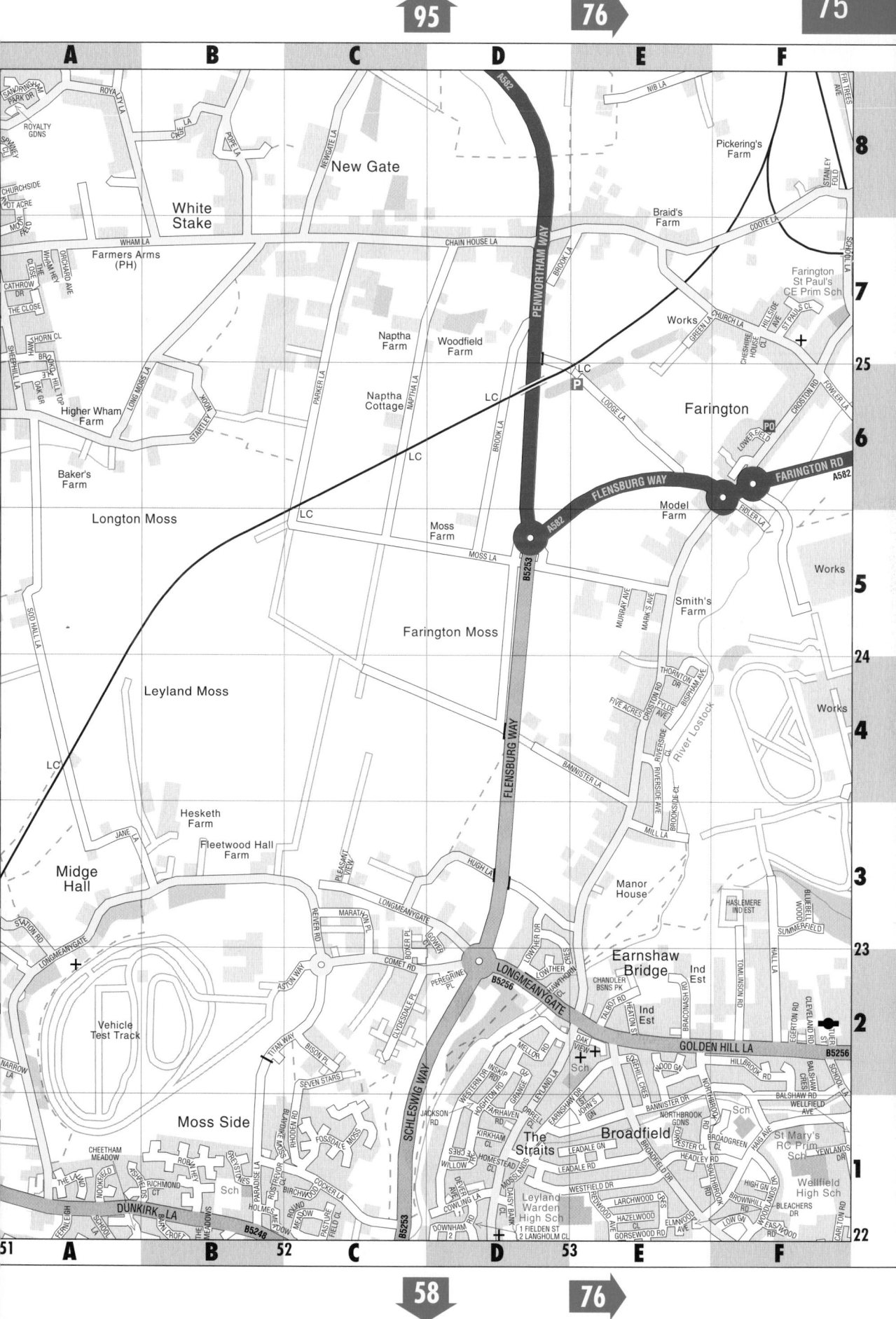

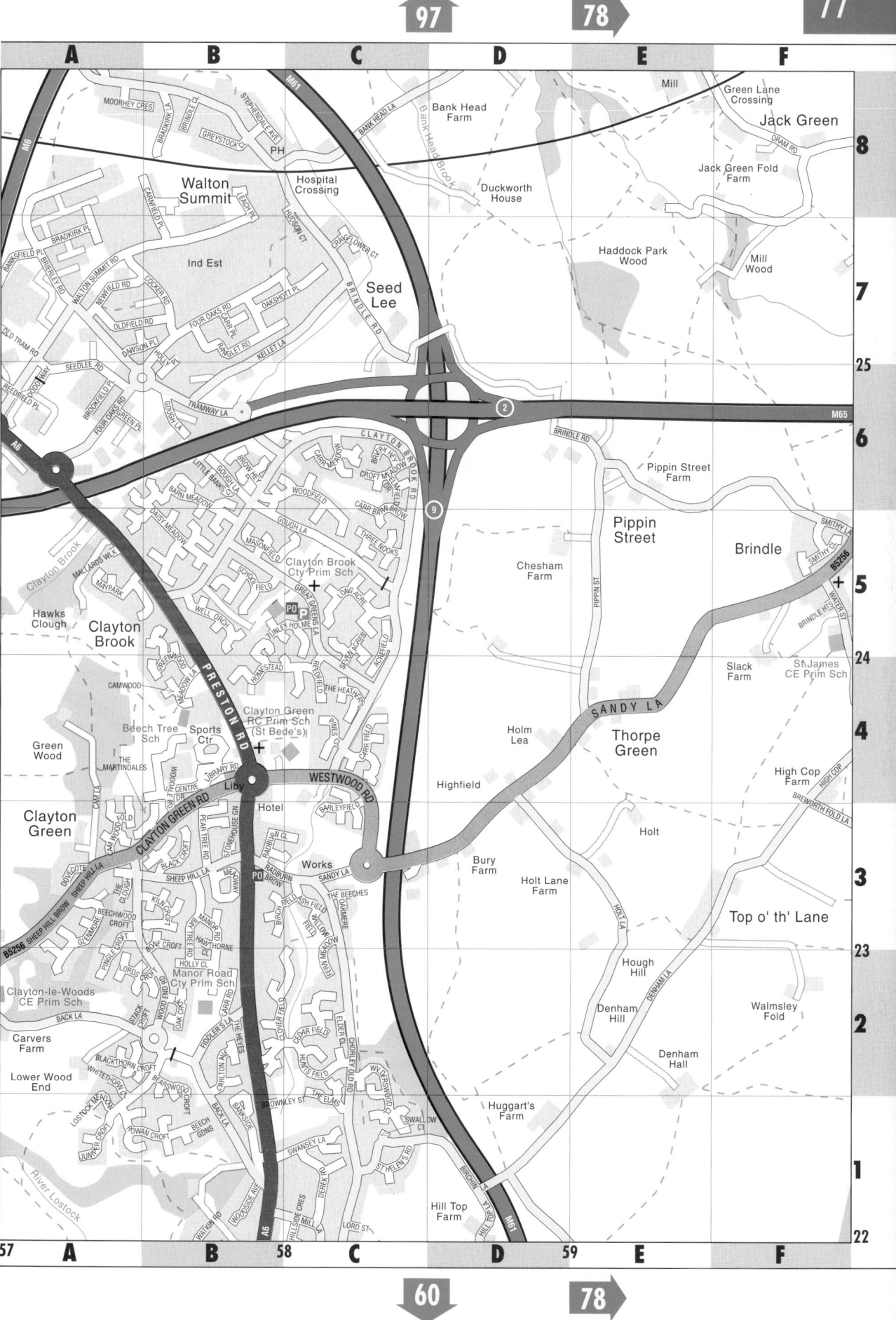

A B C D E F

8
7
25
6
5
24
4
3
23
2
1
22

Millstone Farm
Yew Tree Farm
Dover Farm
Green Lane Farm
Riley Green
Causeway Farm
Back Lane Farm
Royal Oak Hotel (PH)
Grimshaw Farm
Silcock Farm
RILEY GREEN SWITCH RD
HOGHTON LA
A675
B5256
BBC Radio Station
Mast
A6061
Windmill Hill
Moss Farm
Riley Green Bridge
The Boatyard Inn (PH)
Town House Farm
SANDY LA
Head-o-th'-Marsh
BOLTON RD
M65
STONY BANK
Bateson's Farm
Leigh Farm
Brimmicroft Farm
A675
M65
B5256
MARSH LA
Ollerton Bridge No 1
Leeds & Liverpool Canal
A674
PH
Sewage Works
Ollerton Bridge No 2
Ollerton Fold
Laund Fold
Marsh Lane Farm
Knowles Farm
Calvert's Farm
HILTON'S BROW
Lower Hilton's
Ollerton Bridge No 3
Ollerton Hall
OLLERTON LA
LAUND LA
CHORLEY RD
SCHOOL LA
Lark Hill
BREWORTH FOLD LA
Withnell Fold
OLLERTON TERR
BURY LA
Breworth Fold
PARKE MEWS
MILL WOOD
THE CLOSE
Withnell House (Home for the Aged)
Withnell Fold Prim Sch
Cross Fields
THIRLMERE DR
OAKMERE AVE
Snape's Heights
Lower Hill Farm
WITHNELL FOLD OLD RD
LAWTON CL
BLACKBURN RD
PENNY LA
Flash Green Farm
PH
BETT LA
Lower Simpson Fold
Higher Wheelton
BUCKHOLES LA
Pike Lowe
WHINS LA
A674
Woodruff Farm

River Darwen
Witton Weavers Way
GREEN LA

60 61 62

F2

1 NELSON ST	10 MELROSE ST
2 DOBSON ST	11 MATLOCK ST
3 FRANCES ST	12 HIGHER LAWRENCE
4 BROUGHTON ST	13 ROBERT ST
5 FINCH ST	
6 DERWENT ST	
7 ALEXANDRA VIEW	
8 ALEXANDRA RD	
9 WOOD STREET LIVESEY FOLD	

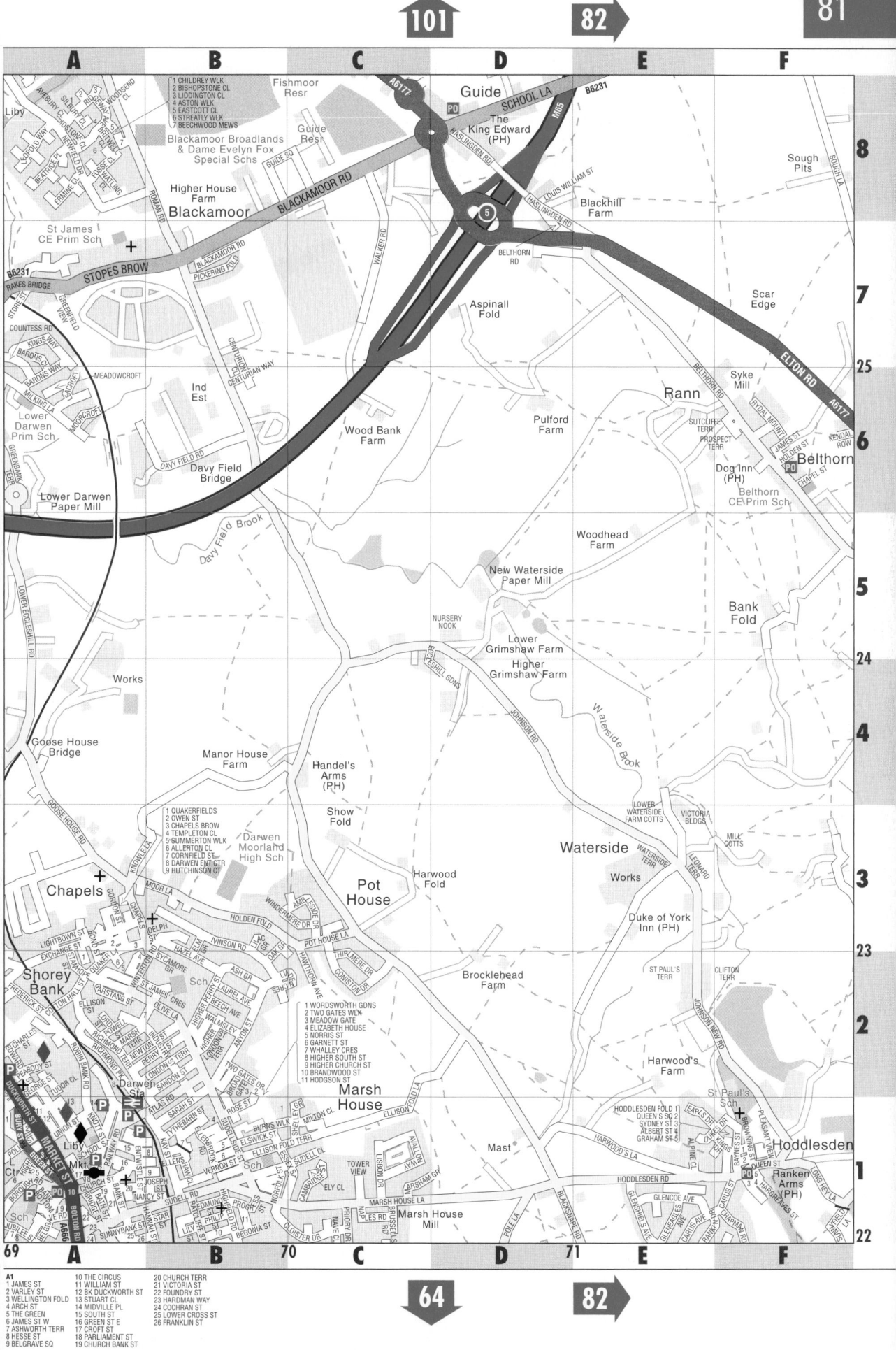

A   B   C   D   E   F

8

7

25

6

5

24

4

3

23

2

1

22

A1
1 JAMES ST
2 VARLEY ST
3 WELLINGTON FOLD
4 ARCH ST
5 THE GREEN
6 JAMES ST W
7 ASHWORTH TERR
8 HESSE ST
9 BELGRAVE SQ
10 THE CIRCUS
11 WILLIAM ST
12 BK DUCKWORTH ST
13 STUART CL
14 MIDVILLE PL
15 SOUTH ST
16 GREEN ST E
17 CROFT ST
18 PARLIAMENT ST
19 CHURCH BANK ST
20 CHURCH TERR
21 VICTORIA ST
22 FOUNDRY ST
23 HARDMAN WAY
24 COCHRAN ST
25 LOWER CROSS ST
26 FRANKLIN ST

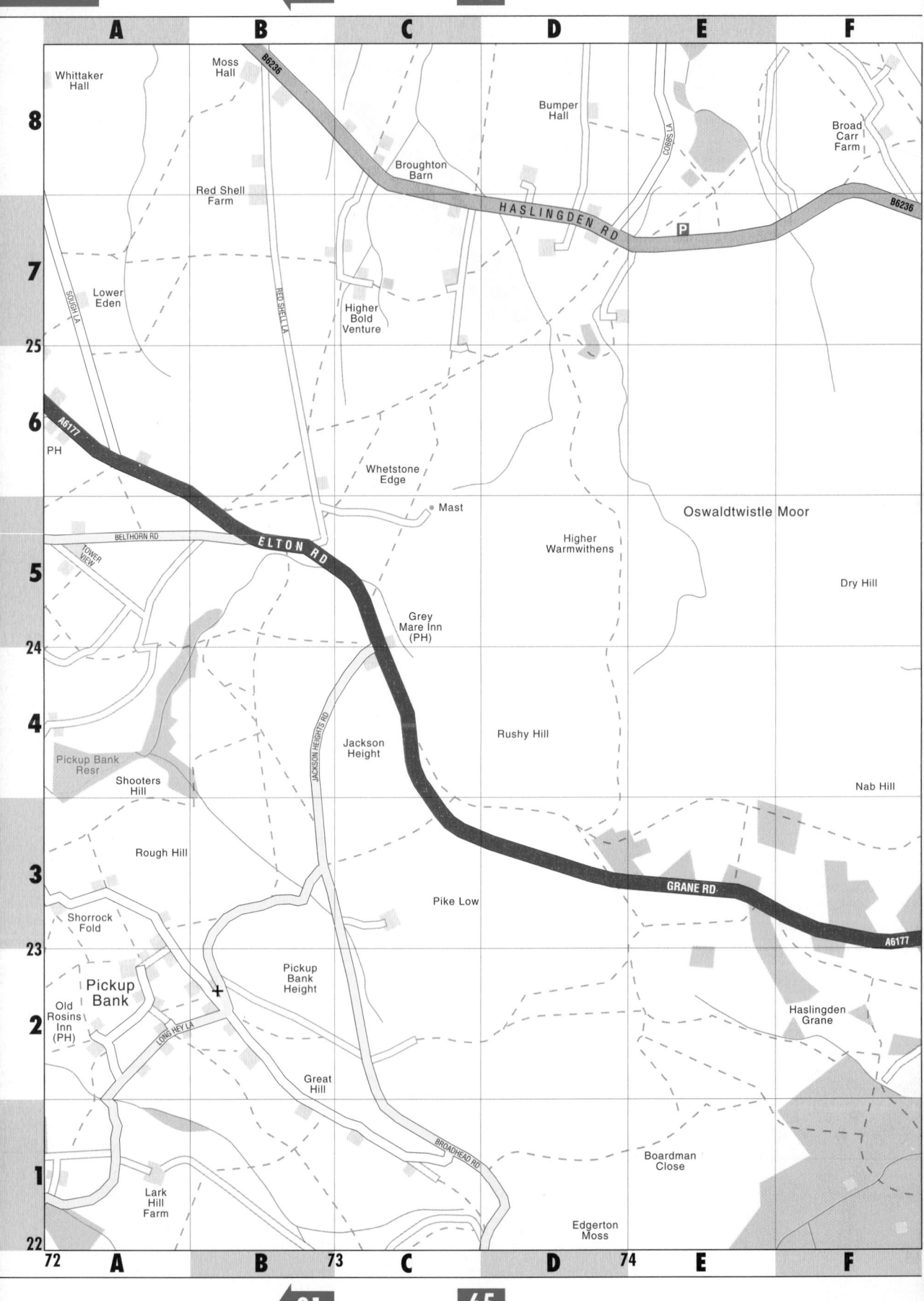

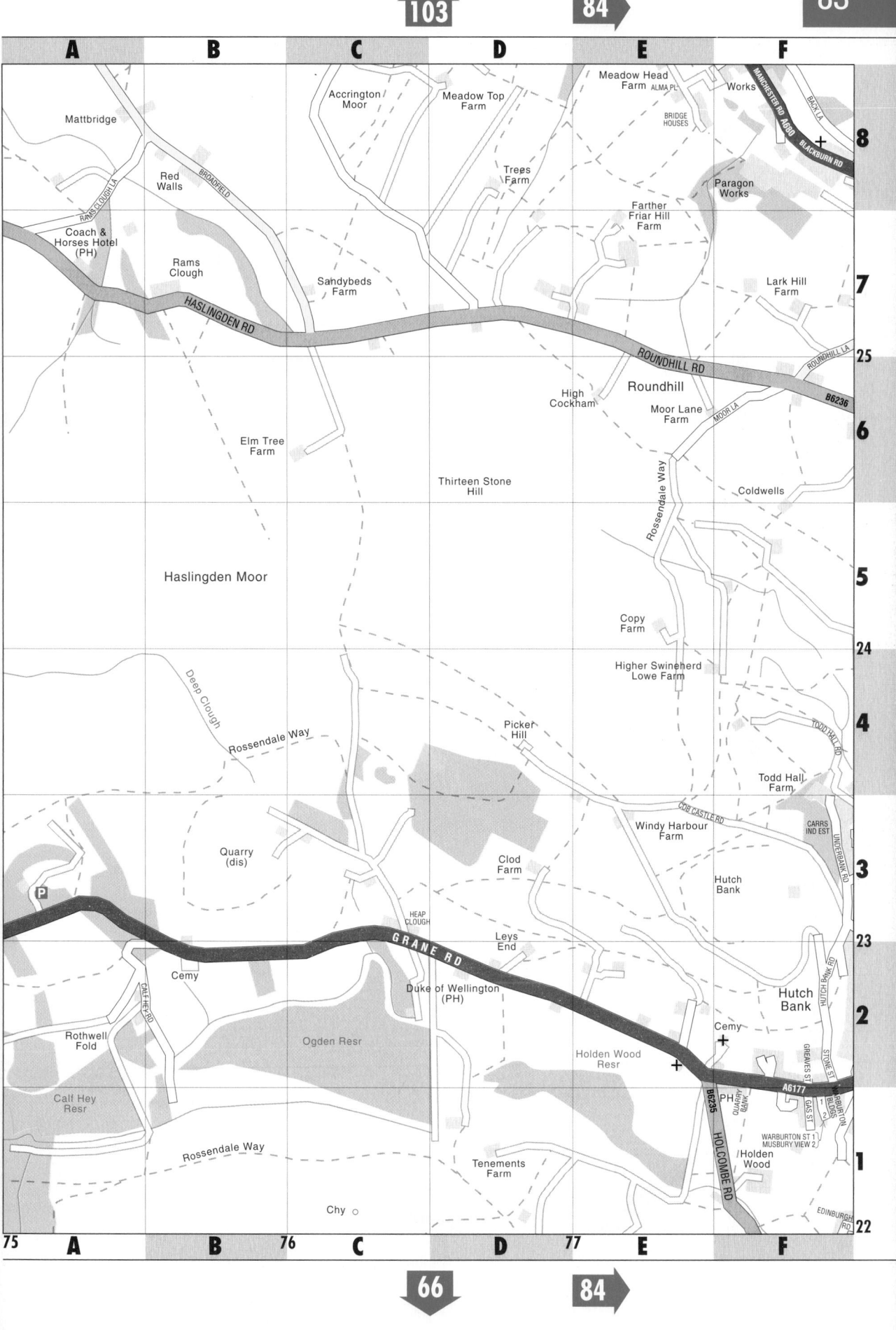

A   B   C   D   E   F

8

Mattbridge

Meadow Head Farm   ALMA PL.   Works   MANCHESTER RD A680   BACK LA   BLACKBURN RD

BRIDGE HOUSES

Accrington Moor   Meadow Top Farm

Red Walls   BROADFIELD

Paragon Works

Trees Farm

Coach & Horses Hotel (PH)   RAMS CLOUGH LA   Farther Friar Hill Farm   Lark Hill Farm   7

Rams Clough   Sandybeds Farm

HASLINGDEN RD   ROUNDHILL RD   ROUNDHILL LA   25

High Cockham   Roundhill   B6236

Moor Lane Farm   MOOR LA   6

Elm Tree Farm   Rossendale Way   Coldwells

Thirteen Stone Hill

Haslingden Moor   5

Copy Farm

24

Higher Swineherd Lowe Farm

Deep Clough   TODD HILL RD   4

Rossendale Way   Picker Hill

Todd Hall Farm

COB CASTLE RD

CARRS IND EST   UNDERBANK RD

Quarry (dis)   Windy Harbour Farm

Clod Farm   Hutch Bank   3

P   HEAP CLOUGH   Leys End   23

GRANE RD

Cemy   HUTCH BANK RD   Hutch Bank   2

CALF HEY RD   Duke of Wellington (PH)   Cemy

Rothwell Fold   Ogden Resr   GREAVES ST   STONE ST

Holden Wood Resr   A6177   WARBURTON BLDGS

Calf Hey Resr   B6235   PH   GAS ST

QUARRY BANK   WARBURTON ST 1   MUSBURY VIEW 2

Rossendale Way   HOLCOMBE RD   Holden Wood   1

Tenements Farm

Chy   EDINBURGH RD   22

A1
1 JUBILEE CT
2 SANDRINGHAM GR
3 HELMCROFT
4 CLARENCE AVE
A3
1 UNDERBANK WAY
2 LINCOLN ST
3 QUEEN ANNE ST
4 THOMAS ST

5 MARSDEN ST
6 SUNNYBANK ST
B1
1 HELMCROFT CT
2 BEAUMARIS CL
3 CRICCIETH CL

B2
1 GREENFIELD GDNS
2 HAZELDENE AVE

3 BANK MILL ST
4 NORTHCOTE ST
5 SIZE HOUSE VILLAGE
6 ST PETER'S PL
7 WHITECROFT AVE
B3
1 HARTLEY ST
2 BACK REGENT ST
3 ST JAMES CL
4 DAVITT CL

B3
5 BURGESS ST
6 RATCLIFFE FOLD
7 CENTRAL SQ
8 SMITHY ST
9 RATCLIFFE ST
10 COAL HEY ST
11 NEW ST
12 SALISBURY ST
13 BEACONSFIELD ST

B3
14 STORE ST
15 ROCK ST
16 LACEY CT
17 SOUTH VIEW

E2
1 OSBORNE TERR
2 AMBLESIDE AVE
3 EGYPT TERR
4 OLD ROW
5 SPRING TERR S
6 GARNALL'S BLDGS
7 ALMSHOUSES

F1
1 SYCAMORE CRES
2 HILL VIEW
3 SHAWFIELD
4 BARLOWS BLDGS
5 DALE VIEW
6 CARR MOUNT

A   B   C   D   E   F

8

Forest
Holme

Peersclough Farm

Crawshawbooth
Cty Prim
Sch

FOLLY
TERR

Bottomley Bank
Farm

Liby

Crawshawbooth

ALBERT RD

PEERS CLOUGH RD

LOWER HOUSE GN

B6238

7

Crown
Farm

A7
1 WOOD NOOK
2 MANSION HOUSE BLDGS
3 CO-OPERATION ST
4 BACK LORD ST
5 ST JOHN'S CL
6 KERSHAW CL
7 PARROCK ST
8 BOULDER ST
9 ROCK TERR
10 SPENCER ST
11 MINOR ST
12 DRIVER ST
13 BACK HILL ST
14 CROSS ST

Swinshaw Moor

Bank
Top

BRIDGE
HOUSES

25

Rake Foot

Height Side
Farm

Higher Bank
Top

Hargreaves
Arms
(PH)

6

1 RUSHBED COTTS
2 REEDSHOLME CL
3 STABLES CL

Rush Bed

Reeds Farm

Higher
Walls

Lumb

SHORT CLOUGH LA

Bonfire Hill

Wheat Head

Mast

HARGREAVES LA

PINCH CLOUGH RD

Salisbury
Farm

5

Higher
Constablelee

The Height

ALBERT ST 1
HARGREAVES ST 2
SAGAR HOLME TERR 3

Works

Whitewell
Bottom

EDGE VALE LA

ROCK RD

WEST VIEW ST

BURNLEY RD E

24

1 WORSTON CL
2 CHATBURN CL
3 ABBOTS CL

Constable
Lee

Alder Grange
High Sch

Chapel Hill
Farm

Meadowhead

Top o' th'
Height

PHILLIPSTOWN
CRABTREE BLDGS 1
CRABTREE ST 2
HIGHTOWN RD 3
OSBORNE TERR 4
LAWRENCE ST 5
ELIZABETH ST 6

PO

Brock Clough
Farm

4

CHAPEL HILL LA

SCHOOL LA

BROCK CLOUGH RD

LUMB LA

FOXHILL

7 HOLLIN CL
8 ROSEACRE CL

Cemy

HURST LA

Myrtle Earth
Farm

EDGE LA

SLINGER HEIGHT LA

WELL ST 1
ODDFELLOWS TERR 2
TATTERSHALL SQ 3
PIERCY MEADOW 4
PIERCY MOUNT 5
PIERCY TERR 6
VIEW TERR 7

SCOUT RD

SHAW CLOUGH RD

ST ANNE'S
CRES

3

WAINGATE

1 HOLMES ST
2 NUTTALL ST
3 GRANGE AVE
4 ALDER ST

Spring Side

Marl Pits
Sports Complex

Far Height
Side

Scout

ASHWORTH LA

23

Mkt

HURST CRES

ROSE BANK

WAINGATE RD

GREEN ST

WAINGATE CL

Higher
Cloughfold

Seat
Naze

WALL ST
ROSE ST

CHARLES ST

TOM LA

CRABTREE AVE

FAIRFIELD AVE

EDGESIDE LA

Piercy

2

BURNLEY RD

ST MARY'S WAY

SPRINGFIELD RD

GRANGE RD

PLANTATION ST

GREENBANK ST

NEWCHURCH RD

CO-OPERAT

BRICK CRES

1 ROSE VALE ST
2 LEVER ST
3 WHEATHOLME ST

Lower
Cloughfold

JOHNNY BARN
COTTS

DOBBIN CL

DOBBIN LA

LEA BANK

HEIGHTSIDE
MEWS

St Peter's RC
Prim Sch

CO-OPERATION ST 1
PARADISE ST 2
CLARKE HOLME ST 3
NAZE VIEW AVE 4
NEWBIGGING AVE 5

NAZE RD

PO

BRIDLEWAY

Newchurch

Edgeside

WALES TERR

WALES RD

1 EASTWOOD ST
2 EASTWOOD CRES
3 DOBBIN CT

Sch

PEEL ST

BRANT LA

BACK CHURCH

Cloughfold

Hareholme

STAGHILLS RD

RECTORY CL

PRIORY CL

BROW

WINDSOR AVE

NORTH ST

SOUTH ST

KIRKDALE AVE

CHAPEL ST

CHURCH ST

TURNPIKE

OLD ST

1

Longholme

Mill

BACUP RD

FALLBARN RD

River Irwell

DAM
TOP

ALBERT
TERR

UNION
TERR

VICTORIA ST

BARON ST

HOPE ST

HILL END

BROOKLAND ST

GILBERT ST

STAGHILLS RD

NORSIDE CRES

TOP BARN LA

DEARDEN AVE

CORPORATION ST

CHURCH LA

Staghills

Booth
Fold

Swiss
Clough

Hall Carr

RAWTENSTALL

UPPER
ASHMOUNT

QUEEN HOUSE 1
COBDEN HOUSE 2
ALBERT HOUSE 3
CUNCLIFFE HOUSE 4
WEBER ST 5
ROSTRON'S BLDGS 6

HIGHFIELD RD

Newchurch
CE Prim Sch

BRIDGE CARR

QUEENSWAY

THISTLEMOUNT AVE

GRESHAM ST

PHEASANT VIEW

WALES TERR

PARK VIEW

B6238

GAGHILLS TERR

TORNFIELD

22

A2
1 RABY ST
2 GRANGE ST
3 WARWICK CRES
4 THE VALLEY CTR
5 ANNIE ST
6 ST MARY'S TERR
7 QUEEN'S SQ
8 PARRAMATTA ST
9 LONGHOLME RD

A3
1 ST JAMES ST
2 IVY GR
3 ASH GR
4 PROSPECT HILL
5 ROCKLIFFE ST
6 TAYLOR ST
7 ROBERTS ST
8 CURTIS
9 CRANKSHAW ST

10 WHITEHEAD ST
11 BARLOW ST
12 HALL ST
13 BRIGHT ST
14 BALDWIN'S BLDGS
15 MILL GATE
16 SOUTH ST
17 EAST PAR
18 MILLGATE RD
19 GRANGE TERR

20 ALDER BANK

E1
1 CHOBHAM CT
2 HALMOT CT
3 NAZE CT
4 BOLTON ST
5 BRANDWOOD

F1
1 THE HAWTHORNS
2 MELBOURNE ST
3 GAGHILLS TERR
4 WEST VIEW
5 CLOUGH ST

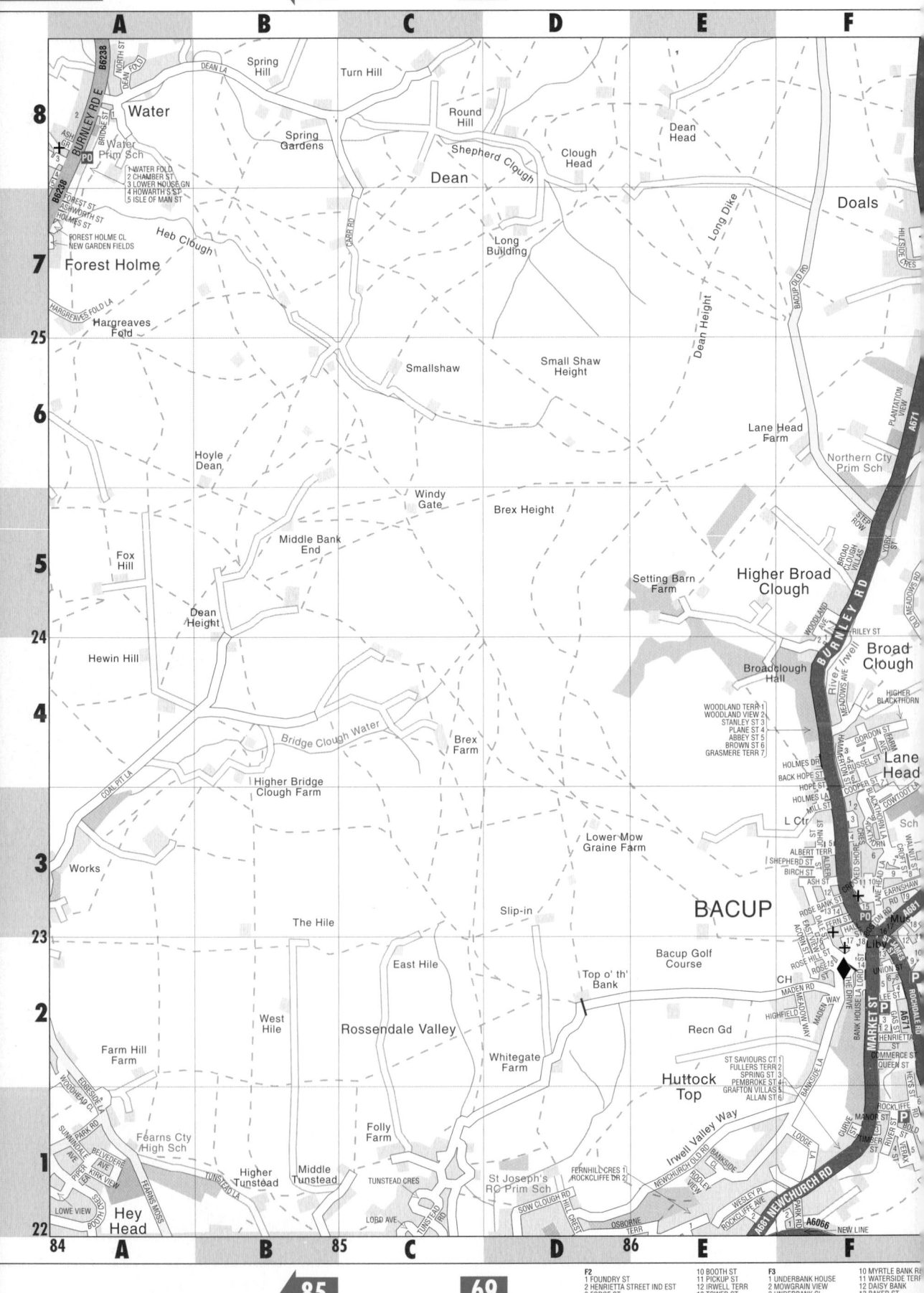

F2		F3	
1 FOUNDRY ST	10 BOOTH ST	1 UNDERBANK HOUSE	10 MYRTLE BANK RD
2 HENRIETTA STREET IND EST	11 PICKUP ST	2 MOWGRAIN VIEW	11 WATERSIDE TERR
3 FORGE ST	12 IRWELL TERR	3 UNDERBANK CL	12 DAISY BANK
4 INDUSTRIAL PL	13 TOWER ST	4 LAUREL ST	13 BAKER ST
5 KING ST	14 BANK ST	5 BACK ST JOHN ST	14 GOOSE HILL ST
6 AUSTIN ST	15 THISTLE ST	6 ST JOHN'S CT	15 HARCOURT ST
7 IRWELL ST	16 LILY ST	7 STANLEY MOUNT	16 ST JAMES SQ
8 KERSHAW ST	17 PRINCESS ST	8 BENTLEY ST	17 YORKSHIRE ST
9 LUMB SCAR	18 MAITLAND ST	9 HIGHER CROSS ROW	18 HAMMERTON GN
			19 EARNSHAW ROW

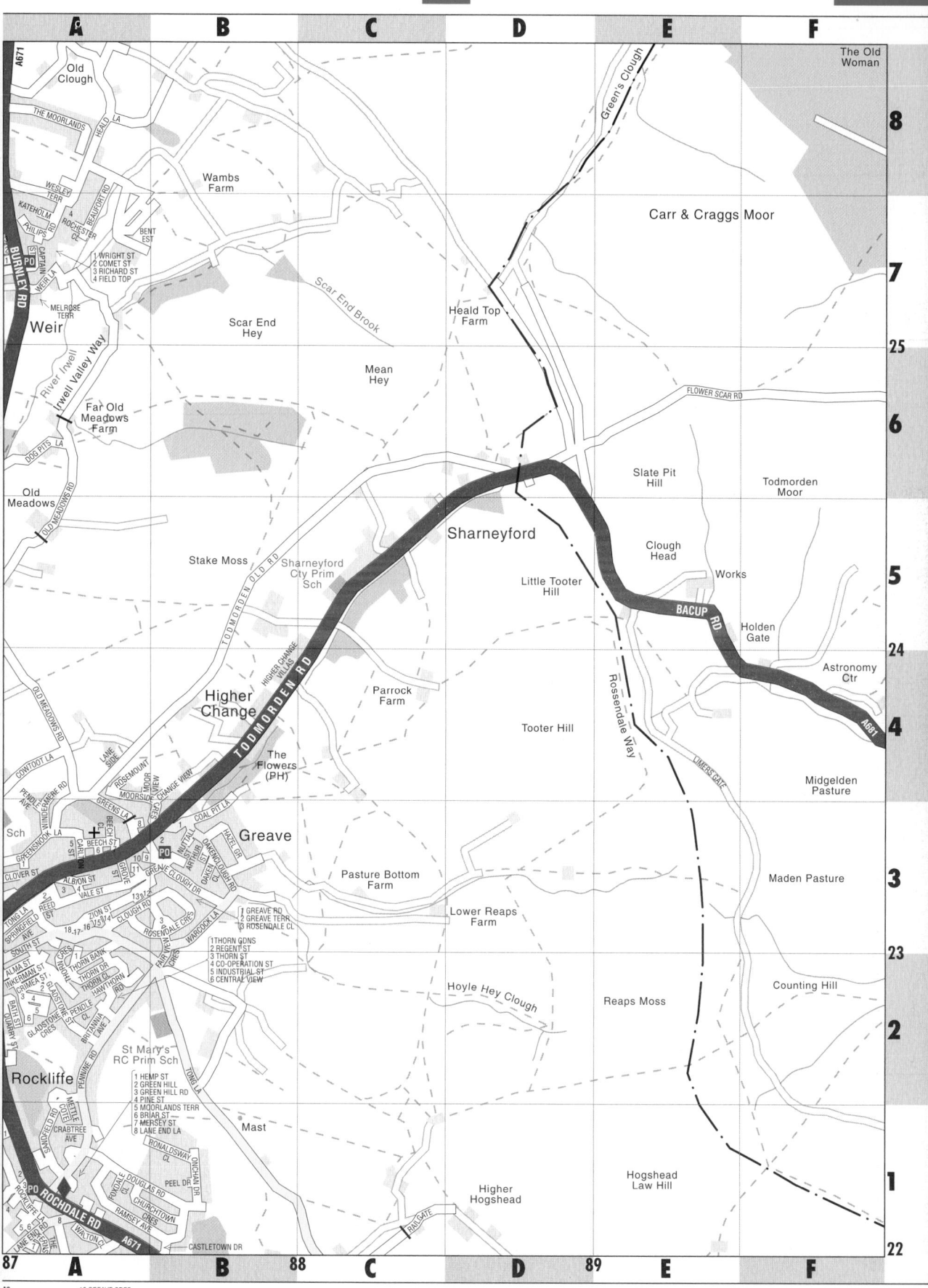

A671
Old Clough
THE MOORLANDS
HEALD LA
WESLEY TERR
KATEHOLM
PHILIPS ST
BEAUFORT RD
ROCHESTER CL
CAPTAIN WEIR LA
BURLEY PO
BURNLEY RD
MELROSE TERR
Weir
BENT EST
1 WRIGHT ST
2 COMET ST
3 RICHARD ST
4 FIELD TOP
Wambs Farm
Scar End Brook
Scar End Hey
Heald Top Farm
Green's Clough
The Old Woman
Carr & Craggs Moor

8

7

River Irwell
Irwell Valley Way
Far Old Meadows Farm
DOG PITS LA
Old Meadows
OLD MEADOWS RD
Mean Hey
FLOWER SCAR RD

25

6

Stake Moss
TODMORDEN OLD RD
Sharneyford Cty Prim Sch
Sharneyford
Slate Pit Hill
Little Tooter Hill
Clough Head
Works
Todmorden Moor
Holden Gate
BACUP RD
Astronomy Ctr
A681

5

24

4

HIGHER CHANGE WLKS
HIGHER CHANGE RD
TODMORDEN RD
Higher Change
Parrock Farm
The Flowers (PH)
Tooter Hill
Rossendale Way
ULMERS GATE
Midgelden Pasture

CONTOOT LA
OLD MEADOWS RD
LANE SIDE
ROSEMOUNT VIEW
MOORSIDE CHANGE VIEW CRES
PENDLE GREENE AVE
PENNINE AVE
GREENS LA
BEECH LA
BEECH ST
CARLTON ST
Sch
GREENSNOOK LA
CLOVER ST
TONG LA
REED ST
ALBION ST
VALE ST
ZION ST
CLOUGH RD
Greave
PO
MULTA ST
ARTHUR ST
BACKING CLOUGH DR
DACEN ST
HAZEL GR
GROVE ST
WARCOCK LA
ROSENDALE CRES
1 GREAVE RD
2 GREAVE TERR
3 ROSENDALE CL
Pasture Bottom Farm
Lower Reaps Farm
Maden Pasture

3

Sch
SPRINGFIELD AVE
SOUTH ST
ALMA ST
INKERMAN ST
GRIMEA ST
GLADSTONE ST
GLADSTONE CRES
BATTISTON ST
QUARRY ST
THORN BAIN
THORN DR
THORN ST
HAWTHORN RD
PENDLE ST
BRITANNIA CL
FAIR VIEW
LANE CL
1 THORN GDNS
2 REGENT ST
3 THORN ST
4 CO-OPERATION ST
5 INDUSTRIAL ST
6 CENTRAL VIEW
Hoyle Hey Clough
Reaps Moss
Counting Hill

23

2

Rockliffe
GREENSFIELD RD
METTLE COTE ST
CRABTREE AVE
PENNINE ST
St Mary's RC Prim Sch
RONALDSWAY CL
DOUGLAS DR
RONTALE CL
CHURCHTOWN
ONCHAN DR
PEEL DR
RAMSEY AVE
1 HEMP ST
2 GREEN HILL
3 GREEN HILL RD
4 PINE ST
5 MOORLANDS TERR
6 BRIAR ST
7 MERSEY ST
8 LANE END LA
TONG LA
Mast
Higher Hogshead
Hogshead Law Hill

PO
ROCHDALE RD
A671
CASTLETOWN DR
RAILGATE

1

22

A3
1 GREENSNOOK TERR
2 SPRING GDNS
3 BEECH IND EST
4 CROSS ST
5 GREENSNOOK MEWS
6 CHRIST CHURCH ST
7 ELM ST
8 THE COURTYARD
9 GREAVE CLOUGH CL
10 GREAVE CRES
11 GREEN END CL
12 EDWARD ST
13 BEAVER TERR
14 HANNAH ST
15 ASHWORTH ST
16 COWGILL ST
17 WARKWORTH TERR
18 VENTURE ST

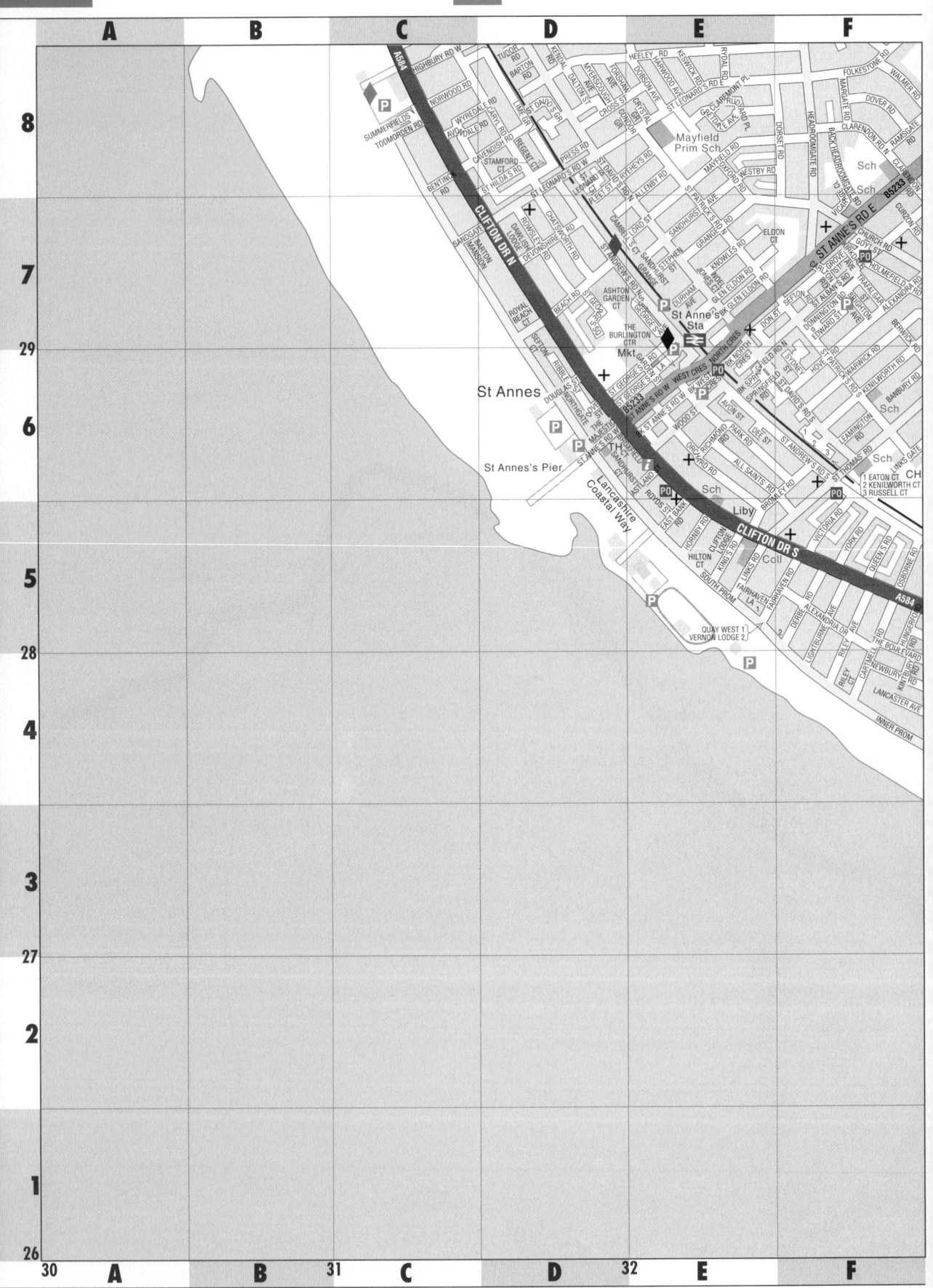

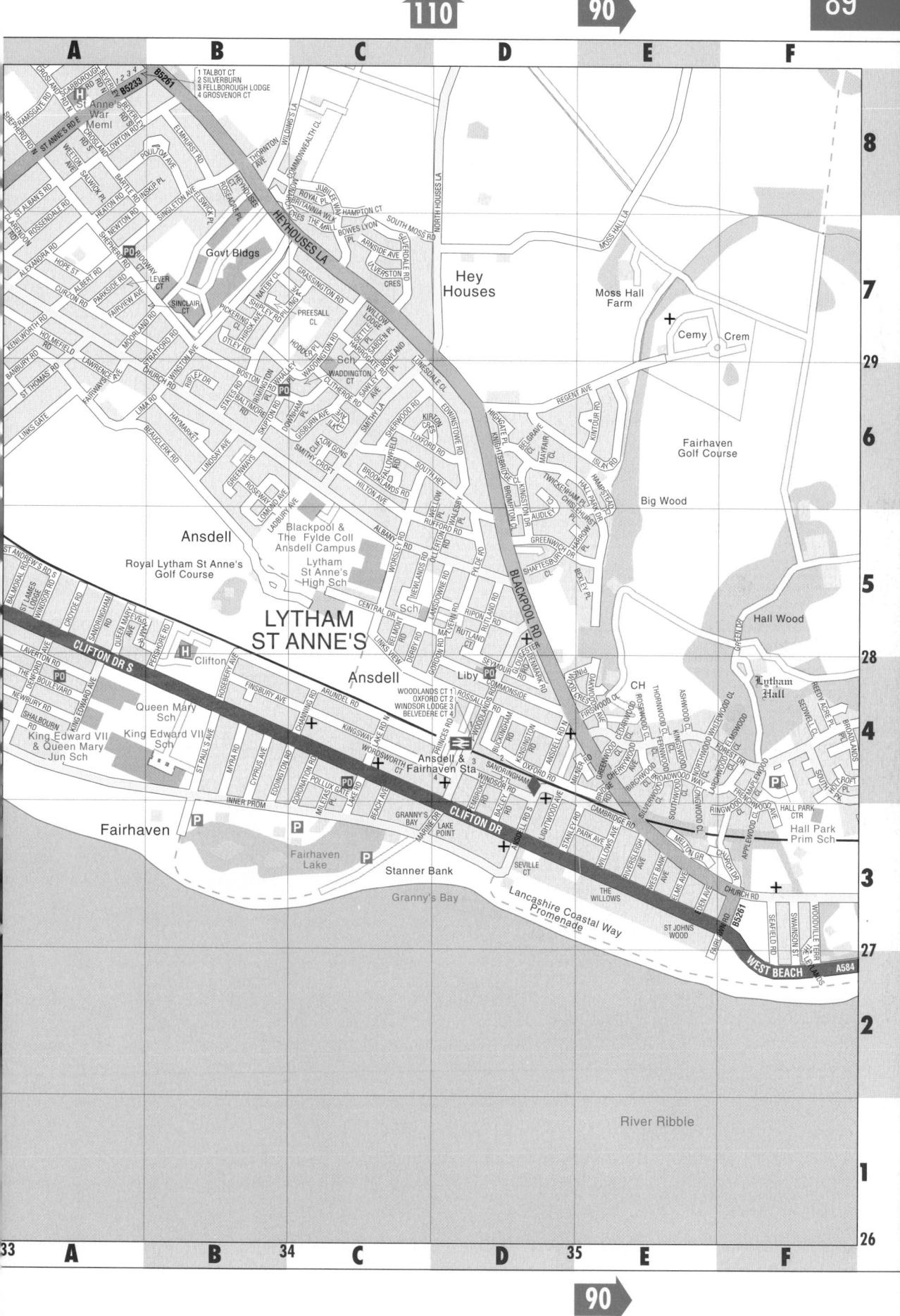

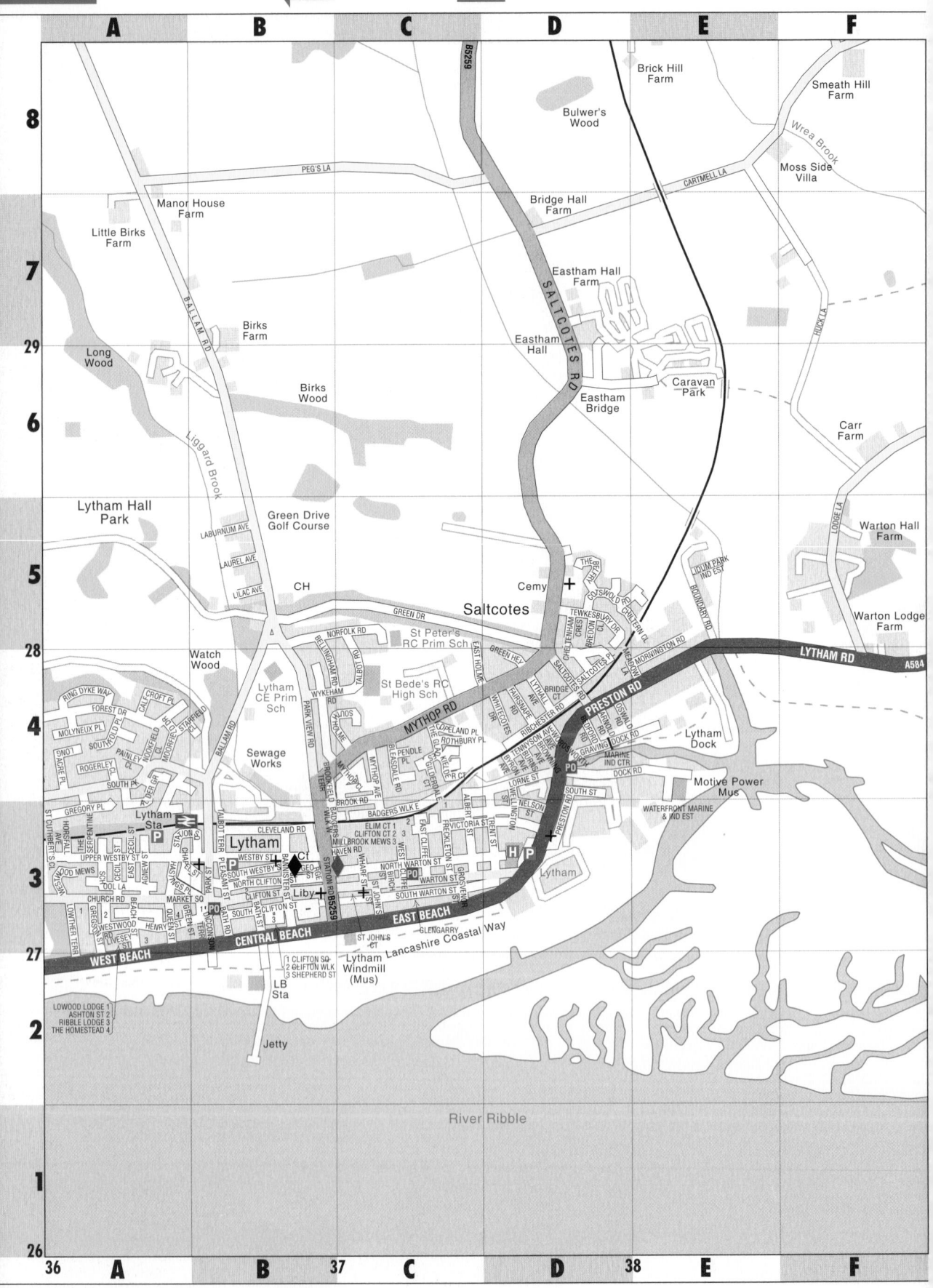

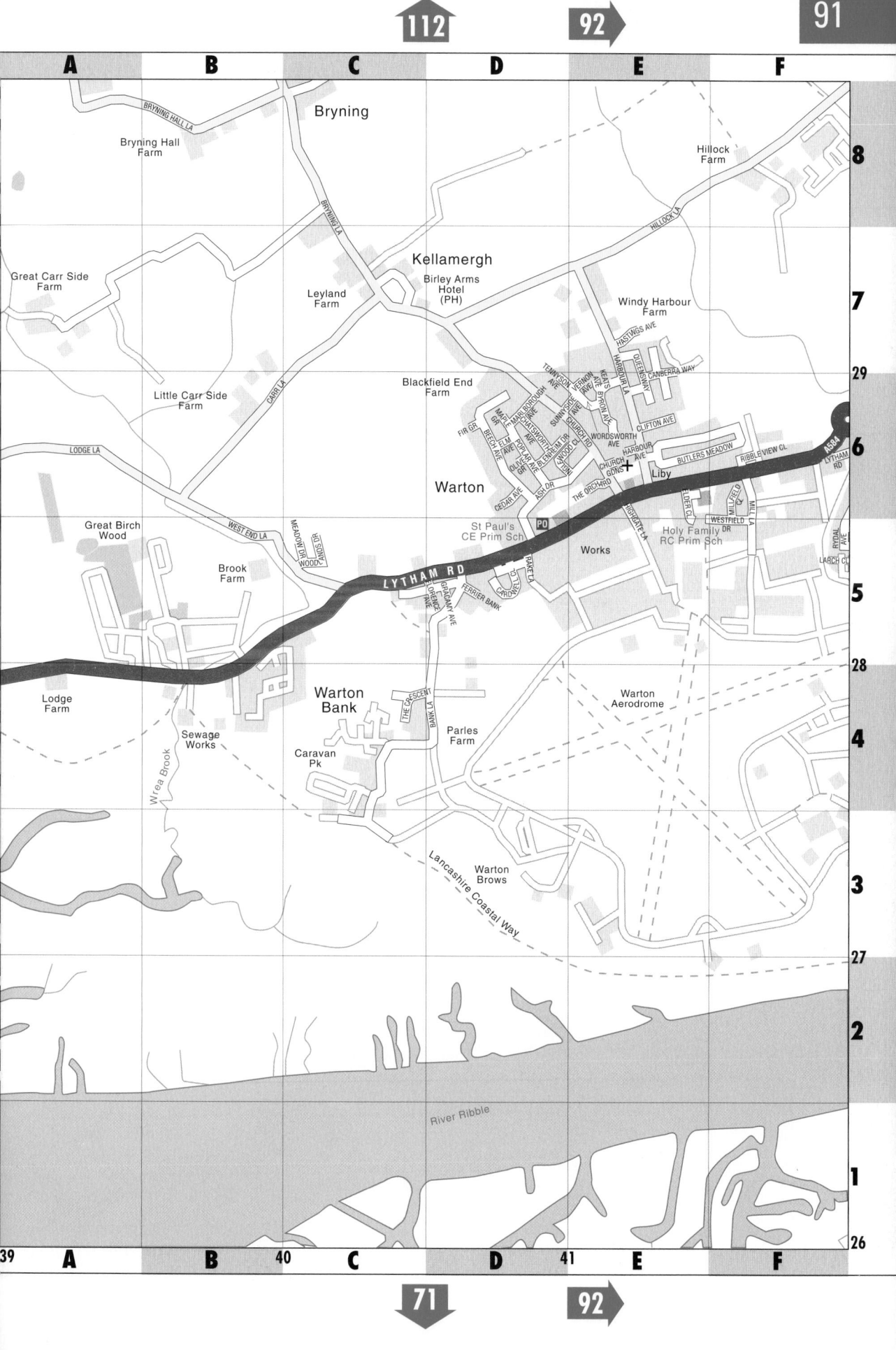

A B C D E F

8

Bryning Hall La

Bryning

Bryning Hall Farm

Hillock Farm

Great Carr Side Farm

Kellamergh

7

Leyland Farm

Birley Arms Hotel (PH)

Bryning La

Windy Harbour Farm

29

Little Carr Side Farm

Carr La

Blackfield End Farm

Hastings Ave

6

Lodge La

Tennyson Ave
Marlborough Ave
Chatsworth Ave
Sunnyside Ave
Vernon Ave
Byron Ave
Keats Ave
Queensway
Harbour La
Canberra Way
Clifton Ave

Fir Gr
Maple Gr
Beech Ave
Elm Ave
Poplar Ave
Olive Gr
Church Rd
West Dr
Wood Cl
Blenheim Dr
Wordsworth Ave
Church Gdns
Harbour Ave
Butlers Meadow
Ribble View Cl
A584
Lytham Rd

Warton

Cedar Ave
Ash Dr
The Orchard
Liby
Elder Cl
Westfield
Mill La

West End La

Meadow Dr
Songs Rd
Woods Rd

St Paul's CE Prim Sch

PO
Rake La

Holy Family RC Prim Sch

Highgate La

Rydal Ave

Great Birch Wood

Brook Farm

Works

Works

Larch Cl

5

28

Lodge Farm

Florence Ave
Granary Ave
Ferrier Bank
Cardens Rd

Warton Bank

The Crescent
Bank La

Warton Aerodrome

4

Caravan Pk

Parles Farm

Sewage Works

Wrea Brook

3

Warton Brows

Lancashire Coastal Way

27

2

River Ribble

1

26

39 A B 40 C D 41 E F

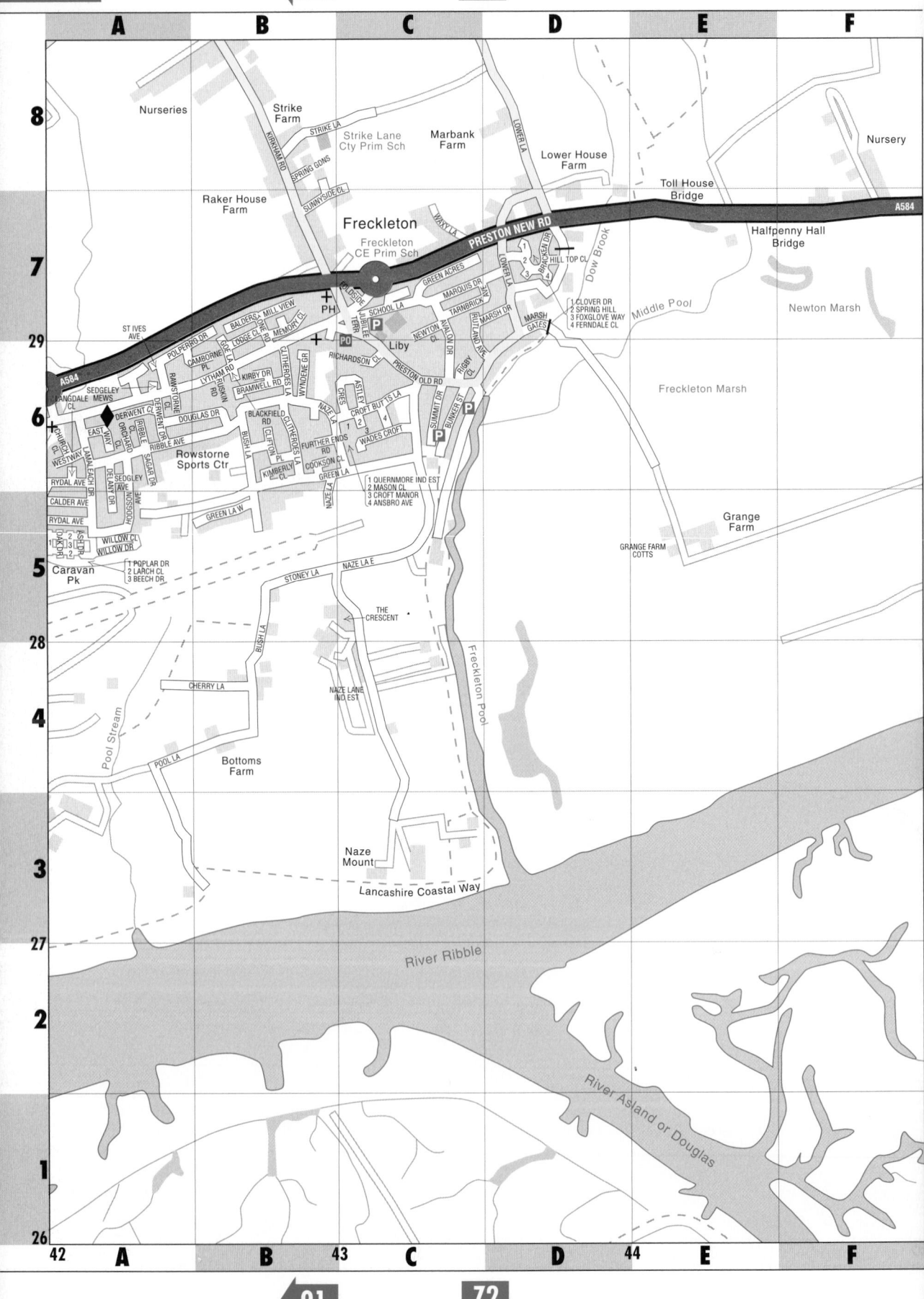

A B C D E F

8 Nurseries · Strike Farm · STRIKE LA · Strike Lane Cty Prim Sch · Marbank Farm · LOWER LA · Lower House Farm · Toll House Bridge · Nursery

KIRKHAM RD · SPRING GDNS · SUNNYSIDE CL · A584 · Halfpenny Hall Bridge

Raker House Farm · Freckleton · PRESTON NEW RD · Dow Brook

Freckleton

Freckleton CE Prim Sch · WYXIA · Newton Marsh

7 · Middle Pool · BRACKEN DR · HILL TOP CL

1 · 2 · 3 · 4 FERNDALE CL

St Ives Ave · PH · SCHOOL LA · GREEN ACRES · MARQUIS DR · TARNBRICK · MARSH DR

1 CLOVER DR
2 SPRING HILL
3 FOXGLOVE WAY
4 FERNDALE CL

29 · POLPERRO DR · BALDERS · MILL VIEW · LODGE CL · MEMORY CL · Liby · RICHARDSON CL · NEWTON · AVALON DR · RUTLAND AVE · RIGBY CL · MARSH GATES

CAMBORNE PL · LYTHAM RD · CLITHEROES LA · WYNDENE GR · PRESTON OLD RD

SEDGELEY · LANGDALE MEWS · RAWSTORNE

A584 · Freckleton Marsh

6 CHURCH CL · DERWENT CL · DOUGLAS DR · ASTLEY CRES · CROFT BUTTS LA · SUMMIT DR · BUNKER ST

EAST WAY · ORCHARD · RIBBLE AVE · BLACKFIELD RD · CLIFTON · FURTHER ENDS RD · WADES CROFT

WESTWAY · ALMEACH DR · SEDGLEY AVE · SUGAR LA · KIMBERLY CL · COOKSON CL

RYDAL AVE · HOODSON · BUSH LA · GREEN LA

CALDER AVE · Rowstorne Sports Ctr · NAZE LA

RYDAL AVE · GREEN LA W · 1 QUERNMORE IND EST
2 MASON CL
3 CROFT MANOR
4 ANSBRO AVE

Grange Farm

WILLOW CL · WILLOW DR

1 OAK DR
2
3 · ASH DR

GRANGE FARM COTTS

5 Caravan Pk · 1 POPLAR DR
2 LARCH CL
3 BEECH DR · NAZE LA E

STONEY LA · NAZE LA E

THE CRESCENT

28 · BUSH LA · Freckleton Pool

CHERRY LA · NAZE LANE IND EST

4 · POOL LA · Bottoms Farm

Pool Stream

3 · Naze Mount · Lancashire Coastal Way

27 · River Ribble

2 · River Asland or Douglas

1

26

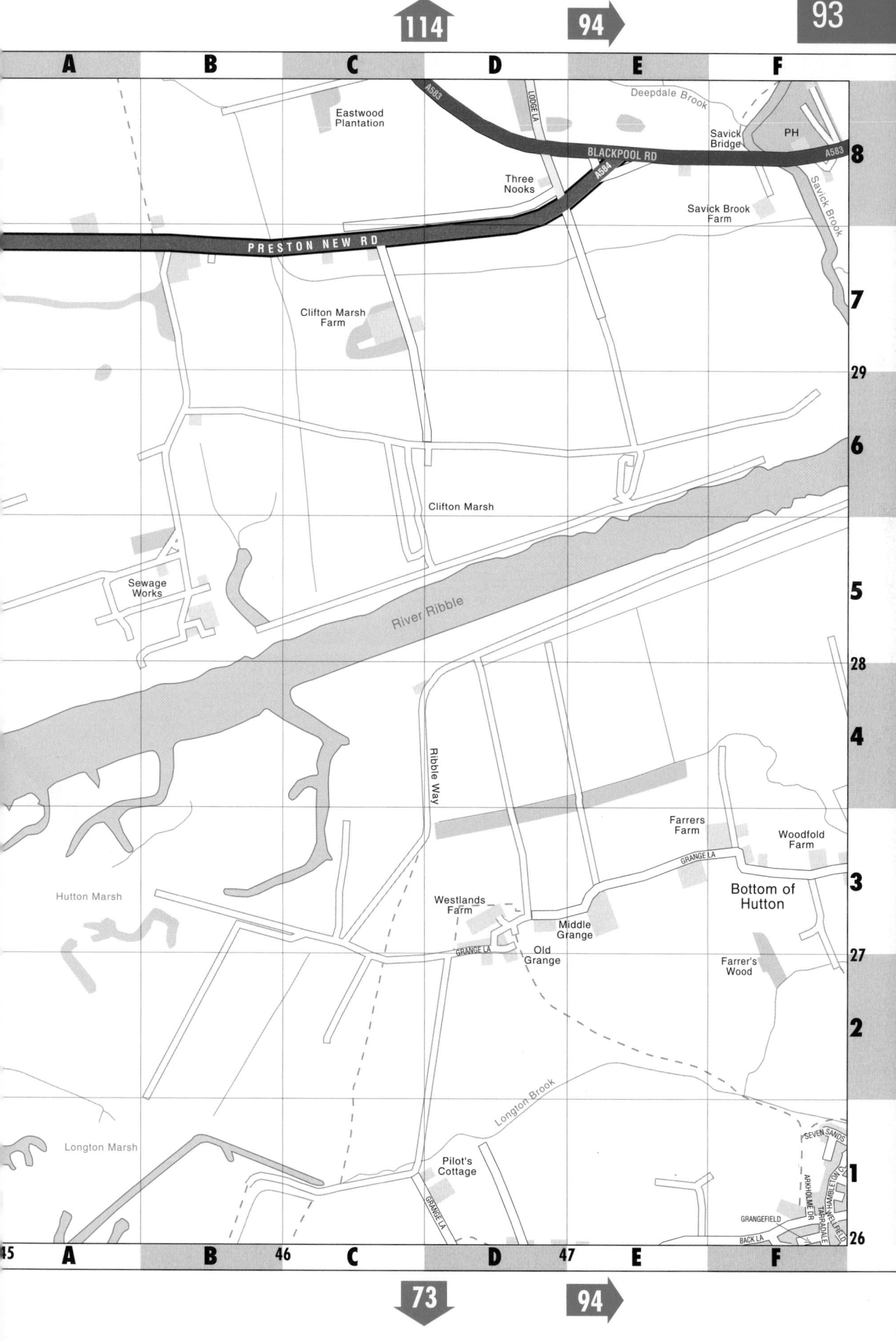

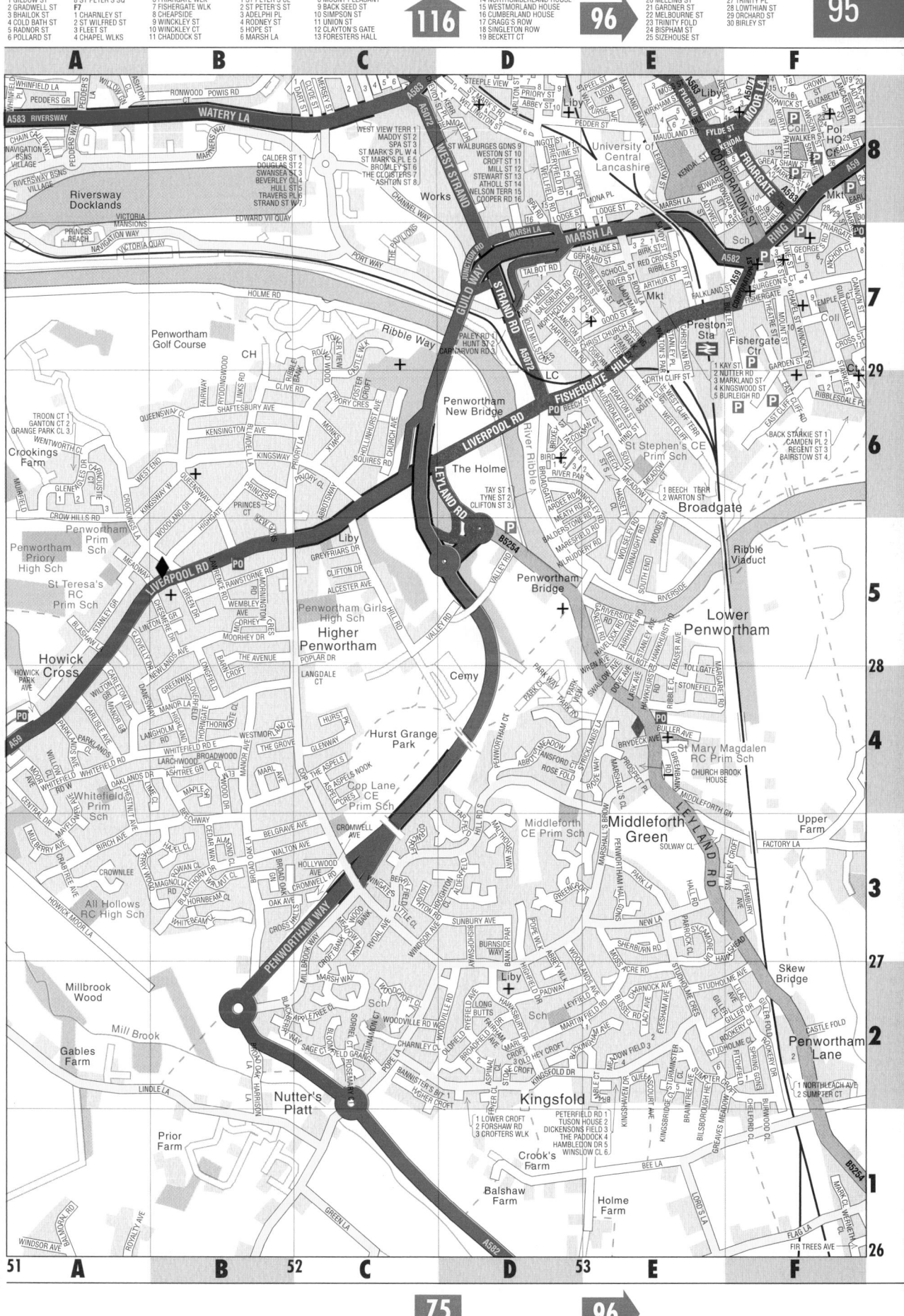

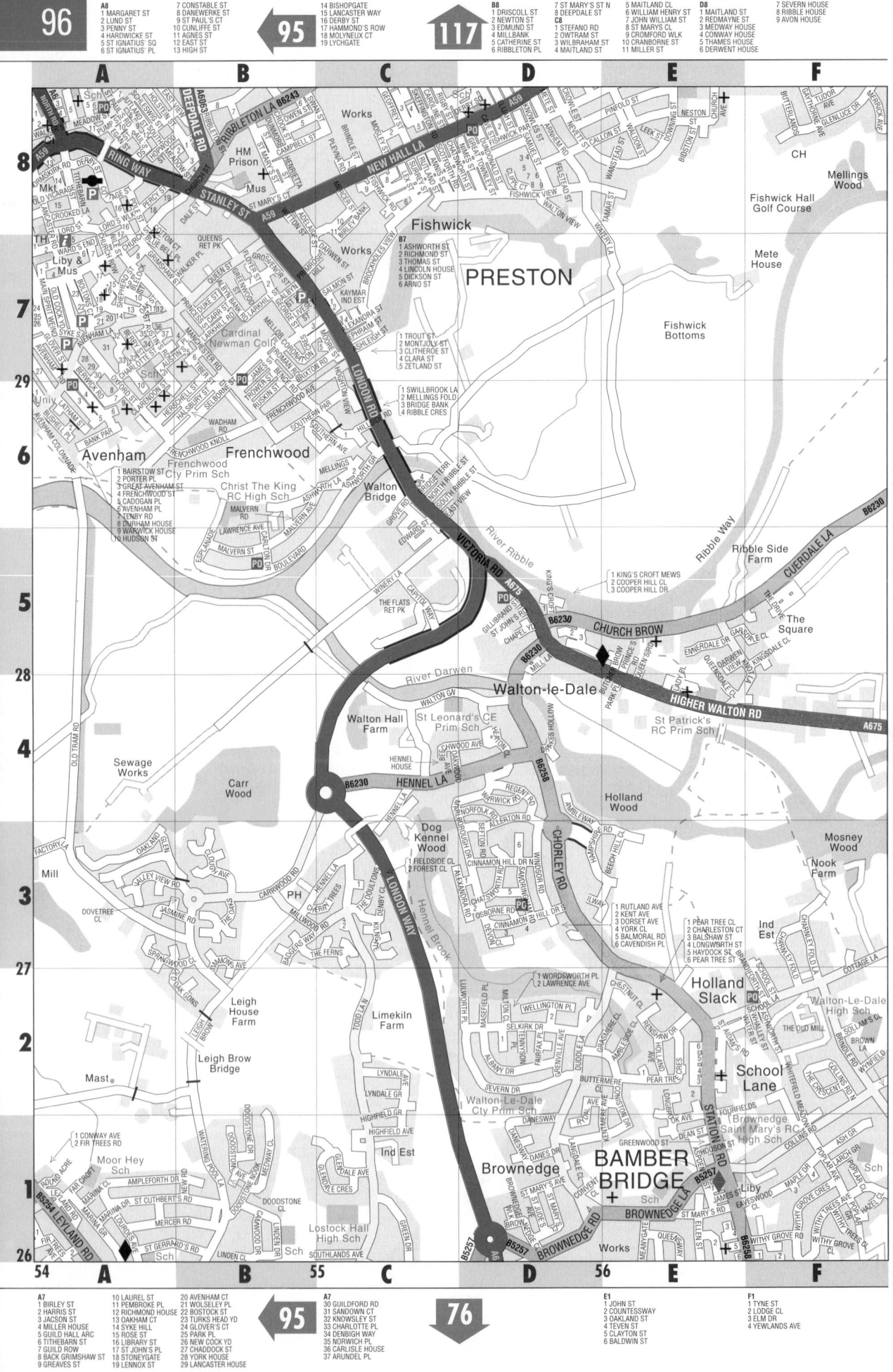

A8
1 MARGARET ST
2 LUND ST
3 PENNY ST
4 HARDWICKE ST
5 ST IGNATIUS' SQ
6 ST IGNATIUS' PL

7 CONSTABLE ST
8 DANEWERKE ST
9 ST PAUL'S CT
10 CUNLIFFE ST
11 AGNES ST
12 EAST ST
13 HIGH ST

14 BISHOPGATE
15 LANCASTER WAY
16 DERBY ST
17 HAMMOND'S ROW
18 MOLYNEUX CT
19 LYCHGATE

B8
1 DRISCOLL ST
2 NEWTON ST
3 EDMUND ST
4 MILLBANK
5 CATHERINE ST
6 RIBBLETON PL

7 ST MARY'S ST N
8 DEEPDALE ST
C8
1 STEFANO RD
2 OWTRAM ST
3 WILBRAHAM ST
4 MAITLAND ST

5 MAITLAND CL
6 WILLIAM HENRY ST
7 JOHN WILLIAM ST
8 ST MARYS CL
9 CROMFORD WLK
10 CRANBORNE ST
11 MILLER ST

D8
1 MAITLAND CL
2 REDMAYNE ST
3 MEDWAY HOUSE
4 CONWAY HOUSE
5 THAMES HOUSE
6 DERWENT HOUSE

7 SEVERN HOUSE
8 RIBBLE HOUSE
9 AVON HOUSE

A7
1 BIRLEY ST
2 HARRIS ST
3 JACSON ST
4 MILLER HOUSE
5 GUILD HALL ARC
6 TITHEBARN ST
7 GUILD ROW
8 BACK GRIMSHAW ST
9 GREAVES ST

10 LAUREL ST
11 PEMBROKE PL
12 RICHMOND HOUSE
13 OAKHAM CT
14 IVY SYKE HILL
15 ROSE ST
16 LIBRARY ST
17 ST JOHN'S PL
18 STONEYGATE
19 LENNOX ST

20 AVENHAM CT
21 WOLSELEY PL
22 BOSTOCK ST
23 TURKS HEAD YD
24 GLOVER'S CT
25 PARK PL
26 NEW COCK YD
27 CHADDOCK ST
28 YORK ROW
29 LANCASTER HOUSE

A7
30 GUILDFORD RD
31 SANDOWN CT
32 KNOWSLEY CT
33 CHARLOTTE PL
34 DENBIGH WAY
35 NORWICH PL
36 CARLISLE HOUSE
37 ARUNDEL PL

E1
1 JOHN ST
2 COUNTESSWAY
3 OAKLAND ST
4 TEVEN ST
5 CLAYTON ST
6 BALDWIN ST

F1
1 TYNE ST
2 LODGE CL
3 ELM DR
4 YEWLANDS AVE

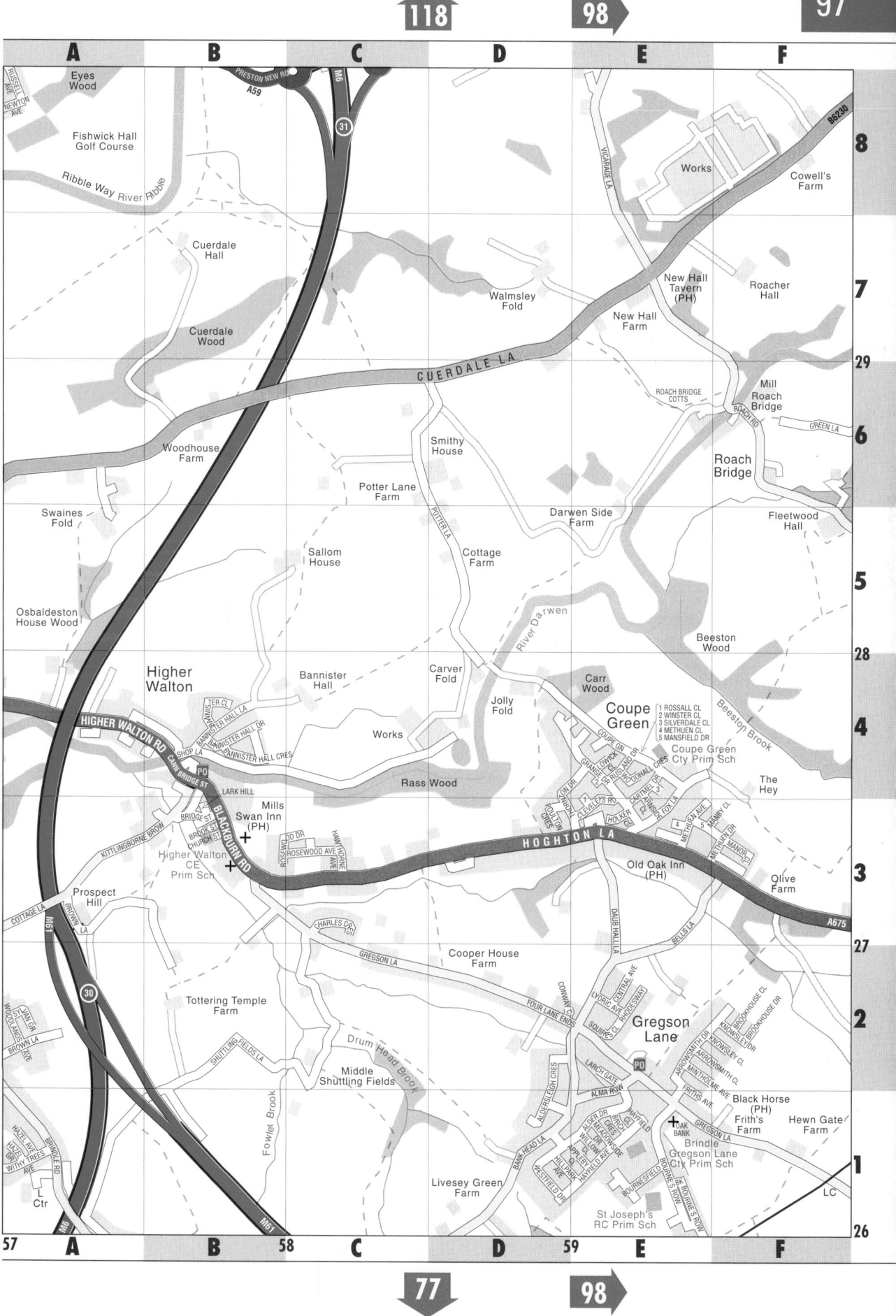

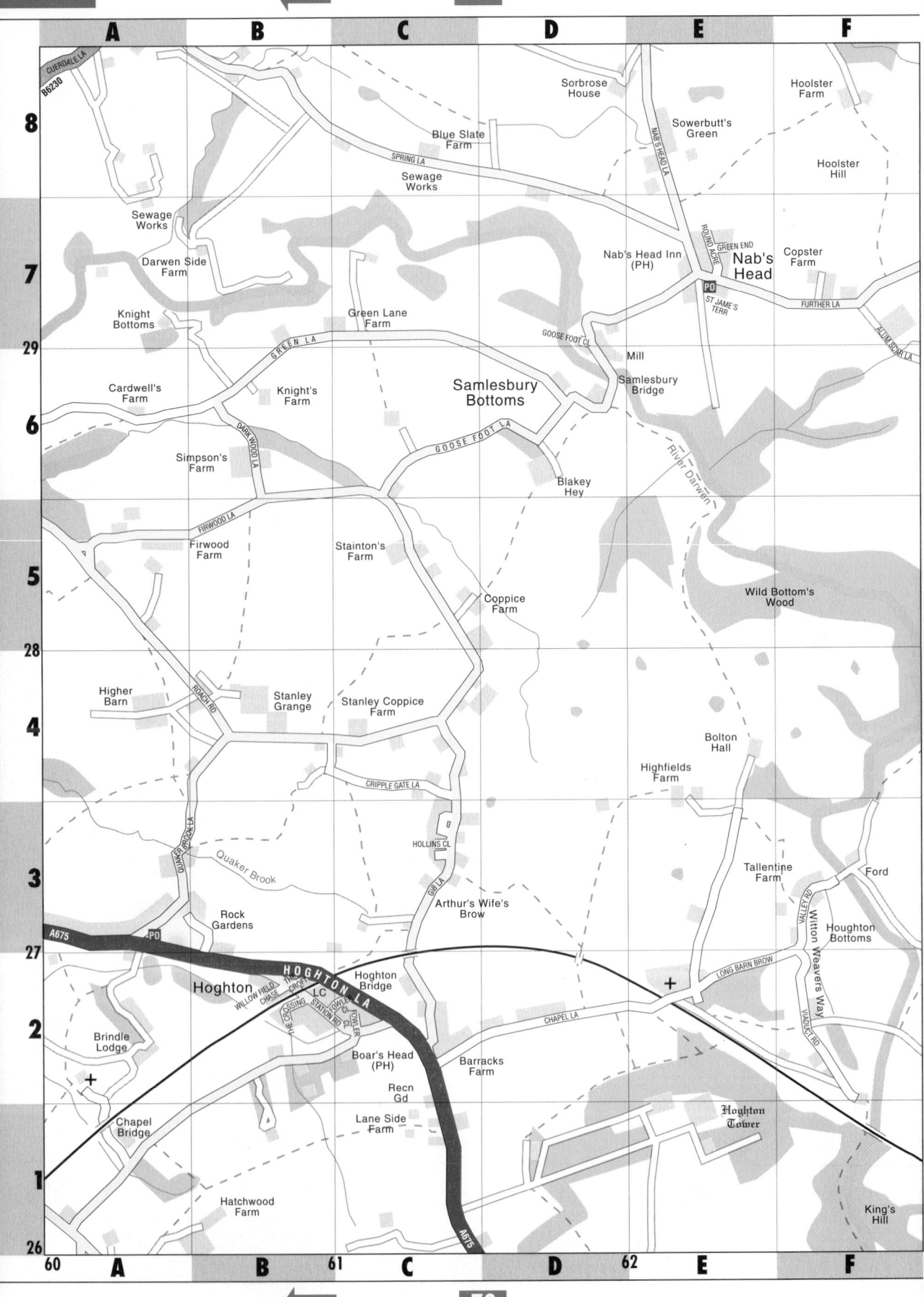

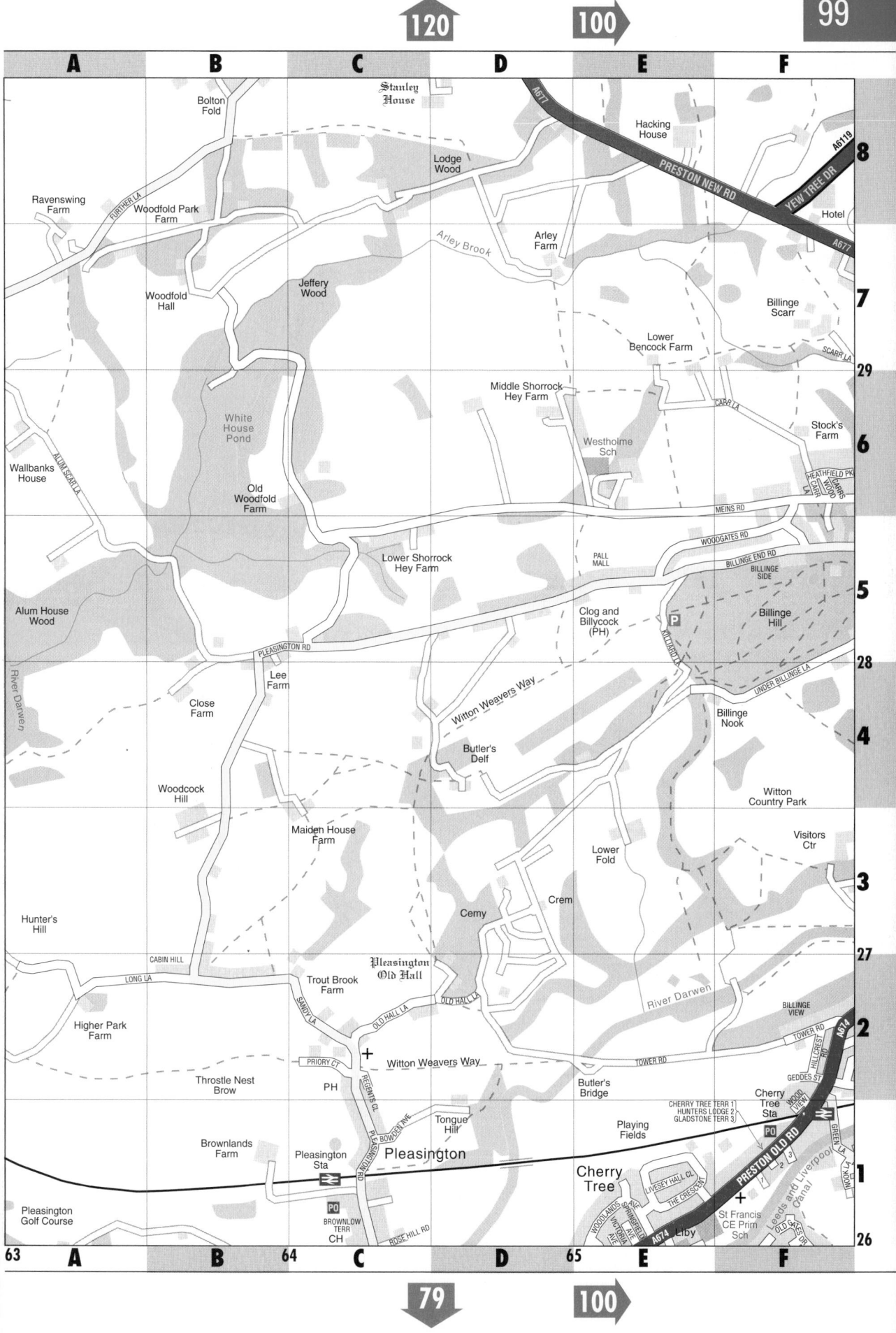

A B C D E F

8
7
29
6
5
28
4
3
27
2
1
26

Ravenswing Farm
Bolton Fold
FURTHER LA
Woodfold Park Farm
Stanley House
Lodge Wood
PRESTON NEW RD
A677
Hacking House
A6119
YEW TREE DR
A677
Hotel

Woodfold Hall
Jeffery Wood
Arley Brook
Arley Farm
Billinge Scarr
SCARR LA

Lower Bencock Farm
Middle Shorrock Hey Farm
CARR LA
29

Wallbanks House
ALUM SCARR LA
White House Pond
Old Woodfold Farm
Westholme Sch
Stock's Farm
HEATHFIELD PK
CARRS WOOD
6

MEINS RD
WOODGATES RD
BILLINGE END RD
BILLINGE SIDE

Alum House Wood
Lower Shorrock Hey Farm
PLEASINGTON RD
PALL MALL
Clog and Billycock (PH)
P
KILLIARD LA
Billinge Hill
5

River Darwen
Lee Farm
Witton Weavers Way
UNDER BILLINGE LA
28

Close Farm
Butler's Delf
Billinge Nook
4

Woodcock Hill
Witton Country Park

Maiden House Farm
Lower Fold
Visitors Ctr

Hunter's Hill
Crem
3

CABIN HILL
Cemy
River Darwen
27

LONG LA
Pleasington Old Hall
Trout Brook Farm
OLD HALL LA
BILLINGE VIEW
A574
TOWER RD

Higher Park Farm
SANDY LA
OLD HALL LA
Witton Weavers Way
TOWER RD
HILLCREST RD
GEDDES ST
2

PRIORY CT
REGENTS CL
Butler's Bridge
Cherry Tree Sta
MOOR VIEW

Throstle Nest Brow
PH
PLEASINGTON RD
BOWGREAVE
Tongue Hill
CHERRY TREE TERR 1
HUNTERS LODGE 2
GLADSTONE TERR 3
PO
GREEN LA
MOOR LA

Brownlands Farm
Pleasington Sta
Pleasington
Playing Fields
PRESTON OLD RD
A574
1

Pleasington Golf Course
PO
BROWNLOW TERR
CH
ROSE HILL RD
Cherry Tree
LIVESEY HALL CL
THE CRESCENT
St Francis CE Prim Sch
A574 Liby
Leeds and Liverpool Canal
OLD OAKS DR
26

63 A 64 B C 65 D E F

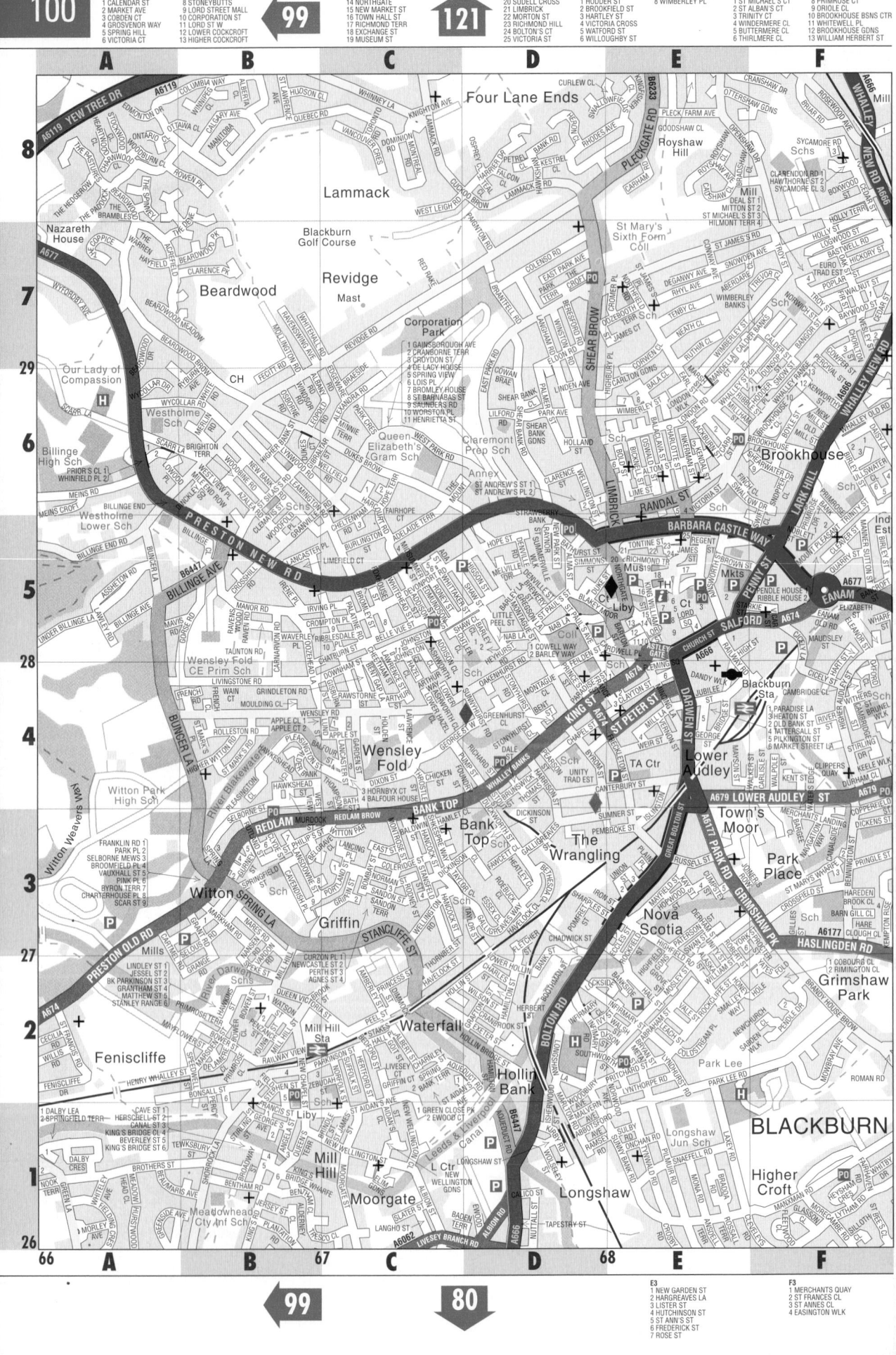

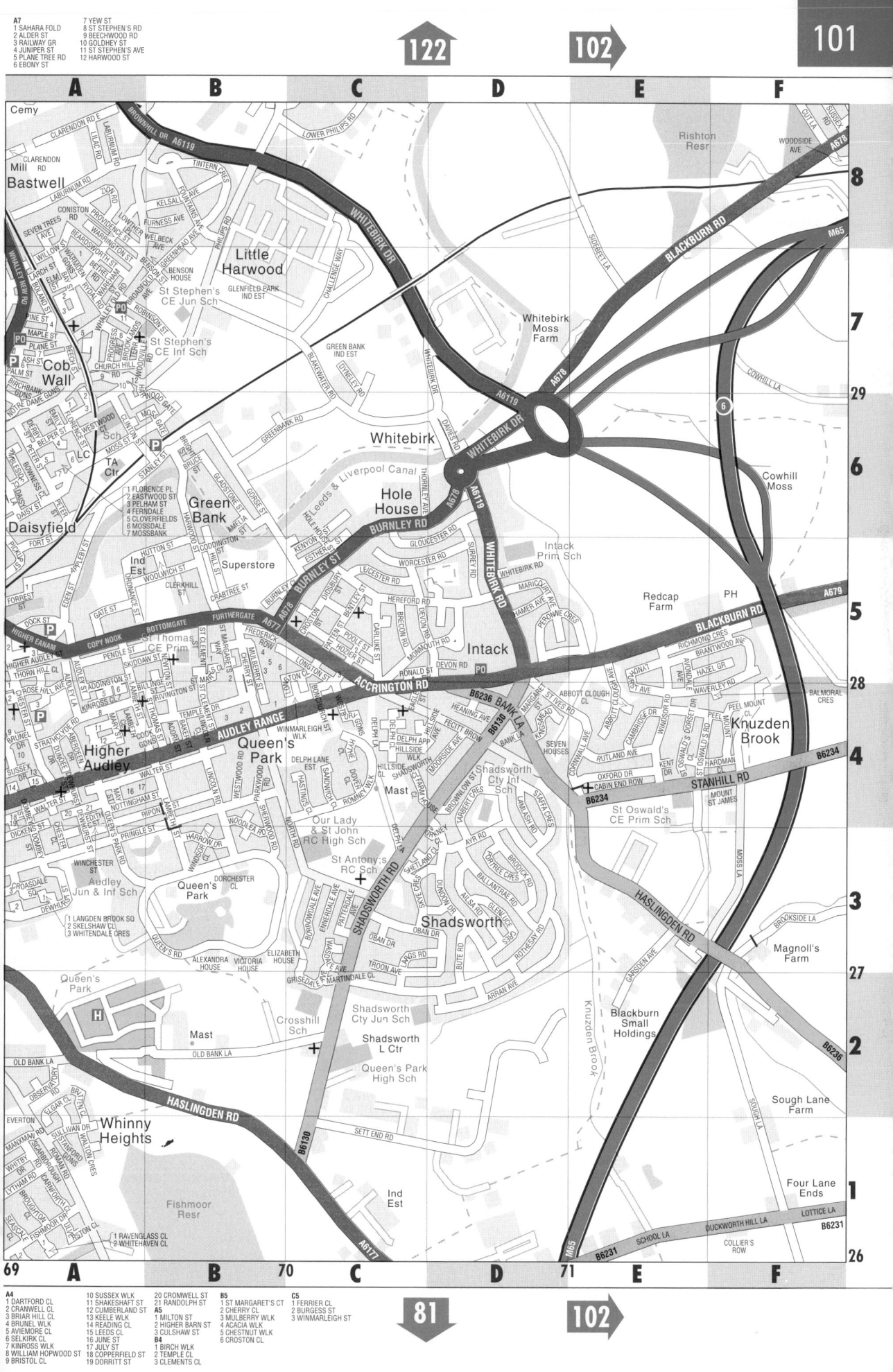

A7
7 YEW ST
1 SAHARA FOLD
8 ST STEPHEN'S RD
2 ALDER ST
9 BEECHWOOD RD
3 RAILWAY GR
10 GOLDHEY ST
4 JUNIPER ST
11 ST STEPHEN'S AVE
5 PLANE TREE RD
12 HARWOOD ST
6 EBONY ST

A   B   C   D   E   F

Cemy

Mill
Bastwell

CLARENDON RD E
CLARENDON RD
BROWNHILL DR A6119
LOWER PHILIPS RD

CONISTON RD
SEVEN TREES AVE
WILLOW ST
LILAC RD
LABURNUM RD
TINTERN CRES
KELSALL AVE
FURNESS AVE

Little Harwood

WHITEBIRK DR

BENSON HOUSE
St Stephen's CE Jun Sch
GLENFIELD PARK IND EST

Whitebirk Moss Farm

A6119   A678

BLACKBURN RD   M65

WOODSIDE AVE

Rishton Resr

CUT LA   SUSSEX RD

A678

8

7

29

6

P
Cob Wall

PO
St Stephen's CE Inf Sch
CHURCH HILL RD

GREEN BANK IND EST

BLACKWATER RD
GREENBANK RD
DYNELEY RD
DAVIES RD

Whitebirk

Leeds & Liverpool Canal

Hole House

WHITEBIRK DR

COWHILL LA

Cowhill Moss

6

Daisyfield

1 FLORENCE PL
2 EASTWOOD ST
3 PELHAM ST
4 FERNDALE
5 CLOVERFIELDS
6 MOSSDALE
7 MOSSBANK

Green Bank

Superstore

HUTTON ST
WOOLWICH ST
CLERKHILL ST
CRABTREE ST

BURNLEY RD
KENYON ST
ESTHER ST
GLOUCESTER RD
WORCESTER RD

THORNLEY AVE
A678   A6119

SURREY RD

WHITEBIRK RD

HAMER AVE

Intack Prim Sch

MARICOURT AVE
PERONNE CRES

Redcap Farm
PH

BLACKBURN RD   A679

5

Ind Est

GATE ST
APPLEBY ST
ROMANCE ST

FURTHERGATE   A677

FREDERICK ROW
LEICESTER RD
HEREFORD RD
BRECON RD
DEVON RD
MONMOUTH RD

POOLE ST

Intack

PO

RICHMOND CRES
ADVISNAL AVE
HAZEL GR
BRANTWOOD AVE

BALMORAL CRES

28

HIGHER EANAM
COPY NOOK
St Thomas CE Prim
PENDLE ST
SKIDDAW ST
CHERRY ST
MULBERRY ST
CLITON ST
LONGTON ST
RONALD ST

ACCRINGTON RD

B6236   BANK LA

B6236

ABBOTT CLOUGH CL
ST IVES RD
WINDSOR CL
CAMBRIDGE DR
RUTLAND AVE
KENT DR
OXFORD DR
CABIN END ROW

MONAT AVE

PEEL MOUNT CL
PEEL CL

Knuzden Brook

B6234

4

HIGHER AUDLEY
THORN HILL CL
ROSE HILL AVE
KINROSS CL
ADDINGTON ST
BILLINGE ST
RIVINGTON ST
TEMPLE DR
BAKER ST
COOK ST

AUDLEY RANGE

LINCOLN RD
WESTWOOD RD

WINMARLEIGH WLK
DELPH WLK
HILLSIDE WLK
HILLSIDE
SHADSWORTH CLARM RD

HEANING AVE
FECITT BROW
BANK LA
MOORSIDE AVE

Shadsworth City Inf Sch

SEVEN HOUSES

CORNWALL AVE

ST OSWALD'S RD
HARDMAN CL
MOUNT ST JAMES

STANHILL RD
MOSS LA

B6234

Higher Audley

BRUNEL ST
STRATHCLYDE RD
DUNDEE CL
SUSSEX RD

WALTER ST
WALTER ST
CHESTER ST
DICKENS ST
DOWREY ST
EDITH ST
NOTTINGHAM ST
RIPON ST
HARROW DR

Queen's Park

WINDSOR DR
PARKWOOD DR
NOODLE RD
PRINGLE ST
NORTH RD
QUEEN'S PARK RD

DELPH LANE EST
Mast
HASTINGS CL
DOVER CL
ROMNEY ST

Our Lady & St John RC High Sch

St Antony's RC Sch

SHADSWORTH RD

BROWNLOW ST
KARBERT CRES
BROOK CL
THREE OAKS CL
BALLANTRAE RD
GLEN JUICE
AYR RD
ALSA RD
BUTE RD
ROTHESAY RD

St Oswald's CE Prim Sch

HASLINGDEN RD

3

1 LANGDEN BROOK SQ
2 SKELSHAW CL
3 WHITENDALE CRES

Audley Jun & Inf Sch

DORCHESTER CL

Queen's Park

WINCHESTER ST

CROASDALE SQ
DEWHURST

ALEXANDRA HOUSE
VICTORIA HOUSE
ELIZABETH HOUSE

BROWNHALL AVE
ENNERDALE AVE
PATTERDALE
GRISEDALE
MARTINDALE CL
KOSWM

OBAN DR
OBAN DR
SHETLAND CL
DUNCAN RD
LAGGS RD
TROON AVE
ARRAN AVE

GARSDEN AVE

BROOKSIDE LA

Magnoll's Farm

27

Queen's Park

H

Mast

OLD BANK LA

OLD BANK LA

Crosshill Sch

Shadsworth

Shadsworth City Jun Sch

Shadsworth L Ctr

Queen's Park High Sch

Knuzden Brook

Blackburn Small Holdings

B6236

2

OBSERVA
BRITTON CL
ELGAR CL
SULLIVAN DR
ST STAMFORDS

Whinny Heights

HASLINGDEN RD

B6130

SETT END RD

Sough Lane Farm

SOUGH LA

1

EVERTON
MAXWAY
WHITBY
DR
SCARBOROUGH RD
ROMAN RD
WALTON CRES
LYTHAM RD
BRIGHTON DR

Fishmoor Resr

Ind Est

Four Lane Ends

26

1 RAVENGLASS CL
2 WHITEHAVEN CL

A6177

M65   B6231

B6231   SCHOOL LA

COLLIER'S ROW

DUCKWORTH HILL LA   LOTTICE LA

B6231

A4
1 DARTFORD CL
2 CRANWELL CL
3 BRIAR HILL CL
4 BRUNEL WLK
5 AVIEMORE CL
6 SELKIRK CL
7 KINROSS WLK
8 WILLIAM HOPWOOD ST
9 BRISTOL CL
10 SUSSEX WLK
11 SHAKESHAFT ST
12 CUMBERLAND ST
13 KEELEY WLK
14 READING CL
15 LEEDS CL
16 JUNE ST
17 JULY ST
18 COPPERFIELD ST
19 DORRIT ST
20 CROMWELL ST
21 RANDOLPH ST

A5
1 MILTON ST
2 HIGHER BARN ST
3 CULSHAW ST

B4
1 BIRCH WLK
2 TEMPLE CL
3 CLEMENTS CL

B5
1 ST MARGARET'S CT
2 CHERRY CL
3 MULBERRY WLK
4 ACACIA WLK
5 CHESTNUT WLK
6 CROSTON CL

C5
1 FERRIER CL
2 BURGESS ST
3 WINMARLEIGH ST

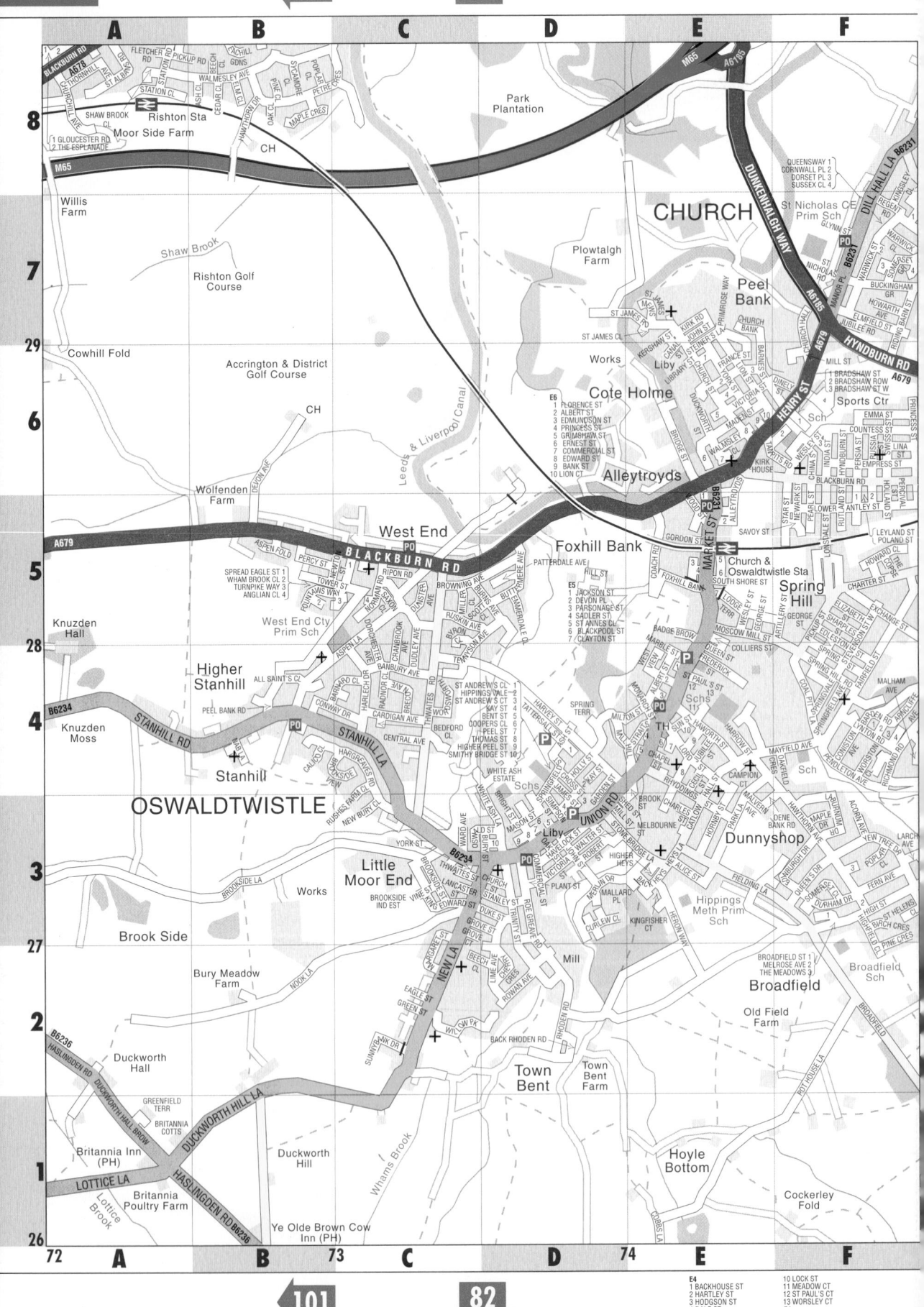

E4
1 BACKHOUSE ST
2 HARTLEY ST
3 HODGSON ST
4 DALE ST
5 SPRING ST
6 MOUNT PLEASANT ST
7 OFF MOUNT PLEASANT ST
8 WATSON ST
9 PADDOCK ST

10 LOCK ST
11 MEADOW CT
12 ST PAUL'S CT
13 WORSLEY CT
F4
1 GAYLE WAY
2 BURNSALL RD
3 REETH WAY
4 BUCKDEN RD

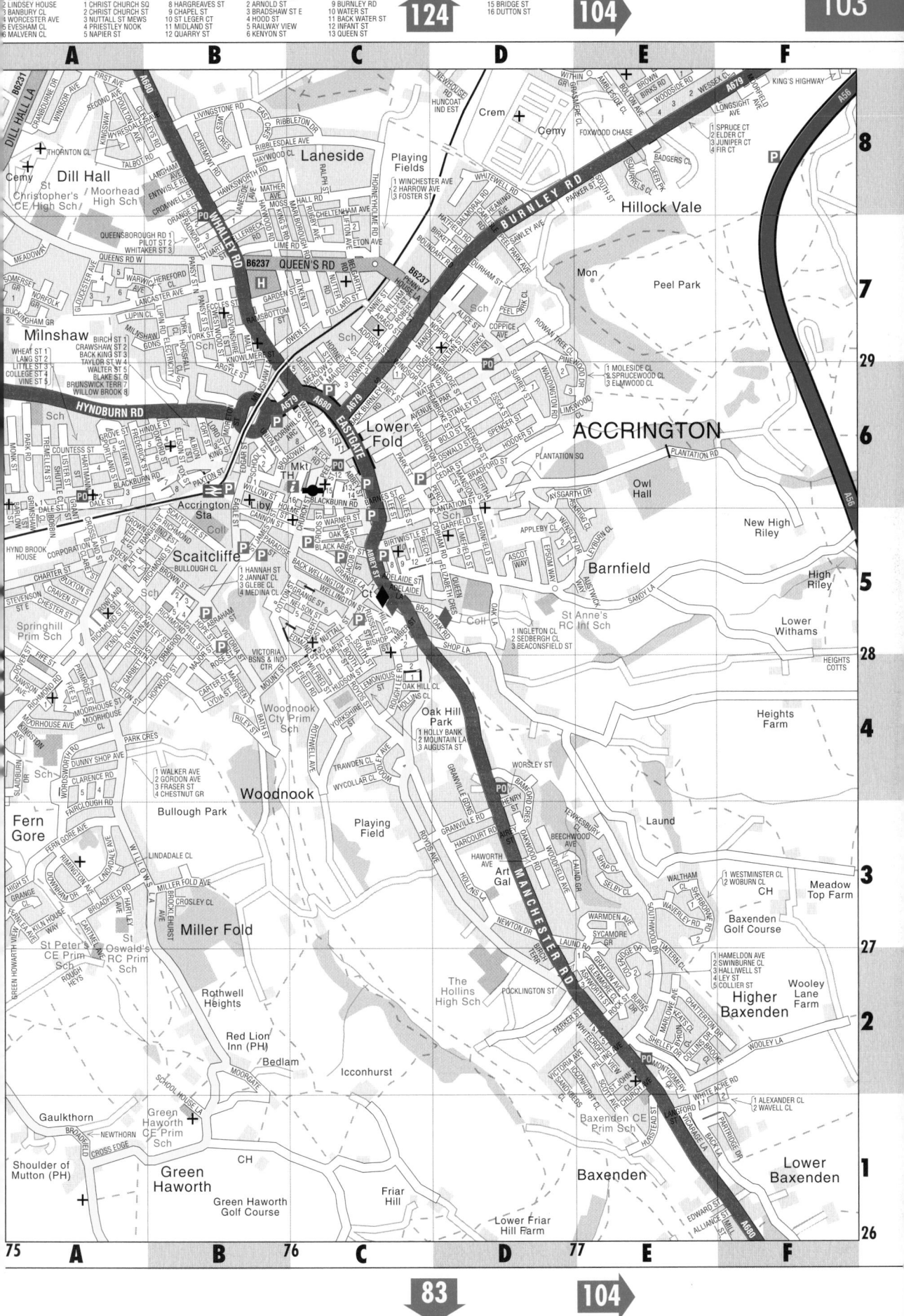

A7
1 LINCOLN CT
2 LINDSEY HOUSE
3 BANBURY CL
4 WORCESTER AVE
5 EVESHAM CL
6 MALVERN CL

C5
1 CHRIST CHURCH SQ
2 CHRIST CHURCH ST
3 NUTTALL ST MEWS
4 PRIESTLEY NOOK
5 NAPIER ST

7 STRATFORD WAY

6 WELLINGTON CT
7 SPRING GDNS
8 HARGREAVES ST
9 CHAPEL ST
10 ST LEGER ST
11 MIDLAND ST
12 QUARRY ST

C6
1 MANOR BROOK
2 ARNOLD ST
3 BRADSHAW ST E
4 HOOD ST
5 RAILWAY VIEW
6 KENYON ST

7 MASON ST
8 CORNHILL
9 BURNLEY RD
10 WATER ST
11 BACK WATER ST
12 INFANT ST
13 QUEEN ST

C6
14 TASKER ST
15 BRIDGE ST
16 DUTTON ST

A B C D E F

8
Cronker
Plantation

Thorny
Bank

Thorny Bank
Wood

Hameldon
Scouts

7
Snipe Rake

Hameldon Common

Hapton Park

Windy
Harbour

Great Slack

29
Park Scout

Moleside Moor

Great Hameldon

Great Hill

6
Moleside End
Farm

King's Highway

Burnley Way

Masts

SANDY LA

A56

5
West
Farm

New Laithe
Height

28
Heights
Farm

Higher
Hey

Higher Moor

Snipe Hole

Great Clough

4
Great
Clough

Mitchell's House
Resrs

3
Black
Moss

Higher
Withens

Rossendale Way

Rough Hill
Farm

Works

27
King's Highway

Hen Heads
Farm

Goodshaw Hill

SILVER CLOUGH RD

Goodshaw
Fold

LOVE CLOUGH RD

2
SPRINGBANK
GDNS

GOODSHAW FOLD RD

New Barn

Fair Banks

Limy Water

Lane Top
Farm

1
GOODSHAW LA

Cross Edge
Farm

Gin Clough

Pewit
Hall

A56

26
78 A 79 B C 79 D 80 E F

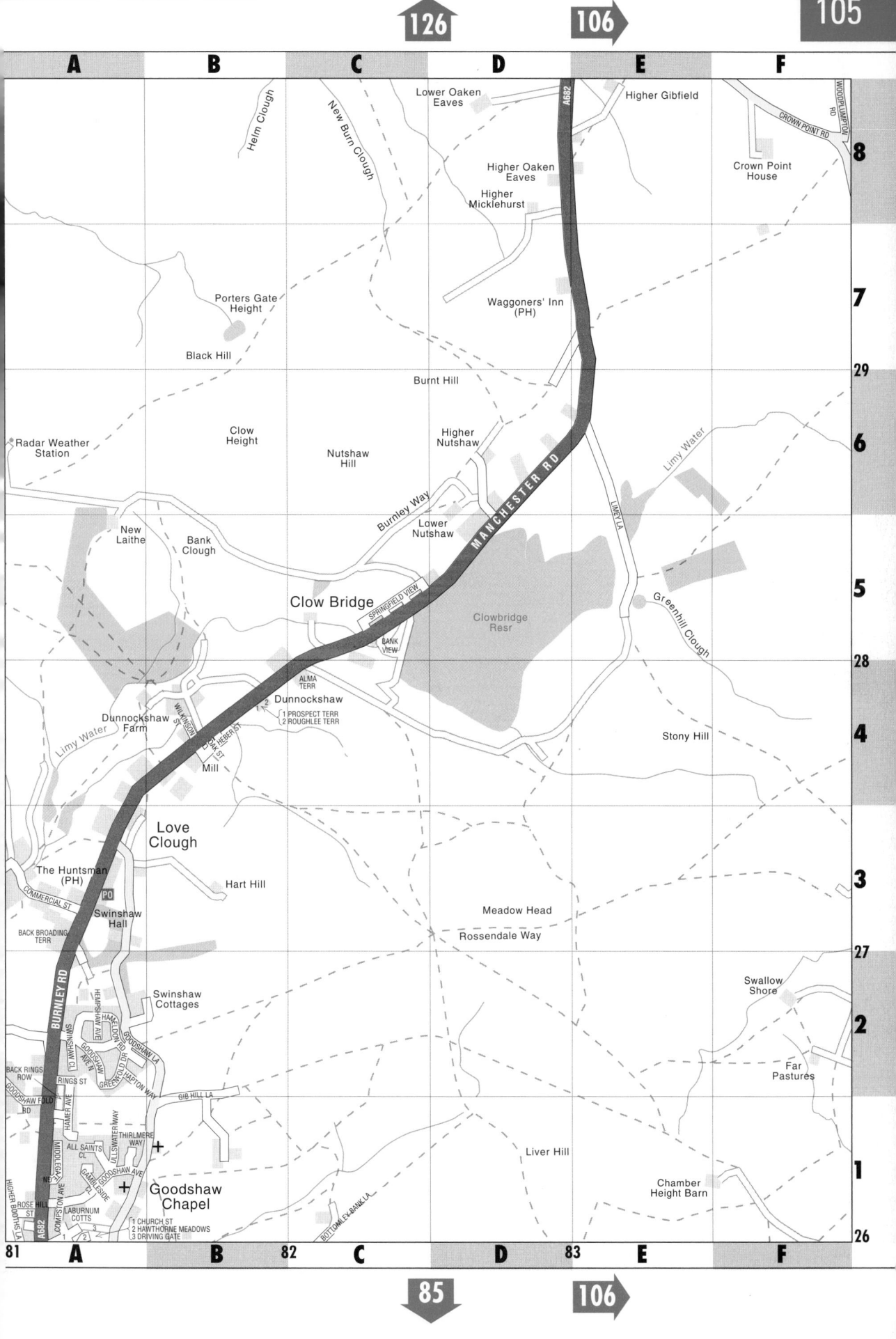

A B C D E F

8
7
29
6
5
28
4
3
27
2
1
26

Lower Oaken Eaves
Higher Gibfield
WOODPLUMPTON RD
CROWN POINT RD
Higher Oaken Eaves
Crown Point House
Helm Clough
New Burn Clough
Higher Micklehurst
A682
Waggoners' Inn (PH)
Porters Gate Height
Black Hill
Burnt Hill
Clow Height
Higher Nutshaw
Limy Water
Radar Weather Station
Nutshaw Hill
MANCHESTER RD
LIMEY LA
Burnley Way
Lower Nutshaw
New Laithe
Bank Clough
SPRINGFIELD VIEW
Clow Bridge
BANK VIEW
Clowbridge Resr
Greenhill Clough
ALMA TERR
Dunnockshaw
1 PROSPECT TERR
2 ROUGHLEE TERR
Stony Hill
WILKINSON ST
Limy Water
Dunnockshaw Farm
OAK ST
HEBER ST
Mill
Love Clough
Hart Hill
Meadow Head
The Huntsman (PH)
PO
COMMERCIAL ST
Swinshaw Hall
BACK BROADING TERR
Rossendale Way
Swallow Shore
BURNLEY RD
Swinshaw Cottages
Far Pastures
HEMPSHAW AVE
HAMELDON AVE
GOODSHAW AVE
GREENFOLD DR
GOODSHAW LA
HAPTON WAY
BACK RINGS ROW
RINGS ST
HAMER AVE
GOODSHAW FOLD RD
GIB HILL LA
Liver Hill
THIRLMERE WAY
ULLSWATER WAY
ALL SAINTS CL
GOODSHAW AVE
GAMBLESIDE CL
Chamber Height Barn
HIGHER BOOTHS LA
COMPSTON AVE
LABURNUM COTTS
Goodshaw Chapel
BOTTOMLEY BANK LA
ROSE HILL ST
MIDDLE
A682
1 CHURCH ST
2 HAWTHORNE MEADOWS
3 DRIVING GATE

105
127

A B C D E F

8

7

29

6

5

28

4

3

27

2

1

26

Burnley Way

Everage Clough

A671

Sagar Fold

RUSH HEY BANK

Dixon Hill

HANE ROW

Towneley Arms (PH)

Buck Clough

CROWN POINT RD

Crown Point

Dyneley Knoll

BACUP RD

P

Long Shay

Quarry

Easden Clough

White Hill

B6238

Red Moss

BURNLEY RD

Bent Hill Rough

Bent Hill

Clough Bottom Resr

Clough Bottom

Windy Bank

Near Pastures

BURNLEY RD E

Whitewell Brook

GRAVER WEIR TERR

TERRA COTTA BLDGS

EAST BANK

B6238

Meadows Farm

Nabb Farm

Rossendale Way

Clifton

Deerplay Hill Syke

Deerplay Moor

Deerplay Hill

BURNLEY RD

Mon

Irwell Spring

Croft Farm

Deerplay Inn (PH)

Irwell Valley Way

A671

BACUP OLD RD

HARROW STILES LA

Height End

LONGFIELD TERR

A646

PO

PH

Walk Mill

BURNLEY RD

CO-OPERATIVE BLDGS

River Calder

Calf Banks Wood

Burnley Way

Spring Gardens

Dyneley Farm

Burnley Way

STONE HOUSE FOLD

Dodbottom Wood

Stone House Edge

Cow Side

Black Clough

HINEY HOLME LA

A646

84 A B 85 C 86 D E F

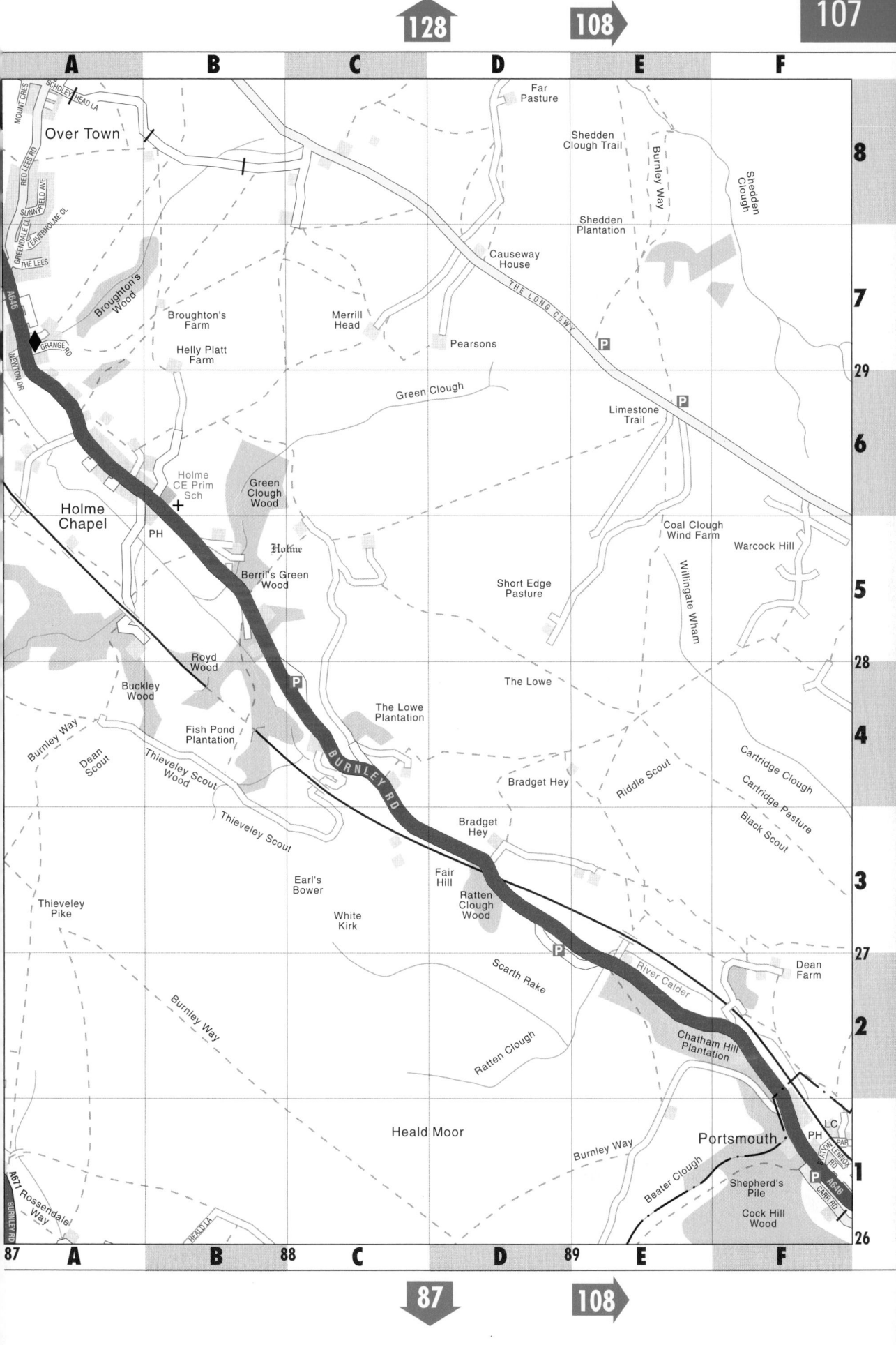

128
108

A　　B　　C　　D　　E　　F

8

7

29

6

5

28

4

3

27

2

1

26

MOUNT CRES
SCHOLEY HEAD LA
Over Town
RED LEES RD
GREENDALE CL
SLANN CL
LEAVERHOLME CL
FIELD AVE
THE LEES
A646
NEWTOWN DR
GRANGE RD

Broughton's Wood
Broughton's Farm
Helly Platt Farm

Merrill Head

Far Pasture
Shedden Clough Trail
Burnley Way
Shedden Clough
Shedden Plantation

Causeway House
THE LONG CSWY
Pearsons

Green Clough

Limestone Trail

Holme CE Prim Sch
Holme Chapel
PH

Green Clough Wood
Holme
Berril's Green Wood

Coal Clough Wind Farm
Warcock Hill

Royd Wood
Buckley Wood

Short Edge Pasture

Willingate Wham

Burnley Way
Dean Scout
Thieveley Scout Wood
Fish Pond Plantation
Thieveley Scout

BURNLEY RD
The Lowe Plantation
The Lowe

Bradget Hey
Riddle Scout
Cartridge Clough
Cartridge Pasture
Black Scout

Earl's Bower
White Kirk
Bradget Hey
Fair Hill
Ratten Clough Wood

Thieveley Pike

River Calder
Dean Farm

Scarth Rake

Chatham Hill Plantation

Ratten Clough

A671 Rossendale Way
BURNLEY RD
HEALD LA

Heald Moor

Burnley Way

Portsmouth
LC
PH
RAILWAY RD
CARR RD
A646
Beater Clough
Shepherd's Pile
Cock Hill Wood

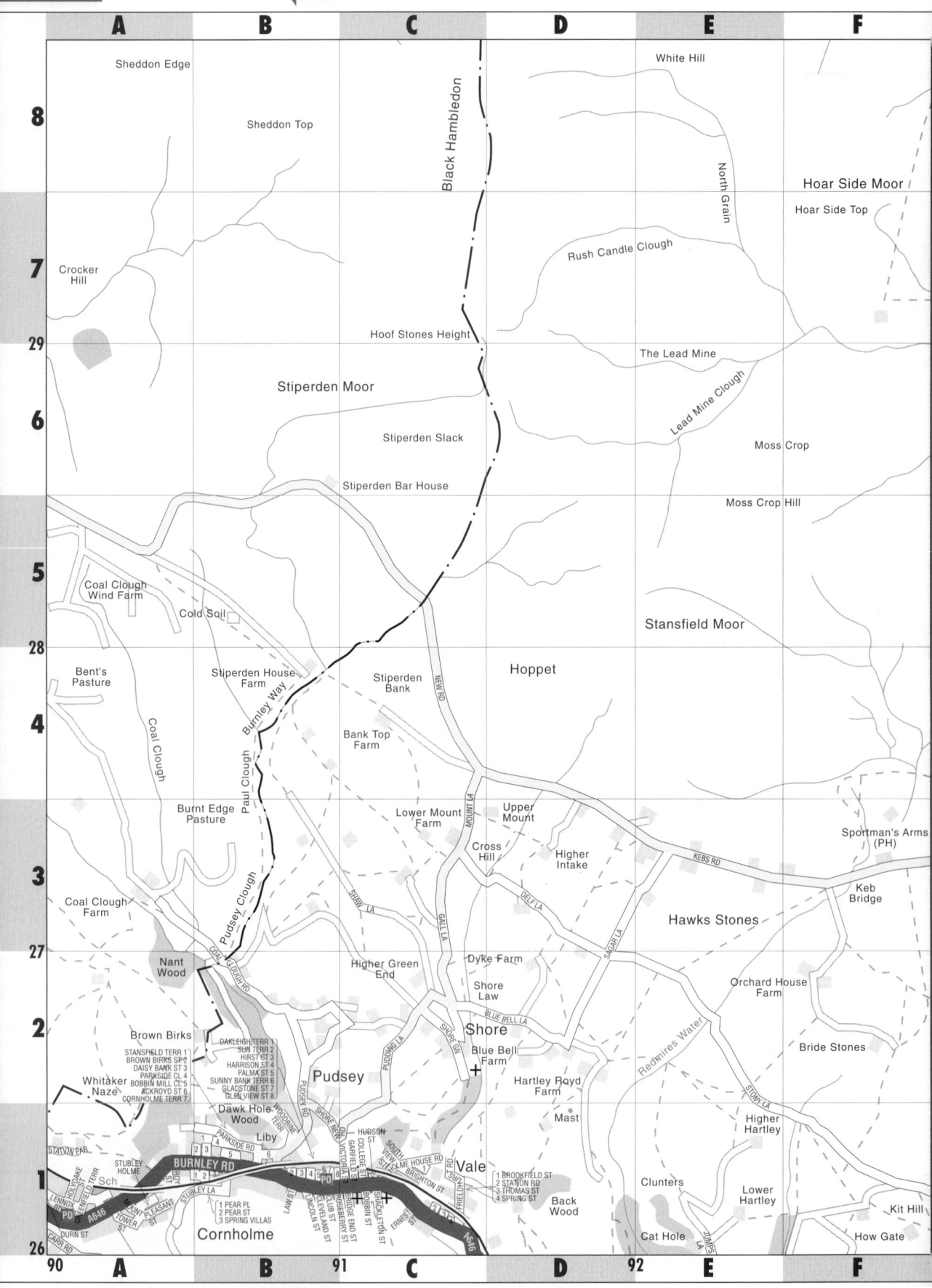

Sheddon Edge

Sheddon Top

Black Hambledon

White Hill

Hoar Side Moor

Hoar Side Top

North Grain

Crocker Hill

Rush Candle Clough

29

Hoof Stones Height

Stiperden Moor

The Lead Mine

Lead Mine Clough

Moss Crop

6

Stiperden Slack

Stiperden Bar House

Moss Crop Hill

5

Coal Clough Wind Farm

Cold Soil

Stansfield Moor

28

Bent's Pasture

Stiperden House Farm

Stiperden Bank

Hoppet

NEW RD

Burnley Way

Coal Clough

Bank Top Farm

4

Paul Clough

Burnt Edge Pasture

Lower Mount Farm

Upper Mount

MOUNT LA

Sportman's Arms (PH)

KEBS RD

Cross Hill

Higher Intake

DELF LA

GALL LA

Keb Bridge

3

Coal Clough Farm

Pudsey Clough

COAL CLOUGH RD

SHAW LA

Hawks Stones

SAGAR LA

27

Nant Wood

Higher Green End

Dyke Farm

Shore Law

Orchard House Farm

SHORE GRN

BLUE BELL LA

REDMIRES WATER

2

Brown Birks

OAKLEIGH TERR 1
SUN TERR 2
HIRST ST 3
HARRISON ST 4
PALMA ST 5
SUNNY BANK TERR 6
GLADSTONE ST 7
GLEN VIEW ST 8

Shore

Blue Bell Farm

Hartley Royd Farm

Bride Stones

STANSFIELD TERR 1
BROWN BIRKS ST 2
DAISY BANK ST 3
PARKSIDE CL 4
BOBBIN MILL CT 5
ACKROYD ST 6
CORNHOLME TERR 7

PUDSEY LA

Pudsey

Whitaker Naze

WOODBINE TERR

PUDSEY RD

Mast

STONY LA

JUMPS LA

Higher Hartley

Dawk Hole Wood

Liby

HUDSON ST

SHORE GRN

Clunters

Lower Hartley

Kit Hill

PARKSIDE RD

SMITH ST

Vale

1 BROOKFIELD ST
2 STATON RD
3 THOMAS RD
4 SPRING ST

1

STATION PAR

STUBLEY HOLME

Sch

HOLME HOUSE RD

Back Wood

Cat Hole

How Gate

LENNO...

PO

DURN ST

A646

TOWER

MOUNT

PLEASANT

STUBLEY LA

1 PEAR PL
2 PEAR ST
3 SPRING VILLAS

LAW ST

LINCOLN ST

CLUB LAND

CLEVELAND ST

ROSEBERY ST

COLLEGE ST

GARFIELD ST

SHACKLETON ST

VICTORIA ST

BOBBIN ST

BRIGHTON ST

GABLE END ST

ERNEST ST

FRIELD...

A646

Cornholme

CARR RD

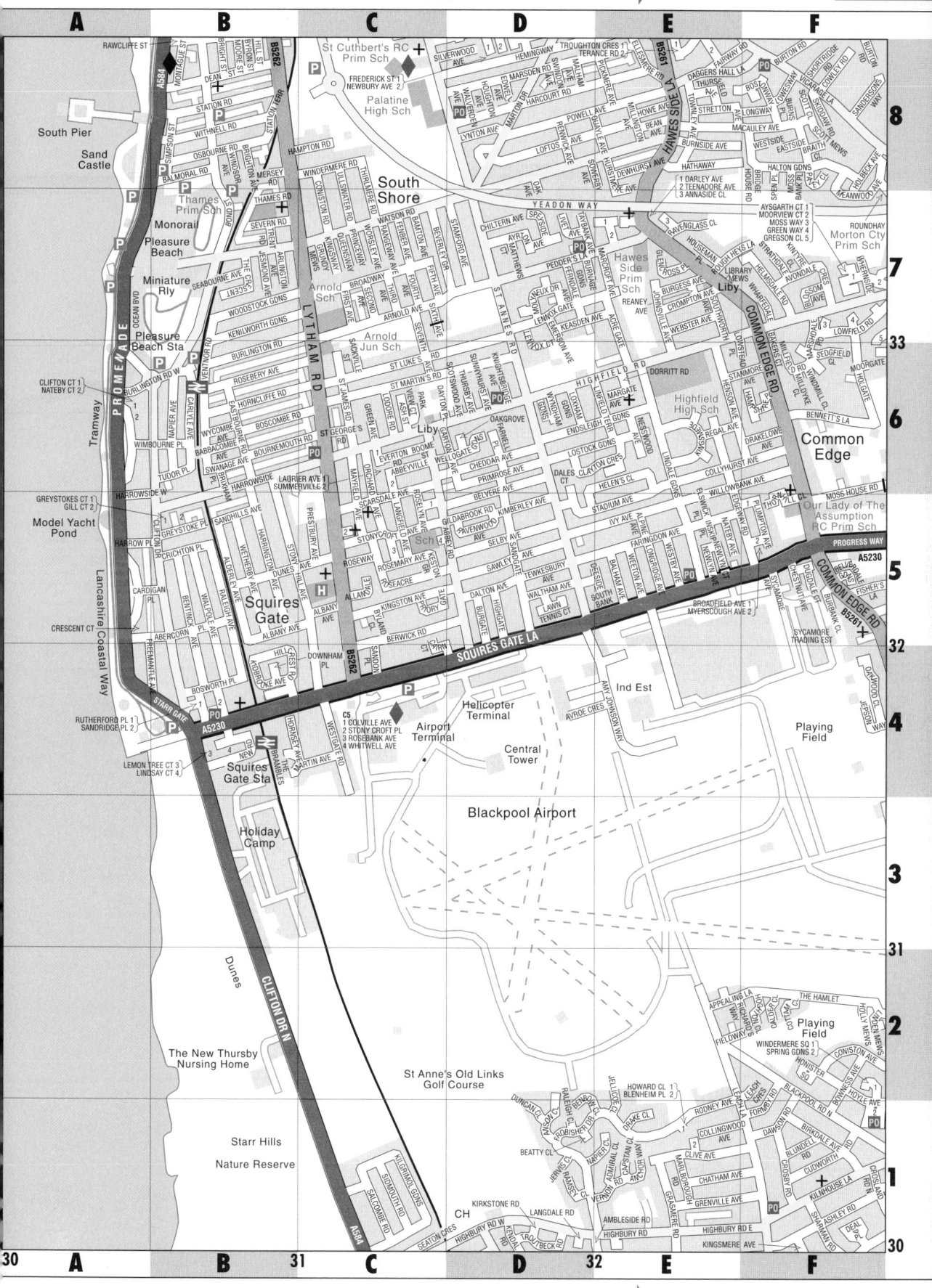

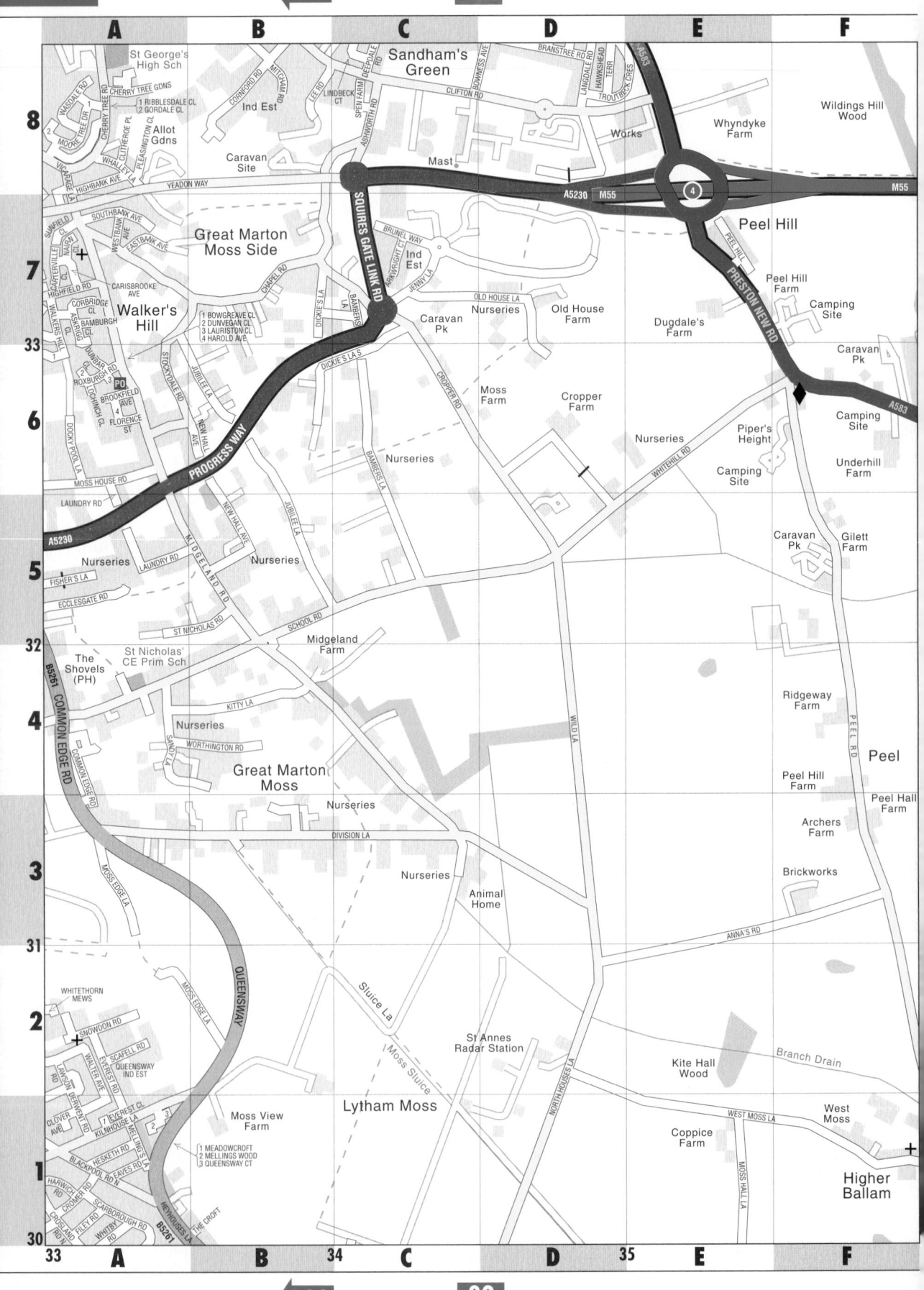

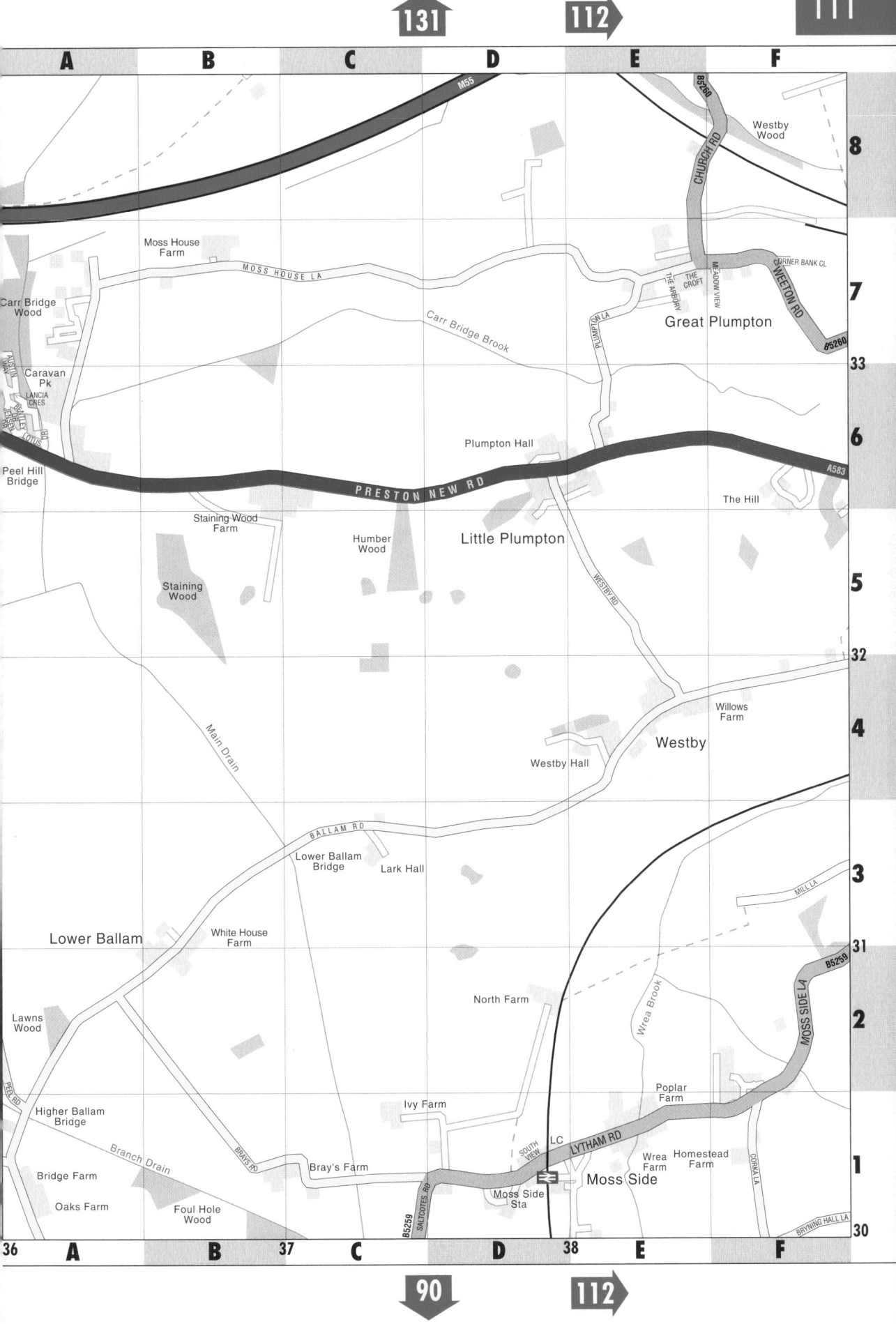

A   B   C   D   E   F

131   112

8

M55

Westby Wood

CHURCH RD

B5260

Moss House Farm

MOSS HOUSE LA

Carr Bridge Wood

Carr Bridge Brook

THE ARBORY

THE CROFT

MEADOW VIEW

CORNER BANK CL

SWEETON RD

Great Plumpton

B5260

7

33

Caravan Pk

LANCIA CRES

BENTLEY

LOTUS

PLUMPTON LA

Plumpton Hall

6

A583

Peel Hill Bridge

PRESTON NEW RD

The Hill

Staining Wood Farm

Humber Wood

Little Plumpton

WESTBY RD

5

Staining Wood

32

Willows Farm

Main Drain

Westby

4

Westby Hall

BALLAM RD

Lower Ballam Bridge

Lark Hall

MILL LA

3

Lower Ballam

White House Farm

31

B5259

Lawns Wood

North Farm

Wrea Brook

MOSS SIDE LA

2

PEEL RD

BRAYS RD

Higher Ballam Bridge

Branch Drain

Bray's Farm

Ivy Farm

SOUTH VIEW

LC

LYTHAM RD

Poplar Farm

CORKA LA

1

Bridge Farm

Oaks Farm

Foul Hole Wood

B5259

SALTCOTES RD

Moss Side Sta

Moss Side

Wrea Farm

Homestead Farm

BRYNING HALL LA

30

90   112

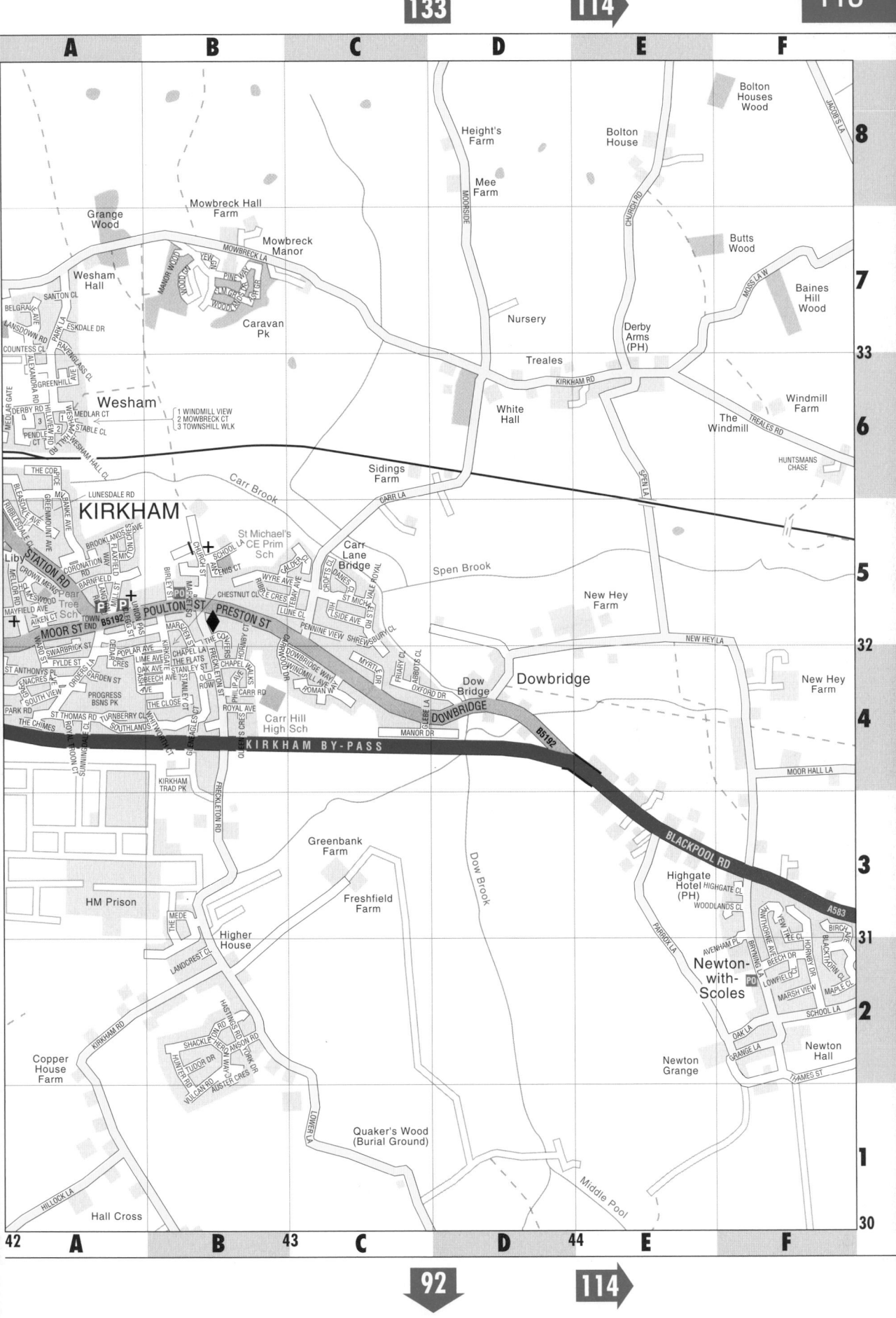

A **B** **C** **D** **E** **F**

8

Bolton
Houses
Wood

Height's
Farm

Bolton
House

Mee
Farm

MOORSIDE

Grange
Wood

Mowbreck Hall
Farm

Butts
Wood

CHURCH RD

7

Mowbreck
Manor

MOWBRECK LA

MOSS LA W

Wesham
Hall

YEW GN

PINE WAY

Baines
Hill
Wood

MANOR WOOD

WOODS LA

Nursery

Derby
Arms
(PH)

33

Caravan
Pk

Treales

KIRKHAM RD

Windmill
Farm

BELGRAVE
AVE

SANTON CL

TREALES RD

LANSDOWN RD

ESKDALE DR

Wesham

1 WINDMILL VIEW
2 MOWBRECK CT
3 TOWNSHILL WLK

White
Hall

The
Windmill

6

COUNTESS CL

ALEXANDRA RD

RAVENGLASS CL

GREENHILL

SPEN LA

HUNTSMANS
CHASE

MEDLAR GATE

MEDLAR CT

DERBY RD

HILLVIEW RD

STABLE CL

THE COPICE

Sidings
Farm

PENDLE
CT

WESHAM HALL RD

LUNESDALE RD

Carr Brook

CARR LA

5

PLEASURE AVE

GREENMOUNT AVE

BROOKLANDS AVE

KIRKHAM

St Michael's
CE Prim
Sch

Carr
Lane
Bridge

Spen Brook

New Hey
Farm

FIBRE ESDALE CL

CORONATION RD

SCHOOL LA

DENIS CT

ST MICHA

CALDER

CROFTS CL

ST MICHAELS

VALE ROYAL

Liby

CROWN MEWS

PEAR TREE

CHURCH ST

WYRE AVE

TEBAY AVE

OAKES CL

DANES CL

NEW HEY LA

MELLOR RD

MAYFIELD AVE

AIKEN CT

PO

POULTON ST

CHESTNUT CL

LUNE CL

HILLSIDE AVE

SHREWSBURY CL

32

B5192

TOWN END

Preston St

PENNINE VIEW

New Hey
Farm

SWARBRICK ST

MOOR ST

MARKET ST

WINDMILL AVE

CROMWELL DR

FYLDE ST

POPLAR AVE

LIME AVE

CHAPEL LA

DOWBRIDGE WAY

FRIARY CL

MYRTLE

ST ANTHONYS

CEDAR

OAK AVE

STANLEY

OLD ROW

OXFORD DR

GLEBE LA

Dowbridge

DR

New Hey
Farm

SOUTH VIEW

BEECH AVE

GARDEN ST

THE CLOSE

CARR CL

ROMAN W

Dow
Bridge

DOWBRIDGE

4

PARK RD

ST THOMAS RD

PROGRESS
BSNS PK

CRANBERRY CL

SOUTHLANDS

Carr Hill
High Sch

MANOR DR

B5192

MOOR HALL LA

THE CHIMES

ROYAL RD

SUNNINGDALE CL

WHITWORTH CT

FRECKLETON RD

KIRKHAM BY-PASS

KIRKHAM
TRAD PK

3

HM Prison

THE MEDE

Greenbank
Farm

BLACKPOOL RD

Highgate
Hotel
(PH)

HIGHGATE CL

A583

LANDCREST CL

Freshfield
Farm

WOODLANDS CL

BIRCH

31

Higher
House

Dow Brook

PARROX LA

AVENHAM PL

BRYNING

BEECH DR

HAWTHORNE AVE

HORNBY DR

BLACKTHORN CL

2

SHACKLETON RD

HESKETH RD

HENSON RD

Newton-
with-
Scoles

PO

LOWFIELD

MARSH VIEW

MAPLE CL

SCHOOL LA

Copper
House
Farm

KIRKHAM RD

HASTINGS RD

HERON WAY

TUDOR DR

AUSTER CRES

Newton
Grange

OAK LA

GRANGE LA

Newton
Hall

HUNTER RD

VULCAN RD

THAMES ST

1

HILLOCK LA

Hall Cross

LOWER LA

Quaker's Wood
(Burial Ground)

Middle Pool

30

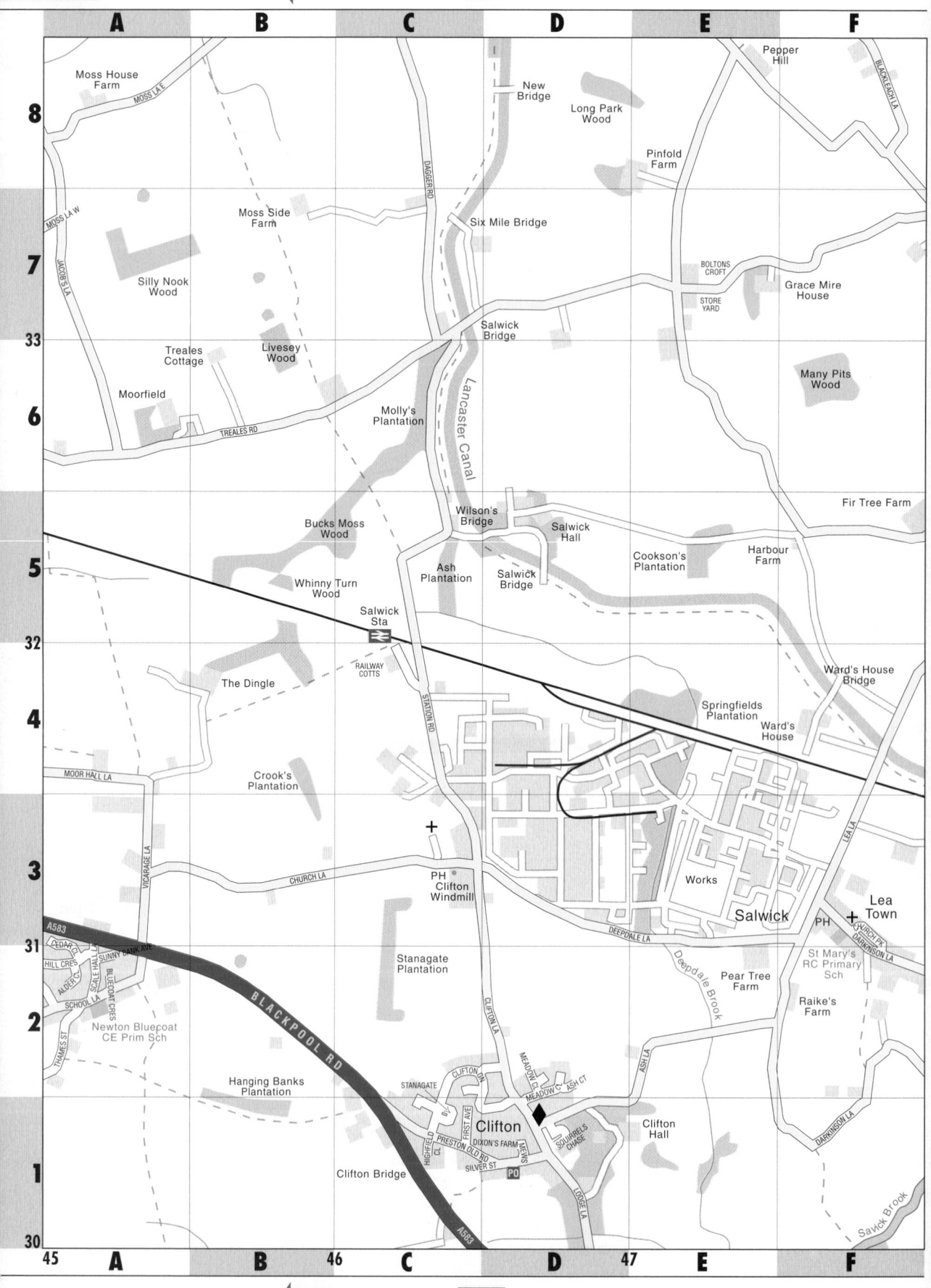

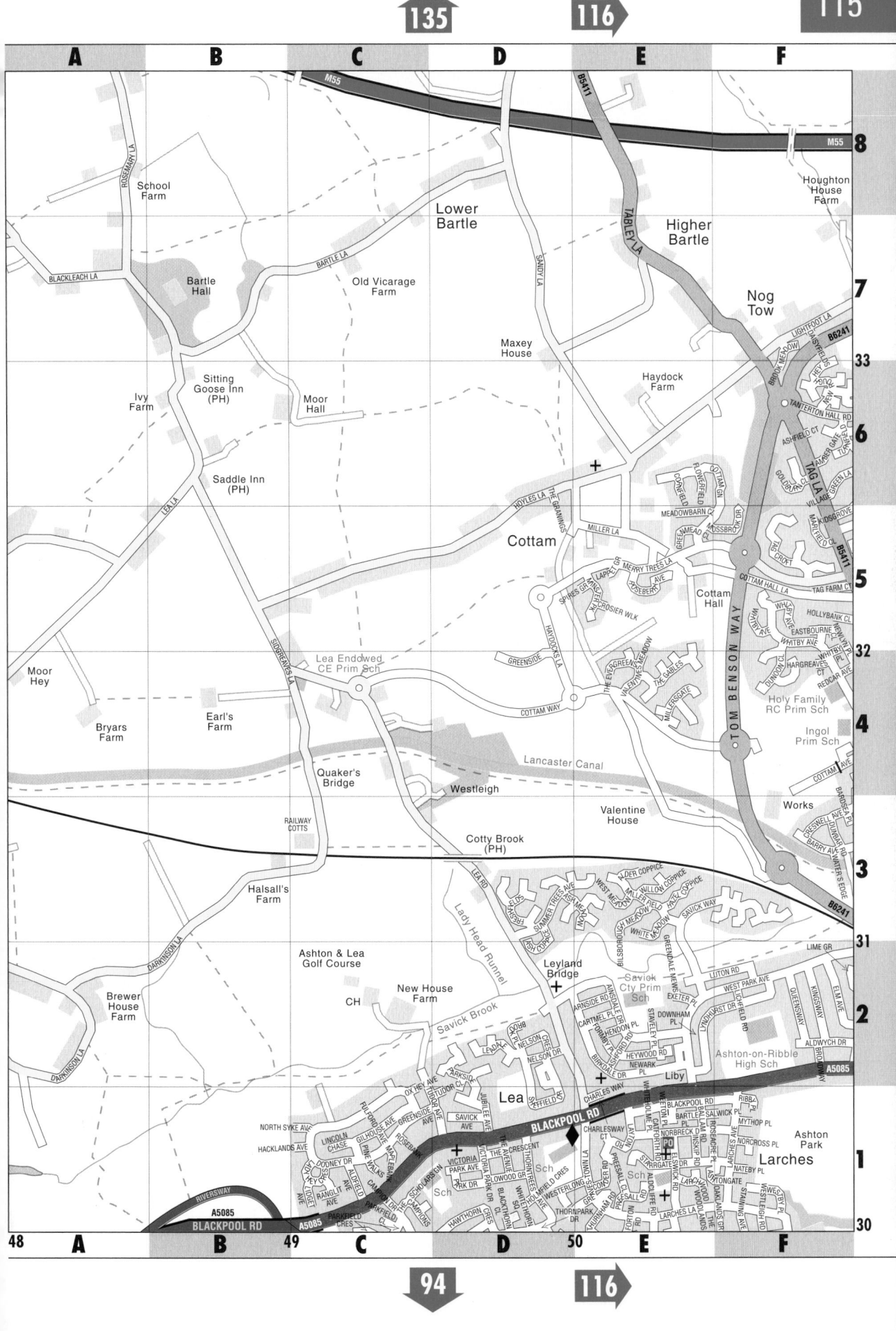

A B C D E F

M55

School Farm

ROSEMARY LA

BLACKLEACH LA

Lower Bartle

BARTLE LA

Old Vicarage Farm

B5411

TABLEY LA

Higher Bartle

Houghton House Farm

8

Nog Tow

7

33

Bartle Hall

Ivy Farm

Sitting Goose Inn (PH)

Moor Hall

Maxey House

Haydock Farm

LIGHTFOOT LA

BRIDA MEADOW

TANTERTON HALL RD

B6241

ASHFIEL CT

6

Saddle Inn (PH)

LEA LA

HOYLES LA

THE GRAININGS

MILLER LA

Cottam

CROSIER WLK

MERRY TREES LA

LAPSC

ROSEBERY

TAG LA

VILLAGE

GOLD LA

KIDSGROVE

MARLFIELD CL

B5411

5

Moor Hey

Earl's Farm

Bryars Farm

SIDGREAVES LA

Lea Endowed CE Prim Sch

GREENSIDE

HAYDOCKS LA

COTTAM WAY

SPIRES GR

MACROSIER WLK

VALENTINE MEADOW

THE EVERGREENS

THE GABLES

MILLERSGATE

Cottam Hall

COTTAM HALL LA

TAG FARM CT

HOLLYBANK CL

EASTBOURNE

WHITBY AVE

HARGREAVES CT

WHITBY PL

REDCAR AVE

TOM BENSON WAY

Holy Family RC Prim Sch

Ingol Prim Sch

COTTAM AVE

32

4

Quaker's Bridge

Lancaster Canal

Westleigh

Valentine House

Works

CRESNELL AVE

DUNBAR RD

BARDSEA PL

BARRY AVE

WINTER'S EDGE

RAILWAY COTTS

Cotty Brook (PH)

LEA RD

N-DER COPPICE

MILLER RD

WILLOW COPPICE

HAZ COPPICE

SAVICK WAY

WEST MEADOW

WHITE MEADOW

GREENDALE MEWS

B6241

3

31

Halsall's Farm

DARKINSON LA

Ashton & Lea Golf Course

LADY HEAD RUNNEL

New House Farm

CH

Leyland Bridge

Savick Brook

SUMMER TREES AVE

RIBORBOROUGH

ARNSIDE RD

CARTMEL PL

HENDON PL

STAVELEY PL

Savick Cty Prim Sch

EXETER PL

DOWNHAM PL

HEYWOOD PL

NEWARK

LYNDHURST DR

LITTON RD

WEST PARK AVE

KINGSWAY

QUEENSWAY

ELM AVE

LIME GR

2

Brewer House Farm

DARKINSON LA

Lea

OX HEY AVE

FILDRID HOUSE AVE

GILHOUSE AVE

GREENSIDE

TUDOR RD

SAVICK AVE

SAVICK CL

SHEFFIELD

JUBILEE AVE

NELSON DR

NELSON CRES

PARKSIDE

LENDAL

BROCK

CHARLES WAY

Liby

Ashton-on-Ribble High Sch

BROADWAY

ALDWYCH DR

A5085

Ashton Park

NORTH SYKE AVE

HACKLANDS AVE

LINCOLN CHASE

DODNEY DR

ALDFIELD AVE

RANGLIT AVE

CAMPBELL

THE SCHOLARS

GREENSIDE

ROSEBERY

THE AVENUE

SCHOLARS GN

VICTORIA PARK AVE

Sch

PARK DR

Sch

BLACKPOOL RD

CHARLESWAY

NORBRECK RD

CATFORTH RD

ELSWICK RD

SALWICK RD

MYTHOP PL

NORCROSS PL

ASHTONGATE

NATEBY PL

PO

Larches

CRESCENT

VICTORIA AVE

THE GARDENS

LOWOOD GR

THORNTREES AVE

WHITETHORN CRES

THORNPARK DR

WESTERLONG AVE

PRESTALL RD

STARGATE

LARCHES LA

WOODLANDS

WESTLEIGH RD

OAKLANDS AVE

1

RIVERSWAY

A5085

BLACKPOOL RD

A5085

PARKFIELD CRES

HAWTHORN

30

48 A B 49 C D 50 E F

← 115   136 ↑

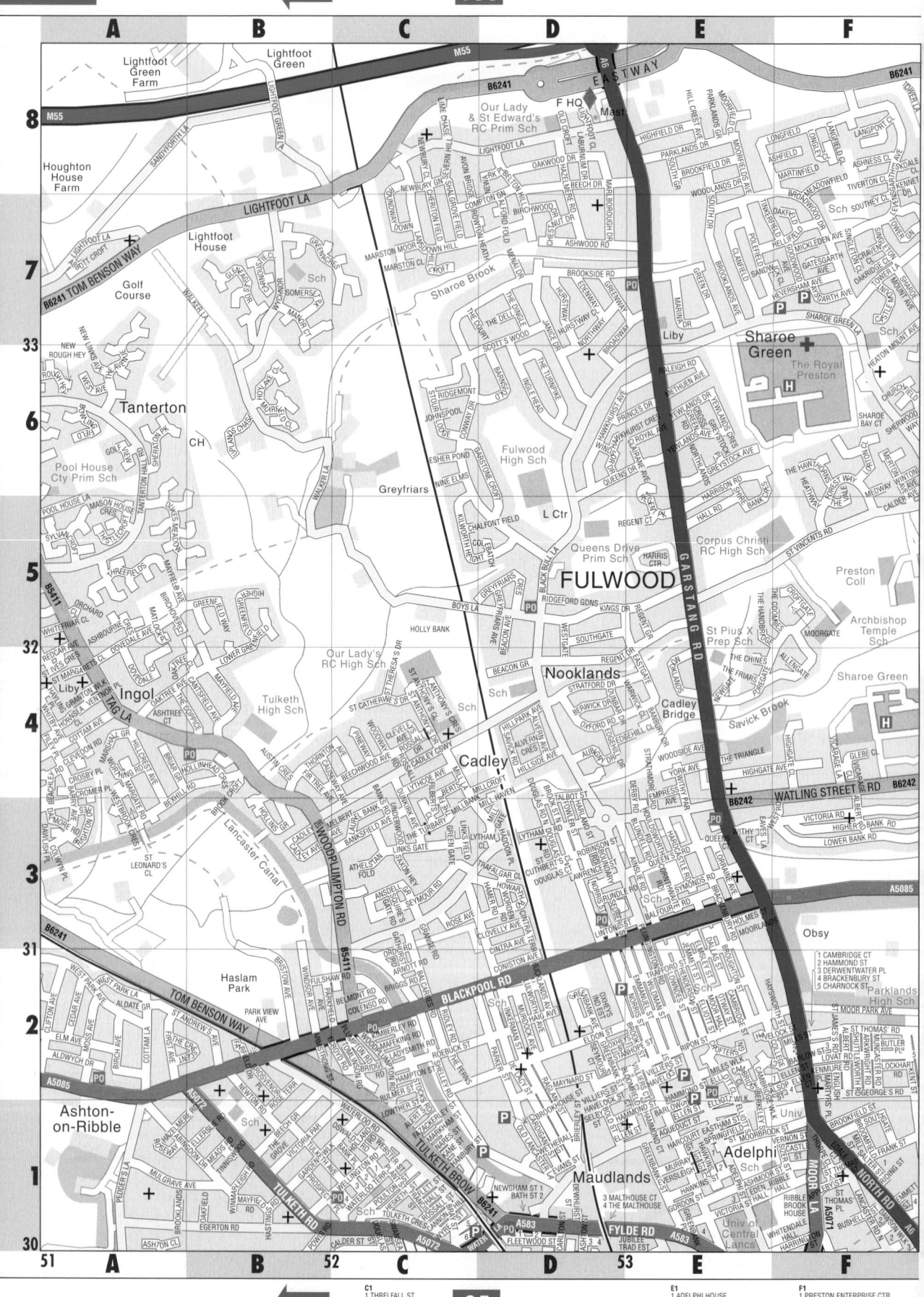

← 115   95

C1
1 THRELFALL ST
2 BRAMPTON ST
3 ELTON ST
4 BRUNSWICK PL
5 PECHELL ST
6 BLANCHE ST

E1
1 ADELPHI HOUSE
2 AUGHTON WLK
3 DERWENT HALL
4 TOWN BROOK HOUSE

F1
1 PRESTON ENTERPRISE CTR
2 MUNASTER CT
3 BECKETT CT
4 HANOVER ST

A B C D E F

8
7
33
6
5
32
4
3
31
2
1
30

Moss Leach Brook

Works

EASTWAY

Sherwood

Mason's Wood

Sherwood Cty Prim Sch

Preston Golf Course

Moss Leach Brook

Boundary Wood

Long Clough Wood
Haighton House

Highton Park Wood

Fulwood Park Wood

Londonderry Bridge

Fernyhalgh Bridge

Clock House Farm

FULWOOD ROW

Road under construction

M6

Savick Brook

1 FERNYHALGH CT
2 FERNYHALGH PL
3 FERNYHALGH GDNS
4 WOOKEY CL

Fulwood Hall

Fulwood Hall (CH)

Fulwood Barracks

Highfield Prim Sch

St Maria Goretti RC Prim Sch

1 WHARFEDALE AVE
2 ELLERBECK AVE
3 AMBLESIDE WLK

Brookfield Prim Sch

Longsands Cty Prim Sch

1 PORTREE CL
2 MARYBANK CL
3 CARLOWAY AVE

Brookfield

1 LANGCLIFFE RD 1
MALHAM PL 2
BRAYSHAW PL 3
TRAWDEN CRES 4

Eaves Brook

WATLING STREET RD

Holme Slack Prim Sch

B6241

Superstore

Holme Slack

Sherburn Sch

The Serpentine

Moor Park

Elms Sch

Moorfield Sch

Deepdale

1 MILNER ST
2 CHARNOCK ST
3 CHARNOCK FOLD
4 VARLEY ST
5 ST STEPHEN'S RD

Moor Park High Sch

North End Football Ground

TA Ctr

DEEPDALE RD

BLACKPOOL RD

RIBBLETON AVE

Woodlands Sch

Cemy

Ribbleton

Farringdon Park

Ribbleton Hall High Sch

LEAGRAM CRES

Ribbleton Park

RIBBLETON LA

NEW HALL LA

A59

Liby

Liby

B6243

Longridge Rd / LONGRIDGE RD

1
SHAW ST
TURNER ST
CROMWELL ST
ALICE SQ
ALEXANDRA PAVILION
ELIZABETH SQ
ALBERT TERR
EDWARD SQ
STAFFORD RD

B1
1 ISHERWOOD ST
2 STRUTT ST
3 ANSDELL ST

C1
1 ST JOSEPH'S TERR
2 HERMON ST
3 BULLFINCH RD
4 GRAHAM ST
5 HOLMAN ST
6 GILLETT ST
7 CURWEN ST
8 WIGNALL ST
9 ST LUKE'S PL

10 ALEXANDRA HOUSE

D1
1 ASHELDON ST
2 BRADDON ST
3 BEENLAND ST
4 TUNBRIDGE ST
5 SALISBURY ST
6 CALVERLEY ST
7 TUNBRIDGE PL
8 TRURO PL

96

D1
9 WELLS ST
10 GRIMSARGH ST
11 CANTERBURY RD
12 LEVENS ST

118

E1
1 HAWARDEN RD
2 CAVENDISH RD
3 IDDESLEIGH RD
4 MANNING RD

F3
1 AINSCOUGH BROOK HOUSE
2 RIBBLETON HALL CRES

F4
1 LAUDERDALE CRES
2 EDLESTON LODGE
3 LEICESTER LODGE
4 HOLLAND LODGE
5 ROTHWELL LODGE
6 SHERBORNE LODGE

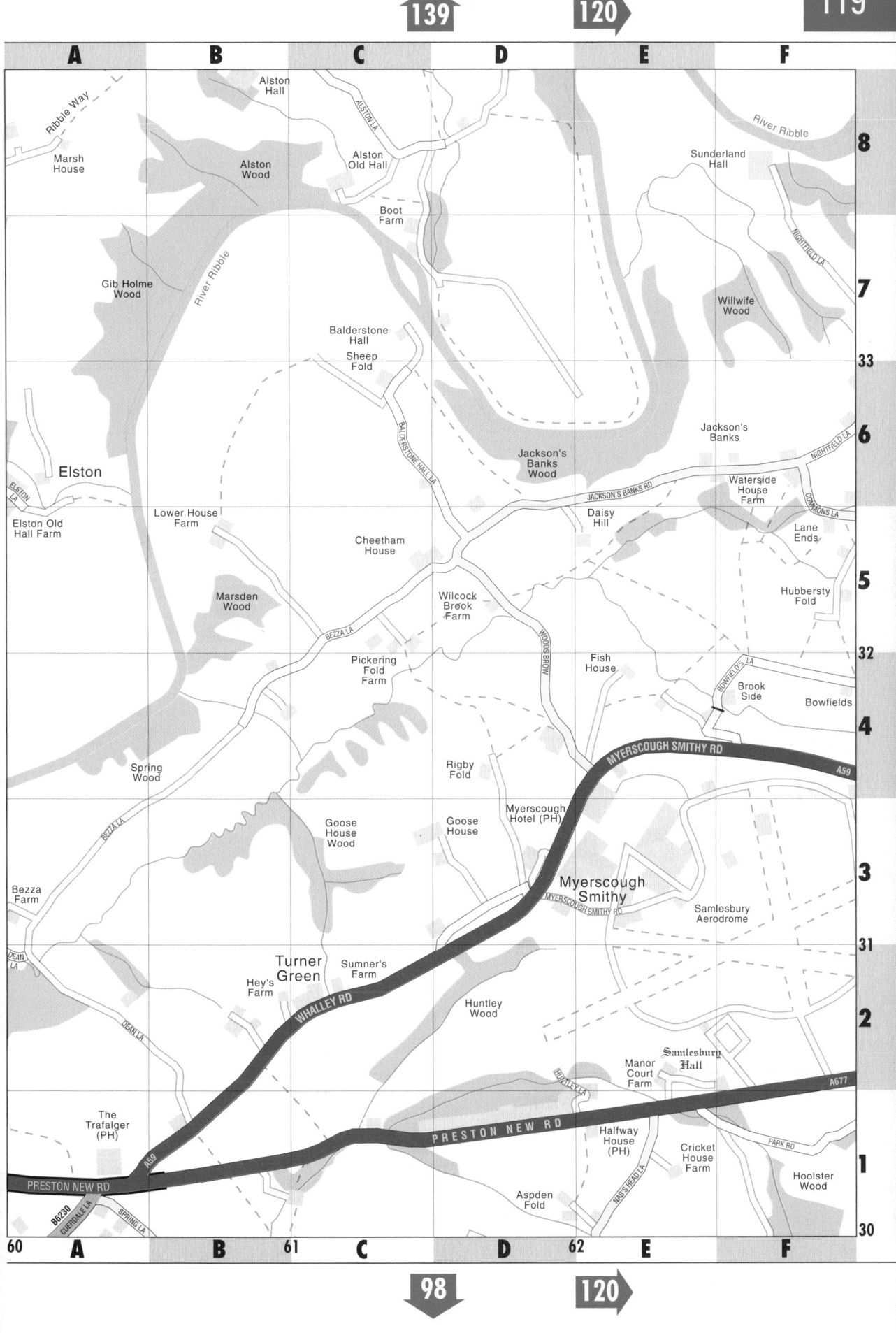

A B C D E F

8
7
33
6
5
32
4
3
31
2
1
30

60 A B 61 C D 62 E F

Ribble Way

Marsh House

Alston Hall

Alston Wood

Alston Old Hall

ALSTON LA

Boot Farm

River Ribble

Sunderland Hall

River Ribble

NIGHTFIELD LA

Gib Holme Wood

River Ribble

Willwife Wood

Balderstone Hall

Sheep Fold

BALDERSTONE HALL LA

Jackson's Banks Wood

Jackson's Banks

NIGHTFIELD LA

Elston

ELSTON LA

Lower House Farm

Cheetham House

JACKSON'S BANKS RD

Daisy Hill

Waterside House Farm

Lane Ends

COMMONS LA

Elston Old Hall Farm

Marsden Wood

BEZZA LA

Wilcock Brook Farm

WOODS BROW

Fish House

Hubbersty Fold

Pickering Fold Farm

ROWFIELD'S LA

Brook Side

Bowfields

Spring Wood

BEZZA LA

Rigby Fold

MYERSCOUGH SMITHY RD

A59

Goose House Wood

Goose House

Myerscough Hotel (PH)

Bezza Farm

DEAN LA

Myerscough Smithy

MYERSCOUGH SMITHY RD

Samlesbury Aerodrome

DEAN LA

Turner Green

Hey's Farm

Sumner's Farm

WHALLEY RD

Huntley Wood

HUNTLEY LA

Manor Court Farm

Samlesbury Hall

A677

The Trafalger (PH)

A59

PRESTON NEW RD

Halfway House (PH)

NAB'S HEAD LA

Cricket House Farm

PARK RD

Hoolster Wood

PRESTON NEW RD

B6230

GUERDLE LA

SPRING LA

Aspden Fold

119
140

A **B** **C** **D** **E** **F**

River Ribble

Dobridding
Wood

Flashers
Wood

Burr
Green

New
House

Showley
Hall

8

Mercyfield
Wood

Old Park
Wood

Lower
Studlehurst

Oxendale
Hall

Mire
Wood

7

Sandiford
Wood

Park
Gate

Higher
Studlehurst

33

Nightfield
Gate

Fletcher Fold
Farm

Robert's
House
Farm

6

Pewter
House
Fold

Osbaldeston
Green

Carr House
Farm

A59

Balderstone

Smalley
Fold

Rush
Paddock

Tottering Brook

Hawkshaw
Fold

5

Balderstone
CE Prim Sch

COMMONS LA

Balderstone
Grange

Sharples
Farm

Birley
Fold

BOWFIELD'S LA

NIGHTFIELD LA

OSBALDESTON LA

32

St Mary's
RC Prim Sch

Cockerham
Hall

4

Holmes
Farm

Bay Horse
Hotel
(PH)

LONGSIGHT RD

Osbaldeston

Moor
Edge

Mammon
Wood

HIGHER COMMONS LA

Abbott
House

**Mellor
Moor**

A59

Mellor Brook

Sykes
Holt

Calf
House

ABBOTT BROW

Ward's
Farm

MYERSCOUGH SMITHY RD

Thurstons

MYERSCOUGH SMITHY RD

WHALLEY RD

Old Dad's
House

3

PH

**Mellor
Brook**

ELSWICK GDNS

STOOPS FOLD

Millstone
Inn
(Hotel)

MELLOR LA

PO

WOODFLD CL

BROADTREE CL

MELLOR BROW

Brundhurst
Farm

Brundhurst Fold

St Mary's
CE Prim Sch

ARLEY RISE

P

31

BRANCH RD

BOSBURN DR

ELSWICK CLOSE

Liby

STANLEY GATE

NICKEY LA

HOB GN

Mellor

2

INTACK LA

LOXLEY MEADOW

Windmill
Hotel
(PH)

CHURCH LA

PO

ST MARY'S GDNS

BROOKFIELD

FOURACRE

CARTER FOLD

Ottie Green
Farm

A677

PARK RD

PRESTON NEW RD

YERBURGH RD
THWAITES AVE 2

CHURCH CL

GLENDALE DR

GLENDALE

WHITECROFT LA

Balshaw Fold
Farm

MIRE ASH BROW

Dick
Dadds

Park
Farm

Higher Park
Farm

Moss Hall
Farm

1

Old
Doozes

FURTHER LA

A677

30

119
99

A B C D E F

8

White Holme

Eden Holme

B6245

RIBCHESTER RD

Oakes Bridge

OAKS BAR

Oaks Farm

ALBANY DR

Copster Green

Langho Colony

Dewhurst House

LONGSIGHT RD

Brook Cottage

Oaks Farm

Clayton-Le-Dale

Lovely Hall

Ashes Farm

7

Mire Fold

OAKS BROW

Low Farm

LOVELY HALL LA

Nook House

DURHAM RD

SHETLAND CL

BERKSHIRE DR

33

Royal Oak Inn (PH)

Salesbury CE Prim Sch

1 CHURCH VIEW
2 HAZELMOOR

THE HAZELS

VICARAGE LA

SHROPSHIRE

ELY CL

SHOWLEY RD

PH

CLAYTON BR

PO

A666

6

Harwood Fold

St PETER'S CL

RIBCHESTER RD

Clayton Hey Fold Farm

Salesbury

BEECH CL

MAPLE CL

SHOWLEY CT

KNOWSLEY RD W

THE HAWTHORNS

SOMERSET AVE

BRYER'S CROFT

GROSVENOR LODGE

CH

FAIRWAYS CT

Showley Fold

Tottering Brook

Showley Brook

Wilpshire

VALLEY RD

B6245

WHALLEY RD

HOLLOWHEAD LA

BEAVER CL

HOLLOWHEAD AVE

5

Blue Slate Farm

Midge Hall

Hagg's Hall

Ramsgreave Wood

Bottoms Farm

BROOKLYN RD

WOODCREST

KNOWSLEY RD

MAYFAIR CRES

WILPSHIRE BANKS

HOLLOWHEAD CL

32

SACARY LA

CLIFTON GR

STATION CL

Wardfall

Mountain Ash Farm

Ramsgreave and Wilpshire Sta

4

Cunliffe Moss Farm

Ramsgreave Hall Farm

RAMSGREAVE RD

ISLE OF MAN

WAVERLEY AVE

PARIS

WALDEN

PARSONAGE RD

PRIMROSE HILL

Longworth's House

MAYFIELD RD

GLENGREAVE AVE

MAYFIELD AVE

WHALLEY NEW RD

BEECH MOUNT

WILLOW

KEMP

BROWNHILL RD

YORK CL

CAMBRIAN CL

EAST LANCASHIRE RD

REVINGTON AVE

Brownhill Farm

3

Primrose Hill

ZECHARIAH BROW

HIGHER RAMSGREAVE RD

Collinson's Farm

HASTON LEE AVE

CHURCH BANK

BANK OF HEY LA

St GABRIEL'S RD

PO

31

Spread Eagle (PH)

MELLOR LA

BARNES LA

Top of Ramsgreave

LONG ROW

Kay Fold Farm

Roe Lee Park Prim Sch

BROWNHILL DR

OPAL

ROE LEE PK

ALDWYCH PL

AMETHYST

CORAL ST

AGATE ST

SONNE AVE

OPAL ST

Brownhill

A6119

2

Kingbank Farm

Vine House Farm

Stone's Farm

RAMSGREAVE DR

BROADWAY

PLECKGATE RD

FURTHER WILWORTH

St GABRIEL'S CE PRIM SCH

LOWER WILWORTH

WILWORTH CRES

Holy Souls RC Prim Sch

EMERALD AVE

BERYL AVE

EMBER AVE

PERIDOT CL

EMERALD ST

JASPER ST

PEARL ST

WHALLEY NEW RD

DOUGLAS PL

HIGHBANK AVE

1

Lower Reaps

Bullion Moss

WHINNEY LA

LAMMACK RD

PO

Roe Lee

BLENHEIM CL

PEMBERTON

ROYAL OAK AVE

HAYDOCK CL

HARDY ST

CAMPBELL ST

SAPPHIRE ST

AGATE ST

Cemy

YEW TREE DR

A6119

GRASMERE AVE

Lammack Prim Sch

WILLOW TREES DR

Pleckgate

Pleckgate High Sch

PLECKGATE FOLD

NORTH BANK AVE

BARMOUTH CRES

B6233

WOODSHAW

HILL VIEW

PENSHAW AVE

THORNWOOD

ROSEWOOD AVE

A666

PO

30

66 A B 67 C D 68 E F

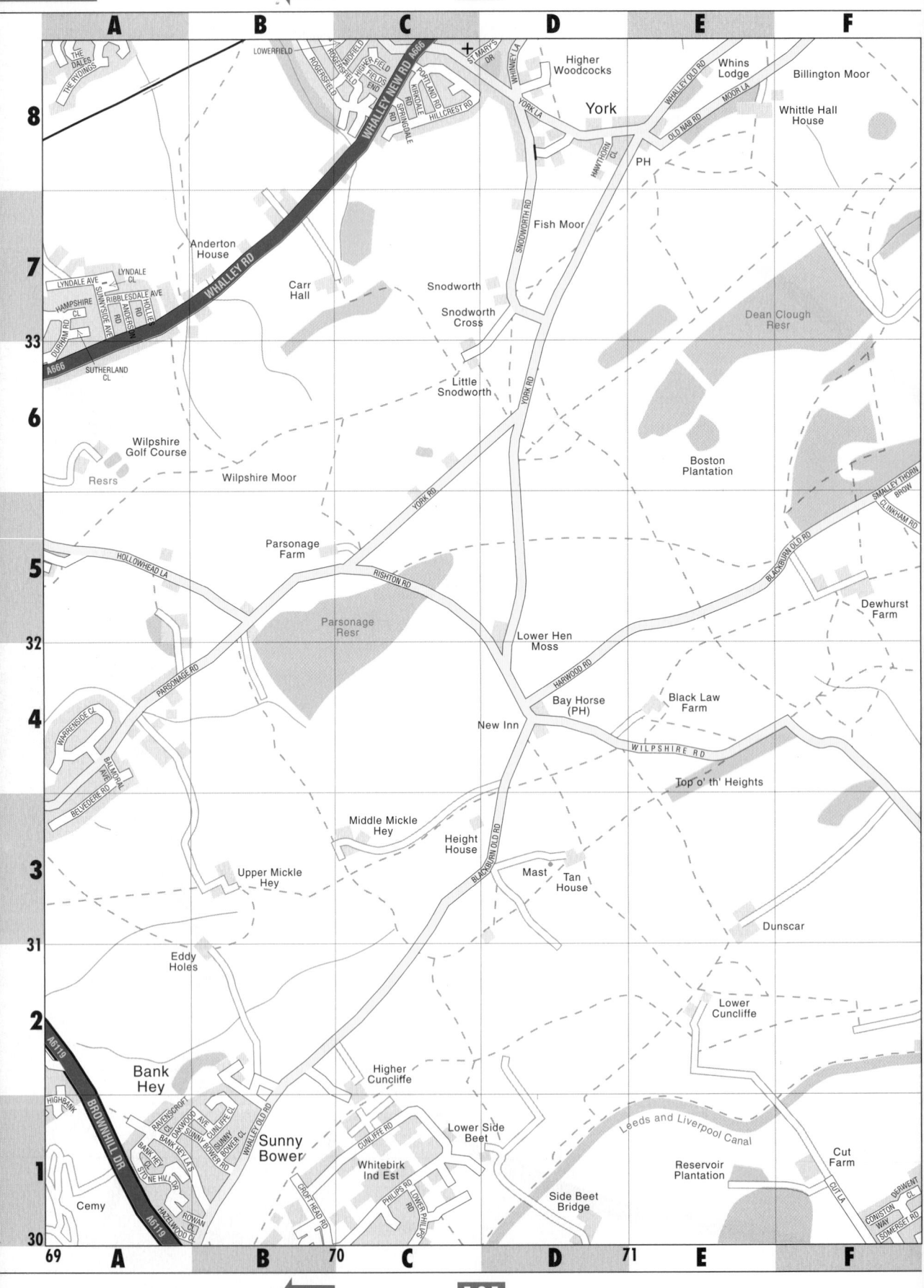

THE DALES
THE RYDINGS

LOWERFIELD

Anderton
House

WHALLEY RD

Carr
Hall

WHALLEY NEW RD A666

ROGERSFIELD

ASGERBY

HIGHER FIELD

HIGHER FIELDS END

SPRINGDALE

HILLCREST RD

PORTLAND RD

KIRKDALE

ST MARY'S DR

WHINNET LA

Higher
Woodcocks

York

YORK LA

HAWTHORN CL

WHALLEY OLD RD

OLD MAB RD

MOOR LA

Whins
Lodge

Billington Moor

Whittle Hall
House

PH

Fish Moor

SNODWORTH RD

Snodworth

Snodworth
Cross

Little
Snodworth

YORK RD

Dean Clough
Resr

Wilpshire
Golf Course

Resrs

Wilpshire Moor

HOLLOWHEAD LA

Parsonage
Farm

RISHTON RD

Parsonage
Resr

Boston
Plantation

SMALLEY THORN BROW

CT INNHAM RD

BLACKBURN OLD RD

Dewhurst
Farm

PARSONAGE RD

WARRENSIDE CL

BALMORAL AVE

BELVEDERE RD

Lower Hen
Moss

HARWOOD RD

Bay Horse
(PH)

New Inn

Black Law
Farm

WILPSHIRE RD

Top o' th' Heights

Middle Mickle
Hey

Height
House

Upper Mickle
Hey

BLACKBURN OLD RD

Mast

Tan
House

Dunscar

Eddy
Holes

Lower
Cuncliffe

A6119

HIGHBANK

BROWNHILL DR

Bank
Hey

RAVENSCROFT

OAKWOOD AVE

SUNNY CL

CUNLIFFE CL

WHALLEY OLD RD

SUNNY BOWER CL

SUNNY BOWER RD

BANK HEY LA S

Higher
Cuncliffe

CUNLIFFE RD

Sunny
Bower

Lower Side
Beet

Leeds and Liverpool Canal

Cut
Farm

CUT LA

Reservoir
Plantation

Cemy

HAZELWOOD CL

ROWAN CL

STONE HILL DR

A6119

Whitebirk
Ind Est

CROFT HEAD RD

PHILIPS RD

LOWER PHILIPS RD

Side Beet
Bridge

DERWENT CL

CONISTON WAY

SOMERSET RD

LYNDALE AVE

LYNDALE CL

HAMPSHIRE CL

SUNNYSIDE AVE

HOLLIES

RIBBLESDALE AVE

ANDERSON RD

DURHAM RD

A666

SUTHERLAND CL

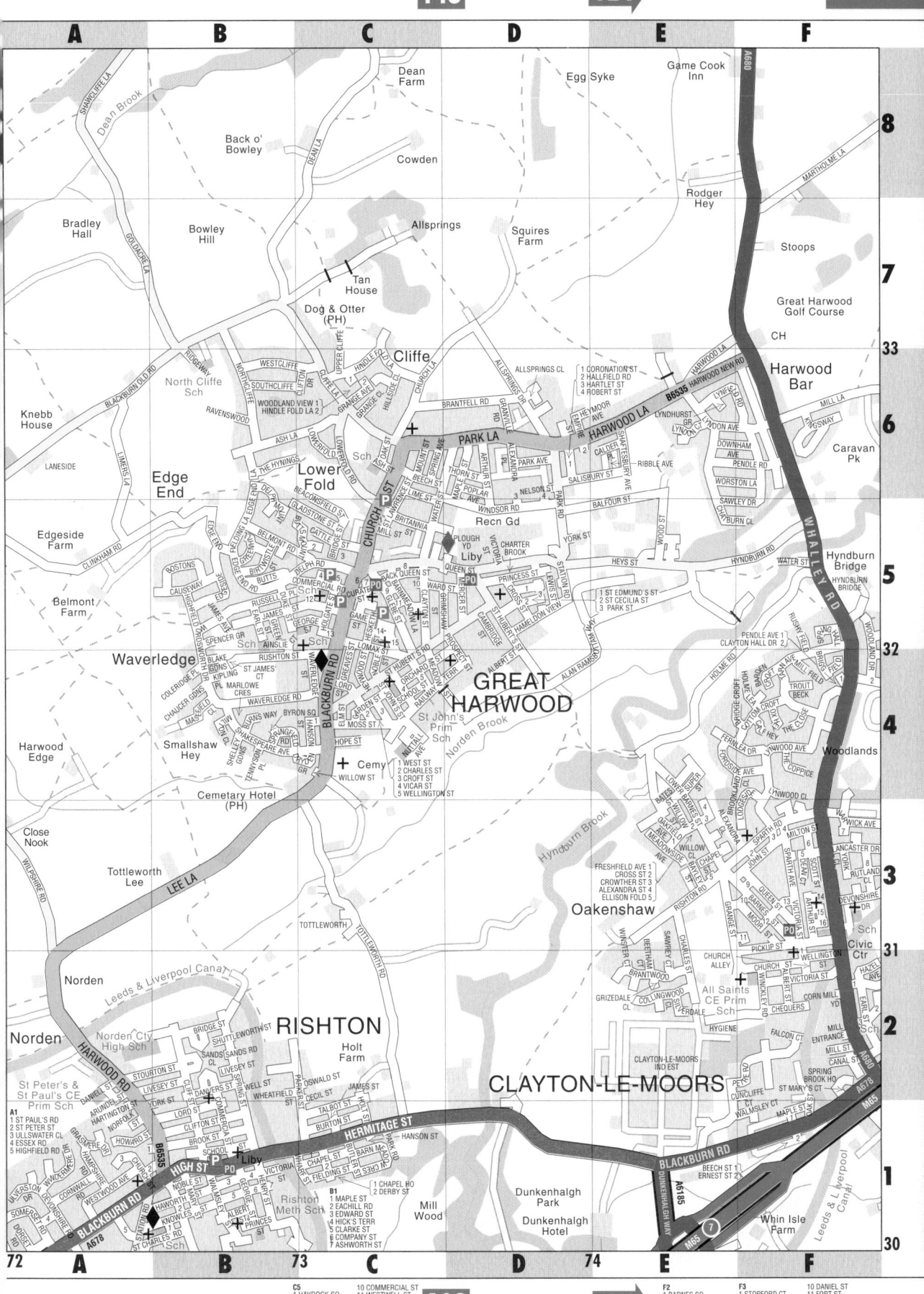

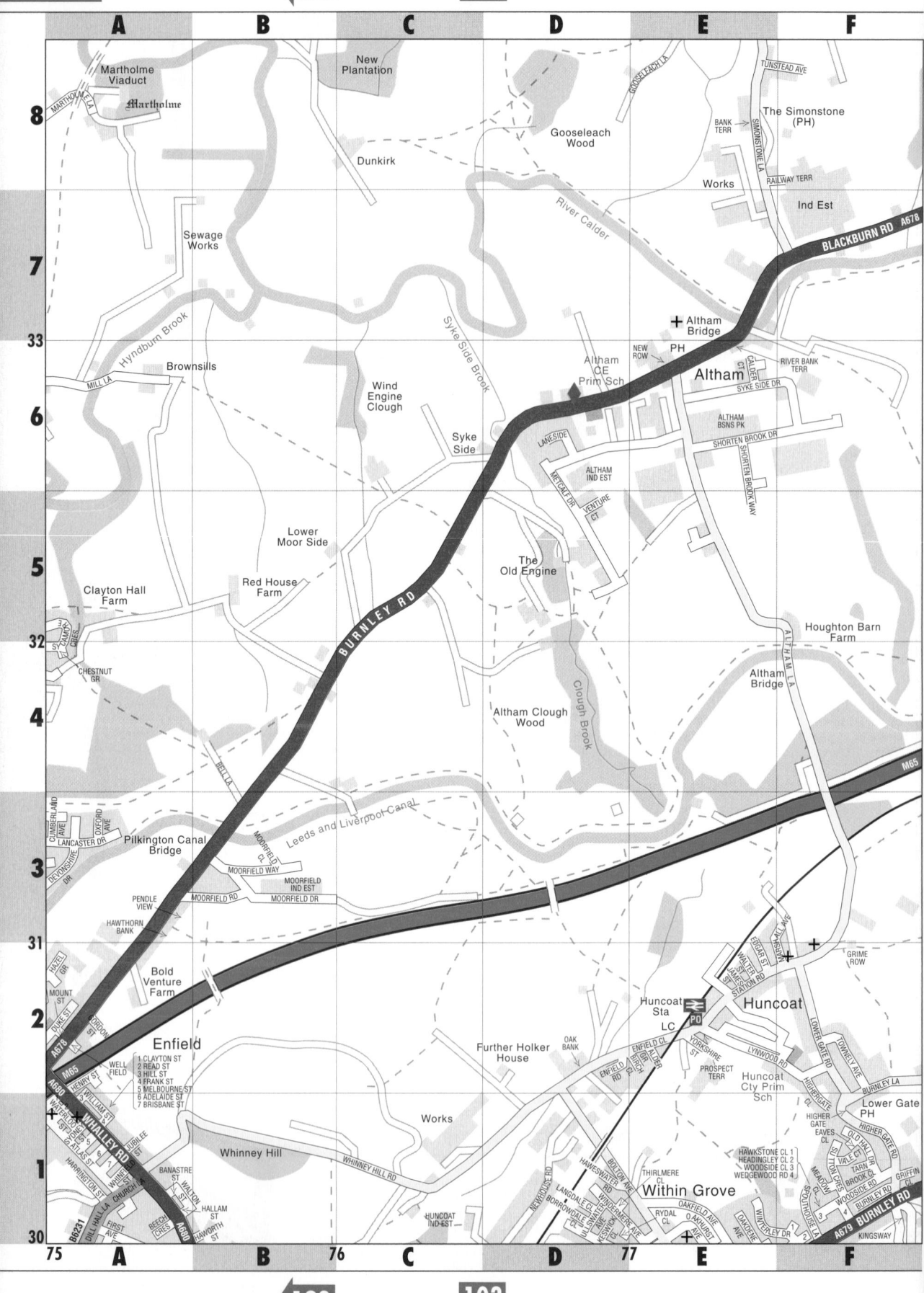

A B C D E F

PADIHAM

WHALLEY RD
CHURCH ST
BLACKBURN RD
A671
A6068
A578

Craggs
DOUBLE ROW 1
ARBORIES AVE 2
Cemy
Striking Hill Farm
Power Sta (Disused)
River Calder
Padiham Green CE Sch
St John the Baptist RC Sch

Liby
Waterside Mews

8 MYTTON ST
DARWEN ST
WYRE ST
HOLME ST
FLEETWOOD RD
LUNE ST
RIBBLE ST

RIVER DR
STOCKBRIDGE DR

Padiham Prim Sch South Dr
BURNLEY RD

Padiham Cty Prim Sch
Gawthorpe High Sch
Gawthorpe Edge Pk

D8
1 TATTERSALL ST
2 WADDINGTON ST
3 ST JAMES PL
4 BACK ALTHAM ST
5 ALTHAM ST
6 WESLEY ST
7 CROSS BANK
8 HOPE ST
9 PITT ST

Bronte Way
HABERGHAM DR
Pit Plantation

PADIHAM RD
A671
A46
HAMBLEDON VIEW
Habergham High Sch
Habergham
Ivy Bank High Sch

Lowerhouse
GREENBROOK CL
LOWERHOUSE LA
WELLESLEY ST
GREENBROOK RD

C8
1 PARISH ST
2 DAME FOLD
3 BACK ALBERT ST
4 INKERMAN ST
5 DRAGON ST
6 SHUTTLEWORTH ST
7 ECCLESHILL ST
8 CLITHEROE ST

Cemy
CEMETERY RD

D7
1 GRAHAM ST
2 HATHAWAY FOLD
3 WYTHAM ST
4 ALBION ST
5 RUTLAND PL

STONE MOOR BOTTOM
FENNYFOLD TERR

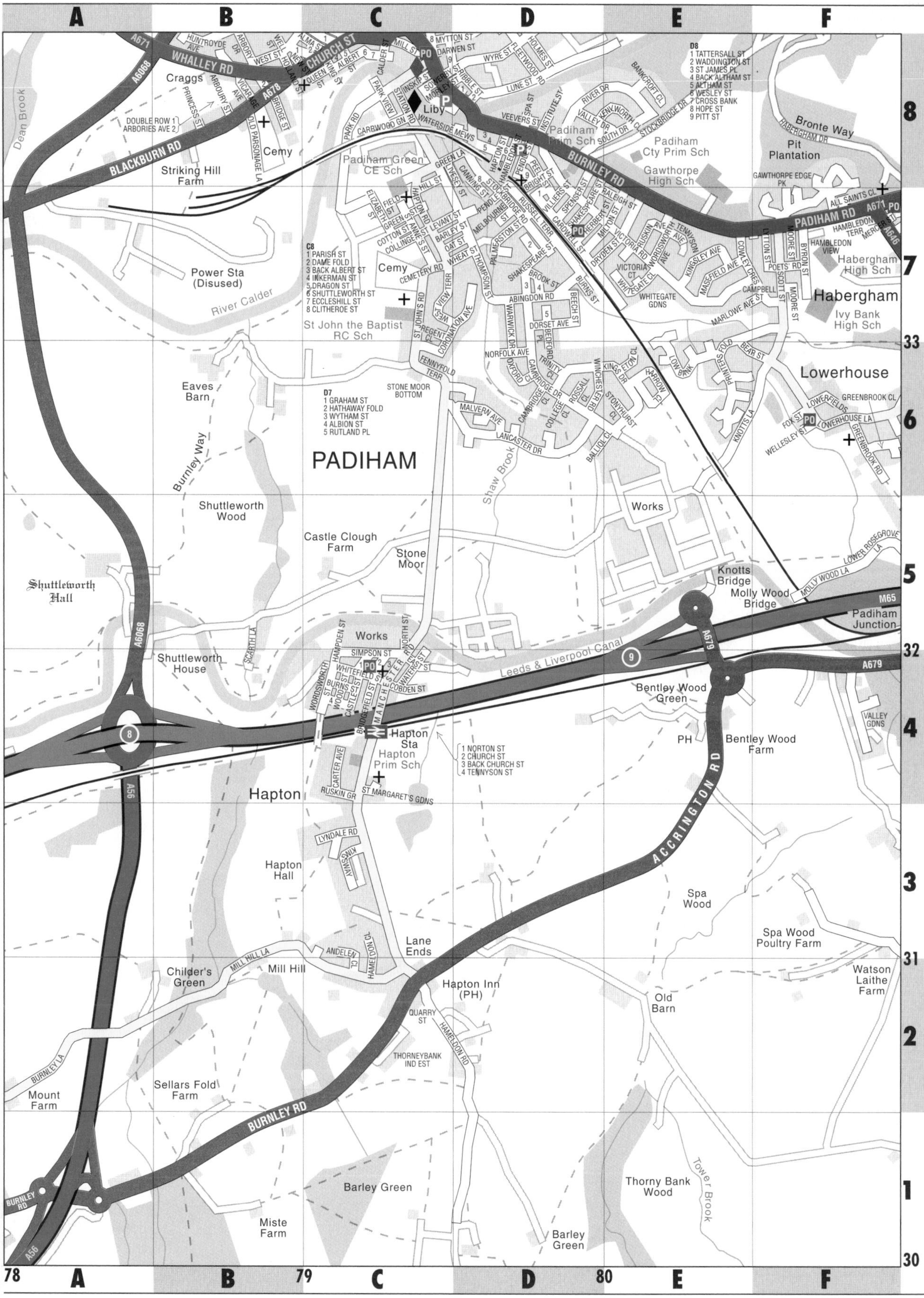

Eaves Barn
Burnley Way
Shuttleworth Wood

Castle Clough Farm
Stone Moor

Works

MALVERN AVE
LANCASTER DR
Shaw Brook

Knotts Bridge
Molly Wood Bridge
LOWER ROSE GROVE LA
MOLLY WOOD LA
M65
Padiham Junction

Shuttleworth Hall
A6068

Shuttleworth House

Works
SIMPSON ST
WHITEFIELD RD
COBDEN ST
HAMPDEN ST
WORDSWORTH
CASTLE ST
BURNS ST
MANCHESTER RD

PO

Leeds & Liverpool Canal
9

Bentley Wood Green
PH
Bentley Wood Farm
A679

VALLEY GDNS

Hapton Sta
Hapton Prim Sch
St Margaret's Gdns
Hapton

1 NORTON ST
2 CHURCH ST
3 BACK CHURCH ST
4 TENNYSON ST

CARTER AVE
RUSKIN GR

8
A56
A679

ACCRINGTON RD

Hapton Hall
LYNDALE RD
KINGSWAY
HAMELDON DL

Spa Wood

Spa Wood Poultry Farm

Watson Laithe Farm

Childer's Green
Mill Hill
MILL HILL LA
ANDELEN
Lane Ends

Hapton Inn (PH)
QUARRY ST
HAMELDON RD

Old Barn

Sellars Fold Farm

BURNLEY LA
Mount Farm
A56

THORNEYBANK IND EST

BURNLEY RD

Barley Green
Miste Farm

Barley Green

Thorny Bank Wood
Tower Brook

8 7 33 6 5 32 4 3 31 2 1 30

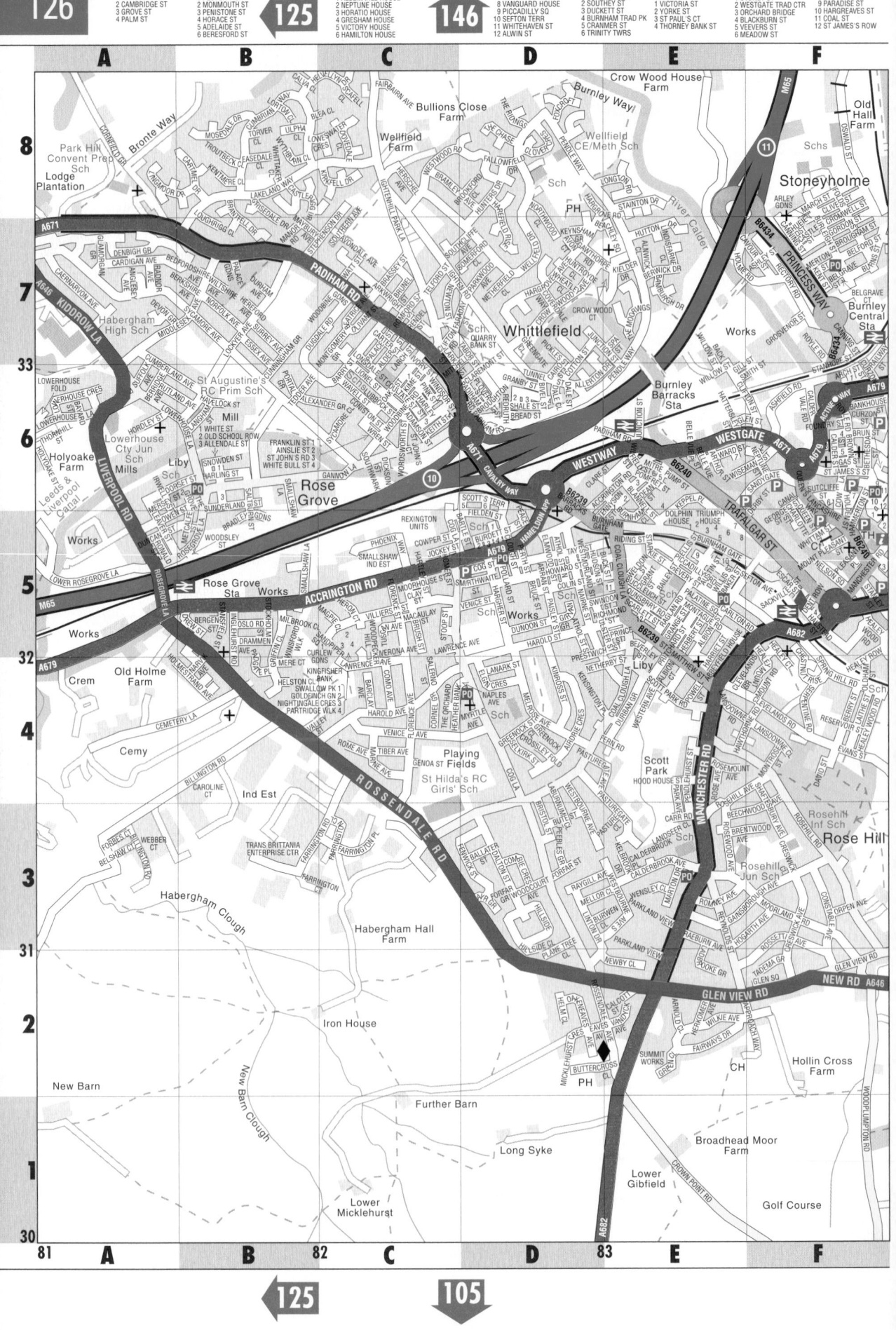

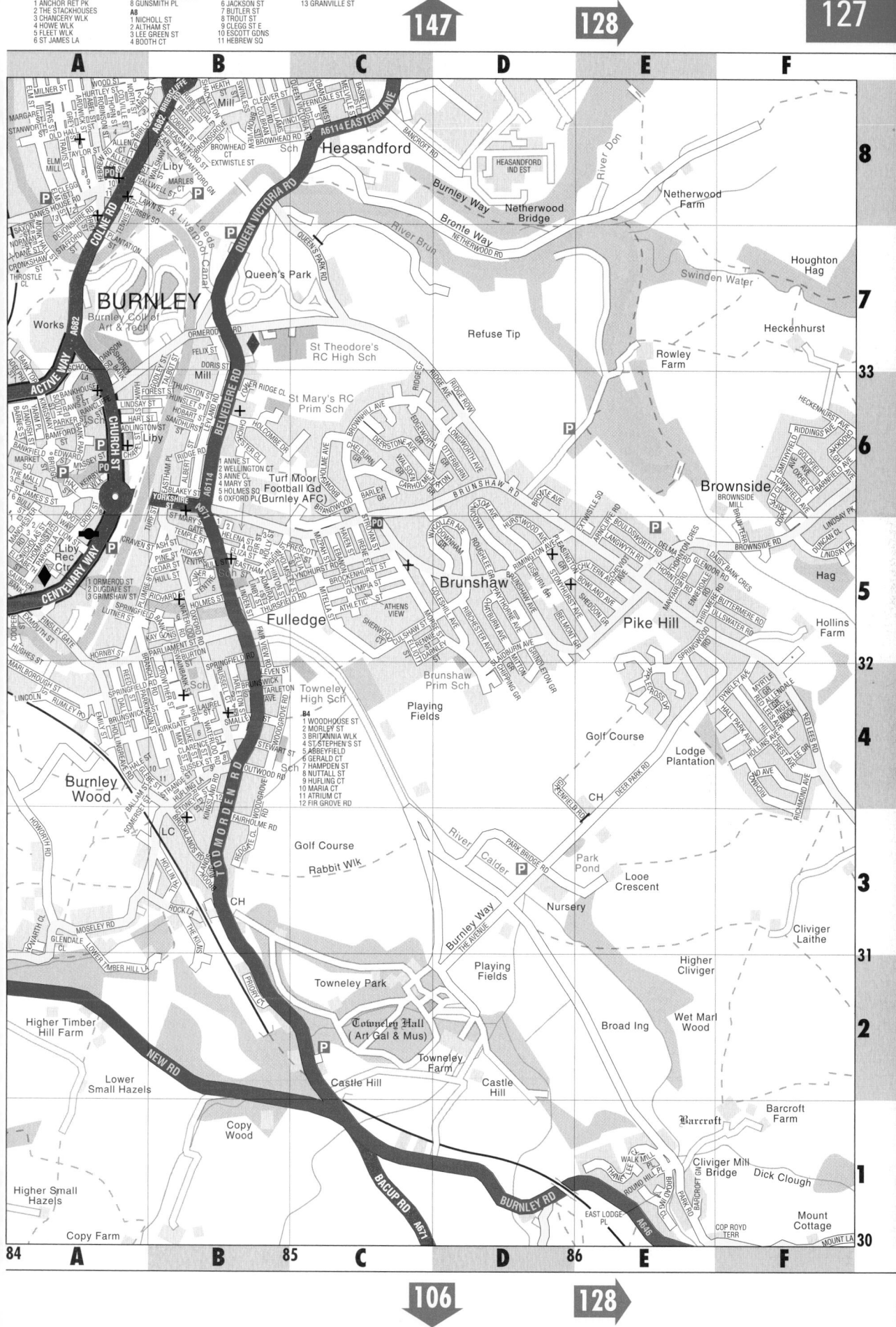

147
128
106
128

A6
1 ANCHOR RET PK
2 THE STACKHOUSES
3 CHANCERY WLK
4 HOWE WLK
5 FLEET WLK
6 ST JAMES LA

7 BURNLEY BSNS CTR
8 GUNSMITH PL
A8
1 NICHOLL ST
2 ALTHAM ST
3 LEE GREEN ST
4 BOOTH CT

5 BARRETT ST
6 JACKSON ST
7 BUTLER ST
8 TROUT ST
9 CLEGG ST E
10 ESCOTT GDNS
11 HEBREW SQ

12 BOND ST
13 GRANVILLE ST

B4
1 WOODHOUSE ST
2 MORLEY ST
3 BRITANNIA WLK
4 ST STEPHEN'S ST
5 ABBEYFIELD
6 GERALD CT
7 HAMPDEN ST
8 NUTTALL ST
9 HUFLING CT
10 MARIA CT
11 ATRIUM CT
12 FIR GROVE RD

BURNLEY

Heasandford

HEASANDFORD
IND EST

Netherwood
Bridge

Netherwood
Farm

Houghton
Hag

Heckenhurst

Rowley
Farm

Refuse Tip

Brownside

BROWNSIDE
MILL

Hag

Queen's Park

St Theodore's
RC High Sch

St Mary's RC
Prim Sch

Hollins
Farm

Turf Moor
Football Gd
(Burnley AFC)

Brunshaw

Pike Hill

Fulledge

Brunshaw
Prim Sch

Playing
Fields

Golf Course

Lodge
Plantation

Burnley
Wood

Towneley
High Sch

River
Calder

Park
Pond

Looe
Crescent

Nursery

Golf Course

Rabbit Wlk

Burnley Way
THE AVENUE

Playing
Fields

Cliviger
Laithe

Higher
Cliviger

Towneley Park

Higher Timber
Hill Farm

Towneley Hall
(Art Gal & Mus)

Towneley
Farm

Broad Ing

Wet Marl
Wood

Lower
Small Hazels

Castle Hill

Castle
Hill

Barcroft

Barcroft
Farm

Copy
Wood

Cliviger Mill
Bridge

Dick Clough

Higher Small
Hazels

EAST LODGE
PL

Mount
Cottage

Copy Farm

127
148

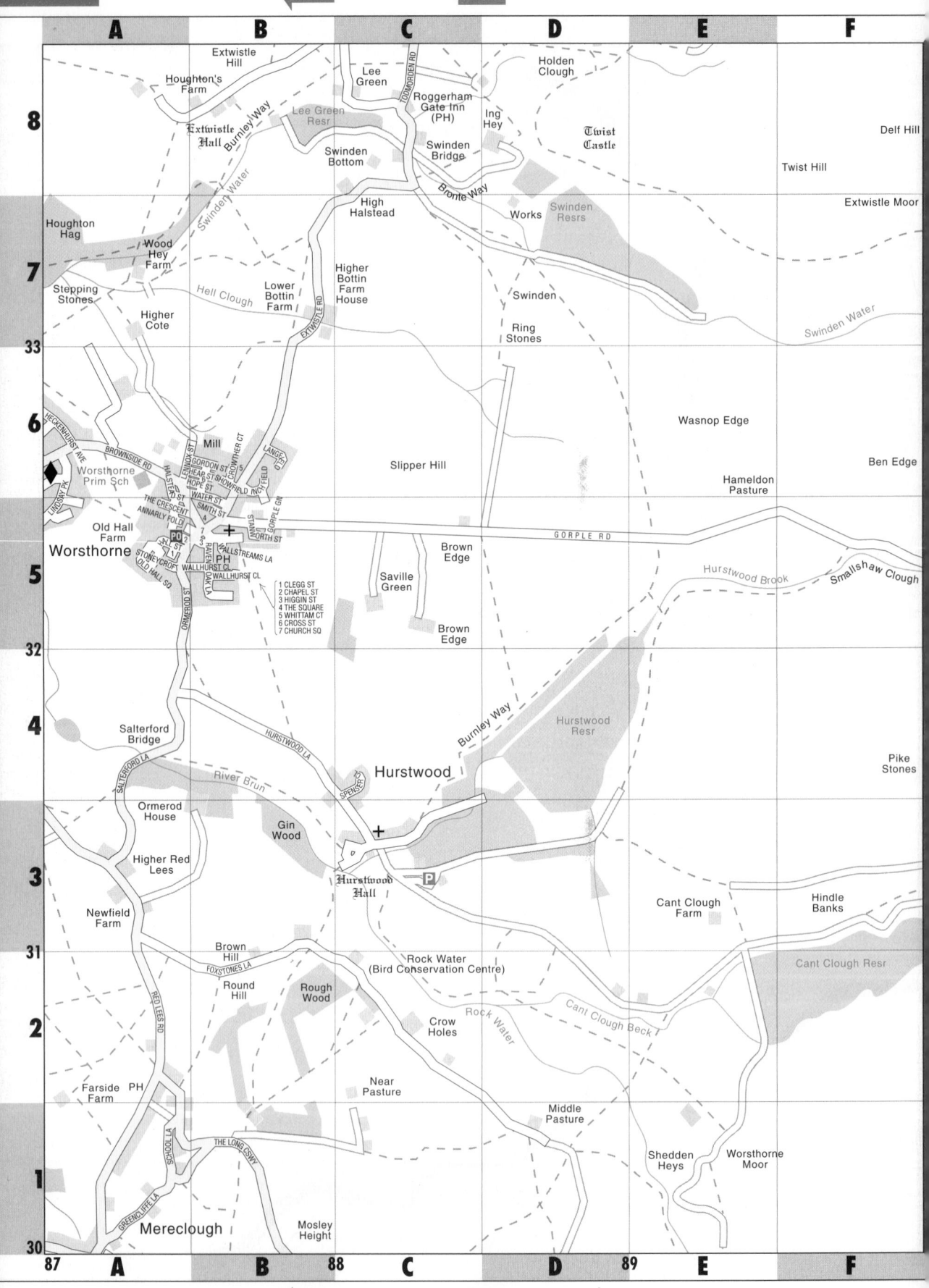

127
107

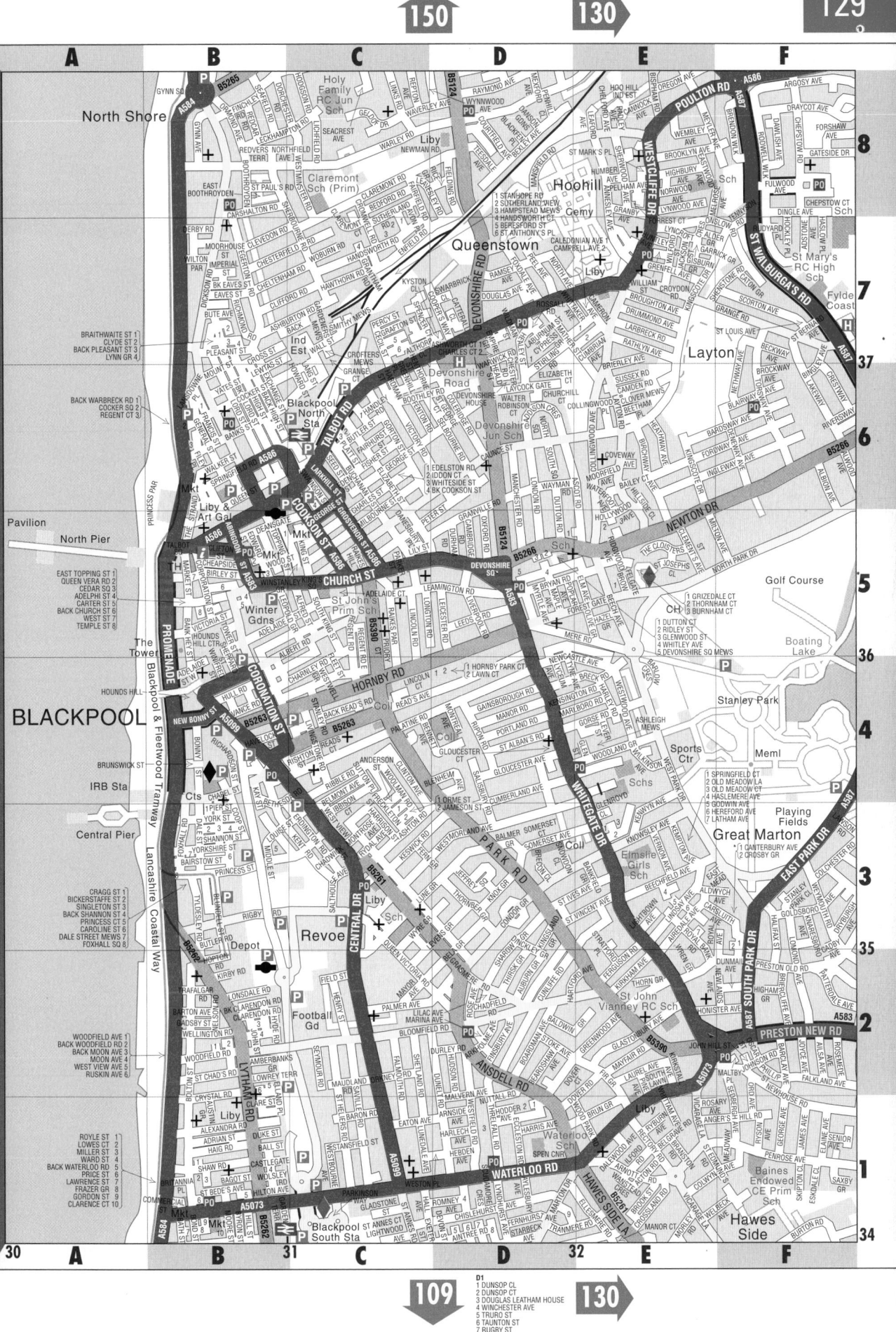

130

A8
1 ARGOSY CT
2 GATESIDE CT
3 FURNESS CT
4 CHIPPING CT
5 SLAIDBURN WLK

129 151

A B C D E F

8

7

37

6

5

36

4

3

35

2

1

34

High Cross
Fylde Sch

Hardhorn

LONGHOUSE LA

Puddle House Farm

FAIRFIELD RD B5266

Fairfield Nurseries

NORMOSS RD

Normoss

Cowburns Farm

Hardhorn Village

Grange Park Cty Prim Sch

NEWTON DR

Newton Lodge

Clinkum Wood

Christ The King RC Prim Sch

Convent
FOUR LANE ENDS

Riversway
B5266

Staining Windmill

Moons Farm

Staining

Staining CE Sch

PH

Stanley Park Golf Course

Victoria

Mere Brook

Dover Lodge

WOODSIDE DR

Dover House

Zoological Gardens

Hotel

Mushroom Farm

Sewage Works

Chain Bridge

EAST PARK DR

Marton Mere

Allot Gdns

LAWSON RD

1 PITTSDALE AVE
2 PRESCOT PL
3 BOLEYN PL
4 CLEVES CT
5 ALLENBURY PL

Mushroom Farm

Caravan Pk

Mythop Grange

QUERNMORE AVE

MYTHOP RD

Mythop Village

PRESTON NEW RD

Metropolitan Bsns Pk

Stanley Prim & Inf Sch

1 BASSENTHWAITE RD
2 DOVEDALE AVE

Gypsy Hole Wood

A583

Mereside

Little Marton

1 ST MONICA'S WAY
2 ACORN MEWS

Caravan Pk

Little Marton Windmill (dis)

Little Marton Moss Side

1 RADWORTH CRES
2 CHERRY TREE CT

Ind Est

33 A B 34 C D 35 E F

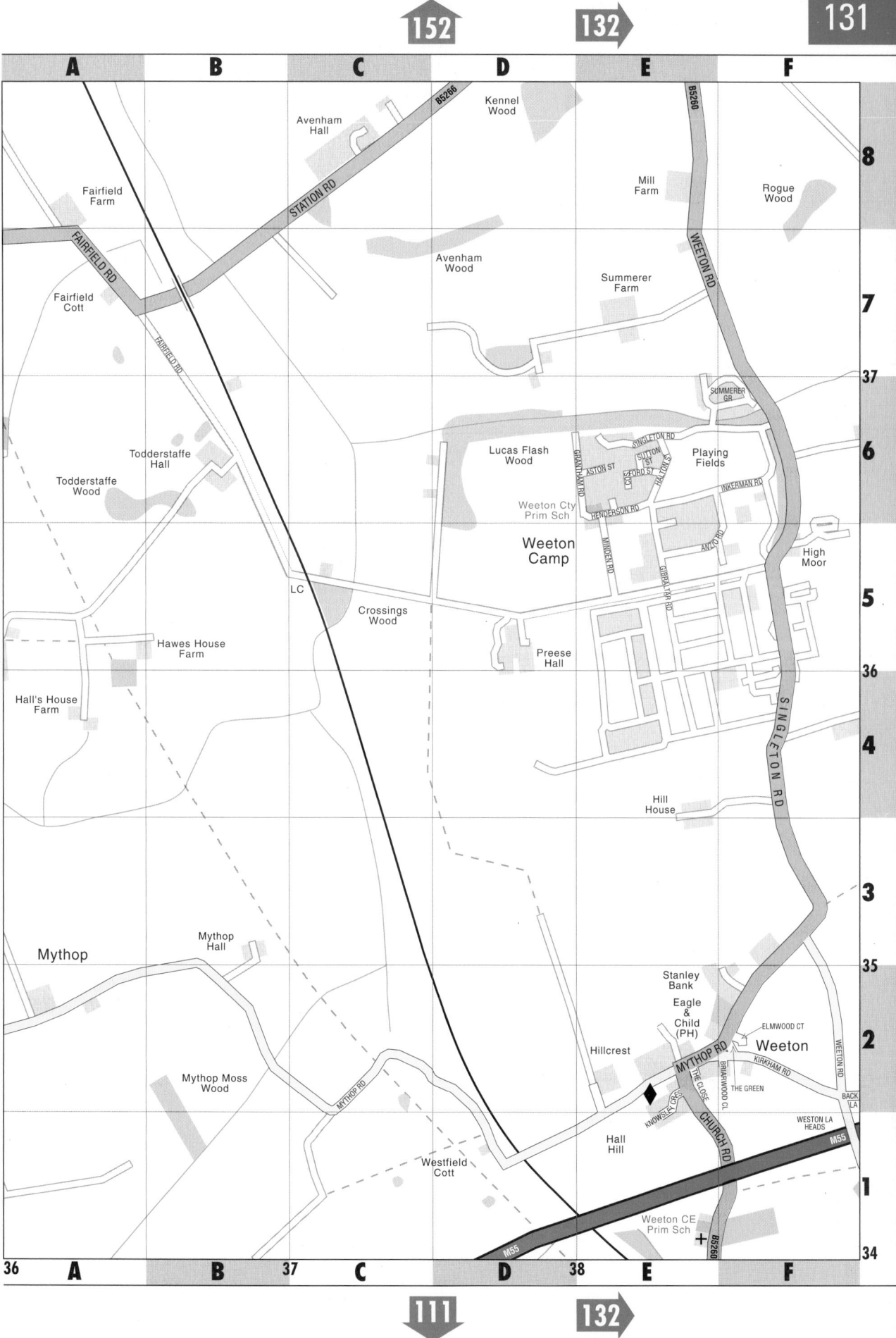

A B C D E F

8
7
37
6
5
36
4
3
35
2
1
34

Kennel
Wood

Avenham
Hall

STATION RD

B5266

Fairfield
Farm

FAIRFIELD RD

Fairfield
Cott

FAIRFIELD RD

Avenham
Wood

Mill
Farm

WEETON RD

B5260

Rogue
Wood

Summerer
Farm

SUMMERER
GR

Lucas Flash
Wood

SINGLETON RD

SUTTON
ST

OXFORD ST

ASTON ST

GRANTHAM RD

HENDERSON RD

Weeton Cty
Prim Sch

Playing
Fields

INKERMAN RD

ANZIO RD

MINDEN RD

Weeton
Camp

GIBRALTAR RD

High
Moor

Todderstaffe
Hall

Todderstaffe
Wood

LC

Crossings
Wood

Preese
Hall

Hawes House
Farm

Hall's House
Farm

Hill
House

SINGLETON RD

Mythop

Mythop
Hall

MYTHOP RD

Mythop Moss
Wood

Stanley
Bank

Eagle
&
Child
(PH)

ELMWOOD CT

Weeton

WEETON RD

MYTHOP RD

Hillcrest

KIRKHAM RD

THE GREEN

BRIARWOOD CL

THE CLOSE

BACK
LA

KNOWSLEY CRES

CHURCH RD

WESTON LA
HEADS

M55

Hall
Hill

Westfield
Cott

M55

Weeton CE
Prim Sch

B5260

A   B   C   D   E   F

8

Copthorn
Wood

Thistleton

THISTLETON RD
B5269

Thistleton
Lodge

Smithy
Farm

Mill Hill
Wood

Elswick Grange
Farm

A585

Brackenscales
Farm

7

37

Moss House
Farm

6

Thistleton Brook

Nursery

Scholar
Bridge

Syke
Hall

Esprick

FLEETWOOD RD

5

Greenhalgh

36

Tunsteads

Medlar
Hall

Swarbrick
Hall

4

Kirby's
Farm

GREENHALGH LA

MEDLAR LA

Medlar Brook

Snipe
Wood

Blue Anchor
(PH)

Leyland
Hall

BACK LA

Pedders
House

3

Beech
Grove

FLEETWOOD OLD RD

35

Pheasant
Wood

M55

3

M55

2

Windmill
Farm

Green Bank
Farm

BRADSHAW LA

Moss Hall
Farm

Corner
Row

FLEETWOOD RD

Nurseries

M55

1

WEETON RD

Whitprick
Hill

Demming

A585

34

39   A   B   40   C   D   41   E   F

A B C D E F

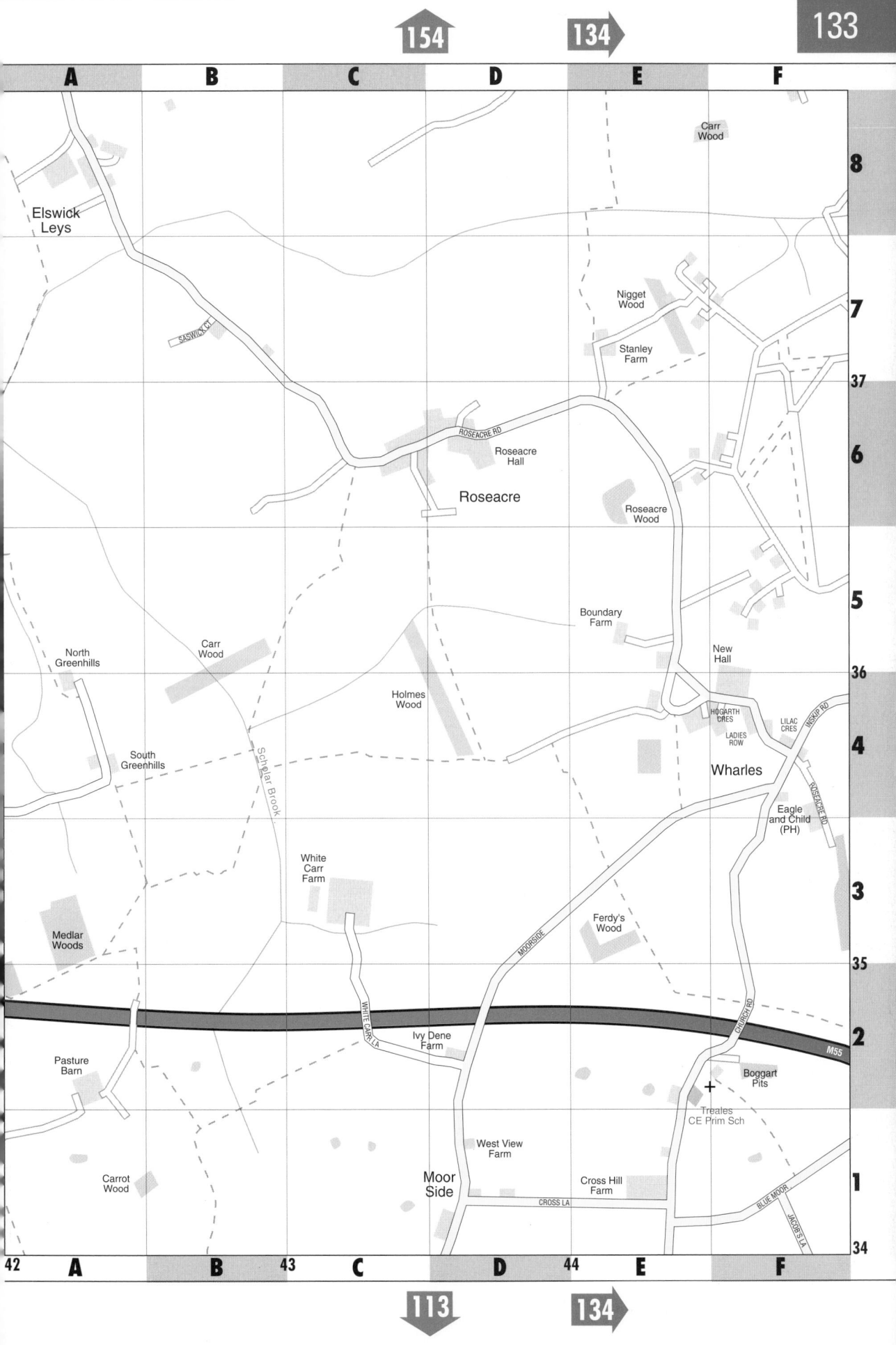

Carr
Wood

Elswick
Leys

Nigget
Wood

SASWICK LA

Stanley
Farm

ROSEACRE RD

Roseacre
Hall

Roseacre

Roseacre
Wood

Boundary
Farm

North
Greenhills

Carr
Wood

New
Hall

HOGARTH
CRES

LILAC
CRES

INSKIP RD

South
Greenhills

Holmes
Wood

LADIES
ROW

Wharles

Schollar Brook

ROSEACRE RD

Eagle
and Child
(PH)

White
Carr
Farm

Ferdy's
Wood

Medlar
Woods

MOORSIDE

CHURCH RD

WHITE CARR LA

M55

Pasture
Barn

Ivy Dene
Farm

Boggart
Pits

Treales
CE Prim Sch

West View
Farm

Carrot
Wood

Moor
Side

Cross Hill
Farm

BLUE MOOR

JACOB S LA

CROSS LA

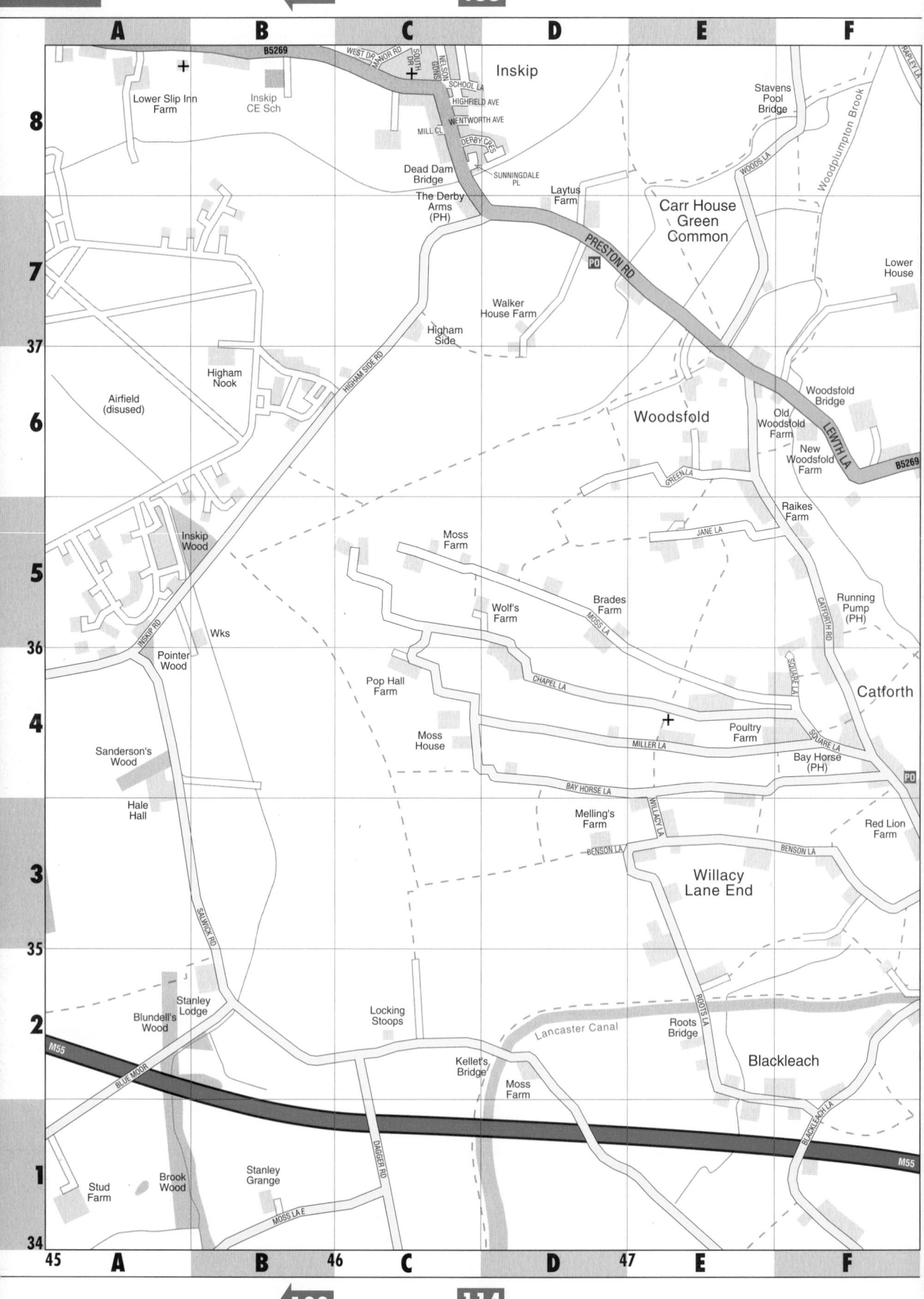

8

Lower Slip Inn Farm

Inskip CE Sch

B5269

WEST DR

MANOR RD

SOUTH DR

NELSON GDNS

SCHOOL LA

HIGHFIELD AVE

WENTWORTH AVE

MILL CL

DERBY CRES

SUNNINGDALE PL

Inskip

Stavens Pool Bridge

WOODS LA

Woodplumpton Brook

Dead Dam Bridge

The Derby Arms (PH)

Laytus Farm

PRESTON RD

PO

Carr House Green Common

7

Lower House

37

Higham Side

Walker House Farm

6

Airfield (disused)

Higham Nook

HIGHAM SIDE RD

Woodsfold

GREEN LA

Old Woodsfold Farm

New Woodsfold Farm

Woodsfold Bridge

LEWTH LA

B5269

Raikes Farm

JANE LA

Running Pump (PH)

CATFORTH RD

5

Inskip Wood

Moss Farm

Wolf's Farm

Brades Farm

MOSS LA

SQUARE LA

36

INSKIP RD

Wks

Pointer Wood

Pop Hall Farm

CHAPEL LA

Poultry Farm

Catforth

PO

4

Sanderson's Wood

Moss House

MILLER LA

Bay Horse (PH)

SQUARE LA

Red Lion Farm

Hale Hall

BAY HORSE LA

Melling's Farm

WILLACY LA

BENSON LA

3

SALWICK RD

Willacy Lane End

BENSON LA

35

Stanley Lodge

Locking Stoops

Lancaster Canal

Roots Bridge

ROOTS LA

2

Blundell's Wood

Kellet's Bridge

Moss Farm

Blackleach

M55

BLUE MOOR

DAGGER RD

BLACKLEACH LA

M55

1

Stud Farm

Brook Wood

Stanley Grange

MOSS LA E

34

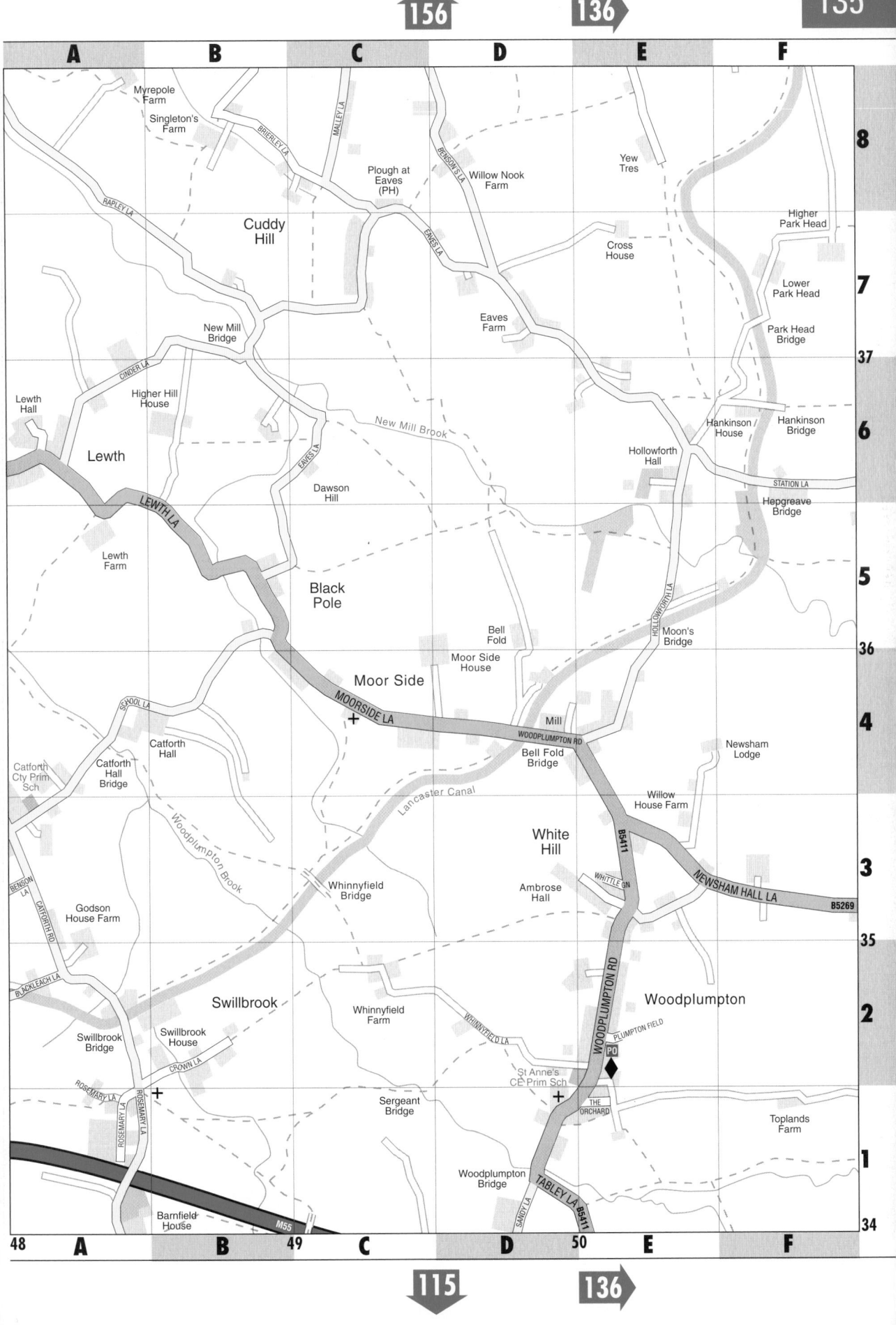

A B C D E F

8

Myrepole Farm

Singleton's Farm

BRIERLEY LA

MALLEY LA

Plough at Eaves (PH)

Willow Nook Farm

BENSON'S LA

Yew Tres

Higher Park Head

RAPLEY LA

Cuddy Hill

EAVES LA

Cross House

7

Lower Park Head

Park Head Bridge

37

New Mill Bridge

CINDER LA

Eaves Farm

Higher Hill House

Lewth Hall

EAVES LA

New Mill Brook

Hankinson House

Hankinson Bridge

6

Lewth

LEWTH LA

Dawson Hill

Hollowforth Hall

STATION LA

Hepgreave Bridge

Lewth Farm

Black Pole

HOLLOWFORTH LA

5

Bell Fold

Moor Side House

Moon's Bridge

36

SCHOOL LA

Moor Side

MOORSIDE LA

WOODPLUMPTON RD

Mill

Newsham Lodge

4

Catforth Cty Prim Sch

Catforth Hall

Catforth Hall Bridge

Bell Fold Bridge

Willow House Farm

Lancaster Canal

White Hill

B5411

BENSON LA

CATFORTH RD

Woodplumpton Brook

Whinnyfield Bridge

Ambrose Hall

WHITTLE GN

NEWSHAM HALL LA

3

B5269

35

BLACKLEACH LA

Godson House Farm

Swillbrook

Whinnyfield Farm

WHINNYFIELD LA

WOODPLUMPTON RD

Plumpton Field

Woodplumpton

2

Swillbrook Bridge

Swillbrook House

CROWN LA

PO

St Anne's CE Prim Sch

THE ORCHARD

ROSEMARY LA

ROSEMARY LA

Sergeant Bridge

Toplands Farm

1

M55

Barnfield House

Woodplumpton Bridge

SANDY LA

TABLEY LA B5411

34

48 A B 49 C D 50 E F

135
157

135
116

Westfield Brook

Westfield Wood

Cross House

Rigby Wood

Eaves Green Hall

EAVES GREEN LA

Middleton Hall

Eaves Green

8

Little Westfield

MILL LA

Field Foot Farm

7

GOOSNARGH LA

Oliverson's CE Prim Sch

Bushell's

37

OAKLEAF C

MILL LA

H

CAMFORTH HALL LA

WILLOW GR

NOOK FIELD
GREEN ACRE
NORTHGATE
CHURCHGATE
PARGATE

Bushell's Arms (PH)

Grindlestone Ct

Cumeragh Village

6

Goosnargh

CHURCH LA
THE CROFT
BEACON DR

BLEASDALE RD

THE SQUARE

Meadowcroft

PO

+

Stags Head (PH)

Cemetery ++

CUMERAGH LA B5269

Mast

WHITTINGHAM LA

+

5

Parkinson's House

Whittingham Hall

+

Dean House

Whittingham House

36

New Field

Chingle Hall

H

4

Cowell's Farm

Whittingham

PUDDING PIE NOOK LA

Works

3

Pudding Pie Nook

Blundle Brook

Cockshoot Wood

35

New Chingle Hall

Haighton Manor

32

Haighton Green

2

Boyse's Farm

HAIGHTON GREEN LA

M55

D'URTON LA

Sea Mark

Savick Brook

1

Haighton Top

M6

LIDGERY LA

FERNYHALGH LA

+

34

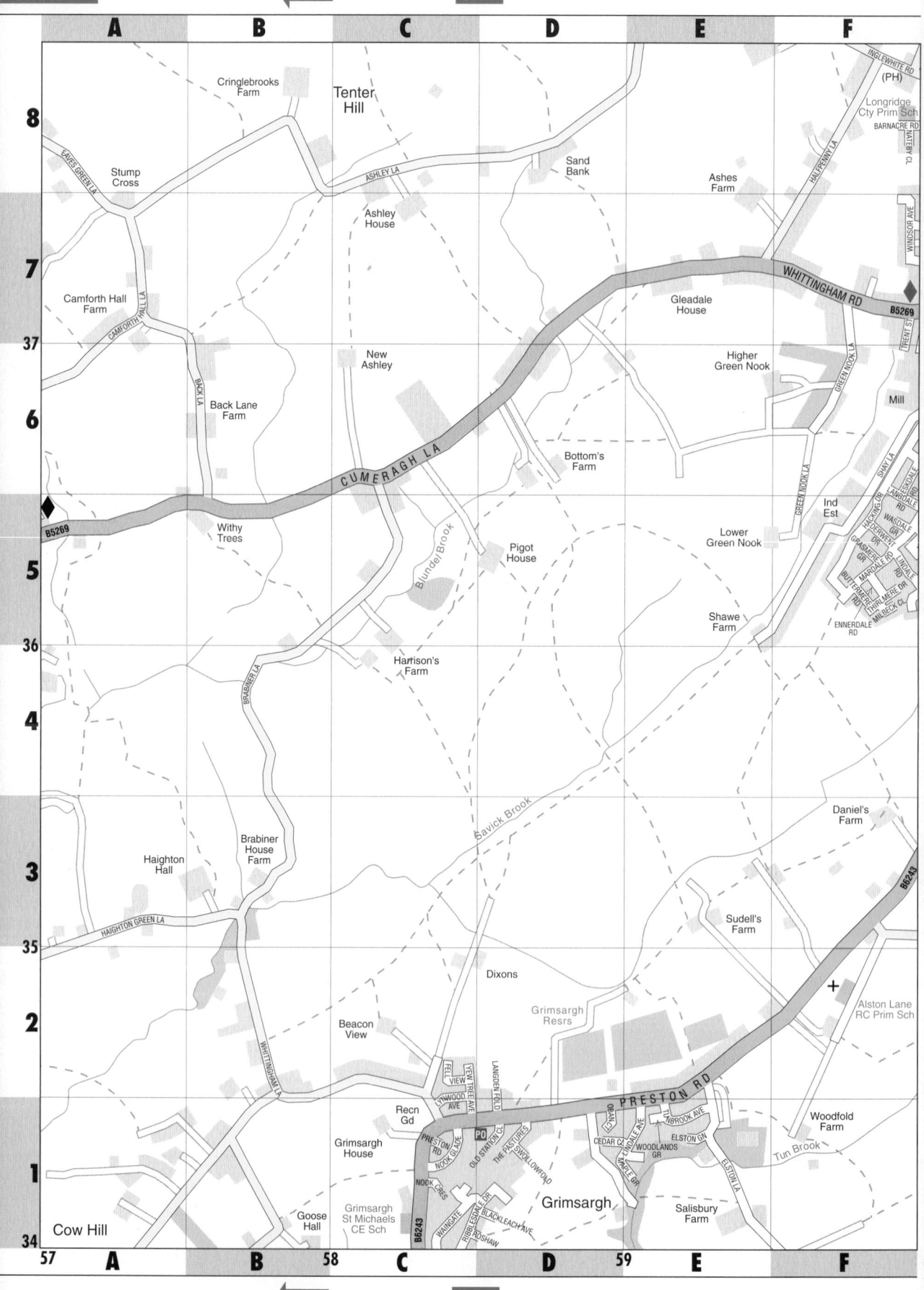

A | B | C | D | E | F

LONGRIDGE

1 MARY ST W
2 GEORGE ST
3 GAS ST

Willows
Farm

Tootle
Height

Written Stone
Farm

Written
Stone

B6243

8

Spade Mill
Resrs

KNOWLE GREEN RD

WARD GREEN LA

LANE
ENDS

Page Brook

7

PH

Dilworth
House

1 BLEASDALE CT
2 SWARBRICK CT
3 FLEMMING SQ

DILWORTH LA B5269 BLACKBURN RD

B6245

Elm
House

Longridge
CE Primary
Sch

King St

Liby

37

Hillside
Autistic Centre

PRESTON RD

Simmy
Nook

KESTOR LA

Higher
College
Farm

Alston
Lodge

Frances
Green

B6245

FLEET STREET LA

6

LOWER LA

1 ALEXANDRA RD
2 CHARLES GR
3 BLACKPOOL RD
4 STONEBRIDGE TERR

HOSPITAL
COTTS

H
Ribchester

St Cecilio's
RC High
Sch

Moss
Farm

Alston
Grange

DOCTORS
ROW

1 2
3 4

Chapel Hill

New
Town

1 CROSS ST
2 SOUTHERN CL
3 THE BACKS
4 LODGE VIEW

Walton Fold
Farm

Alston
Brow

College
Wood

Lower
College
Farm

Lower
Cockhill
Farm

5

Alston Resrs

36

COLLEGE CL

PINFOLD LA

Falicon
Farm

INDALE RD

PRESTON RD

Spout
Farm

Meadow
Head

HOTHERSALL LA

Butcher
Fold

Eatoughs
Farm

4

Charnley
Farm

Bury's
Farm

Pinfold
Farm

The
Greenwood

Bolton
Fold

Ox Hey

Norcross
Wood

Granham
House

3

PH

Manor
House

35

TUN BROOK

Thorn
Lane
Farm

THORN LA

Jinkinson's
Farm

Norcross

Woodland's
Farm

HOTHERSALL LA

2

ALSTON LA

King
Wood

Stubbin's
Nook

Hothersall
Lodge

Alston
Cottage
Farm

Lower
Yew Tree
Farm

Ribble Way

Ribble
View
Farm

Stubbin's
Wood

1

River Ribble

34

A B C D E F

KNOWLE GREEN RD B6243

Mill House

Mill House LA

CLAY HILL LA

Moor House

Seed Green

B6243

Moor Cock Farm

DEAN BROW B6243

Pope's Farm

HUNTINGDON HALL RD

8

Springs Farm

Kellets

GREEN MOOR LA

Cox Farm

Old Buckley

OLD BUCKLEY LA

Davies Gate Wood

Duddel Hill

Duddel Wood

Duddel Brook

7

Scott House

COCK GREEN LA

37

Ward Hall

WARD GREEN CROSS

WARD GREEN LA

Cross Keys Inn (PH)

FLEET STREET LA

B6245

WOOD'S BROW

STONYGATE LA

Phillip's Farm

Stydd Wood

6

Buckley Gate

Buckley Hall

Buckley Wood

5

Lord's Farm

Pinfold Farm

PRESTON RD

Ashmoor House

Oak Bank

Cherry Yate

Stydd Manor

Little Stydd Wood

Higher Alston

Dale Hey Farm

36

Boyce's Farm

Stydd

STYDD LA

4

Eatoughs Wood

Singleton House

Boyce's Brook

New House

CHESTER BROOK

EASTGATE

RIBBLESDALE RD

PH

CLAYTONHALGH

PO

BLACKBURN RD B6245

Stone Bridge

GALLOWS LA

Little Town

3

Parsonage Wood

CHURCH ST

CHURCH ST

MANOR AVE

Ribchester

SUNNYSIDE AVE

PARSONAGE AVE

FORT AVE

WATER ST

GREENSIDE

CHURCH ST

P

P

Parsonage Farm

Ribchester CE Prim Sch

Hothersall Wood

35

Mus

BREMETENNACVM ROMAN FORT

Anchor Hill

Lower Madgell Bank

Hothersall Hall

Red Bank

Boat House

Lower Barn Farm

HOTHERSALL LA

2

River Ribble

Ribble Way

Osbaldeston Hall

Catterall

1

34

63 A 64 B C 65 D E F

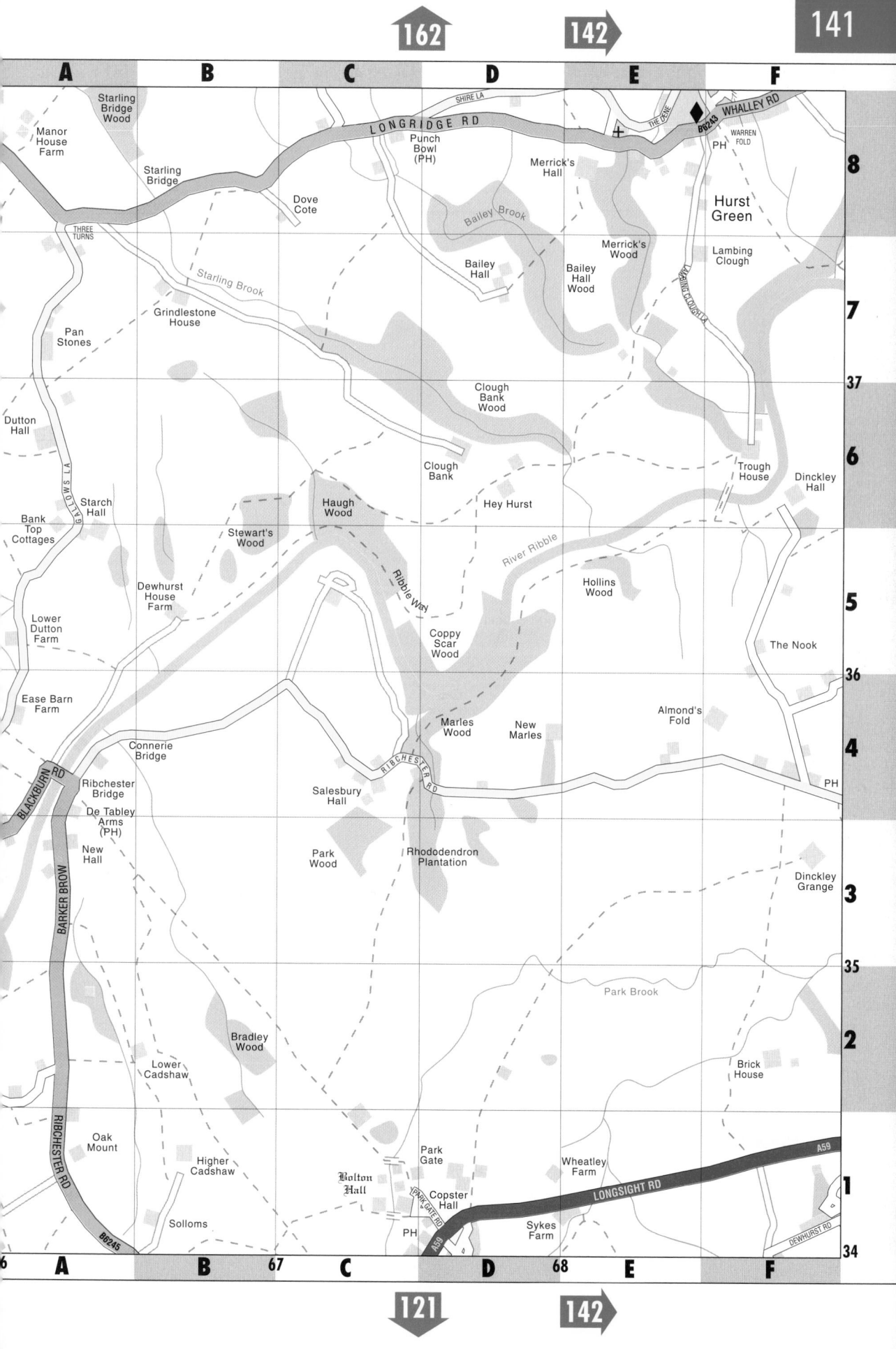

141
163

A B C D E F

8

Ribble Way
Jumbles

Jumbles
Rocks

Mitton
Wood

Brockhall
Wood

River Ribble

7

H
Calderstones

Brockhall
Farm

Hacking
Barn

River Calder

37

Sewage
Works

Hacking
Wood

Hacking
Hall

Mill
Wood

Bank End
Barn

6

Potter Ford
House

Bushburn
Bridge

Chew
Mill

ELKER LA

5

Cravens

LARGHILL

Brockhall
Village

Bushburn Brook

Sewage
Works

Aspinalls

BROOKSIDE

OLD LANGHO RD

36

Dinckley Brook

Black Bull Hotel
(PH)

Old
Langho

Sudell's
Farm

Lower
Elker

4

Gabbott's
Farm

Hillock
Farm

Skenning
Bridge

St Augustine's
RC High Sch

ELKER
COTTS

Wardfall

RIBCHESTER RD

NORTHCOTE RD

Higher
Elker

ELKER
MEWS

3

Lower
Fold

Foxfields
Hotel

WHALLEY NEW RD

35

Rileys

CHAPEL LA

Lower Fold
Wood

Petre Arms
(PH)

St Leonard's
CE Sch

2

Monks
Barton

Laycock's
Farm

A666

LONGSIGHT RD

Hollin Hall
Farm

Smalley's
Farm

Cunliffe
House Wood

Langholme

WHALLEY RD

St Mary's
RC Sch

Doctor's Rake

Woodside

LONGSIGHT RD

A59

Wade
Plat

WHITEHALGH LA

Langho
Sta

WHALLEY NEW RD

4 Spring Terr
5 Taylor's Bldgs

CORONATION TERR 1
BIRTWISTLE TERR 2
PRIMROSE TERR 3

1

THE RYDING

Home
Farm

BUSHBURN DR

RONSHAW DR

MIDFIELD DR

HACKING CL

MOORLAND RD

TUDOR
CL

CLAYTON
ROW

ST MARY'S DR

WHINNEY LA

Cronshaw

WHALLEY OLD RD

MOOR LA

34

PO

A666

St Mary's
RC Sch

Langho

ROGERSFIELD

69 A 70 B C 71 D E F

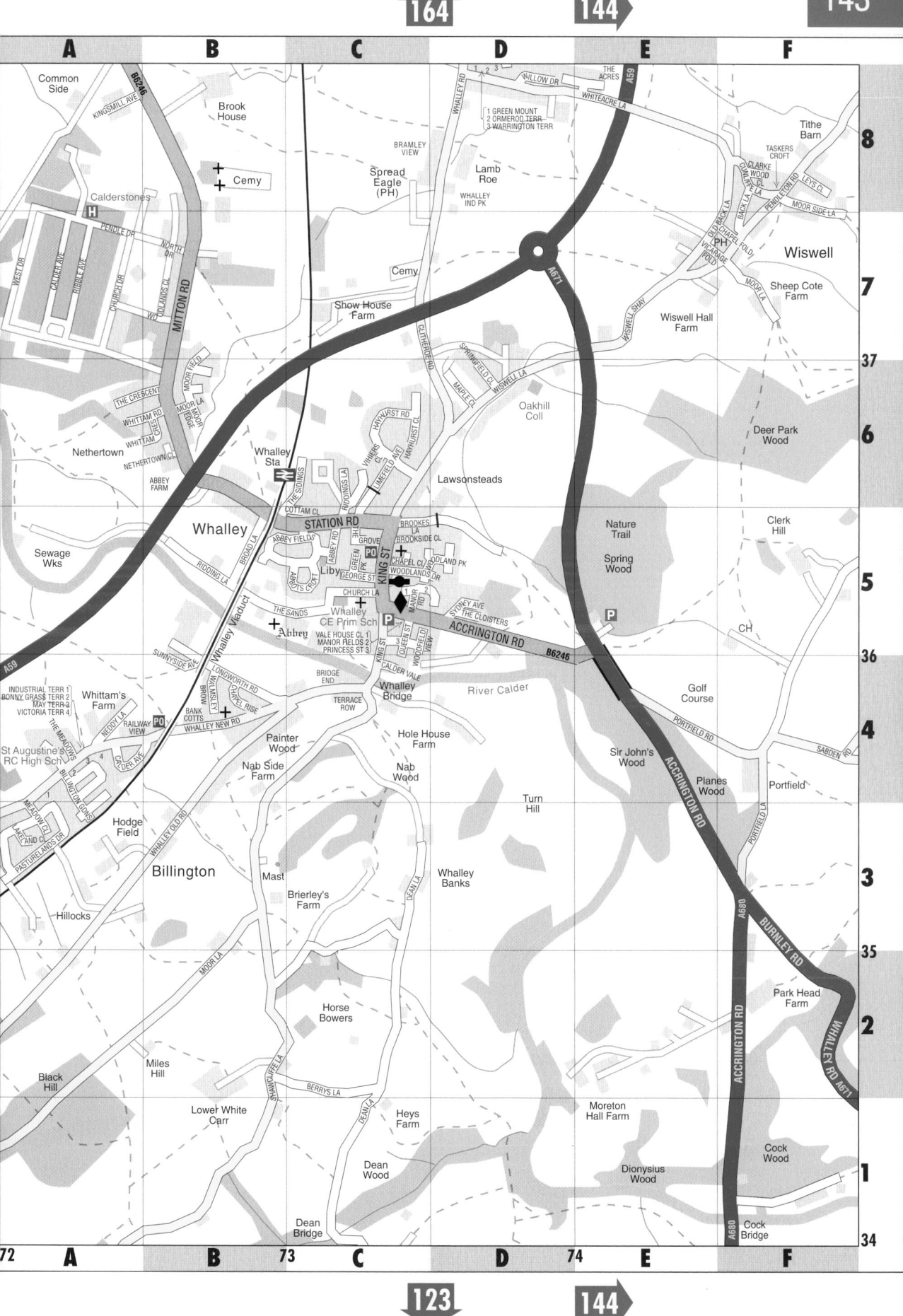

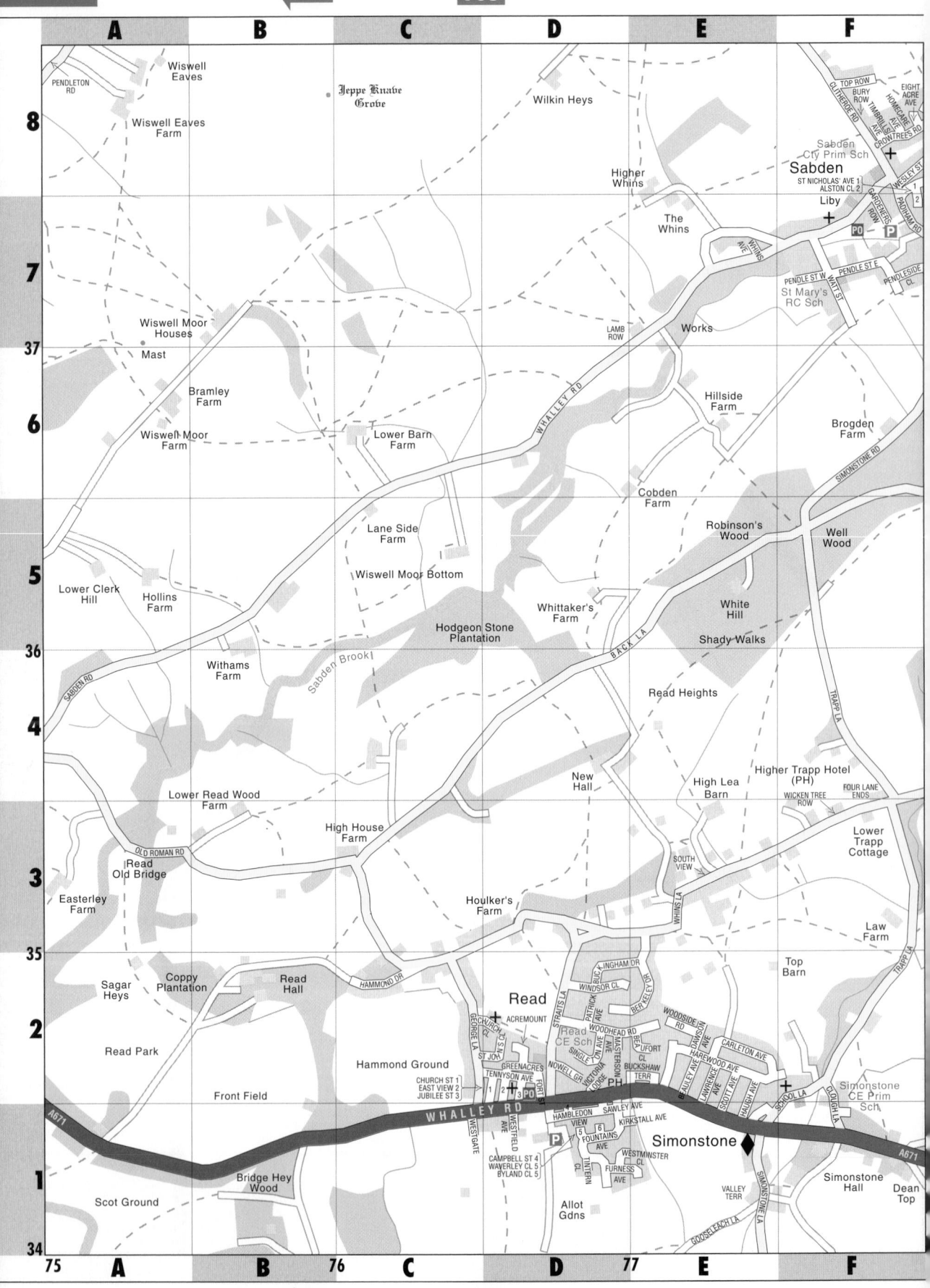
PENDLETON RD
Wiswell Eaves
Wiswell Eaves Farm

8

Jeppe Knave Grove
Wilkin Heys

Higher Whins

Sabden
Cty Prim Sch
TOP ROW
BURY ROW
CLITHEROE RD
HOMEGATE AVE
TIMBRELL'S
CROWTREES DR
EIGHT ACRE AVE
PADIHAM RD
WESLEY ST
GARDENERS ROW

Sabden
ST NICHOLAS' AVE 1
ALSTON CL 2
Liby
PO
P

The Whins

7

St Mary's RC Sch
PENDLE ST W
WHINS AVE
WINDSOR AVE
WITT ST
PENDLE ST E
PENDLESIDE CL

37

Wiswell Moor Houses

Mast

Bramley Farm

Wiswell Moor Farm

Lower Barn Farm

WHALLEY RD

LAMB ROW

Works

Hillside Farm

Brogden Farm

SIMONSTONE RD

6

Cobden Farm

Lane Side Farm

Robinson's Wood

Well Wood

5

Lower Clerk Hill
Hollins Farm

Wiswell Moor Bottom

Whittaker's Farm

White Hill

36

SABDEN RD

Withams Farm

Sabden Brook

Hodgeon Stone Plantation

BACK LA

Shady Walks

TRAPP LA

Read Heights

4

Lower Read Wood Farm

New Hall

High Lea Barn

Higher Trapp Hotel (PH)
WICKEN TREE ROW
FOUR LANE ENDS

OLD ROMAN RD

High House Farm

SOUTH VIEW

Lower Trapp Cottage

3

Easterley Farm

Read Old Bridge

Houlker's Farm

WHINS LA

Law Farm

TRAPP LA

35

Sagar Heys

Coppy Plantation

Read Hall

HAMMOND DR

Read

LINGHAM DR
WINDSOR CL
STRAITS LA
PATRICK AVE
BUC...
WOODSIDE RD
HAWKIN...
CARLETON AVE

Top Barn

2

Read Park

Hammond Ground

Read CE Sch
GEORGE LA
ST JON...
ACREMOUNT
SINGLE...
NOWELL GR
VICTORIA
WOODHEAD RD
MASTERSON...
BEAUFORT CL
Buckshaw TERR
BAILEY AVE
LAWRENCE AVE
HAREWOOD AVE
SCOTT AVE
HAWSON...

Simonstone CE Prim Sch

Front Field

CHURCH ST 1
EAST VIEW 2
JUBILEE ST 3
TENNYSON AVE
PO
PH
HAUGH LA
SCHOOL LA

A671

WHALLEY RD

WESTGATE

HAMBLEDON VIEW
SAWLEY AVE
KIRKSTALL AVE
FOUNTAINS AVE
Simonstone

1

Bridge Hey Wood

P
CAMPBELL ST 4
WAVERLEY CL 5
BYLAND CL 5
WESTFIELD
WESTMINSTER CL
FURNESS AVE
TINTERN...
VALLEY TERR
SIMONSTONE LA
Simonstone Hall
Dean Top

Scot Ground

Allot Gdns

GOOSE LEACH LA

A671

34

75 76 77

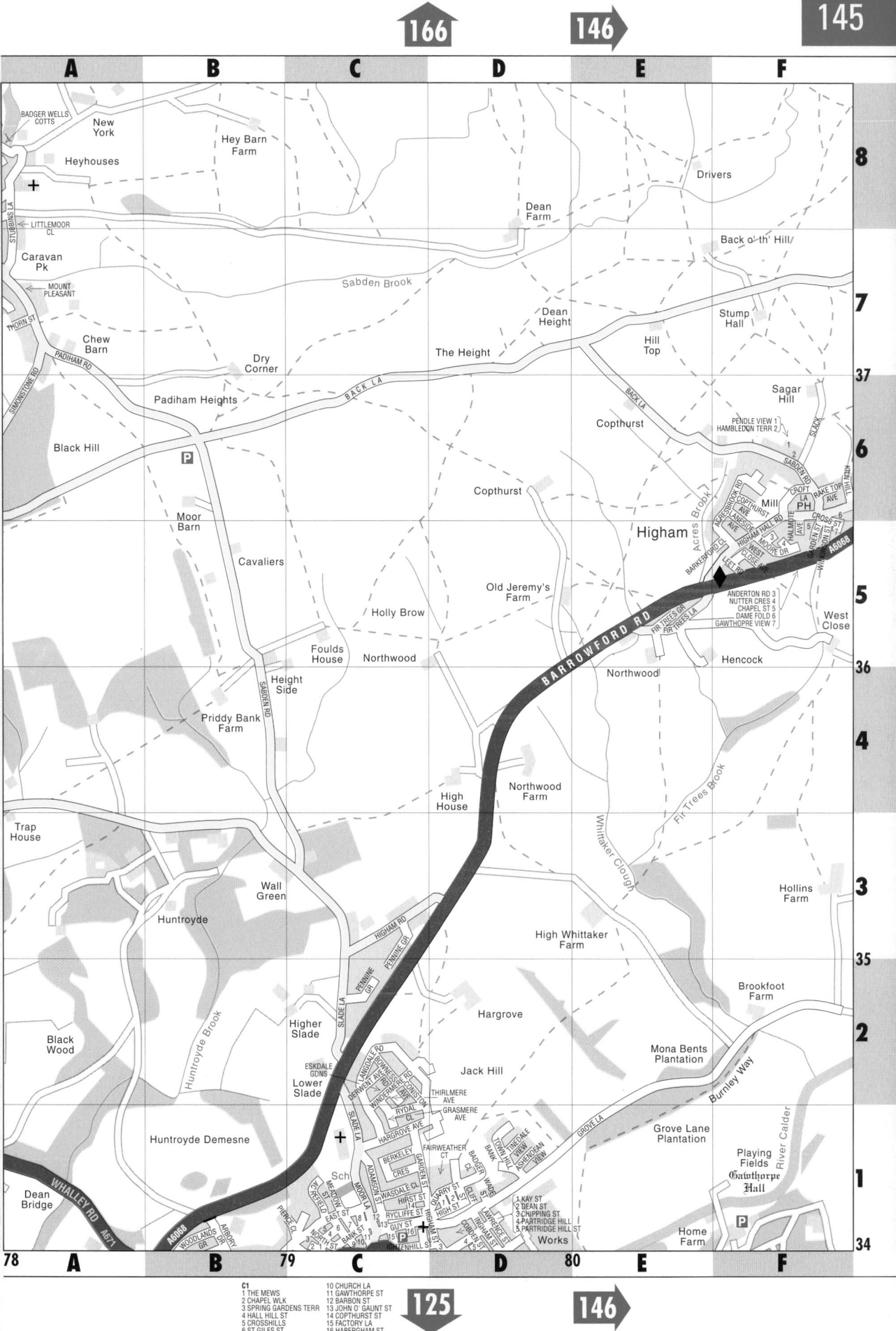

8

BADGER WELLS COTTS
New York
Heyhouses
Drivers
Back o' th' Hill
LITTLEMOOR CL
STUBBINS LA
Caravan Pk
MOUNT PLEASANT
THORN ST
Dean Farm
Stump Hall
7
Sabden Brook
Dean Height
Chew Barn
PADIHAM RD
Hill Top
SIMONSTONE RD
Dry Corner
The Height
Sagar Hill
37
Padiham Heights
BACK LA
Copthurst
BACK LA
PENDLE VIEW 1
HAMBLEDON TERR 2
SLACK
Black Hill
P
Copthurst
Mill
CROFT LA
RAKE TOP AVE
NORTH AVE
SABDEN RD
6
Moor Barn
Copthurst
Higham
COPTHURST AVE
LANSIDE AVE
ACRESBROOK RD
HIGHAM HALL RD
HALMOTE AVE
WEST CLOSE
MOORE DR
GARDEN ST
CROSS
PH
A6068
Cavaliers
Acres Brook
BARKSFORD CS
LEE L RD
WILKINSON ST
ANDERTON RD 3
NUTTER CRES 4
CHAPEL ST 5
DAME FOLD 6
GAWTHORPE VIEW 7
5
Holly Brow
Old Jeremy's Farm
West Close
Height Side
Foulds House
Northwood
Hencock
BARROWFORD RD
Northwood
36
SABDEN RD
Priddy Bank Farm
FIR TREES GR
FIR TREES LA
Northwood
4
High House
Northwood Farm
Fir Trees Brook
Trap House
Hollins Farm
3
Wall Green
HIGHAM RD
High Whittaker Farm
Whittaker Clough
Huntroyde
PENNINE GR
PENNINE GR
Brookfoot Farm
35
SLADE LA
Higher Slade
Hargrove
Mona Bents Plantation
Burnley Way
2
Black Wood
Huntroyde Brook
ESKDALE GDNS
Lower Slade
ANGDALE RD
DERWENT AVE
BOWNESS RD
CONISTON
WINDERMERE RD
RYDAL CL
THIRLMERE AVE
GRASMERE AVE
Jack Hill
SLADE LA
TINEDALE VIEW
TOWN HILL
ASHENDEAN VIEW
GROVE LA
Grove Lane Plantation
River Calder
Sch
HARGROVE AVE
BERKELEY CRES
GARDEN ST
FAIRWEATHER CT
BADGER WADE
BANK
Playing Fields
Gawthorpe Hall
Huntroyde Demesne
MEADOW
PIERCE CL
AIDANSON ST
SWASDALE CL
MOORL
EAST ST
BANK ST
HIRST ST
RYCLIFFE ST
QUARRY ST
HIGH ST
CLIFF ST
THOMAS ST
LAURENCE ST
1 KAY ST
2 DEAN ST
3 CHIPPING ST
4 PARTRIDGE HILL
5 PARTRIDGE HILL
1
Dean Bridge
WHALLEY RD
A671
A6068
WOODLANDS GR
ARBURY
NORTH ST
IGHTENHILL ST
P
P
Home Farm
Works
34

78 A B 79 C D 80 E F

C1
1 THE MEWS
2 CHAPEL WLK
3 SPRING GARDENS TERR
4 HALL HILL ST
5 CROSSHILLS
6 ST GILES ST
7 ST LEONARD'S ST
8 CLAYBANK
9 HAVELOCK ST
10 CHURCH LA
11 GAWTHORPE ST
12 BARBON ST
13 JOHN O' GAUNT ST
14 COPTHURST ST
15 FACTORY LA
16 HABERGHAM ST

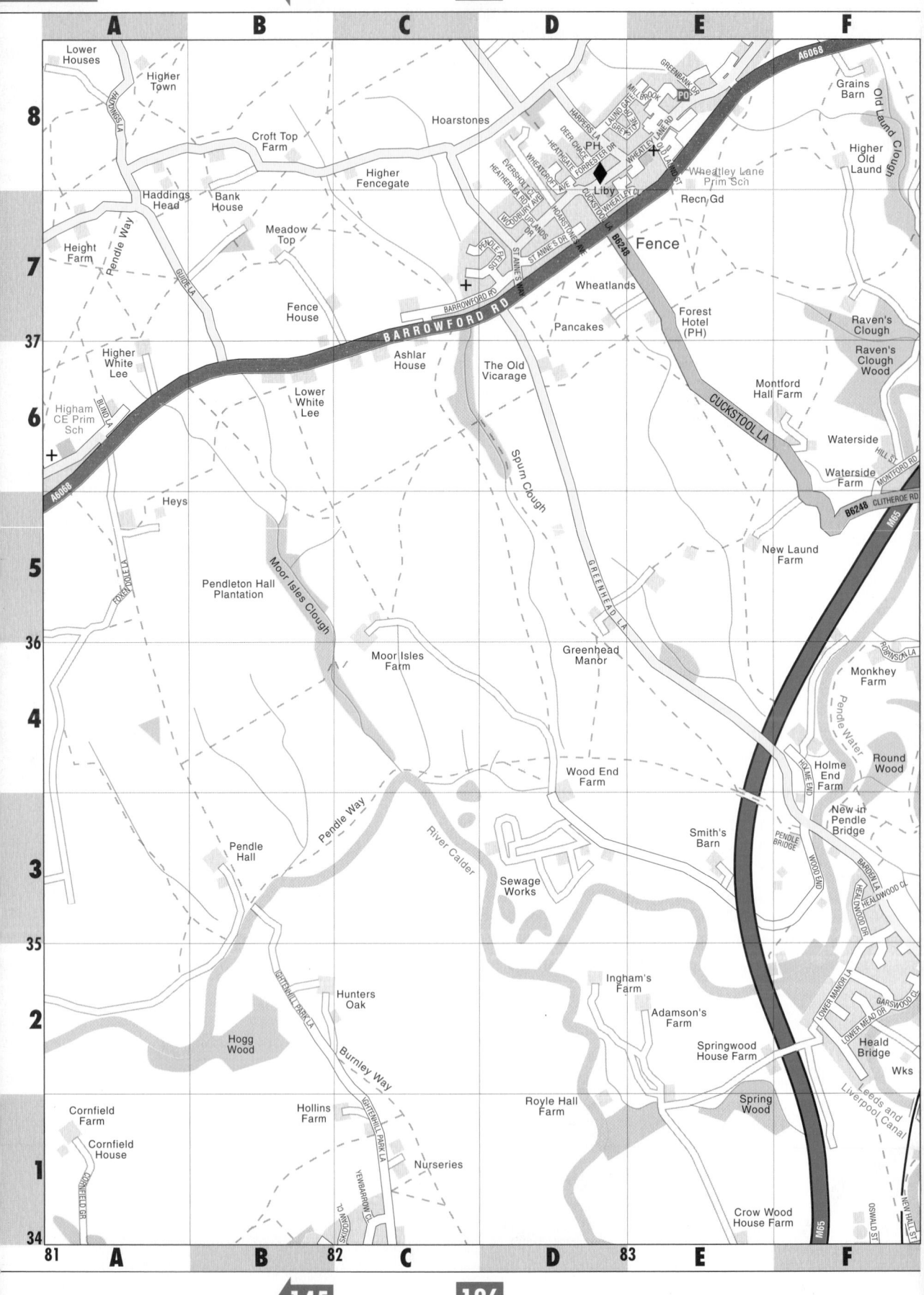

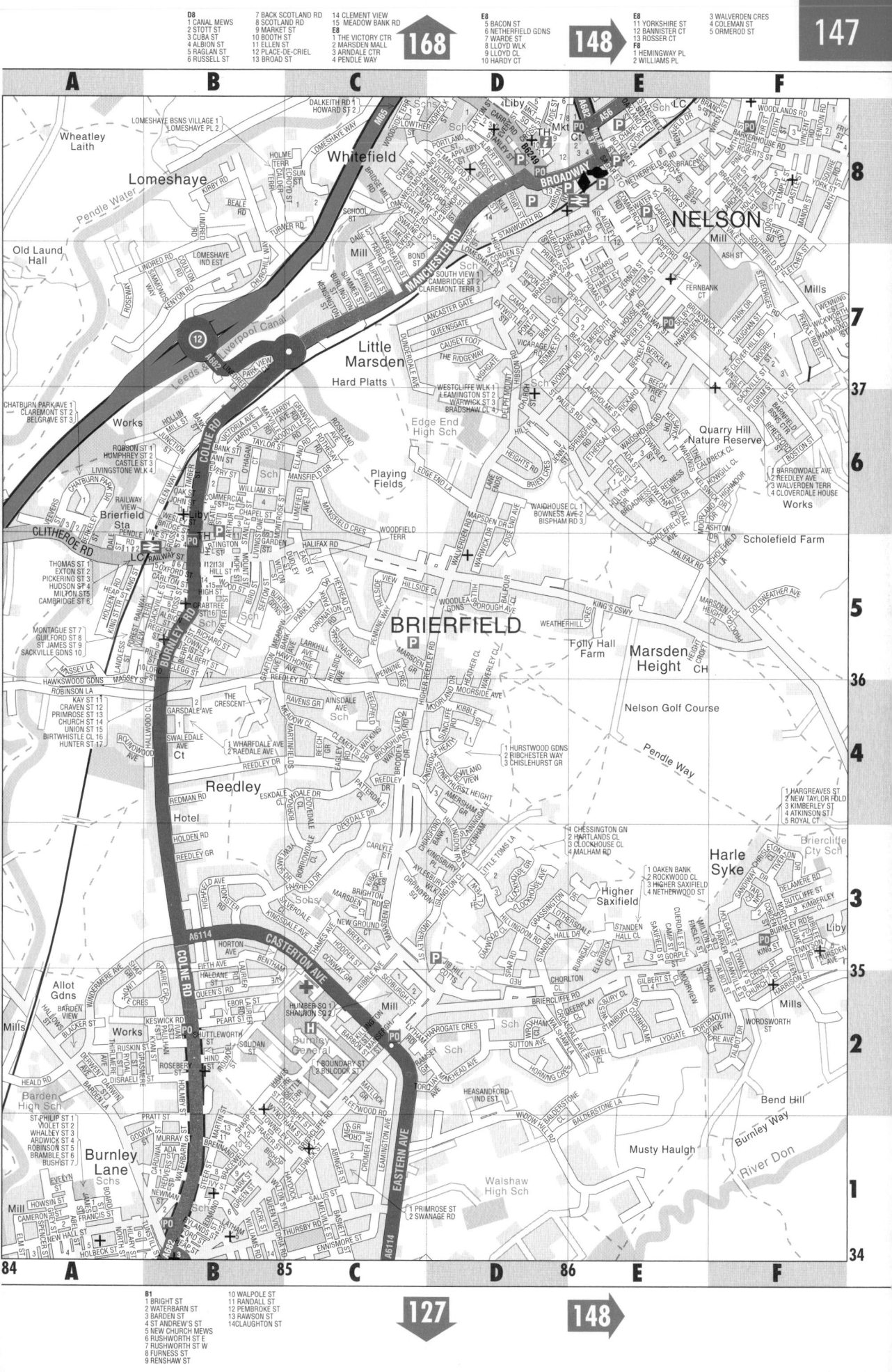

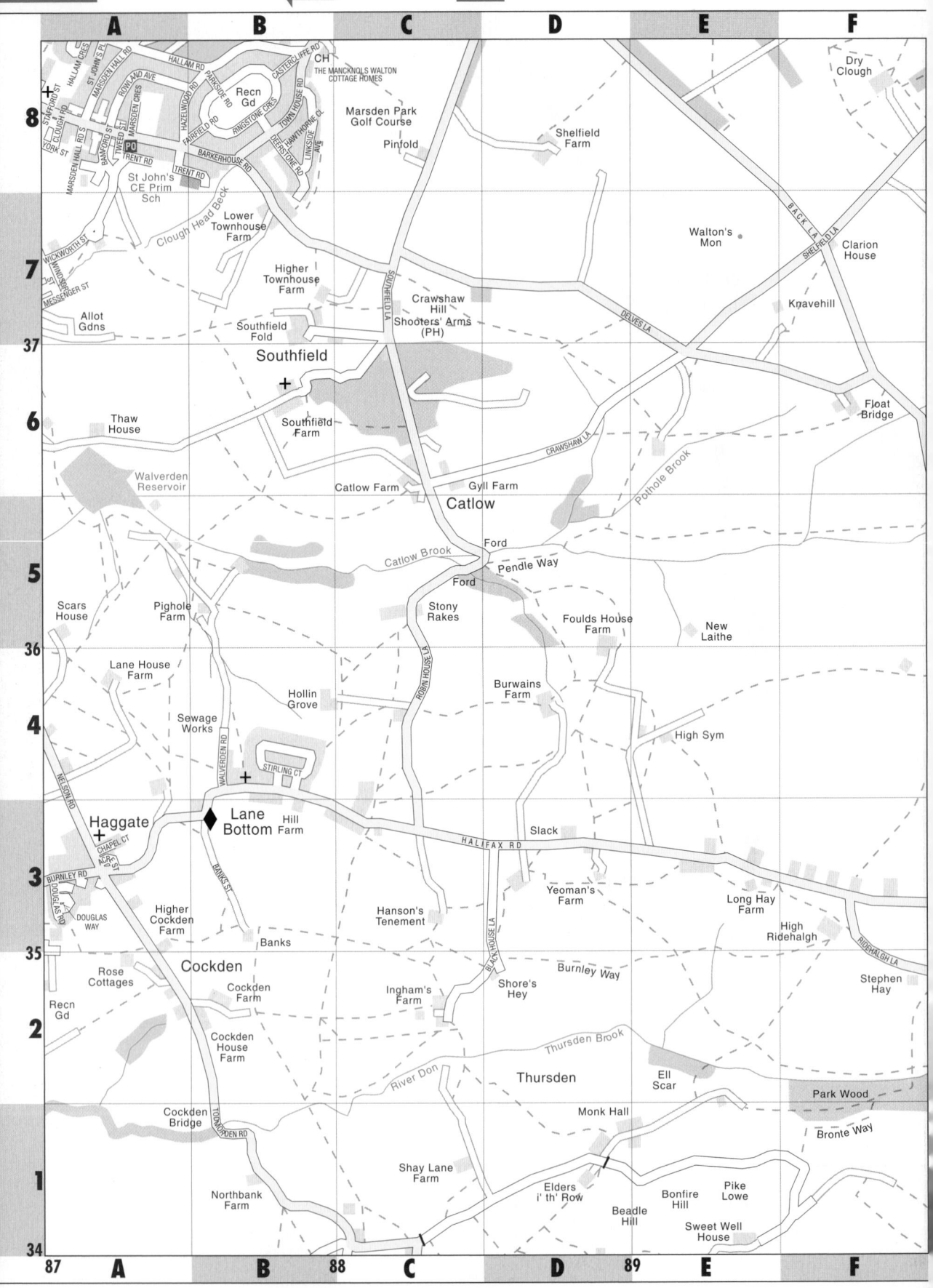

A B C D E F

8

Dry Clough

Recn Gd

CH
THE MANCKNOLS WALTON
COTTAGE HOMES

Marsden Park
Golf Course

Shelfield
Farm

Pinfold

7

Walton's
Mon

Clarion
House

Clough Head Beck

Lower
Townhouse
Farm

Higher
Townhouse
Farm

Crawshaw
Hill
Shooters' Arms
(PH)

Knavehill

37

Allot
Gdns

Southfield
Fold

Southfield

6

Thaw
House

Southfield
Farm

Crawshaw La

Float
Bridge

Pothole Brook

Walverden
Reservoir

Catlow Farm

Gyll Farm

Catlow

Ford

5

Scars
House

Pighole
Farm

Catlow Brook

Pendle Way

Ford

Stony
Rakes

Foulds House
Farm

New
Laithe

36

Lane House
Farm

Robin House La

Burwains
Farm

4

Sewage
Works

Hollin
Grove

High Sym

Stirling Ct

Haggate

Lane
Bottom

Hill
Farm

Halifax Rd

Slack

Yeoman's
Farm

Long Hay
Farm

Chapel Ct

3

Burnley Rd

Higher
Cockden
Farm

Hanson's
Tenement

Black House La

High
Ridehalgh

Ridhalgh La

Douglas
Way

Banks

35

Cockden

Rose
Cottages

Cockden
Farm

Ingham's
Farm

Shore's
Hey

Burnley Way

Stephen
Hay

Recn
Gd

2

Cockden
House
Farm

Thursden Brook

Ell
Scar

Park Wood

River Don

Thursden

Cockden
Bridge

Torsden Rd

Monk Hall

Bronte Way

1

Northbank
Farm

Shay Lane
Farm

Elders
i' th' Row

Beadle
Hill

Bonfire
Hill

Pike
Lowe

Sweet Well
House

34

87 A B 88 C D 89 E F

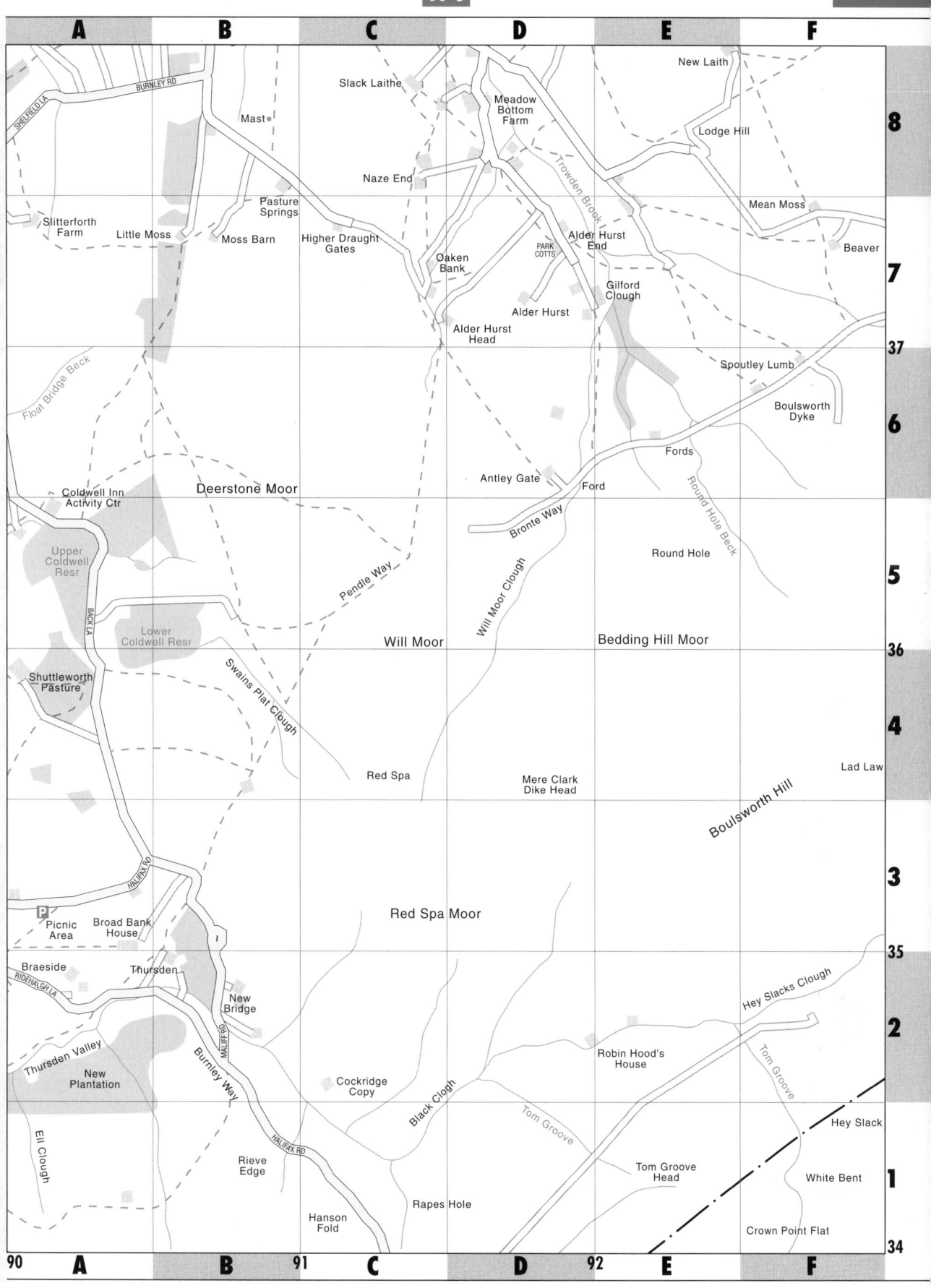

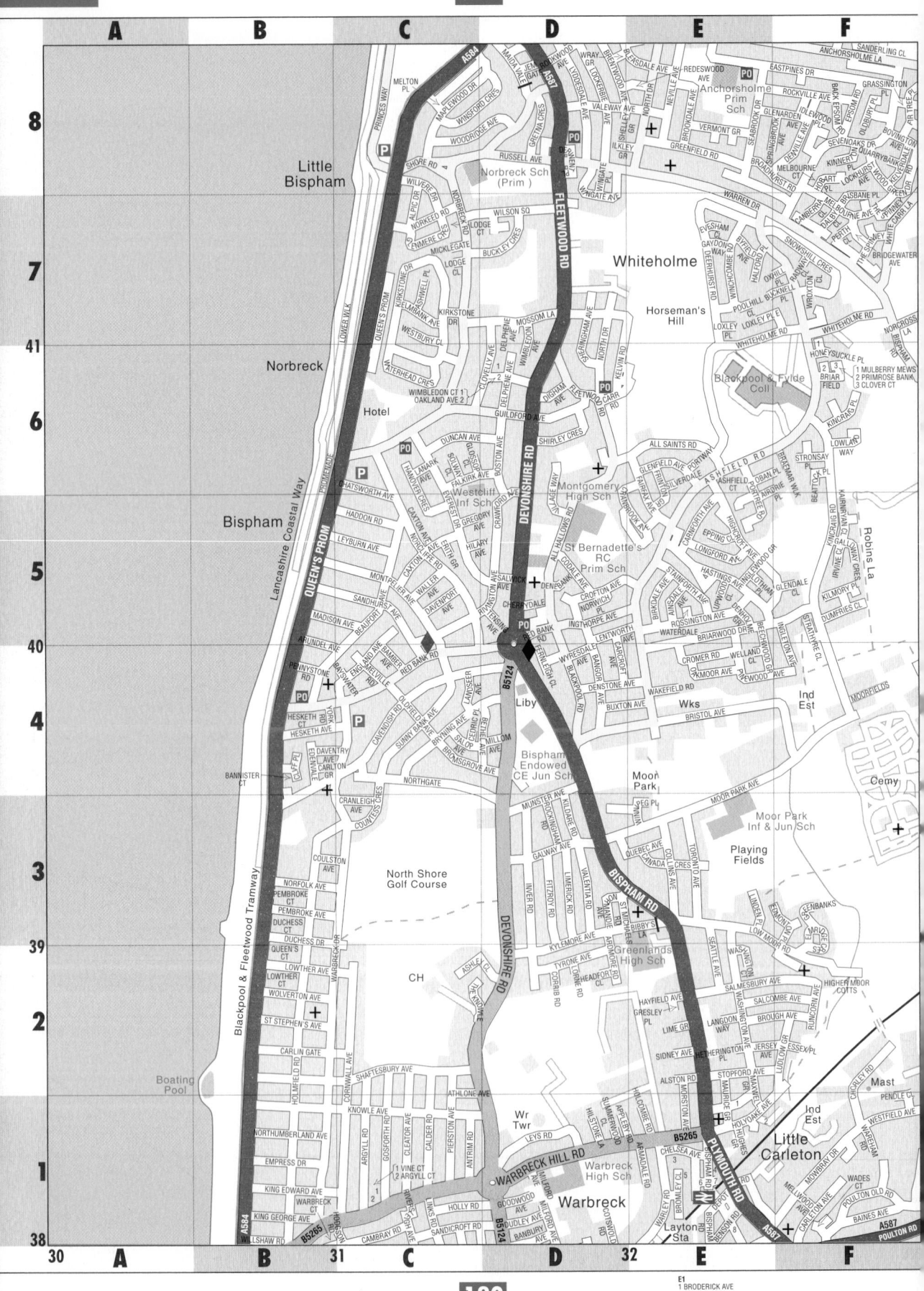

E1
1 BRODERICK AVE
2 FOX IND EST
3 CHELSEA MEWS
4 CHELSEA CT
5 BROMLEY CT
6 PEARL AVE
7 HENLEY CT
8 DELAWARE RD

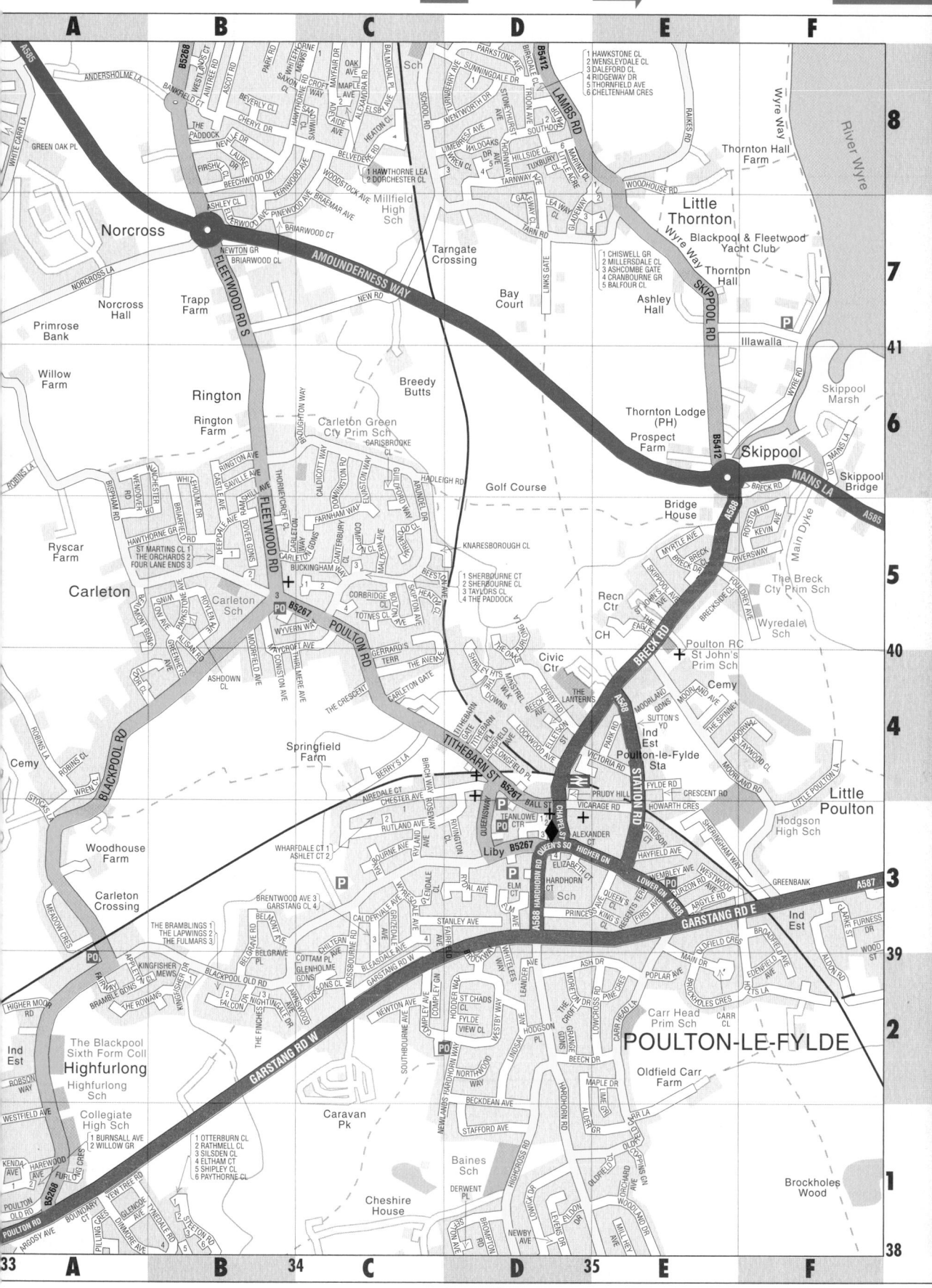

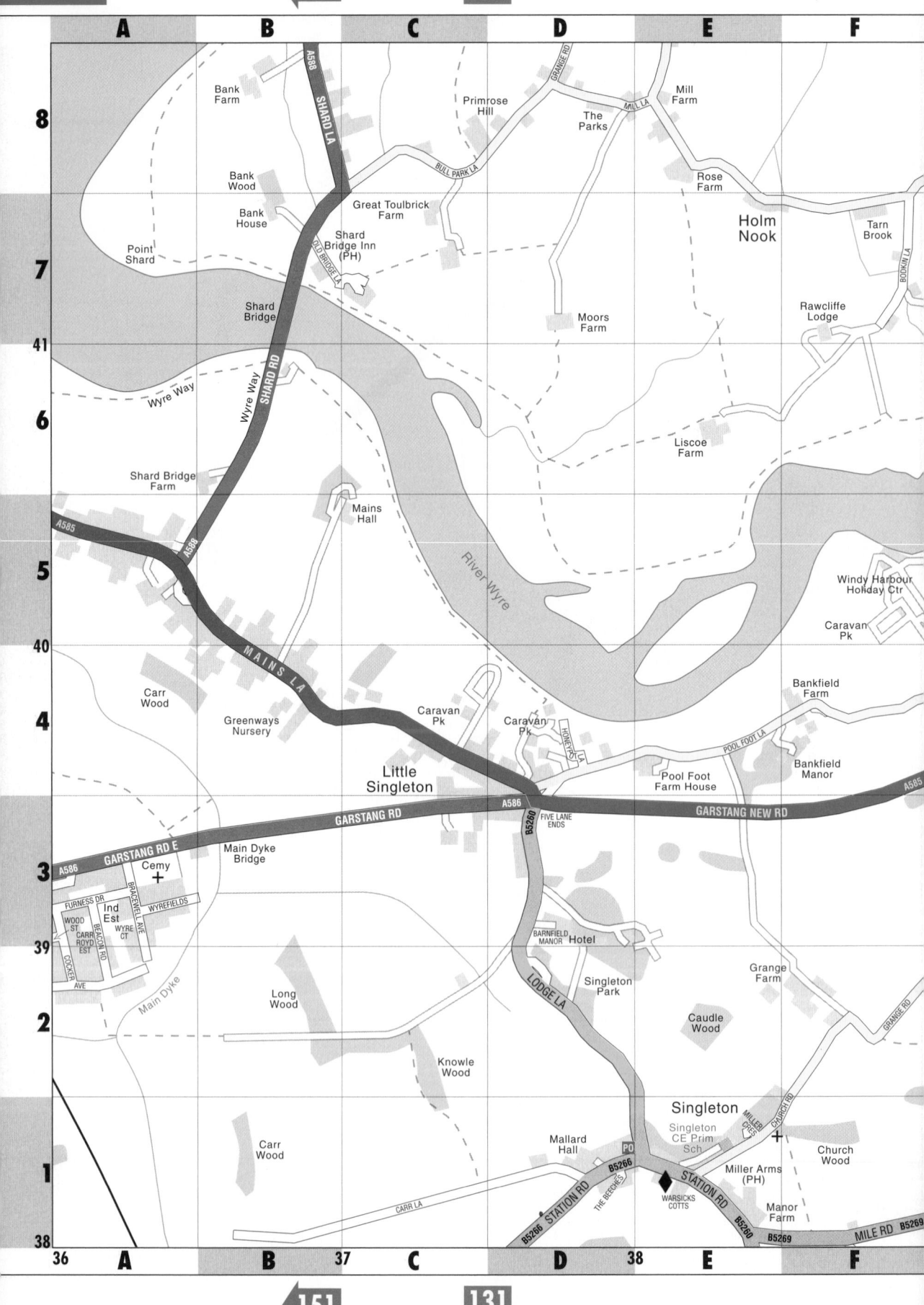

151
174

A B C D E F

8

Bank Farm

Primrose Hill

GRANGE RD

Mill Farm

Bank Wood

BULL PARK LA

MILL LA

The Parks

Rose Farm

Holm Nook

Tarn Brook

7

Bank House

Great Toulbrick Farm

Shard Bridge Inn (PH)

BOON LA

Rawcliffe Lodge

Point Shard

Shard Bridge

ALT BRIDGE LA

Moors Farm

41

Wyre Way

Wyre Way

SHARD RD

Liscoe Farm

6

A585

Shard Bridge Farm

A588

Mains Hall

River Wyre

Windy Harbour Holiday Ctr

5

MAINS LA

Caravan Pk

40

Carr Wood

Greenways Nursery

Caravan Pk

Caravan Pk

HONEYS LA

Pool Foot Farm House

POOL FOOT LA

Bankfield Farm

Bankfield Manor

A585

4

Little Singleton

GARSTANG RD

A586

Five Lane Ends

B5260

GARSTANG NEW RD

Main Dyke Bridge

3

A586

GARSTANG RD E

Cemy

Ind Est

WYREFIELDS

BRACEWELL AVE

BEACON RD

WYRE CT

FURNESS DR

WOOD ST

CARR ROYD EST

COCKER AVE

Main Dyke

BARNFIELD MANOR

Hotel

Singleton Park

Grange Farm

GRANGE RD

39

Long Wood

LODGE LA

Caudle Wood

2

Knowle Wood

Singleton

MILLER CRES

Singleton CE Prim Sch

CHURCH RD

Church Wood

1

Carr Wood

Mallard Hall

PO

Singleton

THE BEECHES

B5266

STATION RD

WARSICKS COTTS

Miller Arms (PH)

STATION RD

Manor Farm

B5269

MILE RD B5269

CARR LA

B5266 STATION RD

B5260

38

36 A B 37 C D 38 E F

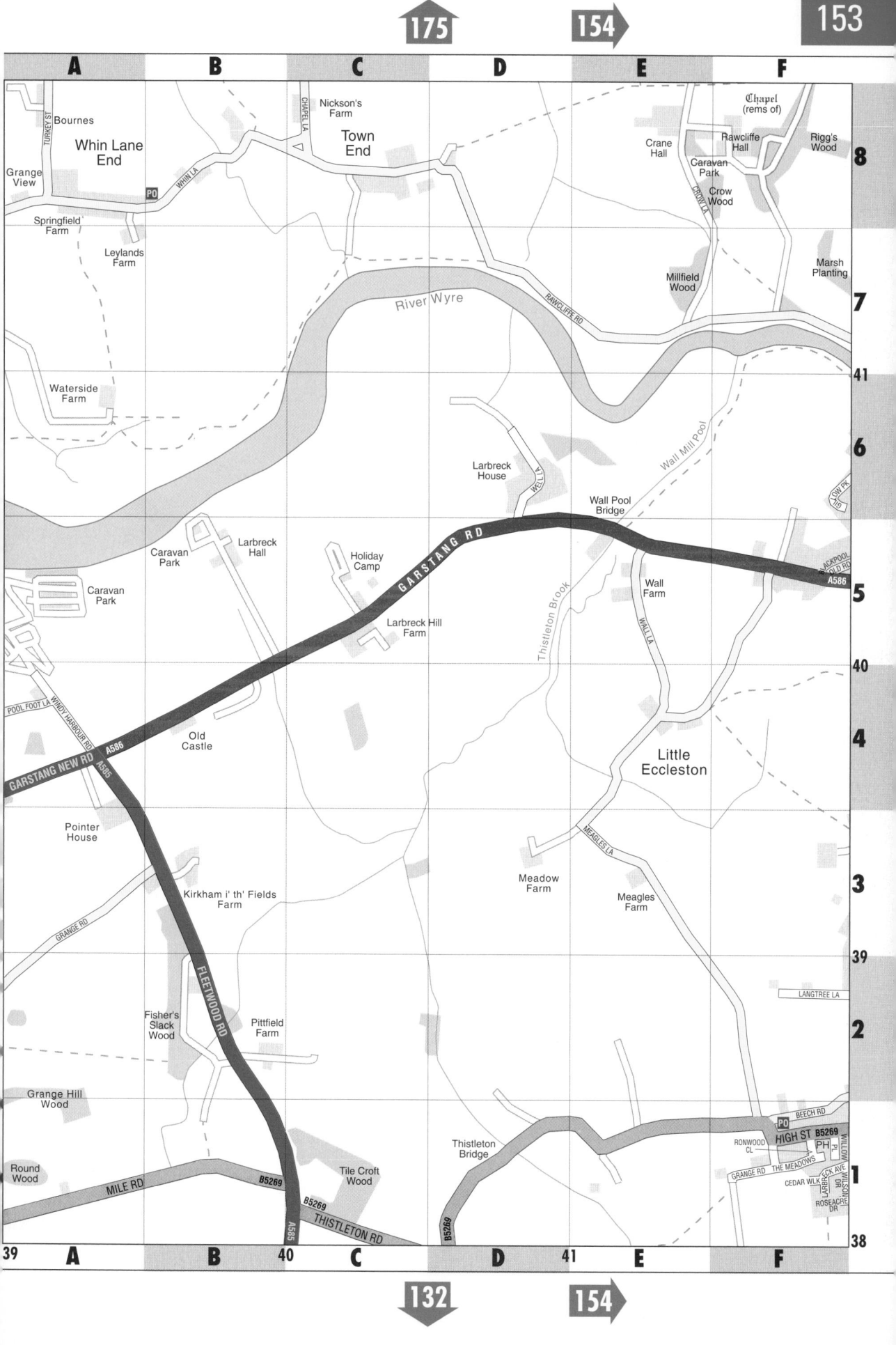

153
176

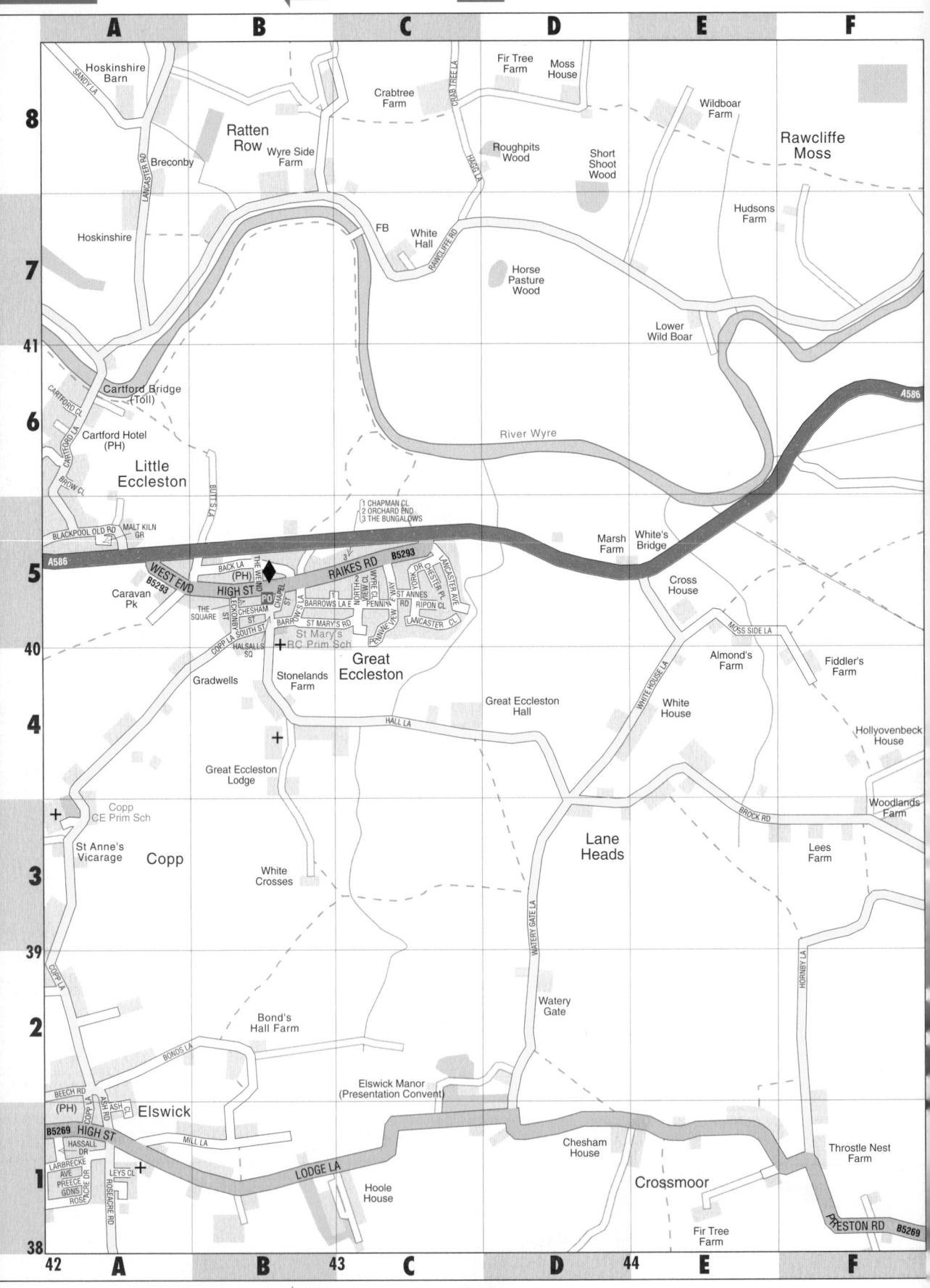

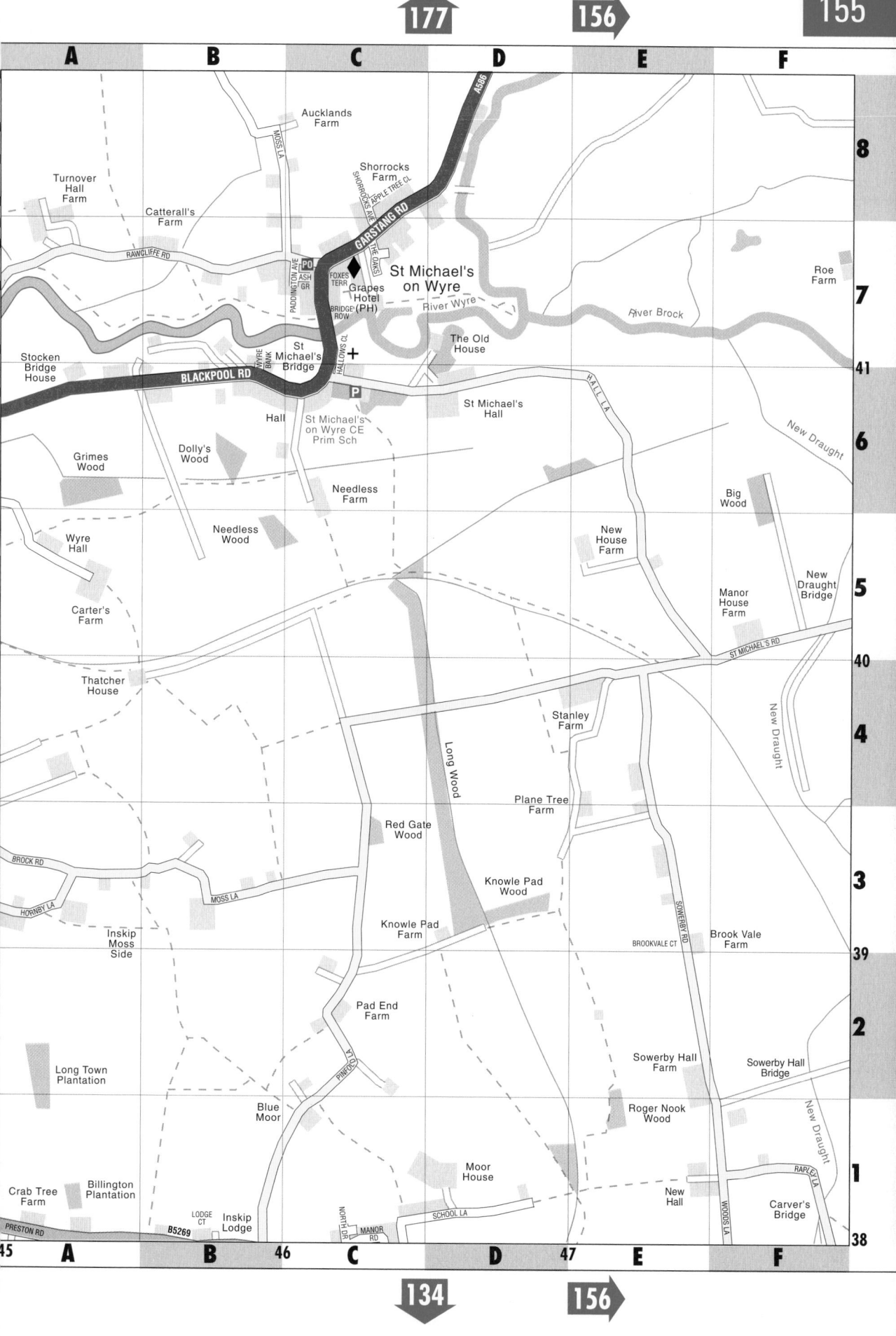

A B C D E F

8
7
41
6
5
40
4
3
39
2
1
38

Aucklands Farm
Shorrocks Farm
St Michael's on Wyre
Turnover Hall Farm
Catterall's Farm
RAWCLIFFE RD
MOSS LA
SHORROCKS AVE
APPLE TREE CL
GARSTANG RD
A586
THE OAKS
PADDINGTON AVE
PO
ASH GR
FOXES TERR
BRIDGE ROW
Grapes Hotel (PH)
River Wyre
The Old House
Roe Farm
River Brock
Stocken Bridge House
St Michael's Bridge
WYRE BANK
HALLOWS CL
BLACKPOOL RD
Hall
St Michael's on Wyre CE Prim Sch
St Michael's Hall
HALL LA
New Draught
P
Grimes Wood
Dolly's Wood
Needless Farm
New House Farm
Big Wood
New Draught Bridge
Wyre Hall
Needless Wood
Manor House Farm
Carter's Farm
ST MICHAEL'S RD
Thatcher House
Long Wood
Stanley Farm
New Draught
Plane Tree Farm
Red Gate Wood
BROCK RD
HORNBY LA
MOSS LA
Knowle Pad Wood
SOWERBY RD
BROOKVALE CT
Brook Vale Farm
Inskip Moss Side
Knowle Pad Farm
Pad End Farm
Long Town Plantation
PINFOLD LA
Sowerby Hall Farm
Sowerby Hall Bridge
Blue Moor
Roger Nook Wood
New Draught
Crab Tree Farm
Billington Plantation
Moor House
New Hall
WOODS LA
RAPLEY LA
Carver's Bridge
PRESTON RD
B5269
LODGE CT
Inskip Lodge
NORTH DR
MANOR RD
SCHOOL LA

45 A B 46 C D 47 E F 38

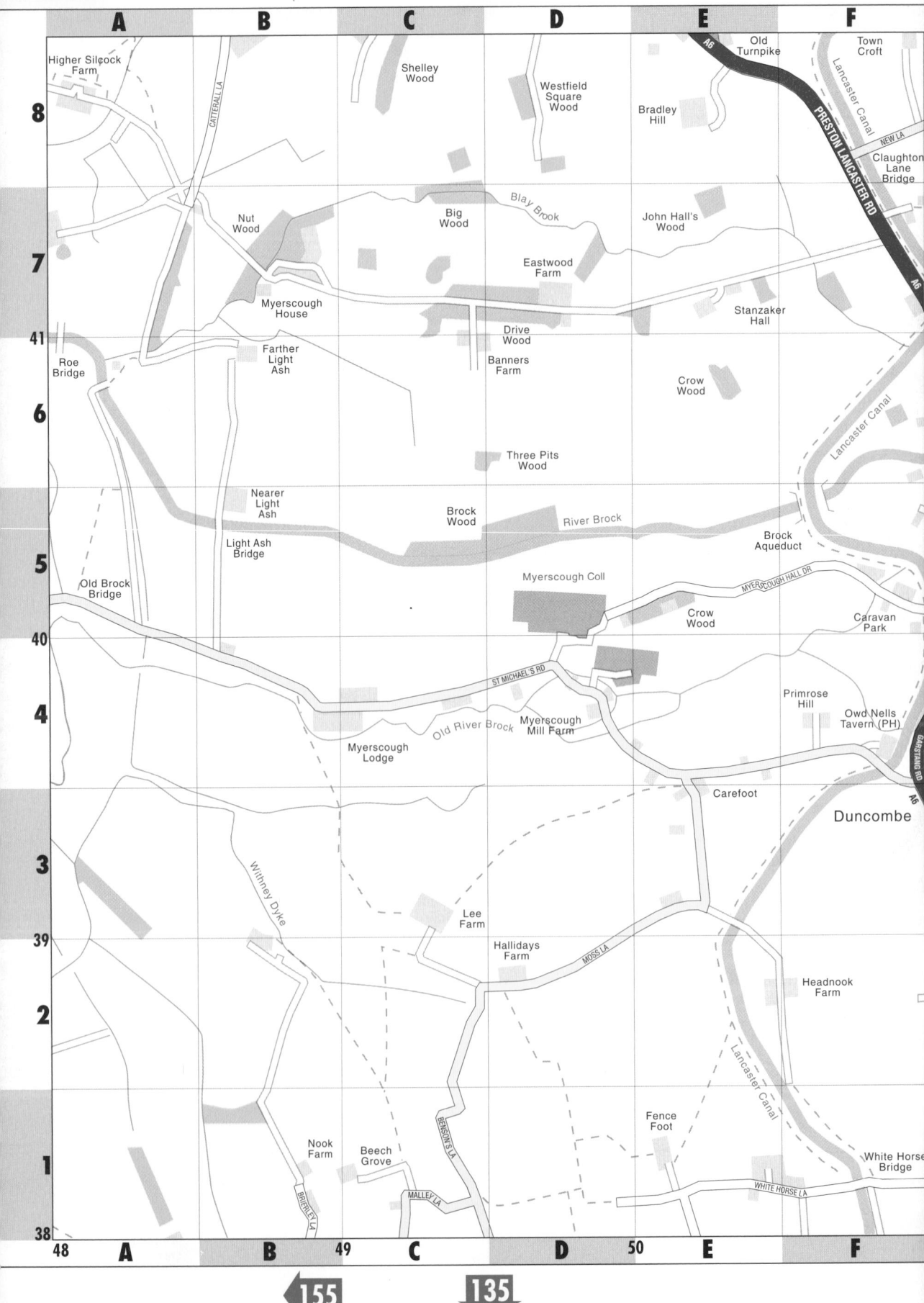

A B C D E F

8

Higher Silcock Farm

CATTERALL LA

Shelley Wood

Westfield Square Wood

Bradley Hill

A6

Old Turnpike

Town Croft

NEW LA

Claughton Lane Bridge

Lancaster Canal

PRESTON LANCASTER RD

7

Nut Wood

Big Wood

Blay Brook

John Hall's Wood

Eastwood Farm

Myerscough House

Stanzaker Hall

A6

41

Farther Light Ash

Drive Wood

Banners Farm

Crow Wood

Roe Bridge

6

Lancaster Canal

Three Pits Wood

Nearer Light Ash

Brock Wood

River Brock

Brock Aqueduct

Light Ash Bridge

5

Old Brock Bridge

Myerscough Coll

MYERSCOUGH HALL DR

Crow Wood

Caravan Park

40

St MICHAEL'S RD

Primrose Hill

4

Myerscough Lodge

Old River Brock

Myerscough Mill Farm

Owd Nells Tavern (PH)

GARSTANG RD

Carefoot

Duncombe

3

Witney Dyke

Lee Farm

A6

39

Hallidays Farm

MOSS LA

Headnook Farm

2

Lancaster Canal

Nook Farm

Beech Grove

BENSON'S LA

Fence Foot

1

BRIERLEY LA

MALLEY LA

White Horse Bridge

WHITE HORSE LA

38

48 A B 49 C D 50 E F

A B C D E F

8

7

41

6

5

40

4

3

39

2

1

38

Carter House
Old Heronry Wood
Bowman House Farm
Manor House Farm
Whinny Plantation
Cloughton House
Lofthouse
Duckett's Farm
Brow Top
Lower Brock Wood
Walmsley Bridge
River Brock
Poulton's Wood
Brock Side
Higher Barn
Matshead
New Bridge
Lower House Wood
LYDIATE LA
BROCK SIDE
Green Man Inn (PH)
Lower House
Brock
Bull Brook
BOURNE BROW
BILSBORROW LA
BILSBORROW SCOTCH GREEN
Bilsborough Hall
Wrights Farm
Spaddock Hall
Bilsborrow
THE GROVE
BEECH AVE
SYCAMORE RD
BALLET HILL CRES
John Cross CE Prim Sch
40
P
CHURCH LA
Bilsborrow Hall Farm
Roebuck Inn (PH)
BILSBORROW LA
Duncombe
FB
Raby's Farm
GREEN LA
Green Lane Farm
Bacchus Brook
Anderton Fold
North Planks
Mount Pleasant Farm
Fisher's Farm
MYERSCOUGH PLANKS
GREEN LA
Abbotts Farm
Jack Nook Farm
Park House
South Planks
Jack Wood
Beesley's Farm
Myerscough Cottage
Manor House
Spatling Brook
Blake Hall
White Horse Hotel (PH)
Barton Old Hall Farm
WHITE HORSE LA
GARSTANG RD
LANGLEY LA
A6
Hall
Hoole Fold
M6

PRESTON LANCASTER RD
GARSTANG RD
LODGE RD
NEW LA

← 157
↑ 180

A **B** **C** **D** **E** **F**

Throstles Nest

Cloggers Farm

Lower Stanalee

BLEASDALE RD

Higher Oaken Head

8

Old Samuels

Whitechapel

Fell Side

Lower Trotter Hill

Whitechapel Prim Sch

+

7

Winn House

Great Plane Tree

Cross Keys Inn (PH)

CHURCH LA

BUTTON ST

41

Patrick House

Higher Fairhurst

Lower Barker

Factory Brook

Ryeheads

Ashes Farmhouse

6

Scotch Green

SCOTCH GREEN LA

Lower Fairhurst

Syke House

5

Little Brooks House

Higher Barker

Plane Tree

Factory Bridge

Whitechapel Brook

40

CARRON LA

BILSBORROW LA

Green Man Hotel

Inglewhite

+

Sparling Brook

Isles Field Farm

SYKE HOUSE LA

Fir Trees

4

Park Head

Cliftons Farm

Palegate Farm

INGLEWHITE RD

Well Wood Stream

Lotus Hall Farm

Turner House

Higher Beesley

Whinnyclough

3

SILK MILL LA

Inglewhite Lodge

Silk Mill Bridge

Longley House Barn

Lower Beesleys

39

Pointer House

CURWEN LA

MILL LA

Whinnyclough Brook

FORD LA

2

LANGLEY LA

Goosnargh Lodge

New House

Ford

BROADITH LA

1

Gardner's Farm

Golden Cliff

Brook Farm

Brook Bridge

Lodge Wood

Townley Wood

Goosnargh Mill

Mill Brook

HORNS LA

EAVES GREEN LA

Brook Cottage

38

54 **A** **B** **55** **C** **D** **56** **E** **F**

← 157
137 ↓

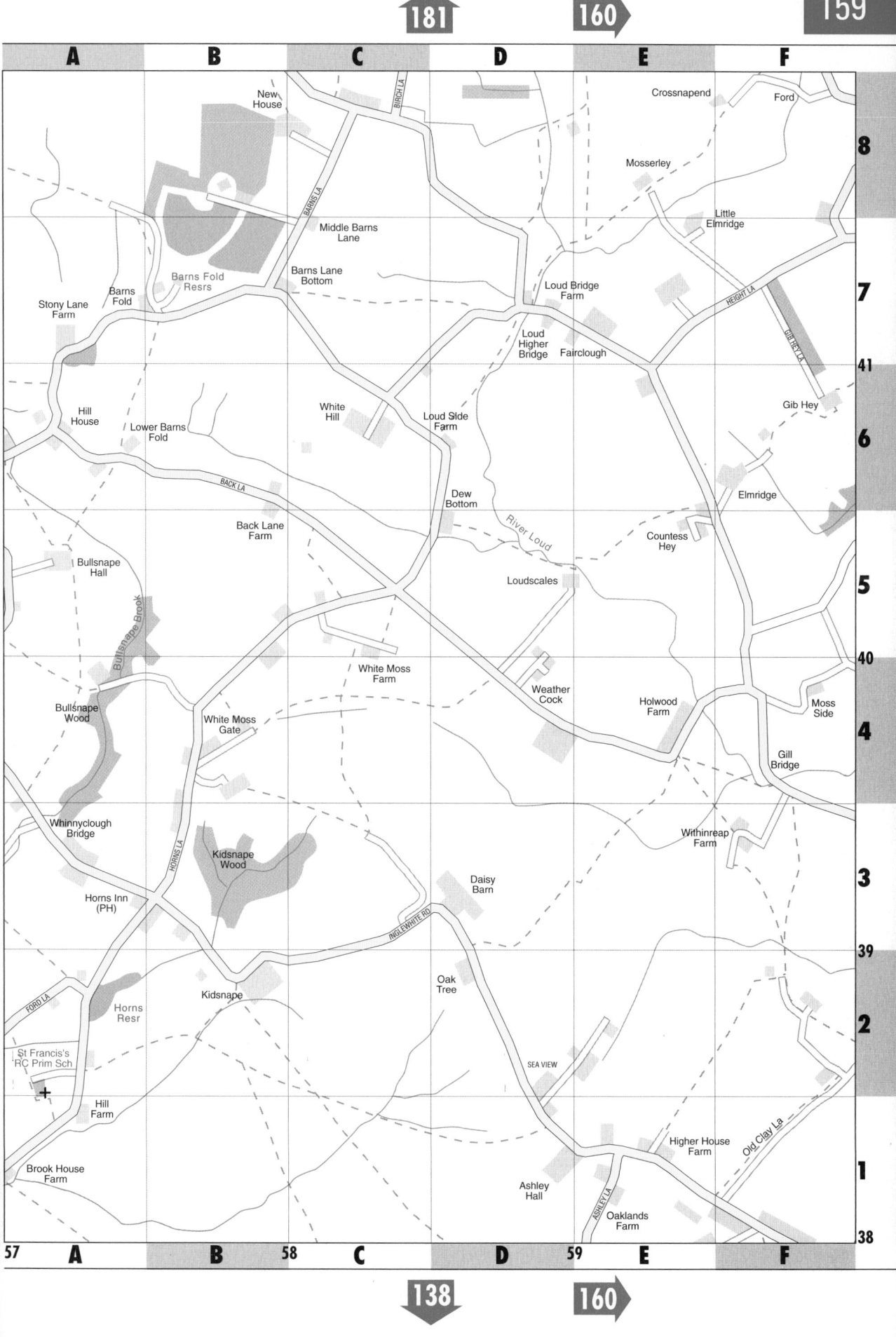

159
182

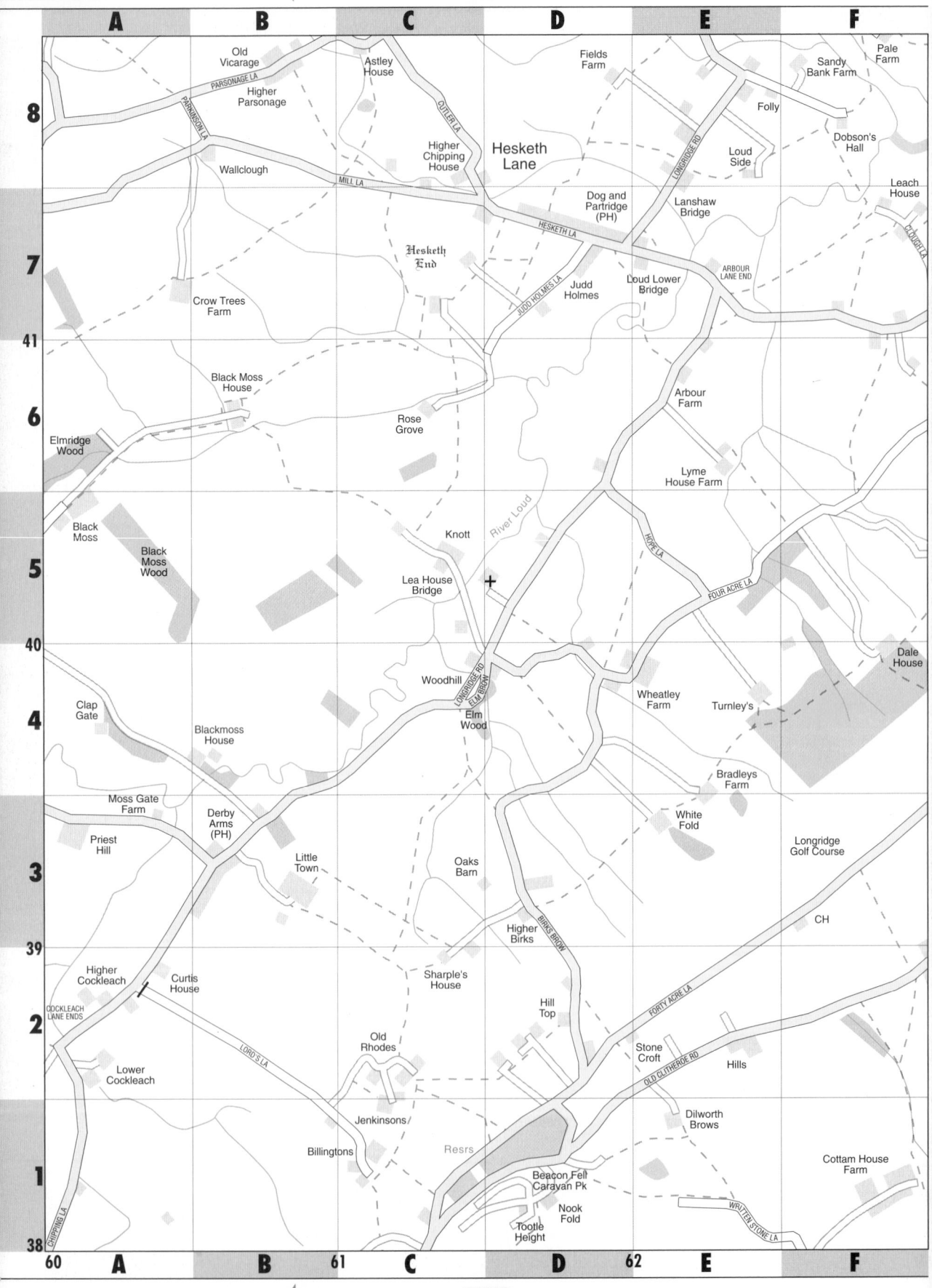

159
139

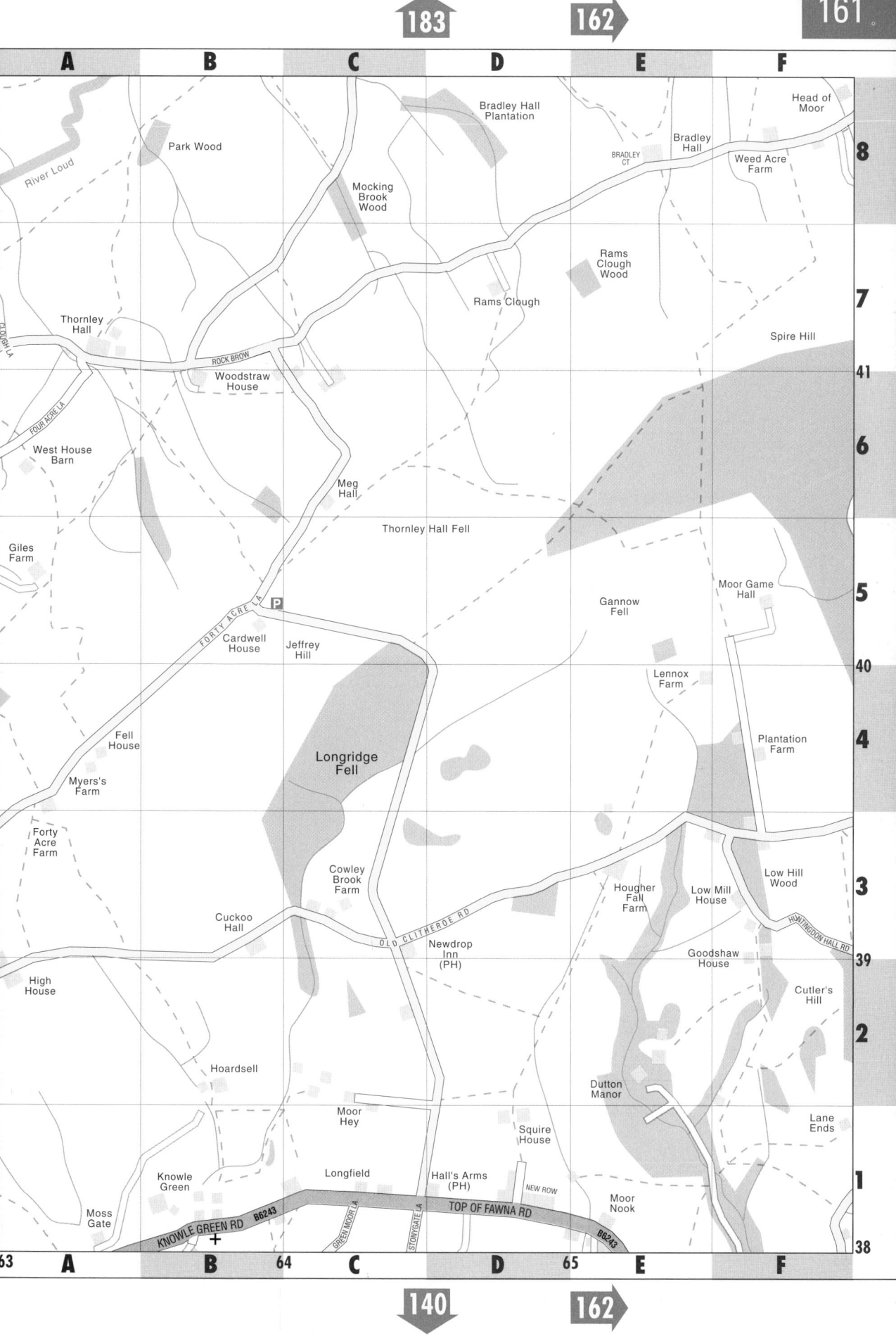

A B C D E F

Head of Moor

Bradley Hall Plantation

Bradley Hall

BRADLEY CT

Weed Acre Farm

Park Wood

Mocking Brook Wood

River Loud

Rams Clough Wood

Rams Clough

Spire Hill

Thornley Hall

ROCK BROW

CLOUGH LA

Woodstraw House

FOUR ACRE LA

West House Barn

Meg Hall

Thornley Hall Fell

Giles Farm

FORTY ACRE LA

Moor Game Hall

Gannow Fell

P

Cardwell House

Jeffrey Hill

Lennox Farm

Plantation Farm

Fell House

Longridge Fell

Myers's Farm

Forty Acre Farm

Cowley Brook Farm

Hougher Fall Farm

Low Mill House

Low Hill Wood

HUNTINGDON HALL RD

Cuckoo Hall

OLD CLITHEROE RD

Newdrop Inn (PH)

Goodshaw House

Cutler's Hill

High House

Hoardsell

Dutton Manor

Lane Ends

Moor Hey

Squire House

Knowle Green

Longfield

Hall's Arms (PH)

NEW ROW

Moor Nook

Moss Gate

KNOWLE GREEN RD

B6243

GREEN MOOR LA

STONYGATE LA

TOP OF FAWNA RD

B6243

63 64 65

8 7 41 6 5 40 4 3 39 2 1 38

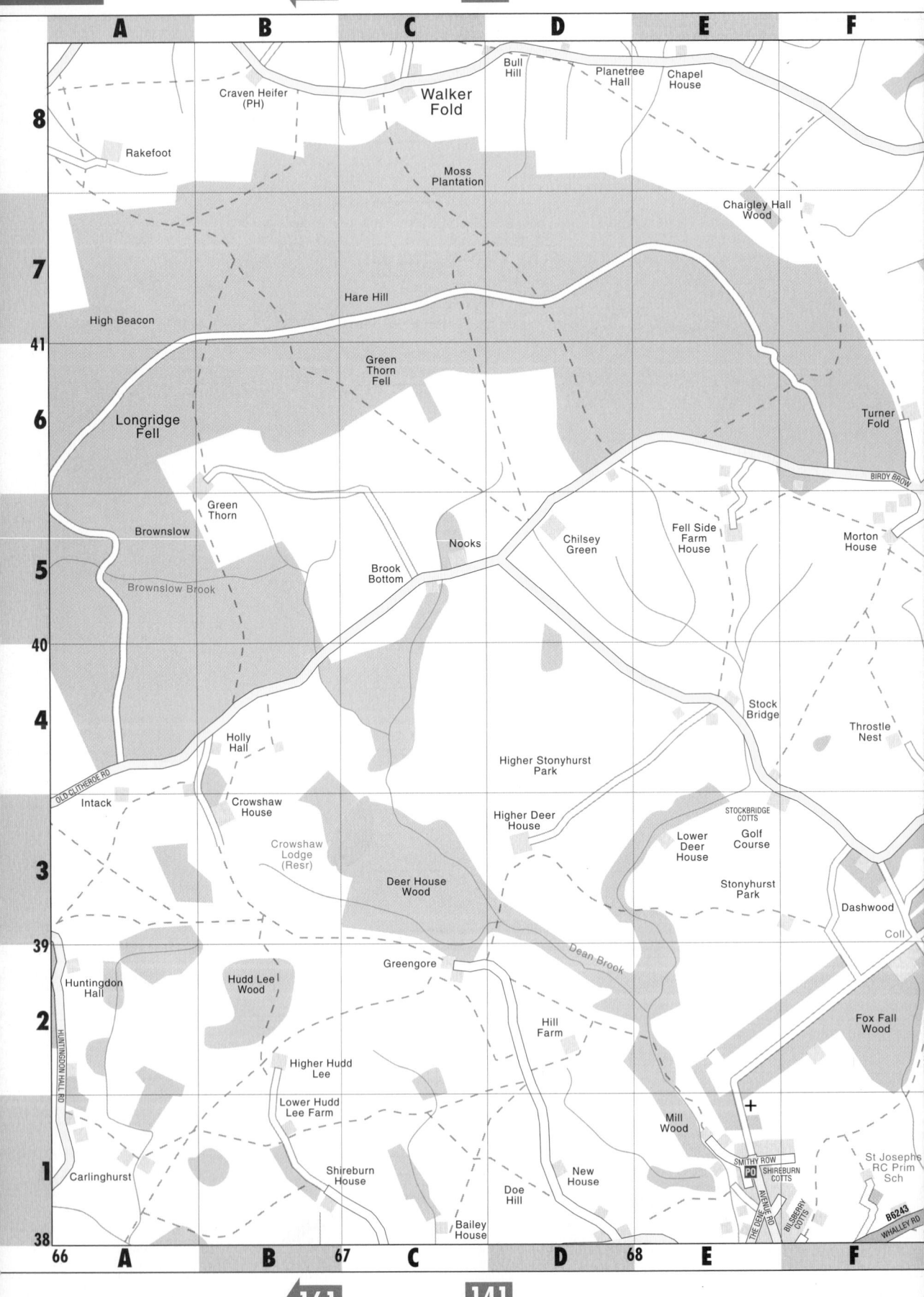

A · B · C · D · E · F

8
Craven Heifer (PH)
Walker Fold
Bull Hill
Planetree Hall
Chapel House
Rakefoot
Moss Plantation
Chaigley Hall Wood

7
Hare Hill
High Beacon
41
Green Thorn Fell

6
Longridge Fell
Turner Fold
BIRDY BROW

Green Thorn
Brownslow
Nooks
Chilsey Green
Fell Side Farm House
Morton House

5
Brownslow Brook
Brook Bottom

40
Stock Bridge
Throstle Nest

4
Holly Hall
Higher Stonyhurst Park
STOCKBRIDGE COTTS
Golf Course

OLD CLITHEROE RD
Intack
Crowshaw House
Higher Deer House
Lower Deer House

3
Crowshaw Lodge (Resr)
Deer House Wood
Stonyhurst Park
Dashwood Coll

39
Greengore
Dean Brook

2
Huntingdon Hall
HUNTINGDON HALL RD
Hudd Lee Wood
Hill Farm
Fox Fall Wood

Higher Hudd Lee
Mill Wood
+

1
Lower Hudd Lee Farm
SMITHY ROW
PO
SHIREBURN COTTS
St Josephs RC Prim Sch
Carlinghurst
Shireburn House
Doe Hill
New House
THE DENE RD
AVENUE RD
BILSBERRY COTTS

38
Bailey House
B6243
WHALLEY RD

66 · A · B · 67 · C · D · 68 · E · F

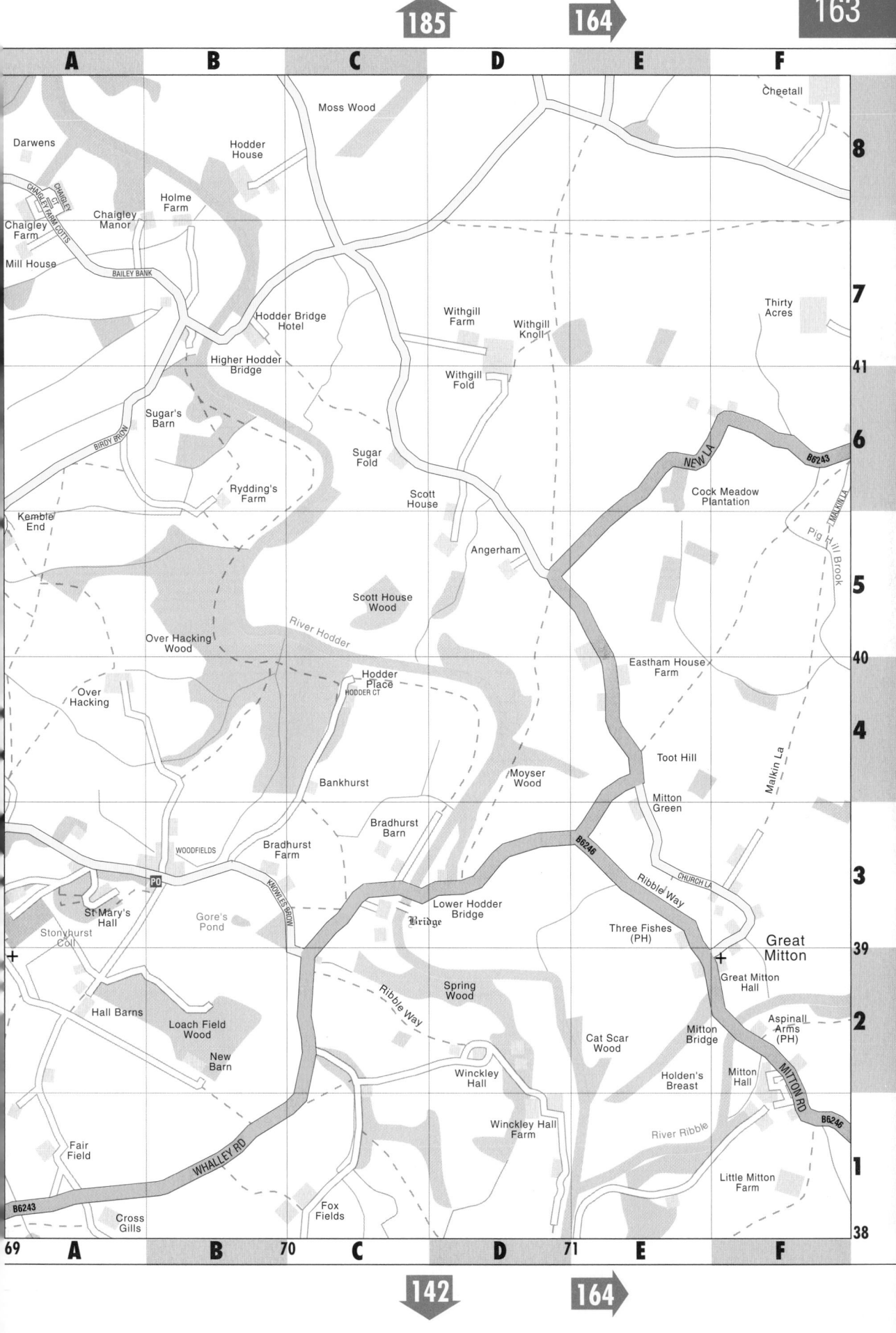

A B C D E F

8

Cheetall

Darwens

Hodder
House

Moss Wood

Holme
Farm

CHAIGLEY

CHAIGLEY PARK COTTS

Chaigley
Manor

Chaigley
Farm

Mill House

7

Thirty
Acres

BAILEY BANK

Hodder Bridge
Hotel

Withgill
Farm

Withgill
Knoll

41

Higher Hodder
Bridge

Withgill
Fold

6

NEW LA

B6243

MALKIN LA

Sugar's
Barn

BIRDY BROW

Rydding's
Farm

Sugar
Fold

Scott
House

Cock Meadow
Plantation

Pig Hill Brook

Kemble
End

Angerham

5

Scott House
Wood

Over Hacking
Wood

River Hodder

40

Eastham House
Farm

Over
Hacking

Hodder
Place

HODDER CT

4

Moyser
Wood

Toot Hill

Malkin La

Bankhurst

Mitton
Green

Bradhurst
Barn

B6246

CHURCH LA

3

WOODFIELDS

Bradhurst
Farm

Lower Hodder
Bridge

Ribble Way

KNOWLES BROW

Bridge

Three Fishes
(PH)

Great
Mitton

PO

Gore's
Pond

39

St Mary's
Hall

Stonyhurst
Coll

Great Mitton
Hall

Spring
Wood

Aspinall
Arms
(PH)

2

Hall Barns

Ribble Way

Loach Field
Wood

Cat Scar
Wood

Mitton
Bridge

New
Barn

Winckley
Hall

Holden's
Breast

Mitton
Hall

MITTON RD

B6246

Fair
Field

Winckley Hall
Farm

River Ribble

1

WHALLEY RD

Little Mitton
Farm

B6243

Cross
Gills

Fox
Fields

38

69 A B 70 C D 71 E F

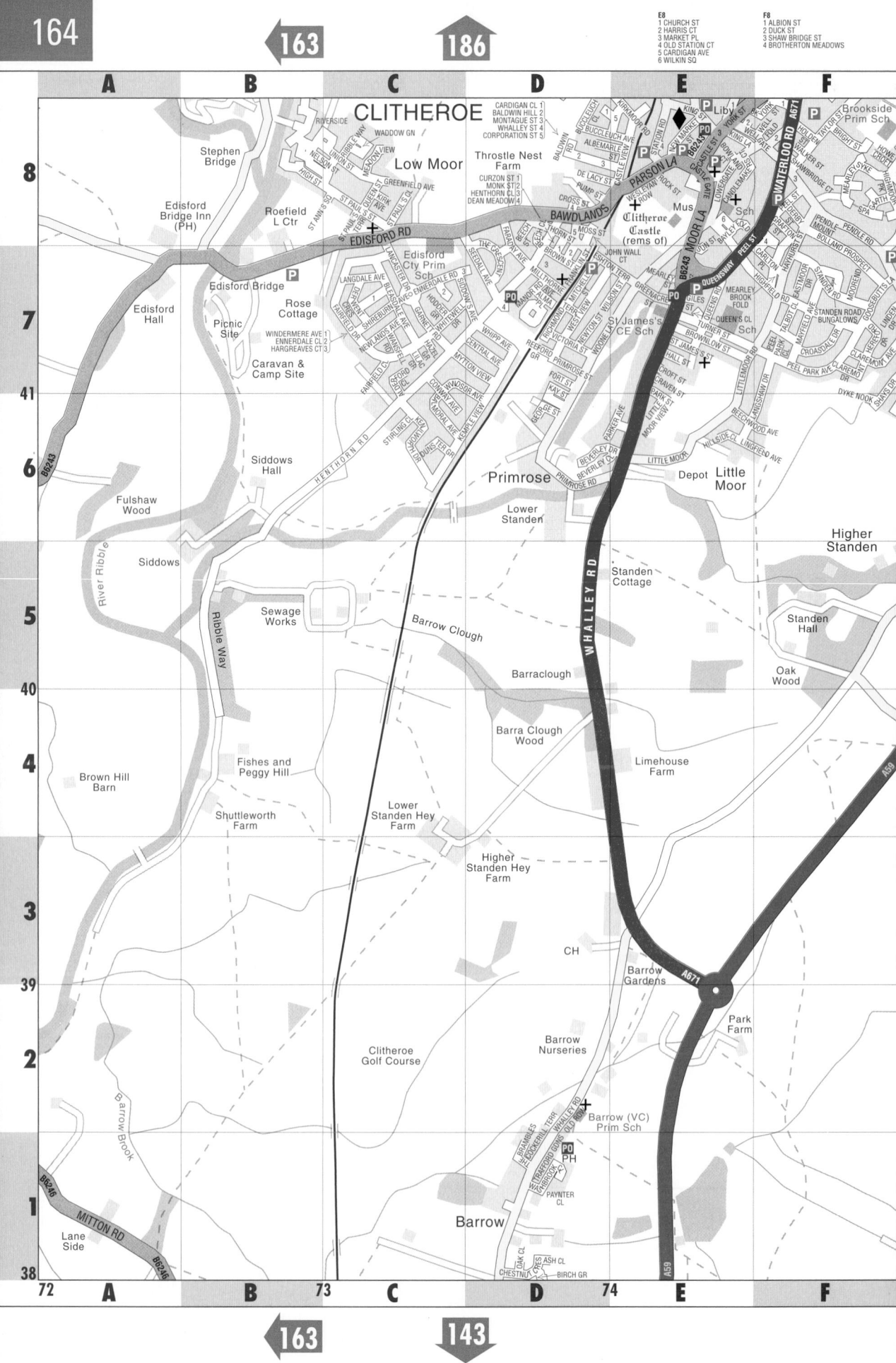

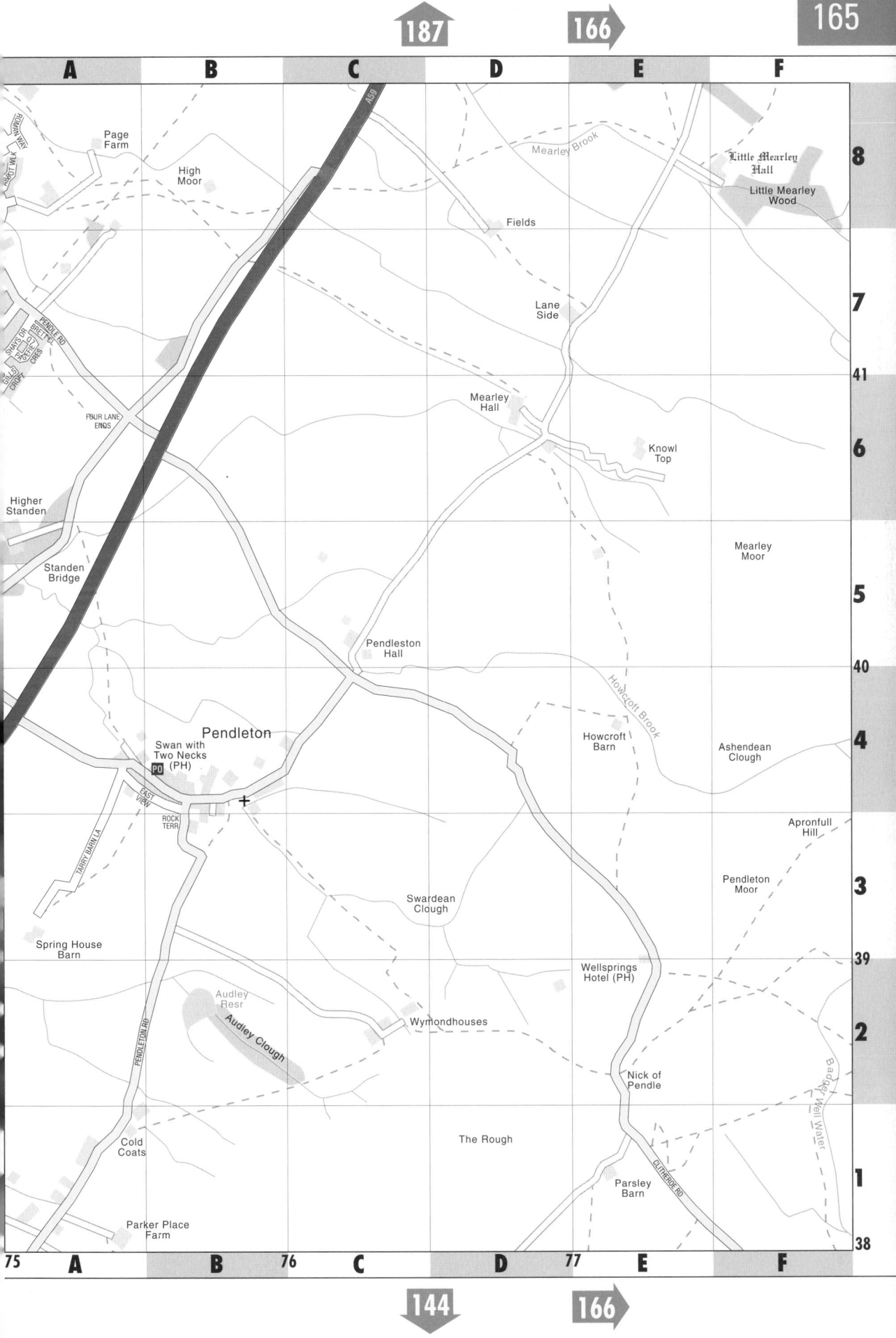

A B C D E F

8
7
41
6
5
40
4
3
39
2
1
38

ROMAN WAY
ABBOT WLK
Page Farm
High Moor
Mearley Brook
Little Mearley Hall
Little Mearley Wood
Fields
Lane Side
A59
SNAYS DR
PENDLE RD
BRETT ST
GT
FOSTER
GIBSON
CROFT
FOUR LANE ENDS
Mearley Hall
Knowl Top
Higher Standen
Mearley Moor
Standen Bridge
Pendleston Hall
Howcroft Brook
Pendleton
Swan with Two Necks (PH)
PO
EAST VIEW
ROCK TERR
Howcroft Barn
Ashendean Clough
Apronfull Hill
Pendleton Moor
TARR BARN LA
Spring House Barn
Swardean Clough
Wellsprings Hotel (PH)
PENDLETON RD
Audley Resr
Audley Clough
Wymondhouses
Nick of Pendle
Badger Well Water
Cold Coats
The Rough
CLITHEROE RD
Parsley Barn
Parker Place Farm

75 A B 76 C D 77 E F

165
188

	A	B	C	D	E	F

8

Worston Moor

Pendle Hill

Beacon or Big End

Pendle Way

Pendle House

7

Pendle Moor

41

Turn Head

Ogden Clough

6

Barley Moor

Under Pendle

Mearley Moor

5

Howcroft Brook

White Slacks

Ogden Hill

Dry Clough

Buttock

40

Cat Holes

New Fields

4

Black Hill

Ogden Clough

Fox Holes

Pendle Way

Ogden Clough

Badger Wells Hill

Upper Ogden Resr

Spence Moor

3

Deerstones

Cock Dole

Driver Height

Craggs Dole

39

Cock Clough Plantation

2

Bank Hill

Wood House Dale

Lower Dale

Stainscomb Dale

Calf Hill

Churn Clough Resr

Sabden Fold

Wood House Brook

1

Rotten Clough

Stainscomb

Lower Lane

Churn Clough

Wood House

The Old House

38

78	A		B	79	C		D	80	E		F

165
145

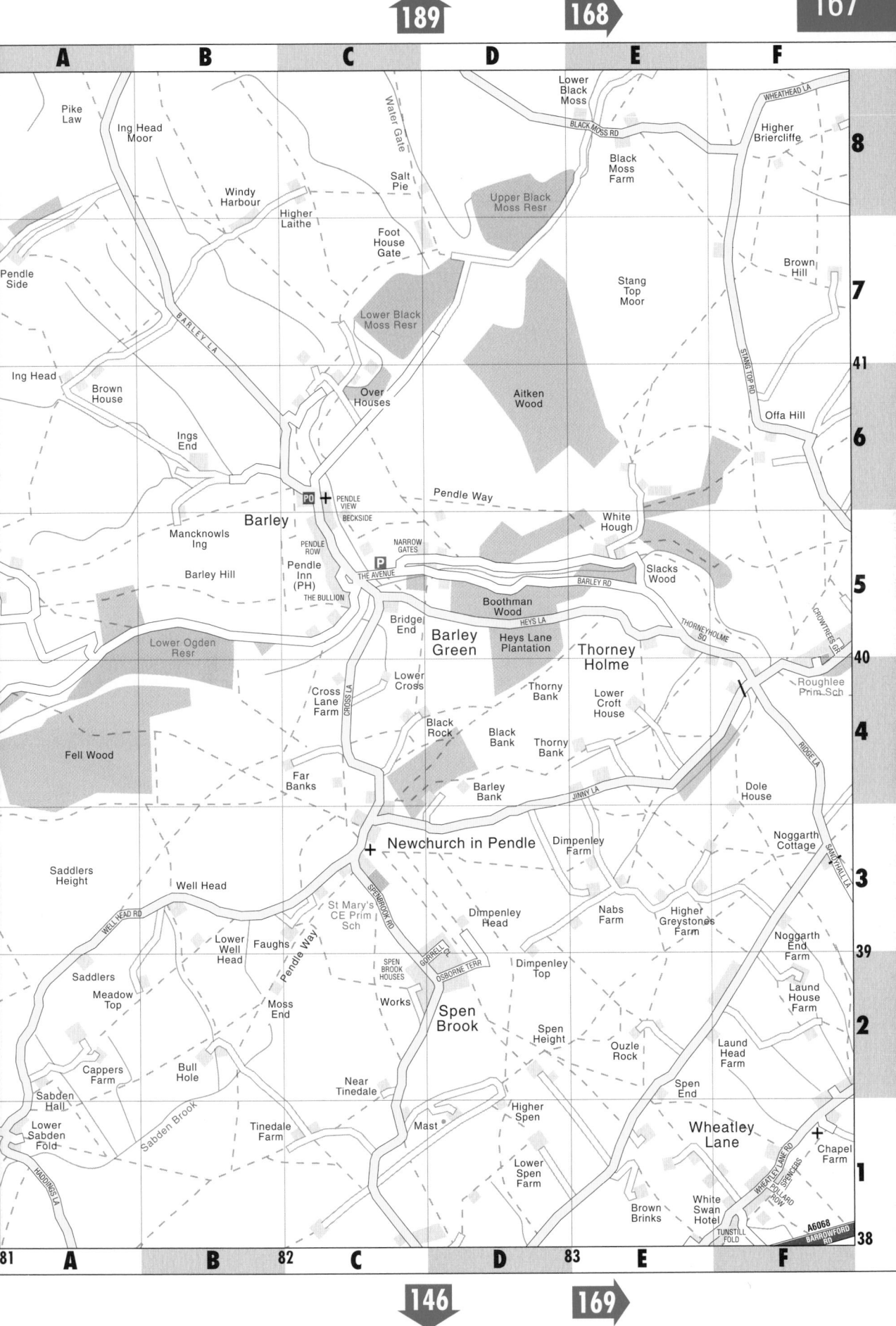

8

Wheathead La

Pike Law

Ing Head Moor

Windy Harbour

Higher Laithe

Salt Pie

Lower Black Moss

Black Moss Rd

Black Moss Farm

Higher Briercliffe

Brown Hill

Pendle Side

Foot House Gate

Upper Black Moss Resr

Stang Top Moor

7

41

Ing Head

Brown House

Barley La

Lower Black Moss Resr

Aitken Wood

Stang Top Rd

Offa Hill

6

Ings End

Over Houses

Pendle Way

White Hough

PO Pendle View

Barley BECKSIDE

Mancknowls Ing

Barley Hill

PENDLE ROW

Pendle Inn (PH)

THE BULLION

NARROW GATES

P THE AVENUE

Barley Rd

Slacks Wood

Crowtrees Gr

Thorneyholme Sq

5

Bridge End

Barley Green

Boothman Wood

HEYS LA

Heys Lane Plantation

Thorney Holme

40

Lower Ogden Resr

Cross Lane Farm

CROSS LA

Lower Cross

Thorny Bank

Lower Croft House

Roughlee Prim Sch

4

Fell Wood

Black Rock

Black Bank

Thorny Bank

Ridge La

Dole House

Far Banks

Barley Bank

Jinny La

Noggarth Cottage

Sabhall La

3

Saddlers Height

Well Head

Newchurch in Pendle

Dimpenley Farm

St Mary's CE Prim Sch

Nabs Farm

Higher Greystones Farm

Noggarth End Farm

WELL HEAD RD

Lower Well Head

Faughs

Pendle Way

SPENBROOK RD

Dimpenley Head

39

Saddlers

Meadow Top

Moss End

SPEN BROOK HOUSES

GORRELL RD

OSBORNE TERR

Works

Dimpenley Top

Laund House Farm

2

Cappers Farm

Bull Hole

Spen Brook

Spen Height

Ouzle Rock

Laund Head Farm

Sabden Hall

Near Tinedale

Mast

Higher Spen

Spen End

Wheatley Lane

Chapel Farm

1

Lower Sabden Fold

HADDINGS LA

Sabden Brook

Tinedale Farm

Lower Spen Farm

Brown Brinks

White Swan Hotel

WHEATLEY LANE RD

SPENCERS POLLARD ROW

A6068 BARROWFORD RD

TUNSTILL FOLD

38

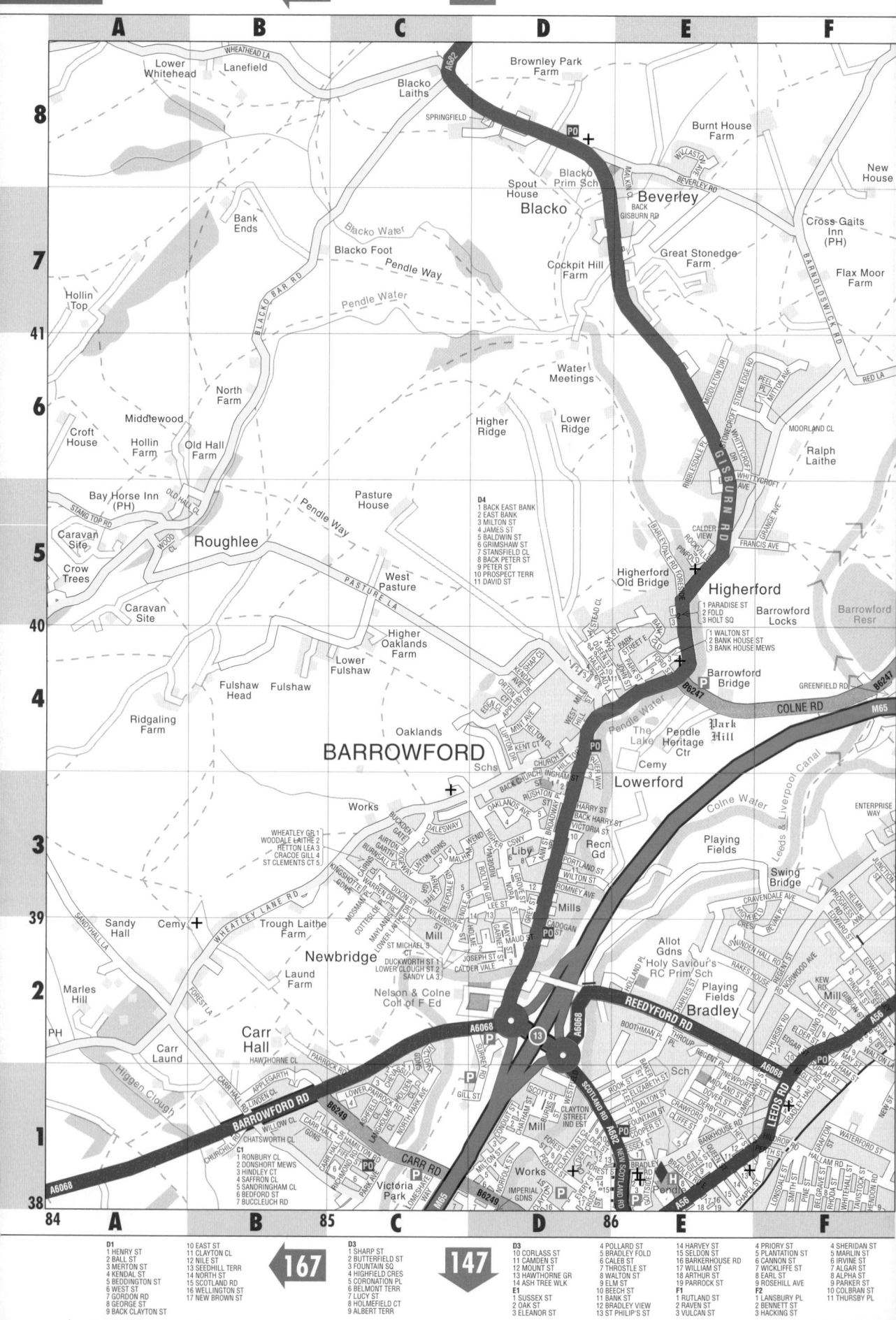

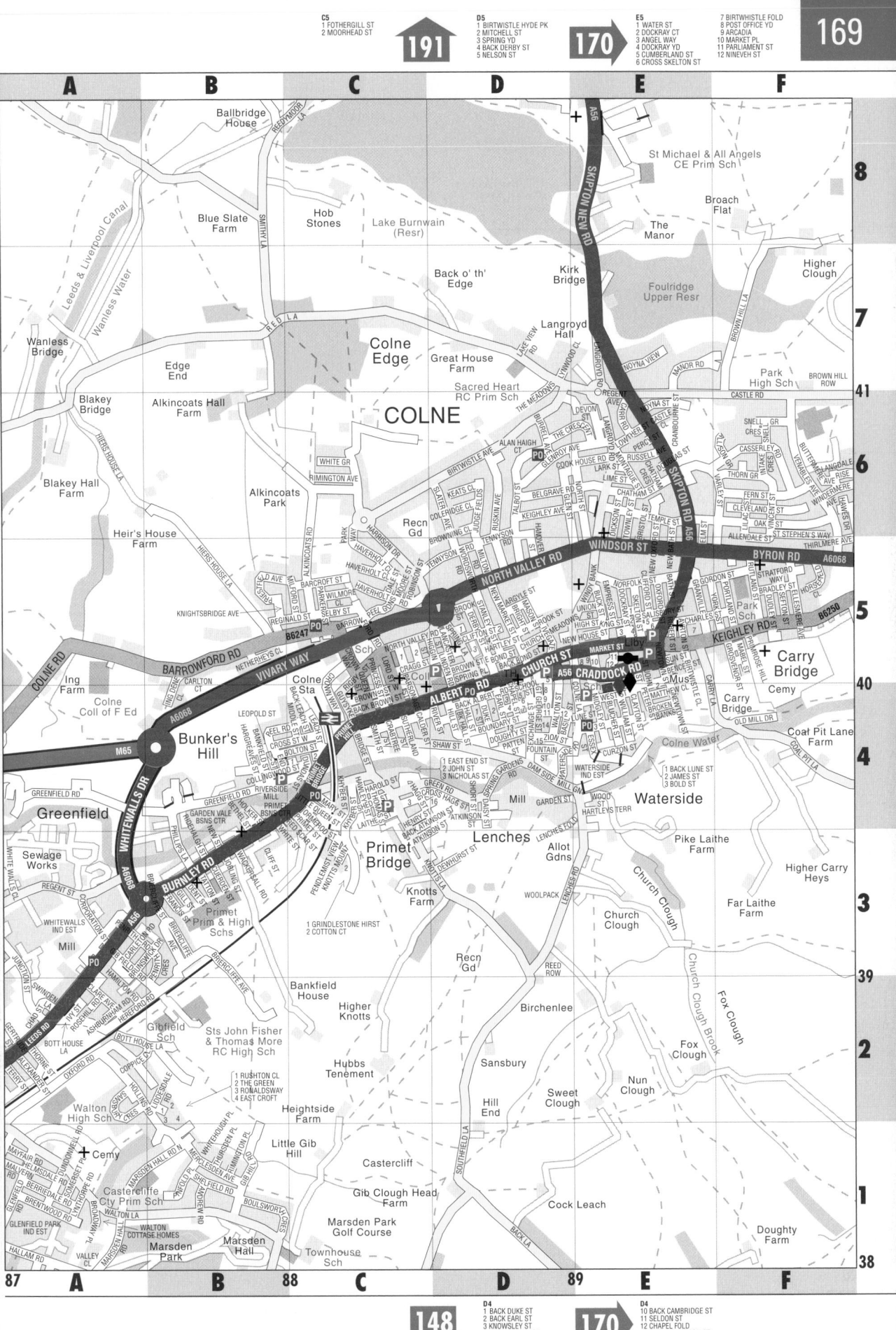

169
192

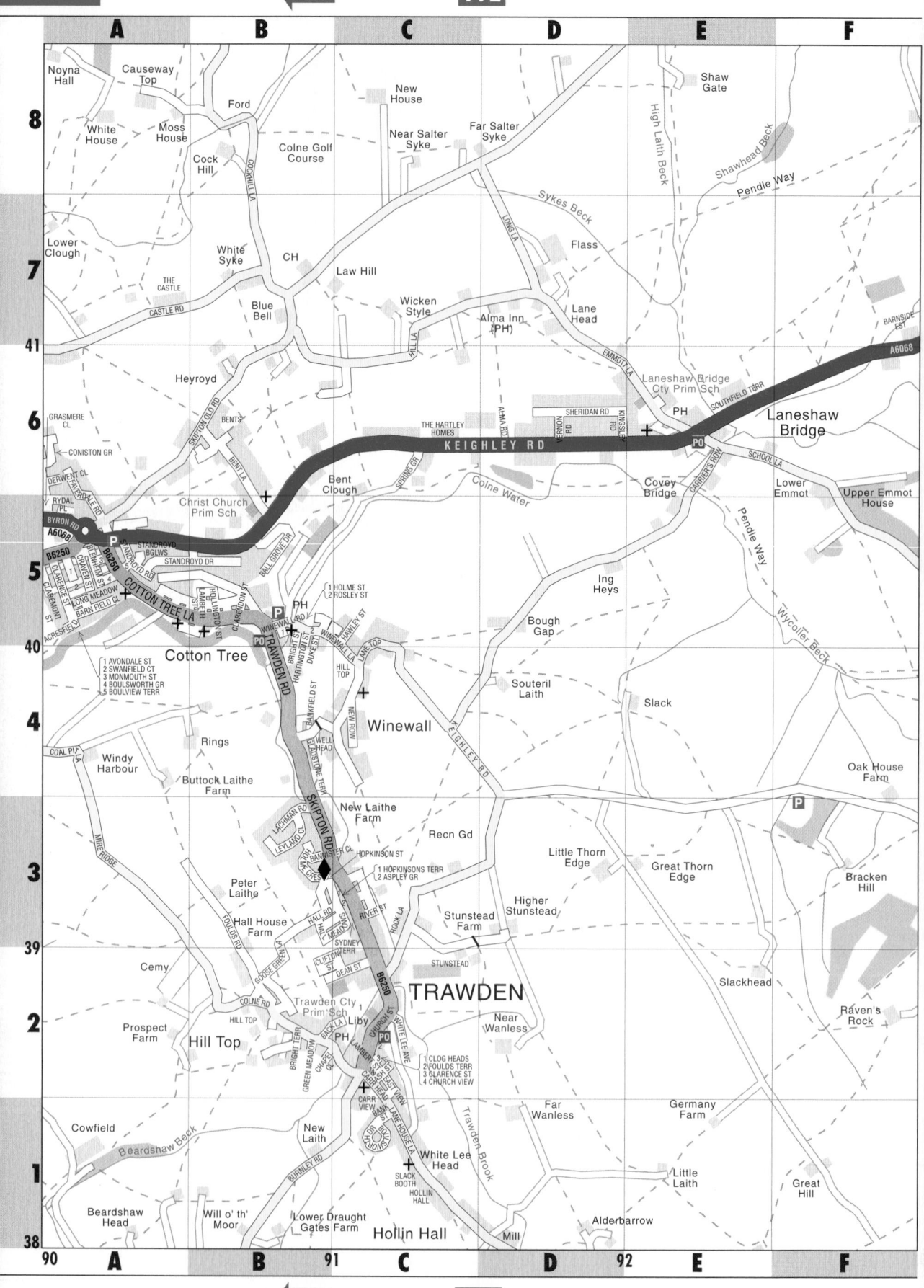

169
149

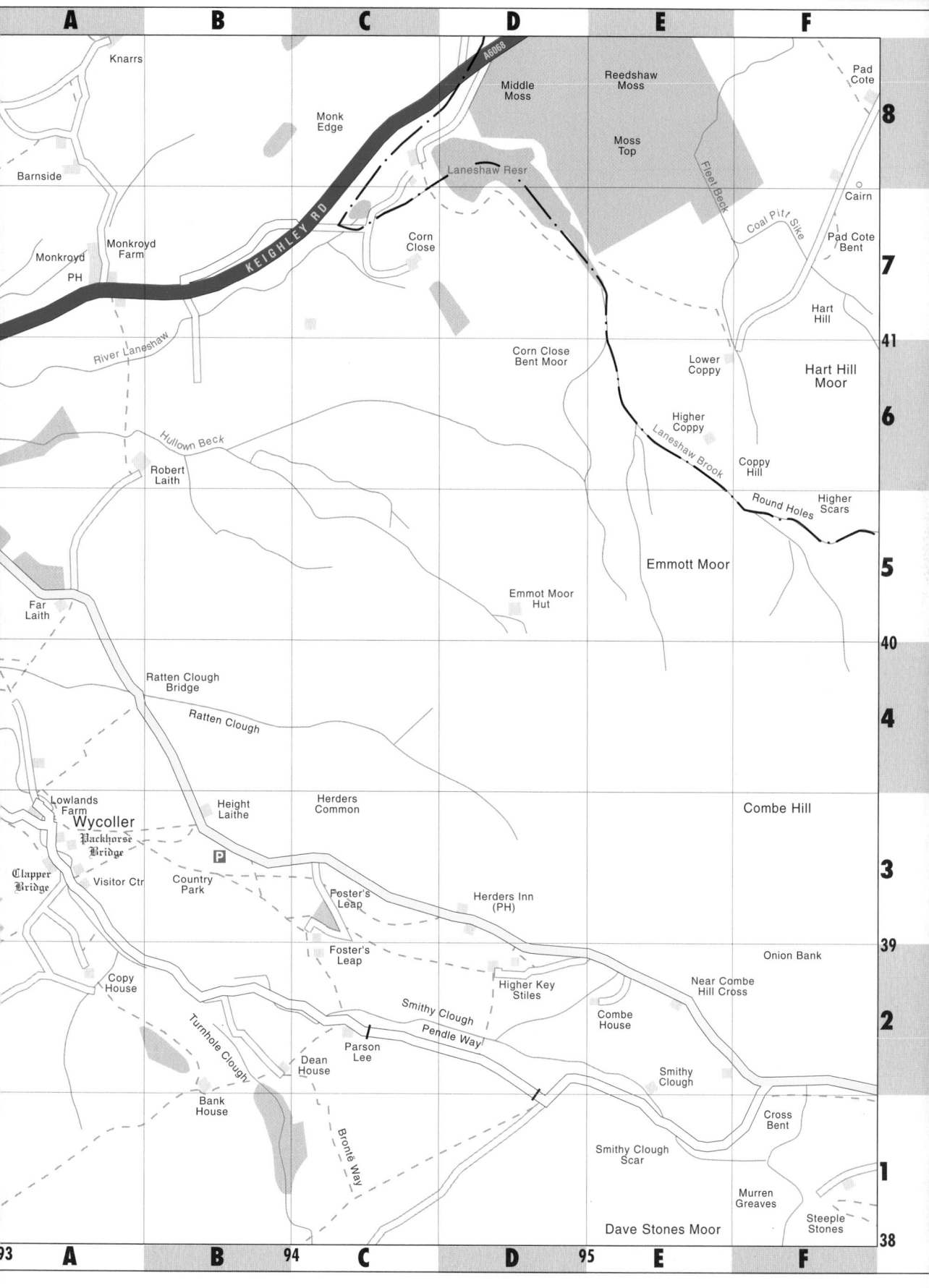

A B C D E F

8

Knarrs

Middle
Moss

Reedshaw
Moss

Pad
Cote

Barnside

Monk
Edge

Moss
Top

Laneshaw Resr

Cairn

Fleet Beck

KEIGHLEY RD

A6068

Coal Pitt Sike

Monkroyd
PH

Monkroyd
Farm

Corn
Close

Pad Cote
Bent

7

41

River Laneshaw

Corn Close
Bent Moor

Lower
Coppy

Hart
Hill

Hart Hill
Moor

Hullown Beck

Higher
Coppy

6

Robert
Laith

Laneshaw Brook

Coppy
Hill

Higher
Scars

Round Holes

Far
Laith

Emmott Moor

5

Emmot Moor
Hut

40

Ratten Clough
Bridge

4

Ratten Clough

Lowlands
Farm

Height
Laithe

Herders
Common

Combe Hill

Wycoller

Packhorse
Bridge

P

3

Clapper
Bridge

Visitor Ctr

Country
Park

Foster's
Leap

Herders Inn
(PH)

Onion Bank

39

Copy
House

Foster's
Leap

Higher Key
Stiles

Near Combe
Hill Cross

Turnhole Clough

Smithy Clough

Combe
House

2

Pendle Way

Parson
Lee

Smithy
Clough

Dean
House

Cross
Bent

Bank
House

Smithy Clough
Scar

1

Brontë Way

Murren
Greaves

Steeple
Stones

Dave Stones Moor

38

93 A B 94 C D 95 E F

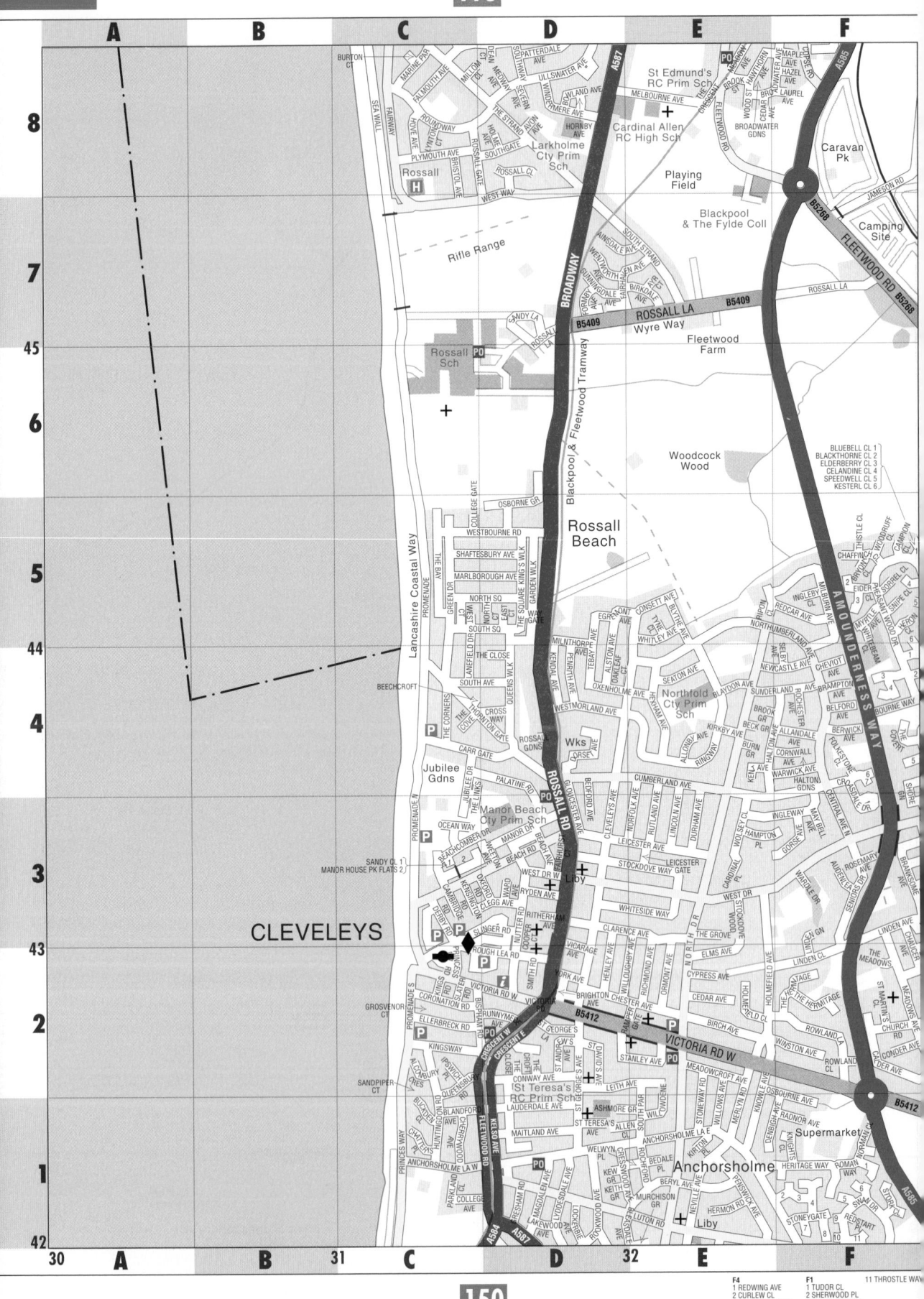

	A	B	C	D	E	F

8

BURTON CT
MARINE PDE
FALMOUTH AVE
MILTON AVE
DEAN MEDWAY AVE
PATTERDALE AVE
ULLSWATER AVE
WINDERMERE AVE
SEVERN AVE
WYLAND AVE
HORNBY AVE
MELBOURNE AVE

St Edmund's RC Prim Sch
MAPLE AVE
HAWTHORN
HAZEL AVE
LAUREL AVE
BROOK
WOODS
CEDAR AVE
BROADWATER GDNS

Caravan Pk

SEA WALL
FAIRWAY
ROUNDWAY
HOVE AVE
PLYMOUTH AVE
SOUTHGATE
HOLME
RUSSELL GATE
RUSSELL CL
THE STRAND
Larkholme Cty Prim Sch

Cardinal Allen RC High Sch

Rossall
H
WEST WAY
Playing Field

FLEETWOOD RD

Blackpool & The Fylde Coll

JAMESON RD

Camping Site

B5268

7

Rifle Range

BROADWAY

A587

AINSDALE AVE
WENTWORTH
WREN AVE
FAIRHAVEN AVE
BIRKDALE
SOUTH STRAND

B5409
ROSSALL LA
Wyre Way
B5409

ROSSALL LA

B5268

FLEETWOOD RD

45

Rossall Sch
PO
ROSSALL LA
SANDY LA

Fleetwood Farm

Blackpool & Fleetwood Tramway

6

+

Woodcock Wood

BLUEBELL CL 1
BLACKTHORNE CL 2
ELDERBERRY CL 3
CELANDINE CL 4
SPEEDWELL CL 5
KESTER CL 6

A MOUNDERNESS WAY

THISTLE CL
WOODRUFF
CAMPION
CHAFFINCH
EIDER CL
SORREL CL

5

Lancashire Coastal Way

PROMENADE

GREEN DR
THE HILL
COLLEGE GATE
WESTBOURNE RD
OSBORNE GR
SHAFTESBURY AVE
MARLBOROUGH AVE
THE SQUARE KING'S WLK
GARDEN WLK
NORTH SQ
NORTH CT
EAST CT
WAY GATE

Rossall Beach

INGLEBY
REDCAR AVE
CONSET AVE
EGREMONT AVE
BLYTHE AVE
WHITLEY AVE
NORTHUMBERLAND AVE
SELBY AVE
NEWCASTLE AVE
CHEVIOT
BRAMPTON AVE
BELFORD AVE
BERWICK AVE

44

BEECHCROFT
SOUTH SQ
QUEENS WLK
SOUTH AVE
THE CLOSE
CROSS WAY
MILNTHORPE AVE
TEBAY AVE
ALSTON AVE
SEATON AVE
BLAYDON AVE
Northfold Cty Prim Sch
SUNDERLAND AVE
ROCHESTER AVE
ALLANDALE

4

THE CORNERS
P
COVE AVE
THORNTON GATE
CARR GATE
Jubilee Gdns
JUBILEE DR
THE LINKS
PALATINE RD
ROSSALL RD
WESTMORLAND AVE
KENDAL AVE
OXENHOLME AVE
HEYSHAM AVE
Wks
ALLONBY AVE
KIRKBY AVE
BURN GR
CORNWALL AVE
WARWICK AVE
HALTON GDNS
FOLKESTONE
CROSSDALE DR

3

OCEAN WAY
P
Manor Beach Cty Prim Sch
BEACHCOMBER DR
MANOR DR
MANOR RD
SANDY CL 1
MANOR HOUSE PK FLATS 2
WEST DR W
RYDEN AVE
GLEGG AVE
CLEVELEYS AVE
NORFOLK AVE
LINCOLN AVE
DURHAM AVE
Liby
LEICESTER AVE
STOCKDOVE WAY GATE
WEST DR
WOLSELY CL
HAMPTON PL
GORSE CL
INGLEWAY
MAY BELL AVE
CARNFIELD PL
ROSEMARY AVE
GLADSTONE AVE
LINDEN AVE

CLEVELEYS

43

SLINGER RD
ROUGH LEA RD
P
CAMBRIDGE RD
KENSINGTON RD
DERBY RD
WARD
RITHERHAM AVE
COOPERS WAY
WHITESIDE WAY
CLARENCE AVE
ELMS AVE
VICARAGE AVE
HENLEY AVE
WILLOUGHBY AVE
RICHMOND AVE
ORMONT AVE
CYPRESS AVE
LINDEN CL
THE MEADOWS
THE HERMITAGE
CHALCER AVE

2

GROSVENOR CT
CORONATION RD
ELLERBRECK RD
PROMENADE S
RUNNYMEAD
VICTORIA RD W
SMITH RD
YORK AVE
BRIGHTON AVE
B5412
CHESTER AVE
CEDAR AVE
BIRCH AVE
VICTORIA RD W
WINSTON AVE
ROWLAND CL
B5412

KINGSWAY
ST GEORGE'S
ST ANDREW'S AVE
STANLEY AVE
MEADOWCROFT RD
ROWLAND AVE
CONDER AVE

1

SANDPIPER CT
ALDENBURY
IPSWICH
QUEENSWAY
CONWAY AVE
LEITH AVE
ST TERESA'S AVE
ST GEORGE'S AVE
ST Teresa's RC Prim Sch
LAUDERDALE AVE
ASHMORE GR
SOUTH PAR
WILLOWS AVE
STONEWAY
MERLIN RD
KNOWLE AVE
OSBORNE AVE
RADNOR AVE
DERBISH RD
Supermarket
A585

PRINCES WAY
BUCKTON
BLANDFORD
QUINTINGDON
CHATTERIS
FLEETWOOD RD
KELSO AVE
ANCHORSHOLME LA W
MAITLAND AVE
WELWYN
KEW
BEDALE
DHOOM
ANCHORSHOLME LA E
NIRTON RD
Anchorsholme
HERITAGE WAY
ROMAN WAY
STONEYGATE
REDSTART

42

GRESHAM AVE
MAGDALENE AVE
LYDSDALE AVE
COLLEGE AVE
PARKLAND AVE
CLYDESDALE AVE
LAKEWOOD AVE
BERYL AVE
KEITH GR
MURCHISON GR
NEVILLE
HERMON RD
LUTON RD
Liby
NEVILLE
A587
A584

	A	B	C	D	E	F

30   31   32

F4
1 REDWING AVE
2 CURLEW CL
3 WHITECREST AVE
4 BARNFIELD CL
5 WIDGEON CL
6 COLCHESTER DR
7 PORTSMOUTH CL

F1
1 TUDOR CL
2 SHERWOOD PL
3 RICHARDS WAY
4 GLADSTONE WAY
5 POCHARD PL
6 DOVE CL
7 INGLENOOK CL
8 HERIOT CL
9 BUNTING PL
10 SANDPIPER PL

11 THROSTLE WAY

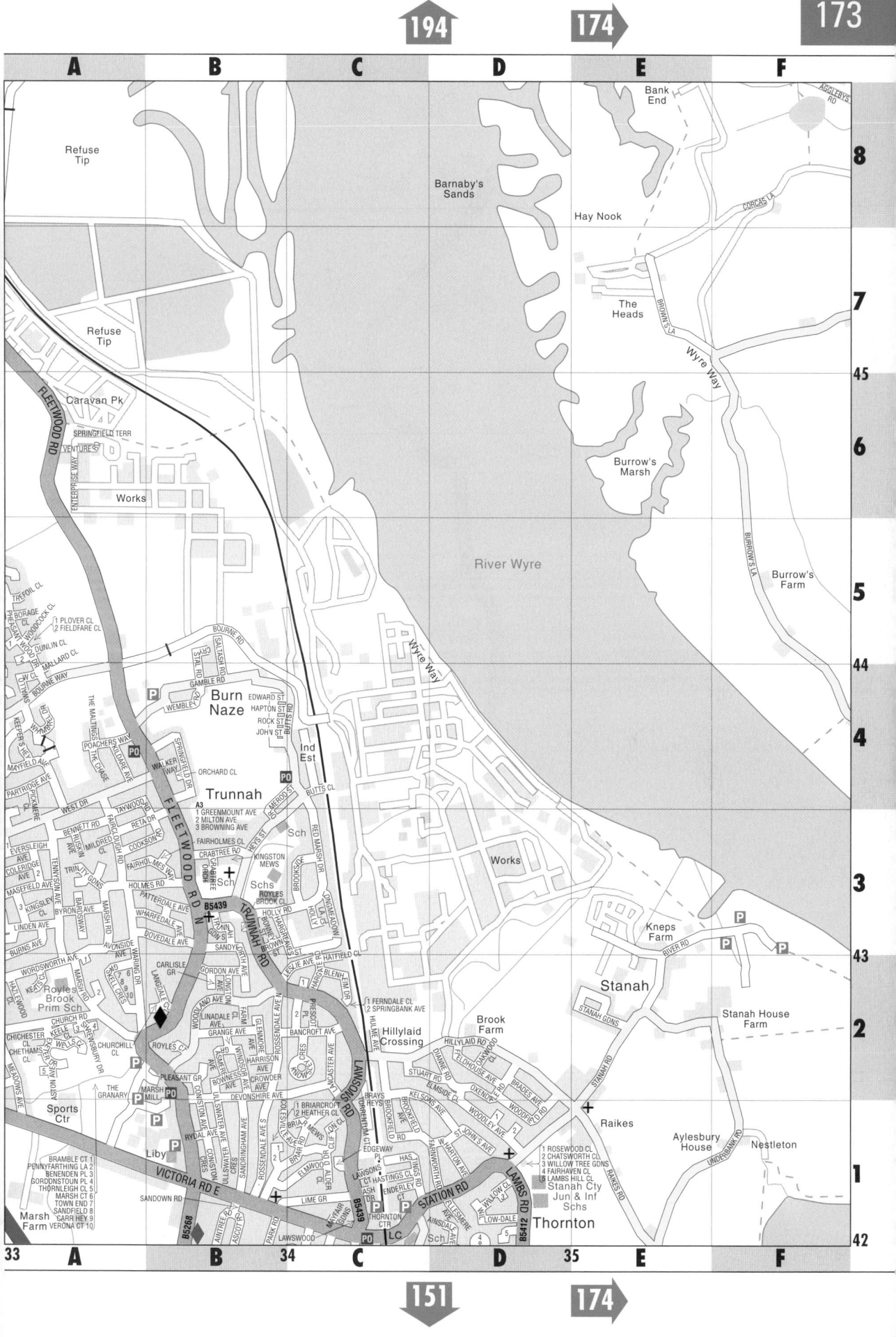

173
195

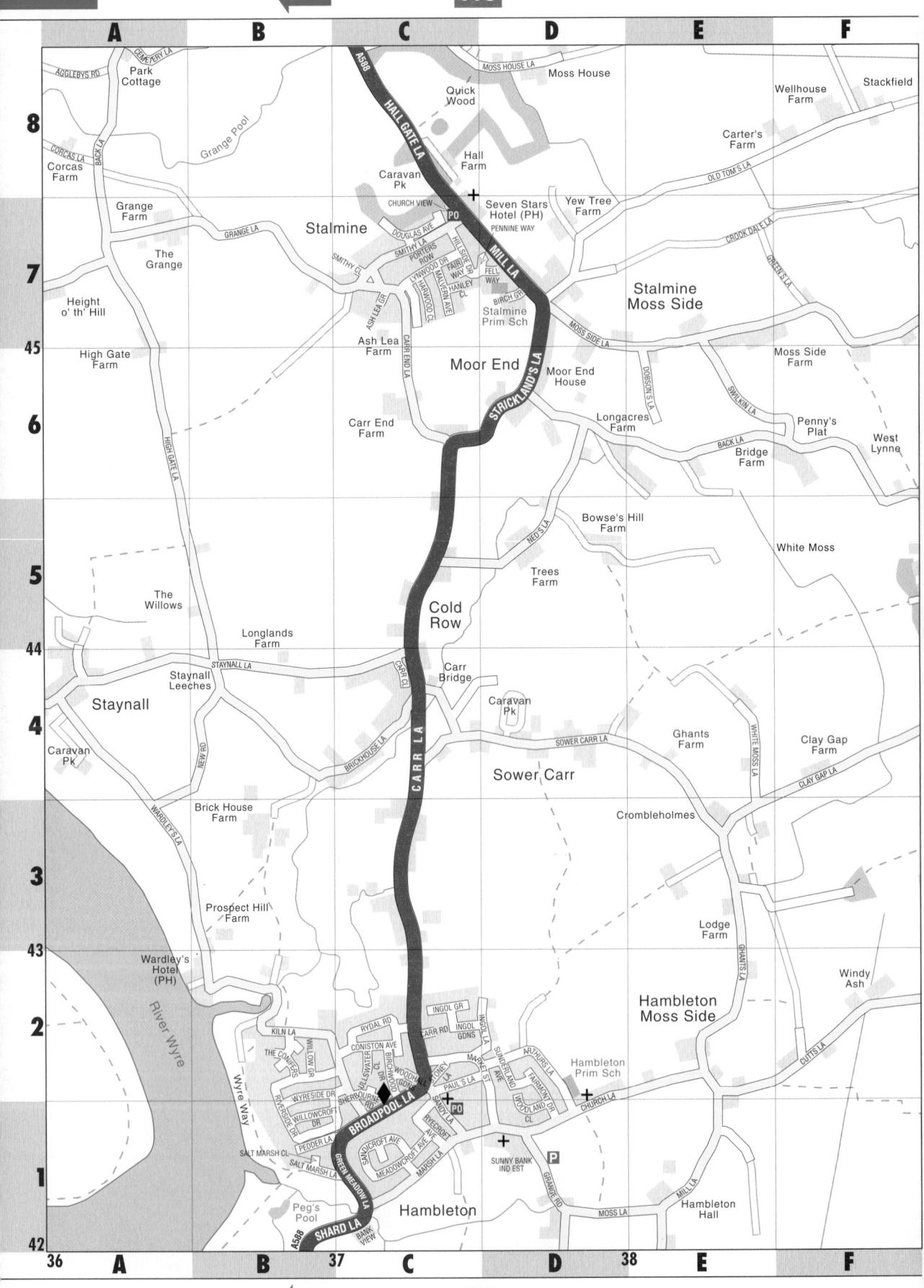

173
152

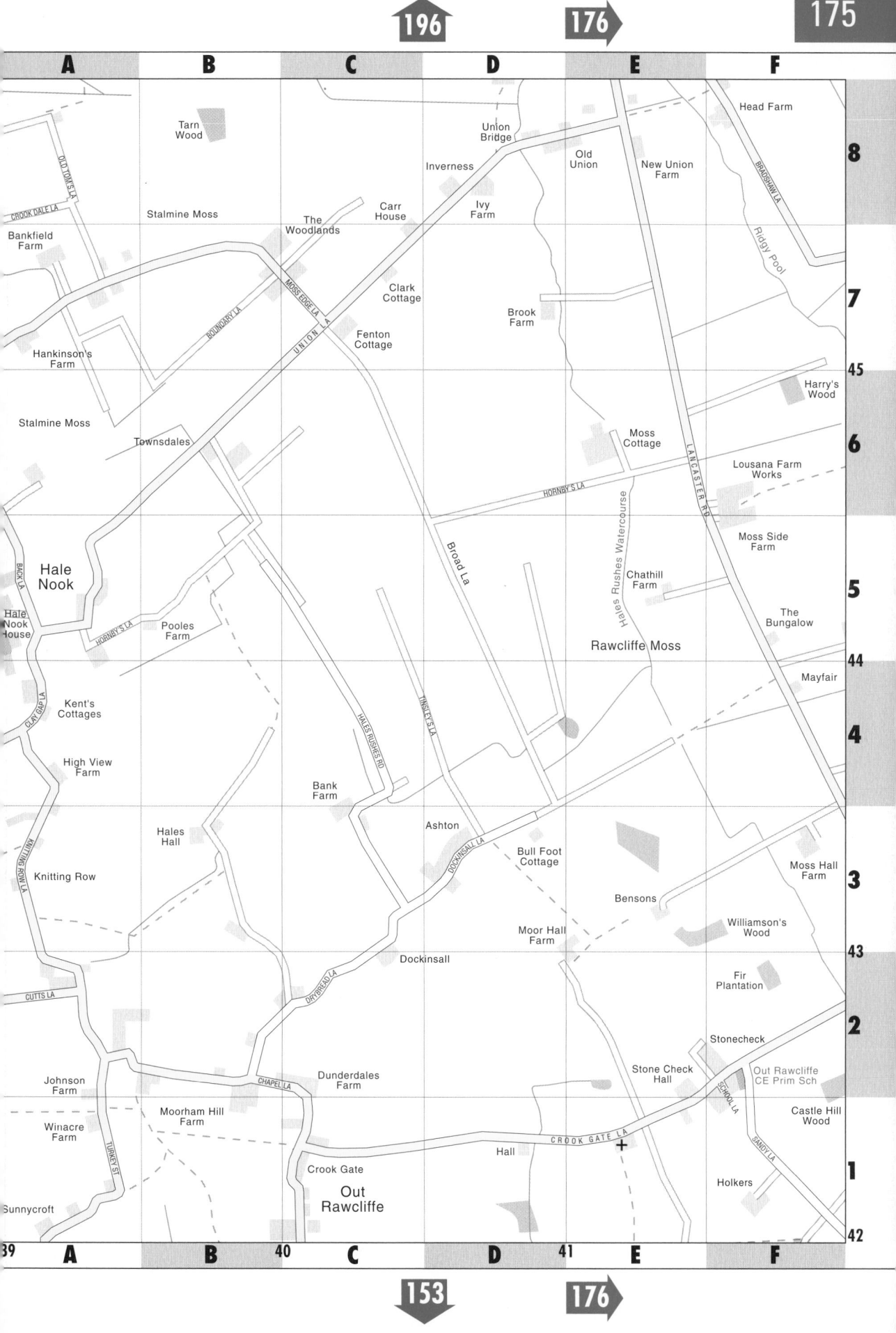

A B C D E F

8
7
45
6
5
44
4
3
43
2
1
42

Head Farm
Tarn Wood
Union Bridge
Inverness
Old Union
New Union Farm
Stalmine Moss
Carr House
The Woodlands
Ivy Farm
Bankfield Farm
Clark Cottage
Brook Farm
Fenton Cottage
Hankinson's Farm
Harry's Wood
Stalmine Moss
Townsdales
Moss Cottage
Lousana Farm Works
Hornby's La
Moss Side Farm
Broad La
Chathill Farm
Rawcliffe Moss
Hale Nook
The Bungalow
Hale Nook House
Pooles Farm
Hornby's La
Mayfair
Kent's Cottages
High View Farm
Hales Rushes Rd
Tinsley's La
Bank Farm
Ashton
Hales Hall
Moss Hall Farm
Bull Foot Cottage
Knitting Row
Dockinsall La
Bensons
Williamson's Wood
Moor Hall Farm
Fir Plantation
Dockinsall
Drybread La
Cutts La
Stonecheck
Johnson Farm
Dunderdales Farm
Stone Check Hall
Out Rawcliffe CE Prim Sch
Chapel La
School La
Castle Hill Wood
Moorham Hill Farm
Winacre Farm
Crook Gate La
Sandy La
Turkey St
Hall
Holkers
Crook Gate
Out Rawcliffe
Sunnycroft

Old Tom's La
Crook Dale La
Moss Edge La
Union La
Boundary La
Back La
Clay Gap La
Knitting Row La
Bradshaw La
Ridgy Pool
Lancaster Rd
Hales Rushes Watercourse

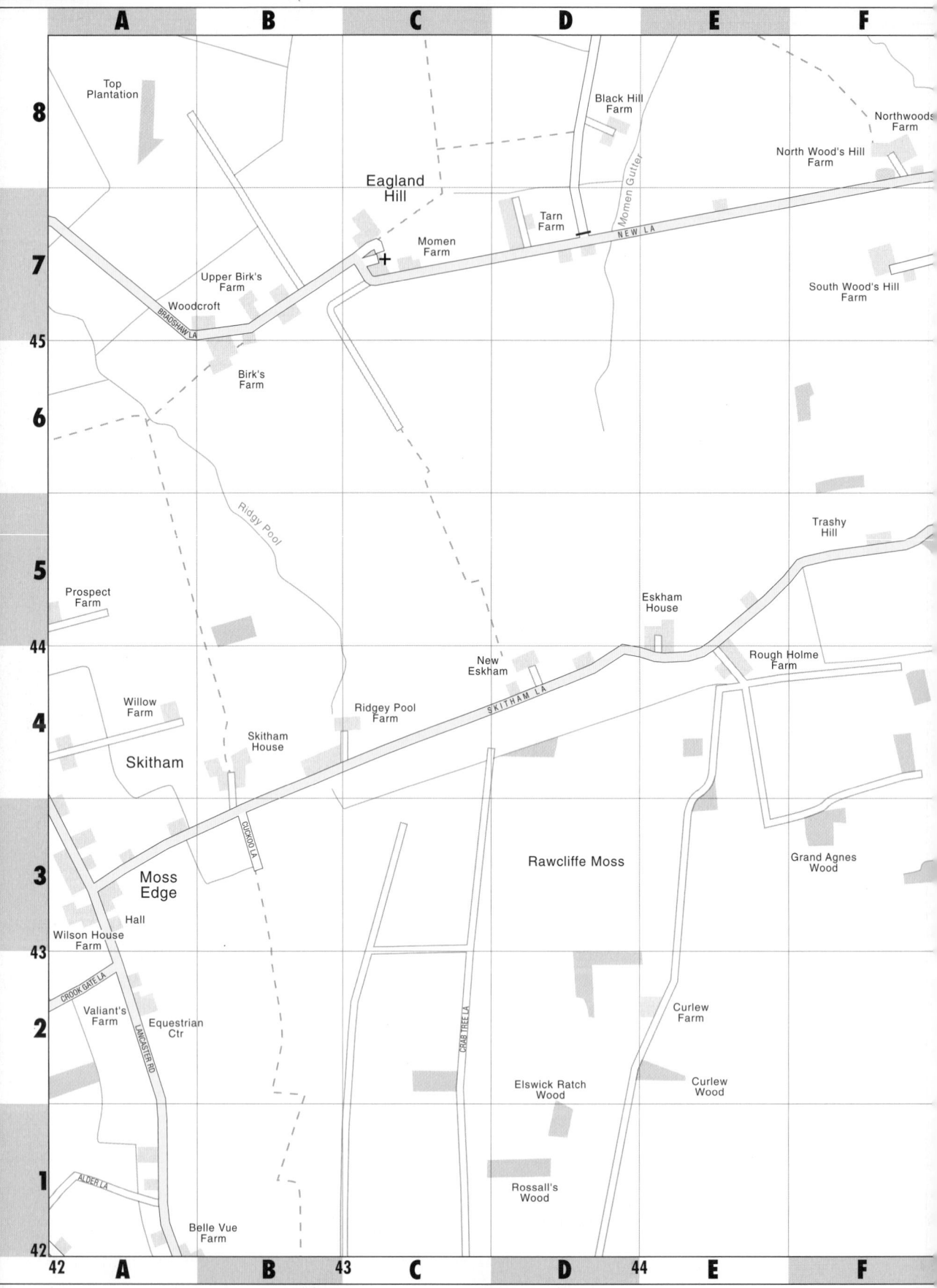

175
197

A B C D E F

8

Top
Plantation

Black Hill
Farm

Northwoods
Farm

North Wood's Hill
Farm

Eagland
Hill

Momen Gutter

Tarn
Farm

NEW LA

7

Upper Birk's
Farm

Momen
Farm

South Wood's Hill
Farm

BRADSHAW LA

Woodcroft

45

Birk's
Farm

6

Ridgy Pool

Trashy
Hill

5

Prospect
Farm

Eskham
House

44

New
Eskham

Rough Holme
Farm

SKITHAM LA

Willow
Farm

Ridgey Pool
Farm

4

Skitham
House

Skitham

CUCKOO LA

Rawcliffe Moss

Grand Agnes
Wood

3

Moss
Edge

Hall

Wilson House
Farm

43

CROOK GATE LA

Curlew
Farm

Valiant's
Farm

LANCASTER RD

Equestrian
Ctr

CRAB TREE LA

2

Elswick Ratch
Wood

Curlew
Wood

1

ALDER LA

Rossall's
Wood

Belle Vue
Farm

42

42 A B 43 C D 44 E F

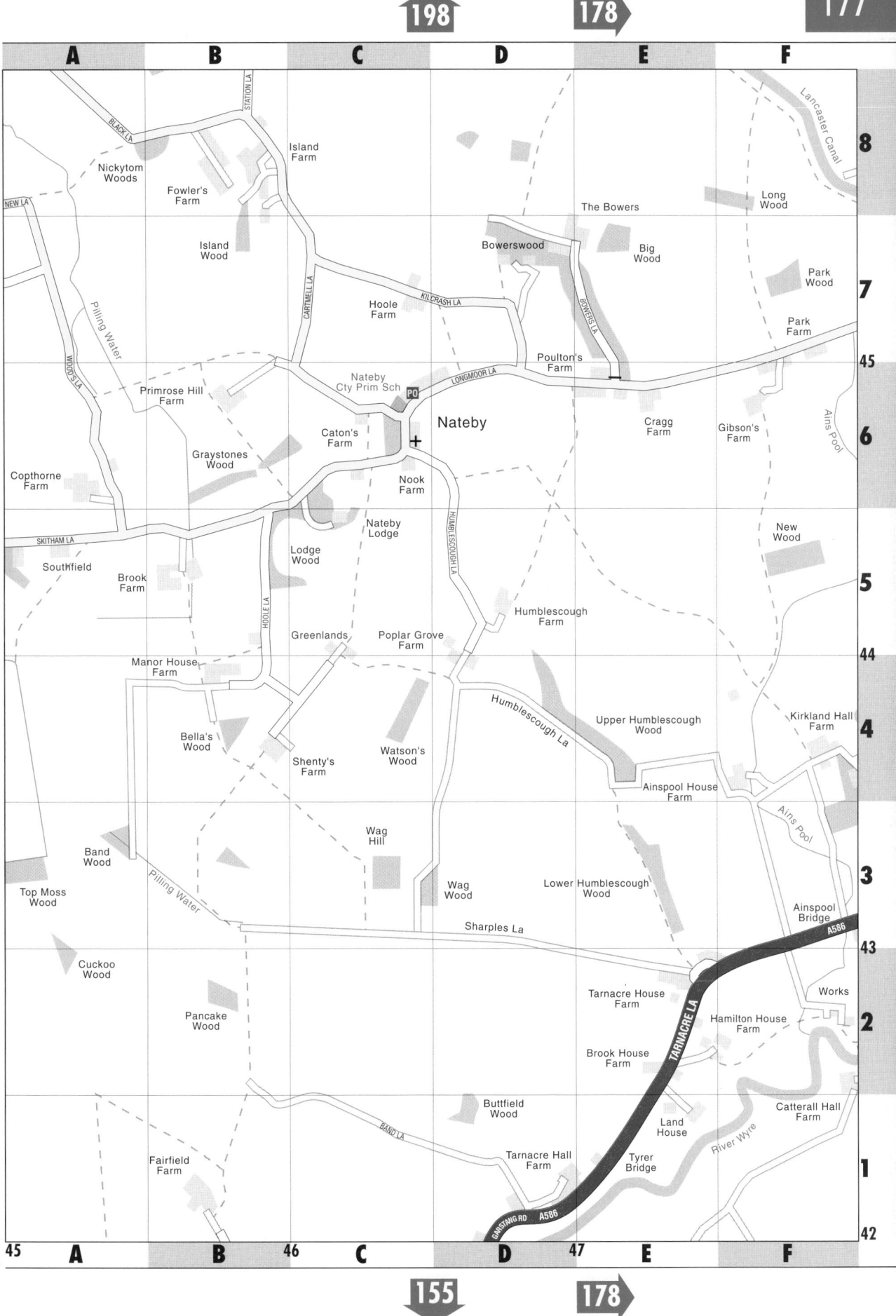

A B C D E F

8

7

45

6

5

44

4

3

43

2

1

42

Nickytom Woods

Island Farm

Fowler's Farm

Island Wood

BLACK LA

NEW LA

STATION LA

CARTMELL LA

KILCRASH LA

Hoole Farm

The Bowers

Bowerswood

Big Wood

Long Wood

Park Wood

BOWERS LA

Park Farm

Pilling Water

WOOD'S LA

Primrose Hill Farm

Nateby Cty Prim Sch

PO

LONGMOOR LA

Poulton's Farm

Ains Pool

Copthorne Farm

Caton's Farm

Nateby

Graystones Wood

Nook Farm

Cragg Farm

Gibson's Farm

SKITHAM LA

Southfield

Brook Farm

Lodge Wood

HOOLE LA

Nateby Lodge

HUMBLESCOUGH LA

Humblescough Farm

New Wood

Greenlands

Poplar Grove Farm

Manor House Farm

Bella's Wood

Shenty's Farm

Watson's Wood

Humblescough La

Upper Humblescough Wood

Kirkland Hall Farm

Ainspool House Farm

Ains Pool

Band Wood

Pilling Water

Wag Hill

Wag Wood

Lower Humblescough Wood

Ainspool Bridge

A586

Top Moss Wood

Cuckoo Wood

Sharples La

43

Tarnacre House Farm

TARNACRE LA

Works

Pancake Wood

Hamilton House Farm

Brook House Farm

BAND LA

Buttfield Wood

Land House

River Wyre

Catterall Hall Farm

Fairfield Farm

Tarnacre Hall Farm

Tyrer Bridge

GARSTANG RD

A586

45 A 46 B C 47 D E F

Lancaster Canal

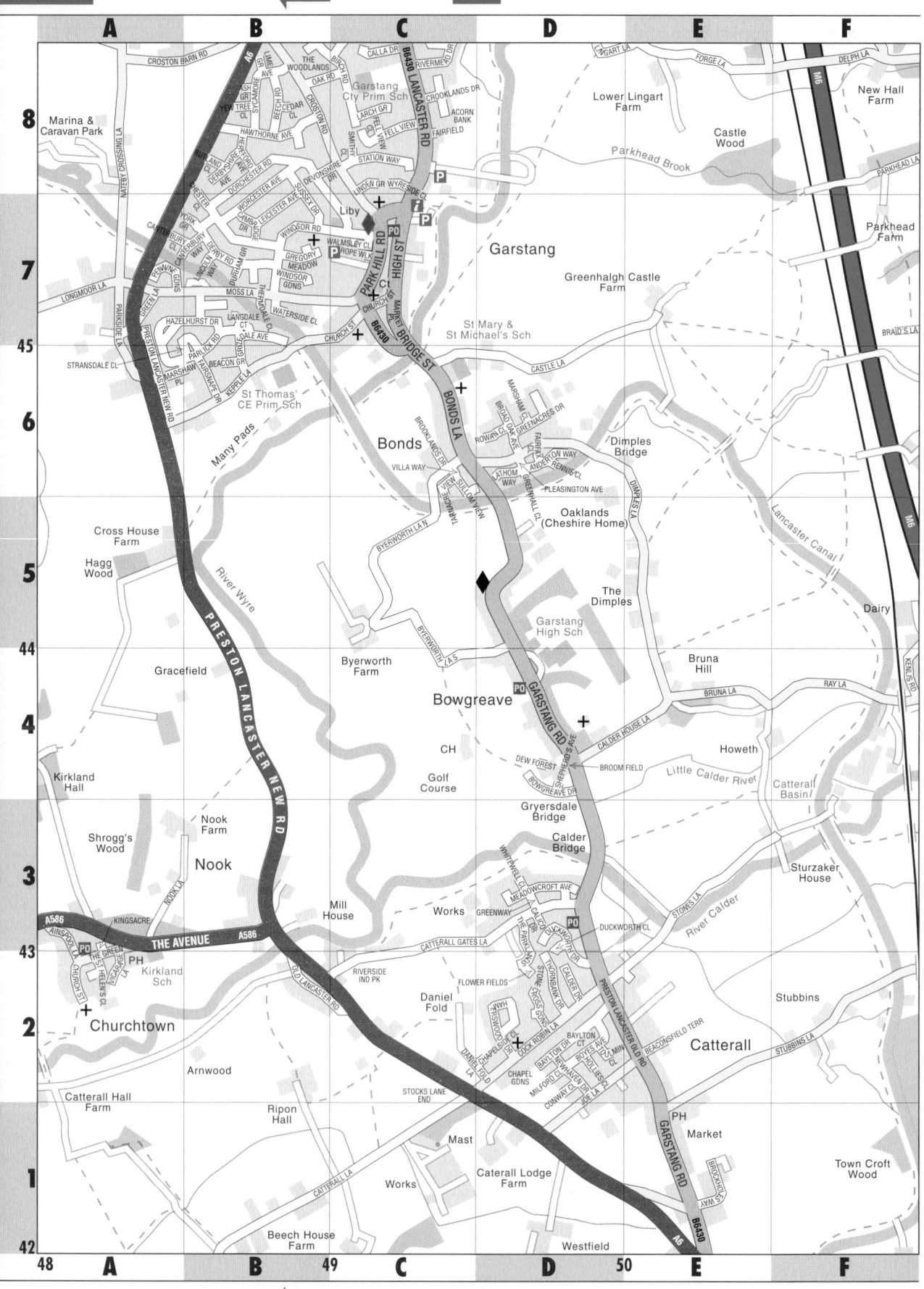

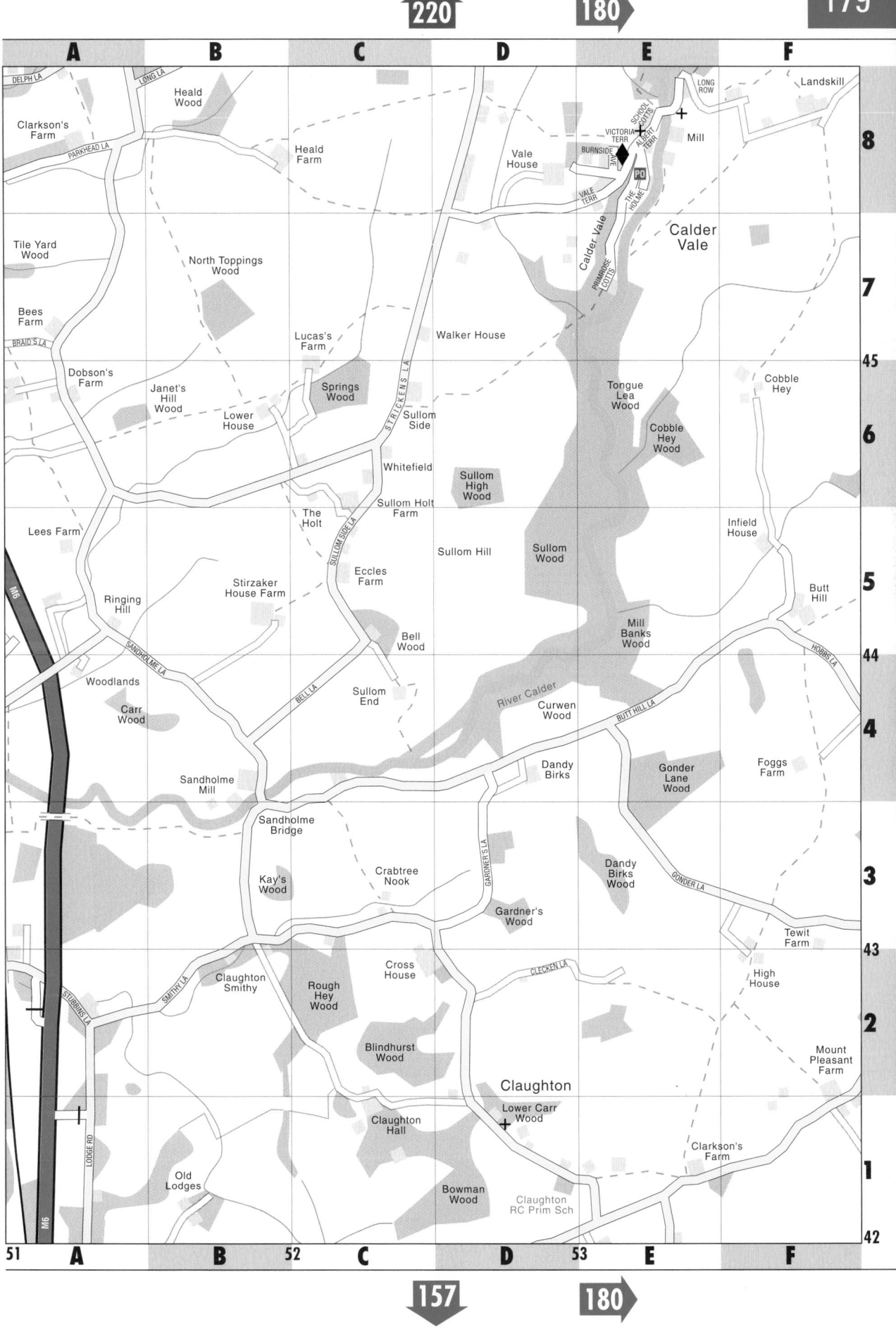

220

180

DELPH LA
LONG LA
Heald
Wood
Clarkson's
Farm
PARKHEAD LA
Heald
Farm
Vale
House
SCHOOL
COTTS
Mill
LONG
ROW
Landskill
VICTORIA
TERR
ALBERT
TERR
BURNSIDE
AVE
THE
HOLMS
PO
VALE
TERR
Calder
Vale

8

Tile Yard
Wood
North Toppings
Wood
Calder Vale
PRIMROSE
COTTS

7

Bees
Farm
BRAID'S LA
Dobson's
Farm
Lucas's
Farm
Walker House
Tongue
Lea
Wood
Cobble
Hey

45

Janet's
Hill
Wood
Springs
Wood
STRICKENS LA
Sullom
Side
Cobble
Hey
Wood

6

Lower
House
Whitefield
Sullom
High
Wood

Lees Farm
The
Holt
SULLOM SIDE LA
Sullom Holt
Farm
Sullom Hill
Sullom
Wood
Infield
House

Stirzaker
House Farm
Eccles
Farm
Butt
Hill

5

Ringing
Hill
Mill
Banks
Wood
HOBBS LA

44

Woodlands
SANDHOLME LA
BELL LA
Bell
Wood
River Calder
Curwen
Wood
BUTT HILL LA

Carr
Wood
Sullom
End

4

Sandholme
Mill
Dandy
Birks
Gonder
Lane
Wood
Foggs
Farm

M6

Sandholme
Bridge
GARDNER'S LA
Dandy
Birks
Wood
GONDER LA

3

Kay's
Wood
Crabtree
Nook
Gardner's
Wood
Tewit
Farm

43

Claughton
Smithy
SMITH LA
Rough
Hey
Wood
Cross
House
CLECKEN LA
High
House

2

STUBBINS LA
Blindhurst
Wood
Claughton
Lower Carr
Wood
Clarkson's
Farm

LODGE RD
Claughton
Hall
Mount
Pleasant
Farm

1

Old
Lodges
Bowman
Wood
Claughton
RC Prim Sch

M6

157

180

179
220

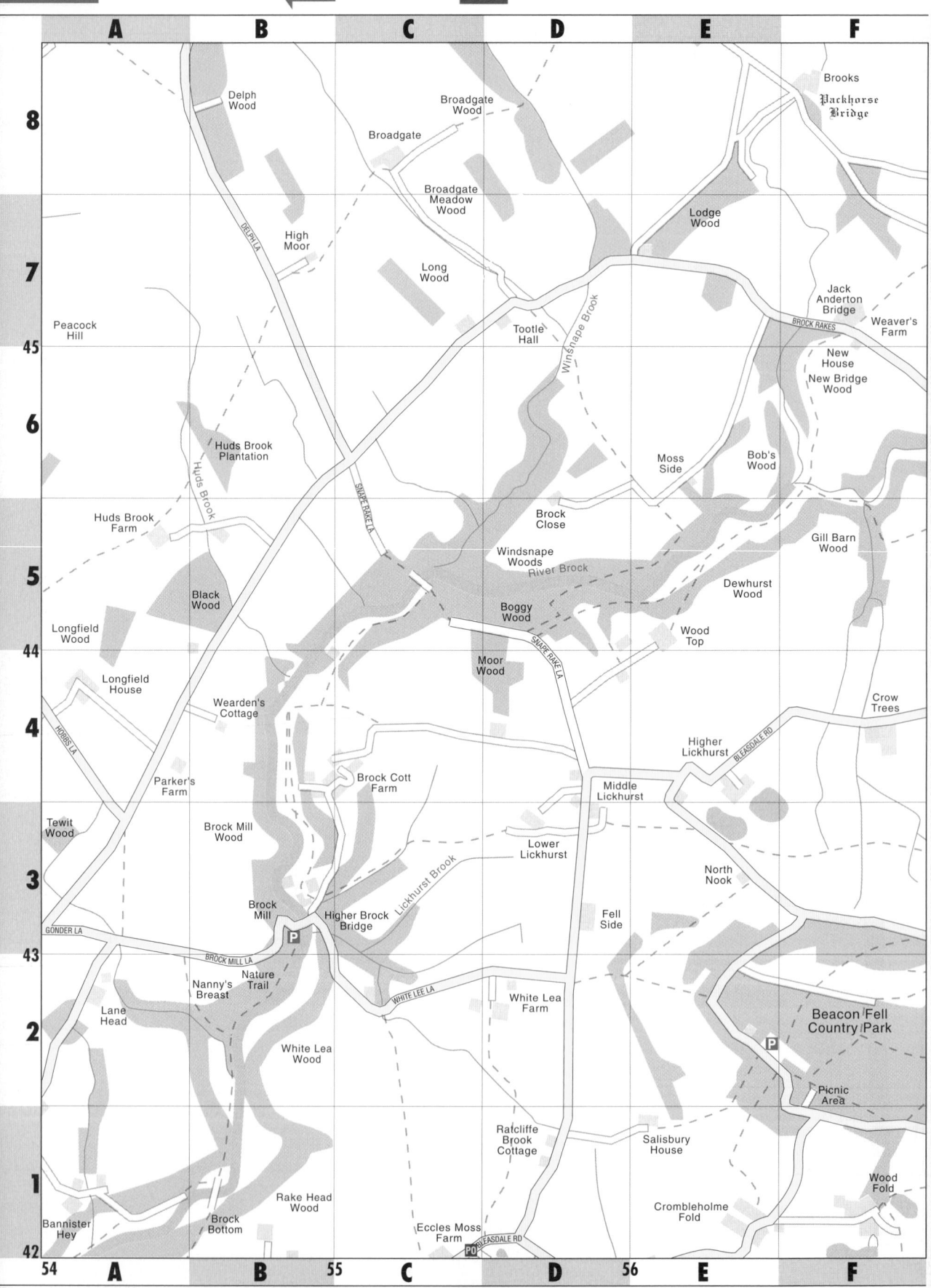

179
158

221
182

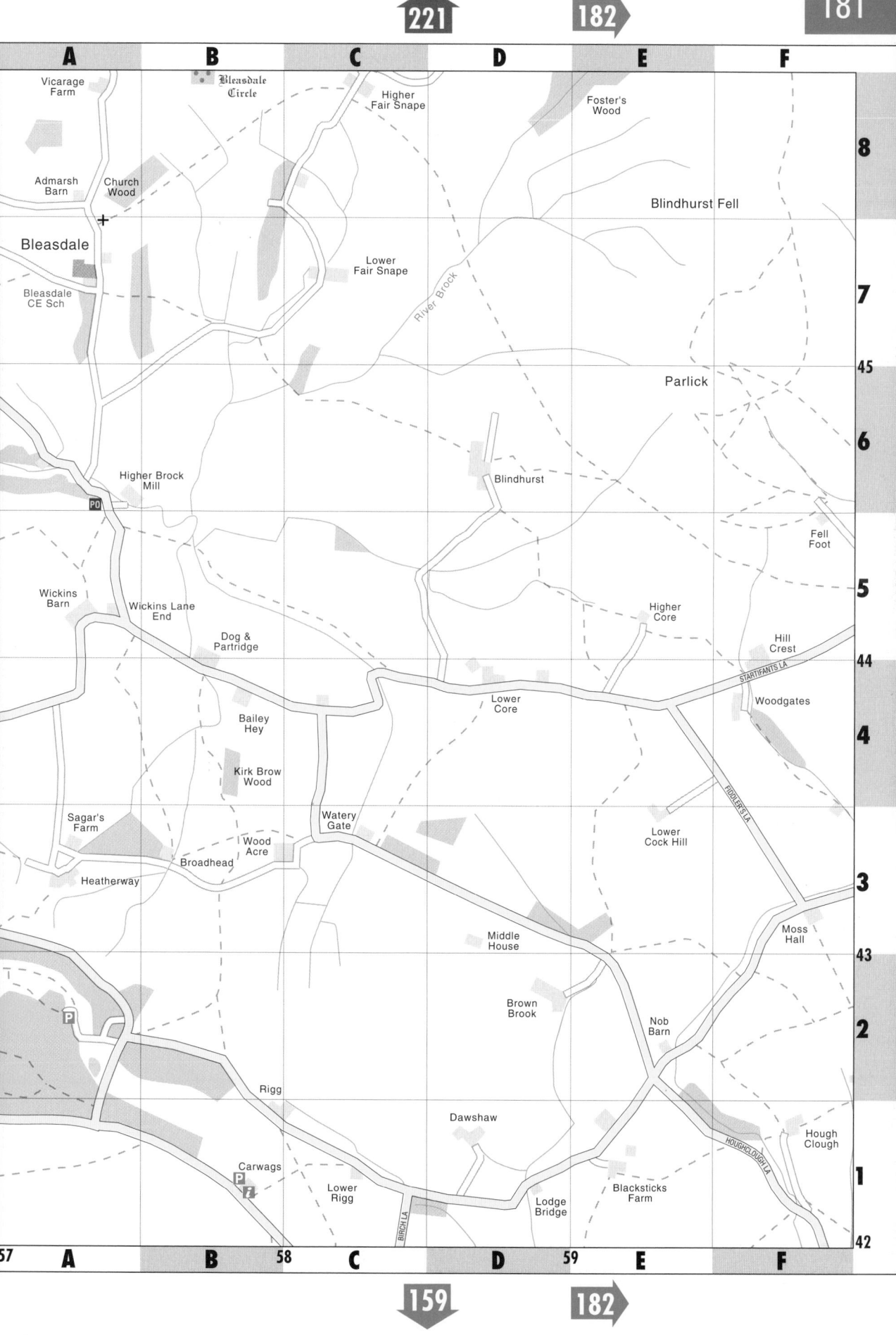

A B C D E F

8

7

45

6

5

44

4

3

43

2

1

42

Ward's End

Stanley

Ginney Hey

Park Gate

Greenough Clough

High Barn

Chipping Brook

Saddle End Farm

Dobson's Brook

Birchen Lee

Wolfen Hall

Bradley

Windy Hill Farm

Laund Farm

Wolfen Hall Plantation

Peacock Hey Farm

Leagram Hall

STARTIFANTS LANE END

Nan King's Farm

STARTIFANTS LA

Windy Harbour

FISH HOUSE LA

Fish House

After Lee

TWEEDY CT

Works

Works

Crag House

Out Lane Head

Lingey Hill

Clark House

OLD HIVE

MALT KILN BROW

CHURCH RAIKE

PH

Springs House

KIRKFIELD

KIRKLANDS

CLUB LA

P

TALBOT ST

PO

WINDY ST

STANLEY CT

GREEN LA

Green Slack

P

St Mary's Prim Sch

Chipping

BROAD MEADOW

Brabins Endowed Sch

BROOKFIELD CT

BROOKLANDS

Handlesteads Farm

COLLIN'S HILL LA

Ferry Butts

Blackhall

GARSTANG RD

Cold Coates

Cuthbert Hill

Isaac's Farm

Chipping Brook

LONGRIDGE RD

Startifants

Richmond Houses

Holton Hill

Daub Hall

New House

Sewage Works

Abbot Barn

BLACK HOUSE LA

PARSONAGE LA

Radcliffe Hall

Chipping Dairy

Hall Trees Farm

Dairy Farm

MOSS LA

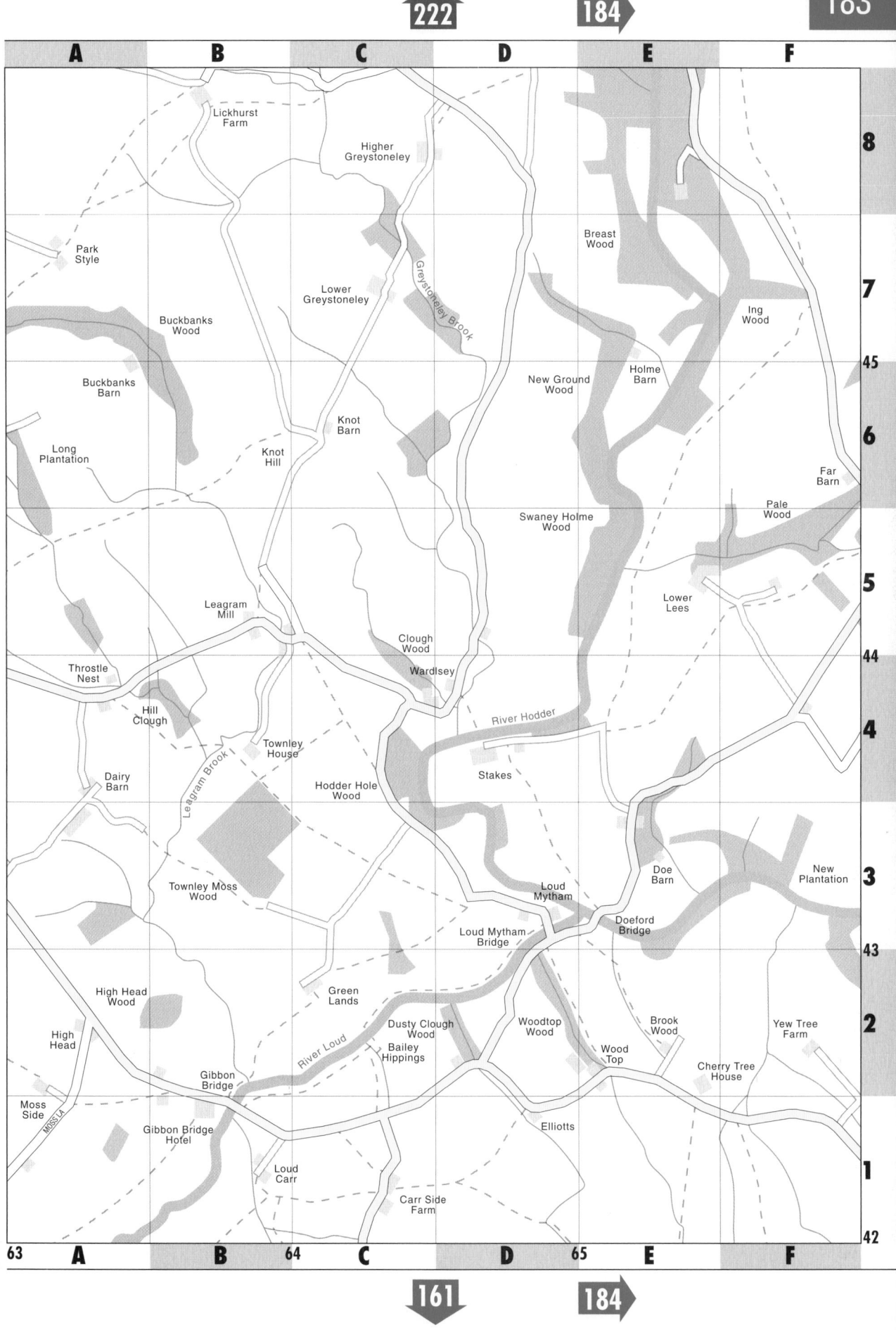

A B C D E F

8

Lickhurst
Farm

Higher
Greystoneley

Park
Style

7

45

Lower
Greystoneley

Breast
Wood

Ing
Wood

Buckbanks
Wood

Greystoneley Brook

New Ground
Wood

Holme
Barn

Buckbanks
Barn

6

Knot
Barn

Far
Barn

Long
Plantation

Knot
Hill

Swaney Holme
Wood

Pale
Wood

5

Leagram
Mill

Lower
Lees

44

Clough
Wood

Throstle
Nest

Wardlsey

River Hodder

4

Hill
Clough

Leagram Brook

Townley
House

Hodder Hole
Wood

Stakes

Dairy
Barn

New
Plantation

3

Doe
Barn

Townley Moss
Wood

Loud
Mytham

Doeford
Bridge

43

Loud Mytham
Bridge

Green
Lands

High Head
Wood

Dusty Clough
Wood

Woodtop
Wood

Brook
Wood

Yew Tree
Farm

2

High
Head

River Loud

Bailey
Hippings

Wood
Top

Cherry Tree
House

Moss
Side

MOSS LA

Gibbon
Bridge

Gibbon Bridge
Hotel

Elliotts

1

Loud
Carr

Carr Side
Farm

42

183
222

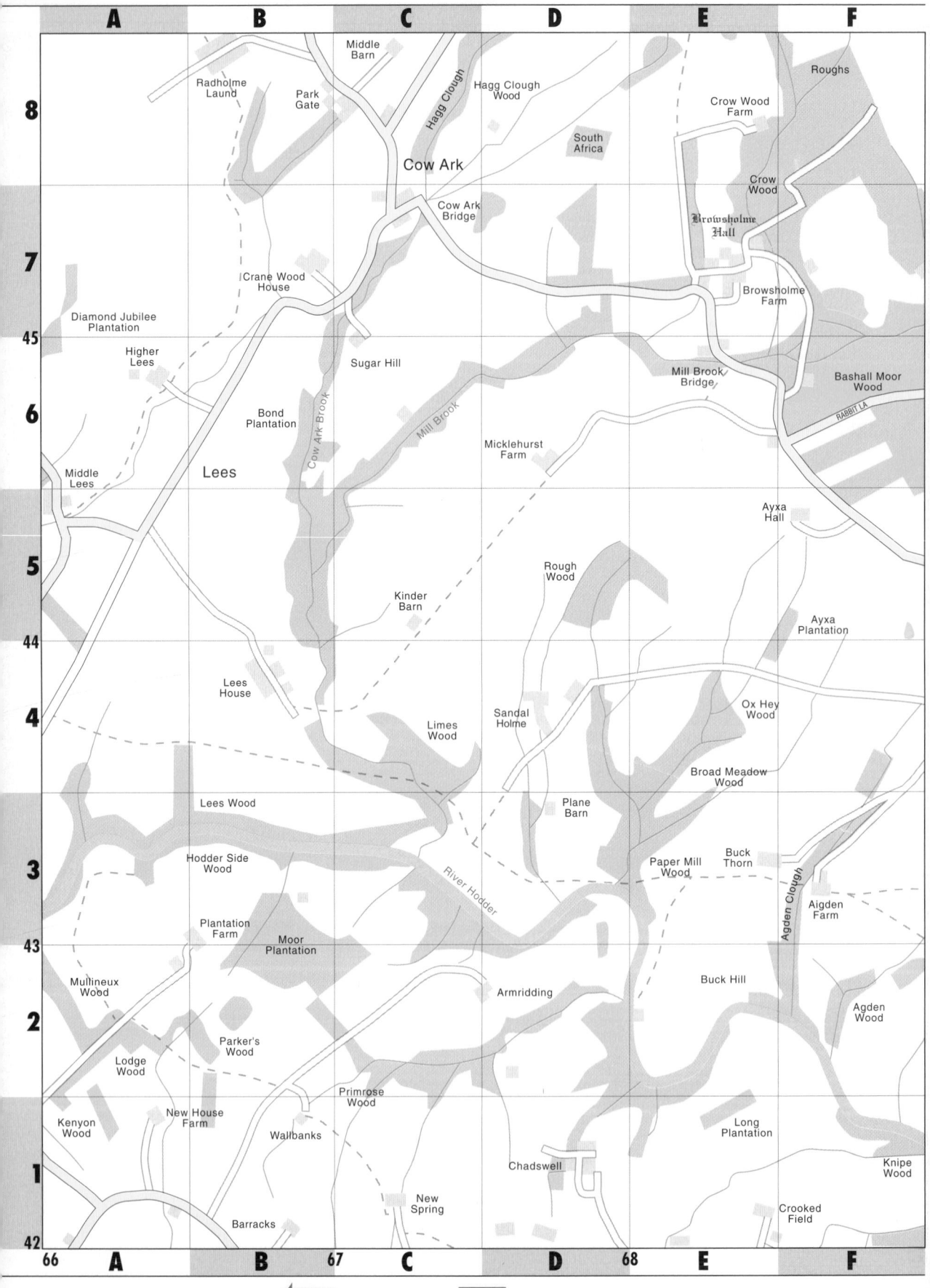

183
162

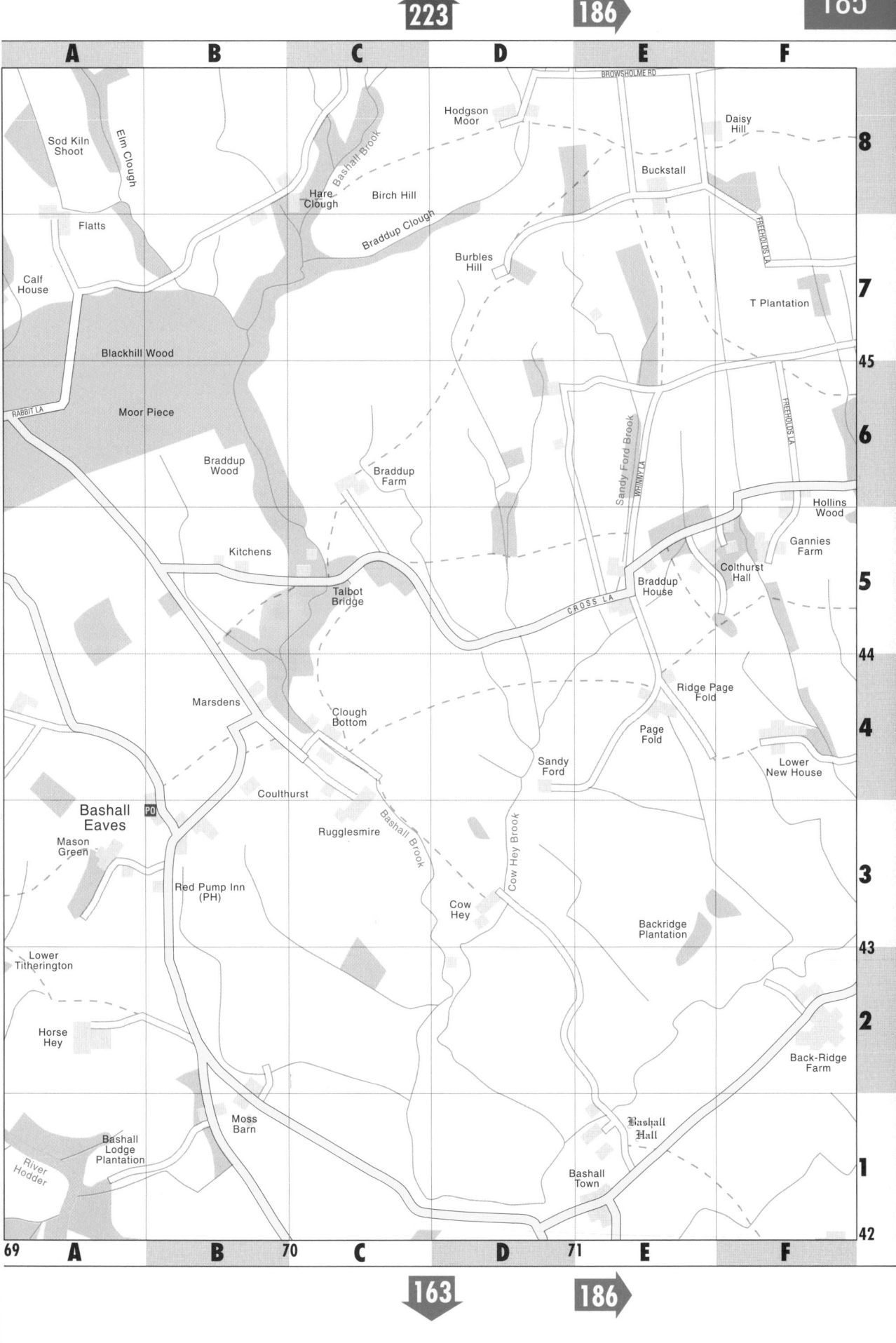

A B C D E F

8
7
45
6
5
44
4
43
2
1
42

69 70 71

Sod Kiln Shoot
Elm Clough
Flatts
Calf House
Blackhill Wood
RABBIT LA
Moor Piece
Braddup Wood
Kitchens
Talbot Bridge
Marsdens
Clough Bottom
Coulthurst
Bashall Eaves
Mason Green
PO
Red Pump Inn (PH)
Ruggatesmire
Lower Titherington
Horse Hey
Bashall Lodge Plantation
River Hodder
Moss Barn

Hare Clough
Bashall Brook
Birch Hill
Braddup Clough
Braddup Farm
Bashall Brook

Hodgson Moor
Burbles Hill
Sandy Ford Brook
Cross La
Braddup House
Sandy Ford
Ridge Page Fold
Page Fold
Cow Hey Brook
Cow Hey
Backridge Plantation
Bashall Hall
Bashall Town

BROWSHOLME RD
Buckstall
Daisy Hill
FREEHOLDS LA
T Plantation
FREEHOLDS LA
Hollins Wood
Gannies Farm
Colthurst Hall
Whinny La
Lower New House
Back-Ridge Farm

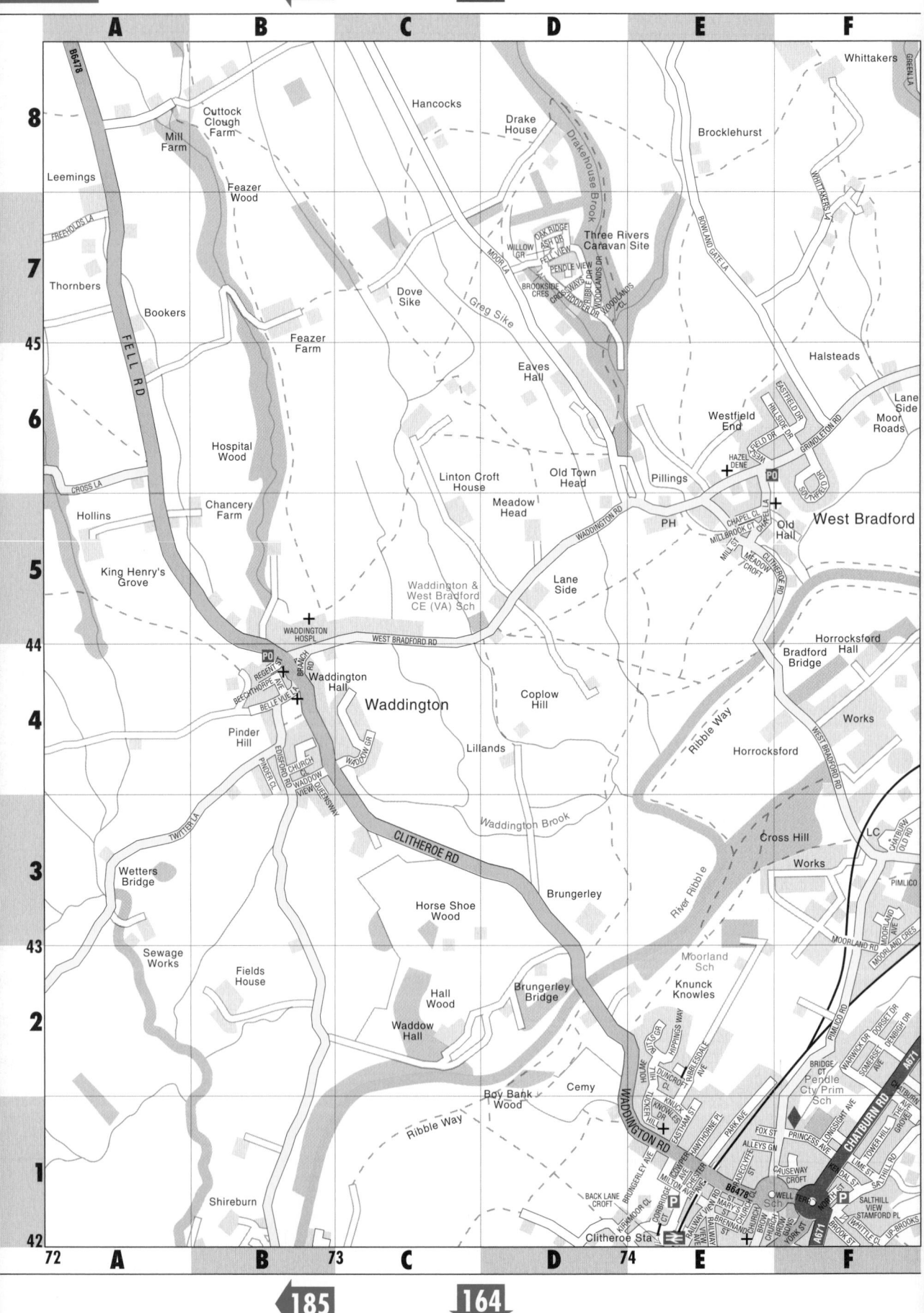

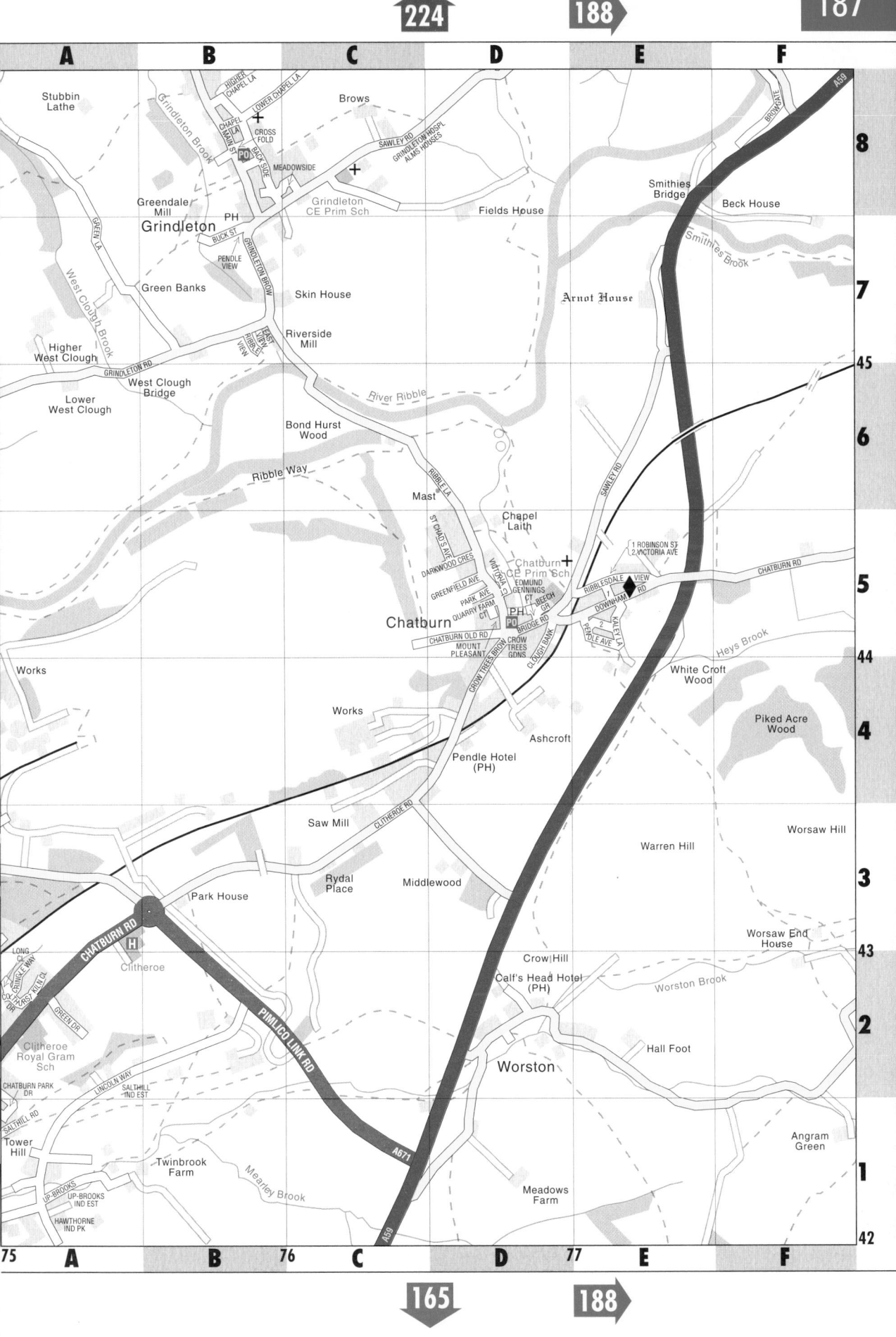

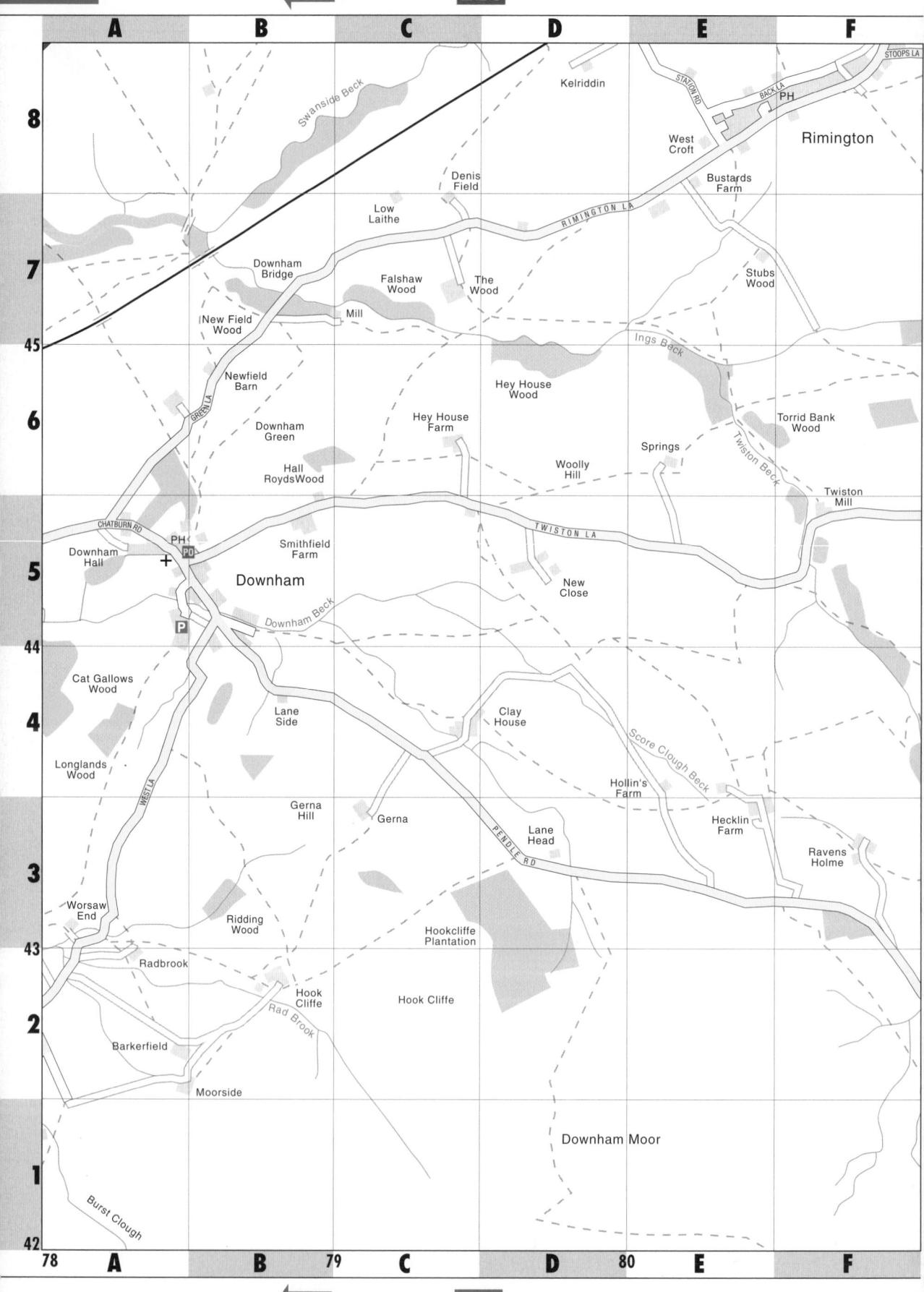

8

Swanside Beck

Kelriddin

Station Rd · Back La · PH
Stoops La

West Croft
Rimington

Denis Field

Bustards Farm

Low Laithe

Rimington La

Downham Bridge

7

Falshaw Wood

The Wood

Stubs Wood

New Field Wood

Mill

45

Ings Beck

Newfield Barn

Green La

Hey House Wood

6

Downham Green

Hey House Farm

Torrid Bank Wood

Hall Royds Wood

Woolly Hill

Springs

Twiston Beck

Twiston Mill

Chatburn Rd

Twiston La

Downham Hall

PH PO

Smithfield Farm

Downham

New Close

5

P

44

Downham Beck

Cat Gallows Wood

Lane Side

Clay House

Score Clough Beck

4

West La

Longlands Wood

Hollin's Farm

Hecklin Farm

Gerna Hill

Gerna

Lane Head

Pendle Rd

Ravens Holme

3

Worsaw End

Ridding Wood

Hookcliffe Plantation

43

Radbrook

Rad Brook

Hook Cliffe

Hook Cliffe

2

Barkerfield

Moorside

Downham Moor

1

Burst Clough

42

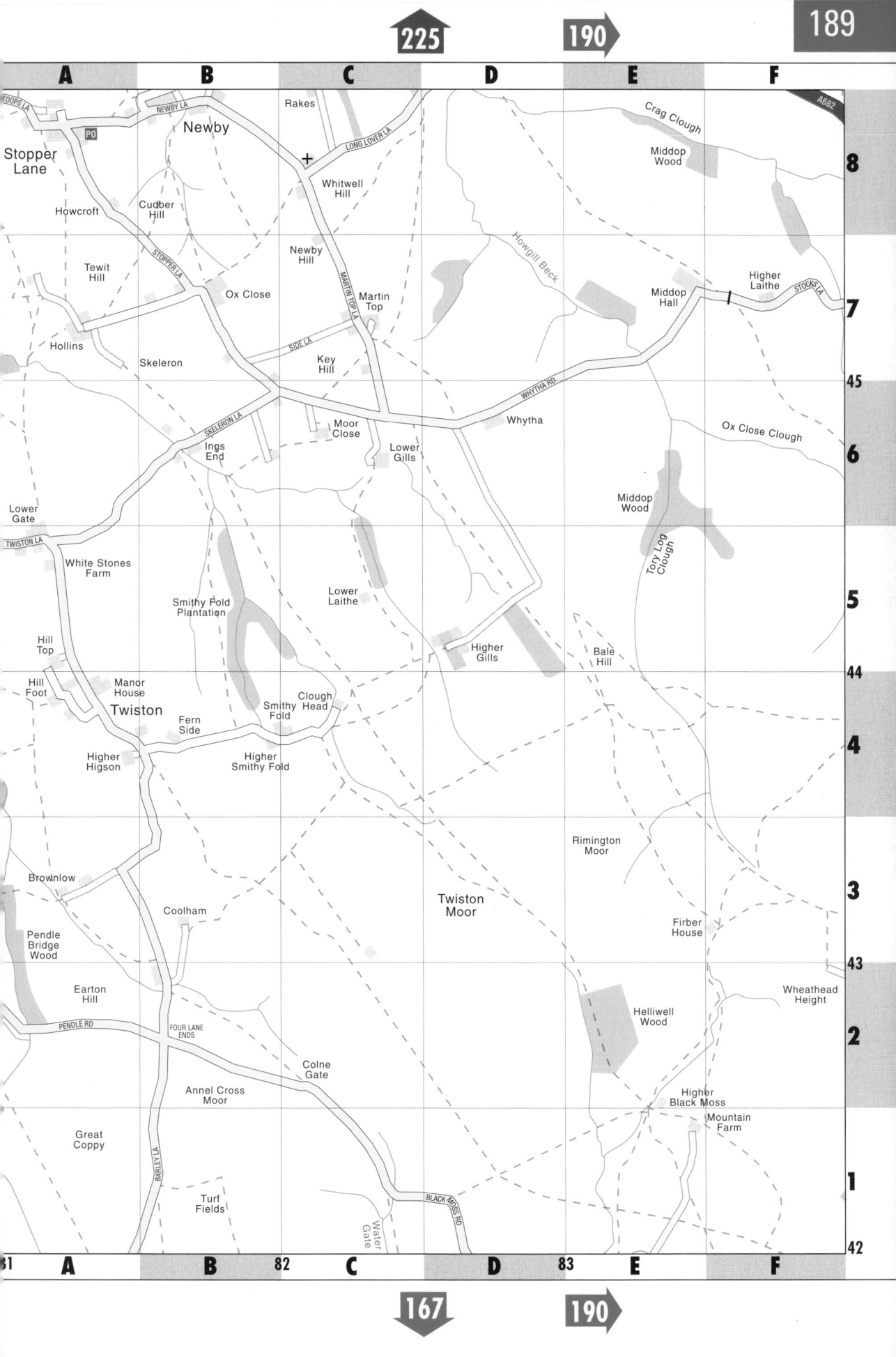

225
190

A B C D E F

A682

STOOPS LA

Stopper
Lane

PO

NEWBY LA

Newby

Rakes

Long Lover La

Crag Clough

Middop
Wood

8

Howcroft

Cudber
Hill

Whitwell
Hill

STOPPER LA

Tewit
Hill

Newby
Hill

Martin Top La

Howgill Beck

Higher
Laithe

Stocks La

Ox Close

Martin
Top

Middop
Hall

7

Hollins

SIDE LA

Key
Hill

45

Skeleron

SKELERON LA

Moor
Close

WHYTHA RD

Whytha

Ox Close Clough

6

Ings
End

Lower
Gills

Lower
Gate

TWISTON LA

Middop
Wood

White Stones
Farm

Smithy Fold
Plantation

Lower
Laithe

Tory Log Clough

5

Hill
Top

Higher
Gills

Bale
Hill

44

Hill
Foot

Manor
House

Clough
Head

Twiston

Fern
Side

Smithy
Fold

4

Higher
Higson

Higher
Smithy Fold

Rimington
Moor

Brownlow

Coolham

Twiston
Moor

Firber
House

3

Pendle
Bridge
Wood

43

Earton
Hill

Wheathead
Height

PENDLE RD

FOUR LANE
ENDS

Helliwell
Wood

2

BARLEY LA

Annel Cross
Moor

Colne
Gate

Higher
Black Moss

Mountain
Farm

Great
Coppy

Turf
Fields

BLACK MOSS RD

1

Water
Gate

42

81 A B 82 C D 83 E F

189
225

A   B   C   D   E   F

8
Little Middop
Lane Side
COAL PIT LA
BROGDEN LA
Higher Clough
Brown Hill
Far New Field Edge
Hill Cloughs
FOLLY LA

7
STOCKS LA
Stocks House
COAL PIT LA
New House
New Field Edge Hall Farm
Weets
Higher View Farm

45
GISBURN OLD RD
Ridge of Weets
Level of Weets
Weets Hill
Prospect House

6
Crag
Crag Clough
Duck Pond
FOLLY LA

5
Sunny Bank
Cold Weather House
Weets House Farm

44
Craven Laithe
Greystone Moor
Sandyford
Star Hall
LISTER WELL RD

4
Greystone
Pendle Way

3
Jackson Slack Hill
Burn Moor
Moorcock Inn (PH)
Admergill Pasture
Peel's House
GISBURN OLD RD
Wham Clough

43
Jackson's House
Wicken Clough
Greenbank Farm
Brown House

2
Burn Moor End
Admergill Water
Higher Admergill

1
Higher Wheathead
Claude's Clough
Lower Admergill Farm
Tower Farm
Stansfield Tower
Malkin Tower
Pasture Head Farm

Height House
Blacko Hill
A682
Blacko Hill Side
Hollin Hall

84   A   85   B   C   85   D   86   E   F

A682

189
168

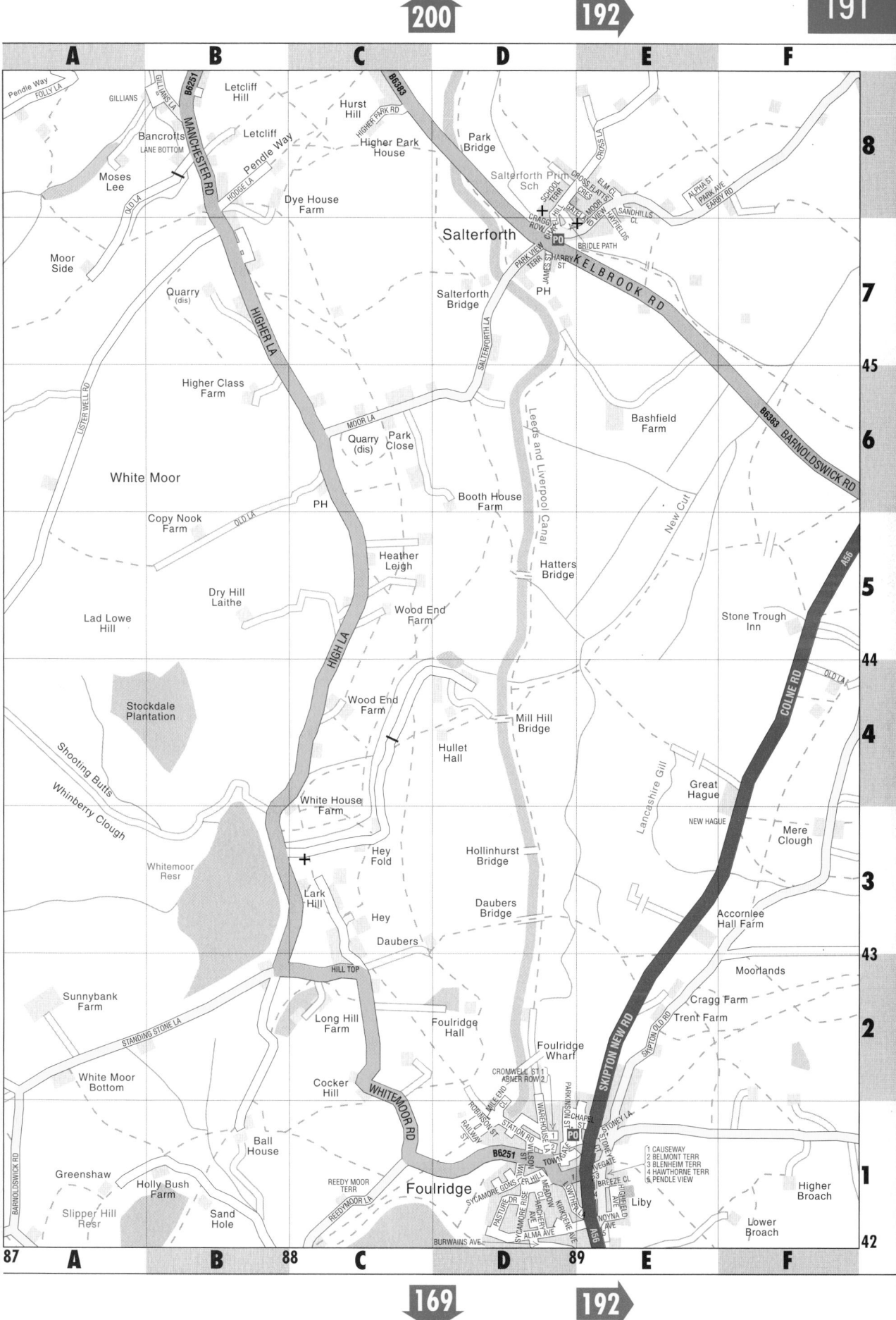

191 201

A B C D E F

8
Moor Hall
KEN WORTH
PARK SIDE
Higher Verjuice Bank
Sough
CLIFTON ST
HOLME CL
ARTHUR ST
SOUGH LA
New Cut
Bleara Moor
Bleara Lowe

7
COLNE RD
Sough Bridge
Tunstead Farm
Shuttleworth Moor
BLEARA RD
Bleara
Broom

45
CHURCH LA
Heads House
Kelbrook
HEADS LA
Copy House
Steney Bank Farm
Bleara Side

6
VICARAGE RD
Craven Heifer Inn
MAIN ST
HARDEN RD
HIGH FOLD
LOW FOLD
DOCLIFFE RD
Paris Farm
Pendle Way
Out Laithe
Harden Old House
PO
UNITY ST
SCHOOL ST
WATERLOO RD
Kelbrook Prim Sch
Harden Beck

5
A56
OVERMOOR DR
YELLOW HALL
OLD STONE TROUGH LA
Thick Bank
Harden New Hall
Brown Hill
Lower Burnt Hill
Higher Burnt Hill

44
OLD STONE BROW
Old Stone Trough
OLD LA
Moor Gate
Kitchen
Harden Clough

4
COB LA
Hard Clough
Roger Moor
Sheep Hill
Kelbrook Wood
Burnt Hill
Hague House
Kelbrook Moor
Scald Bank

3
Hague
Laycock
The Hill
Kelbrook Wood
Copy House
Hare & Hounds Inn (PH)
WARLEY WISE LA
BLACK LANE ENDS
Oxenards
Piked Edge

43
Ambwell
Earl Hall
Great Edge
Piked Edge
Throstle Nest
Shaw Clough

2
Noyna Hill
Noyna End
Great Edge
Jerusalem
Pasture
High Clough

1
Noyna Bottom
White House Farm
Close House
Cornshaw Brook
Flass Bent
Shaw Head Farm
SHAY HEAD COTTS
Shawhead Beck
Bent Laithe

42

90 A B 91 C D 92 E F

F2
1 WESTHEAD WLK
2 HATFIELD MEWS
3 GREGSON DR
4 EDMONDSEN PL
5 ARMISTEAD WAY
6 FORSHAW CL
7 CROOKALL CL
8 ARMISTEAD CT
9 NOBLETT CT

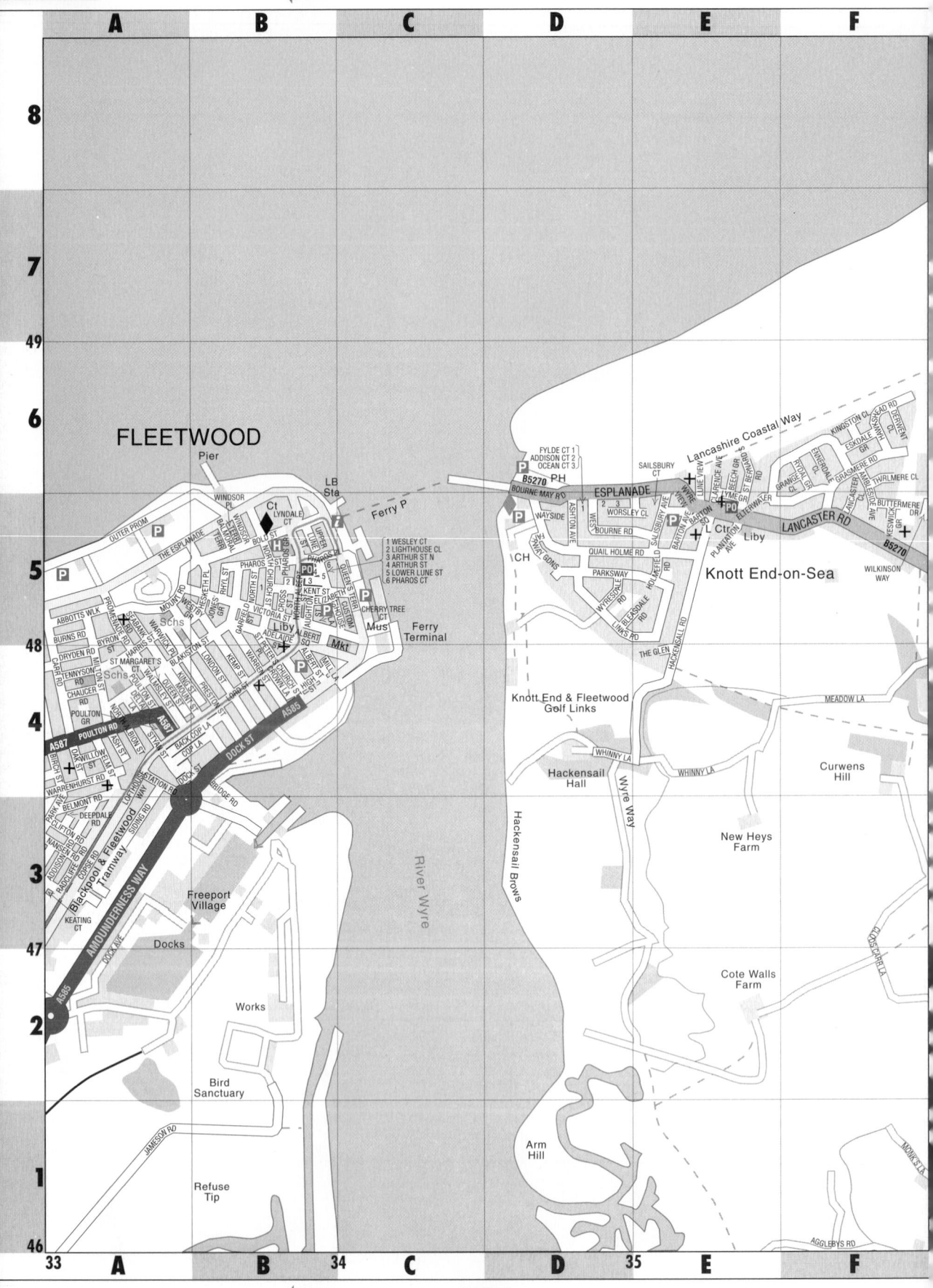

FLEETWOOD

Knott End-on-Sea

A	B	C	D	E	F

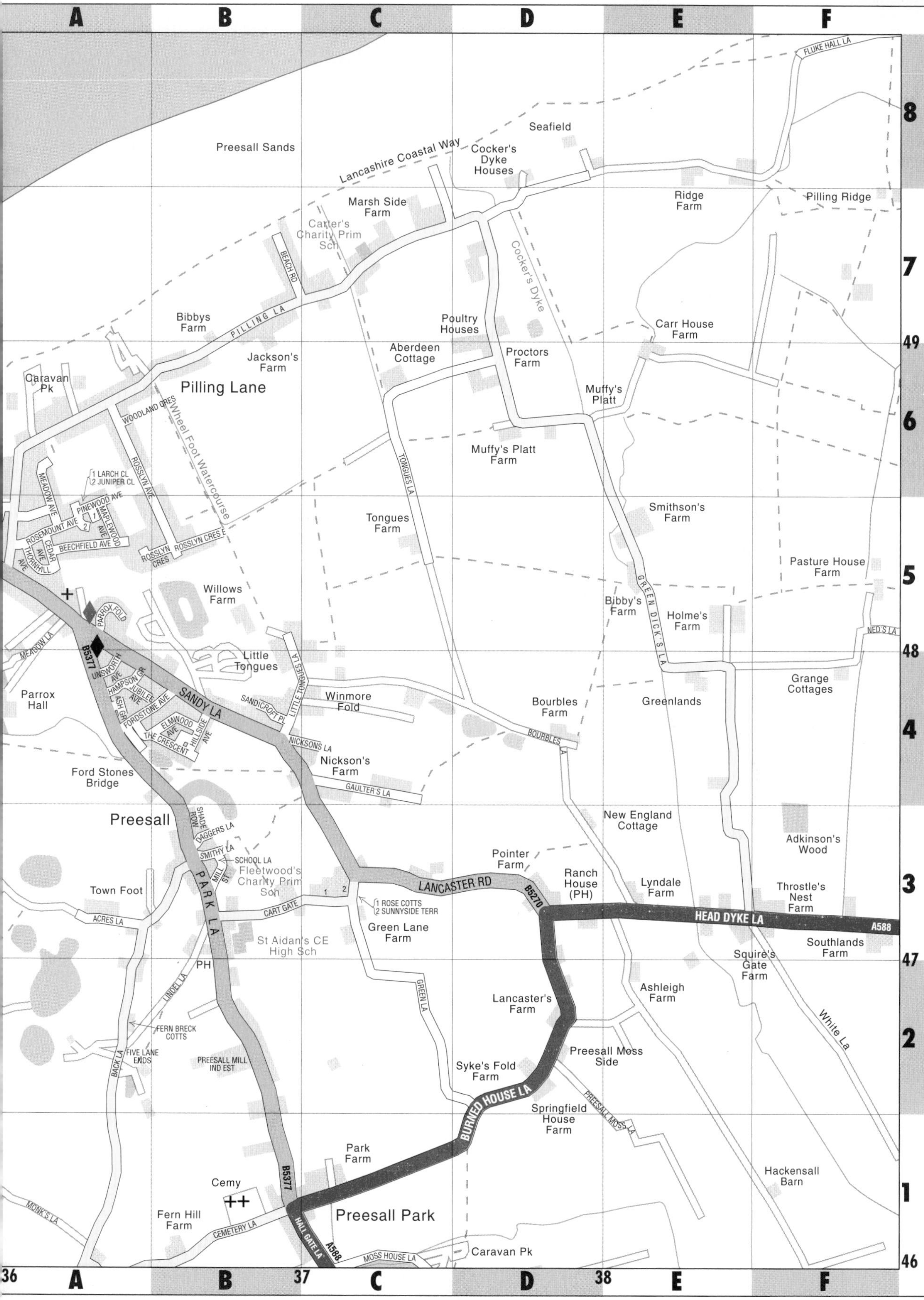

8

Fluke Hall La

Preesall Sands

Lancashire Coastal Way

Seafield

Cocker's Dyke Houses

Ridge Farm

Pilling Ridge

Marsh Side Farm

Carter's Charity Prim Sch

Beach Rd

Pilling La

7

Bibbys Farm

Jackson's Farm

Poultry Houses

Carr House Farm

49

Caravan Pk

Pilling Lane

Aberdeen Cottage

Proctors Farm

Muffy's Platt

6

Woodland Cres

Wheel Foot Watercourse

Rosslyn Ave

1 Larch Cl
2 Juniper Cl

Pinewood Ave

Maplewood Ave

Tongues La

Muffy's Platt Farm

Meadow Ave

Cedar Ave

Thornhill Ave

Rosemount Ave

Beechfield Ave

Rosslyn Cres

Rosslyn Cres E

Tongues Farm

Smithson's Farm

Green Dick's La

Pasture House Farm

5

Willows Farm

Bibby's Farm

Holme's Farm

Ned's La

Meadow La

Parrox Fold

Little Tongues

Little Tongues La

48

B5377

Unsworth

Parrox Hall

Hampson

Jubilee

Sandy La

Sandicroft Pl

Winmore Fold

Bourbles Farm

Greenlands

Grange Cottages

4

Ash La

Fordstone Ave

Elmwood Ave

The Crescent

Hillside Ave

Nicksons La

Nickson's Farm

Bourbles

Ford Stones Bridge

Gaulter's La

New England Cottage

Adkinson's Wood

3

Preesall

Shade Row

Daggers La

Smithy La

School La

Fleetwood's Charity Prim Sch

Pointer Farm

Ranch House (PH)

Lyndale Farm

Throstle's Nest Farm

Town Foot

Mill St

Park La

Cart Gate

Lancaster Rd

B5270

Head Dyke La

A588

Acres La

1 2

1 Rose Cotts
2 Sunnyside Terr

Green Lane Farm

St Aidan's CE High Sch

Green La

Ashleigh Farm

Squire's Gate Farm

Southlands Farm

47

Lindel La

PH

Lancaster's Farm

White La

2

Back La

Fern Breck Cotts

Five Lane Ends

Preesall Mill Ind Est

Syke's Fold Farm

Preesall Moss Side

Preesall Moss La

Hackensall Barn

Monk's La

B5377

Park Farm

Burned House La

Springfield House Farm

1

Cemy

++

Fern Hill Farm

Cemetery La

Hall Gate La

A588

Preesall Park

Moss House La

Caravan Pk

46

195

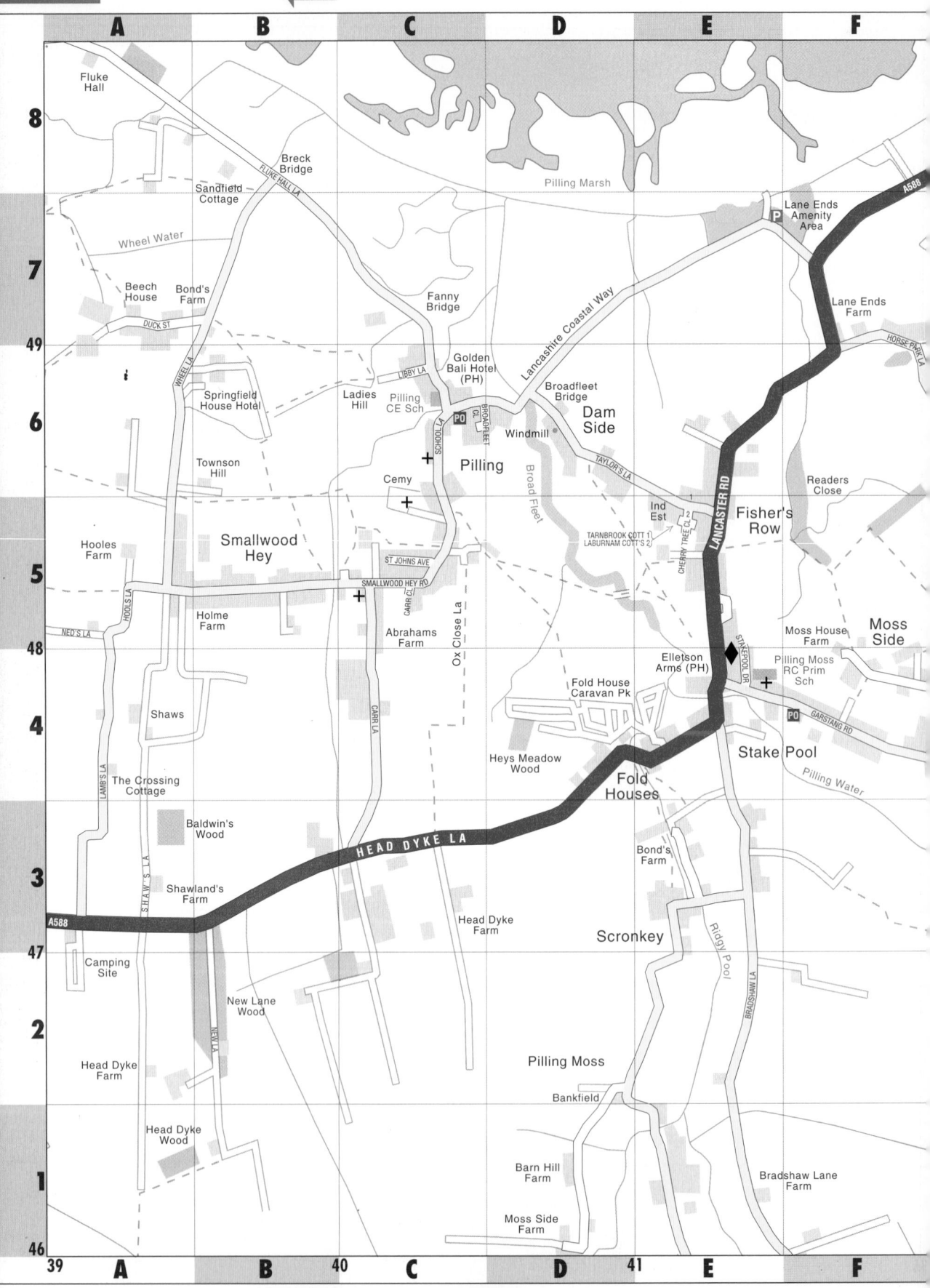

175

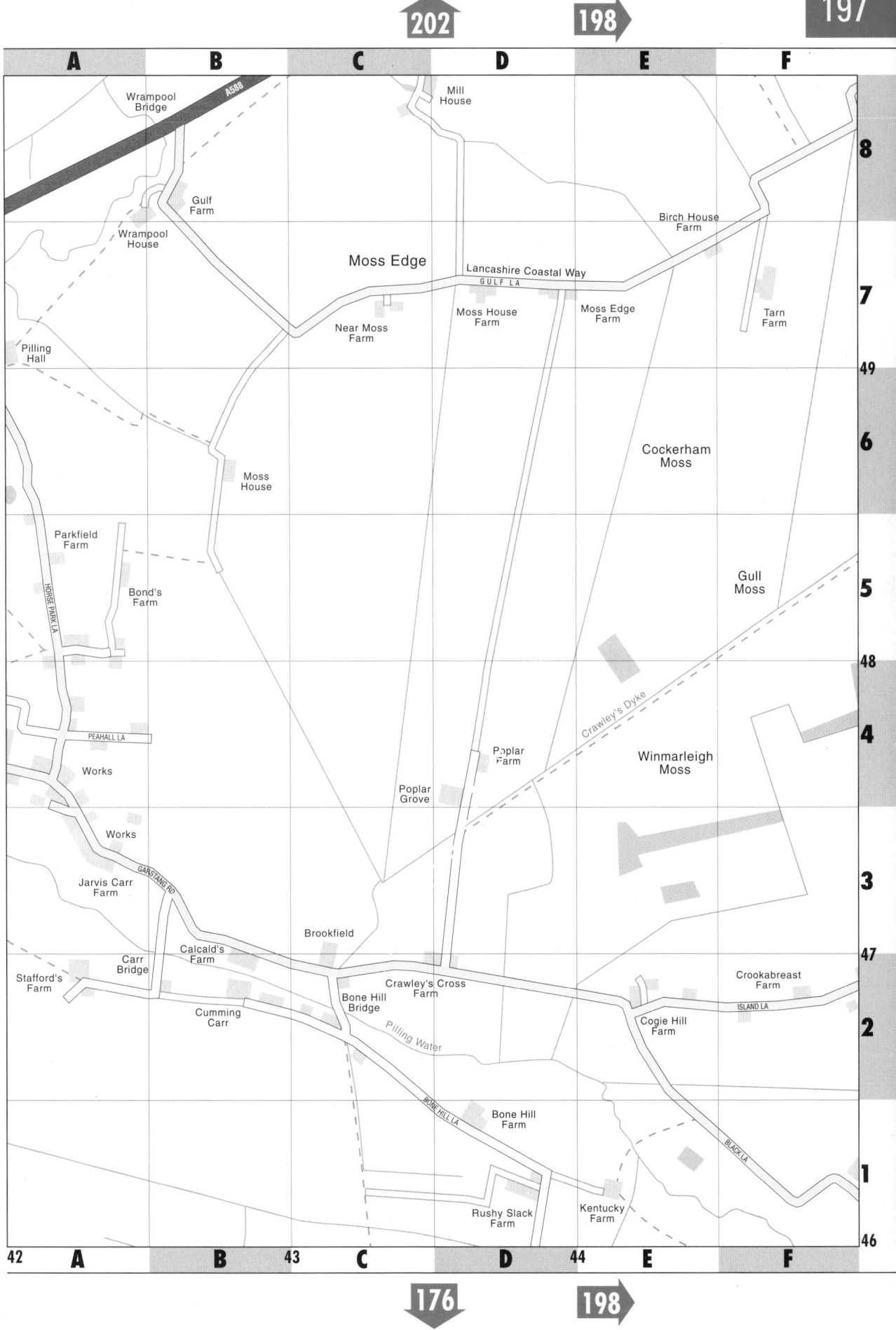

A B C D E F

8

Wrampool
Bridge

A588

Gulf
Farm

Wrampool
House

Mill
House

Birch House
Farm

Moss Edge

Lancashire Coastal Way

GULF LA

7

Near Moss
Farm

Moss House
Farm

Moss Edge
Farm

Tarn
Farm

Pilling
Hall

49

Cockerham
Moss

6

Moss
House

Parkfield
Farm

HORSE PARK LA

Bond's
Farm

Gull
Moss

5

48

Crawley's Dyke

4

PEAHALL LA

Works

Poplar
Farm

Poplar
Grove

Winmarleigh
Moss

Works

GARSTANG RD

Jarvis Carr
Farm

3

Brookfield

47

Calcald's
Farm

Crawley's Cross
Farm

Crookabreast
Farm

Carr
Bridge

Stafford's
Farm

Bone Hill
Bridge

ISLAND LA

Cogie Hill
Farm

2

Cumming
Carr

Pilling Water

BONE HILL LA

Bone Hill
Farm

BLACK LA

1

Rushy Slack
Farm

Kentucky
Farm

46

42 A B 43 C D 44 E F

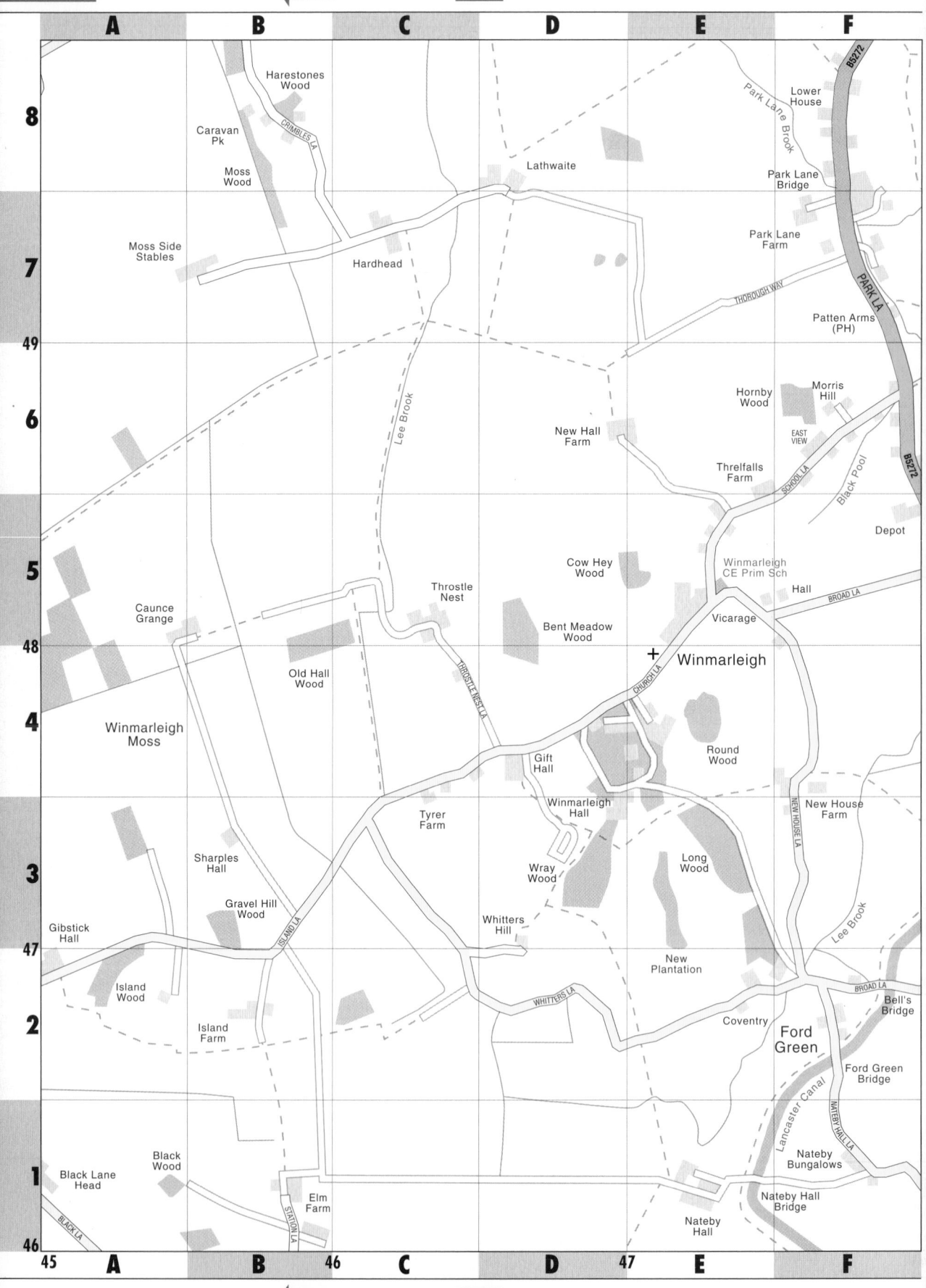

A B C D E F

8

Harestones Wood

Caravan Pk

Moss Wood

CRIMBLES LA

Lathwaite

Park Lane Brook

Lower House

B5272

Park Lane Bridge

Park Lane Farm

7

Moss Side Stables

Hardhead

THOROUGH WAY

PARK LA

Patten Arms (PH)

49

Lee Brook

6

New Hall Farm

Hornby Wood

Morris Hill

EAST VIEW

Threlfalls Farm

SCHOOL LA

Black Pool

B5272

Depot

5

Caunce Grange

Throstle Nest

Cow Hey Wood

Winmarleigh CE Prim Sch

Hall

BROAD LA

48

Old Hall Wood

Bent Meadow Wood

Vicarage

Winmarleigh

4

Winmarleigh Moss

THROSTLE NEST LA

CHURCH LA

Round Wood

New House Farm

NEW HOUSE LA

Gift Hall

Winmarleigh Hall

3

Sharples Hall

Tyrer Farm

Wray Wood

Long Wood

Lee Brook

Gravel Hill Wood

ISLAND LA

Whitters Hill

Gibstick Hall

47

New Plantation

BROAD LA

Bell's Bridge

Island Wood

WHITTERS LA

Coventry

Ford Green

2

Island Farm

Ford Green Bridge

Lancaster Canal

NATEBY HALL LA

Black Wood

Nateby Bungalows

1

Black Lane Head

Elm Farm

Nateby Hall Bridge

BLACK LA

STATION LA

Nateby Hall

46

45 A 46 C D 47 E F

B C D E F

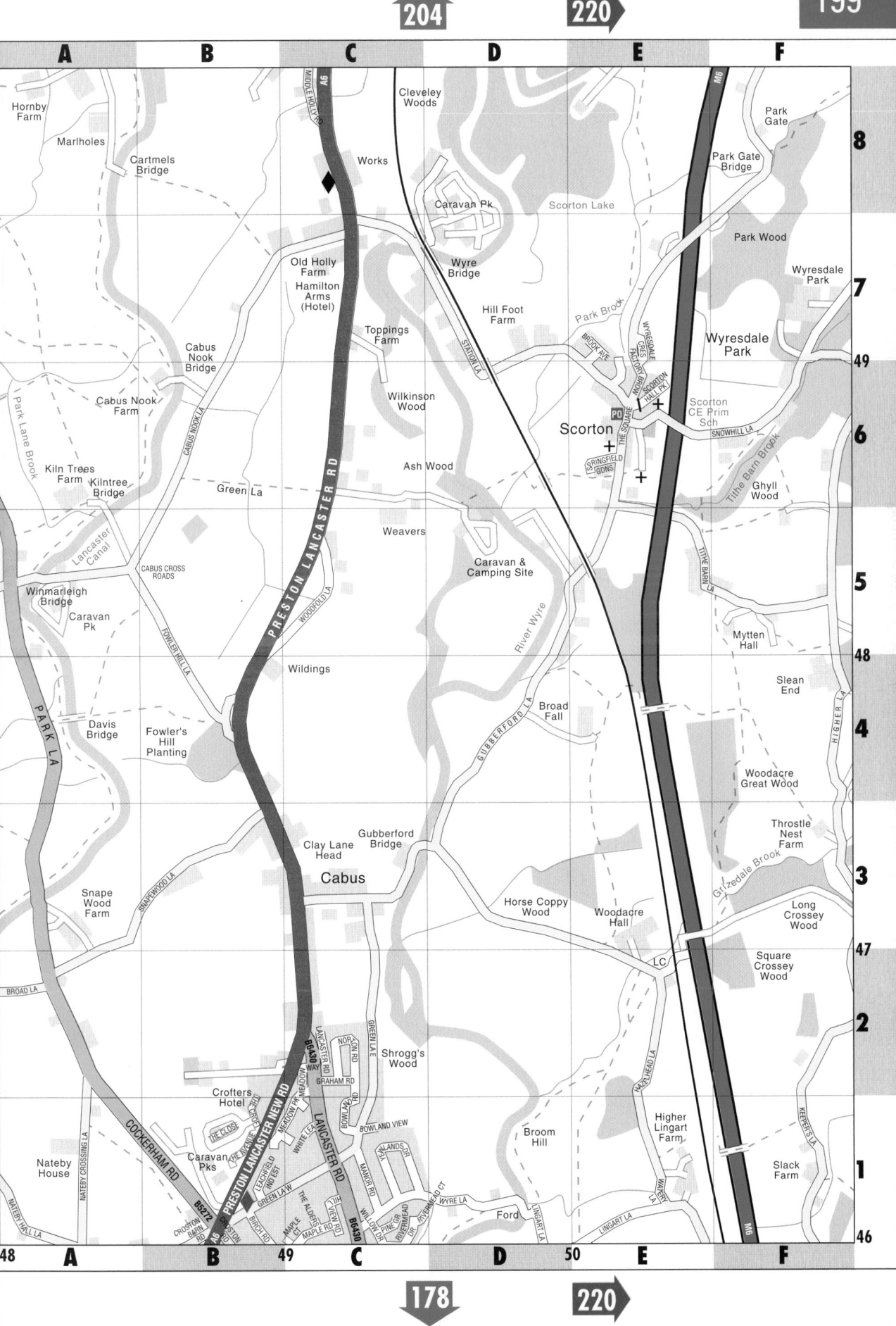

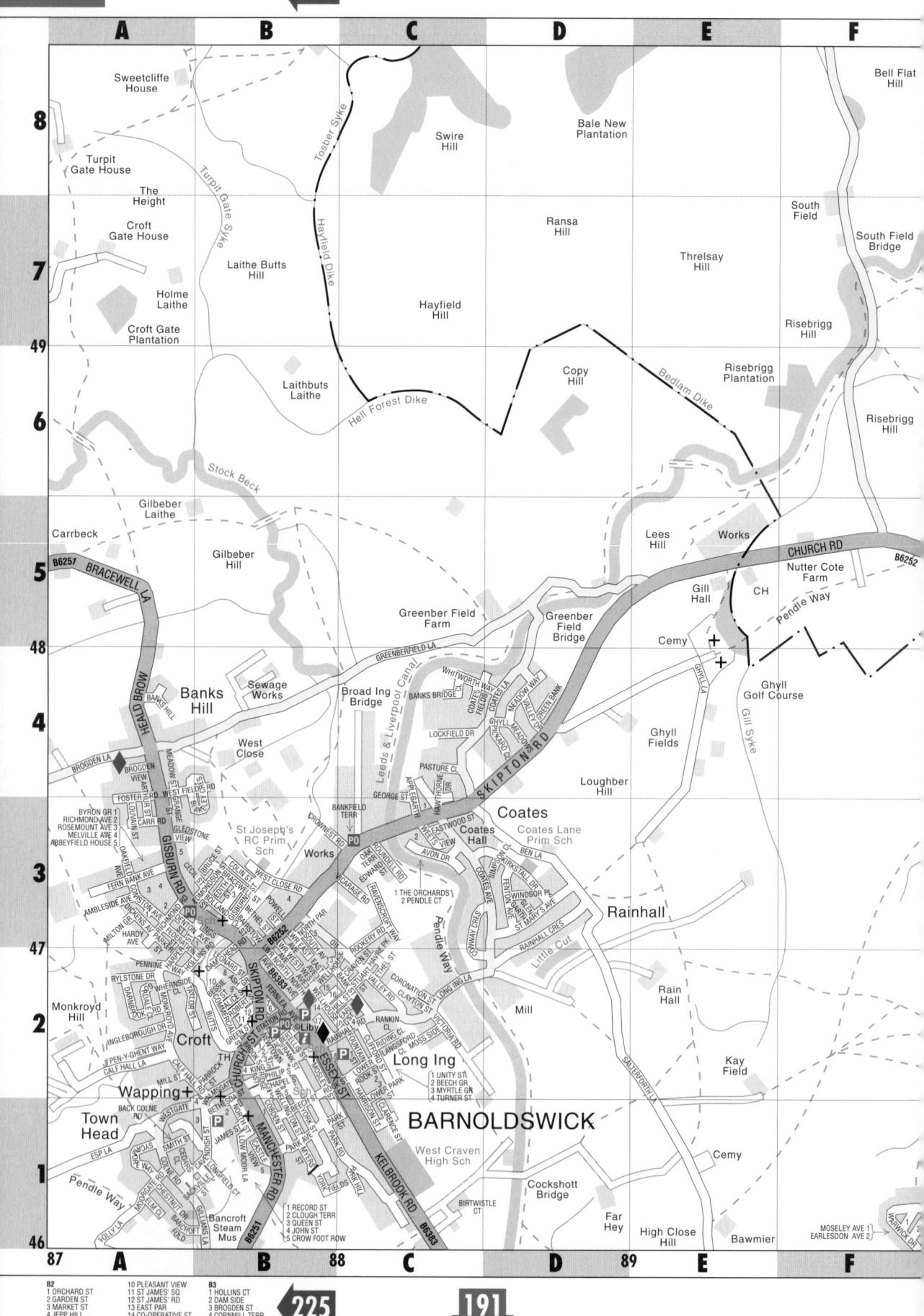

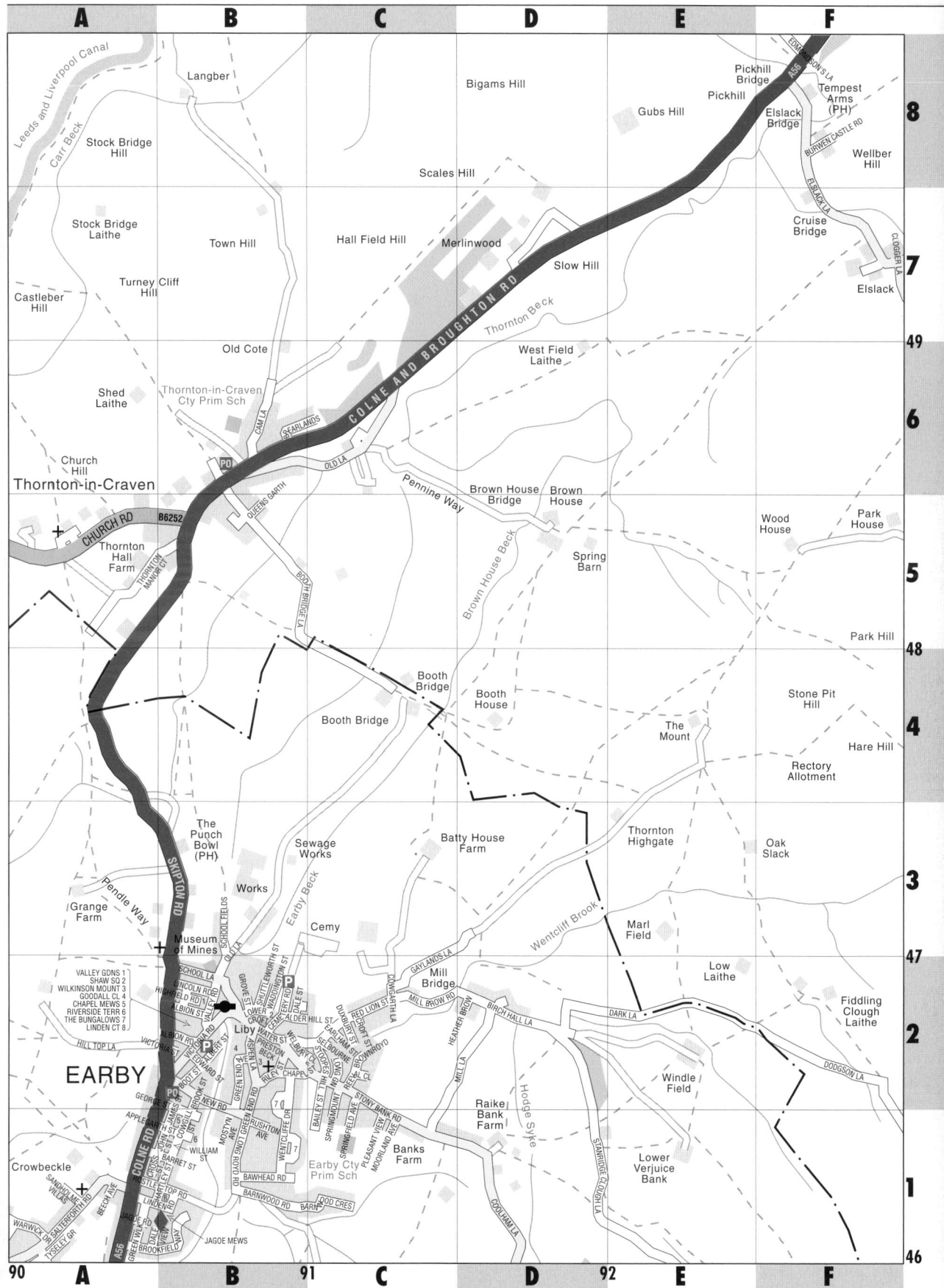

A B C D E F

8
7
49
6
5
48
4
3
47
2
1
46

Leeds and Liverpool Canal
Carr Beck
Langber
Stock Bridge Hill
Stock Bridge Laithe
Turney Cliff Hill
Castleber Hill
Town Hill
Old Cote
Shed Laithe
Church Hill
Thornton-in-Craven
Thornton Hall Farm
CHURCH RD
B6252
THORNTON MANOR CT
QUEENS GARTH
CAM LA
SEARLANDS
PO
OLD LA
BOOTH BRIDGE LA
Thornton-in-Craven Cty Prim Sch
COLNE AND BROUGHTON RD
Bigams Hill
Scales Hill
Hall Field Hill
Merlinwood
Slow Hill
Thornton Beck
West Field Laithe
Pennine Way
Brown House Bridge
Brown House Beck
Brown House
Spring Barn
Gubs Hill
Pickhill Bridge
Pickhill
Elslack Bridge
Tempest Arms (PH)
Wellber Hill
Cruise Bridge
Elslack
EDMONDSON'S LA
A56
BURWEN CASTLE RD
ELSLACK LA
CLOGGER LA
Wood House
Park House
Park Hill
Stone Pit Hill
Hare Hill
Rectory Allotment
Booth Bridge
Booth House
Booth Bridge
The Mount
Thornton Highgate
Oak Slack
The Punch Bowl (PH)
SKIPTON RD
Sewage Works
Works
Batty House Farm
Wentcliff Brook
Marl Field
Low Laithe
Fiddling Clough Laithe
Pendle Way
Grange Farm
Museum of Mines
Cemy
Earby Beck
GAYLANDS LA
Mill Bridge
COWGARTH LA
MILL BROW RD
BIRCH HALL LA
DARK LA
DODGSON LA
VALLEY GDNS 1
SHAW SQ 2
WILKINSON MOUNT 3
GOODALL CL 4
CHAPEL MEWS 5
RIVERSIDE TERR 6
THE BUNGALOWS 7
LINDEN CT 8
SCHOOL FIELDS
SCHOOL LA
LINCOLN RD
HIGHFIELD RD
ALBION ST
GROVE RD
OLD LA
SHUTTLEWORTH ST
WADDINGTON ST
RED LION ST
DUXBURY ST
MAPLE AV
SEL BOURNE
BIRCH CL
CONWY CRES
HILL TOP LA
ALBION RD
Liby
VICTORIA RD
HOWARD ST
RILEY ST
CHAPEL ST
GREEN END RD
NEW RD
WENTCLIFFE DR
BAILEY ST
SPRINGMOUNT
STONY BANK RD
PLEASANT VIEW
MOORLAND AVE
HEATHER BROW
MILL LA
HODGE SYKE
STANRIDGE CLOUGH LA
COOLHAM LA
Windle Field
Lower Verjuice Bank
EARBY
Crowbeckle
COLNE RD
A56
BEECH AVE
GREEN WAY
LINDEN RD
DALE WAY
BROOKFIELD
JAGOE RD
JAGOE MEWS
GEORGE ST
APPLETREE
PRESTON CROSS
SANDHOLME LA
WARWICK DR
TYSELEY GR
SALTERFORTH RD
BARRET ST
WILLIAM ST
BAWHEAD RD
BARNWOOD RD
DOD CRES
Earby Cty Prim Sch
Banks Farm
Raike Bank Farm
Thornton Beck

205

Cockersand
Abbey
(remains of)

Thursland
Hill

Bank
Houses

Caravan
Pks

Higher Bank
House

Bank
End

HILLAM LA

Lancashire Coastal Way

Cockerham
Marsh

A588

Braides

Sand
Side

Sand Villa
Cottages

Sweetings

Sand
Side

Beechfield

Sand
Villa

A588

Mill House
Bridge

A588

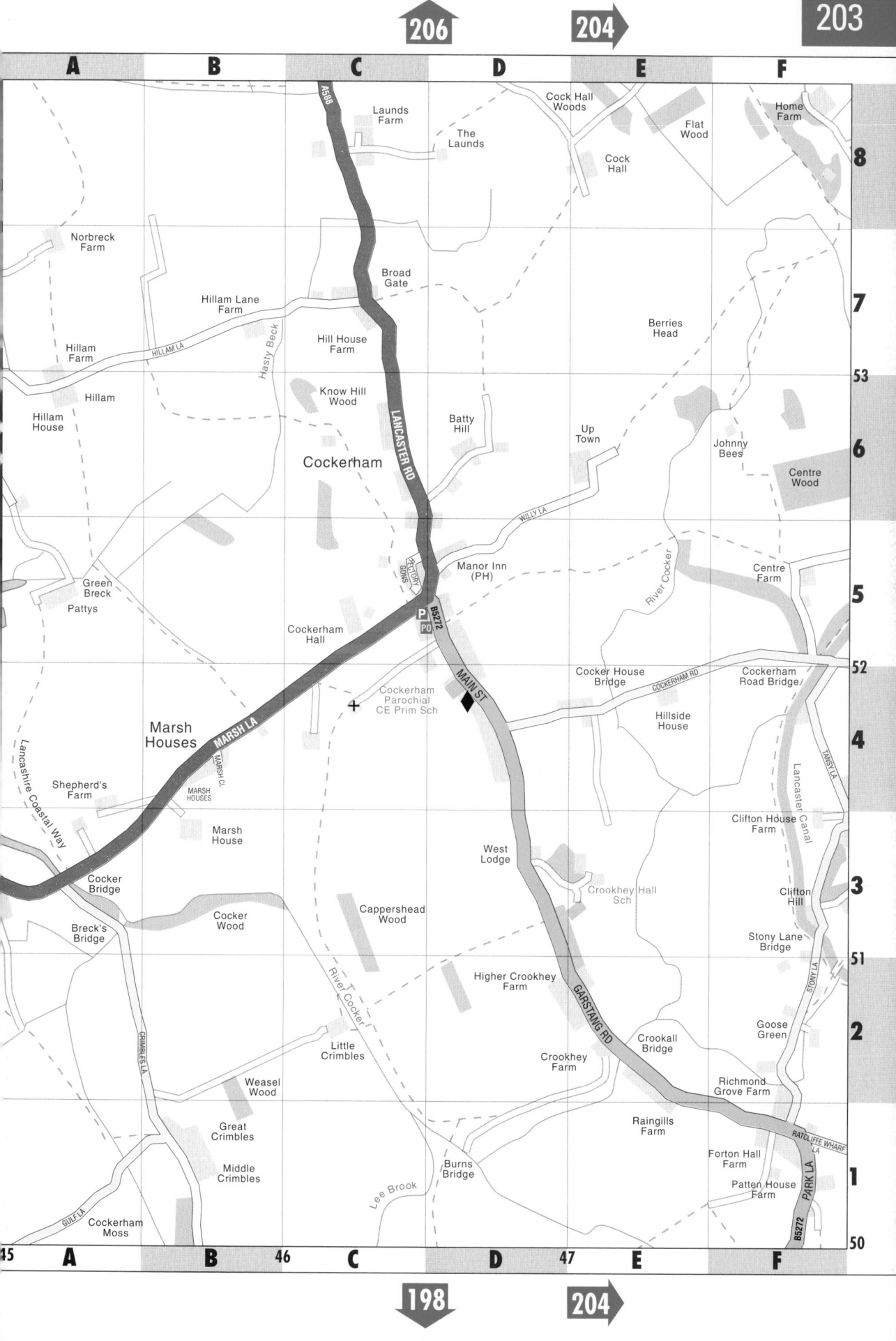

A   B   C   D   E   F

8

7

53

6

A588

Launds Farm

The Launds

Cock Hall Woods

Flat Wood

Home Farm

Cock Hall

Norbreck Farm

Broad Gate

Hillam Lane Farm

Berries Head

Hill House Farm

Hasty Beck

HILLAM LA

Hillam Farm

Hillam

Know Hill Wood

Johnny Bees

Batty Hill

Centre Wood

Hillam House

LANCASTER RD

Cockerham

Up Town

River Cocker

WILLY LA

Centre Farm

Green Breck

Pattys

Manor Inn (PH)

RECTORY GDNS

5

Cockerham Hall

P
B5272
PO

Cocker House Bridge

COCKERHAM RD

Cockerham Road Bridge

52

Cockerham Parochial CE Prim Sch

MAIN ST

Hillside House

Marsh Houses

MARSH LA

+

Lancashire Canal

Clifton House Farm

4

MARSH CL

MARSH HOUSES

Shepherd's Farm

Marsh House

West Lodge

Crookhey Hall Sch

Clifton Hill

TANSY LA

Lancashire Coastal Way

Cocker Bridge

Stony Lane Bridge

51

Breck's Bridge

Cocker Wood

Cappershead Wood

Higher Crookhey Farm

GARSTANG RD

Goose Green

STONY LA

3

River Cocker

Crookall Bridge

Richmond Grove Farm

2

CRIMBLES LA

Little Crimbles

Crookhey Farm

Weasel Wood

Raingills Farm

RATCLIFFE WHARF LA

Great Crimbles

Forton Hall Farm

PARK LA

Middle Crimbles

Burns Bridge

Patten House Farm

1

GULF LA

Cockerham Moss

Lee Brook

B5272

50

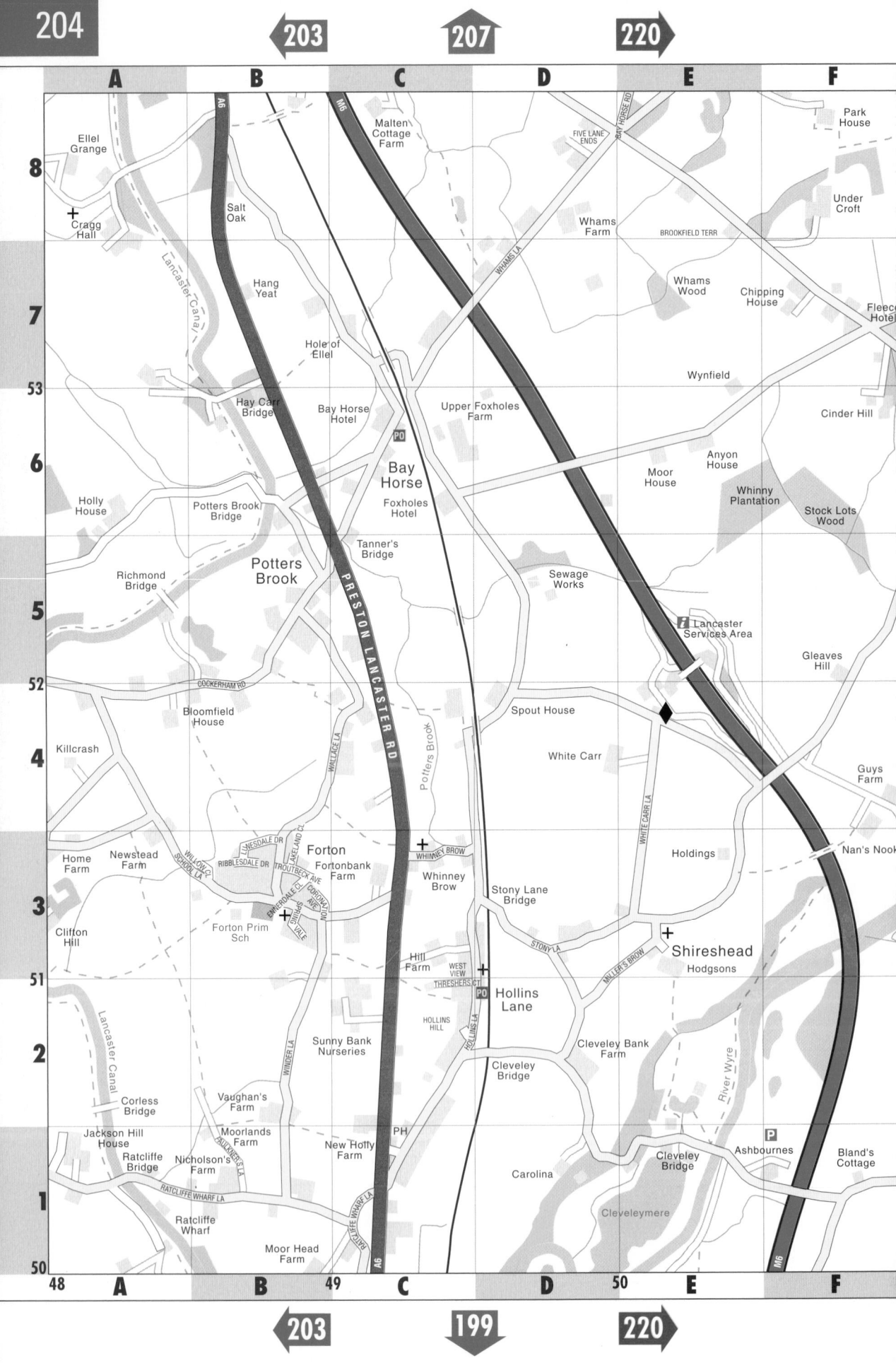

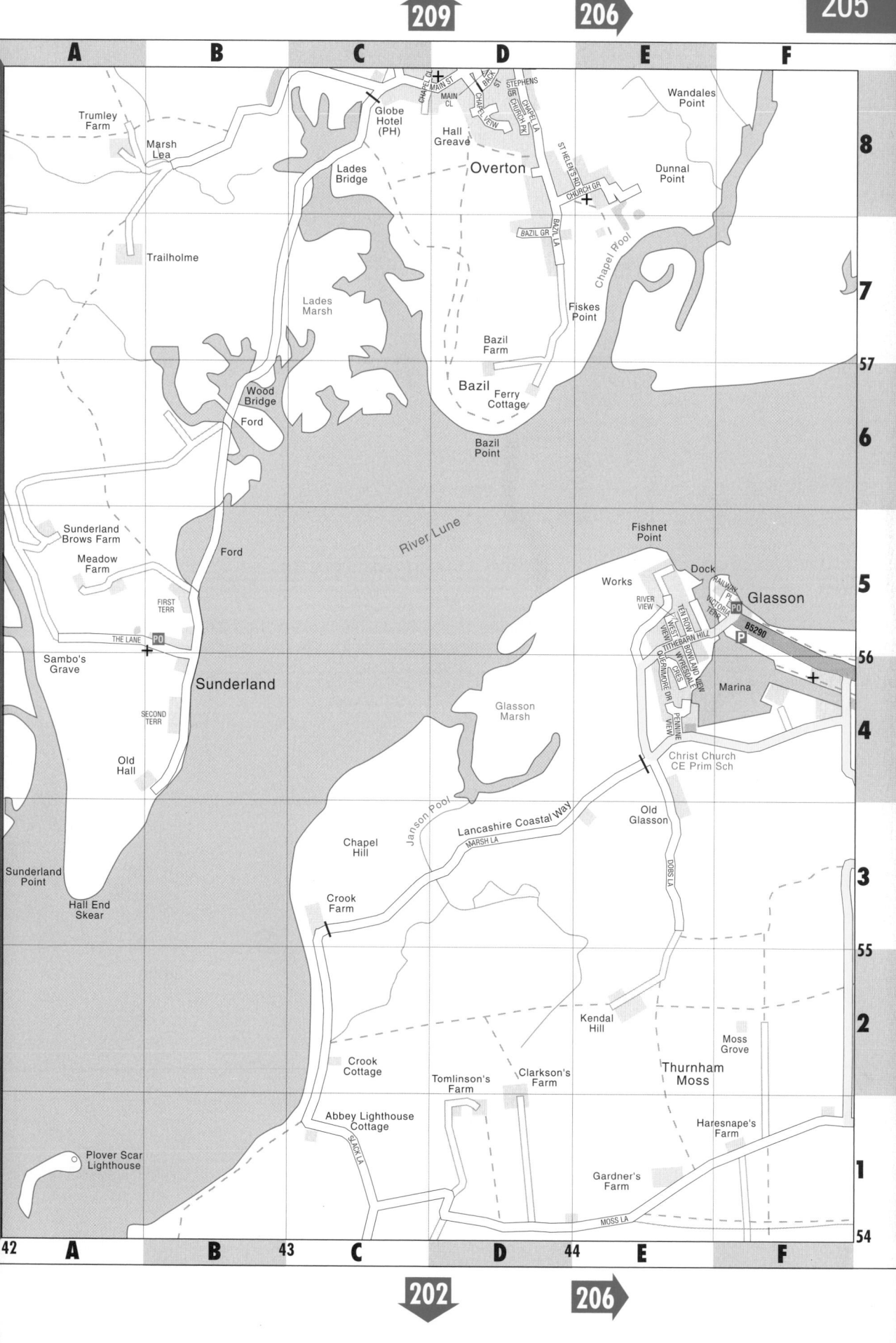

A   B   C   D   E   F

8

7

57

6

5

56

4

3

55

2

1

54

42   A   B   43   C   D   44   E   F

Trumley Farm
Marsh Lea
Trailholme
Lades Bridge
Globe Hotel (PH)
Hall Greave
Overton
CHAPEL CL
MAIN ST
MAIN CL
BACK ST
STEPHENS
CHAPEL VIEW
CHURCH PK
CHAPEL LA
ST HELEN'S RD
CHURCH GR
Wandales Point
Dunnal Point
Chapel Pool
BAZIL GR
BAZIL LA
Fiskes Point
Lades Marsh
Bazil Farm
Bazil
Ferry Cottage
Wood Bridge
Ford
Bazil Point
River Lune
Sunderland Brows Farm
Meadow Farm
Ford
Ford
FIRST TERR
THE LANE   PO
Sambo's Grave
Sunderland
SECOND TERR
Old Hall
Sunderland Point
Hall End Skear
Fishnet Point
Works
Dock
RIVER VIEW
TITHEBARN HILL
TEXT ROW
WEST
WIRRESDALE
BOWLAND VIEW
CRES
QUERNMORE DR
PENNINE VIEW
VICTORIA TERR
RAILWAY PO
Glasson
B5290
P
Marina
Christ Church CE Prim Sch
Glasson Marsh
Old Glasson
Janson Pool
Lancashire Coastal Way
MARSH LA
DOBS LA
Chapel Hill
Crook Farm
Kendal Hill
Moss Grove
Thurnham Moss
Crook Cottage
Tomlinson's Farm
Clarkson's Farm
Abbey Lighthouse Cottage
SLACK LA
Haresnape's Farm
Gardner's Farm
MOSS LA
Plover Scar Lighthouse

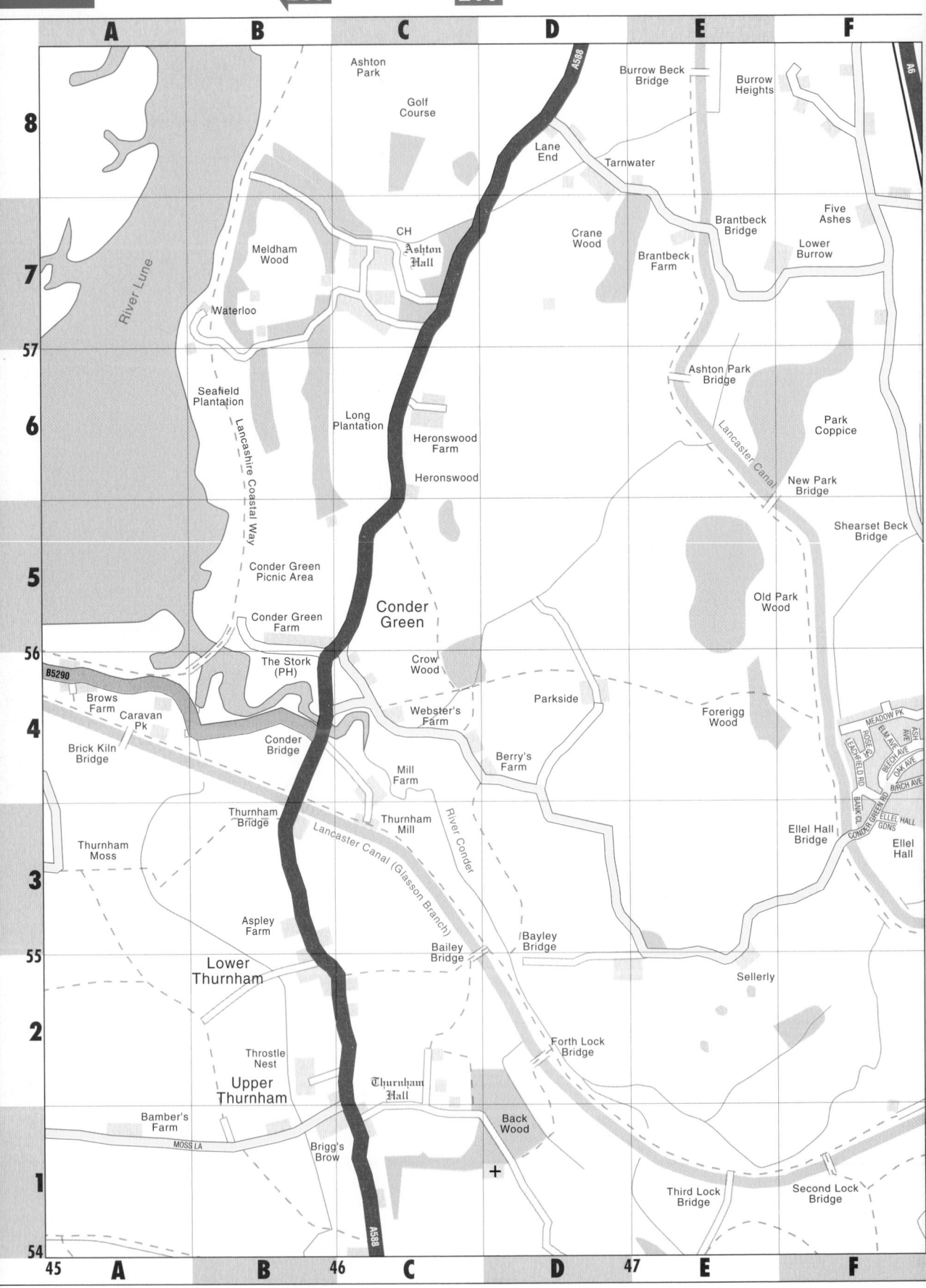

A588

A6

8

A6

Ashton
Park

Golf
Course

Lane
End

Burrow Beck
Bridge

Burrow
Heights

Tarnwater

7

Meldham
Wood

CH

Ashton
Hall

Crane
Wood

Brantbeck
Farm

Brantbeck
Bridge

Five
Ashes

Lower
Burrow

Waterloo

River Lune

57

Seafield
Plantation

Ashton Park
Bridge

6

Lancashire Coastal Way

Long
Plantation

Heronswood
Farm

Heronswood

Lancaster Canal

Park
Coppice

New Park
Bridge

Shearset Beck
Bridge

5

Conder Green
Picnic Area

Conder
Green

Old Park
Wood

Conder Green
Farm

56

The Stork
(PH)

Crow
Wood

B5290

Brows
Farm

Caravan
Pk

Webster's
Farm

Parkside

Forerigg
Wood

MEADOW PK
ROSE SQ
ELM AVE
ASH AVE
BEECH AVE
LEACHFIELD RD
OAK AVE
BIRCH AVE

4

Brick Kiln
Bridge

Conder
Bridge

Berry's
Farm

BANK CL
CONDER GREEN RD
ELLEL HALL
GDNS

Ellel Hall
Bridge

Ellel
Hall

Thurnham Moss

Thurnham
Bridge

Mill
Farm

Thurnham
Mill

Lancaster Canal (Glasson Branch)

River Conder

3

Aspley
Farm

Bailey
Bridge

Bayley
Bridge

Sellerly

55

Lower
Thurnham

2

Throstle
Nest

Forth Lock
Bridge

Upper
Thurnham

Thurnham
Hall

Bamber's
Farm

Back
Wood

MOSS LA

Brigg's
Brow

1

Third Lock
Bridge

Second Lock
Bridge

A588

54

A **B** **C** **D** **E** **F**

Mast
Met Sta

Dam Head
Bridge

Dam Head
Farm

Thorn
Hill

LONG LA

Cander
Bank

Old School
House

PROCTER MOSS RD

Hazelrigg

Eastrigg

Condergarth

Lane
Side

LONG LANE
END

Thornfield

Banton
House

Brandrigg

Barrow
Greaves

River Conder

Higher Kit
Brow

KIT BROW LA

Sefton's
Farm

Whitley Beck

Higher
Knowe Hill

Barker
House

Kitchen
Grange

Univ of
Lancaster

GREEN LA

Leach
House

Knowe
Hill

Ward
Farm

Ward
Houses

Lower Kit
Brow

LANGSHAW LA

Lunds
Green

Pipe
House

Cocker Clough
Wood

Ellel

SCHOOL VILLAS
DAMSIDE COTTS

Boldens

CHURCH LA

GALGATE SILK
MILLS IND EST

Cockshades
Hill

Crag
End

BAY HORSE RD

LEACHFIELD CL

VERNON
PK JOHN ST

Galgate

MAKINSONS ROW

Cockshades

St John's CE
Prim Sch

CHAPEL ST

LIME AVE
BEECH AVE
OAK AVE
BIRCH AVE

Whitley Beck

SCREEN LA

Walker's-i'-
th'-Fields

Brunstow

Brunstow
Wood

VERNON

SALFORD RD

Railway
Farm

MAIN RD

STONEY LA

Skew
Bridge

Smith
Green

Smith Green
Farm

Cocker
Bridge

Galgate
Bridge

School
House

River Cocker

Borbles
Hall

Ellel
Crag

Lane
House

PRESTON LANCASTER RD

Coppy House
Barn

Junction
Bridge

Double
Bridge

Lancaster Canal

Hampson
Green

HAMPSON LA

HAMPSON
COTTS

A6

M5

Chatburn
House

Nuthurst
Farm

Newland
Hall

Newland Home
Farm

SCOTFORTH RD A6

PRESTON LANCASTER RD A6

M6

HIGHLAND BROW

P

8 **7** **57** **6** **5** **56** **4** **55** **3** **2** **1** **54**

48 **A** **B** **49** **C** **D** **E** **50** **F**

HEYSHAM

A **B** **C** **D** **E** **F**

Lower Heysham

TARNBROOK RD 1
KNOWLYS DR 2
BACK KNOWLYS RD 3

ST MARY'S RD 1
HESKETH RD 2

Lib

PO

Chapel Hill

Barrows

St Peter's Prim Sch

Heysham Head

Higher Heysham

Half Moon Bay

GLEN VIEW AVE 1
ST MILDRED'S WAY 2
CURWEN AVE 3
CHERRY TREE CL 4
HEATHFOOT DR 5
PENHALE CT 6

Near Naze

PO

PENNINGTON CT

ROTHESAY RD

TRUMACAR LA

MIDDLETON WAY

BELL-AIRE PARK HOMES

Custom House

North Wharf

McDONALD RD

Trumacar Cty Prim Sch

A683

Heysham Harbour

Fish Quay

Heysham Sta

South Quay

PRINCESS ALEXANDRA WAY

A589

North Round Head

Nature Reserve

CH

South Jetty

PH
Caravan Pk

Heysham Banks

P

Heysham Golf Course

Nuclear Power Stas

MIDDLETON RD

Mast

Whittam Hill

Caravan Pk

MAIN AVE

Ind Est

Middleton Tower Holiday Ctr

Greendales Farm

Greendales L Pk

39 **A** **B** **40** **C** **D** **41** **E** **F**

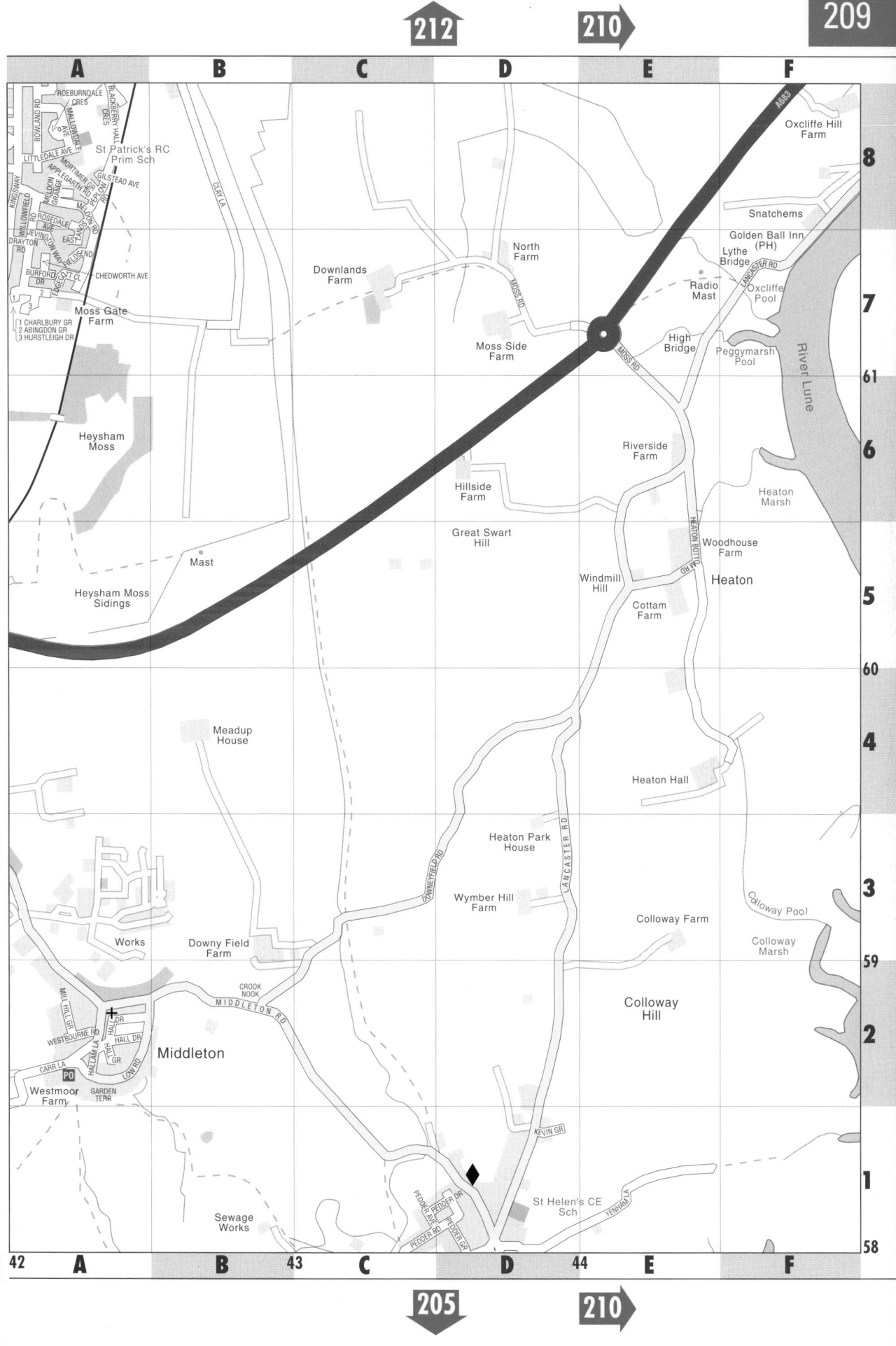

8

7

61

6

5

60

4

3

59

2

1

58

A   B   C   D   E   F

Top labels (left to right):
ROEBURNDALE CRES
BLACKBERRY HALL CRES
BOWLAND RD
MALHAMDALE AVE
LITTLEDALE AVE
St Patrick's RC Prim Sch
MORTIMER GR
APPLEGARTH RD
GILSTEAD AVE
KINGSWAY
WILLOWFIELD
ROSEDALE AVE
MELDON
GRANGE
EAST
DRAYTON RD
BURFORD DR
EDGECROFT CL
CHEDWORTH AVE
LEGEND
Moss Gate Farm
1 CHARLBURY GR
2 ABINGDON GR
3 HURSTLEIGH DR

CLAY LA

Downlands Farm

North Farm

MOSS RD

Radio Mast

A683

Oxcliffe Hill Farm

Snatchems

Golden Ball Inn (PH)
Lythe Bridge
LANCASTER RD
Oxcliffe Pool

High Bridge

Peggymarsh Pool

River Lune

Moss Side Farm

Heysham Moss

Riverside Farm

Heaton Marsh

Hillside Farm

Great Swart Hill

Windmill Hill

HEATON BOTTO RD

Woodhouse Farm

Heaton

Cottam Farm

Mast

Heysham Moss Sidings

Heaton Hall

Meadup House

DOWNEYFIELD RD

Heaton Park House

LANCASTER RD

Colloway Farm

Colloway Pool

Colloway Marsh

Works

Downy Field Farm

Wymber Hill Farm

Colloway Hill

CROOK NOOK
MIDDLETON RD

MILL HILL GR
HALL DR
HALL GR
HALL LA
LOW RD
WESTBOURNE RD
CARR LA
PO
GARDEN TERR
Westmoor Farm
Middleton

Sewage Works

PEDDER AVE
PEDDER RD
PEDDER DR
PEDDER GR

KEVIN GR

St Helen's CE Sch

YENHAM

E8
1 KELLET CT
2 COVELL HOUSE
3 CHENNEL HOUSE
4 KELNE HOUSE
5 WHEATFIELD CT
6 ST JAMES CT

F7
1 HIGH MOUNT HOUSE
2 HIGH MOUNT CT
3 GEORGE ST
4 MARTON ST
5 PETER ST
6 VICTORIA PL

F8
1 WOOD ST
2 BUTTERFIELD ST
3 CHAPEL ST
4 ALEXANDRA CT
5 NILE ST

7 BACK QUEEN ST

209

213

7 BACK QUEEN ST

6 DYE HOUSE LA
7 CALKELD LA
8 ROSEMARY LA
9 BACK SUN ST
10 MARKET SQ
11 CHEAPSIDE
12 ASHTON WLK

13 ST NICHOLAS ARCS
14 LANCASTER GATE
15 RENDSBURG WAY
16 PERPIGNON WAY
17 STONEWELL
18 ST ANNE'S PL
19 BREWERY LA

20 GREAT JOHN ST
21 BRIDGET ST
22 FRIARS PAS
23 FRIAR ST
24 BRYER ST
25 ST CATHERINES CT
26 SIR SIMON'S ARC

27 MARKET GATE
28 SLIP INN LA
29 JAMES ST
30 FFRANCES PAS
31 GAGE ST
32 MOOR ST
33 KINGS ARMS CL

34 ALMSHOUSES
35 WINDYHILL
36 COMMON GDN ST
37 RUSSELL ST
38 SPRING GDN ST
39 BREWERY ARC
40 ROBERT ST

River Lune

Marsh

LANCASTER

Abraham
Heights

Brookholme
Farm

Aldcliffe
Marsh

Lancaster Coastal Way

Aldcliffe

Haverbreaks

Royal
Albert

Royal Albert
Farm

Lancaster Canal

Heaton
Marsh

Arna
Wood

River Lune

Deep Cutting
Farm

Deep Cutting
Bridge

Cemy

Colloway
Marsh

Low
Wood

Sewage
Works

Stodday

Grange
Farm

Lunecliffe
Hall

Whinney
Carr

Jansteval

Lawson's
Bridge

Burrow Beck
Bridge

Burrow Beck

Burrow
Bridge

Waterside
Farm

Hamilton
Plantation

The Greaves

Kensington House 1
THE HASTINGS 2
CHELTENHAM RD 3
VICTORIA AVE 4
HEATON HOUSE 5
FRANKLIN ST 6
DEVONSHIRE ST 7

1 MORNINGSIDE
2 ALDCLIFFE PL

GREATHWAITE CT 1
SIZERGH CT 2

LARCH GR 1
HOLLY WLK 2
HAZEL GR 3
LIME GR 4
ROWAN PL 5
ASHBROOK ST 6
STANLEY PL 7
BEECH ST 8

BINYON CT 1
PICKARD ST 2

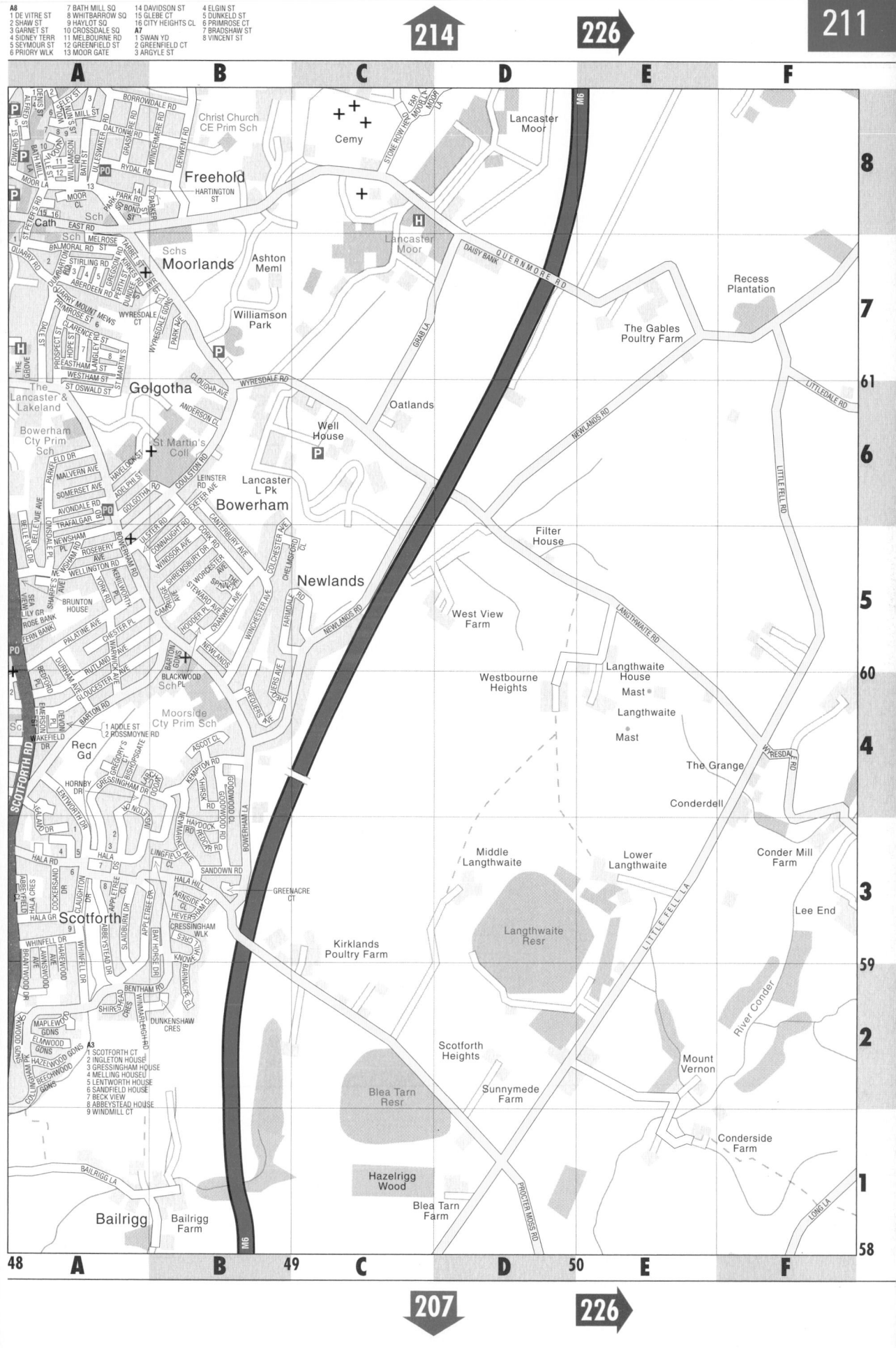

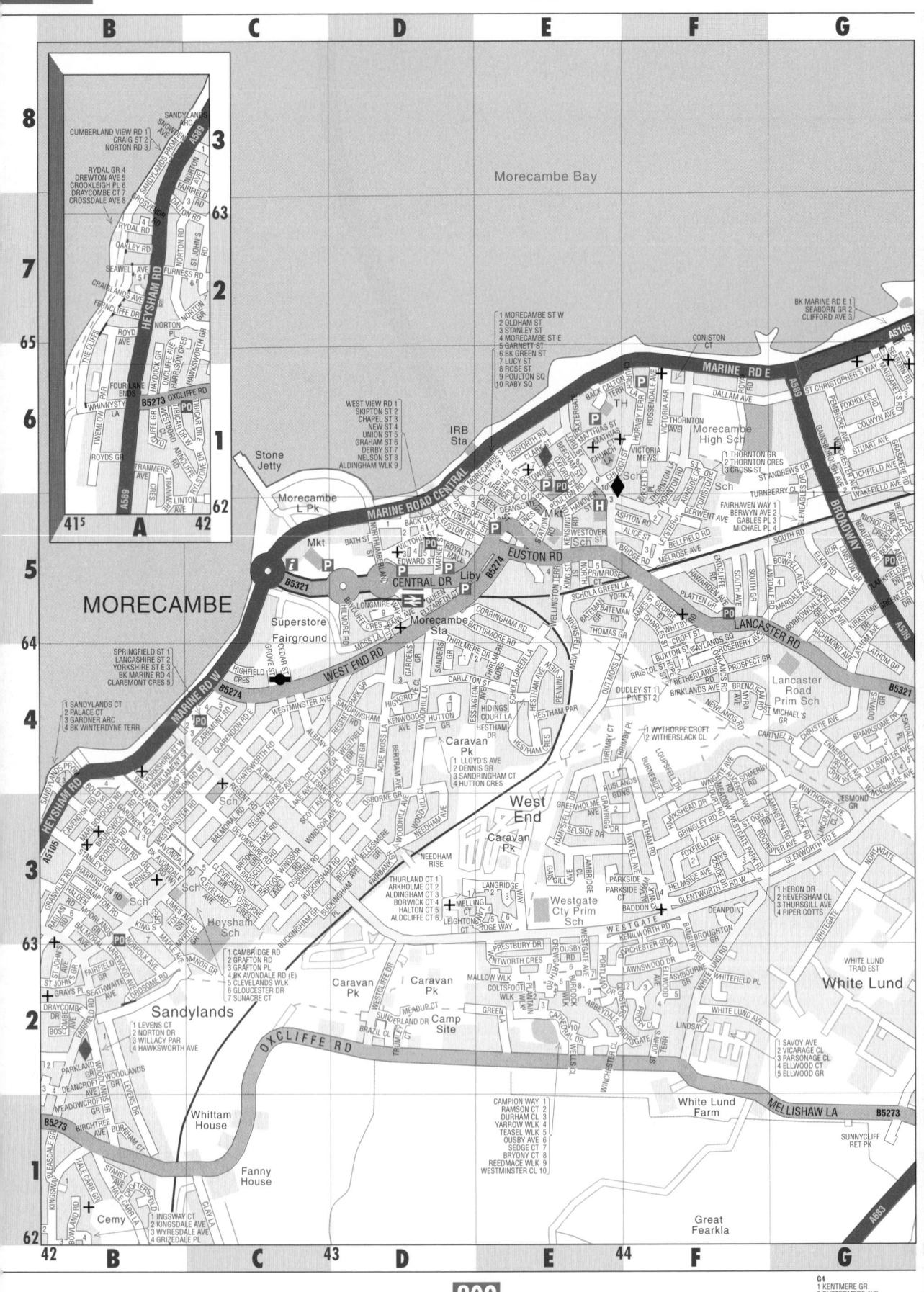

E5
1 BK QUEEN ST
2 BK LINES ST
3 RABY ST
4 RIBBLESDALE CT
5 PRIMROSE ST

MORECAMBE

Morecambe Bay

West End

White Lund

Sandylands

G4
1 KENTMERE GR
2 BUTTERMERE AVE
3 BLEA TARN PL
4 WINDERMERE CT
5 LOWESWATER DR

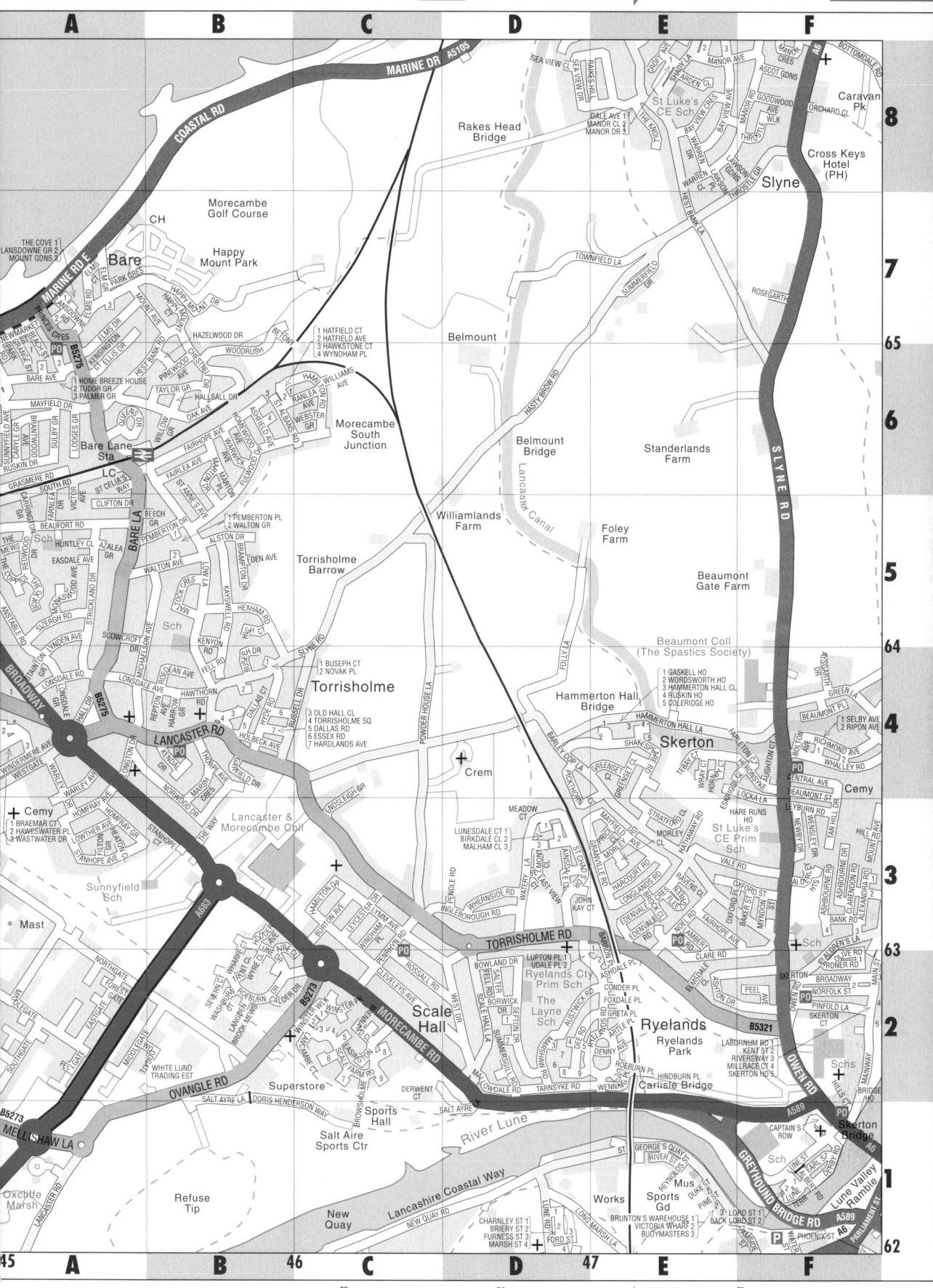

A **B** **C** **D** **E** **F**

MARINE DR A5105

COASTAL RD

Rakes Head Bridge

SEA VIEW DR
RAKES HILL
CROFT HILL
MANOR AVE
ASCOT GDNS
BOTTOMDALE RD
A6

St Luke's CE Sch
THE WAGL
MANOR CL 2
MANOR DR 3
DALE AVE 1
BAY VIEW AVE
GOODWOOD AVE
ORCHARD CL
Caravan Pk

8

THE COVE 1
LANSDOWNE GR 2
MOUNT GDNS 2
CH
Morecambe Golf Course
Happy Mount Park
WARREN CRES
WARREN DR
BAY VIEW CL
MANOR RD
LANSON GDNS
LANSON GR
THROSTLE GR
Cross Keys Hotel (PH)
Slyne

7

Bare
MARINE RD E
ELMS RD
PARK CRES
ELM GR
HAZELWOOD DR
BELTONY
TOWNFIELD LA
ROSEGARTH

65

NEWMARKET
PRINCES GR
BREEZE'S LA
ACRE'S LA
PO
B5275
HEST BANK LA
SUMMERFIELD DR
SLYNE RD

HAWTHORN
WILLOW
QUEENS DR
PINEWOOD
CHESTNUT GR
RAINLEA GR
HAMILTON GR
WEBSTER GR
WILLIAMS AVE
1 HATFIELD CT
2 HATFIELD AVE
3 HAWKSTONE CT
4 WYNDHAM PL
Belmount
6

Bare Lane Sta
LC
ST CELIA'S
FAIRHOPE AVE
FAIRLEA AVE
ST ANNE'S AVE
EDEN AVE
FULWOOD AVE
Morecambe South Junction
Belmount Bridge
HASTY BROW RD
Standerlands Farm

BEECH GR
PEMBERTON GR
BRAMPTON DR
1 PEMBERTON PL
2 WALTON GR
Williamlands Farm
Lancaster Canal
Beaumont Gate Farm
5

SCH
AZALEA GR
WALTON AVE
LOW LA
ALSTON DR
Torrisholme Barrow
Foley Farm

64

MAYLOCK CRES
KAYSWELL RD
HEXHAM DR
KENYON RD
FELL DR
SLYNE RD
1 BUSEPH CT
2 NOVAK PL
Beaumont Coll (The Spastics Society)

REPTON GR
HARROW GR
DALLAS CT
HYDE RD
Torrisholme
1 GASKELL HO
2 WORDSWORTH HO
3 HAMMERTON HALL CL
4 RUSKIN HO
5 COLERIDGE HO
BEAUMONT PL
1 SELBY AVE
2 RIPON AVE
4

HAWTHORN
BOLBECK RD
HOLBECK AVE
3 OLD HALL CL
4 TORRISHOLME SQ
5 DALLAS RD
6 ESSEX RD
7 HARDLANDS AVE
Hammerton Hall Bridge
HAMMERTON HALL LA
SHAKESPEARE
Skerton
WHALLEY RD
Cemy

LANCASTER RD
PO
KENDAL
THORPE AVE
ENFIELD DR
POWDER HOUSE LA
BARLEY COP LA
PICKTHORN
GREENSET CL
HERDSIDE
PO
CENTRAL AVE
BEAUMONT CT

Cemy
1 BRAEMAR CT
2 HAWESWATER PL
3 WASTWATER DR
WINDERMERE AVE
WESTGATE
WARLEY RD
LONGTON DR
NORWOOD DR
MARSH CRES
Crem
MEADOW CT
STRATFORD RD
MORLEY
RAVENS CL
HARCOURT RD
LONGLANDS RD
OXFORD ST
LEYBURN RD
HILL RD
3

Lancaster & Morecambe Coll
THE WAY
STANHOPE CT
EASDALE GR
HAMILTON RD
BURTON AVE
LEICESTER AVE
LYMM AVE
INGLEBOROUGH RD
WHERNSIDE RD
LUNESDALE CT 1
BIRKDALE RD 2
MALHAM CL 3
WATERY LA
ST CHAD'S
JOHN KAY CT
MAYFIELD AVE
GRANVILLE RD
EDENVALE RD
FAIRHOPE AVE
ST LUKE'S CE Prim Sch
VALE RD
ASHBOURNE DR
CLARENDON RD

A683
Sunnyfield Sch
Mast
PENDLE RD
EAST VIEW
AINSDALE RD
HARBOUR RD
DENNY AVE
BANK RD
SCH
DRY'S AVE
63

NORTHGATE
FOREST
GATE
EASTGATE
B5273
WHARFE CT
TREN CL
CALDER DR
WINSTER CL
ROEBURN DR
LANGDEN
BROOK MEWS
ROSSALL RD
WEST DR
CLEVELEYS AVE
Scale Hall
MORECAMBE RD
TORRISHOLME RD
BOWLAND DR
FELL RD
SALTER
BORWICK
SCOTFORTH RD
LUPTON PL 1
UDALE PL 2
ASHDALE PL
CONDER PL
FOXDALE PL
GRETA PL
PO
BROADWAY
NORFOLK ST
PINFOLD LA
SKERTON
CT
2

White Lund Trading Est
WHARFE CT
SWINSER WK
MAX
LEASINGHAM
ASHTON DR
CLARE RD
EASDALE
Ryelands City Prim Sch
The Layne Sch
Ryelands
LABURNUM RD 1
KENT ST 2
RIVERSWAY 3
MILLRACE CT 4
SKERTON HO 5

OVANGLE RD
Superstore
DERWENT CT
BROWSHOLME LA
SALT AYRE LA
MAXWELL DR
TARNSYKE RD
WENNA
ARTLE RD
ROEBURN PL
HINDBURN PL
Ryelands Park
Carlisle Bridge
Schs
Skerton Bridge
A6

B5273
MELLISHAW LA
DORIS HENDERSON WAY
SALT AYRE
Sports Hall
CAPTAIN'S ROW
Lune Valley Ramble
1

Salt Aire Sports Ctr
River Lune
GEORGE'S QUAY
LINE ST
DUKE ST
PHOENIX ST
A589

Oxcliffe Marsh
Refuse Tip
New Quay
Lancashire Coastal Way
NEW QUAY RD
LONG MARSH LA
Works
Mus Sports Gd
Brunton's Warehouse 1
Victoria Wharf 2
Buoymasters 3
GREYHOUND BRIDGE RD
PARLIAMENT ST
A6
62

CHARNLEY ST 1
BRIERY ST 2
FURNESS ST 3
MARSH ST 4
LINE END RD
FORD ST

45 **A** 46 **B** **C** 47 **D** **E** **F**

C2
1 KEER BANK
2 GILPIN CL
3 BELA CL
4 CRAKE BANK
5 GREGARETH CL
6 WINDHOLME
7 CROASDALE
8 WHITENDALE
9 BRINDLE CL

D2
1 BURNFELL RD
2 TARNBROOK RD
3 RAYGILL PL
4 AUSTWICK RD
5 RAWTHEY RD
6 MEARBECK PL
7 CROSSHILL PL
8 BROWGILL PL
9 WHITERAY RD

F3
1 BULLER ST
2 RUSKIN RD
3 DAISY ST
4 ASHBOURNE CL

A   B   C   D   E   F

8

Ancliffe Hall

BOTTOMDALE RD

7

FOUR LANE
ENDS

FOUNDRY LA

Beaumont
Grange

Haverbreaks
Farm

65

St Wilfrid's CE
Prim Sch

Halton

KELLET LA

GREEN LA

Dale
Wood

St
Wilfrid's
Sch

Town End
Mill

PH

Halton
Mills

6

Carus
Lodge

FOUNDRY LA

CHURCH ST

CHURCH BROW

RIVERSIDE CL

MILL LA

Carus
House

Bulk
Bridge

Halton
Training
Camp

River Lune

Lune Valley Ramble

P

Denny
Beck
Farm

A683

5

Halton
Road
Bridge

Hotel

Cottam's
Farm

34

DENNY BANK

Denny Bank

64

Lune
Aqueduct

RIVERSIDE PARK
IND EST

♦

Long Bank
Wood

Denny Beck

CH

Works

Golf Course

Moss Syke
Wood

Old
Parkside
Farm

CATON RD

Lancaster Canal

4

3

LANSIL
IND EST

NEWTON
TERR

Ridge
Wood

Davies's
Farm

Moor
Side

63

Lune
Riverside
Park

GREGEDALE RD

Ridge
Farm

GRIMESHAW LA

Old Parkside
Fell

Newton

Ridge

Newton Beck

RIDGE LA

2

THE RAMPARTS

LANGDALE
PL

TA
Ctr

Trading
Est

P

KINGSWAY

A683

P

The
Ridge
Prim Sch

Central
Lancaster
High Sch

HM Prison

MOOR LA

Stanley Farm
Fell

1

Sports
Ctr

A6 CATON RD

Ridge Lea

FAR MOOR LA

M6

Stanley
Farm

Bulk

62

48   A   B   49   C   D   50   E   F

A1
1 GLADSTONE TERR
2 FACTORY HILL
3 ST LEONARD CT
4 DE VITRE ST

B1
1 HERLEBECK RISE
2 MONTHALL RISE
3 RIDGE SQ
4 KESWICK CT
5 KESWICK WLK
6 THIRLMERE CT
7 BUTTERMERE CT

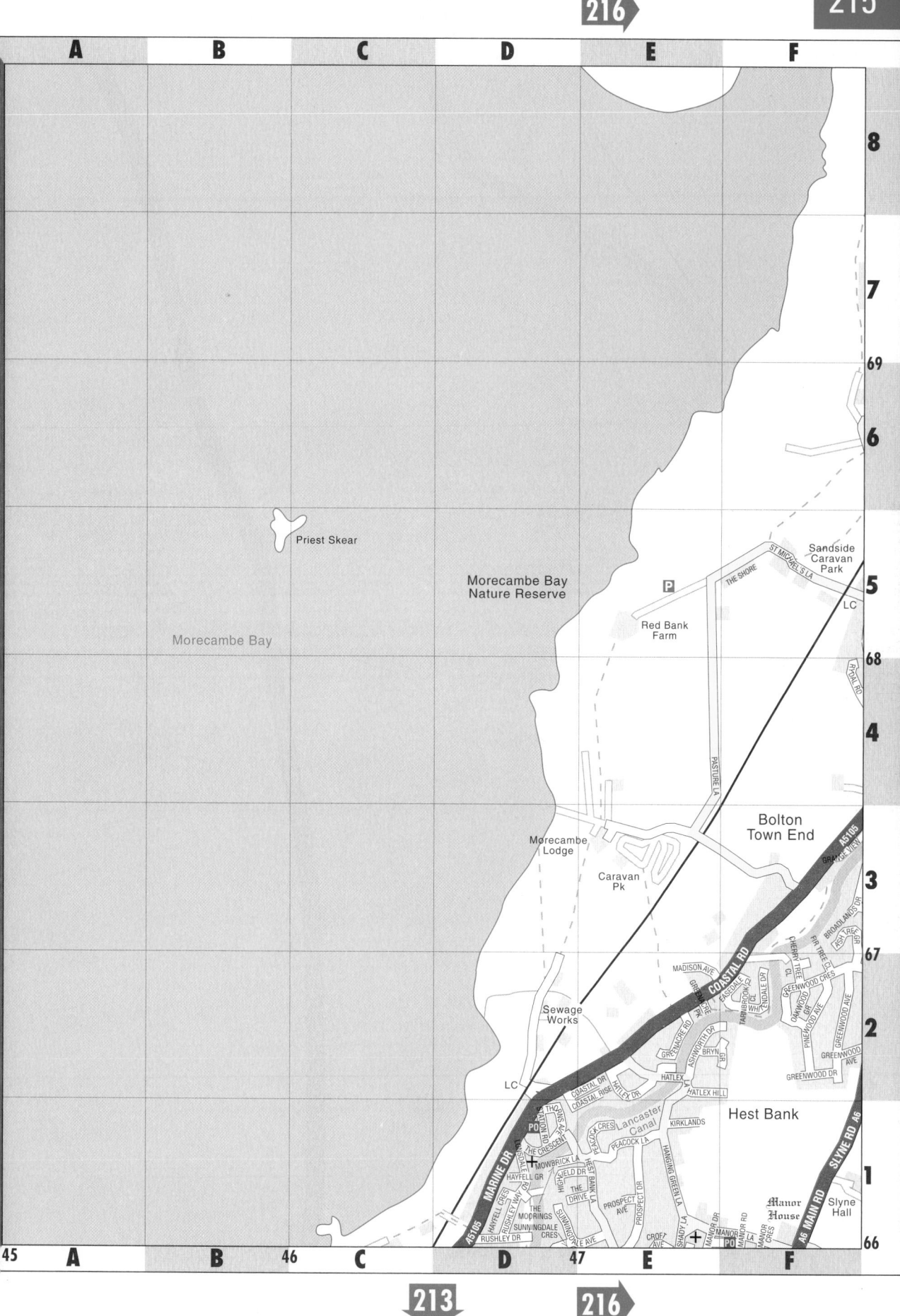

A   B   C   D   E   F

8

7

69

6

Priest Skear

Morecambe Bay
Nature Reserve

Sandside
Caravan
Park

ST MICHAEL'S LA

THE SHORE

P

LC

5

Morecambe Bay

Red Bank
Farm

PASTURE LA

PROAL RD

68

4

Bolton
Town End

A5105

GRANGE VIEW

Morecambe
Lodge

Caravan
Pk

BROADLANDS DR

ASH TREE

3

MADISON AVE

COASTAL RD

CHERRY TREE CL

FIR TREE

67

GREENACRE RD

EASTDALE

ZINDALE DR

OAKWOOD DR

GREENWOOD CRES

PINEWOOD DR

GREENWOOD AVE

Sewage
Works

TARNBROOK WHI

GREENACRE RD

ASHWORTH DR

BRYN

HATLEX

GREENWOOD
AVE

2

GREENACRE RD

HATLEX DR

Hest Bank

LC

COASTAL DR

COASTAL RISE

HATLEX HILL

GREENWOOD DR

Lancaster Canal

KIRKLANDS

THO...

CRES

PLAY...

PEACOCK LA

HANGING GREEN LA

MARINE DR

PO

MOWBRICK LA

THE CRESCENT

HEST BANK LA

PROSPECT
AVE

PROSPECT DR

Manor
House

A6 MAIN RD

SLYNE RD A6

Slyne
Hall

1

A5105

HAYFELL GR

RUSHLEY WAY

THE
MODRINGS

SUNNINGDALE
CRES

HIGH...

YIELD DR

THE DRIVE

SHADY LA

MANOR RD

MANOR
CRES

PO

RUSHLEY DR

SUNNINGDALE AVE

CROFT
AVE

MANOR LA

66

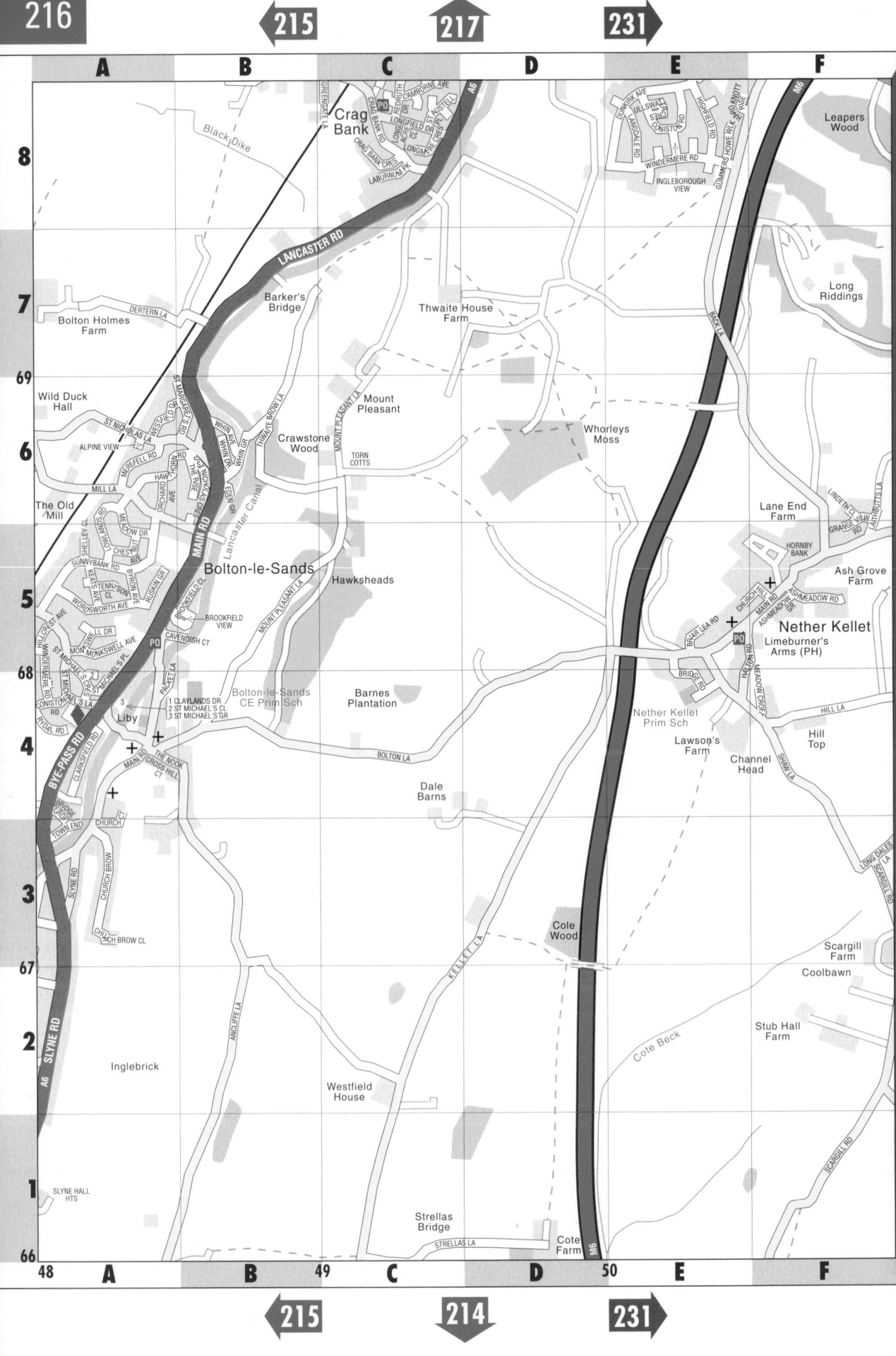

215
217
231
215
214
231

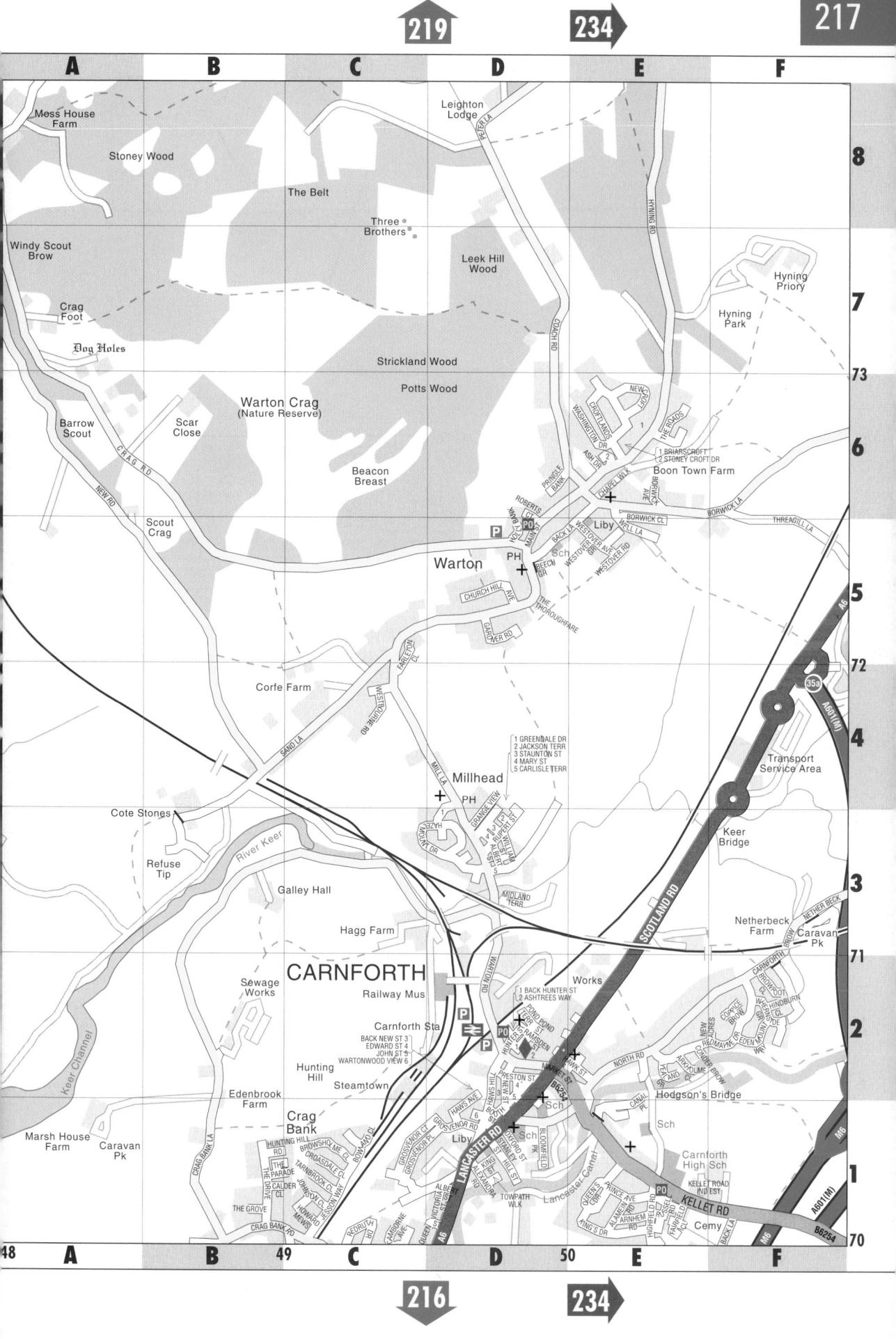

A B C D E F

8
73
7
6
5
72
4
3
71
2
1
70

Moss House Farm
Stoney Wood
The Belt
Leighton Lodge
PETER LA
HYNING RD
Hyning Priory
Hyning Park
Three Brothers
Leek Hill Wood
Windy Scout Brow
Strickland Wood
Potts Wood
CHURCH RD
Crag Foot
Dog Holes
Warton Crag
(Nature Reserve)
Barrow Scout
Scar Close
Beacon Breast
NEW RD
CRAG RD
Scout Crag
Corfe Farm
1 BRIARSCROFT
2 STONEY CROFT DR
Boon Town Farm
THE ROADS
NEW C
CROFT LANDS
WASHINGTON DR
ASH DR
PRINGLE BANK
CHAPEL WLK
BORWICK'S AVE
Liby
BORWICK CL
THREAGILL LA
BORWICK LA
ROBERTS
BACK LA
MAIN ST
PO
WESTOVER AVE
Sch
WELL LA
WESTOVER RD
WESTOVER RD
BEECH GR
Warton
PH
THE THOROUGHFARE
CHURCH HILL
GARDEN RD
CARE COM CL
WESTBOURNE RD
SAND LA
MILL LA
1 GREENDALE DR
2 JACKSON TERR
3 STAUNTON ST
4 MARY ST
5 CARLISLE TERR
Millhead
PH
A6
A601(M)
35a
Transport Service Area
Keer Bridge
SCOTLAND RD
GRANGE VIEW
HAZEL
MOWN DR
WILLIAM
RUPERT ST
Cote Stones
River Keer
Refuse Tip
Galley Hall
Hagg Farm
MIDLAND TERR
Netherbeck Farm
Caravan Pk
CARNFORTH BROW
CARNFORTH
Railway Mus
WARTON RD
Works
1 BACK HUNTER ST
2 ASHTREES WAY
Sewage Works
Carnforth Sta
BACK NEW ST 3
EDWARD ST 4
JOHN ST 5
WARTONWOOD VIEW 6
PO
PO
POND SOND
HINTONS MARSDEN
BROWFOOT
HINDBURN
NEW ACRES
REDMAYNE
MOUNT PD
COPPICE BROW
EDEN
Hodgson's Bridge
Sch
Carnforth High Sch
Hunting Hill
Steamtown
Crag Bank
Liby
HAWS AVE
PRESTON ST
GROSVENOR CT
GROSVENOR PL
K'SMITH ST
HIGH SMITH
HAWK ST
MARKET ST
NORTH RD
B6254
Sch
CANAL TER
ARKHOLME
COLNE BROW
ABBEYSTEAD
Sch
ST KING ST
ST ALEXANDRA
Sch
BLOOMFIELD
OXFORD ST
SEFTON
KELLET RD
Carnforth High Sch
M6
Marsh House Farm
Caravan Pk
Edenbrook Farm
CRAG BANK LA
HUNTING HILL RD
THE PARADE
THE DRIVE
CALDER CL
THE GROVE
BROWSHQ'ME CL
CROASDALE CL
TARNBROOK CL
JOHNSTON CL
HOWARD MEWS
SESSION WAY
CARBORNE LANE
BORWICK RD
REDRUTH RD
QUEEN'S DR
QUEEN VICTORIA
CARNFORTH RD
ALBERT
CRAG BANK RD
LANCASTER RD
A6
TOWPATH WLK
Lancaster Canal
QUEEN'S CT
PRINCE AVE
ARNHEM RD
HIGHFIELD DR
ALAMEIN
RUSSELL
TARFIELD
KELLET RD
BACK LA
Cemy
KELLET ROAD IND EST
PO
KING'S DR
A601(M)
B6254

237

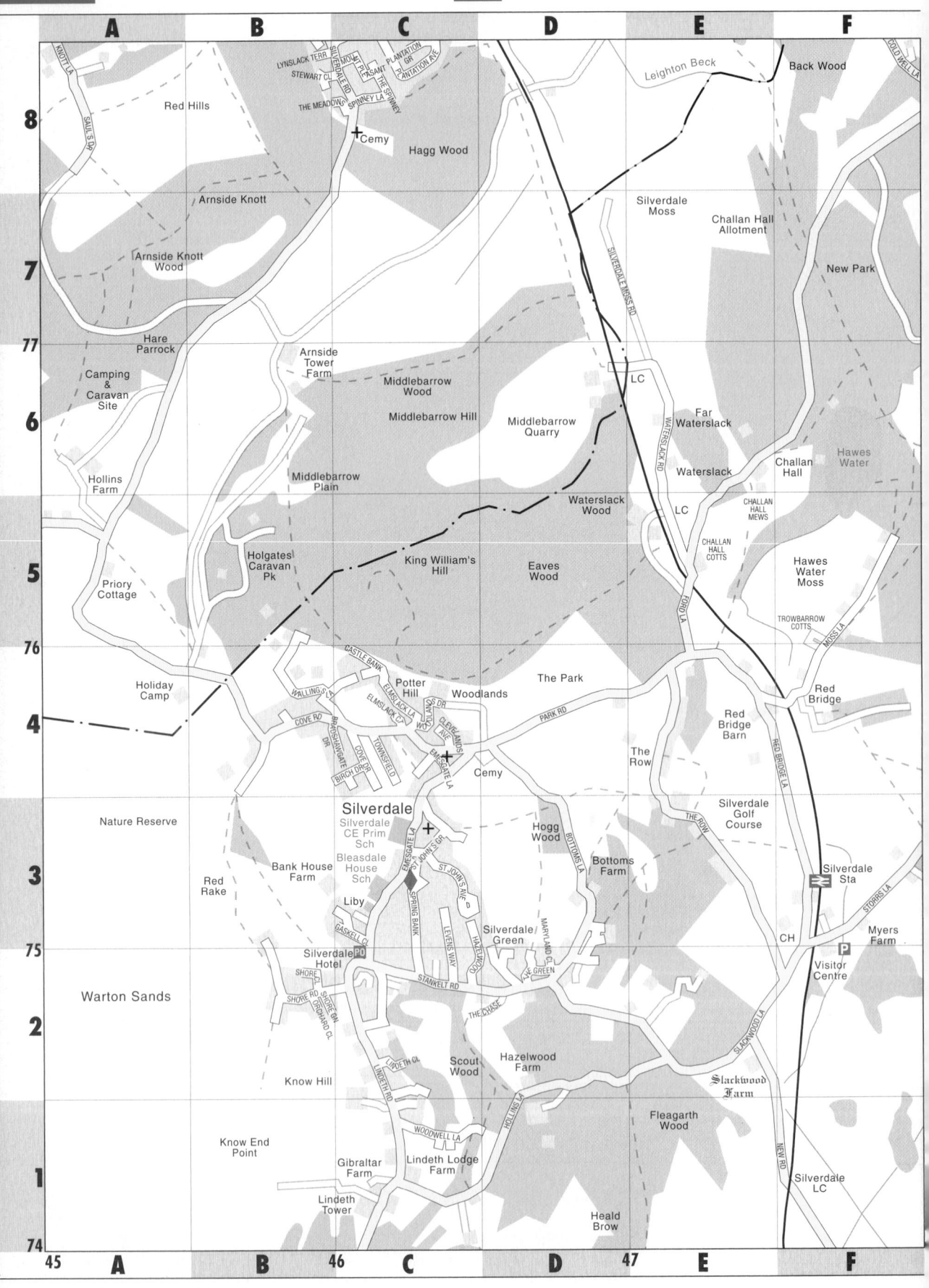

Map showing Silverdale and surrounding area with grid references A–F (horizontal) and 1–8 (vertical).

Labels visible on the map:

KNOTT LA, Red Hills, LYNSLACK TERR, PLANTATION GR, STEWART CL, THE SPINNEY, PLANTATION AVE, Back Wood, COLD WELL LA, Leighton Beck, THE MEADOWS, SPINNEY LA, Hagg Wood, Silverdale Moss, Challan Hall Allotment, SAUL'S DR, Cemy, Arnside Knott, Silverdale Moss, New Park, SILVERDALE MOSS RD, Arnside Knott Wood, Arnside Tower Farm, Middlebarrow Wood, Middlebarrow Hill, Middlebarrow Quarry, LC, Far Waterslack, WATERSLACK RD, Hare Parrock, Camping & Caravan Site, Middlebarrow Plain, Middlebarrow Quarry, Waterslack, Challan Hall, Hawes Water, Hollins Farm, Holgates Caravan Pk, Waterslack Wood, CHALLAN HALL MEWS, LC, CHALLAN HALL COTTS, Priory Cottage, King William's Hill, Eaves Wood, FORD LA, Hawes Water Moss, TROWBARROW COTTS, MOSS LA, Holiday Camp, CASTLE BANK, Potter Hill, Woodlands, The Park, Red Bridge Barn, Red Bridge, WALLING'S LA, ELMSLACK LA, ELMSLACK CL, COLLINS DR, PARK RD, The Row, RED BRIDGE LA, COVE RD, BRAMSHAUGATE DR, COVE RD, TOWNSFIELD, EMESGATE LA, Cemy, Silverdale Golf Course, BIRCH DR, Nature Reserve, Silverdale, Silverdale CE Prim Sch, Bleasdale House Sch, Hogg Wood, BOTTOMS LA, Bottoms Farm, THE ROW, Silverdale Sta, STORRS LA, Red Rake, Bank House Farm, Liby, ST JOHN'S GR, ST JOHN'S AVE, Silverdale Green, MARYLAND, CH, Myers Farm, GASKELL CL, EMESGATE LA, SPRING BANK, LEVENS WAY, HALDOOD, THE GREEN, P Visitor Centre, Warton Sands, Silverdale Hotel, SHORE, SHORE RD, STANKELT RD, THE CHASE, SLACKWOOD LA, SHORE RD, SHORE BM, ORCHARD CL, LINDETH RD, Scout Wood, Hazelwood Farm, Slackwood Farm, Know Hill, POETH CL, HOLLINS LA, Fleagarth Wood, NEW RD, Know End Point, WOODWELL LA, Gibraltar Farm, Lindeth Lodge Farm, Silverdale LC, Lindeth Tower, Heald Brow

Grid numbers: 45, 46, 47 (bottom); 74, 75, 76, 77 (left, lower); 8, 7, 6, 5, 4, 3, 2, 1 (left)

A B C D E F

Leighton House
Leighton Beck Bridge
Beetham Caravan Pk
Silver Ridge Caravan Pk
Fell End Caravan Pk
BRACKENTHAITE RD
Leighton Beck
Hall More Farm
Hale Moss
8
Gait Barrows (Nature Reserve)
Brackenthwaite Farm
Hall More Caravan Pk
Main Drain
7
East Coppice
Thrang End Wood
Thrang End Farm
Hazel Grove
77
A6
6
West Coppice
THRANG BROW LA
Thrang Coppice
Thrang Moss
White Moss
Birch Cottage
Yealand Hall Allotment
5
Trough Plantation
Yealand Storrs
Yealand Hall
SILVERDALE RD
76
The Trough
STORRS LA
Brow Foot Farm
EIGHT ACRE LA
NINETEEN ACRE LA
4
Storrs Moss
Round Top
Yealand Redmayne
MEADOWS CL
THE
SANDGATE
PO
WELL LA
Leighton Moss (Nature Reserve)
Cringlebarrow Wood
Storrs Farm
FOOTERAN LA
Yealand Conyers CE Prim Sch
3
FLAT LA
75
Grisedale Farm
Deepdale Wood
Old Hall Farm
ROSE ACRE LA
The Pool
New Inn (PH)
Dykes Farm
A6
2
Leighton Hall Home Farm
Yealand Manor
YEALAND RD
DYKES LA
Dykes House
Grisedale Wood
Yealand Conyers
Leighton Hall
Leighton Park
1
Hermitage Wood
PETER LA
HYNING RD
SNAPE LA
74

48 A B 49 C D 50 E F

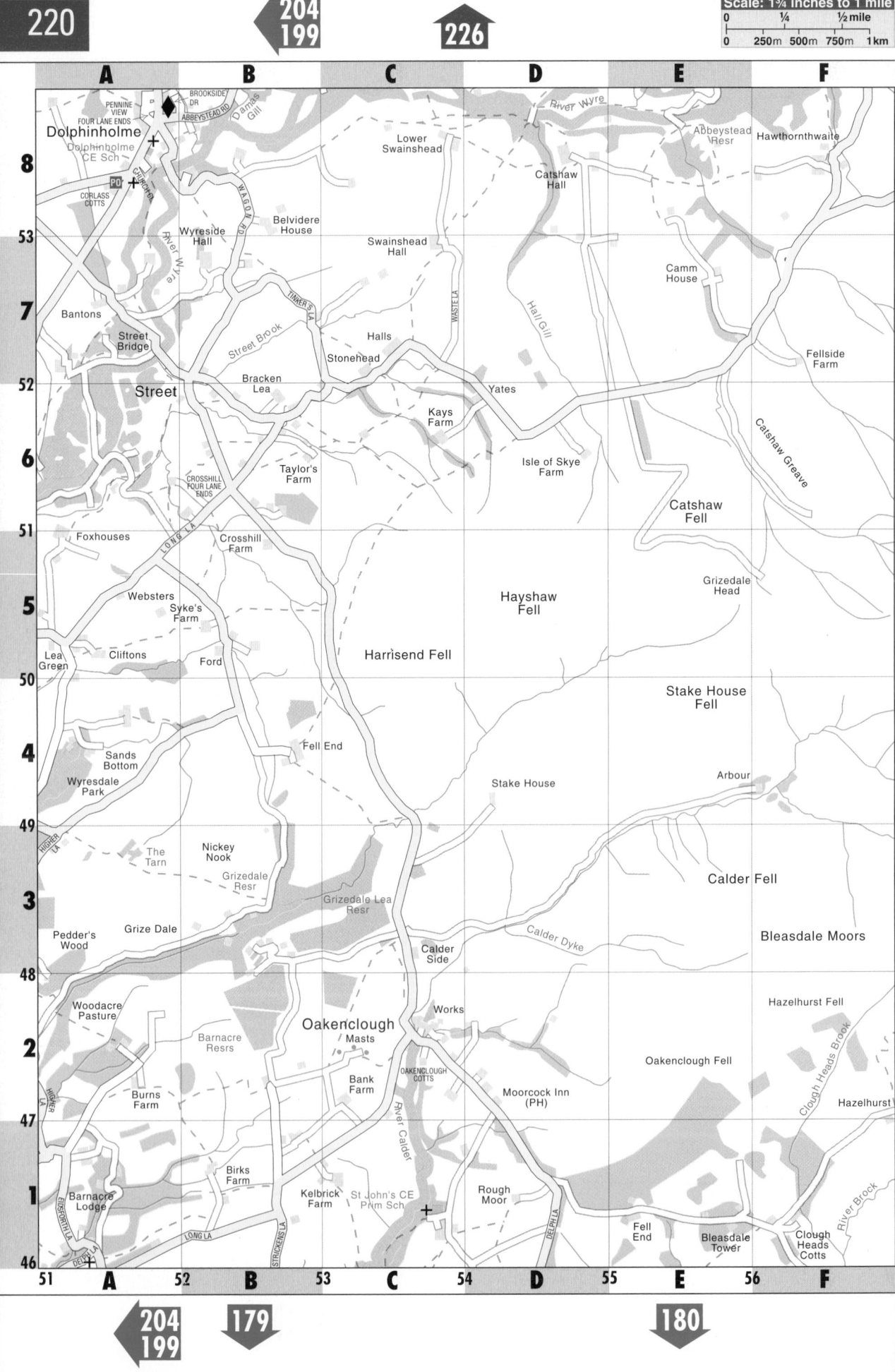

204
199

226

Scale: 1¾ inches to 1 mile

0   ¼   ½ mile

0   250m   500m   750m   1km

A   B   C   D   E   F

PENNINE VIEW
FOUR LANE ENDS
BROOKSIDE DR
ABBEYSTEAD RD
Damas Gill
River Wyre
Abbeystead Resr
Hawthornthwaite

Dolphinholme
Dolphinholme CE Sch
PO
CORLASS COTTS
CHURCH LA
WAGON RD
Lower Swainshead
Catshaw Hall

8

Wyreside Hall
Belvidere House
Swainshead Hall
Camm House

53

Bantons
Street Bridge
Street Brook
TINKER'S LA
Halls
Stonehead
WASTE LA
Hall Gill
Fellside Farm

7

Street
Bracken Lea
Yates
Catshaw Greave

52

Kays Farm

6

Taylor's Farm
Isle of Skye Farm
Catshaw Fell

51

Foxhouses
LONG LA
Crosshill Farm
CROSSHILL FOUR LANE ENDS
Hayshaw Fell
Grizedale Head

5

Websters
Syke's Farm
Harrisend Fell
Stake House Fell

50

Lea Green
Cliftons
Ford

4

Sands Bottom
Wyresdale Park
Fell End
Stake House
Arbour

49

HIGHER LA
The Tarn
Nickey Nook
Grizedale Resr
Grizedale Lea Resr
Calder Dyke
Calder Fell

3

Pedder's Wood
Grize Dale
Calder Side
Bleasdale Moors

48

Woodacre Pasture
Barnacre Resrs
Works
Hazelhurst Fell

2

HIGHER LA
Oakenclough
Masts
OAKENCLOUGH COTTS
Bank Farm
Moorcock Inn (PH)
Oakenclough Fell
Clough Heads Brook
Hazelhurst

Burns Farm

47

Birks Farm
River Calder
Rough Moor
DELPH LA
Fell End
Bleasdale Tower
River Brook

1

ELMSWORTH LA
Barnacre Lodge
LONG LA
Kelbrick Farm
STRICKENS LA
St John's CE Prim Sch
Clough Heads Cotts

DELPH LA

46

51   A   52   B   53   C   54   D   55   E   56   F

204
199

179

180

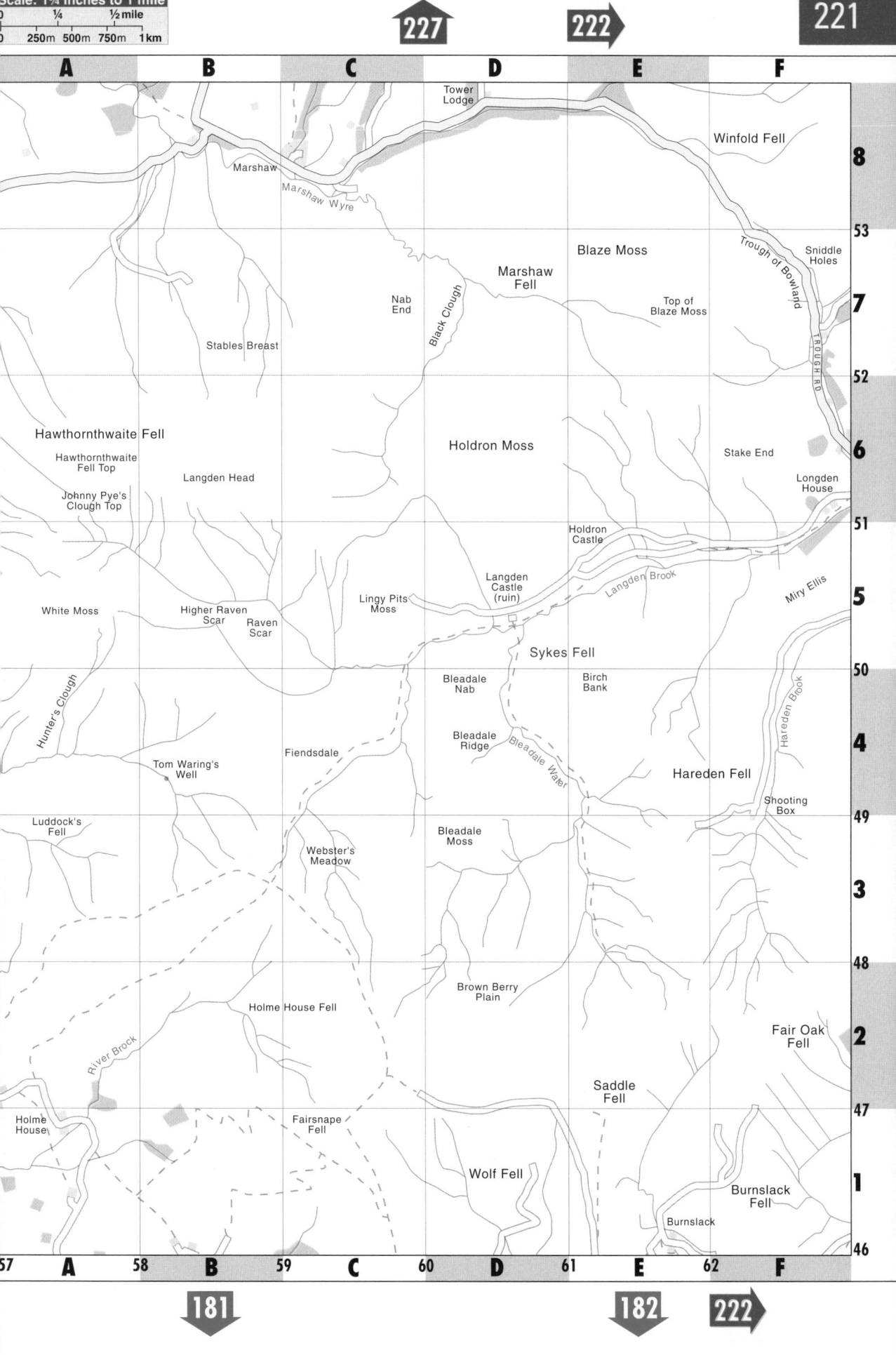

Scale: 1¾ inches to 1 mile
¼ ½ mile
250m 500m 750m 1km

227

222

221

A   B   C   D   E   F

8
Tower Lodge
Winfold Fell
Marshaw
Marshaw Wyre
53
Blaze Moss
Trough of Bowland
Sniddle Holes
Marshaw Fell
7
Nab End
Black Clough
Top of Blaze Moss
Stables Breast
52
TROUGH RD
Hawthornthwaite Fell
Holdron Moss
6
Stake End
Hawthornthwaite Fell Top
Langden Head
Longden House
Johnny Pye's Clough Top
51
Holdron Castle
White Moss
Higher Raven Scar
Lingy Pits Moss
Langden Castle (ruin)
Langden Brook
Miry Ellis
5
Raven Scar
Sykes Fell
Bleadale Nab
Birch Bank
50
Hunter's Clough
Bleadale Ridge
Bleadale Water
Hareden Brook
4
Tom Waring's Well
Fiendsdale
Hareden Fell
Shooting Box
Luddock's Fell
49
Bleadale Moss
Webster's Meadow
3
48
Brown Berry Plain
River Brock
Holme House Fell
Fair Oak Fell
2
Saddle Fell
47
Holme House
Fairsnape Fell
Wolf Fell
Burnslack Fell
1
Burnslack
46

A   B   C   D   E   F
57 58 59 60 61 62

Scale: 1¾ inches to 1 mile

0   ¼   ½ mile
0 250m 500m 750m 1km

A   B   C   D   E   F

Burn
Side

Whins Brow

Whin Fell

Costy Clough

Burn
Fell

8

Brennand River

53

Beatrix
Fell

Burn
House

Calder
Moor

7

Rams Clough

The
Hey

New
Biggin

52

Staple Oak
Fell

River Dunsop

Oxenhurst

Brunghill
Moor

BACK LA

6

Sykes Farm

Sykes
Nab

Bishops
House

Beatrix

Back of
Hill Barn

Gamble Hole
Farm

51

Hareden
Farm

TROUGH RD

Closes
Barn

Low
Barn

Knot or
Sugar Loaf

Moor
End

Heaning

5

Hareden Brook

Dunsop
Bridge

Mossthwaite

Boarsden

Brown
Nab

Bowland Forest
RC Sch

THE
CRESCENT PO P

FORESTRY
HOUSES

Root

Thorneyholme

Knowlmere
Manor

Fober
Farm

50

Mellor
Knoll

River Hodder

Hodder Bank
Fell

4

Totridge

New Hay
Farm

Langden
Bridge

Birkett

49

Ing
Barn

Hodder Bank
Farm

Burholme

Birkett
Fell

3

Whitmore

Crag
House

48

Burholme
Bridge

Lower
Fence Wood

Marl
Hill

2

Higher
Fence Wood

Reed Barn
Cottage

Higher
Whitewell

Crimpton

Dinkling Green
Farm

New
Laund

Whitewell

Marl Hill
Moor

47

The Inn at
Whitewell

HALL HILL

New Laund
Hill

Spire
Farm

1

Seedalls

Fair
Oak

Wilsons

46

63   A   64   B   65   C   66   D   67   E   68   F

A   B   C   D   E   F

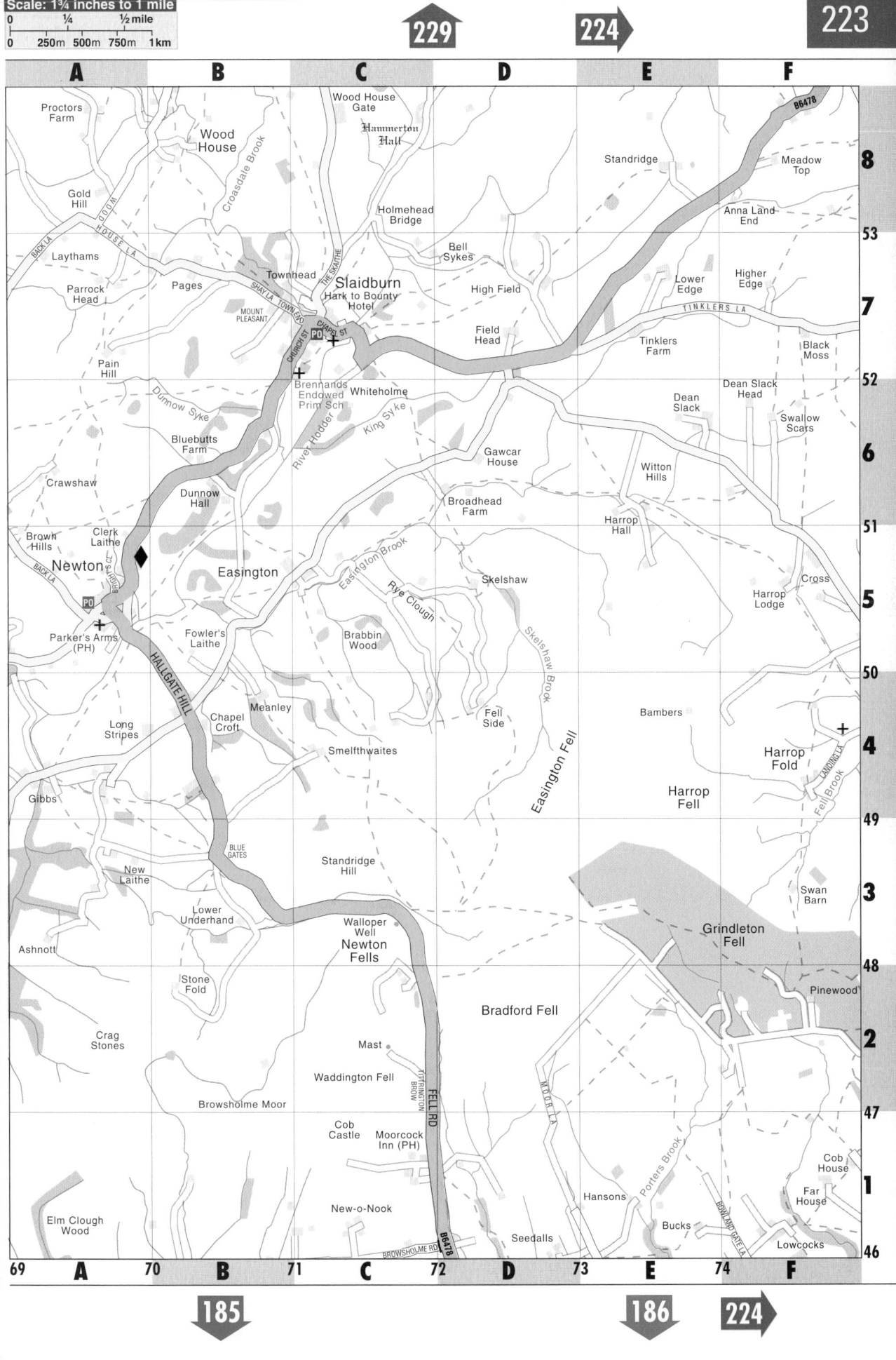

Proctors Farm
Wood House
Wood House Gate
Hammerton Hall
Standridge
Meadow Top

8

Gold Hill
WOOD HOUSE LA
Croasdale Brook
Holmehead Bridge
Anna Land End
B6478

53

Laythams
BACK LA
Townhead
THE SKAITHE
Bell Sykes
Lower Edge
Higher Edge
TINKLERS LA

Parrock Head
Pages
SHAY LA
TOWN END
Slaidburn
Hark to Bounty Hotel
High Field
Tinklers Farm
Black Moss

7

Pain Hill
MOUNT PLEASANT
CHAPEL ST
PO
Field Head
Dean Slack Head
52

Dunnow Syke
CHURCH ST
Brennands Endowed Prim Sch
Whiteholme
King Syke
Gawcar House
Dean Slack
Swallow Scars

Bluebutts Farm
RIVER HODDER
Witton Hills

6

Crawshaw
Dunnow Hall
Broadhead Farm
Harrop Hall

51

Brown Hills
Clerk Laithe
Easington
Easington Brook
Rye Clough
Skelshaw
Cross

Newton
BACK LA
♦
Harrop Lodge

5

PO
Fowler's Laithe
Brabbin Wood
Skelshaw Brook
Bambers

Parker's Arms (PH)
Meanley
Fell Side
Easington Fell
Harrop Fold

50

Long Stripes
Chapel Croft
Smelfthwaites
Harrop Fell
LANDING LA

4

Gibbs
HALLGATE HILL
Fell Brook

49

New Laithe
BLUE GATES
Standridge Hill
Swan Barn

3

Lower Underhand
Grindleton Fell

Ashnott
Walloper Well
Newton Fells
Pinewood

48

Stone Fold
Bradford Fell

Crag Stones
Mast

2

Waddington Fell
AITHRINGTON BROW
FELL RD
MOOR LA
Porters Brook
BOWLAND GATE LA

Browsholme Moor

47

Cob Castle
Moorcock Inn (PH)
Cob House

Hansons
Far House

1

Elm Clough Wood
New-o-Nook
Bucks
Lowcocks

Seedalls
BROWSHOLME RD
B6478

46

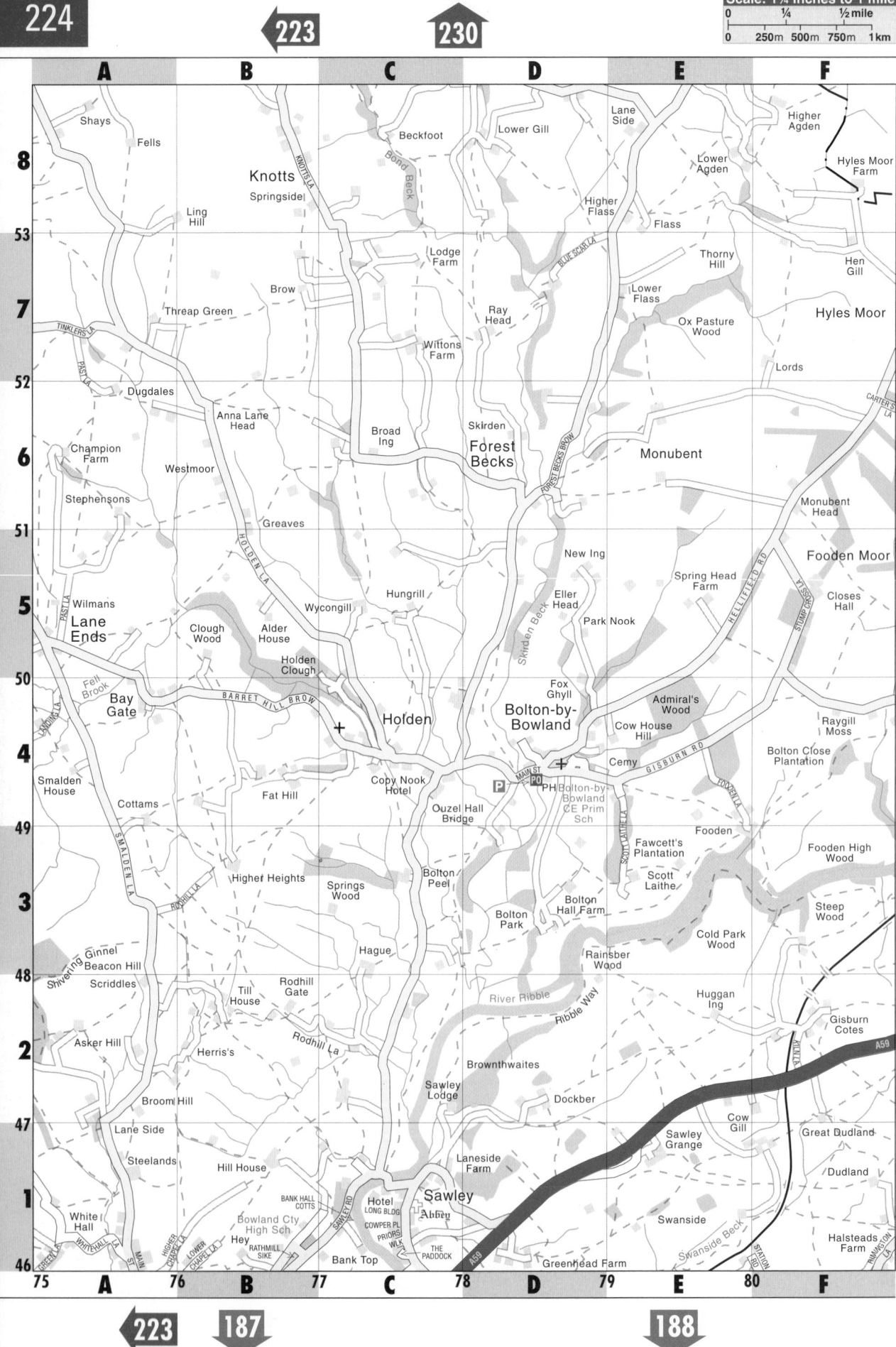

Scale: 1¾ inches to 1 mile

| 0 | ¼ | ½ mile |
| 0 | 250m | 500m | 750m | 1km |

A **B** **C** **D** **E** **F**

Shays

Fells

8

Knotts

Springside

Ling
Hill

Beckfoot

Lower Gill

Lane
Side

Higher
Agden

Hyles Moor
Farm

53

Lodge
Farm

Brow

Threap Green

Higher
Flass

Lower
Agden

Flass

Blue Scar La

Thorny
Hill

Hen
Gill

7

Dugdales

Wittons
Farm

Ray
Head

Lower
Flass

Ox Pasture
Wood

Hyles Moor

Tinklers La
Past La

52

Anna Lane
Head

Broad
Ing

Skirden

Lords

Carter's La

6

Champion
Farm

Westmoor

Forest
Becks

Monubent

Forest Becks Brow

Monubent
Head

Stephensons

Greaves

New Ing

Fooden Moor

Hellitfield Rd

Stump Cross

51

Holden La

Hungrill

Eller
Head

Spring Head
Farm

Closes
Hall

5

Wilmans

Lane
Ends

Clough
Wood

Wycongill

Alder
House

Park Nook

Skirden Beck

Past La

Fell Brook

Holden
Clough

Fox
Ghyll

Admiral's
Wood

Raygill
Moss

50

Bay
Gate

Barret Hill Brow

Holden

Bolton-by-
Bowland

Cow House
Hill

Bolton Close
Plantation

Fooden La

4

Smalden
House

Cottams

Fat Hill

Copy Nook
Hotel

P

Main St
PO
PH

Cemy

Gisburn Rd

Bolton-by-
Bowland
CE Prim
Sch

Smalden La

Ouzel Hall
Bridge

Fawcett's
Plantation

Fooden

Fooden High
Wood

49

Rodhill La

Higher Heights

Springs
Wood

Bolton
Peel

Scott Laithe La

Scott
Laithe

Steep
Wood

3

Shivering Ginnel
Beacon Hill

Hague

Bolton
Park

Bolton
Park

Bolton Hall
Farm

Rainsber
Wood

Cold Park
Wood

48

Scriddles

Till
House

Rodhill
Gate

River Ribble

Huggan
Ing

Gisburn
Cotes

2

Asker Hill

Herris's

Rodhill La

Ribble Way

Brownthwaites

Dockber

A59

Great Dudland

Broom Hill

Sawley
Lodge

Sawley
Grange

Cow
Gill

Dudland

47

Lane Side

Steelands

Hill House

Bank Hall
Cotts

Laneside
Farm

Swanside Beck

Station Rd

Halsteads
Farm

1

White
Hall

Bowland Cty
High Sch

Hey

Hotel
LONG BLDG
COWPER PL
PRIORS
WLK

Sawley
Abbey

Swanside

Whitehall La

Higher Chapel La

Lower Chapel La

Main St

Sawley Rd

Rathmill
Sike

Bank Top

THE
PADDOCK

A59

Greenhead Farm

Swanside Beck

Gisburn La

Grimmington La

46

Green La

75 **A** **76** **B** **77** **C** **78** **D** **79** **E** **80** **F**

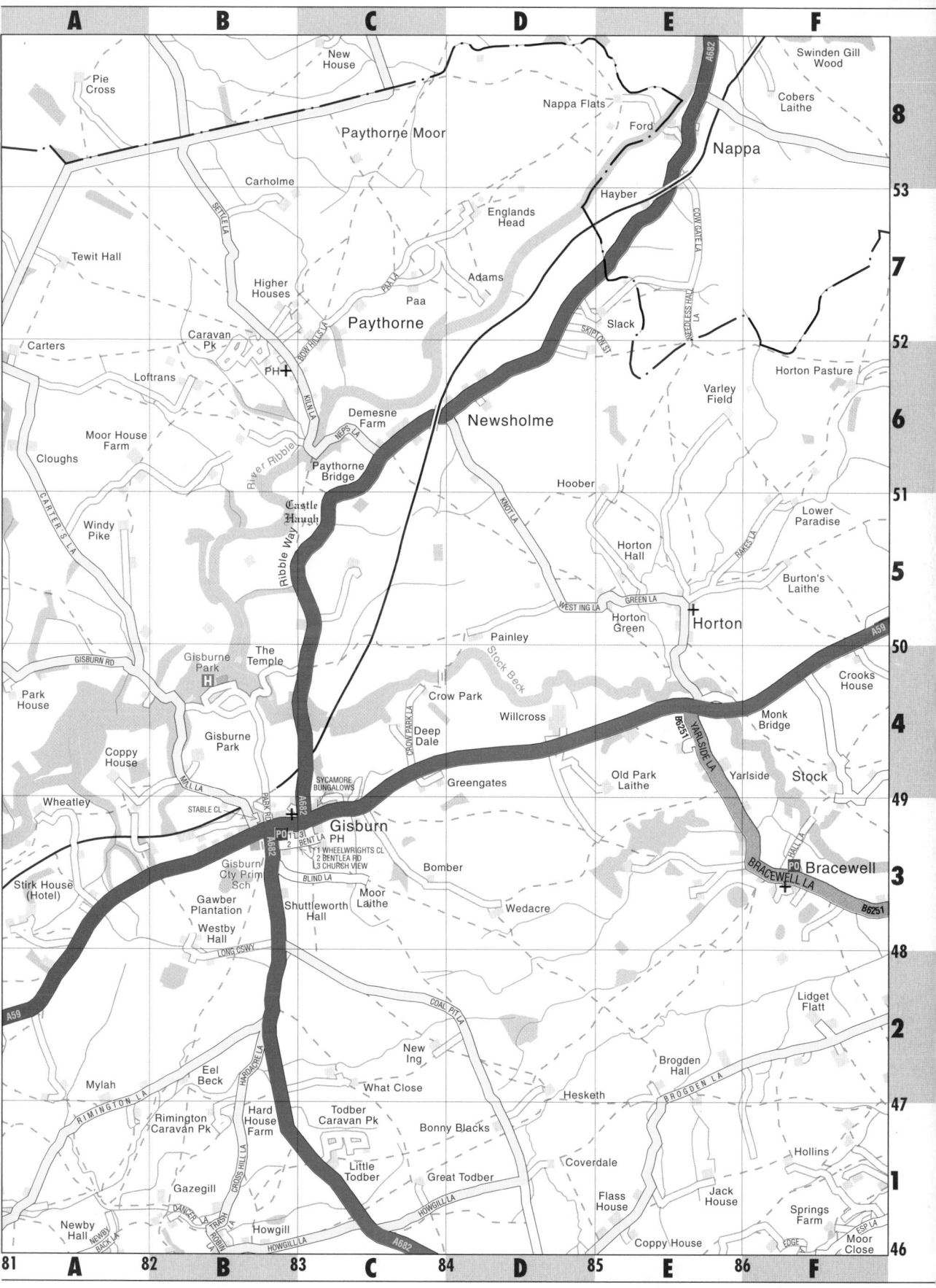

Scale: 1¾ inches to 1 mile

0   ¼   ½ mile
0 250m 500m 750m 1km

A **B** **C** **D** **E** **F**

8
53
7
52
6
51
5
50
4
49
3
48
2
47
1
46

Pie Cross

New House

Swinden Gill Wood

Paythorne Moor

Nappa Flats

Cobers Laithe

Ford

Carholme

Nappa

Tewit Hall

Englands Head

Hayber

Carters

Higher Houses

Adams

Slack

Horton Pasture

Loftrans

Caravan Pk

Paa

Paythorne

Varley Field

PH

Demesne Farm

Newsholme

Moor House Farm

Cloughs

Hoober

Lower Paradise

River Ribble

Paythorne Bridge

Horton Hall

Burton's Laithe

Windy Pike

Castle Haugh

Horton

Ribble Way

West Ing La

Green La

Horton Green

Crooks House

Park House

Gisburne Park

The Temple

Painley

Stock Beck

Monk Bridge

Coppy House

Gisburne Park

Crow Park

Willcross

Old Park Laithe

Yarlside

Stock

Wheatley

Deep Dale

Greengates

Stirk House (Hotel)

Gisburn

Bomber

Wedacre

Bracewell

Gawber Plantation

Shuttleworth Hall

Moor Laithe

Westby Hall

Lidget Flatt

New Ing

Mylah

Eel Beck

What Close

Hesketh

Brogden Hall

Rimington Caravan Pk

Hard House Farm

Todber Caravan Pk

Bonny Blacks

Hollins

Gazegill

Little Todber

Great Todber

Coverdale

Flass House

Jack House

Springs Farm

Newby Hall

Howgill

Coppy House

Moor Close

81 **A** 82 **B** 83 **C** 84 **D** 85 **E** 86 **F** 46

189   190   200

Scale: 1¾ inches to 1 mile

0   ¼   ½ mile
0 250m 500m 750m 1km

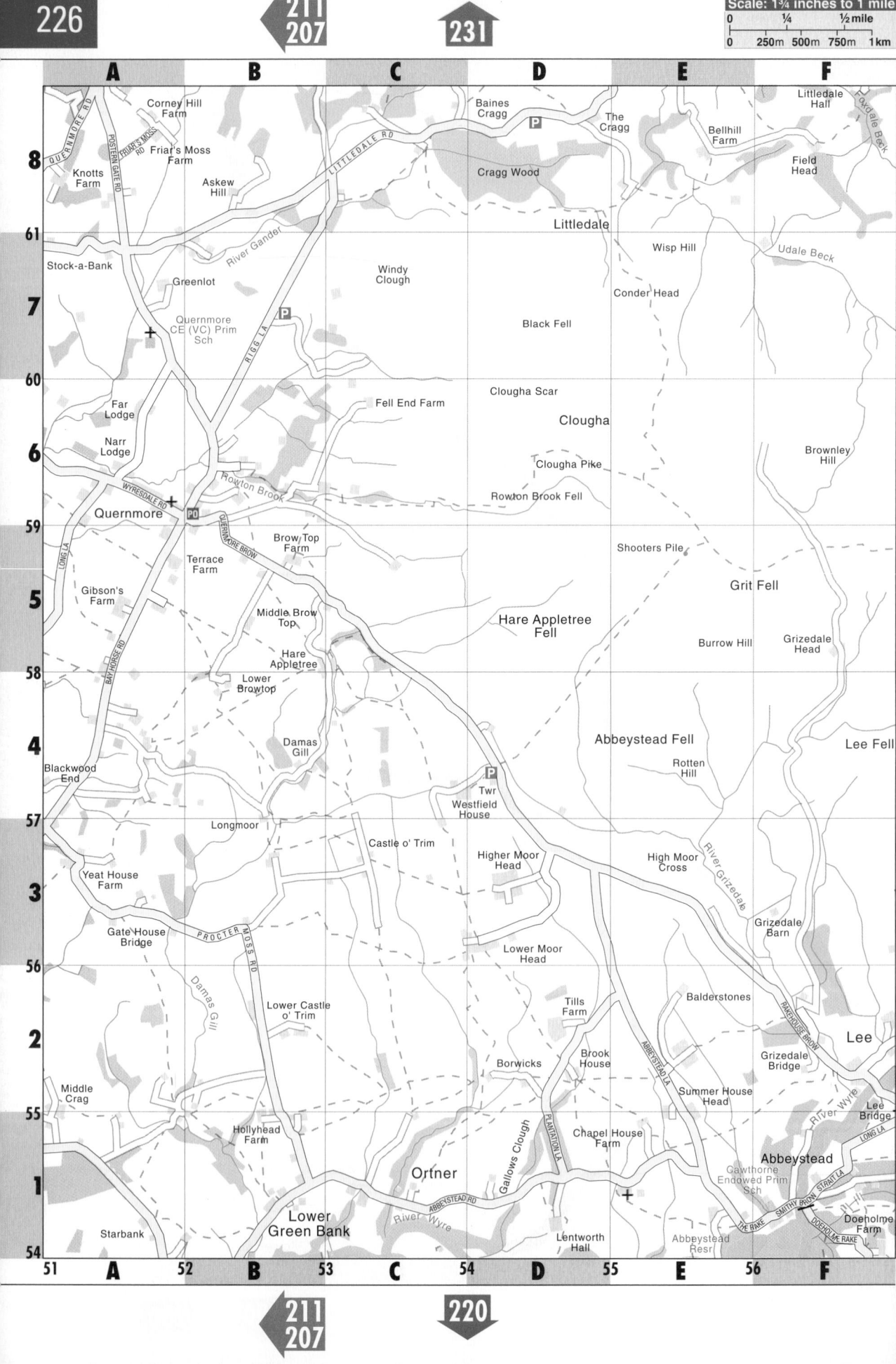

A   **B**   **C**   **D**   **E**   **F**

Quernmore Rd
Postern Gate Rd
Friar's Moss Rd
Corney Hill Farm
Friar's Moss Farm
Baines Cragg
P
The Cragg
Littledale Hall
Oakdale Beck
Bellhill Farm
Field Head

Knotts Farm
Askew Hill
Littledale Rd
Cragg Wood

8

Littledale

61

Stock-a-Bank
River Gander
Windy Clough
Wisp Hill
Udale Beck
Conder Head

Greenlot
P
Rigg La
Quernmore CE (VC) Prim Sch
Black Fell

7

60

Far Lodge
Fell End Farm
Clougha Scar
Clougha
Brownley Hill

Narr Lodge
Clougha Pike

6

Wyresdale Rd
Rowton Brook
Rowton Brook Fell

Long La
Quernmore
PO
Quernmore Brow
Brow Top Farm
Shooters Pile
Grit Fell

59

Terrace Farm

Gibson's Farm
Middle Brow Top
Hare Appletree Fell
Burrow Hill
Grizedale Head

5

Bay Horse Rd
Hare Appletree
Lower Browtop

58

Damas Gill
Abbeystead Fell
Rotten Hill
Lee Fell

4

Blackwood End
P
Twr
Westfield House

57

Longmoor
Castle o' Trim
Higher Moor Head
High Moor Cross
River Grizedale
Grizedale Barn

3

Yeat House Farm
Procter Moss Rd
Gate House Bridge
Lower Moor Head
Balderstones
Racehouse Brow
Lee

56

Damas Gill
Lower Castle o' Trim
Tills Farm
Grizedale Bridge

2

Middle Crag
Borwicks
Brook House
Abbeystead La
Summer House Head
River Wyre
Lee Bridge
Long La

55

Hollyhead Farm
Plantation La
Gallows Clough
Chapel House Farm
Abbeystead
Cawthorne Endowed Prim Sch
Strait La

1

Ortner
Abbeystead Rd
River Wyre
Lentworth Hall
Abbeystead Resr
The Rake
Smithy Brow
Doeholme Rake
Doeholme Farm

Starbank
Lower Green Bank

54

51 **A** **52** **B** **53** **C** **54** **D** **55** **E** **56** **F**

A   B   C   D   E   F

Mallowdale

Goodber
Fell

Haylot Fell

High Salter
Close

8

River Roeburn

61

Blanch
Fell

Foxdale Beck

Gallows
Hill

Mallowdale
Pike

7

Whitespout Gutter

High Stephen's
Head

60

Marking Fold
Hill

Rushbed Gutter

6

Shooting
Box

Lary Syke

59

Mallowdale Fell

Ward's
Stone

Brown
Syke

5

Ward's Stone
Breast

58

Hare Syke

Dunkenshaw Fell

4

Tarnbrook Fell

Luncheon
Huts

Thorn
Crag

57

Coppy
Heads

Black Side of
Tarnbrook Fell

Gavells Clough

Long
Crag

Stick Close Beck

Tarnsyke Clough

Thrush Clough

Gables Clough

3

Tarnsyke
Barn

Brennand
Great Hill

Brennand River

Dog
Crag

56

White Side of
Tarnbrook Fell

Swine
Crag

White
Crag

Brennand Round
Hill

Dunkenshaw

2

FLINTRON BROW

HIGHER SYKE

Tarnbrook Wyre

Deer Clough

Millers
House

Lower
Emmetts

Ouzel
Thorn

Tarnbrook

Greenside Hill

55

Higher
Emmetts

Greenside

White Moor

Brennand
Tarn

1

Marshaw Wyre

Border
Side

Hangington Clough
Bridge

Threaphaw
Fell

54

57   A   58   B   59   C   60   D   61   E   62   F

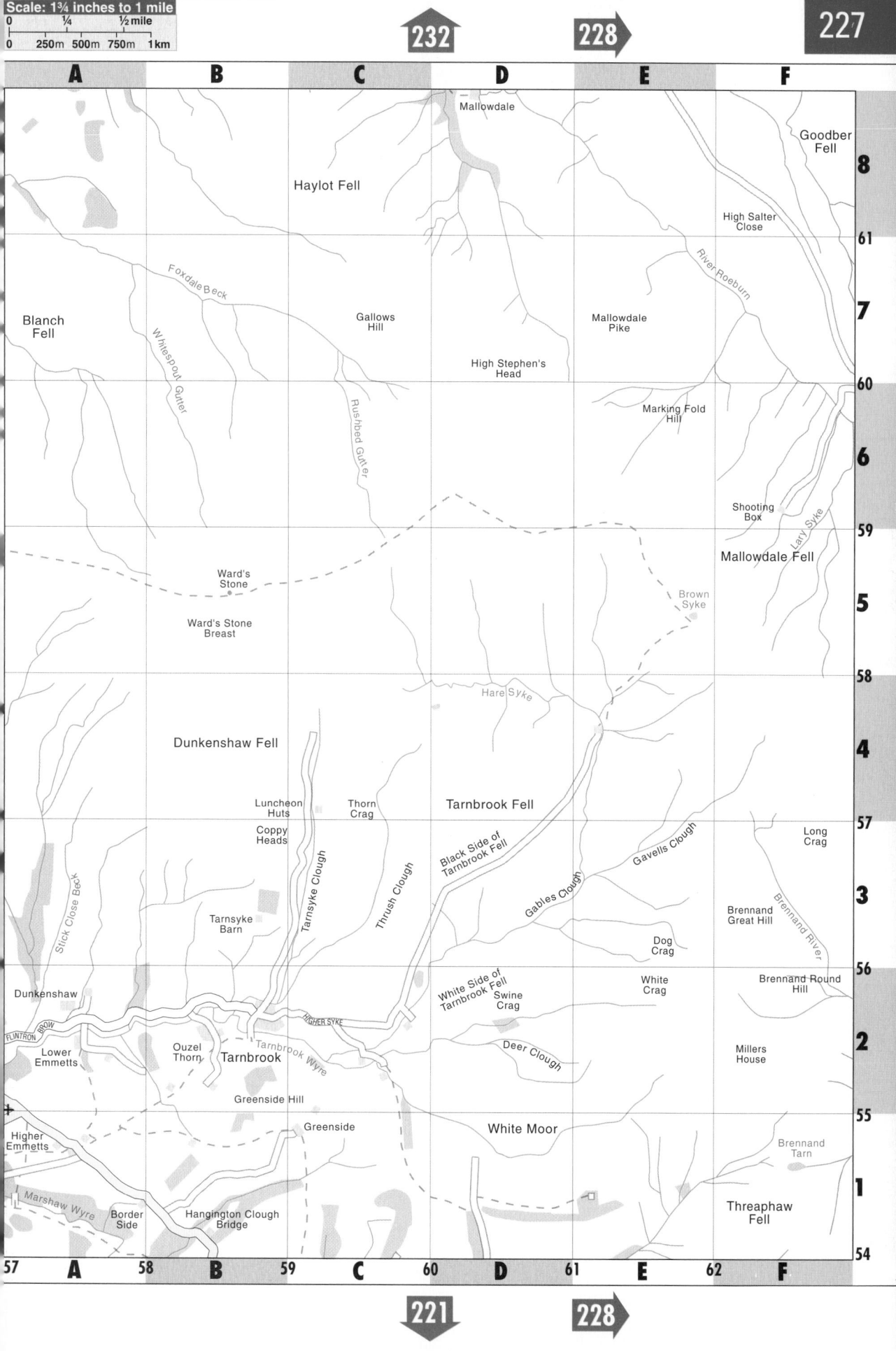

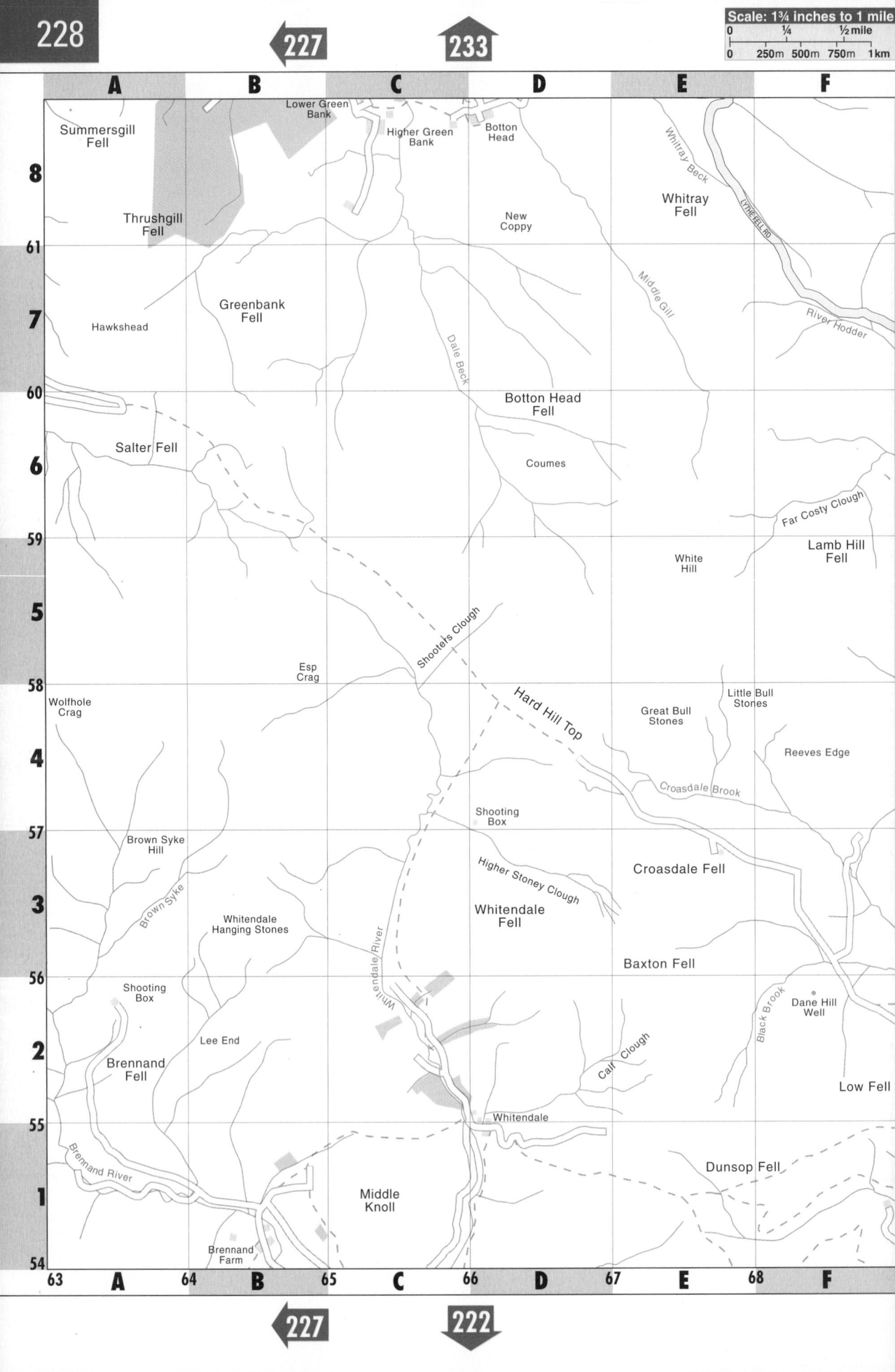

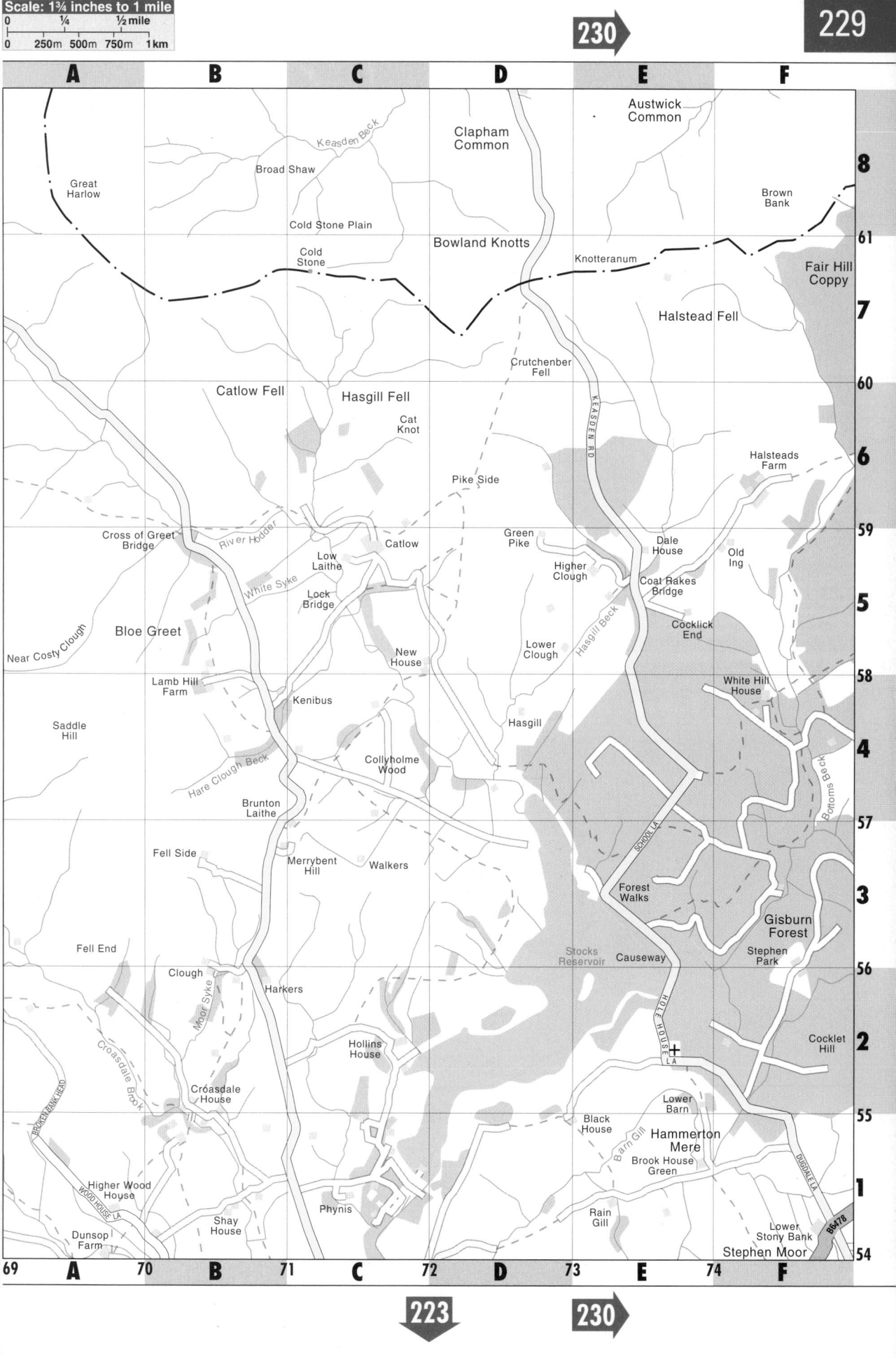

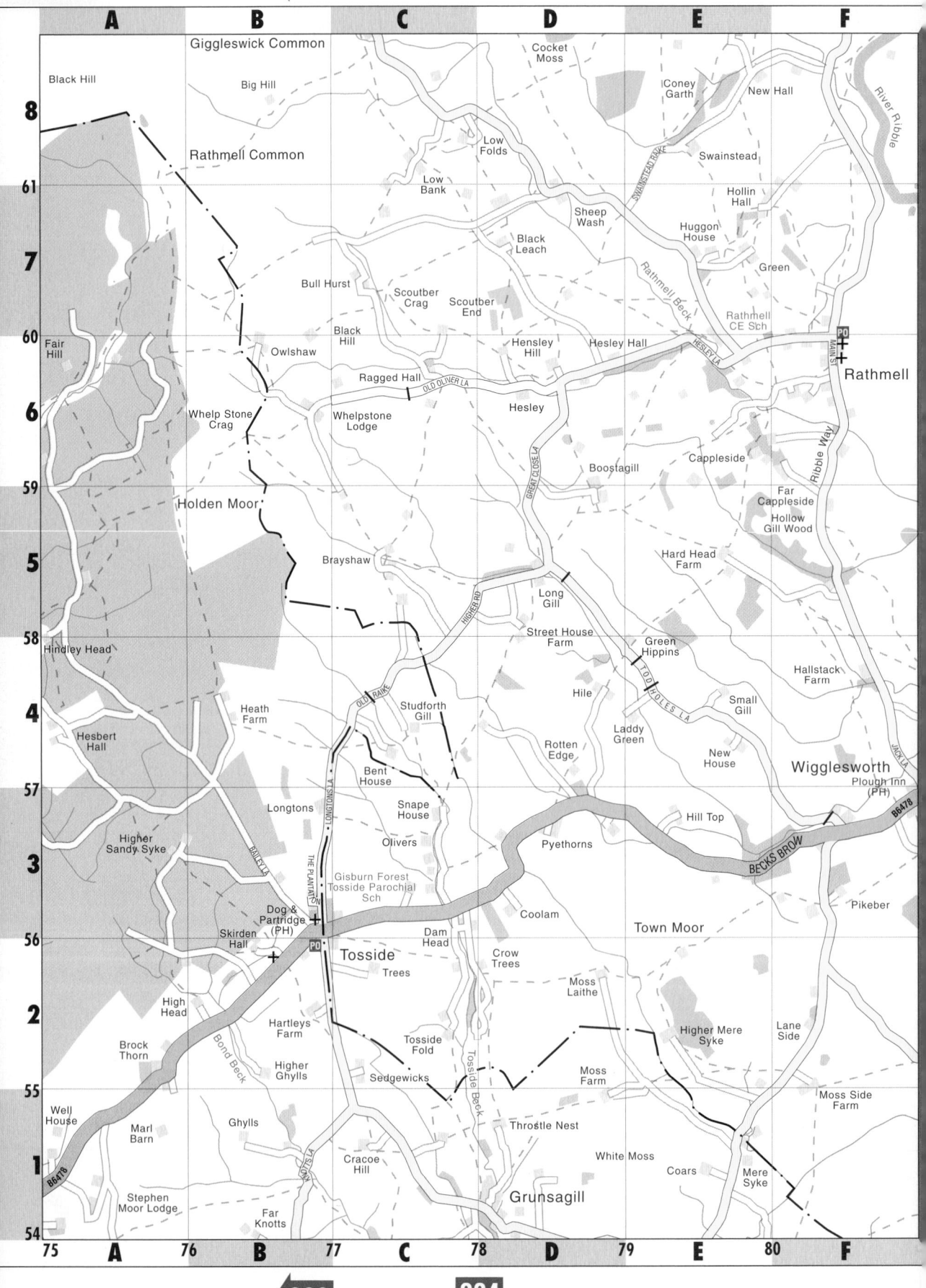

Scale: 1¾ inches to 1 mile

0   ¼   ½ mile
0 250m 500m 750m 1km

A   B   C   D   E   F

Giggleswick Common

Black Hill

Big Hill

Cocket Moss

Coney Garth

New Hall

River Ribble

8

Rathmell Common

Low Folds

Swainstead

61

Low Bank

Sheep Wash

Hollin Hall

7

Black Leach

Huggon House

Green

Bull Hurst

Scoutber Crag

Scoutber End

60

Fair Hill

Owlshaw

Black Hill

Hensley Hill

Hesley Hall

Rathmell CE Sch

PO

Rathmell

6

Whelp Stone Crag

Ragged Hall

OLD OLIVER LA

Hesley

Whelpstone Lodge

Boostagill

Cappleside

HESLEY LA

Ribble Way

59

Holden Moor

Brayshaw

Far Cappleside

Hollow Gill Wood

5

Long Gill

Hard Head Farm

58

Hindley Head

HIGHER RD

Street House Farm

Green Hippins

Hallstack Farm

4

Heath Farm

OLD RAIK

Studforth Gill

Hile

TOD HOLES LA

Small Gill

Hesbert Hall

Rotten Edge

Laddy Green

New House

Wigglesworth

57

Higher Sandy Syke

Longtons

Bent House

Snape House

Pyethorns

Hill Top

Plough Inn (PH)

B6478

Olivers

LONGTONS

BECKS BROW

3

BAILEY LA

THE PLANTATN

Gisburn Forest Tosside Parochial Sch

Coolam

Town Moor

Pikeber

Dog & Partridge (PH)

Dam Head

Skirden Hall

PO

Tosside

Crow Trees

56

High Head

Trees

Moss Laithe

Lane Side

2

Brock Thorn

Hartleys Farm

Tosside Fold

Higher Mere Syke

Bond Beck

Higher Ghylls

Sedgewicks

Moss Farm

Moss Side Farm

55

Well House

Ghylls

Tosside Beck

Throstle Nest

Coars

Mere Syke

1

Marl Barn

Cracoe Hill

White Moss

B6478

Stephen Moor Lodge

Far Knotts

Grunsagill

54

75   A   76   B   77   C   78   D   79   E   80   F

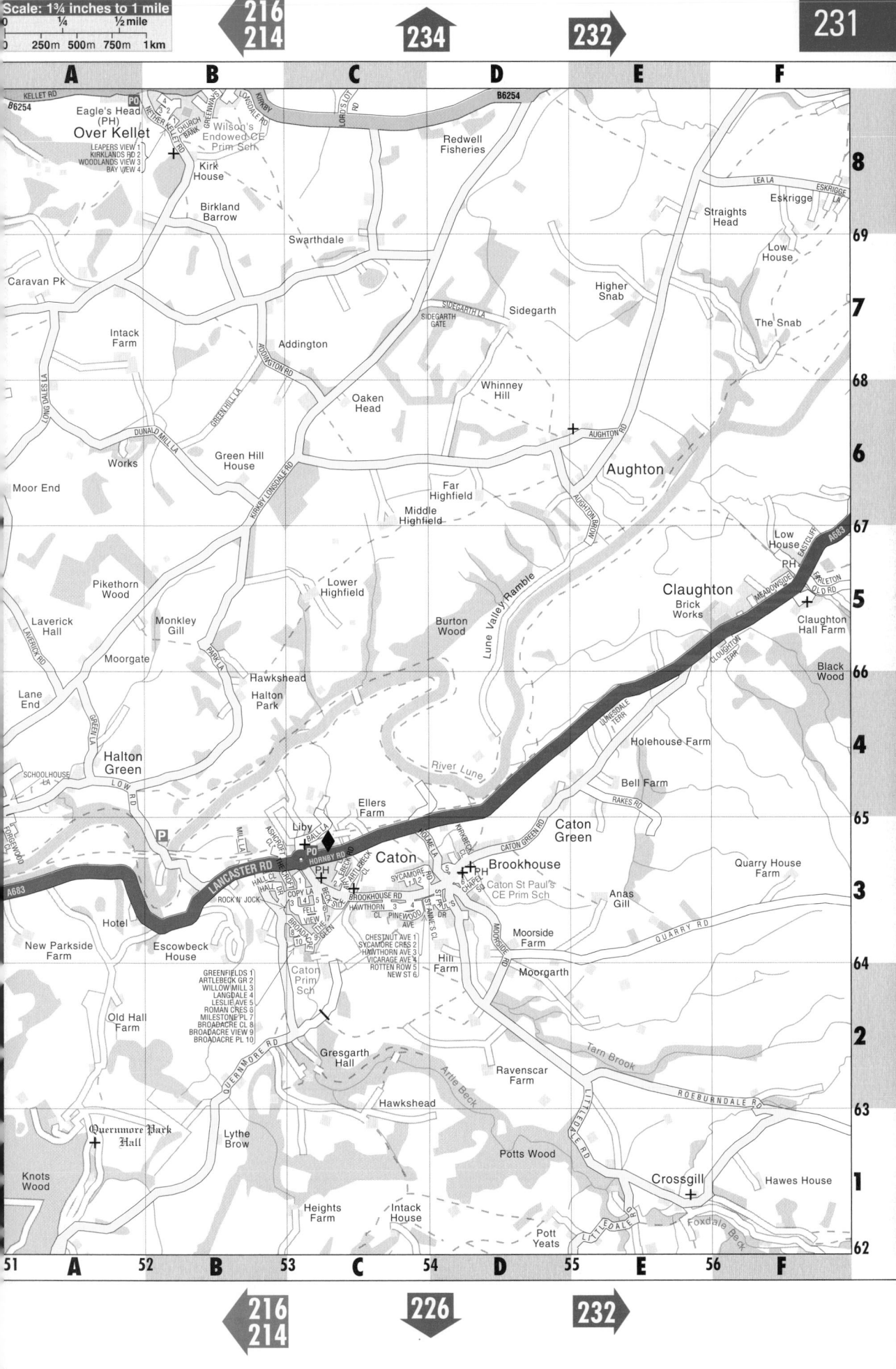

Scale: 1¾ inches to 1 mile

0 ¼ ½ mile
0 250m 500m 750m 1km

216
214

234

232

231

A B C D E F

8
69
7
68
6
67
5
66
4
65
3
64
2
63
1
62

KELLET RD
B6254
Eagle's Head (PH)
Over Kellet
LEAPERS VIEW 1
KIRKLANDS RD 2
WOODLANDS VIEW 3
BAY VIEW 4
PO
NETHER KELLET RD
CHURCH BANK
Kirk House
GREENWAYS
LOVSDALE RD
KIRKBY
Wilson's Endowed CE Prim Sch
LORD'S LOT RD
B6254
Redwell Fisheries

Birkland Barrow
Swarthdale
LEA LA
Straights Head
Eskrigge
ESKRIGGE LA
Low House

Caravan Pk
Higher Snab
The Snab

Intack Farm
Addington
SIDEGARTH LA
SIDEGARTH GATE
Sidegarth

LONG DALES LA
ADDINGTON RD
Oaken Head
Whinney Hill

GREEN HILL LA
DUNALD MILL LA
Green Hill House
Far Highfield
AUGHTON RD
Aughton

Works
Middle Highfield
AUGHTON BROW

Moor End
KIRKBY LONSDALE RD
Low House
EASTCLIFF
A683
PH
MEADOWSIDE
SKLETON OLD RD

Pikethorn Wood
Lower Highfield
Lune Valley Ramble
Claughton
Brick Works
CLOUGHTON TERR
Claughton Hall Farm

Laverick Hall
Monkley Gill
Burton Wood
Black Wood

LAVERICK RD
PARK LA
Hawkshead
LUNESDALE TERR

Moorgate
Halton Park
Holehouse Farm

Lane End
GREEN LA
SCHOOLHOUSE LA
Halton Green
River Lune
Bell Farm
RAKES RD

LOW RD
Ellers Farm
Caton Green
CATON GREEN RD

P
Liby
BALL LA
MILL LA
Quarry House Farm

HORNBY RD
PO
PH
Caton
Brookhouse
KINGBECK
Caton St Paul's CE Prim Sch
Anas Gill
QUARRY RD

ASHCROFT CL
HALL DR
COPY LA
BROOKHOUSE RD
Hawthorn
SYCAMORE AVE
ST ANNE'S CL
ST PAUL'S
CHAPEL
PINEWOOD AVE
Moorside Farm

A683
Hotel
ROCK 'N' JOCK
FELL VIEW
BROADACRE CL
CHESTNUT AVE 1
SYCAMORE CRES 2
HAWTHORN AVE 3
VICARAGE AVE 4
ROTTEN ROW 5
NEW ST 6
ST ANNE'S DR
Hill Farm
MOORSIDE RD
Moorgarth

New Parkside Farm
Escowbeck House
GREENFIELDS 1
ARTLEBECK GR 2
WILLOW MILL 3
LANGDALE 4
LESLIE AVE 5
ROMAN CRES 6
MILESTONE PL 7
BROADACRE CL 8
BROADACRE VIEW 9
BROADACRE PL 10
Caton Prim Sch

Old Hall Farm
QUERNMORE RD
Gresgarth Hall
Hawkshead
Artle Beck
Ravenscar Farm
Tarn Brook
ROEBURNDALE RD

Quernmore Park Hall
Lythe Brow
LITTLEDALE RD
Potts Wood
Crossgill
Hawes House

Knots Wood
Heights Farm
Intack House
LITTLEDALE RD
Pott Yeats
Foxdale Beck

51 A 52 B 53 C 54 D 55 E 56 F

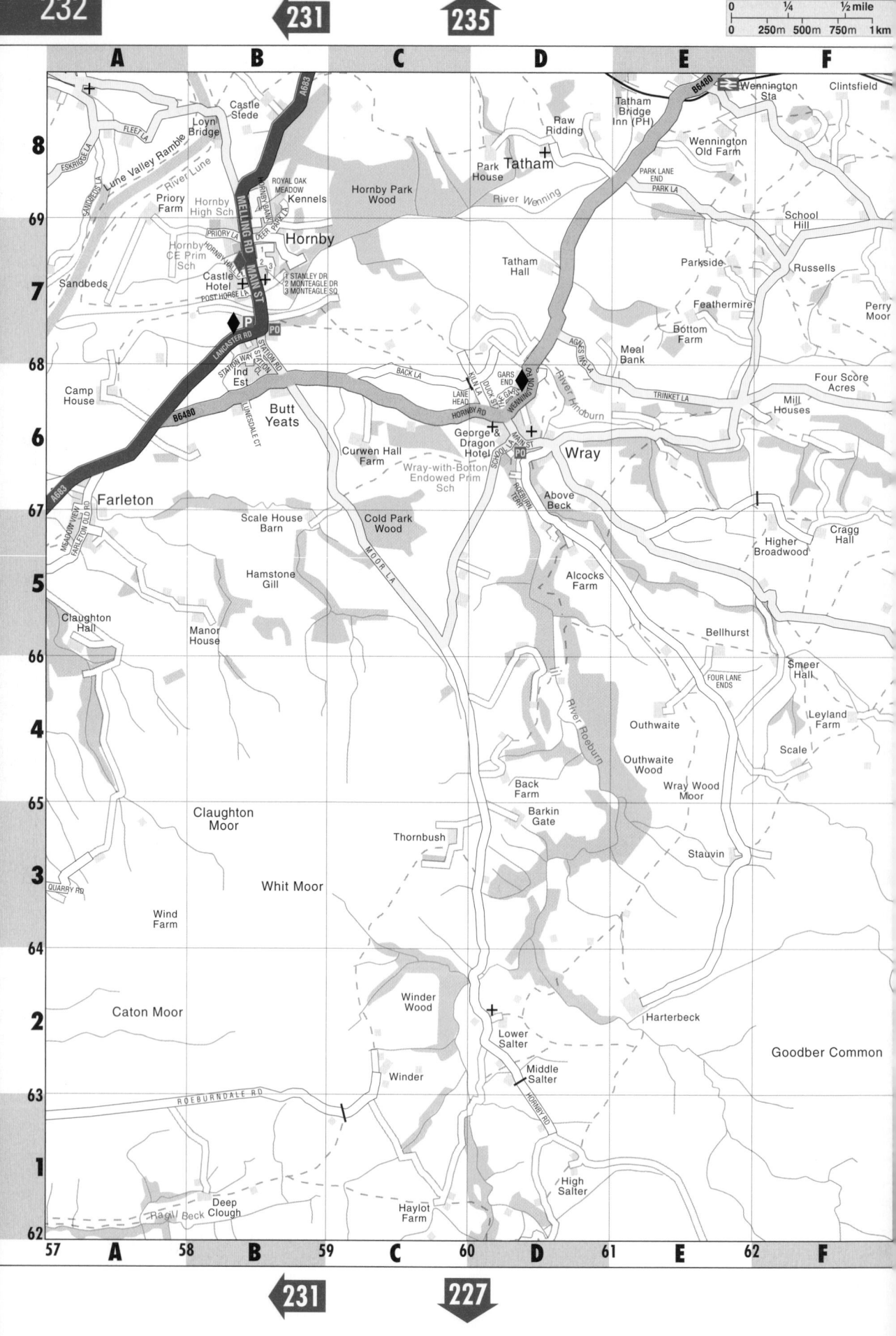

231
235

Scale: 1¾ inches to 1 mile

0 ¼ ½ mile
0 250m 500m 750m 1km

8

Castle Stede
Loyn Bridge
FLEET LA
ESKRIGGE LA
SANDBEDS LA
Lune Valley Ramble
River Lune
A683
Royal Oak Meadow
Hornby High Sch
Kennels
Raw Ridding
Park House
Tatham
Hornby Park Wood
Wennington Sta
B6480
Clintsfield
Tatham Bridge Inn (PH)
Wennington Old Farm

69

Priory Farm
Hornby CE Prim Sch
PRIORY LA
HORNBY HALL
MELLING RD
DEER PARK LA
Hornby
Tatham Hall
River Wenning
PARK LANE END
PARK LA
School Hill
Parkside
Russells

7

Sandbeds
Castle Hotel
POST HORSE LA
1 STANLEY DR
2 MONTEAGLE DR
3 MONTEAGLE SQ
Featermire
Bottom Farm
Perry Moor

68

Camp House
LANCASTER RD
STATION WAY
STATION RD
Ind Est
LIMESDALE CT
BACK LA
LANE HEAD
DUCK ST
GARS END
GARS
HORNBY RD
AGNES ING LA
GARS WENNINGTON
Meal Bank
TRINKET LA
Four Score Acres

6

B6480
Butt Yeats
Curwen Hall Farm
Wray-with-Botton Endowed Prim Sch
George & Dragon Hotel
SCHOOL ST
MAIN ST
HORNBY RD
PO
Wray
River Hindburn
Mill Houses

67

A683
Farleton
MEADOW VIEW
FARLETON OLD RD
Scale House Barn
Cold Park Wood
MOOR LA
Above Beck
Higher Broadwood
Cragg Hall

5

Claughton Hall
Manor House
Hamstone Gill
Alcocks Farm
Bellhurst

66

FOUR LANE ENDS
Smeer Hall
Leyland Farm
Scale

4

Outhwaite
Outhwaite Wood
River Roeburn
Wray Wood Moor

65

Claughton Moor
Thornbush
Back Farm
Barkin Gate

3

QUARRY RD
Whit Moor
Stauvin

64

Wind Farm

2

Caton Moor
Winder Wood
Harterbeck
Goodber Common

Lower Salter

63

ROEBURNDALE RD
Winder
Middle Salter
HORNBY RD

1

Deep Clough
River Back
Haylot Farm
High Salter

62

231
227

A 57 B 58 C 59 D 60 E 61 F 62

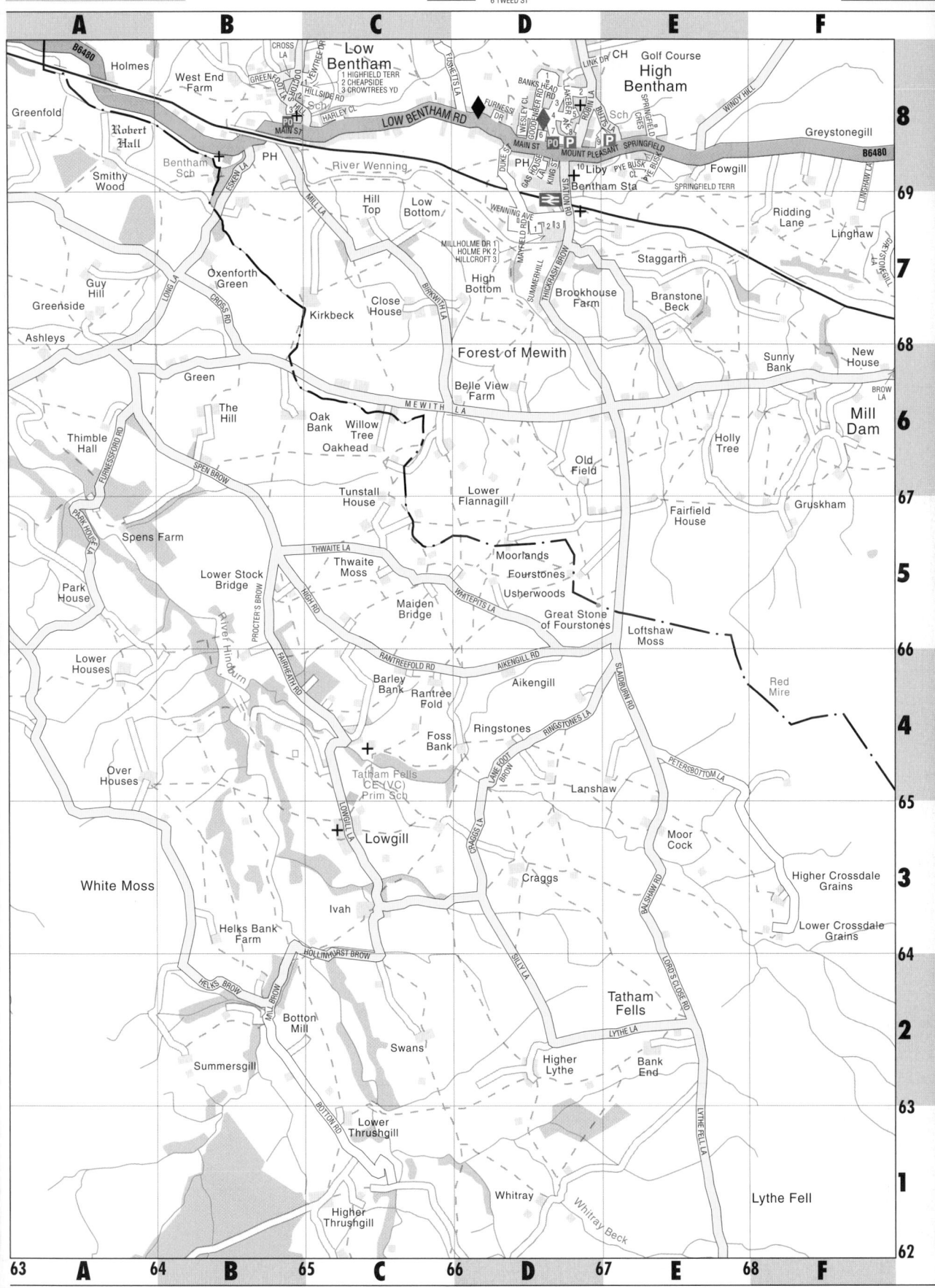

236
D8
1 GOODENBER CRES
2 LAKEBER DR
3 BANKS WAY
4 BANKS RISE
5 LAKEBER CL
6 TWEED ST
7 GRASMERE DR
8 GRASMERE CL
9 LAIRGILL ROW
10 COLLINGWOOD TERR

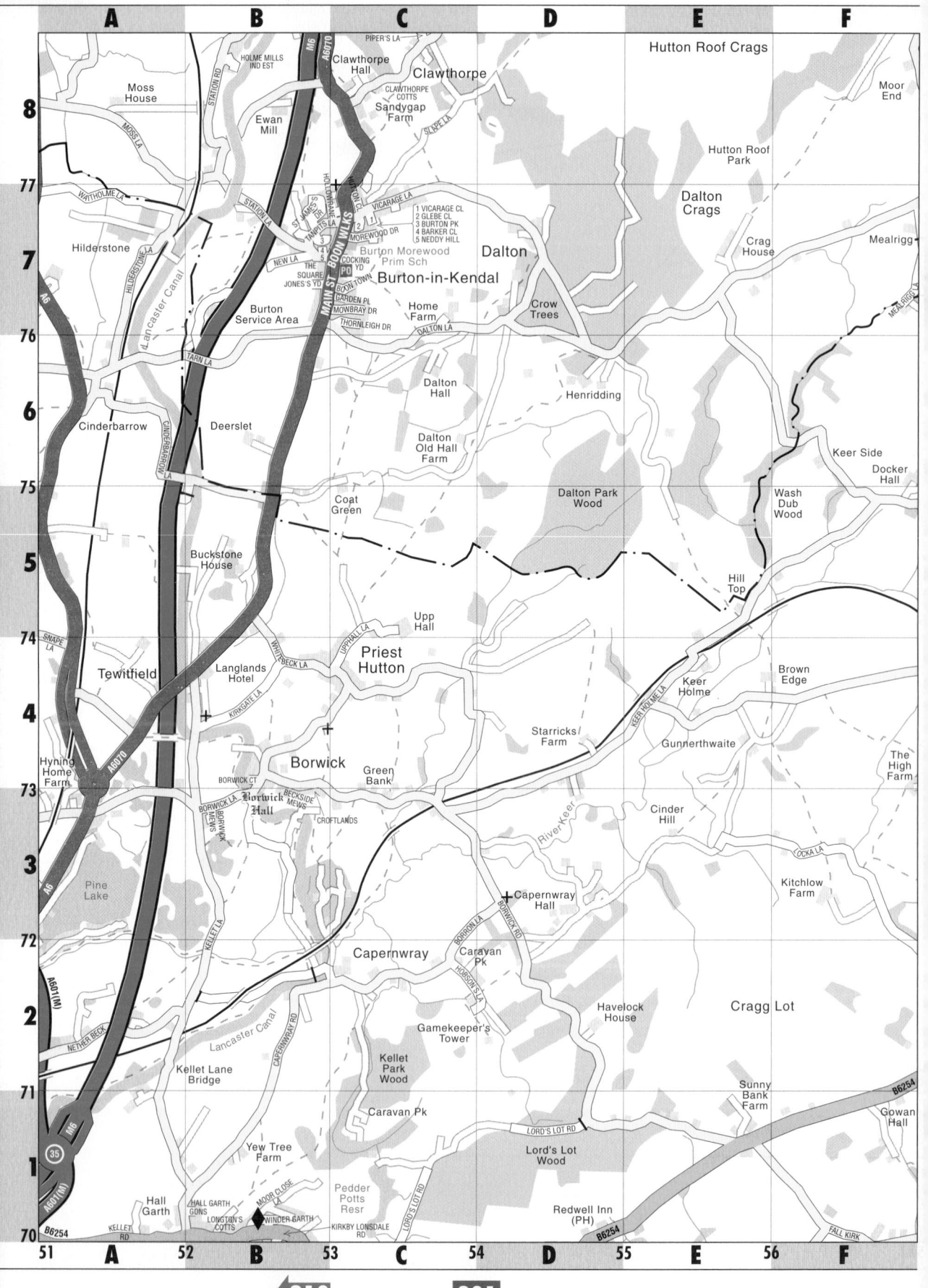

Scale: 1¾ inches to 1 mile

0   ¼   ½ mile
0 250m 500m 750m 1km

A   B   C   D   E   F

Hutton Roof Crags

Moor End

8

Moss House

Holme Mills Ind Est

Clawthorpe Hall

Clawthorpe

Ewan Mill

Clawthorpe Cotts

Sandygap Farm

Hutton Roof Park

77

Whytholme La

Hilderstone

Hilderstone La

Station La

St James's

Tarnpits La

Vicarage La

Dalton Crags

Crag House

Mealrigg

7

Lancaster Canal

New La

The Square

Jones's Yd

Cocking Yd

Boon Town

Morewood Dr

Burton Morewood Prim Sch

Burton-in-Kendal

1 VICARAGE CL
2 GLEBE CL
3 BURTON PK
4 BARKER CL
5 NEDDY HILL

Dalton

Mealrigg

76

A6

Tarn La

Burton Service Area

Garden Pl

Mowbray Dr

Thornleigh Dr

Home Farm

Dalton La

Crow Trees

Keer Side

6

Cinderbarrow

Cinderbarrow La

Deerslet

Dalton Hall

Henridding

Docker Hall

75

Coat Green

Dalton Old Hall Farm

Dalton Park Wood

Hill Top

Wash Dub Wood

5

Buckstone House

Upp Hall

74

Snape La

Tewitfield

Langlands Hotel

Whitbeck La

Upphall La

Priest Hutton

Keer Holme La

Keer Holme

Brown Edge

4

A6070

Kirkgate La

Borwick

Green Bank

Starricks Farm

Gunnerthwaite

The High Farm

73

Hyning Home Farm

Borwick Ct

Borwick La

Borwick Mews

Borwick Hall

Beckside Mews

Croftlands

Riverkeer

Cinder Hill

Ocka La

3

A6

Pine Lake

Kellet La

Capernwray Hall

Kitchlow Farm

72

A601(M)

Nether Beck

Lancaster Canal

Capernway Rd

Capernwray

Borron La

Caravan Pk

Borwick Rd

Horson La

Havelock House

Cragg Lot

2

Kellet Lane Bridge

Gamekeeper's Tower

Kellet Park Wood

Sunny Bank Farm

B6254

71

Caravan Pk

Lord's Lot Rd

Gowan Hall

1

M6

35

A601(M)

Hall Garth

Kellet Rd

Hall Garth Gdns

Longton's Cotts

Yew Tree Farm

Moor Close La

Winder Garth

Pedder Potts Resr

Kirkby Lonsdale Rd

Lord's Lot Rd

Lord's Lot Wood

Redwell Inn (PH)

B6254

Fall Kirk

70

B6254

51   52   53   54   55   56

A   B   C   D   E   F

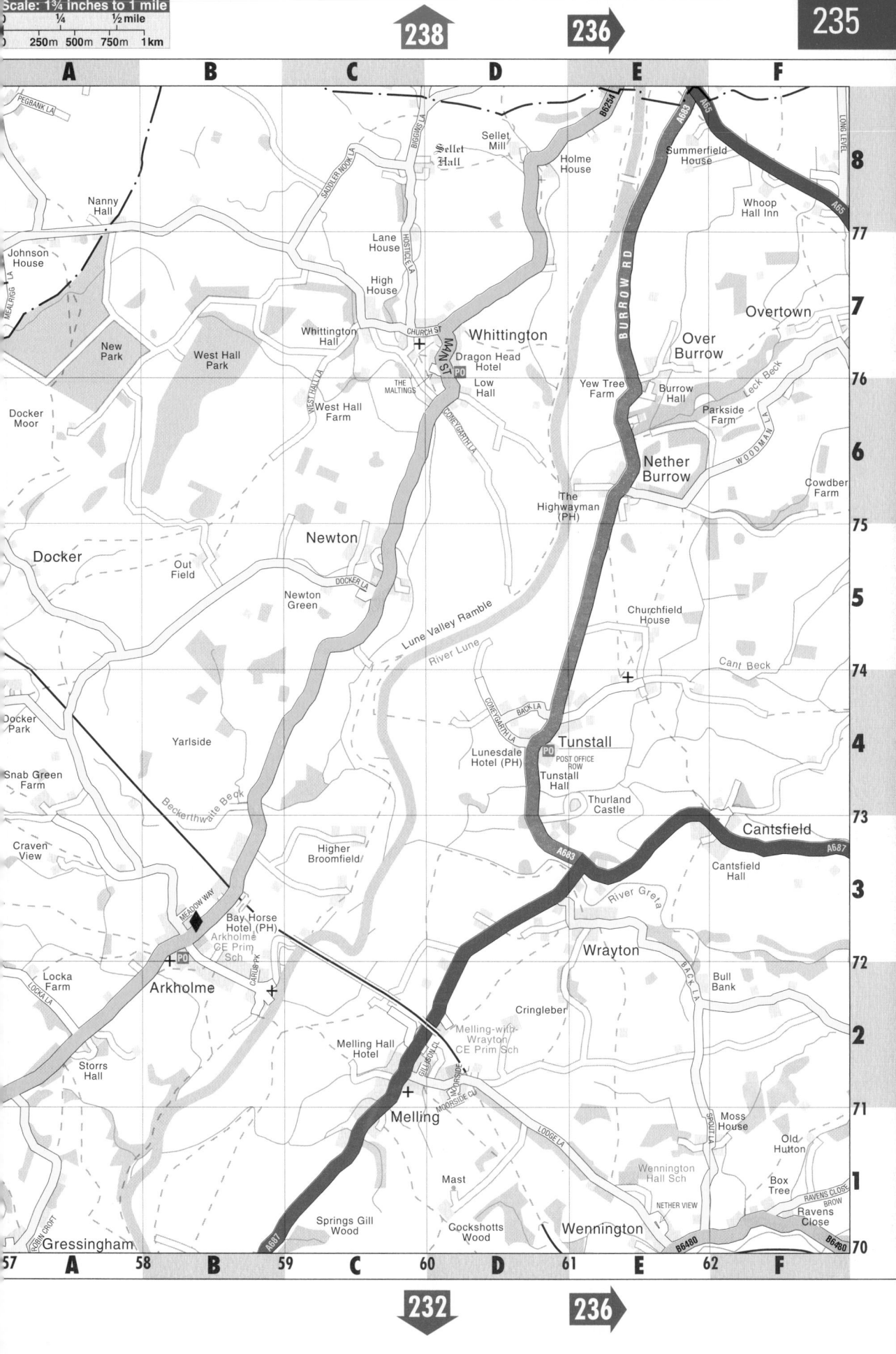

235

Scale: 1¾ inches to 1 mile

0 ¼ ½ mile
0 250m 500m 750m 1km

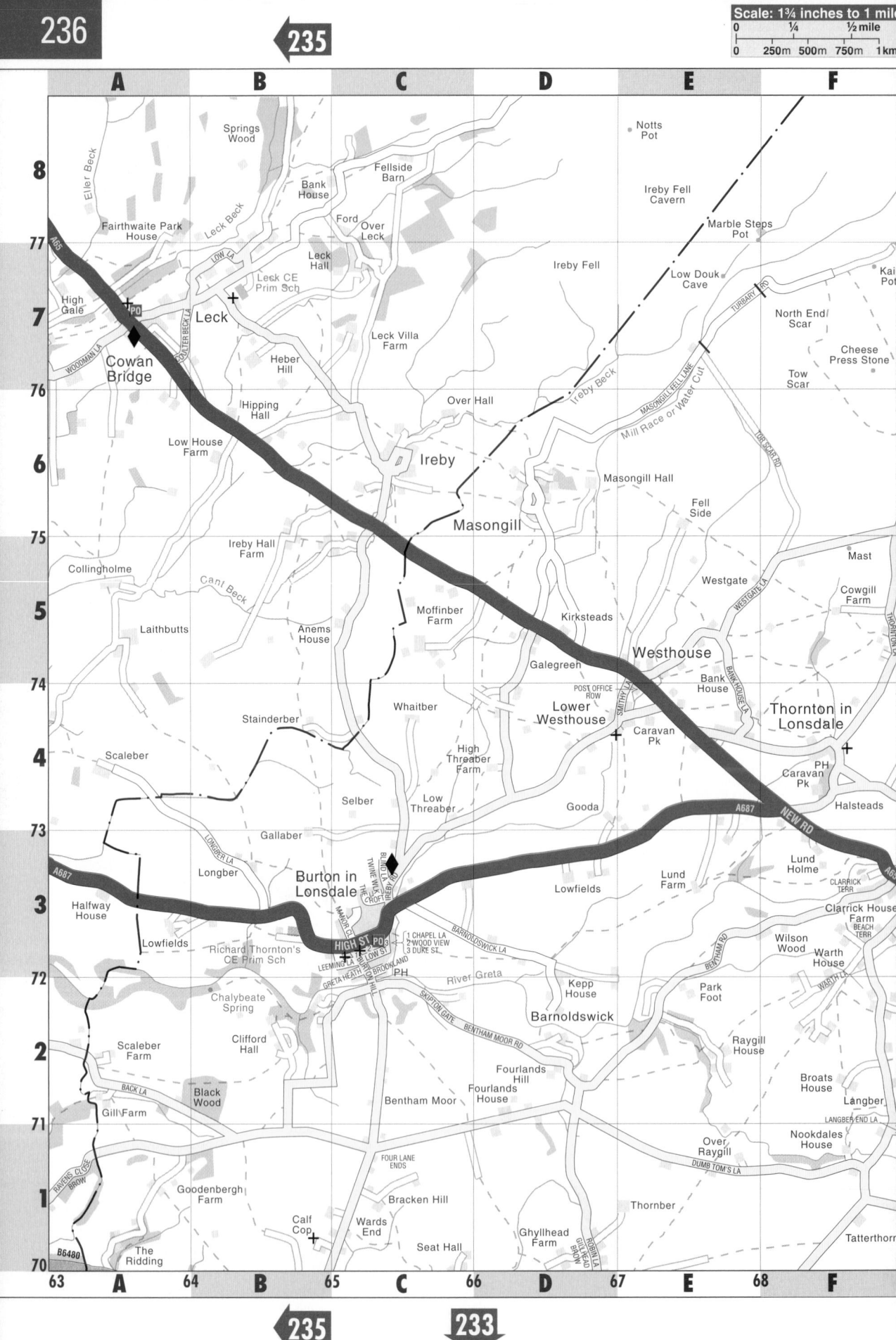

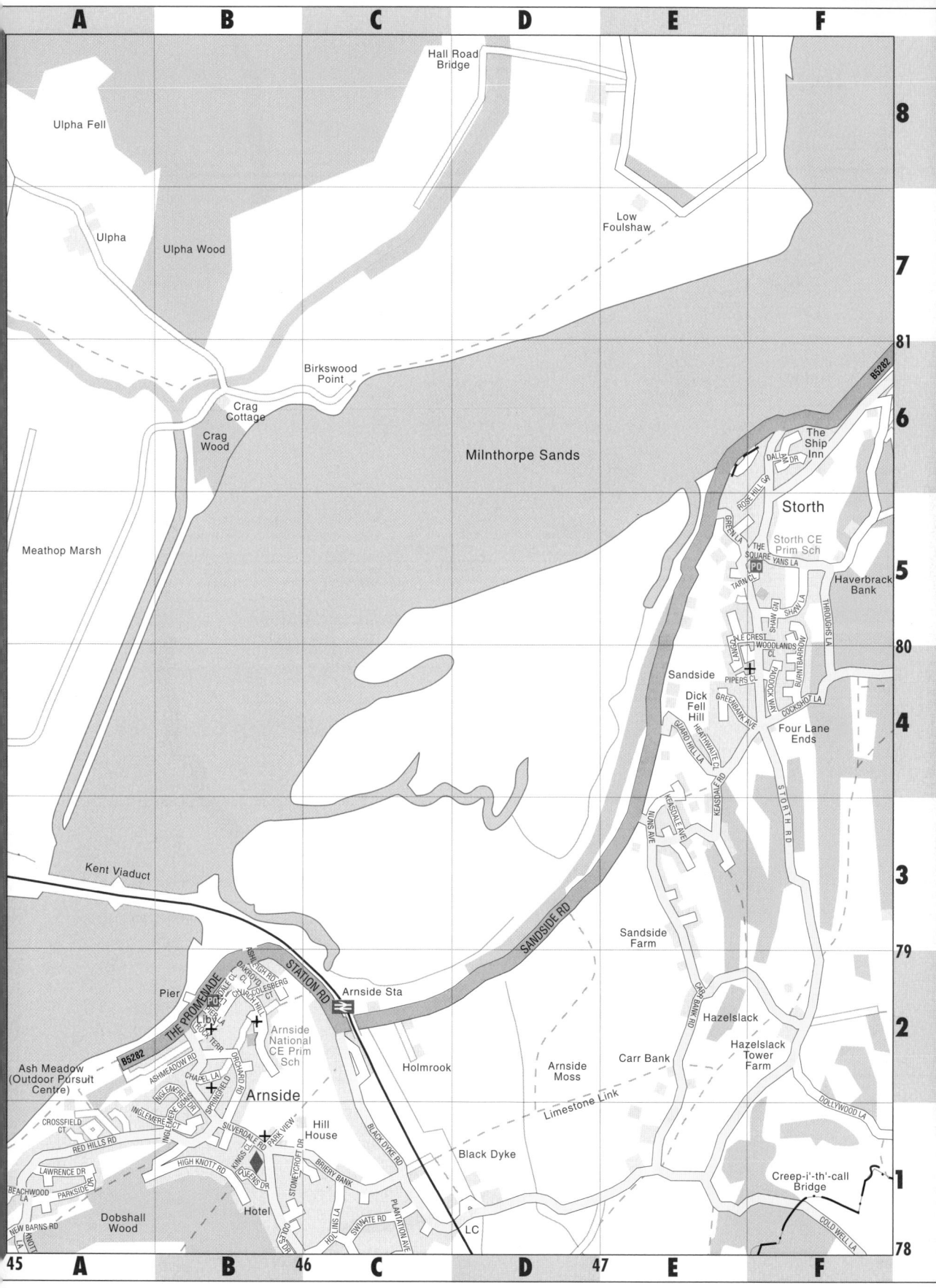

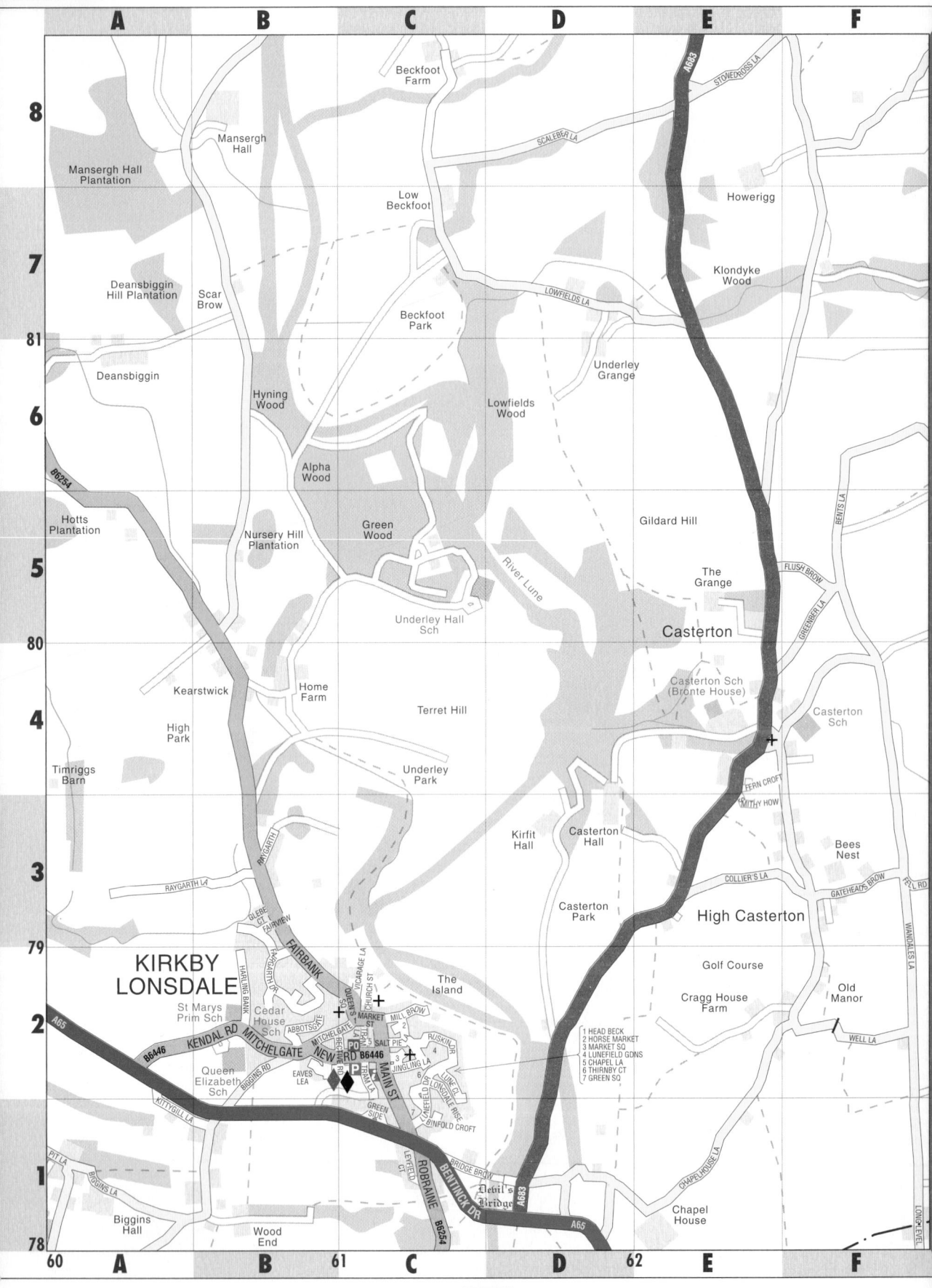

KIRKBY
LONSDALE

Casterton

High Casterton

1 HEAD BECK
2 HORSE MARKET
3 MARKET SQ
4 LUNEFIELD GDNS
5 CHAPEL LA
6 THIRNBY CT
7 GREEN SQ

Street names are listed alphabetically and show the locality, the Postcode District, the page number and a reference to the square in which the name falls on the map page

Winchester Ave. 4 Blackpool FY4 .... **129** D1

Grid square in which the centre of the street falls

Page number of the map on which the street name appears

Postcode District for the street name

Town, village or locality in which the street falls.

Full street name This may have been abbreviated on the map

Location Number If present, this indicates the street's position on a congested area of the map instead of the name

Schools, hospitals, sports centres, railway stations, shopping centres, industrial estates, public amenities and other places of interest are also listed. These are highlighted in magenta

Abbreviations used in the index

App	Approach	Cl	Close	Espl	Esplanade	Orch	Orchard	Sq	Square
Arc	Arcade	Comm	Common	Est	Estate	Par	Parade	Strs	Stairs
Ave	Avenue	Cnr	Corner	Gdns	Gardens	Pk	Park	Stps	Steps
Bvd	Boulevard	Cotts	Cottages	Gn	Green	Pas	Passage	St	Street, Saint
Bldgs	Buildings	Ct	Court	Gr	Grove	Pl	Place	Terr	Terrace
Bsns Pk	Business Park	Ctyd	Courtyard	Hts	Heights	Prec	Precinct	Trad Est	Trading Estate
Bsns Ctr	Business Centre	Cres	Crescent	Ind Est	Industrial Estate	Prom	Promenade	Wlk	Walk
Bglws	Bungalows	Dr	Drive	Intc	Interchange	Ret Pk	Retail Park	W	West
Cswy	Causeway	Dro	Drove	Junc	Junction	Rd	Road	Yd	Yard
Ctr	Centre	E	East	La	Lane	Rdbt	Roundabout		
Cir	Circus	Emb	Embankment	N	North	S	South		

Albyn St E. PR1 96 B7
Alcester Ave. PR1 95 C5
Alconbury Cres. FY5 172 C2
Aldate Gr. PR2 116 A2
Aldcliffe Cotts. LA1 210 D5
Aldcliffe Ct. LA4 212 E3
Aldcliffe Mews. LA1 210 D5
Aldcliffe Pl. LA1 210 E7
Aldcliffe Rd. Lancaster LA1 210 E6
Aldcliffe Rd. Preston PR2 115 E1
Alden Rd. BB4 & BL8 66 F5
Alden Rise. BB4 67 A6
Alder Ave. Bury BL9 32 C3
Alder Ave. Rawtenstall BB4 85 B2
Alder Bank. Blackburn BB2 100 B4
Alder Bank. 20 Rawtenstall BB4 85 A3
Alder Cl. Leyland PR5 58 B8
Alder Cl. Newton-with-S PR4 114 A2
Alder Cl. Thornton FY5 173 C1
Alder Coppice. PR4 115 E3
Alder Ct. FY7 193 C2
Alder Dr. Charnock Richard PR7 41 D3
Alder Dr. Gregson Lane PR5 97 E1
Alder Gr. Blackpool FY3 129 E7
Alder Gr. Coppull PR7 41 F1
Alder Gr. Huncoat BB5 124 E2
Alder Gr. Lancaster LA1 210 D8
Alder Gr. Lytham St Anne's FY8 90 A4
Alder Gr. Poulton-le-F FY6 151 D1
Alder Grange High Sch. BB4 85 A4
Alder Hill St. BB8 201 B2
Alder La. Formby L39 12 E7
Alder La. Moss Edge PR3 176 A1
Alder La. Parbold WN8 26 C1
Alder Meadow Cl. 1 OL12 51 A1
Alder Rd. PR2 118 A4
Alder St. Bacup OL13 86 F3
Alder St. 2 Blackburn BB1 101 A7
Alder St. Burnley BB12 126 C7
Alder St. Rawtenstall BB4 85 B3
Alderbank. BL6 30 F3
Alderbrook Dr. WN8 26 C2
Alderdale Ave. PR8 20 A5
Alderfield. PR1 95 D3
Alderford Cl. BB7 164 C7
Alderley. WN8 9 C6
Alderley Ave. FY4 109 B5
Alderley Hts. LA1 213 F3
Alderman Foley Dr. OL12 51 A2
Alderney Cl. BB2 100 B1
Alders The. PR3 199 C1
Aldersleigh Cres. PR5 97 D1
Alderson Cres. L37 11 F4
Alderway. BL0 67 C1
Alderwood Gr. BL0 67 D4
Aldfield Ave. PR2 115 C1
Aldingham Ct. LA4 212 E3
Aldingham Wlk. LA4 212 D5
Aldon Gr. PR4 94 A1
Aldon Rd. FY6 151 F2
Aldren's La. LA1 213 F3
Aldwych Ave. FY3 129 E3
Aldwych Dr. Bamber Bridge PR5 76 B7
Aldwych Dr. Preston PR2 116 A2
Aldwych Pl. BB1 121 E2
Alert St. PR1 116 C1
Alexander Cl. Accrington BB5 103 E1
Alexander Cl. Burscough L40 24 F3
Alexander Ct. FY6 151 D3
Alexander Dr. L31 5 D3
Alexander Gr. BB12 126 B6
Alexander St. BB9 169 A2
Alexandra Cl. BB5 123 E3
Alexandra Ct. 4 LA1 210 F8
Alexandra House. Blackburn BB1 101 B3
Alexandra House. 10 Preston PR1 117 C1
Alexandra Mews. 1 L39 15 E6
Alexandra Pavilion. 5 PR1 117 A1
Alexandra Pl. BB6 123 D6
Alexandra Rd. Bamber Bridge PR5 96 D3
Alexandra Rd. Blackburn BB2 100 C6
Alexandra Rd. Blackpool FY1 129 B1
Alexandra Rd. Burscough L40 24 D4
Alexandra Rd. Carnforth LA5 217 D1
Alexandra Rd. 8 Darwen BB3 80 F2
Alexandra Rd. Formby L37 11 B1
Alexandra Rd. Kirkham PR4 113 A6
Alexandra Rd. Lancaster LA1 213 F3
Alexandra Rd. Longridge PR3 139 A7
Alexandra Rd. Lytham St Anne's FY8 89 A7
Alexandra Rd. Morecambe LA3 212 B3
Alexandra Rd. Southport PR9 34 D8
Alexandra Rd. Thornton FY5 151 C8
Alexandra St. Clayton-le-M BB5 123 E3
Alexandra St. Preston PR1 96 C7
Alexandra View. 7 BB3 80 F2
Alexandria Dr. FY8 88 F5
Alexandria St. BB4 84 F4
Alford Fold. PR2 116 D7
Alfred St. Blackpool FY1 129 C5
Alfred St. Bury BL9 32 A1
Alfred St. Darwen BB3 64 B6
Alfred St. Egerton BL7 46 D3
Alfred St. Lancaster LA1 211 A8
Alfred St. 10 Ramsbottom BL0 49 B5
Alfred St. Whitworth OL12 70 D2
Algar St. 7 BB9 168 F2
Alice Ave. PR5 76 A1
Alice Sq. 4 PR1 117 A1
Alice St. Accrington BB5 103 D7
Alice St. Barnoldswick BB8 200 B2
Alice St. 7 Darwen BB3 64 A8
Alice St. Morecambe LA4 212 F5
Alice St. Oswaldtwistle BB5 102 E3
Alicia Ct. OL12 51 E1
Alicia Dr. OL12 51 E1
Alisan Rd. FY6 151 B5
Alker La. PR7 60 B3
Alker St. PR7 42 C7
Alkincoats Rd. BB8 169 C5
All Hallows Rd. FY2 150 D5
All Hallows RC High Sch. PR1 95 A3
All Saint's Cl. BB5 102 B4
All Saints CE Prim Sch. Appley Bridge WN6 27 C1
All Saints CE Prim Sch. Chorley PR7 42 B5
All Saints CE Prim Sch. Clayton-le-M BB5 123 F2
All Saints Cl. Padiham BB12 125 F7
All Saints Cl. Rawtenstall BB4 105 A1
All Saints RC High Sch. BB4 84 D1
All Saints Rd. Blackpool FY2 150 E6
All Saints' Rd. Lytham St Anne's FY8 88 E6
Allan St. OL13 86 F1
Allandale. FY4 109 C5
Allandale Ave. FY5 172 F4
Allen Cl. Cleveleys FY5 172 D1
Allen Cl. Fleetwood FY7 193 D2
Allen Ct. BB10 127 A8
Allen St. BB10 127 A8
Allen Way. FY7 193 D2
Allenbury Pl. FY3 130 A2
Allenby Ave. PR2 117 B4
Allenby Rd. FY8 88 E8
Allendale Gr. BB10 127 F4
Allendale St. Burnley BB12 126 B6
Allendale St. Colne BB8 169 F5
Allengate. PR1 116 F4
Allerton Cl. BB3 81 A2
Allerton Dr. BB12 126 D6
Allerton Rd. Bamber Bridge PR5 96 D4
Allerton Rd. Southport PR9 52 E1
Alleys Gn. BB7 186 E1
Alleytroyds. BB5 102 E5
Alliance St. BB5 103 F1
Allison Gr. BB8 169 F6
Allonby Ave. FY5 172 E4
Allsprings Cl. BB6 123 D6
Allsprings Dr. BB6 123 D6
Alma Ave. BB8 191 D1
Alma Cl. WN8 10 C7
Alma Ct. Southport PR8 20 F7
Alma Ct. Up Holland WN8 10 C7
Alma Dr. PR7 41 E4
Alma Hill. WN8 10 C7
Alma Ind Est. 25 OL12 51 F1
Alma Par. WN8 10 C7
Alma Pl. Accrington BB5 83 E8
Alma Pl. Clitheroe BB7 164 D7
Alma Rd. Lancaster LA1 210 F6
Alma Rd. Laneshaw Bridge BB8 170 D6
Alma Rd. Southport PR8 34 A4
Alma Rd. Up Holland WN8 10 C7
Alma Row. PR5 97 E1
Alma St. Bacup OL13 87 A2
Alma St. Blackburn BB2 100 D5
Alma St. 9 Clayton-le-M BB5 123 F3
Alma St. Padiham BB12 125 C8
Alma St. Preston PR1 117 A1
Alma St. 13 Rochdale OL12 51 F1
Alma Terr. BB11 105 C4
Almond Ave. Burscough Bridge L40 24 F6
Almond Ave. 4 Bury BL9 32 C3
Almond Brook Rd. WN6 28 C1
Almond Cl. Abbey Village PR7 79 B2
Almond Cl. Fulwood PR2 117 D6
Almond Cl. Penwortham PR1 95 B3
Almond Cres. BB4 67 F8
Almond St. BB3 64 A8
Almshouses. Aughton L39 6 A7
Almshouses. 34 Lancaster LA1 210 F8
Almshouses. 7 Rawtenstall BB4 84 E2
Alnwick Cl. BB12 126 E7
Alpha St. Darwen BB3 64 B8
Alpha St. 8 Nelson BB9 168 F2
Alpha St. Salterforth BB8 191 E8
Alpic Dr. FY5 150 C7
Alpine Ave. Bamber Bridge PR5 76 B7
Alpine Ave. Blackpool FY4 109 E5
Alpine Cl. Bamber Bridge PR5 76 B7
Alpine Cl. Hoddlesden BB3 81 E1
Alpine Gr. BB2 80 B8
Alpine Rd. PR6 60 E3
Alpine View. LA5 216 A6
Alsop St. PR1 116 F2
Alston Ave. FY5 172 D4
Alston Cl. BB7 144 F8
Alston Dr. LA4 213 B5
Alston La. PR2 & PR3 139 A2
Alston Lane RC Prim Sch. PR3 138 F2
Alston Rd. FY2 150 E2
Alston St. PR1 117 D1
Alt Rd. Formby L37 12 B2
Alt Rd. Hightown L38 3 A4
Altcar La. Formby L37 11 F1
Altcar La. Maghull L31 & L39 5 A4
Altcar La. Runshaw Moor PR5 58 E5
Altcar Rd. L37 12 B2
Altham Bsns Pk. BB5 124 E6
Altham CE Prim Sch. BB5 124 D6
Altham Ind Est. BB5 124 D6
Altham La. BB5 124 F4
Altham Rd. Morecambe LA4 212 F3
Altham Rd. Southport PR8 34 E2
Altham St. 2 Burnley BB10 127 A8
Altham St. 5 Padiham BB12 125 D8
Altham Wlk. LA4 212 F3
Althorp Cl. FY1 129 C7
Althorpe Dr. PR8 34 E3
Altom St. BB1 100 E6
Alton Cl. L38 2 F2
Altys La. L39 15 F3
Alum Scar La. BB2 99 A6
Alvern Ave. PR2 116 D4
Alvern Cres. PR2 116 D4
Alwin St. 12 BB11 126 E5
Alwood Ave. FY3 129 F6
Amber Ave. BB1 121 F2
Amber Gate. PR2 115 F6
Amberbanks Gr. FY1 129 B2
Ambergate. WN8 9 B7
Amberley St. BB2 100 C2
Amberwood. PR4 112 F5
Ambleside Ave. Barnoldswick BB8 200 A3
Ambleside Ave. Euxton PR7 59 D1
Ambleside Ave. Knott End-on-S FY6 194 F6
Ambleside Ave. 2 Rawtenstall BB4 84 E2
Ambleside Cl. Bamber Bridge PR5 96 E2
Ambleside Cl. Blackburn BB1 101 A6
Ambleside Cl. Huncoat BB5 103 E8
Ambleside Dr. BB3 81 C3
Ambleside Rd. Blackpool FY4 130 D1
Ambleside Rd. Fulwood PR2 117 E5
Ambleside Rd. Lancaster LA1 214 B2
Ambleside Rd. Lytham St Anne's FY8 109 E1
Ambleside Rd. Maghull L31 5 D2
Ambleside Wlk. PR2 117 E5
Ambleway. PR5 96 C4
Ambrose. PR5 76 B2
Amelia St. BB1 101 B6
Amersham. WN8 9 C7
Amersham Cl. PR4 74 F8
Amersham Gr. BB10 147 D4
Amethyst St. BB1 121 F2
Amounderness Way. Cleveleys FY5 172 F4
Amounderness Way. Fleetwood FY7 194 A3
Amounderness Way. Thornton FY5 151 C7
Ampleforth Dr. PR5 96 A1
Amy Johnson Way. FY4 109 E4
Amy St. OL11 & OL12 51 B1
Ancenis Ct. PR4 113 B5
Anchor Ave. BB3 80 F4
Anchor Ct. PR1 95 F7
Anchor Dr. PR4 94 D2
Anchor Gr. BB3 80 E5
Anchor Rd. BB3 80 F4
Anchor Ret Pk. 1 BB11 127 A6
Anchor St. PR8 & PR9 34 B7
Anchor Way. FY8 109 E1
Anchorage Ave. PR4 71 F1
Anchorsholme La. FY5 150 F8
Anchorsholme La E. FY5 172 E1
Anchorsholme La W. FY5 172 C1
Anchorsholme Prim Sch. FY5 150 E8
Ancliffe La. LA2 & LA5 216 B2
Andelen Cl. BB11 125 C3
Andersholme La. FY5 151 A8
Anderson Cl. LA1 211 B6
Anderson Rd. BB1 122 A7
Anderson St. FY1 129 C4
Anderton Cl. BB4 68 F7
Anderton La. BL6 30 E4
Anderton Prim Sch. PR6 30 B8
Anderton Rd. Euxton PR7 59 D1
Anderton Rd. Higham BB12 145 F5
Anderton St. Adlington PR6 30 A7
Anderton St. Chorley PR6 & PR7 42 C7
Anderton Way. PR3 178 D6
Andertons Way. PR2 117 D5
Andreas Cl. PR8 34 B4
Andrew Ave. BB4 84 F1
Andrew Cl. Blackburn BB2 80 B8
Andrew Cl. Ramsbottom BL8 48 F1
Andrew Rd. BB9 169 B1
Andrew St. Bury BL9 32 A2
Andrew St. Preston PR1 117 C1
Andrews Cl. L37 11 E1
Andrews La. L37 11 E1
Andrews Yort. L37 11 E1
Anemone Dr. BB4 66 F8
Angel Way. 3 BB8 169 E5
Angela St. BB2 100 B1
Anger's Hill Rd. FY4 129 F1
Angle St. BB10 127 A8
Anglesey Ave. BB12 126 A7
Anglesey St. BB2 80 B8
Anglezarke Rd. PR6 30 A7
Anglian Cl. BB5 102 C5
Angus St. OL13 69 C8
Aniline St. PR6 42 E8
Ann St. Barrowford BB9 168 D3
Ann St. Brierfield BB9 147 B6
Ann St. 4 Clayton-le-M BB5 123 F3
Ann St. Lancaster LA1 210 F7
Ann St. Skelmersdale WN8 8 E8
Anna's Rd. FY4 110 E3
Annan Cres. FY4 130 C1
Annandale Gdns. WN8 10 A7
Annarly Fold. BB10 128 A5
Annaside Cl. FY4 109 E7
Anne Ave. PR8 20 E6
Anne Cl. BB10 127 B5
Anne St. BB11 127 B5
Annesley Ave. FY3 129 E8
Annie St. Accrington BB5 103 C7
Annie St. Ramsbottom BL0 49 A4
Annie St. 5 Rawtenstall BB4 85 A2
Annis St. PR1 96 C8
Ansbro Ave. PR4 92 C6
Ansdell Cty Prim Sch. FY8 89 C5
Ansdell & Fairhaven Sta. FY8 89 D4
Ansdell Gr. Fulwood PR2 116 C3
Ansdell Gr. Southport PR9 53 A4
Ansdell Rd. Blackpool FY1 129 D2
Ansdell Rd. Horwich BL6 31 C4
Ansdell Rd N. FY8 89 D4
Ansdell Rd S. FY8 89 D3
Ansdell St. 3 PR1 117 C1
Ansdell Terr. BB2 100 E1
Anshaw Cl. BL7 45 C5
Anson Cl. FY8 109 D1
Anson Rd. PR4 113 B2
Anstable Rd. LA4 213 A5
Anthony Rd. LA1 210 E7
Antrim Rd. FY2 150 C1
Anvil Cl. WN5 10 E5
Anvil St. OL13 69 E8
Anyon St. BB3 81 B2
Anzio Rd. PR4 131 E5
Apiary The. PR5 57 A6
Appealing La. FY8 109 E2
Apple Cl. BB2 100 C4
Apple Ct. BB2 100 C4
Apple St. BB2 100 C4
Apple Tree Cl. PR3 155 C8
Appleby Cl. Accrington BB5 103 D5
Appleby Cl. Gregson Lane PR5 97 E1
Appleby Dr. BB9 168 D4
Appleby Rd. FY2 150 D1
Appleby St. Blackburn BB1 101 A5
Appleby St. Nelson BB9 147 D8
Appleby St. Preston PR1 116 F1
Applecross Dr. BB10 127 E4
Applefields. PR5 59 B7
Applegarth. Barnoldswick BB8 200 C3
Applegarth. Barrowford BB9 168 B1
Applegarth Rd. LA3 209 A8
Applegarth St. BB8 201 B1
Applesike. PR4 94 A1
Appleton Cl. FY6 151 A2
Appleton Rd. WN8 17 F2
Appletree Cl. Lancaster LA1 211 A3
Appletree Cl. Penwortham PR1 95 C2
Appletree Dr. LA1 211 A3
Applewood Cl. FY8 89 F3
Appley Bridge Sta. WN6 19 C7
Appley Cl. WN6 27 C2
Appley La N. Appley Bridge WN6 19 C8
Appley La N. Appley Bridge WN6 27 C1
Appley La S. WN6 & WN8 19 C6
Approach Way. BB11 126 F2
Apsley Brow. L31 5 B1
Apsley Fold. PR3 139 B6
Aqueduct Rd. Blackburn BB2 100 D1
Aqueduct Rd. Blackburn BB2 100 D2
Aqueduct St. PR1 116 E1
Arago St. BB5 103 C7
Aragon Cl. L31 5 E3
Arbories Ave. BB12 125 B8
Arbory Dr. BB12 125 B8
Arbory The. PR4 111 E7
Arbour La. Kirkby L32 & L33 1 B2
Arbour La. Shevington Moor WN6 28 B1
Arbour Lane End. PR3 160 E7
Arbour St. PR8 34 C6
Arboury St. BB12 125 B8
Arcadia. 9 BB8 169 E5
Arcadia Ave. L31 5 D3
Arch St. Burnley BB11 & BB12 126 F6
Arch St. 4 Darwen BB3 81 A1
Archbishop Hutton's Prim Sch. LA5 217 D5
Archbishop Temple Sch. PR2 116 F5
Archery Ave. BB8 191 D1
Arcon Rd. PR7 41 E1
Ardee Rd. PR1 95 D6
Arden Cl. Ainsdale PR8 20 A5
Arden Cl. Hest Bank LA2 213 E8
Arden Gn. FY7 193 E4
Ardengate. LA1 210 F4
Ardleigh Ave. PR8 34 E3
Ardley Rd. BL6 31 C4
Ardmore Rd. FY2 150 D2
Ardwick St. BB10 127 A8
Argameols Cl. PR8 34 F5
Argarmeols Gr. L37 11 E5
Argarmeols Rd. L37 11 E6
Argosy Ave. FY3 129 F8
Argosy Ct. 1 FY3 130 A8
Argyle Ct. PR9 52 D1
Argyle Rd. 7 Leyland PR5 76 A1
Argyle Rd. Poulton-le-F FY6 151 E3
Argyle Rd. Southport PR9 52 D2
Argyle St. Accrington BB5 103 B6
Argyle St. Colne BB8 169 D5
Argyle St. Darwen BB3 80 F3
Argyle St. Heywood OL10 32 E1
Argyle St. 3 Lancaster LA1 211 A7
Argyll Ct. FY2 150 C1
Argyll Rd. Blackpool FY2 150 C1
Argyll Rd. Preston PR1 117 A1
Ariel Way. FY7 193 E4
Arkholme Ave. FY1 129 D2
Arkholme CE Prim Sch. LA6 235 B3
Arkholme Cl. LA5 217 E2
Arkholme Ct. LA4 212 E3
Arkholme Dr. PR4 93 F1
Arkwright Ct. FY4 110 C7
Arkwright Fold. BB2 80 C8
Arkwright Rd. PR1 116 F2
Arkwright St. Burnley BB12 126 C7
Arkwright St. Horwich BL6 31 C2
Arley Gdns. BB12 126 F7
Arley La. WN1 & WN2 29 D2
Arley Rise. BB2 120 E2
Arley St. PR6 42 D8
Arlington Ave. FY4 109 B7
Arlington Cl. Ainsdale PR8 20 A5
Arlington Cl. Ramsbottom BL9 49 C2
Arlington Rd. BB3 63 F8
Armadale Rd. FY2 150 E1
Armitstead Ct. 8 FY7 193 F2
Armitstead Way. 5 FY7 193 F2
Armstrong St. Horwich BL6 31 C2
Armstrong St. Preston PR1 & PR2 116 B2
Arncliffe Ave. BB5 102 F4
Arncliffe Gr. BB9 168 C3
Arncliffe Rd. Burnley BB10 127 E5
Arncliffe Rd. Morecambe LA3 212 A1
Arndale Cl. FY7 193 C2
Arndale Ctr. 3 BB9 147 E8
Arndale Rd. PR3 139 A7
Arnhem Rd. Carnforth LA5 217 E1
Arnhem Rd. Preston PR1 96 D8
Arnian Ct. L39 6 C7
Arno St. 6 PR1 96 B7
Arnold Ave. FY4 109 C7
Arnold Cl. Burnley BB11 126 E2
Arnold Cl. Fulwood PR2 117 E2
Arnold Jun Sch. FY4 109 C6
Arnold Pl. PR7 42 A5
Arnold Rd. FY8 90 D4
Arnold Sch. FY4 109 C7
Arnold St. 2 BB5 103 C6
Arnott Rd. Blackpool FY4 129 E1
Arnott Rd. Fulwood PR2 116 C2
Arnside Ave. Blackpool FY1 129 D1
Arnside Ave. Lytham St Anne's FY8 89 C7
Arnside Cl. Coupe Green PR5 97 E4
Arnside Cl. Lancaster LA1 211 B3
Arnside Cres. Blackburn BB2 79 E8
Arnside Cres. Morecambe LA4 212 F6
Arnside National CE Prim Sch. LA5 237 B2
Arnside Rd. Broughton PR3 136 D2
Arnside Rd. Preston PR2 115 E2
Arnside Rd. Southport PR9 34 C7
Arnside Sta. LA5 237 C2
Arnside Terr. PR9 34 C7
Arran Ave. BB1 101 D2
Arran Cl. LA3 208 E7
Arran St. BB11 126 D5
Arrow La. LA2 214 F7
Arrowsmith Cl. PR5 97 E2
Arrowsmith Ct. 7 BL6 31 E1
Arrowsmith Dr. PR5 97 E2
Arroyo Way. PR2 117 B4
Arthur St. Bacup OL13 87 B3
Arthur St. Barnoldswick BB8 200 A3
Arthur St. Blackburn BB2 100 C4
Arthur St. Brierfield BB9 147 B6
Arthur St. Burnley BB11 126 E6
Arthur St. Clayton-le-M BB5 123 F3
Arthur St. Fleetwood FY7 194 B5
Arthur St. Great Harwood BB6 123 D6
Arthur St. 18 Nelson BB9 168 E1
Arthur St. Preston PR1 95 E7
Arthur St. Sough BB8 192 A7
Arthur St N. FY7 194 B6
Arthur Way. BB2 100 C4
Arthurs La. FY6 174 D2
Artillery St. BB5 102 F5
Artle Pl. LA1 213 E2
Artlebeck Cl. LA2 231 C3
Artlebeck Gr. LA2 231 C3
Artlebeck Rd. LA2 231 C3
Arundel Ave. FY2 150 B5
Arundel Dr. FY6 151 C5
Arundel Pl. 37 PR1 96 A7
Arundel Rd. Longton PR4 94 A1
Arundel Rd. Lytham St Anne's FY8 89 C4
Arundel Rd. Southport PR8 20 F8
Arundel St. BB1 123 A2
Arundel Way. PR5 & PR6 59 C8
Ascot Cl. Lancaster LA1 211 B4
Ascot Cl. Southport PR8 33 E5
Ascot Gdns. LA2 213 F8
Ascot Rd. Blackpool FY3 129 E6
Ascot Rd. Thornton FY5 151 B8
Ascot Way. BB5 103 D5
Ash Ave. Galgate LA2 206 F4
Ash Ave. Haslingden BB4 84 C3
Ash Ave. Kirkham PR4 113 A4
Ash Bank Cl. PR3 136 B8
Ash Brow. WN8 26 B1
Ash Cl. Appley Bridge WN6 19 D7
Ash Cl. Barrow BB7 164 D1
Ash Cl. Elswick PR4 154 A1
Ash Cl. Ormskirk L39 15 D5
Ash Cl. Rishton BB1 102 B8
Ash Coppice. PR4 115 D2
Ash Ct. PR4 114 D2
Ash Dr. Freckleton PR4 92 A5
Ash Dr. Poulton-le-F FY6 151 E2
Ash Dr. Thornton FY5 173 C1
Ash Dr. Warton PR4 91 D6
Ash Dr. Warton LA5 217 E6
Ash Dr. West Bradford BB7 186 D7
Ash Field. PR6 77 C3
Ash Gr. Bamber Bridge PR5 96 F1
Ash Gr. Barnoldswick BB8 200 B2
Ash Gr. Chorley PR7 42 C5
Ash Gr. Darwen BB3 81 B2
Ash Gr. Formby L37 11 C1
Ash Gr. Garstang PR3 178 B8
Ash Gr. 8 Horwich BL6 31 B4
Ash Gr. Kirkham PR4 113 B7
Ash Gr. Lancaster LA1 210 F5
Ash Gr. Longton PR4 73 F8
Ash Gr. New Longton PR4 74 F6

Back St Anne's Rd W. FY8 88 E6
Back St Anne's St. BL9 32 A4
Back St John St. 5 OL13 86 F3
Back Stanley St. BL0 49 B5
Back Starkie St. PR1 95 F6
Back Sun St. 9 LA1 210 F8
Back Teak St. 5 BL9 32 B2
Back Tinline St. 11 BL9 32 A2
Back Union St. BL7 46 D2
Back Virginia St. PR8 34 B6
Back Walmersley Rd E. BL9 32 A3
Back Warbreck Rd. FY1 129 B6
Back Wash La. BL9 32 B2
Back Wash La S. 6 BL9 32 A2
Back Water St. 11 Accrington BB5 103 C6
Back Water St. Egerton BL7 46 D2
Back Waterloo Rd. FY1 129 B1
Back Wellington St. BB5 103 C5
Back West Cres. FY8 88 E6
Back Willow St. BB12 126 E6
Back Winterdyne Terr. LA3 212 B4
Back Wood St. BL6 31 C3
Back Woodfield Rd. FY1 129 B2
Back Wright St. BL6 31 B4
Back York St. Clitheroe BB7 164 F8
Back York St. Rawtenstall BB4 85 A7
Back Zion St. 15 BB8 169 D4
Backhouse St. 1 BB5 102 E4
Backs The. PR3 139 A6
Bacon St. 5 BB9 147 E8
Bacup Golf Course. OL13 86 E2
Bacup Holy Trinity Stacksteads CE Sch. OL13 69 C8
Bacup Old Rd. OL13 86 F7
Bacup & Rawtenstall Gram Sch. BB4 68 F8
Bacup Rd. Rawtenstall BB4 85 C2
Bacup Rd. Sharneyford OL14 87 E5
Bacup Rd. Walk Mill BB11 106 E6
Baddon Cl. LA4 212 F3
Baden Terr. BB2 100 D1
Badge Brow. BB5 102 E5
Badger Cl. BB12 145 D1
Badger Rd. PR5 76 A4
Badger St. BL9 32 A3
Badger Wells Cotts. BB7 145 A8
Badgers Cl. BB5 103 E8
Badgers Croft. PR1 117 F1
Badgers Rake. L37 11 C5
Badgers Way. PR5 96 B3
Badgers Wlk E. FY8 90 C3
Badgers Wlk W. FY8 90 B3
Bagganley La. PR6 60 F2
Bagnold Rd. PR1 117 D1
Bagot St. FY1 129 B1
Baildon Rd. OL11 & OL12 51 B1
Bailey Bank. BB7 163 A7
Bailey Ct. FY3 129 E6
Bailey La. Heysham LA3 208 E8
Bailey La. Tosside BD23 230 B3
Bailey St. Burnley BB11 126 E5
Bailey St. Earby BB8 201 C2
Bailrigg La. LA1 211 A1
Baines Ave. FY3 150 F1
Baines Endowed CE Prim Sch. FY4 129 F1
Baines' Endowed Cty Prim Sch. FY5 173 C1
Baines Sch. FY6 151 D1
Bairstow St. Barnoldswick BB8 200 B3
Bairstow St. Blackpool FY1 129 B3
Bairstow St. Preston PR1 & PR0 95 F7
Baker St. 13 Bacup OL13 86 F3
Baker St. Blackburn BB1 101 B4
Baker St. Burnley BB11 126 E5
Baker St. Lancaster LA1 213 F3
Baker St. 4 Leyland PR5 76 B2
Baker St. Nelson BB9 168 E1
Baker St. Ramsbottom BL0 49 B5
Baker's La. PR9 53 A3
Bakers Ct. FY4 109 F7
Bala Cl. BB1 100 E6
Balaclava St. BB1 100 E6
Balcarres Cl. PR5 76 A1
Balcarres Pl. PR5 59 A8
Balcarres Rd. Chorley PR7 42 B5
Balcarres Rd. Leyland PR5 59 A8
Balcarres Rd. 5 Leyland PR5 76 B1
Balcarres Rd. Preston PR1 & PR2 116 C2
Balderstone CE Prim Sch. BB2 120 A5
Balderstone Cl. BB10 147 D2
Balderstone Hall La. BB2 119 C6
Balderstone La. BB10 147 E2
Balderstone Rd. Freckleton PR4 92 B7
Balderstone Rd. Preston PR1 95 D5
Baldwin Gr. FY1 129 D2
Baldwin Hill. BB7 164 D8
Baldwin Rd. BB7 164 D8
Baldwin St. Bacup OL13 69 B8
Baldwin St. 6 Bamber Bridge PR5 96 E1
Baldwin St. 5 Barrowford BB9 168 D4
Baldwin St. Blackburn BB2 100 C4
Baldwin's Bldgs. 14 BB4 85 A3
Balfour Cl. Brierfield BB9 147 D5
Balfour Cl. Thornton FY5 151 D7
Balfour House. BB2 100 C4
Balfour Rd. Fulwood PR2 116 E3
Balfour Rd. Southport PR8 34 E5
Balfour Rd. 6 Spotland Fold OL12 51 C1
Balfour St. Blackburn BB2 100 C4
Balfour St. Great Harwood BB6 123 E5
Balfour St. Leyland PR5 76 A1
Balham Ave. FY4 109 E5
Ball Grove Dr. BB8 170 B5
Ball La. LA2 231 C3
Ball St. Blackpool FY1 129 B1
Ball St. 2 Nelson BB9 168 D1
Ball St. Poulton-le-F FY6 151 D3
Ball's Pl. PR8 34 B7
Balladen Prim Sch. BB4 67 F8
Ballam Rd. Lower Ballam PR4 111 C3
Ballam Rd. Lytham St Anne's FY8 90 B4
Ballam Rd. Preston PR2 115 E1
Ballam St. BB11 127 A4
Ballantrae Rd. BB1 101 D3
Ballater St. BB11 126 D3
Balle St. BB3 64 A8
Ballet Hill Cres. PR3 157 A5
Balliol Cl. BB12 125 D6
Balm St. BL0 49 A4
Balmer Gr. FY1 129 D3
Balmoral. PR7 29 E6
Balmoral Ave. Blackburn BB1 122 A4
Balmoral Ave. Clitheroe BB7 164 C6
Balmoral Ave. Leyland PR5 59 C8
Balmoral Ave. Morecambe LA3 212 B3
Balmoral Cl. Horwich BL6 31 E2
Balmoral Cl. Ramsbottom BL8 49 A1
Balmoral Cres. BB1 101 F4
Balmoral Dr. Brinscall PR6 61 E8
Balmoral Dr. Formby L37 11 E1
Balmoral Dr. Southport PR9 53 B3
Balmoral Pl. FY5 151 C8
Balmoral Rd. Accrington BB5 103 D7
Balmoral Rd. Bamber Bridge PR5 96 D3
Balmoral Rd. Blackpool FY4 109 B8
Balmoral Rd. Chorley PR7 42 B8
Balmoral Rd. Darwen BB3 64 B6
Balmoral Rd. Eccleston PR7 40 C7
Balmoral Rd. Haslingden BB4 84 A1
Balmoral Rd. Lancaster LA1 211 A7
Balmoral Rd. Lytham St Anne's FY8 89 A5
Balmoral Rd. Maghull L31 5 C1
Balmoral Rd. Morecambe LA3 & LA4 212 C3
Balmoral Rd. New Longton PR4 95 A1
Balmoral Terr. FY7 194 B5
Balmore Ct. OL10 32 E1
Balniel Cl. PR7 42 A7
Balshaw Ave. PR7 59 D2
Balshaw Cres. PR5 75 F2
Balshaw La. PR7 59 D1
Balshaw Lane Cty Prim Sch. PR7 59 E1
Balshaw Rd. Leyland PR5 75 F1
Balshaw Rd. Lowgill LA2 233 E3
Balshaw St. PR5 96 E2
Balshaw's High Sch. PR5 59 B7
Baltic Rd. BB4 68 E8
Baltimore Rd. FY8 89 B6
Bamber Ave. FY2 150 C4
Bamber Bridge Meth Prim Sch. PR5 76 F8
Bamber Bridge Sta. PR5 76 E8
Bamber Gdns. PR9 35 A8
Bamber St. PR7 42 B5
Bamber's Wlk. PR4 112 E7
Bambers La. Blackpool FY4 110 C6
Bambers La. Blackpool FY4 110 C7
Bamburgh Cl. FY4 110 A7
Bamburgh Dr. BB12 126 E7
Bamford Cl. BL9 32 E4
Bamford Cres. BB5 103 D4
Bamford Pl. OL12 51 E1
Bamford Rd. BL0 50 B6
Bamford St. Burnley BB11 127 A6
Bamford St. Nelson BB9 148 A8
Bamfords Fold. PR5 56 F5
Bamton Ave. FY4 109 C7
Banastre. PR7 60 A2
Banastre Rd. PR8 34 B5
Banastre St. BB5 124 A1
Banbury Ave. Blackpool FY2 150 D1
Banbury Ave. Oswaldtwistle BB5 102 C4
Banbury Cl. 3 Accrington BB5 103 A7
Banbury Cl. Blackburn BB2 79 F8
Banbury Dr. PR2 116 E4
Banbury Rd. Longshaw WN5 10 D2
Banbury Rd. Lytham St Anne's FY8 89 A6
Banbury Rd. Morecambe LA3 & LA4 212 F3
Bancroft Ave. FY5 173 C2
Bancroft Fold. BB8 200 A1
Bancroft Rd. BB10 127 C8
Bancroft St. BB1 100 F5
Bancroft Steam Mus. BB8 200 B1
Band La. PR3 177 D1
Bangor Ave. FY2 150 D4
Bangor St. BB1 100 F7
Bank Ave. WN5 10 D5
Bank Bottom. BB3 81 A1
Bank Bridge. PR4 56 B5
Bank Brow. WN8 19 C5
Bank Cl. Galgate LA2 206 F3
Bank Cl. Longton PR4 74 A8
Bank Cotts. BB7 143 B4
Bank Croft. PR4 74 A8
Bank Fold. BB9 168 E4
Bank Hall Cotts. BB7 224 C1
Bank Head La. PR5 97 D1
Bank Hey Cl. BB1 122 A1
Bank Hey La N. BB1 121 F1
Bank Hey La S. BB1 122 A1
Bank Hey Sch. BB2 80 C7
Bank Hey St. FY1 129 B5
Bank House La. Bacup OL13 86 F2
Bank House La. Westhouse LA6 236 E4
Bank House St. BB9 168 E4
Bank La. Blackburn BB1 101 D4
Bank La. Warton PR4 91 D4
Bank Meadow. BL6 31 C4
Bank Mill St. 3 BB4 84 B2
Bank Par. Burnley BB11 127 A6
Bank Par. Penwortham PR1 95 D3
Bank Par. Preston PR1 96 A6
Bank Pas. PR8 34 A7
Bank Pl. PR1 116 C1
Bank Rd. Lancaster LA1 213 F3
Bank Rd. Shevington Vale WN8 19 D4
Bank Sq. PR8 34 B8
Bank St. Accrington BB5 103 C5
Bank St. Adlington PR6 30 A7
Bank St. 14 Bacup OL13 86 F2
Bank St. Bank Lane BL0 49 E7
Bank St. Barnoldswick BB8 200 C2
Bank St. Brierfield BB9 147 B6
Bank St. Chapeltown BL7 47 C4
Bank St. Chorley PR7 42 C8
Bank St. 9 Church BB5 102 E6
Bank St. Darwen BB3 81 A1
Bank St. Haslingden BB4 84 B3
Bank St. 11 Nelson BB9 168 E1
Bank St. Padiham BB12 145 C1
Bank St. Rawtenstall BB4 85 A2
Bank St. Trawden BB8 170 C1
Bank Terr. Simonstone BB12 124 E8
Bank Terr. Whitworth OL12 51 C8
Bank Top. Baldingstone BL9 49 F1
Bank Top. Blackburn BB2 100 C4
Bank Top. Burnley BB11 127 A6
Bank View. Hambleton FY6 174 C1
Bank View. Rawtenstall BB11 105 C5
Bankcroft Cl. BB12 125 E8
Bankfield. Burnley BB11 127 A6
Bankfield. Skelmersdale WN8 9 C7
Bankfield Ct. FY5 151 B8
Bankfield Gr. FY1 129 E3
Bankfield La. PR9 53 B2
Bankfield St. Bacup OL13 69 D8
Bankfield St. Colne BB8 169 B4
Bankfield St. Colne BB8 170 B4
Bankfield Terr. 1 Bacup OL13 69 D8
Bankfield Terr. Barnoldswick BB8 200 C3
Bankhouse Rd. BB9 168 E1
Bankhouse St. Burnley BB11 126 F6
Bankhouse St. Burnley BB11 127 A6
Banks Bridge Cl. BB8 200 C4
Banks Cres. LA3 208 F6
Banks Head Rd. LA2 233 D8
Banks Hill. BB8 200 A4
Banks Meth Prim Sch. PR9 54 B7
Banks Rd. Fulwood PR2 116 C3
Banks Rd. Southport PR9 53 D6
Banks Rise. 4 LA2 233 D8
Banks St. Blackpool FY1 129 B6
Banks St. Lane Bottom BB10 148 B3
Banks Way. 3 LA2 233 D8
Banksbarn. WN8 9 C7
Banksfield Ave. PR2 116 C3
Banksfield Pl. PR5 77 A7
Bankside. Blackburn BB2 100 E2
Bankside. Clayton Green PR6 77 B1
Bankside. Hightown L38 2 F3
Bankside. Parbold WN8 26 B2
Bankside Cl. OL13 86 E1
Bankside La. OL13 86 F2
Bankwood. WN6 19 E6
Banner Cl. PR7 40 B6
Bannerman Terr. PR6 60 D2
Bannister Brow. L40 & WN8 26 E6
Bannister Cl. Higher Walton PR5 97 B4
Bannister Cl. Trawden BB8 170 B3
Bannister Ct. Blackpool FY2 150 B4
Bannister Ct. 12 Nelson BB9 147 E8
Bannister Dr. PR5 75 E1
Bannister Gn. PR7 40 C3
Bannister Hall Cres. PR5 97 B4
Bannister Hall Dr. PR5 97 B4
Bannister Hall La. PR5 97 B4
Bannister La. Eccleston PR7 40 C5
Bannister La. Hill Dale L40 & WN8 26 E6
Bannister La. Leyland PR5 75 E4
Bannister St. 10 Chorley PR7 42 C7
Bannister St. Lytham St Anne's FY8 90 B3
Bannister's Bit. PR1 95 C2
Bannistre Ct. PR4 56 A6
Bar St. BB10 127 B8
Bar Terr. OL12 51 C7
Barbara Castle Way. BB1 & BB2 100 E5
Barberry Bank. BL7 46 E2
Barbon Pl. LA1 213 E2
Barbon St. Burnley BB10 147 C2
Barbon St. 12 Padiham BB12 145 C1
Barbrook Cl. WN6 28 B2
Barclay Ave. Blackpool FY4 129 F2
Barclay Ave. Burnley BB11 126 C4
Barclay Rd. PR3 139 A7
Barcroft Gn. BB10 127 E1
Barcroft St. BB8 169 C5
Barden Croft. BB5 123 F4
Barden Cty Inf Sch. BB10 147 A1
Barden High Sch. BB10 147 A1
Barden Jun Sch. BB10 147 A1
Barden La. BB10 & BB12 147 A2
Barden Pl. PR2 117 D4
Barden Rd. BB5 102 F4
Barden St. 3 BB10 147 B1
Barden View. BB10 147 A2
Bardsea Pl. PR2 115 F3
Bardsley Cl. WN8 10 A7
Bardsway. FY5 173 A3
Bardsway Ave. FY3 129 F6
Bare Ave. LA4 213 A6
Bare La. LA4 213 A5
Bare Lane Sta. LA4 213 A6
Barford Cl. Ainsdale PR8 20 A6
Barford Cl. Hall Green WN8 10 A7
Barford Gr. BL6 31 F1
Bargee Cl. BB1 100 F3
Barker Brow. BB1 & PR3 141 A3
Barker Cl. LA6 234 B7
Barker La. BB1 & BB2 121 C2
Barkerford Cl. BB12 145 F5
Barkerhouse Rd. Nelson BB10 & BB9 148 B8
Barkerhouse Rd. 16 Nelson BB9 168 E1
Barkfield Ave. L37 11 E4
Barkfield La. L37 11 D4
Barley Bank St. BB3 80 F2
Barley Cl. BB2 100 D5
Barley Cop La. LA1 213 D4
Barley Gr. BB10 127 C6
Barley Holme Rd. BB4 85 A8
Barley La. Barley BB12 & BB9 & BB7 167 B7
Barley La. Blackburn BB2 100 D5
Barley Rd. BB12 167 E5
Barley St. BB12 125 C7
Barley Way. BB2 100 D5
Barleydale Rd. BB9 168 E5
Barleyfield. PR5 & PR6 77 C3
Barlow Cres. FY3 129 E4
Barlow Ct. BL7 47 E5
Barlow St. Accrington BB5 103 A6
Barlow St. Bacup OL13 69 B7
Barlow St. Bury BL9 32 A2
Barlow St. Horwich BL6 31 C2
Barlow St. Preston PR1 116 E1
Barlow St. Preston PR1 116 F2
Barlow St. 11 Rawtenstall BB4 85 A3
Barlow's La. L39 21 D5
Barlows Bldgs. 4 BB4 84 F1
Barmouth Ave. FY3 130 A3
Barmouth Cres. BB1 121 E1
Barmskin La. PR7 40 B2
Barn Acre. BL6 30 E1
Barn Cl. PR4 55 A2
Barn Croft. Leyland PR5 75 B1
Barn Croft. Penwortham PR1 95 B4
Barn Field Cl. BB8 170 A5
Barn Gill Cl. BB1 100 F3
Barn Hey. PR4 94 A1
Barn Hey Rd. L33 1 A2
Barn Meadow. Clayton Brook PR5 77 B6
Barn Meadow. Edgworth BL7 47 D5
Barn Meadow Cres. BB1 123 C1
Barnacre Cl. Fulwood PR2 117 A8
Barnacre Cl. Lancaster LA1 211 B2
Barnacre Rd. PR3 139 A8
Barnard Cl. BB5 102 C4
Barnbrook St. BL9 32 A3
Barncroft Dr. BL6 31 F3
Barnes Ave. BB4 84 F2
Barnes Cl. BL0 49 A3
Barnes Dr. L31 5 C3
Barnes Rd. Morecambe LA3 212 B3
Barnes Rd. Ormskirk L39 15 E3
Barnes Rd. Skelmersdale WN8 17 E1
Barnes Sq. 1 BB5 123 F2
Barnes St. Accrington BB5 103 C6
Barnes St. Burnley BB11 127 A6
Barnes St. Church BB5 102 E6
Barnes St. Clayton-le-M BB5 123 F3
Barnes St. Haslingden BB4 84 B4
Barnfield. Bamber Bridge PR5 76 A8
Barnfield. Kirkham PR4 113 A5
Barnfield. Much Hoole PR4 73 E3
Barnfield Ave. BB10 127 F6
Barnfield Bsns Ctr. BB9 147 F6
Barnfield Cl. Egerton BL7 46 E2
Barnfield Cl. 4 Thornton FY5 172 F4
Barnfield Dr. WN8 9 E7
Barnfield Manor. FY6 152 D3
Barnfield St. Accrington BB5 103 D5
Barnfield St. Lower Healey OL12 51 F2
Barnmeadow La. BB6 123 C5
Barnoldswick CE Prim Sch. BB8 200 B2
Barnoldswick La. LA6 236 D3
Barnoldswick Rd. Beverley BB8 & BB9 168 F7
Barnoldswick Rd. Kelbrook BB8 191 F6
Barns La. PR3 159 C8
Barns The. L37 12 A1
Barnsfold. PR2 116 D6
Barnside. Euxton PR7 59 C3
Barnside. Whitworth OL12 51 B8
Barnside Est. BB8 170 F7
Barnwood Cres. BB8 201 C1
Barnwood Rd. BB8 201 B1
Baron Rd. FY1 129 C1
Baron St. Darwen BB3 80 F2
Baron St. Rawtenstall BB4 85 D1
Barons Cl. BB3 81 A7
Barons Way. Blackburn BB3 81 A6
Barons Way. Euxton PR7 59 D2
Barracks Rd. BB11 126 D6
Barracks The. L39 22 C2
Barret Hill Brow. BB7 224 B4
Barret St. BB8 201 A1
Barrett Ave. PR8 34 A2
Barrett Ct. 5 BL9 32 A2
Barrett Rd. PR8 34 A2
Barrett St. 5 BB10 127 A8
Barrington Dr. PR8 20 B5
Barrison Gn. L40 23 E2
Barritt Rd. BB4 84 F2
Barronwood Ct. PR4 56 A5
Barrow Nook La. L39 7 E2
Barrow (VC) Prim Sch. BB7 164 D2
Barrow's La. PR3 154 B5
Barrowdale Ave. BB9 147 F7
Barrowford Rd. Barrowford BB9 168 B1
Barrowford Rd. Colne BB8 169 B5
Barrowford Rd. Fence BB12 & BB9 146 C7
Barrows La. LA3 208 E7
Barrows La E. PR3 154 B5
Barry Ave. PR2 116 A3
Barry Gr. LA3 208 F6
Barry St. BB12 126 C7
Bartle La. PR4 115 C7
Bartle Pl. PR2 115 E1
Bartle Rd. FY8 89 A8
Bartle St. BB11 126 D5
Barton Ave. Blackpool FY1 129 B2
Barton Ave. Knott End-on-S FY6 194 E5
Barton Gdns. LA1 211 B5
Barton Heys Rd. L37 11 D1
Barton La. PR3 136 E7
Barton Mansion. FY8 88 C7
Barton Rd. Lancaster LA1 211 A4
Barton Rd. Lytham St Anne's FY8 88 D8
Barton Sq. FY6 194 E5
Barton St. BB2 100 E5
Barton Streety. BB2 100 E5
Bashall Gr. PR5 76 B3
Basil St. Colne BB8 169 D4
Basil St. Preston PR1 117 C2
Basnett St. BB10 147 C1
Bass La. BL9 49 D3
Bassenthwaite Rd. FY3 130 C2
Bassett Way. OL12 51 E2
Bastwell Rd. BB1 100 F7
Bateman Gr. LA4 212 E5
Bateman Rd. LA4 212 E5
Bateman St. BL6 31 D2
Bates St. BB5 123 E3
Bath Mill La. LA1 211 A8
Bath Mill Sq. 7 LA1 211 A8
Bath Rd. FY8 90 B3
Bath Springs. L39 15 F5
Bath St. Accrington BB5 103 B4
Bath St. Blackburn BB2 100 C4
Bath St. Blackpool FY4 129 B1
Bath St. Colne BB8 169 E5
Bath St. Darwen BB3 81 A1
Bath St. Lancaster LA1 211 A8
Bath St. Lytham St Anne's FY8 90 B3
Bath St. Morecambe LA4 212 D5
Bath St. Nelson BB9 147 F8
Bath St. Preston PR1 116 D1
Bath St. Southport PR8 34 B8
Bath St N. PR8 & PR9 34 B8
Bathurst Ave. FY3 130 A7
Bathurst St. BB2 100 D5
Batridge Rd. BL7 47 A7
Battersby St. BL9 32 D3
Battismore Rd. LA4 212 E5
Battle Way. L37 12 B2
Bawdlands. BB7 164 D8
Bawhead Rd. BB8 201 B1
Baxenden CE Prim Sch. BB5 103 E1
Baxenden Golf Course. BB5 103 F3
Baxter St. WN6 28 F1
Baxtergate. LA4 212 E6
Bay Cl. LA3 208 D6
Bay Horse Dr. LA1 211 B3
Bay Horse La. PR4 134 D4
Bay Horse Rd. LA2 207 E4
Bay Rd. Fulwood PR2 117 E2
Bay Rd. Heysham LA3 208 D6
Bay St. BB1 101 A7
Bay The. FY5 172 C5
Bay Tree Farm. PR2 94 D8
Bay Tree Rd. PR6 77 B3
Bay View. LA6 231 B8
Bay View Ave. LA2 213 E8
Bay View Cres. LA2 213 E8
Bayard St. BB12 126 A6
Baycliffe Cres. LA4 212 D5
Bayley Fold. BB7 164 E8
Bayley St. BB5 123 E3
Baylton Ct. PR3 178 D2
Baylton Dr. PR3 178 D2
Baynes St. BB3 81 F1
Bayswater. FY2 150 C4
Baytree Cl. Bamber Bridge PR5 76 C8
Baytree Cl. Southport PR9 53 D5
Baytree Gr. BL0 49 B2
Baytree Wlk. OL12 70 C1
Baywood St. BB1 100 F7
Bazil Gr. LA3 205 D7
Bazil La. LA3 205 D7
Bazley Rd. FY8 89 D3
Beach Ave. Cleveleys FY5 172 D3
Beach Ave. Lytham St Anne's FY8 89 C3
Beach Priory Gdns. PR8 34 A6
Beach Rd. Cleveleys FY5 172 D3
Beach Rd. Fleetwood FY7 193 E3
Beach Rd. Lytham St Anne's FY8 88 D7
Beach Rd. Pilling Lane PR3 195 B7
Beach Rd. Southport PR8 33 F6
Beach St. Lytham St Anne's FY8 90 A3
Beach St. Morecambe LA4 213 A7
Beach Terr. LA6 236 F3
Beacham Rd. PR8 34 E7
Beachcomber Dr. FY5 172 C3
Beachley Rd. PR2 116 A4
Beachley Sq. BB12 126 D7
Beachmews. PR8 33 F6
Beachwood La. LA5 237 A1
Beacon Ave. PR2 116 D5
Beacon Crossing. WN8 26 C2
Beacon Ctry Pk. WN8 18 E2

Beacon Dr. PR3 137 D6
Beacon Fell Ctry Pk. PR3 180 F2
Beacon Gr. Fulwood PR2 116 D4
Beacon Gr. Garstang PR3 178 B6
Beacon La. L40 & WN8 18 D4
Beacon Rd. Poulton-le-F FY6 152 A3
Beacon Rd. Shevington Moor WN6 28 B2
Beacon St. PR6 & PR7 42 D7
Beacon View. WN6 19 C8
Beacon View Dr. WN8 10 B7
Beacons The. WN6 19 D7
Beaconsfield Ave. PR1 117 E1
Beaconsfield Rd. PR9 34 F6
Beaconsfield St. Accrington BB5 103 D5
Beaconsfield St. Great Harwood BB6 123 C5
Beaconsfield St. 13 Haslingden BB4 84 B3
Beaconsfield Terr. Catterall PR3 178 E2
Beaconsfield Terr. Chorley PR6 60 D2
Beale Rd. BB9 147 B8
Beamont Dr. PR1 & PR2 95 D8
Bean Ave. FY4 109 E8
Bear St. BB12 125 F6
Beardshaw Ave. FY1 129 D2
Beardsworth St. BB1 101 A7
Beardwood. BB2 100 A8
Beardwood Brow. BB2 100 B7
Beardwood Dr. BB2 100 A7
Beardwood Meadow. BB2 100 A7
Beardwood Pk. BB2 100 B7
Bearncroft. WN8 9 D6
Bearswood Croft. PR6 77 B2
Beatie St. BB9 147 B6
Beatrice Ave. BB12 126 C7
Beatrice Mews. 9 BL6 31 B4
Beatrice Pl. BB2 81 A8
Beattock Pl. FY2 150 F6
Beatty Ave. PR7 42 B6
Beatty Cl. FY8 109 D1
Beatty Rd. PR8 34 E5
Beauclerk Rd. FY8 89 B6
Beaufort. L37 12 A2
Beaufort Ave. FY2 150 C5
Beaufort Cl. BB12 144 E2
Beaufort Gr. LA4 212 G5
Beaufort Rd. Morecambe LA4 213 A5
Beaufort Rd. Weir OL13 87 A7
Beaufort St. Nelson BB9 147 E7
Beaufort St. Spotland Fold OL12 51 C1
Beauley Ave. BB12 144 E2
Beaumaris Ave. BB2 100 A1
Beaumaris Cl. 2 BB4 84 B1
Beaumaris Rd. PR5 59 C8
Beaumont Ave. BL6 31 C4
Beaumont Coll (The Spastics Society). LA1 213 F4
Beaumont Cres. L39 15 D2
Beaumont Gdns. FY6 151 A5
Beaumont Pl. LA1 213 F4
Beaumont Rd. BL6 31 C4
Beaumont St. LA1 213 F4
Beaver Cl. BB1 121 F5
Beaver Terr. 13 OL13 87 A3
Beavers La. WN8 9 D6
Bebles Rd. L39 15 C3
Becconsall La. PR4 72 F3
Beck Ct. FY7 193 D1
Beck Gr. FY5 172 E4
Beck Side. LA2 231 C3
Beck View. 7 LA1 211 A3
Beckdean Ave. FY6 151 D2
Beckenham Ct. BB10 147 D3
Beckett Ct. 19 PR1 95 F8
Beckett St. 4 BB3 64 A8
Becks Brow. BD23 230 F3
Beckside. BB12 167 C5
Beckside Mews. LA6 234 B3
Beckway Ave. FY3 129 F7
Bective Rd. LA6 238 C2
Bedale Pl. FY5 172 E1
Beddington St. 5 BB9 168 D1
Bedford Ave. FY5 172 D3
Bedford Cl. BB5 102 C4
Bedford Pl. Lancaster LA1 211 A4
Bedford Pl. Padiham BB12 125 D7
Bedford Rd. Blackpool FY1 129 C8
Bedford Rd. Fulwood PR2 117 A4
Bedford Rd. Lytham St Anne's FY8 90 D4
Bedford Rd. Southport PR8 34 A2
Bedford St. 6 Barrowford BB9 168 C1
Bedford St. Blackburn BB2 100 C2
Bedford St. Darwen BB3 80 F4
Bedford St. Egerton BL7 46 D2
Bedford Terr. Bury BL9 32 A4
Bedford Terr. Haslingden BB4 67 A8
Bedfordshire Ave. BB12 126 B7
Bee La. PR1 & PR5 95 E1
Beech Ave. Adlington PR6 30 B8
Beech Ave. Bilsborrow PR3 157 A5
Beech Ave. Blackpool FY3 129 E5
Beech Ave. Darwen BB3 81 B2
Beech Ave. Earby BB8 201 A1
Beech Ave. Euxton PR7 59 C4
Beech Ave. Galgate LA2 206 F4
Beech Ave. Horwich BL6 31 E1
Beech Ave. Kirkham PR4 113 B4
Beech Ave. Leyland PR5 59 A7
Beech Ave. Parbold WN8 26 C2
Beech Ave. Poulton-le-F FY6 151 D4
Beech Ave. Warton PR4 91 D6
Beech Cl. Bacup OL13 87 A3
Beech Cl. Clitheroe BB7 164 D8
Beech Cl. Oswaldtwistle BB5 102 C2
Beech Cl. Rishton BB1 102 B8
Beech Cl. Rufford L40 38 C4
Beech Cl. Skelmersdale WN8 17 E1
Beech Cl. Whitworth OL12 70 C1
Beech Cl. Wilpshire BB1 121 E6
Beech Cres. BB5 124 A1
Beech Dr. Formby L37 11 D4
Beech Dr. Freckleton PR4 92 A5
Beech Dr. Fulwood PR2 116 D8
Beech Dr. Haslingden BB4 84 C2
Beech Dr. Longridge PR3 139 A7
Beech Dr. Newton-with-S PR4 113 F2
Beech Dr. Poulton-le-F FY6 151 D2
Beech Gdns. PR6 77 B1
Beech Gr. Accrington BB5 103 A4
Beech Gr. Barnoldswick BB8 200 C2
Beech Gr. Brierfield BB10 147 C4
Beech Gr. Chatburn BB7 187 D5
Beech Gr. Darwen BB3 80 D6
Beech Gr. Knott End-on-S FY6 194 E6
Beech Gr. Morecambe LA4 213 A5
Beech Gr. Preston PR1 116 B1
Beech Gr. Ramsbottom BL8 49 A1
Beech Gr. Southport PR9 34 F7
Beech Gr. Warton LA5 217 D5
Beech Grove Cl. BL9 32 B4
Beech Hill Cl. PR5 96 E3
Beech Ind Est. 3 OL13 87 A3
Beech Meadow. L39 16 A4
Beech Mount. BB1 121 F3
Beech Rd. Elswick PR4 153 F1
Beech Rd. Garstang PR3 178 B8
Beech Rd. Halton LA2 214 E7
Beech Rd. Holt Green L39 6 A6
Beech Rd. Leyland PR5 76 A2
Beech St. Accrington BB5 103 C5
Beech St. Bacup OL13 87 A3
Beech St. Barnoldswick BB8 200 B1
Beech St. Blackburn BB1 101 A7
Beech St. Bury BL9 32 B2
Beech St. Clayton-le-M BB5 123 F1
Beech St. Clitheroe BB7 164 D8
Beech St. Edgworth BL7 47 D5
Beech St. Great Harwood BB6 123 C6
Beech St. Lancaster LA1 210 D8
Beech St. 10 Nelson BB9 168 E1
Beech St. Padiham BB12 125 D7
Beech St. Preston PR1 95 D6
Beech St. Ramsbottom BL0 49 C3
Beech St. Rawtenstall BB4 85 A3
Beech St S. PR1 95 E6
Beech Terr. PR1 95 E6
Beech Tree Ave. WN6 19 D8
Beech Tree Cl. BB9 147 E7
Beech Tree Sch. PR5 77 B4
Beechacre. BL0 49 D5
Beecham St. LA4 212 E6
Beechcroft. Cleveleys FY5 172 C4
Beechcroft. Maghull L31 5 C1
Beeches The. Clayton Green PR6 77 C3
Beeches The. Singleton FY6 152 D1
Beeches The. Tarleton PR4 56 A7
Beechfield. Hill Dale WN8 26 C5
Beechfield. Lancaster LA1 210 D7
Beechfield. Maghull L31 5 E1
Beechfield Ave. Blackpool FY3 129 E3
Beechfield Ave. Knott End-on-S FY6 195 A5
Beechfield Ave. Wrea Green PR4 112 C4
Beechfield Ct. PR5 59 B8
Beechfield Gdns. PR8 33 F6
Beechfield Mews. PR9 34 C7
Beechfield Rd. PR5 59 B8
Beechfields. PR7 40 B6
Beeching Cl. LA1 210 F6
Beechthorpe Ave. BB7 186 B4
Beechtrees. WN8 9 D7
Beechway. Fulwood PR2 117 A4
Beechway. Moss Side L31 6 B2
Beechway. Penwortham PR1 95 B3
Beechway Ave. L31 6 B2
Beechwood. WN8 18 C3
Beechwood Ave. Accrington BB5 103 D3
Beechwood Ave. Bamber Bridge PR5 96 D4
Beechwood Ave. Burnley BB11 126 F3
Beechwood Ave. Clitheroe BB7 164 E6
Beechwood Ave. Fulwood PR2 116 C4
Beechwood Ave. Ramsbottom BL0 49 D6
Beechwood Ave. Shevington WN6 19 F5
Beechwood Cres. WN5 10 E6
Beechwood Croft. PR6 77 A3
Beechwood Ct. Maghull L31 5 F1
Beechwood Ct. Skelmersdale WN8 9 D6
Beechwood Dr. Blackburn BB2 79 E8
Beechwood Dr. Formby L37 11 C1
Beechwood Dr. Ormskirk L39 15 D5
Beechwood Dr. Thornton FY5 151 B8
Beechwood Gdns. LA1 211 A2
Beechwood Gr. FY2 150 E4
Beechwood Mews. BB1 81 A8
Beechwood Rd. 9 Blackburn BB1 101 A7
Beechwood Rd. Chorley PR7 42 D6
Beenland St. 3 PR1 117 D1
Beeston Ave. FY6 151 C5
Beetham Ct. BB5 123 E2
Beetham Pl. FY3 129 E6
Begonia St. BB3 81 B1
Beightons Wlk. OL12 51 D4
Bela Cl. 3 LA1 213 C2
Bela Gr. FY1 129 D2
Belfield. WN8 9 D6
Belfield Rd. BB5 103 C4
Belford Ave. FY5 172 F4
Belford St. BB12 126 F7
Belfry Cres. WN6 28 F2
Belfry The. FY8 90 D5
Belgarth Rd. BB5 103 C7
Belgrave Ave. Kirkham PR4 113 A7
Belgrave Ave. Penwortham PR1 95 B3
Belgrave Cl. Blackburn BB2 100 B3
Belgrave Cl. Lytham St Anne's FY8 89 D6
Belgrave Cres. BL6 31 D3
Belgrave Ct. BB12 126 F7
Belgrave Pl. Poulton-le-F FY6 151 B2
Belgrave Pl. Southport PR8 33 F3
Belgrave Rd. Blackpool FY4 129 E1
Belgrave Rd. Colne BB8 169 D6
Belgrave Rd. Darwen BB3 64 A8
Belgrave Rd. 5 Leyland PR5 76 A1
Belgrave Rd. Poulton-le-F FY6 151 B3
Belgrave Rd. Southport PR8 33 F3
Belgrave Sq. 9 BB3 81 A1
Belgrave St. Brierfield BB9 147 A6
Belgrave St. Burnley BB12 126 F7
Belgrave St. Haslingden BB5 84 A8
Belgrave St. Nelson BB9 168 F1
Belgrave St. Spotland Fold OL12 51 D1
Bell La. Bury BL9 32 A3
Bell La. Claughton PR3 179 C4
Bell La. Clayton-le-M BB5 124 B4
Bell St. BB4 84 B3
Bell's Cl. L31 5 C4
Bell's La. L31 5 B3
Bell-Aire Park Homes. LA3 208 F5
Bellamy Ave. LA4 212 D3
Belle Isle Ave. OL12 51 C6
Belle Vue Ave. LA1 211 A5
Belle Vue Dr. LA1 211 A5
Belle Vue La. BB7 186 B4
Belle Vue Pl. BB11 126 E6
Belle Vue St. Blackburn BB2 100 C5
Belle Vue St. Burnley BB11 126 E6
Bellfield Rd. LA4 212 F5
Bellingham Rd. FY8 90 B4
Bellis Ave. PR9 52 F2
Bells La. PR5 97 E3
Belmont Ave. Blackpool FY1 129 C4
Belmont Ave. Fulwood PR2 117 D2
Belmont Ave. Orrell WN5 10 D3
Belmont Ave. Poulton-le-F FY6 151 B3
Belmont Cl. Brinscall PR6 61 E8
Belmont Cl. Burscough L40 24 E3
Belmont Cl. Fulwood PR2 117 D2
Belmont Cl. Lancaster LA1 213 D3
Belmont Cres. PR2 117 D2
Belmont Ct. PR3 139 B7
Belmont Dr. PR6 60 E1
Belmont Gr. BB10 127 D5
Belmont Pl. PR7 28 C6
Belmont Rd. Adlington PR6 30 B7
Belmont Rd. Belmont PR7 & BL7 63 A2
Belmont Rd. Fleetwood FY7 194 A3
Belmont Rd. Fulwood PR2 116 C2
Belmont Rd. Great Harwood BB6 123 B5
Belmont Rd. Horwich BL6 31 C7
Belmont Rd. Leyland PR5 58 D8
Belmont Rd. Lytham St Anne's FY8 89 C5
Belmont Rd. Rivington BL6 44 C3
Belmont Sch. BB4 84 E2
Belmont St. PR8 34 A5
Belmont Terr. 6 Barrowford BB9 168 D3
Belmont Terr. Foulridge BB8 191 E1
Belmont Way. OL12 51 E2
Belper St. BB1 101 A6
Belsfield Dr. PR4 72 E4
Belshaw Ct. BB11 126 A3
Belthorn CE Prim Sch. BB1 81 F6
Belthorn Rd. BB1 81 E6
Belton Hill. PR2 116 D8
Belvedere Ave. Ramsbottom BL8 49 A1
Belvedere Ave. Rawtenstall BB4 86 A1
Belvedere Ct. FY8 89 D4
Belvedere Dr. Chorley PR7 42 B8
Belvedere Dr. Formby L37 11 F1
Belvedere Pk. L39 6 C7
Belvedere Rd. Adlington PR6 30 B8
Belvedere Rd. Ainsdale PR8 20 C5
Belvedere Rd. Blackburn BB1 122 A3
Belvedere Rd. Burnley BB10 & BB11 127 B6
Belvedere Rd. 2 Leyland PR5 76 B2
Belvedere Rd. Thornton FY5 151 C8
Belverdale Gdns. FY4 109 F5
Belvere Ave. FY4 109 D6
Belvoir St. OL12 51 C1
Ben La. Barnoldswick BB8 200 D3
Ben La. Barrow Nook L39 8 A1
Benbow Cl. FY8 109 D2
Bence Rd. PR1 96 B6
Bence St. BB8 169 E5
Bench Carr. OL12 51 E1
Benenden Pl. FY5 173 A2
Bengal St. PR6 60 D1
Bengarth Rd. PR9 34 F8
Benjamin Hargreaves CE Prim Sch. BB5 103 D5
Bennett Ave. FY1 129 C4
Bennett Rd. FY5 173 A3
Bennett St. 2 BB9 168 F2
Bennett's La. FY4 109 F6
Bennington St. BB1 & BB2 100 F3
Benson Ave. LA4 212 G4
Benson House. BB1 101 C8
Benson La. PR4 134 F3
Benson Rd. FY2 150 E1
Benson St. Blackburn BB1 101 B7
Benson St. Bury BL9 32 A1
Benson St. Edgworth BL7 47 E5
Benson's La. PR3 & PR4 156 C1
Bent Est. OL13 87 A7
Bent Gap La. BB2 100 C4
Bent La. Colne BB8 170 B6
Bent La. Gisburn BB7 225 C3
Bent La. Leyland PR5 & PR6 59 C8
Bent St. Blackburn BB2 100 D4
Bent St. Haslingden BB4 67 D8
Bent St. Oswaldtwistle BB5 102 D3
Bentgate Cl. BB4 67 D8
Bentham Ave. Burnley BB10 147 B3
Bentham Ave. Fleetwood FY7 193 A1
Bentham Cl. BB2 100 B1
Bentham Moor Rd. LA6 236 D2
Bentham Pl. WN6 28 F2
Bentham Rd. Barnoldswick LA6 236 E3
Bentham Rd. Blackburn BB2 100 B1
Bentham Rd. Lancaster LA1 211 A2
Bentham Rd. Standish WN6 28 F2
Bentham Sch. LA2 233 B8
Bentham St. Coppull PR7 41 E1
Bentham St. Southport PR8 34 B5
Bentham Sta. LA2 233 D7
Bentham's Way. PR8 34 C2
Bentinck Ave. FY4 109 B5
Bentinck Rd. FY8 88 C8
Bentinck St. 9 OL12 51 C1
Bentlea Rd. BB7 225 C3
Bentley Dr. Kirkham PR4 112 E5
Bentley Dr. Peel Hill FY4 111 A6
Bentley La. Andertons Mill L40 & PR7 40 A1
Bentley La. Baldingstone BL9 50 A1
Bentley La. Bispham Green L40 26 E8
Bentley Park Rd. PR4 73 F7
Bentley St. 8 Bacup OL13 86 F3
Bentley St. Blackburn BB1 101 C5
Bentley St. Darwen BB3 64 C7
Bentley St. Falinge Fold OL12 51 E2
Bentley St. Nelson BB9 147 D7
Bentmeadows. OL12 51 E1
Benton Rd. PR2 117 D4
Bents. BB8 170 B6
Bents La. LA6 238 F5
Bentwood Rd. BB4 84 A3
Beresford Dr. PR9 52 F1
Beresford Gdns. PR9 52 F2
Beresford Rd. BB1 100 D7
Beresford St. Blackpool FY1 129 C7
Beresford St. 6 Burnley BB11 126 D6
Beresford St. Nelson BB9 147 F6
Bergen St. BB11 126 B5
Berkeley Cl. Chorley PR7 42 D5
Berkeley Cl. Nelson BB9 147 E7
Berkeley Cres. BB12 145 C1
Berkeley Dr. Clayton-le-W PR5 76 E4
Berkeley Dr. Simonstone BB12 144 E2
Berkeley St. Brierfield BB9 147 A5
Berkeley St. Nelson BB9 147 E7
Berkeley St. Preston PR1 116 E1
Berkley Cl. PR4 112 E5
Berkshire Ave. BB12 126 B7
Berkshire Cl. BB1 121 F7
Bernard St. OL12 51 E3
Berne Ave. BL6 31 A3
Berridge Ave. BB12 126 A6
Berriedale Rd. BB9 169 A1
Berry Cl. WN8 17 F2
Berry Field. PR1 95 C3
Berry House Rd. L40 37 A4
Berry La. PR3 139 A7
Berry St. Bamber Bridge PR5 76 A8
Berry St. Brierfield BB9 147 B5
Berry St. Burnley BB11 126 F4
Berry St. Preston PR1 96 A7
Berry St. Skelmersdale WN8 17 F2
Berry's La. FY6 151 C4
Berrys La. BB7 143 C1
Bertha St. BB5 103 D6
Bertram Ave. LA4 212 D4
Bertrand Ave. FY3 130 A7
Berwick Ave. Ainsdale PR8 20 D5
Berwick Ave. Cleveleys FY5 172 F4
Berwick Dr. Burnley BB12 126 E7
Berwick Dr. Fulwood PR2 116 D4
Berwick Rd. Blackpool FY4 109 C5
Berwick Rd. Lytham St Anne's FY8 88 F7
Berwick Rd. Preston PR1 96 A6
Berwick St. PR1 117 E1
Berwick Way. LA3 208 E7
Berwyn Ave. LA4 212 G6
Berwyn Cl. BL6 31 C5
Berwyn Ct. PR8 34 D4
Beryl Ave. Blackburn BB1 121 F2
Beryl Ave. Cleveleys FY5 172 E1
Bescar Brow La. L40 22 F7
Bescar La. L40 & PR9 36 B1
Bessie St. BB8 200 B2
Bessie's Well Pl. WN6 28 F1
Best St. PR4 112 F5
Bethel Ave. FY2 150 D4
Bethel Rd. BB1 101 A7
Bethel St. Barnoldswick BB8 200 B1
Bethel St. Colne BB8 169 B4
Bethesda Cl. BB2 100 D3
Bethesda Rd. FY1 129 B3
Bethesda St. Barnoldswick BB8 200 B2
Bethesda St. Burnley BB11 126 F6
Betony. LA4 213 B7
Betony Cl. OL12 51 D3
Bett La. PR6 78 C1
Beulah Ave. LA4 212 G5
Bevan Pl. BB9 168 F2
Beverley Ave. Longshaw WN5 10 E1
Beverley Ave. Poulton-le-F FY6 130 D8
Beverley Cl. Clitheroe BB7 164 E6
Beverley Cl. Preston PR1 95 C8
Beverley Cl. Southport PR9 53 C5
Beverley Cl. Wrea Green PR4 112 A3
Beverley Dr. BB7 164 D6
Beverley Gr. FY4 109 C7
Beverley Rd. BB9 168 E8
Beverley Rd N. FY8 89 A8
Beverley Rd S. FY8 89 A8
Beverley St. Blackburn BB2 100 B1
Beverley St. Burnley BB11 126 E5
Beverly Cl. FY5 151 B8
Bewcastle Dr. L40 16 C3
Bexhill Rd. PR2 116 A4
Bexley Ave. FY3 129 D8
Bexley Pl. FY8 89 E5
Bezza La. BB2 119 C5
Bhailok St. 3 PR1 95 E8
Bibby Dr. FY3 130 E5
Bibby Rd. PR9 53 A1
Bibby's La. FY2 150 E3
Bickerstaffe CE Sch. L39 7 E5
Bickerstaffe St. FY1 129 B3
Bickerton Rd. PR8 33 F4
Bicknell St. BB1 100 E6
Bideford Ave. FY3 130 A6
Bidston St. PR1 96 E8
Big Fold. BL6 30 D2
Bigdale Dr. L33 1 A3
Biggins La. LA6 238 A1
Biggins Rd. LA6 238 B2
Billinge Ave. BB2 100 B5
Billinge Cl. BB2 100 B5
Billinge End. BB2 100 A6
Billinge End Rd. BB2 99 F5
Billinge High Sch. BB2 100 A6
Billinge Side. BB2 99 F5
Billinge St. BB1 101 B4
Billinge View. BB2 99 F2
Billings Hospl. WN5 10 D2
Billington Ave. BB4 85 A5
Billington Gdns. BB6 143 A4
Billington Rd. Burnley BB11 126 A3
Billington Rd. Burnley BB11 126 B4
Billington St. PR4 112 F6
Billington St E. PR4 112 F6
Bilsberry Cotts. BB7 162 F1
Bilsborough Hey. PR1 95 E2
Bilsborough Meadow. PR4 115 E3
Bilsborrow La. Bilsborrow PR3 157 C4
Bilsborrow La. Inglewhite PR3 157 F5
Binbrook Pl. PR7 42 A7
Binfold Croft. LA6 238 C1
Bingley Ave. FY3 129 F6
Binns St. BB4 85 A7
Binyon Ct. LA1 210 F6
Binyon Rd. LA1 210 F5
Birbeck Rd. L33 1 A3
Birbeck Wlk. 8 L33 1 A3
Birch Ave. Burscough L40 24 E4
Birch Ave. Clayton-le-W PR5 76 D3
Birch Ave. Cleveleys FY5 172 E2
Birch Ave. Euxton PR7 59 C4
Birch Ave. Galgate LA2 207 A4
Birch Ave. Haslingden BB4 84 C3
Birch Ave. Newton-with-S PR4 113 F3
Birch Ave. Penwortham PR1 95 A3
Birch Ave. Preston PR2 116 A2
Birch Cl. Huncoat BB5 124 E2
Birch Cl. Maghull L31 5 F1
Birch Cl. Tonacliffe OL12 51 C6
Birch Cres. Gregson Lane PR5 97 E1
Birch Cres. Oswaldtwistle BB5 102 F3
Birch Dr. LA5 218 C4
Birch Field. PR6 77 B3
Birch Gn. L37 11 D4
Birch Gr. Barrow BB7 164 D1
Birch Gr. Lancaster LA1 210 D8
Birch Gr. Ramsbottom BL0 49 A3
Birch Gr. Stalmine FY6 174 D7
Birch Green Rd. WN8 18 C3
Birch Hall Ave. BB3 80 D4
Birch Hall La. BB8 201 D2
Birch La. PR3 181 C1
Birch Rd. Chorley PR6 60 E2
Birch Rd. Coppull PR7 41 E1
Birch Rd. Garstang PR3 178 C8
Birch St. Accrington BB5 103 B6
Birch St. Bacup OL13 86 F3
Birch St. Fleetwood FY7 194 A4
Birch St. Lytham St Anne's FY8 90 C3
Birch St. Skelmersdale WN8 8 E8
Birch St. Southport PR8 34 B4
Birch Terr. BB5 103 D2
Birch Tree Gdns. FY3 130 B2
Birch Tree Way. 4 BL6 31 E1
Birch Way. FY6 151 C4
Birch Wlk. 1 BB1 101 B4
Birchbank Gdns. BB1 101 A7
Birches Rd. BL7 47 D4
Birches The. L37 11 E5
Birchfield. PR4 73 F4
Birchfield Ave. OL10 32 E1
Birchfield Dr. PR3 139 A8
Birchfield Way. L31 5 B5
Birchill Rd. L33 1 C2
Birchin La. PR6 77 D1
Birchover Cl. PR2 116 A5
Birchtree Ave. LA3 212 B1
Birchway Ave. FY3 129 E6
Birchwood. PR5 75 C1
Birchwood Ave. PR4 94 B1
Birchwood Cl. FY8 89 E4
Birchwood Dr. Coppull PR7 41 E2
Birchwood Dr. Fulwood PR2 116 D7
Birchwood Dr. Hambleton FY6 174 C2

Butts. Great Harwood BB6 123 B5
Butts Cl. FY5 173 C4
Butts Gr. BB7 186 E2
Butts La. High Bentham LA2 233 E8
Butts La. Southport PR8 & PR9 34 F5
Butts Mount. BB6 123 C5
Butts Rd. FY5 173 C4
Buxton Ave. FY2 150 D4
Buxton St. Accrington BB5 103 A5
Buxton St. Morecambe LA4 212 F4
Buxton St. Whitworth OL12 70 D3
Bye La. L39 14 C3
Bye Rd. BL0 49 E8
Bye-Pass Rd. LA5 216 A4
Byerworth La N. PR3 178 C5
Byerworth La S. PR3 178 C4
Byfield Ave. FY5 150 E7
Byland Cl. Blackpool FY4 109 C5
Byland Cl. Formby L37 12 B2
Byland Cl. Read BB12 144 D1
Bymbrig Cl. PR5 76 E8
Byrom St. Blackburn BB2 100 D4
Byrom St. Southport PR9 34 F7
Byron Ave. Bolton-le-S LA5 216 A5
Byron Ave. Lytham St Anne's FY8 90 D4
Byron Ave. Thornton FY5 173 A3
Byron Ave. Warton PR4 91 E6
Byron Cl. Accrington BB5 103 E2
Byron Cl. Formby L37 11 F4
Byron Cl. Orrell WN5 10 F7
Byron Cl. Oswaldtwistle BB5 102 C5
Byron Cl. Tarleton PR4 55 F5
Byron Cres. PR7 28 E8
Byron Gr. BB8 200 A3
Byron Rd. Colne BB8 169 F5
Byron Rd. Maghull L31 5 D3
Byron Rd. Morecambe LA3 212 B3
Byron Rd. Ramsbottom BL8 48 F2
Byron Sq. BB6 123 B4
Byron St. Blackpool FY4 129 B1
Byron St. Chorley PR6 42 D8
Byron St. Fleetwood FY7 194 A5
Byron St. Padiham BB12 125 F7
Byron Terr. BB2 100 B3
Byton Wlk. L33 1 A4

Cabin End Row. BB1 101 E4
Cabin Hill. BB2 99 B2
Cabin La. Banks PR9 53 F3
Cabin La. Holmeswood PR4 37 A6
Cabin La. Maghull L31 4 F4
Cabin La. Shirdley Hill L39 21 C5
Cable St. Formby L37 12 A4
Cable St. Lancaster LA1 210 F8
Cable St. Southport PR8 34 B7
Cabus Cross Roads. PR3 199 A5
Cabus Nook La. PR3 199 B6
Cadby Ave. FY3 129 F3
Cadley Ave. PR2 116 B3
Cadley Cswy. PR2 116 C4
Cadley Dr. PR2 116 B3
Cadogan Pl. PR1 96 A6
Cadogan St. BB9 168 D2
Cadshaw Cl. BB1 100 E8
Cadwell Rd. L31 5 B5
Caernarvon Ave. BB12 126 A7
Caernarvon Cl. BL8 48 F1
Caernarvon Rd. BB4 84 A1
Cage La. PR4 75 B8
Cairn Ct. FY4 109 C4
Cairndale Dr. PR5 59 B6
Cairns Cl. BB9 168 C3
Cairnsmore Ave. PR1 117 F1
Cairo St. BB12 126 D6
Caister Cl. WN8 9 E8
Calcott St. BB11 126 E2
Caldbeck Cl. BB9 147 E6
Caldbeck Rd. LA1 214 B1
Calder Ave. Billington BB7 143 A4
Calder Ave. Chorley PR7 42 B5
Calder Ave. Darwen BB3 80 D4
Calder Ave. Fleetwood FY7 193 D3
Calder Ave. Freckleton PR4 92 A5
Calder Ave. Fulwood PR2 116 F6
Calder Ave. Longridge PR3 139 A8
Calder Ave. Ormskirk L39 15 E4
Calder Ave. Thornton FY5 172 F2
Calder Ave. Whalley BB7 143 A7
Calder Ave. Withnell PR6 79 A1
Calder Banks. BB1 100 F7
Calder Cl. Bury BL9 32 A8
Calder Cl. Carnforth LA5 217 B1
Calder Cl. Kirkby L33 1 A6
Calder Cl. Kirkham PR4 113 C5
Calder Cl. Lytham St Anne's FY8 109 F2
Calder Cl. Nelson BB9 168 D1
Calder Ct. BB5 124 E6
Calder Dr. Catterall PR3 178 D2
Calder Dr. Lancaster LA1 213 B2
Calder Dr. Maghull L31 5 F2
Calder House La. PR3 178 D4
Calder Pl. BB6 123 E6
Calder Rd. Blackpool FY2 150 C1
Calder Rd. Rawtenstall BB4 85 A4
Calder St. Blackburn BB1 100 F7
Calder St. Burnley BB11 126 F6
Calder St. Colne BB8 169 C4
Calder St. Nelson BB9 168 D1
Calder St. Padiham BB12 125 C8
Calder St. Preston PR1 116 C1
Calder Terr. BB9 147 B8
Calder Vale. Barrowford BB9 168 D2
Calder Vale. Whalley BB7 143 C4
Calder Vale Rd. BB11 & BB12 126 F6
Calder View. BB9 168 E5
Calderbrook Ave. BB11 126 E3
Calderbrook Pl. BB11 126 E3
Caldershaw Ctr The. OL12 51 B2
Caldershaw La. OL12 51 A2
Caldershaw Prim Sch. OL12 51 A1
Caldershaw Rd. OL11 & OL12 51 A1
Calderstones Hospl. BB7 143 A7
Caldervale Ave. FY6 151 C3
Calderview Sch. BB12 126 F8
Caldicott Way. FY6 151 C6
Caldy Dr. BL8 49 A3
Caleb St. 6 BB9 168 E1
Caledonian Ave. FY3 129 E7
Calendar St. 1 BB1 100 E5
Calf Croft Pl. FY8 90 A4
Calf Hall La. BB8 200 A2
Calf Hall Rd. BB8 200 A2
Calf Hey. BB5 123 F4
Calf Hey Rd. BB4 83 B2
Calfcote La. PR3 139 B7
Calgary Ave. BB2 100 B8
Calico Cl. BB5 102 B4
Calico Dr. PR3 178 D3
Calico St. BB2 100 D1
Calico Wood Ave. WN6 19 F6
Calkeld La. 7 LA1 210 F8
Calla Dr. PR3 178 C8
Callander Sq. OL10 32 F1
Callender St. BL0 49 B6
Callon St. PR1 96 E8
Caltha St. 8 BL0 49 B6
Calva Cl. BB12 126 B8
Calverley St. 6 PR0 & PR1 117 D1
Calverley Way. OL12 51 E4
Calvert Pl. FY3 130 A7
Cam Cl. 1 PR5 76 F8
Cam La. Clayton Green PR5 & PR6 77 A4
Cam La. Thornton-in-C BD23 201 B6
Cam St. PR1 117 C2
Cam Wood Fold. PR5 & PR6 77 A3
Cambell's Ct. FY8 88 E7
Camberley Cl. PR8 33 E5
Camborne Ave. LA5 216 C8
Camborne Ct. FY3 130 B2
Camborne Pl. PR4 92 B6
Cambray Rd. FY1 150 C1
Cambrian Cl. BB1 121 F3
Cambrian Way. BB4 84 B1
Cambridge Arc. PR8 34 B7
Cambridge Ave. Lancaster LA1 211 B5
Cambridge Ave. Southport PR9 52 F2
Cambridge Cl. Blackburn BB1 100 F4
Cambridge Cl. Padiham BB12 125 D6
Cambridge Cl. Preston PR1 116 E2
Cambridge Ct. Preston PR1 116 F2
Cambridge Ct. Southport PR9 52 F2
Cambridge Dr. Blackburn BB1 101 E4
Cambridge Dr. Garstang PR3 178 B7
Cambridge Dr. Padiham BB12 125 D6
Cambridge Gdns. PR9 52 F2
Cambridge Rd. 9
Bamber Bridge PR5 76 F8
Cambridge Rd. Blackpool FY1 129 D5
Cambridge Rd. Cleveleys FY5 172 C3
Cambridge Rd. Fleetwood FY7 193 E3
Cambridge Rd. Formby L37 11 D1
Cambridge Rd.
Lytham St Anne's FY8 89 E3
Cambridge Rd. Morecambe LA3 212 B3
Cambridge Rd. Orrell WN5 10 F8
Cambridge Rd.
Skelmersdale WN8 17 E1
Cambridge Rd. Southport PR9 52 E2
Cambridge St. Accrington BB5 103 D6
Cambridge St. Blackburn BB1 100 E4
Cambridge St. Brierfield BB9 147 B5
Cambridge St. 2 Burnley BB11 126 D5
Cambridge St. 9 Chorley PR6 42 C7
Cambridge St. 9 Colne BB8 169 D4
Cambridge St. Darwen BB3 81 C1
Cambridge St.
Great Harwood BB6 123 D5
Cambridge St. Haslingden BB4 84 B1
Cambridge St. Nelson BB9 147 D7
Cambridge St. Preston PR1 116 E2
Cambridge Wlk. PR1 116 E2
Cambridge Wlks. PR8 34 B7
Camden Pl. PR1 95 F6
Camden Rd. FY3 129 E6
Camden St. 11 Barrowford BB9 168 D3
Camden St. Nelson BB9 147 D7
Cameron Ave. FY3 129 E7
Cameron St. BB10 147 A1
Camforth Hall La. PR3 138 A7
Camms View. BB4 67 A8
Camp St. BB10 147 E3
Campbell Ave. FY3 129 E7
Campbell St. Blackburn BB1 121 F1
Campbell St. Falinge Fold OL12 51 E2
Campbell St. Padiham BB12 125 F7
Campbell St. Preston PR1 96 B8
Campbell St. Read BB12 144 D1
Campion Cl. FY5 172 F5
Campion Ct. BB5 102 E4
Campion Dr. Haslingden BB4 67 A8
Campion Dr. Preston PR2 115 C1
Campion Way. Lower Fold OL12 51 C3
Campion Way. Morecambe LA3 212 E4
Campions The. PR2 115 C1
Camwood. PR5 77 B4
Camwood Dr. PR5 96 B1
Canada Cres. FY2 150 E3
Canada St. BL6 31 B3
Canal Bank. Appley Bridge WN6 19 C7
Canal Bank. New Lane L40 24 B6
Canal Bank. Ring o'Bells L40 25 C2
Canal Bank Cotts. L31 5 C7
Canal Bank Pygons Hill. L31 5 C7
Canal Mews. 1 BB9 147 D8
Canal Pl. LA5 217 E1
Canal Row. WN2 29 D1
Canal St. Adlington PR7 30 A6
Canal St. Blackburn BB2 100 B1
Canal St. Burnley BB11 126 F6
Canal St. Church BB5 102 E6
Canal St. Clayton-le-M BB5 123 F2
Canal Wlk. PR6 42 F8
Canalside. BB1 100 F3
Canberra Cl. FY5 150 F7
Canberra Rd. PR5 59 B8
Canberraway. PR4 91 E7
Candlemakers Ct. BB7 164 E8
Candlestick Pk. BL9 32 D4
Cann Bridge St. PR5 97 B4
Canning Rd. PR9 35 A6
Canning St. Burnley BB12 126 F7
Canning St. Padiham BB12 125 D7
Cannock Ave. FY3 129 E8
Cannock Gn. L31 5 B1
Cannon Hill. PR1 116 C1
Cannon St. Accrington BB5 103 B5
Cannon St. 9 Chorley PR7 42 C8
Cannon St. 6 Nelson BB9 168 F1
Cannon St. Preston PR1 & PR0 95 F7
Cannon St. 6 Ramsbottom BL0 49 A4
Canon Cl. WN6 28 F2
Canon St. BL9 32 A4
Canterbury Ave. Blackpool FY3 129 F3
Canterbury Ave. Lancaster LA1 211 B5
Canterbury Cl. Brinscall PR6 61 E8
Canterbury Cl. Carleton FY6 151 C5
Canterbury Cl. Formby L37 11 F5
Canterbury Cl. Garstang PR3 178 A7
Canterbury Cl. Southport PR8 33 F4
Canterbury Rd. 11 PR1 117 D1
Canterbury St. Blackburn BB2 100 E4
Canterbury St. Chorley PR7 42 E6
Canterbury Way. PR3 178 B7
Cantlow Fold. PR8 20 A4
Cantsfield Ave. PR2 116 B4
Canute St. PR1 117 A1
Cape St. BB4 85 A2
Capernwray Rd. LA6 234 B2
Capilano Pk. L39 6 C8
Capitol Way. PR1 & PR5 96 C5
Capstan Cl. FY8 109 E1
Captain St. Horwich BL6 31 B4
Captain St. Weir OL13 87 A7
Captain's Row. LA1 213 F1
Carawood Cl. WN6 19 D7
Carcroft Ave. FY2 150 D4
Cardale. PR4 94 D2
Cardiff St. WN8 17 D1
Cardigan Ave. Burnley BB12 126 A7
Cardigan Ave. 5 Clitheroe BB7 164 E8
Cardigan Ave.
Oswaldtwistle BB5 102 C4
Cardigan Cl. BB7 164 D8
Cardigan Pl. FY4 109 A5
Cardigan Rd. PR8 33 F1
Cardigan St. Lower Healey OL12 51 E3
Cardigan St. Preston PR1 116 D1
Cardinal Allen RC High Sch.
FY7 172 E8
Cardinal Newman Coll. PR1 96 B7
Cardinal Pl. FY5 172 E3
Cardinal St. BB10 147 B1
Cardwell Cl. PR4 91 D5
Cardwell Pl. BB2 100 E5
Cardwell St. BB12 125 D7
Carfax Fold. OL12 51 B2
Carfax Rd. L33 1 A4
Carfield. WN8 9 E6
Carham Rd. BB1 100 E8
Carholme Ave. BB10 127 C6
Carisbrooke Ave. FY4 110 A7
Carisbrooke Cl. FY6 151 C6
Carisbrooke Dr. PR9 52 F1
Carleton Ave. Blackpool FY3 150 F1
Carleton Ave. Fulwood PR2 117 D4
Carleton Ave. Simonstone BB12 144 E2
Carleton Dr. PR1 95 A4
Carleton Gate. FY6 151 C4
Carleton Gdns. FY6 151 B5
Carleton Green Cty Prim Sch.
FY6 151 C6
Carleton Rd. Great Knowley PR6 60 F3
Carleton Rd. Nelson BB8 169 A3
Carleton Sch. FY6 151 B5
Carleton St. Morecambe LA4 212 D4
Carleton St. Nelson BB9 147 E7
Carleton Way. FY6 151 B5
Carley St. BB3 80 E2
Carlin Gate. FY2 150 B2
Carlisle Ave. Fleetwood FY7 193 D1
Carlisle Ave. Penwortham PR1 95 A4
Carlisle Gr. FY5 173 B2
Carlisle House. 36 PR1 96 A7
Carlisle Pl. PR6 30 A8
Carlisle Rd. Accrington BB5 103 D7
Carlisle Rd. Southport PR8 34 A2
Carlisle St. Blackburn BB1 100 F4
Carlisle St. Lower Healey OL12 51 E3
Carlisle Terr. LA5 217 D3
Carloway Ave. PR2 117 C5
Carlton Ave. Clayton Green PR6 77 B2
Carlton Ave. Hall Green WN8 10 A7
Carlton Cl. BL6 30 D2
Carlton Ct. BB8 169 B5
Carlton Dr. PR1 96 B5
Carlton Gdns. BB1 100 E6
Carlton Gr. Blackpool FY2 150 B4
Carlton Gr. Horwich BL6 31 D1
Carlton Pl. BB7 164 F7
Carlton Rd. Ainsdale PR8 20 C6
Carlton Rd. Burnley BB11 126 E5
Carlton Rd. Leyland PR5 58 F8
Carlton Rd. Lytham St Anne's FY8 88 F7
Carlton St. Bacup OL13 87 A3
Carlton St. Brierfield BB9 147 B5
Carlton St. Preston PR1 95 D8
Carluke St. BB1 101 C5
Carlyle Ave. FY4 109 B6
Carlyle St. BB10 147 C3
Carmel Cl. L39 15 D2
Carnarvon Rd. Blackburn BB2 100 B5
Carnarvon Rd. Preston PR1 95 D7
Carnarvon Rd. Southport PR8 33 F1
Carnfield Pl. PR5 77 B8
Carnforth Ave. FY2 150 E5
Carnforth Brow. LA5 217 F2
Carnforth Cl. BB2 101 A1
Carnforth Dr. BL8 49 A2
Carnforth High Sch. LA5 217 E1
Carnforth Sta. LA5 217 D2
Carnoustie Cl. PR2 116 B7
Carnoustie Ct. PR1 95 A6
Carnoustie Dr. BL0 49 B5
Caroline Cl. LA3 208 F8
Caroline Ct. BB11 126 B4
Caroline St. Blackpool FY1 129 B3
Caroline St. Preston PR1 96 C8
Carr Bank Ave. BL0 49 B7
Carr Bank Dr. BL0 49 B7
Carr Bank Rd. Ramsbottom BL0 49 B7
Carr Bank Rd. Storth LA7 237 E2
Carr Barn Brow. PR5 77 C6
Carr Brook Cl. PR6 60 B8
Carr Cl. Cold Row FY6 174 C4
Carr Cl. Poulton-le-F FY6 151 E2
Carr Cl. Smallwood Hey PR3 196 C5
Carr Dr. PR4 112 E7
Carr End La. FY6 174 C6
Carr Field. PR5 77 C4
Carr Fold. BL0 49 B7
Carr Gate. FY5 172 C4
Carr Hall Dr. BB9 168 C1
Carr Hall Gdns. BB9 168 B1
Carr Hall Rd. BB9 168 B1
Carr Hall St. BB4 84 A5
Carr Head. BB8 170 C2
Carr Head La. FY6 151 E2
Carr Hey. FY5 173 A2
Carr Hill High Sch. PR4 113 B4
Carr House La.
Bretherton PR4 & PR5 56 D6
Carr House La.
Heskin Green PR7 &WN6 40 F1
Carr House La. Ince Blundell L38 3 E4
Carr House La. Lancaster LA1 210 E7
Carr La. Blackburn BB2 99 F6
Carr La. Chorley PR7 42 D5
Carr La. Cold Row FY6 174 C4
Carr La. Croston PR5 & PR7 39 B8
Carr La. Heysham LA3 208 E7
Carr La. Kirkham PR4 113 C6
Carr La. Leyland PR5 76 A3
Carr La. Maghull L31 4 F5
Carr La. Middleton LA3 208 F1
Carr La. Much Hoole PR4 74 A1
Carr La. Newchurch BB4 68 F7
Carr La. Rawtenstall BB4 85 A1
Carr La. Ring o'Bells L40 25 B3
Carr La. Singleton FY6 152 C1
Carr La. Smallwood Hey PR3 196 C4
Carr La. Southport PR8 20 F7
Carr La. Tarleton PR4 55 F7
Carr La. Warton PR4 91 B6
Carr Meadow. PR5 77 C6
Carr Mill St. BB4 84 B5
Carr Moss La. L39 21 D2
Carr Mount. 6 BB4 84 F1
Carr Pl. PR5 77 B7
Carr Rd. Barnoldswick BB8 200 A3
Carr Rd. Blackpool FY5 150 D6
Carr Rd. Burnley BB11 126 E3
Carr Rd. Clayton Green PR6 77 B2
Carr Rd. Colne BB8 169 E6
Carr Rd. Cornholme OL14 107 F1
Carr Rd. Darwen BB3 64 B8
Carr Rd. Fleetwood FY7 194 A4
Carr Rd. Hambleton FY6 174 C2
Carr Rd. Horwich BL6 31 B5
Carr Rd. Kirkham PR4 113 B4
Carr Rd. Nelson BB9 168 C1
Carr Rd. Rawtenstall BB4 84 F1
Carr Rd. Water BB4 86 C7
Carr Royd Est. FY6 152 A3
Carr Side La. L29 & L38 4 A3
Carr St. Bamber Bridge PR5 76 E8
Carr St. Blackburn BB1 100 E6
Carr St. Chorley PR6 60 E1
Carr St. Preston PR1 96 E7
Carr St. Ramsbottom BL0 49 B7
Carr View. BB8 170 C1
Carr's Cres. L37 11 E1
Carr's Cres W. L37 11 D1
Carradice Cl. BB9 147 D8
Carradon Dr. WN6 28 E1
Carrier's Row. BB8 170 E6
Carrington Ave. BB2 80 C8
Carrington Gr. LA4 213 A5
Carrington Rd. Adlington PR7 29 F7
Carrington Rd. Chorley PR7 42 C7
Carrol St. PR1 117 B1
Carroll Cres. L39 15 F7
Carron La. PR3 158 A4
Carrs Ind Est. BB4 84 A4
Carrs Wood. BB2 99 F6
Carrwood Dr. PR4 113 B4
Carrwood Gn. BB12 125 C8
Carrwood Hey. BL0 49 A4
Carrwood Rd. PR1 & PR5 96 B3
Carry La. BB8 169 E4
Carshalton Rd. FY1 129 B8
Carsluith Ave. FY3 129 F3
Carson Rd. FY4 130 A1
Cart Gate. FY6 195 B3
Carter Ave. BB11 125 C4
Carter Fold. BB2 120 E2
Carter St. Accrington BB5 103 B4
Carter St. Blackpool FY1 129 B5
Carter St. Burnley BB12 126 C7
Carter's Charity Prim Sch.
PR3 195 C7
Carter's La. BB7 225 A5
Carterville Cl. FY4 110 A7
Cartford Cl. PR3 154 A6
Cartford La. PR3 154 A6
Cartmel Ave. Accrington BB5 103 A3
Cartmel Ave. Fleetwood FY7 193 D1
Cartmel Ave. Maghull L31 5 E2
Cartmel Cl. PR8 34 F3
Cartmel Dr. Burnley BB12 126 B8
Cartmel Dr. Coupe Green PR5 97 E4
Cartmel Dr. Formby L37 12 B2
Cartmel Pl. Morecambe LA4 212 G4
Cartmel Pl. Preston PR2 115 E2
Cartmel Rd. Blackburn BB2 100 A3
Cartmel Rd. Lancaster LA1 214 B2
Cartmel Rd. Leyland PR5 58 D8
Cartmell La. Moss Side FY8 90 E8
Cartmell La. Nateby PR3 177 C7
Cartmell Rd. Blackpool FY4 130 D1
Cartmell Rd.
Lytham St Anne's FY8 88 F5
Cartwright Ct. LA1 210 E5
Carus Ave. BB3 81 E1
Carus Pk. LA6 235 B2
Carus St. BB3 81 F1
Carvers Brow. PR5 57 B1
Carwood Gr. BL6 31 D1
Carwood La. Whittle-le-W PR6 60 C8
Carwood La. Whittle-le-W PR6 60 D8
Caryl Rd. FY8 88 D8
Caryle Gr. LA4 213 A6
Casserley Rd. BB8 169 F6
Casson Gate. OL12 51 E1
Castercliffe Cty Prim Sch.
BB9 169 B1
Castercliffe Rd. BB9 148 B8
Casterton. PR7 59 C2
Casterton Ave. BB10 147 C3
Casterton Prim Sch. BB10 147 C3
Casterton Sch. LA6 238 F4
Castle Ave. FY6 151 B6
Castle Bank. LA5 218 C4
Castle Cl. BB8 169 E6
Castle Cres. BL6 31 C5
Castle Ct. LA1 210 E8
Castle Dr. Adlington PR7 29 E6
Castle Dr. Formby L37 11 F1
Castle Fold. PR1 95 F2
Castle Gate. BB7 164 E8
Castle Gr. BL0 49 A2
Castle Hill. LA1 210 E8
Castle Hill Rd. BL9 32 D5
Castle House La. PR7 29 E6
Castle La. Bonds PR3 178 D6
Castle La. Staining FY3 130 D5
Castle La. Westhead L40 16 E5
Castle Mount. PR2 116 F7
Castle Park Mews. LA1 210 E8
Castle Pk. LA1 210 E8
Castle Rd. BB8 170 A7
Castle St. Brierfield BB9 147 B6
Castle St. Burnley BB12 126 F7
Castle St. Clitheroe BB7 164 E8
Castle St. Hapton BB12 125 C4
Castle St. Nelson BB9 147 F8
Castle St. Preston PR1 116 F1
Castle St. Ramsbottom BL9 49 C2
Castle St. Southport PR9 34 B8
Castle Sta. LA1 210 E8
Castle The. BB8 170 A7
Castle View. Barnoldswick BB8 200 B1
Castle View. Clitheroe BB7 164 E8
Castle Wlk. Penwortham PR1 95 C7
Castle Wlk. Southport PR8 34 A6
Castlecroft Ave. BL6 30 D2
Castlegate. FY1 129 B1
Castlehey. WN8 9 E6
Castlerigg Dr. BB12 126 B8
Castlerigg Pl. FY4 130 C1
Castleton Rd. PR1 117 B1
Castletown Dr. OL13 87 B1
Cat Tail La. PR8 35 E1
Catches La. OL11 51 B1
Catforth Ave. FY4 130 B1
Catforth Cty Prim Sch. PR4 135 A4
Catforth Rd. Catforth PR4 134 F5
Catforth Rd. Preston PR2 115 E1
Catharine's La. L39 15 F1
Cathedral Dr. LA3 212 E2
Cathedral RC Sch. LA1 211 A7
Catherine Cl. PR4 112 F7
Catherine St. Chorley PR7 42 C6
Catherine St. Kirkham PR4 112 F6
Catherine St. 5 Preston PR1 96 B8
Catherine St E. BL6 31 B4
Catherine St W. BL6 31 B5
Cathrow Dr. PR4 75 A7
Catlow Hall St. BB5 102 E4
Cato St. 4 BL0 49 A4
Caton Ave. FY7 193 D1
Caton Cl. Clayton-le-W PR5 & PR6 76 E2
Caton Cl. Longridge PR3 139 B8
Caton Cl. Southport PR9 52 F4
Caton Gr. FY3 129 F7
Caton Green Rd. LA2 231 D3
Caton Prim Sch. LA2 231 C3
Caton Rd. Lancaster LA1 214 A1

Chindits Way. PR2 117 B4
Chines The. PR2 116 E4
Chingford Bank. BB10 147 D3
Chingle Cl. PR2 117 E6
Chipping Ave. PR8 20 A5
Chipping Ct. 4 FY3 130 A8
Chipping Gr. Burnley BB10 127 D4
Chipping Gr. Normoss FY3 130 A8
Chipping La. PR3 139 A8
Chipping St. BB12 145 D1
Chisacre Dr. WN6 19 D7
Chisholm Cl. WN6 28 B2
Chisholme Cl. BL8 48 F2
Chislehurst Ave. FY4 129 D1
Chislehurst Gr. BB10 147 D4
Chislehurst Pl. FY8 89 E5
Chislett Cl. L40 24 D4
Chisnall Ave. WN6 27 F6
Chisnall La. Coppull Moor PR7 28 C6
Chisnall La. Heskin Green PR7 40 F2
Chisnall La. Mossy Lea PR7 28 A5
Chiswell Gr. FY5 151 D8
Chiswick Gr. FY3 130 B2
Chobham Ct. 1 BB4 85 E1
Chorley Bsns & Tech Ctr. PR7 59 E4
Chorley Cl. PR9 53 F5
Chorley & District Hospl. PR7 60 C2
Chorley Golf Course. PR6 43 A3
Chorley Hall Rd. PR6 & PR7 60 C2
Chorley La. PR7 41 D3
Chorley New Rd. BL6 31 C2
Chorley New Road Inf Sch. BL6 31 D2
Chorley New Road Prim Sch. BL6 31 D2
Chorley North Ind Est. PR6 60 D3
Chorley Old Rd. PR6 77 C2
Chorley Rd. Adlington BL6 & PR6 30 B5
Chorley Rd. Bamber Bridge PR5 96 D3
Chorley Rd. Blackpool FY3 150 F2
Chorley Rd. Blackrod BL6 30 C3
Chorley Rd. Hill Dale L40 & WN8 26 D6
Chorley Rd. Ollerton Fold BB2 & PR6 78 E4
Chorley Rd. Parbold WN8 26 C4
Chorley Rd. Standish WN1 29 C3
Chorley St. PR6 30 B8
Chorley St James CE Prim Sch. PR6 42 E7
Chorley Sta. PR6 42 D8
Chorley West Bsns Pk. PR7 41 F8
Chorlton Cl. BB10 147 D2
Chorlton St. BB1 100 F7
Chrisleton Cl. BB10 147 F3
Christ Church CE Prim Sch. Carnforth LA5 217 D1
Christ Church CE Prim Sch. Glasson LA2 205 E4
Christ Church CE Prim Sch. Lancaster LA1 211 B8
Christ Church CE Prim Sch. Ormskirk L39 15 C3
Christ Church CE Sch. LA1 211 A8
Christ Church Prim Sch. BB8 170 B5
Christ Church Sq. 1 BB5 103 C5
Christ Church St. 2 Accrington BB5 103 C5
Christ Church St. 6 Bacup OL13 87 A3
Christ Church St. Preston PR1 95 E7
Christ The King RC High Sch. PR1 96 B6
Christ The King RC Prim Sch. Blackpool FY3 130 A7
Christ the King RC Prim Sch. Burnley BB11 126 E3
Christ The King Sch. PR8 34 B2
Christian Rd. PR1 95 E7
Christiana Hartley Maternity Hospl. PR8 34 D5
Christie Ave. LA4 212 G4
Christines Cres. L40 24 E4
Church Alley. BB5 123 F2
Church Ave. Accrington BB5 103 E2
Church Ave. Lancaster LA1 210 F4
Church Ave. Penwortham PR1 95 C6
Church Ave. Preston PR1 96 E8
Church Bank. LA6 231 B8
Church Bank St. 19 BB3 81 A1
Church Brook House. PR1 95 E4
Church Brow. Bolton-le-S LA5 216 A3
Church Brow. Clitheroe BB7 186 E1
Church Brow. Halton LA2 214 E6
Church Brow. Walton-le-D PR5 96 E5
Church Brow Cl. LA5 216 A3
Church Brow Gdns. BB7 186 E1
Church Cl. Clitheroe BB7 186 E1
Church Cl. Dolphinholme LA2 220 A8
Church Cl. Formby L37 12 A3
Church Cl. Freckleton PR4 92 A6
Church Cl. Mellor BB2 120 E2
Church Cl. Read BB12 144 D2
Church Cl. Southport PR9 35 A8
Church Cl. Waddington BB7 186 B4
Church Close Ct. L37 12 A3
Church Ct. Bolton-le-S LA5 216 A3
Church Ct. Edenfield BL0 67 D4
Church Dr. Lytham St Anne's FY8 89 F3
Church Dr. Orrell WN5 10 D5
Church Dr. Whalley BB7 143 A7
Church Fields. Bescar L40 22 F7
Church Fields. Ormskirk L39 15 E5
Church Fold. Charnock Richard PR7 41 E4
Church Fold. Coppull PR7 28 F8
Church Gdns. PR4 91 E6
Church Gn. L37 11 C2
Church Gr. LA3 205 E8
Church Hall. BB5 102 F7
Church Hill. Arnside LA5 237 B2
Church Hill. Nether Kellet LA6 216 F5
Church Hill. Whittle-le-W PR6 60 C7
Church Hill Ave. LA5 217 D5
Church Hill Rd. Blackburn BB1 101 A7
Church Hill Rd. Ormskirk L39 15 D6
Church La. Accrington BB5 124 A1
Church La. Aughton L39 6 A7
Church La. Bilsborrow PR3 157 A4
Church La. Broughton PR3 136 D1
Church La. Charnock Richard PR7 41 D4
Church La. Edenfield BL0 67 D4
Church La. Farington PR5 75 F7
Church La. Galgate LA2 207 B4
Church La. Goosnargh PR3 137 D6
Church La. Great Harwood BB6 123 C6
Church La. Great Mitton BB7 163 E3
Church La. Hambleton FY6 174 D1
Church La. Kelbrook BB8 192 A6
Church La. Maghull L39 5 A8
Church La. Mellor BB2 120 E2
Church La. Morecambe LA4 212 E6
Church La. Morecambe LA4 212 F6
Church La. Newchurch BB4 85 E1
Church La. Newton-with-S PR4 114 B3
Church La. 10 Padiham BB12 145 C1
Church La. Whalley BB7 143 C5
Church La. Whitechapel PR3 158 E7
Church La. Winmarleigh PR3 198 E4
Church La. Wrightington Bar WN6 27 D8
Church Meadows. BB8 169 D5
Church & Oswaldtwistle Sta. BB5 102 E5
Church Pk. Lea Town PR4 114 F3
Church Pk. Overton LA3 205 D8
Church Raike. PR3 182 E3
Church Rd. Bamber Bridge PR5 76 E7
Church Rd. Bamber Bridge PR5 76 F6
Church Rd. Banks PR9 54 A6
Church Rd. Bickerstaffe L39 7 E6
Church Rd. Formby L37 12 A5
Church Rd. Kirkham PR4 112 F7
Church Rd. Leyland PR5 59 A8
Church Rd. Lytham FY8 89 F3
Church Rd. Lytham St Anne's FY8 89 B6
Church Rd. Rufford L40 38 C4
Church Rd. Shuttleworth BL0 49 E8
Church Rd. Singleton FY6 152 F1
Church Rd. Skelmersdale WN8 17 F1
Church Rd. Tarleton PR4 56 A5
Church Rd. Thornton FY5 173 A2
Church Rd. Thornton-in-C BB8 & BD23 201 A5
Church Rd. Warton PR4 91 D6
Church Rd. Weeton PR4 131 F1
Church Rd. Wharles PR4 133 F2
Church Row. Preston PR1 96 A7
Church Row. Wrea Green PR4 112 B4
Church Row Chambers. PR4 74 A8
Church Sq. BB10 128 B5
Church St. Accrington BB5 103 C5
Church St. Adlington PR6 30 A7
Church St. Bacup OL13 69 C8
Church St. Barnoldswick BB8 200 B2
Church St. Barrowford BB9 168 D4
Church St. Belmont BL7 45 C4
Church St. Blackburn BB1 100 E5
Church St. Blackpool FY1 129 C5
Church St. Blackrod BL6 30 C2
Church St. Brierfield BB9 147 B5
Church St. Brierfield BB10 147 F2
Church St. Burnley BB11 127 A6
Church St. Bury BL9 32 A3
Church St. Chorley PR6 42 C7
Church St. Church BB5 102 E6
Church St. Churchtown PR3 178 A2
Church St. Clayton-le-M BB5 123 F2
Church St. 1 Clitheroe BB7 164 E8
Church St. Colne BB8 169 D5
Church St. Croston PR5 57 B1
Church St. Darwen BB3 81 A1
Church St. Fleetwood FY7 194 B4
Church St. Garstang PR3 178 C7
Church St. Goodshaw Chapel BB4 105 A1
Church St. Great Harwood BB6 123 C5
Church St. Halton LA2 214 D6
Church St. Hapton BB12 125 C4
Church St. Haslingden BB4 84 B4
Church St. Higher Walton PR5 97 B3
Church St. Horwich BL6 31 C3
Church St. Kirkby Lonsdale LA6 238 C2
Church St. Kirkham PR4 113 B5
Church St. Lancaster LA1 210 F8
Church St. Leyland PR5 76 B2
Church St. Longridge PR3 139 B7
Church St. Morecambe LA4 212 E6
Church St. Nelson BB9 147 D6
Church St. Newchurch BB4 68 E8
Church St. Newchurch BB4 85 E1
Church St. Ormskirk L39 15 E5
Church St. Orrell WN5 10 E5
Church St. Oswaldtwistle BB5 102 D3
Church St. Padiham BB12 125 C8
Church St. 1 Poulton-le-F FY6 151 D3
Church St. Preston PR1 96 A7
Church St. Preston PR1 96 B8
Church St. 5 Ramsbottom BL0 49 C6
Church St. Read BB12 144 D2
Church St. Ribchester BB1 & PR3 140 D3
Church St. Rishton BB1 123 A1
Church St. Slaidburn BB7 223 C7
Church St. Southport PR9 34 C7
Church St. Standish WN6 28 E1
Church St. Trawden BB8 170 C2
Church St. Up Holland WN8 10 C7
Church St. Whittington LA6 235 C7
Church St. Whitworth OL12 51 C8
Church Terr. 20 BB3 81 A1
Church View. Aughton L39 6 A7
Church View. Gisburn BB7 225 C3
Church View. Salesbury BB1 121 E6
Church View. Stalmine FY6 174 C7
Church View. Tarleton PR4 56 A5
Church View. Trawden BB8 170 C2
Church View Ct. L39 15 E5
Church Way. L37 11 C2
Church Wlk. Blackburn BB1 121 F3
Church Wlk. Euxton PR7 59 C2
Church Wlk. Kirkham PR4 112 F7
Church Wlk. Tarleton PR4 56 A6
Church Wlks. L39 15 E5
Churchfield. PR2 116 F6
Churchfields. PR8 33 F3
Churchgate. Goosnargh PR3 137 D6
Churchgate. Southport PR9 52 F1
Churchgate Mews. PR9 53 A1
Churchill Ave. Rishton BB1 102 A8
Churchill Ave. Southport PR9 52 F2
Churchill Cl. FY5 173 B2
Churchill Ct. FY3 129 D6
Churchill Dr. PR2 117 D4
Churchill Rd. Barrowford BB9 168 B1
Churchill Rd. Brinscall PR7 62 A8
Churchill Rd. Fulwood PR2 117 C4
Churchill St. OL11 & OL12 51 C1
Churchill Way. Leyland PR5 76 A2
Churchill Way. Nelson BB9 147 B7
Churchlands La. WN6 28 F1
Churchside. PR4 74 F8
Churchtown Cres. OL13 87 B1
Churchtown Ct. PR9 53 A2
Churchtown Prim Sch. PR9 53 B2
Churchward Sq. BL6 31 C2
Churton Gr. WN6 28 B2
Cicely La. BB1 100 F5
Cicely St. BB1 100 F4
Cinder La. Lancaster LA1 & LA2 210 F3
Cinder La. Lewth PR4 135 A6
Cinder La. Mere Brow PR4 54 F2
Cinderbarrow La. LA5 & LA6 234 A6
Cinnamon Brow. WN8 10 C6
Cinnamon Ct. PR1 95 C2
Cinnamon Hill Dr N. PR5 96 D3
Cinnamon Hill Dr S. PR5 96 D3
Cintra Ave. PR2 116 D3
Cintra Terr. PR2 116 D3
Circus The. 10 BB3 81 A1
City Heights Cl. 16 LA1 211 A8
Clairane Ave. PR2 116 E6
Clairville. PR8 33 F5
Clancut La. PR7 41 F2
Clanfield. PR2 116 E7
Clara St. Preston PR1 96 C7
Clara St. Whitworth OL12 70 D1
Clare Ave. BB8 169 A2
Clare Rd. LA1 213 E2
Clare St. Blackpool FY1 129 B1
Clare St. Burnley BB11 126 E6
Claremont Ave. Chorley PR7 42 B7
Claremont Ave. Clitheroe BB7 164 F7
Claremont Cres. LA4 212 C4
Claremont Ct. FY1 129 C7
Claremont Dr. Clitheroe BB7 164 F7
Claremont Dr. Ormskirk L39 15 D3
Claremont Gdns. PR8 34 A4
Claremont Pl. FY8 88 E8
Claremont Prep Sch. BB1 100 D6
Claremont Rd. Accrington BB5 103 B8
Claremont Rd. Blackpool FY1 129 C8
Claremont Rd. Chorley PR7 42 B5
Claremont Rd. Morecambe LA4 212 C4
Claremont Rd. Southport PR8 34 A4
Claremont Sch (Prim). FY1 129 C8
Claremont St. Brierfield BB9 147 A6
Claremont St. Burnley BB12 126 D6
Claremont St. Colne BB8 170 A5
Claremont Terr. BB9 147 D7
Claremount Ave. PR5 59 B8
Clarence Ave. Cleveleys FY5 172 D3
Clarence Ave. 4 Haslingden BB4 84 A1
Clarence Ave. Knott End-on-S FY6 194 E5
Clarence Ct. FY4 129 B1
Clarence House Sch. L37 11 F6
Clarence Pk. BB2 100 B7
Clarence Rd. Accrington BB5 103 A4
Clarence Rd. Southport PR8 34 A4
Clarence St. Barnoldswick BB8 200 C1
Clarence St. Blackburn BB1 100 D6
Clarence St. Burnley BB11 127 B4
Clarence St. Chorley PR6 42 D7
Clarence St. Colne BB8 170 A5
Clarence St. Darwen BB3 80 F3
Clarence St. Lancaster LA1 211 A7
Clarence St. Leyland PR5 76 B2
Clarence St. Lower Fold OL12 51 D2
Clarence St. Morecambe LA4 212 E5
Clarence St. Rawtenstall BB4 85 A7
Clarence St. Trawden BB8 170 C2
Clarendon Gr. L31 5 C5
Clarendon Rd. Blackburn BB1 100 F8
Clarendon Rd. Blackpool FY1 129 B2
Clarendon Rd. Lancaster LA1 213 F3
Clarendon Rd. Lytham St Anne's FY8 89 A8
Clarendon Rd E. Blackburn BB1 101 A8
Clarendon Rd E. Morecambe LA4 212 C4
Clarendon Rd N. FY8 88 F8
Clarendon Rd W. LA3 & LA4 212 B4
Clarendon St. Accrington BB5 103 D6
Clarendon St. Bury BL9 32 A4
Clarendon St. Chorley PR7 42 E7
Clarendon St. Colne BB8 170 B5
Clarendon St. Preston PR1 96 A6
Claret St. BB5 103 A5
Clark St. LA4 212 E6
Clarke Holme St. BB4 85 F2
Clarke St. Poulton-le-F FY6 151 F3
Clarke St. 5 Rishton BB1 123 B1
Clarke Wood Cl. BB7 143 F8
Clarke's Cotts. L40 26 A8
Clarke's La. OL12 51 E1
Clarkes Croft. BL9 32 C3
Clarkfield Dr. LA4 212 G5
Clarksfield Rd. LA5 216 A4
Clarrick Terr. LA6 236 F3
Claughton Ave. PR6 76 E1
Claughton Dr. LA1 211 A3
Claughton RC Prim Sch. PR3 179 D1
Claughton St. 14 BB10 147 B1
Clawthorpe Cotts. LA6 234 C8
Clay Brow Rd. WN8 9 E6
Clay Gap La. FY6 & PR3 174 F4
Clay Hill La. PR3 140 B8
Clay La. LA3 209 B8
Clay St. BB11 126 C5
Claybank. 8 BB12 145 C1
Clayburn Cl. PR6 60 E2
Claylands Dr. LA5 216 A4
Claypool Prim Sch. BL6 31 F1
Claypool Rd. BL6 31 E1
Clayton Ave. Leyland PR5 58 D7
Clayton Ave. Rawtenstall BB4 67 E8
Clayton Brook Cty Prim Sch. PR5 77 B5
Clayton Brook Rd. PR5 77 C6
Clayton Cl. 11 BB9 168 D1
Clayton Cres. FY4 109 E6
Clayton Ct. PR3 139 B7
Clayton Gdns. L40 24 E4
Clayton Gr. BB1 121 D6
Clayton Green RC Prim Sch (St Bede's). PR5 77 C4
Clayton Green Rd. PR5 & PR6 77 B3
Clayton Hall Dr. BB5 123 F4
Clayton Mews. WN8 17 D1
Clayton Row. BB6 142 D1
Clayton St. 5 Bamber Bridge PR5 96 E1
Clayton St. Barnoldswick BB8 200 C2
Clayton St. Blackburn BB2 100 E4
Clayton St. Colne BB8 169 E4
Clayton St. Enfield BB5 124 A1
Clayton St. Great Harwood BB6 123 C5
Clayton St. Nelson BB9 168 D1
Clayton St. 7 Oswaldtwistle BB5 102 E5
Clayton St. Skelmersdale WN8 17 D1
Clayton Street Ind Est. BB9 168 D1
Clayton's Gate. 12 PR1 95 F8
Clayton-le-Moors Ind Est. BB5 123 E2
Clayton-le-Woods CE Prim Sch. PR6 77 A2
Claytongate. PR7 41 F2
Claytonhalgh. PR3 140 E3
Cleator Ave. FY2 150 C1
Cleaver St. Blackburn BB1 100 F5
Cleaver St. Burnley BB10 127 B8
Clecken La. PR3 179 D2
Clegg Ave. FY5 172 D3
Clegg St. 6 Bacup OL13 69 C8
Clegg St. Brierfield BB9 147 B5
Clegg St. Burnley BB10 127 A8
Clegg St. Haslingden BB4 84 B3
Clegg St. Kirkham PR4 113 A5
Clegg St. Nelson BB9 147 E6
Clegg St. Skelmersdale WN8 17 D1
Clegg St. Whitworth OL12 70 C2
Clegg St. Worsthorne BB10 128 A5
Clegg St E. 9 BB10 127 A8
Clegg's Ct. OL12 70 C2
Clematis St. BB2 100 B6
Clement St. Accrington BB5 103 C5
Clement St. 3 Darwen BB3 64 A8
Clement View. 14 BB9 147 D8
Clementina St. OL12 51 F1
Clements Dr. BB10 147 C4
Clengers Brow. PR9 53 A3
Clent Ave. L31 5 C3
Clent Gdns. L31 5 C3
Clent Rd. L31 5 C3
Clerkhill St. BB1 101 B5
Cleve Way. L37 12 B2
Clevedon Rd. Blackpool FY1 129 B7
Clevedon Rd. Fulwood PR2 116 A4
Cleveland Ave. PR2 117 C4
Cleveland Cl. BL0 49 C3
Cleveland Dr. LA1 210 D7
Cleveland Rd. Leyland PR5 75 F2
Cleveland Rd. Lytham St Anne's FY8 90 B3
Cleveland St. Chorley PR6 42 C8
Cleveland St. Colne BB8 169 F6
Cleveland St. Coppull PR7 41 E1
Cleveland St. Cornholme OL14 108 B1
Clevelands Ave. Morecambe LA3 212 C3
Clevelands Ave. Silverdale LA5 218 C4
Clevelands Gr. Burnley BB11 126 F4
Clevelands Gr. Morecambe LA3 212 C3
Clevelands Rd. BB11 126 F4
Clevelands Wlk. LA3 212 C3
Cleveleys Ave. Cleveleys FY5 172 D3
Cleveleys Ave. Fulwood PR2 116 C4
Cleveleys Ave. Lancaster LA1 213 C2
Cleveleys Ave. Southport PR9 53 A4
Cleveleys Rd. Accrington BB5 103 B8
Cleveleys Rd. Blackburn BB2 100 F1
Cleveleys Rd. Coupe Green PR5 97 E3
Cleveleys Rd. Southport PR9 53 A3
Cleves Ct. FY3 130 A2
Cleves The. L31 5 E3
Clieves Hills La. L39 14 E3
Clieves Rd. L32 1 A1
Clifden Ct. L37 11 F3
Cliff Ave. BL9 49 C2
Cliff Mount. BL0 49 B7
Cliff Pl. FY2 150 B4
Cliff Rd. PR9 52 D1
Cliff St. Colne BB8 169 B3
Cliff St. Padiham BB12 145 D1
Cliff St. Preston PR1 95 E6
Cliff St. Rishton BB1 123 B2
Cliffe Ct. PR1 96 D8
Cliffe Dr. PR6 60 B8
Cliffe La. BB6 123 C6
Cliffe St. BB9 168 E1
Clifford Ave. Longton PR4 94 A1
Clifford Ave. Morecambe LA4 212 G6
Clifford Rd. Blackpool FY1 129 C7
Clifford Rd. Southport PR8 34 A2
Clifford St. Barnoldswick BB8 200 C2
Clifford St. Chorley PR6 42 D8
Clifford St. Colne BB8 169 E5
Cliffs The. LA3 212 A2
Clifton Ave. Accrington BB5 103 C7
Clifton Ave. Blackpool FY4 130 C1
Clifton Ave. Leyland PR5 59 B8
Clifton Ave. Preston PR2 116 A2
Clifton Ave. Warton PR4 91 E6
Clifton Cl. FY5 173 C1
Clifton Cres. Blackpool FY3 130 A2
Clifton Cres. Fulwood PR1 117 C2
Clifton Ct. Blackpool FY4 109 B6
Clifton Ct. Lytham St Anne's FY8 90 C3
Clifton Cty Prim Sch. FY8 89 C6
Clifton Dr. Blackpool FY4 109 B5
Clifton Dr. Blackrod BL6 30 C3
Clifton Dr. Great Harwood BB6 123 C6
Clifton Dr. Lytham St Anne's FY8 89 D3
Clifton Dr. Morecambe LA4 213 A5
Clifton Dr. Penwortham PR1 95 C5
Clifton Dr N. FY8 109 B2
Clifton Dr S. FY8 88 E5
Clifton Gdns. FY8 89 C6
Clifton Gn. PR4 114 C2
Clifton Gr. Chorley PR7 42 B7
Clifton Gr. Fulwood PR1 117 C3
Clifton Gr. Wilpshire BB1 121 F4
Clifton Hospl. FY8 89 B5
Clifton La. PR4 114 D2
Clifton Lodge. FY8 88 E5
Clifton Pl. PR4 92 B6
Clifton Rd. Blackpool FY4 110 C8
Clifton Rd. Brierfield BB9 147 C4
Clifton Rd. Burnley BB12 126 C7
Clifton Rd. Fleetwood FY7 194 A3
Clifton Rd. Formby L37 12 A5
Clifton Rd. Southport PR8 34 F6
Clifton Sq. FY8 90 B3
Clifton St. Accrington BB5 103 A4
Clifton St. Blackpool FY1 129 B5
Clifton St. Burnley BB11 & BB12 126 F6
Clifton St. Colne BB8 169 D5
Clifton St. Darwen BB3 80 F4
Clifton St. Lytham St Anne's FY8 90 B3
Clifton St. Preston PR1 95 D6
Clifton St. Rishton BB1 123 B1
Clifton St. Sough BB8 192 A8
Clifton St. Trawden BB8 170 C2
Clifton Terr. BB3 81 E2
Clifton Wlk. FY8 90 B3
Clinkham Rd. BB6 123 A5
Clinning Rd. PR8 34 A2
Clinton Ave. FY1 129 C4
Clinton St. BB1 101 A6
Clippers Quay. BB1 100 F4
Clitheroe Castle. BB8 164 E8
Clitheroe Hospl. BB7 187 A3
Clitheroe Pl. FY4 110 A8
Clitheroe Rd. Brierfield BB9 147 A5
Clitheroe Rd. Chatburn BB7 187 C3
Clitheroe Rd. Lytham St Anne's FY8 89 C6
Clitheroe Rd. Sabden BB7 165 E1
Clitheroe Rd. Waddington BB7 186 C3
Clitheroe Rd. West Bradford BB7 186 F5
Clitheroe Rd. Whalley BB7 143 C7
Clitheroe Royal Gram Sch. Clitheroe BB7 186 F1
Clitheroe Royal Gram Sch. Clitheroe BB7 187 A2
Clitheroe St. 8 Padiham BB12 125 C8
Clitheroe St. Preston PR1 96 C7
Clitheroe Sta. BB7 186 E1
Clitheroes La. PR4 92 B6
Clive Ave. FY8 109 E1
Clive Lodge. PR8 33 F2
Clive Rd. Penwortham PR1 95 B6
Clive Rd. Southport PR8 33 F2
Clive St. BB12 126 F8
Clockhouse Ave. BB10 147 D3
Clockhouse Ct. BB10 147 D3
Clockhouse Gr. BB10 147 D3
Clod La. BB4 67 C8
Clods Carr La. FY6 194 F3
Clog Heads. BB8 170 C2
Clogger La. BD23 201 F7
Cloister Dr. BB3 81 C1
Cloister Gn. L37 12 B2
Cloisters. LA3 212 F2
Cloisters The. Blackpool FY3 129 E5
Cloisters The. Formby L37 11 F3

Cottage Cl. L39 15 D4
Cottage Fields. PR7 42 B5
Cottage La. Bamber Bridge PR5 96 F3
Cottage La. Ormskirk L39 15 D5
Cottage Mews. L39 15 D5
Cottage St. PR1 96 A8
Cottage Wlk. OL12 51 C4
Cottam Ave. PR2 116 A4
Cottam Cl. Lytham St Anne's FY8 109 F2
Cottam Cl. Whalley BB7 143 C5
Cottam Gn. PR4 115 F6
Cottam Hall La. PR2 & PR4 115 F5
Cottam La. PR2 116 A2
Cottam Pl. FY6 151 C2
Cottam St. PR7 42 C6
Cottam Way. PR2 & PR4 115 D4
Cottesloe Pl. BB9 168 C3
Cottesmore Pl. FY3 130 A6
Cottom Croft. BB5 123 F4
Cotton Ct. Colne BB8 169 C3
Cotton Ct. Preston PR1 96 A8
Cotton Dr. L39 15 D6
Cotton Gn. L37 12 B3
Cotton Hall St. BB3 81 A2
Cotton St. Accrington BB5 103 B5
Cotton St. Burnley BB12 126 D7
Cotton St. Padiham BB12 125 C7
Cotton Tree La. BB8 170 A5
Cottys Brow. PR9 52 F3
Coudray Rd. PR9 52 E1
Coulston Ave. FY2 150 B3
Coulston Rd. LA1 211 B6
Coultate St. BB12 126 C6
Coulter Beck La. LA6 236 A7
Coulthurst St. 1 BL0 49 B6
Coulton Rd. BB9 147 B7
Countess Cl. PR4 113 A7
Countess Cres. FY2 150 C3
Countess Rd. BB3 81 A7
Countess St. BB5 103 A6
Countess Way. PR7 59 D2
Countessway. 2 PR5 96 E1
County Cl. PR5 76 A4
County Rd. Kirkby L32 1 A1
County Rd. Ormskirk L39 15 E6
County St. LA1 210 E8
Coupe Gn. PR5 97 E4
Coupe Green Cty Prim Sch. PR5 97 E4
Coupland St. OL12 51 C8
Courage Low La. WN6 27 D5
Course La. L40 & WN8 25 D1
Court Hey. L31 5 E1
Court Rd. PR9 34 C8
Court The. PR2 116 C7
Courtfield. L39 15 D7
Courtfield Ave. FY3 129 D8
Courtgreen. L39 15 D7
Courtyard The. 8 OL13 87 A3
Courtyard Works. L33 1 C2
Cousin's La. L40 38 A3
Cove Dr. LA5 218 C4
Cove Rd. LA5 218 B4
Cove The. Cleveleys FY5 172 C4
Cove The. Morecambe LA4 213 A7
Covell House. 2 LA1 210 E8
Coventry St. PR7 42 C6
Coverdale Dr. BB2 79 D7
Coverdale Rd. LA1 210 D8
Coverdale Way. BB12 126 D7
Covert The. FY5 172 F4
Coveway Ave. FY3 129 E6
Cow Gate La. BD23 225 E7
Cow Well La. PR6 60 B8
Cowan Brae. BB1 100 D6
Cowell Way. BB2 100 D5
Cowes Ave. BB4 84 C2
Cowgarth La. BB8 201 C2
Cowgill St. 16 Bacup OL13 87 A3
Cowgill St. Earby BB8 201 B1
Cowhill La. BB1 101 F7
Cowley Cres. BB12 125 E7
Cowley Rd. Blackpool FY4 109 F8
Cowley Rd. Fulwood PR2 117 E4
Cowling Brow. PR7 42 E7
Cowling Brow Ind Est. PR7 42 F6
Cowling La. PR5 75 D1
Cowling Rd. PR7 42 F6
Cowm Park Way N. OL12 70 D2
Cowm Park Way S. OL12 70 C1
Cowm St. OL12 70 E5
Cowpe Rd. BB4 68 F7
Cowper Ave. BB7 186 E1
Cowper Pl. BB7 224 C1
Cowper St. Blackburn BB1 100 F7
Cowper St. Burnley BB11 126 C5
Cowslip Way. PR6 60 D2
Cowtoot La. OL13 87 A4
Cox Green Cl. BL7 46 D3
Cox Green Rd. BL7 46 E2
Coxfield. WN6 19 D7
Coyford Dr. PR9 53 A4
Crab Tree La. PR3 176 C2
Crabtree Ave. Bacup OL13 87 A1
Crabtree Ave. Newchurch BB4 85 F2
Crabtree Ave. Penwortham PR1 95 A3
Crabtree Bldgs. BB4 85 F4
Crabtree Cl. L40 24 D4
Crabtree La. L40 24 D6
Crabtree Orch. FY5 173 B3
Crabtree Rd. FY5 173 B3
Crabtree St. Blackburn BB1 101 B5
Crabtree St. Brierfield BB9 147 B5
Crabtree St. Bury BL9 32 B3
Crabtree St. Colne BB8 169 C4
Crabtree St. Whitewell Bottom BB4 85 F4
Cracoe Gill. BB9 168 C3
Craddock Rd. BB8 169 E5
Crag Ave. BL9 49 D2
Crag Bank Cres. LA5 216 C8
Crag Bank La. LA5 217 B1
Crag La. BL9 49 D2
Crag Rd. Lancaster LA1 214 B1
Crag Rd. Warton LA5 217 A6
Cragg Row. BB8 191 D7
Cragg St. Blackpool FY1 129 B3
Cragg St. Colne BB8 169 C5
Cragg's Row. 17 PR1 95 F8
Craggs La. LA2 233 D3
Craig St. LA3 212 A3
Craigflower Ct. PR5 77 C7
Craiglands Ave. LA3 212 A2
Craiglands Ct. LA1 210 C5
Crail Pl. OL10 32 F1
Crake Ave. FY7 193 C2
Crake Bank. 4 LA1 213 C2
Cranberry Cl. BB3 64 D6
Cranberry La. BB3 64 D6
Cranborne Cl. Horwich BL6 31 F1
Cranborne Cl. Standish WN6 28 D1
Cranborne St. 5 Bamber Bridge PR5 76 E8
Cranborne St. 10 Preston PR1 96 C8
Cranborne Terr. BB2 100 C6
Cranbourne Dr. Chorley PR7 42 E7
Cranbourne Dr. Church BB5 103 A8
Cranbourne Gr. FY5 151 E7
Cranbourne St. Chorley PR7 42 D7
Cranbourne St. Colne BB8 169 E6
Cranbrook Ave. Blackpool FY2 150 E5
Cranbrook Ave. Oswaldtwistle BB5 102 C4
Cranbrook St. BB2 100 D2
Crane St. PR7 28 D6
Cranes La. L40 16 E7
Cranfield View. BB3 64 C6
Crank Rd. WN5 10 D1
Crankshaw St. 9 BB4 85 A3
Cranleigh Ave. FY2 150 C3
Cranleigh Cl. BL6 30 D1
Cranmer St. 5 BB11 126 E6
Cranshaw Dr. BB1 100 F8
Cranston Rd. L33 1 C2
Cranwell Ave. LA1 211 B5
Cranwell Cl. 2 BB1 101 A4
Cranwell Ct. PR4 112 F5
Craven Cl. PR2 116 F7
Craven Ct. BL6 31 D2
Craven St. Accrington BB5 103 A5
Craven St. Barnoldswick BB8 200 C2
Craven St. Brierfield BB9 147 B5
Craven St. Burnley BB11 127 A5
Craven St. Bury BL9 32 C3
Craven St. Clitheroe BB7 164 E7
Craven St. Colne BB8 170 A5
Craven St. Nelson BB9 147 C8
Craven St. Rawtenstall BB4 84 F2
Craven St E. BL6 31 D2
Craven's Ave. BB2 80 D6
Craven's Brow. BB2 80 E7
Cravendale Ave. BB9 168 F3
Crawford Ave. Adlington PR7 29 E5
Crawford Ave. Blackpool FY2 150 D5
Crawford Ave. Chorley PR7 42 B7
Crawford Ave. Leyland PR5 59 B8
Crawford Ave. Maghull L31 5 B3
Crawford Ave. Preston PR1 117 F1
Crawford Rd. WA11 & WN8 9 D2
Crawford St. BB9 168 E1
Crawford Village Prim Sch. WN8 9 E3
Crawshaw Dr. BB4 85 A6
Crawshaw La. BB10 148 D6
Crawshaw St. BB5 103 B6
Crawshaw's Bldgs. BB4 85 A1
Crawshawbooth Cty Prim Sch. BB4 85 A8
Crediton Ave. PR9 53 B5
Crediton Cl. BB2 80 C8
Crescent Ave. L37 11 E1
Crescent Ct. FY4 109 A5
Crescent E. FY5 172 D2
Crescent Gn. L39 15 B1
Crescent Rd. Poulton-le-F FY6 151 E4
Crescent Rd. Southport PR8 33 F3
Crescent St. PR1 117 C1
Crescent The. Lostock Hall PR5 76 C8
Crescent The. Bamber Bridge PR5 96 F2
Crescent The. Blackburn BB2 99 E1
Crescent The. Blackpool FY4 109 B7
Crescent The. Brierfield BB10 147 B4
Crescent The. Bury BL9 32 A3
Crescent The. Carleton FY6 151 C4
Crescent The. Chorley PR6 & PR7 60 C2
Crescent The. Clitheroe BB7 164 D7
Crescent The. Colne BB8 169 E6
Crescent The. Dunsop Bridge BB7 222 C5
Crescent The. Fleetwood FY7 172 E8
Crescent The. Freckleton PR4 92 C5
Crescent The. Hest Bank LA2 215 D1
Crescent The. Horwich BL6 31 E1
Crescent The. Preesall FY6 195 B4
Crescent The. Preston PR2 115 D1
Crescent The. Preston PR2 116 B2
Crescent The. Southport PR9 53 C3
Crescent The. Warton PR4 91 C4
Crescent The. Whalley BB7 143 A6
Crescent The. Whitworth OL12 51 E8
Crescent The. Worsthorne BB10 128 A5
Crescent W. FY5 172 D2
Cressell Pk. WN6 28 B1
Cressingham Wlk. LA1 211 B3
Cresswood Ave. FY5 172 D1
Crestway. Blackpool FY3 129 F6
Crestway. Tarleton PR4 56 A8
Creswell Ave. PR2 115 F3
Creswick Ave. BB11 126 F3
Creswick Cl. BB11 126 F3
Crewdson St. BB3 80 F2
Crewgarth Rd. LA3 & LA4 212 E2
Cribden End La. BB4 84 D4
Cribden House Sch. BB4 84 E1
Cribden La. BB4 84 E3
Cribden St. BB4 84 F4
Criccieth Cl. 3 BB4 84 B1
Crichton Pl. FY4 109 B5
Cricket Path. Formby L37 11 F5
Cricket Path. Southport PR8 33 F3
Cricketers Gn. PR7 40 B6
Crimbles La. LA2 203 B2
Crime Well La. LA3 208 E7
Crimea St. OL13 87 A2
Crinan Sq. OL10 32 F1
Cringle Way. BB7 187 A2
Cripple Gate. WN6 28 A2
Cripple Gate La. PR5 98 C4
Croasdale. 7 LA1 213 C2
Croasdale Ave. Brierfield BB10 147 E2
Croasdale Ave. Fulwood PR2 117 E4
Croasdale Cl. LA5 217 C1
Croasdale Dr. Cleveleys FY5 172 F4
Croasdale Dr. Clitheroe BB7 164 F7
Croasdale Dr. Parbold WN8 26 C3
Croasdale Sq. BB1 101 A3
Croasdale Wlk. FY3 130 B8
Crockleford Ave. PR8 34 E3
Crocus Cl. BB4 66 F8
Crocus Field. PR5 59 A7
Croft Acres. BL0 67 D2
Croft Ave. Burscough L40 24 F3
Croft Ave. Hest Bank LA2 213 E8
Croft Ave. Orrell WN5 10 D5
Croft Bank. PR1 95 C3
Croft Butts La. PR4 92 C6
Croft Cl. BB4 85 A5
Croft Ct. FY7 193 E2
Croft Field. L31 5 E1
Croft Head Rd. BB1 122 B1
Croft Hey. L40 38 B4
Croft Heys. L39 15 B1
Croft La. BB12 145 F6
Croft Manor. PR4 92 C6
Croft Meadow. PR5 77 C6
Croft Rd. PR7 42 E7
Croft St. Bacup OL13 86 F3
Croft St. Burnley BB11 127 A5
Croft St. Bury BL9 32 A2
Croft St. Clitheroe BB7 164 E7
Croft St. 17 Darwen BB3 81 A1
Croft St. Earby BB8 201 C2
Croft St. Great Harwood BB6 123 C4
Croft St. Morecambe LA4 212 F5
Croft St. Preston PR1 95 D8
Croft St. Preston PR1 95 E8
Croft The. Blackburn BB1 100 D7
Croft The. Burton in L LA6 236 C3
Croft The. Caton LA2 231 C3
Croft The. Cleveleys FY5 172 D2
Croft The. Eccleston PR7 40 C7
Croft The. Euxton PR7 59 B3
Croft The. Fleetwood FY7 193 E2
Croft The. Garstang PR3 199 B1
Croft The. Goosnargh PR3 137 D6
Croft The. Great Plumpton PR4 111 E7
Croft The. Hoghton PR5 98 B2
Croft The. Lytham St Anne's FY8 110 B1
Croft The. Maghull L31 5 B5
Croft The. Orrell WN5 10 D3
Croft The. Poulton-le-F FY6 151 D2
Croft Way. FY5 151 C8
Crofters Fold. LA3 212 B1
Crofters Gn. Euxton PR7 59 C3
Crofters Gn. Preston PR1 116 E2
Crofters Mews. FY1 129 C7
Crofters Wlk. PR1 95 D2
Croftgate. PR2 116 F5
Croftlands. Borwick LA6 234 B3
Croftlands. Orrell WN5 10 D4
Croftlands. Ramsbottom BL0 49 A3
Croftlands. Warton LA5 217 E6
Crofton Ave. FY2 150 D5
Crofts Cl. PR4 113 C5
Crofts The. PR4 94 A1
Croftson Ave. L39 15 F7
Croichley Fold. BL8 48 D2
Cromarty Sq. OL10 32 F1
Crombleholme Rd. PR1 117 E1
Cromer Ave. BB10 147 C1
Cromer Gr. BB10 147 C1
Cromer Pl. Blackburn BB1 100 E7
Cromer Pl. Fulwood PR2 116 A4
Cromer Rd. Blackpool FY2 150 E4
Cromer Rd. Lytham St Anne's FY8 110 A1
Cromer Rd. Southport PR8 33 E2
Cromer St. OL12 51 E1
Cromfield. L39 15 C2
Cromford Wlk. 9 PR1 96 C8
Crompton Ave. FY4 109 E7
Crompton Pl. BB2 100 C5
Crompton St. PR1 117 C1
Cromwell Ave. PR1 95 C3
Cromwell Cl. L39 15 C2
Cromwell Rd. Blackpool FY1 129 C7
Cromwell Rd. Fulwood PR2 117 D3
Cromwell Rd. Lancaster LA1 210 E6
Cromwell Rd. Penwortham PR1 95 C3
Cromwell St. Accrington BB5 103 B8
Cromwell St. 20 Blackburn BB1 101 A4
Cromwell St. Burnley BB12 126 F8
Cromwell St. Foulridge BB8 191 D1
Cromwell St. 3 Preston PR1 117 A1
Cronkeyshaw Rd. OL12 51 F1
Cronkshaw St. BB10 127 A7
Cronshaw Dr. BB6 142 C1
Crook Dale La. FY6 & PR3 174 E7
Crook Gate La. PR3 175 E1
Crook Nook. LA3 209 B2
Crook St. Adlington PR7 29 F7
Crook St. Chorley PR7 42 B5
Crook St. Preston PR1 96 B8
Crookall Cl. 7 FY7 193 F2
Crooked La. PR1 96 A8
Crooked Shore. OL13 86 F3
Crookfield Rd. PR7 63 B3
Crookhalgh Ave. BB10 127 F6
Crookhey Hall Sch. LA2 203 E3
Crookings La. PR1 95 A6
Crooklands Dr. PR3 178 C8
Crookleigh Pl. LA3 212 A2
Croos St. BB5 103 C5
Cropper Gdns. PR4 72 D3
Cropper Rd. FY4 110 C6
Cropper's La. L39 16 A1
Cropton Rd. L37 11 F3
Crosby Cl. BB3 64 B6
Crosby Gr. FY3 129 F3
Crosby Pl. PR2 116 A4
Crosby Rd. Blackburn BB2 100 E1
Crosby Rd. Lytham St Anne's FY8 109 F1
Crosby Rd. Southport PR8 34 A3
Crosby St. OL12 51 F2
Crosfield Ave. BL9 49 C2
Crosier Wlk. PR4 115 E5
Crosland Rd. L32 1 A1
Crosland Rd N. FY8 89 A8
Crosland Rd S. FY8 89 A8
Crosley Cl. BB5 103 B3
Cross Bank. 7 BB12 125 D8
Cross Barn Gr. BB3 64 B8
Cross Barn La. L38 3 E3
Cross Barn Wlk. BB3 64 B8
Cross Brow. PR7 41 C8
Cross Edge. BB5 103 A1
Cross Field. PR4 94 C1
Cross Flatts Cres. BB8 191 E8
Cross Fold. BB7 187 B8
Cross Gn. L37 12 A2
Cross Green Cl. L37 12 A2
Cross Green Rd. PR2 116 E6
Cross Hagg St. BB8 169 C4
Cross Halls. PR1 95 C3
Cross Helliwell St. 16 BB8 169 D4
Cross Hill Ct. LA5 216 A4
Cross Hill Four Lane Ends. PR3 220 B6
Cross Hill La. BB7 225 B1
Cross La. Barley Green BB12 167 C4
Cross La. Halsall L39 22 C1
Cross La. Low Bentham LA2 233 B8
Cross La. Moor Side PR4 133 D1
Cross La. Orrell WN5 10 D3
Cross La. Ramsbottom BL8 49 A6
Cross La. Salterforth BB8 191 E8
Cross La. Waddington BB7 185 E5
Cross Meanygate. L40 & PR4 37 C5
Cross Rd. LA2 233 B7
Cross School St. 5 BB8 169 D4
Cross Skelton St. 6 BB8 169 E5
Cross St. 4 Bacup OL13 87 A3
Cross St. Blackburn BB3 80 F7
Cross St. Blackpool FY1 129 B7
Cross St. Brierfield BB9 147 B5
Cross St. Brierfield BB10 147 F3
Cross St. Chorley PR6 60 C1
Cross St. Clayton-le-M BB5 123 E3
Cross St. Clitheroe BB7 164 D8
Cross St. Darwen BB3 64 B7
Cross St. Earby BB8 201 A1
Cross St. Fleetwood FY7 194 B5
Cross St. Great Harwood BB6 123 D5
Cross St. Higham BB12 145 F6
Cross St. 3 Leyland PR5 76 B2
Cross St. Longridge PR3 139 A6
Cross St. Lytham St Anne's FY8 88 D8
Cross St. Morecambe LA4 212 F5
Cross St. Nelson BB9 147 D8
Cross St. Oswaldtwistle BB5 102 D4
Cross St. Preston PR0 & PR1 95 F7
Cross St. Ramsbottom BL0 49 C6
Cross St. 14 Rawtenstall BB4 85 A7
Cross St. Southport PR8 34 B6
Cross St. Standish WN6 28 E1
Cross St. Worsthorne BB10 128 B6
Cross St N. BB4 84 B5
Cross St S. BB4 84 B4
Cross St W. BB8 169 B4
Cross Swords Cl. PR7 42 A5
Cross Way. FY5 172 D4
Crossdale Ave. LA3 212 A2
Crossdale Sq. 10 LA1 211 A8
Crosse Hall La. PR6 & PR7 42 F7
Crosse Hall St. PR6 & PR7 42 F7
Crossens CE Prim Sch. PR9 53 C5
Crossens Way. PR9 53 C6
Crossfield Ct. LA5 237 A1
Crossfield St. BB1 & BB2 100 F3
Crosshall Brow. L40 16 C4
Crosshall High Sch. L40 16 B5
Crosshill Pl. 7 LA2 213 D2
Crosshill Rd. BB2 100 B5
Crosshill Sch. BB1 101 C2
Crosshills. 5 BB12 145 C1
Crossing The. PR5 98 B2
Crossland Rd. FY4 129 E1
Crossland St. BB5 103 A5
Crossley Fold. BB11 126 D4
Crossways. BB7 186 D7
Croston Ave. PR6 30 A8
Croston Barn Rd. PR3 178 A8
Croston Cl. 6 BB1 101 B5
Croston Close Rd. BL0 & BL9 50 C4
Croston Dr. L40 38 B6
Croston La. PR7 41 B2
Croston Meth Prim Sch. PR5 57 B2
Croston Rd. Croston L40 38 C7
Croston Rd. Farington PR5 75 F6
Croston Rd. Garstang PR3 178 B8
Croston Rd. Leyland PR5 75 E4
Croston St. BB1 101 C5
Croston Sta. PR5 57 B3
Croston's Brow. PR9 52 F3
Crow Foot Row. BB8 200 B1
Crow Hills Rd. PR1 95 A6
Crow La. Ramsbottom BL0 49 C6
Crow La. Skelmersdale WN8 18 F3
Crow La. Town End PR3 153 E8
Crow Orch Sch. WN8 17 F2
Crow Orchard Rd. WN6 28 A1
Crow Park La. BB7 225 C4
Crow Tree Ave. 5 OL13 69 B8
Crow Trees Brow. BB7 187 D4
Crow Trees Gdns. BB7 187 D5
Crow Trees La. BL7 47 C7
Crow Wood Ave. BB12 126 D7
Crow Wood Ct. BB12 126 E7
Crow Wood Rd. BL0 67 D6
Crowborough Cl. BL6 31 F1
Crowder Ave. FY5 173 B2
Crowland Cl. PR9 35 A6
Crowland St. PR9 35 A6
Crowland Way. L37 12 B2
Crowle St. PR1 96 D8
Crown Cl. L37 12 A2
Crown Gdns. BL7 47 D6
Crown La. Fleetwood FY7 194 B4
Crown La. Horwich BL6 31 A4
Crown La. Swillbrook PR4 135 B2
Crown Mews. PR4 113 A5
Crown Point. BL7 47 D6
Crown Point Rd. BB11 126 E1
Crown St. Accrington BB5 103 B5
Crown St. 3 Chorley PR7 42 C8
Crown St. Darwen BB3 64 A8
Crown St. Leyland PR5 76 B3
Crown St. Preston PR1 95 F8
Crown Way. Colne BB8 169 C4
Crown Way. Colne BB8 169 C5
Crowndale. BL7 47 D7
Crownest Rd. BB8 200 C3
Crownlee. PR1 95 A3
Crowshaw Dr. OL12 51 E3
Crowther St. Burnley BB11 127 B4
Crowther St. Clayton-le-M BB5 123 E3
Crowthorn Rd. BL7 66 A1
Crowthorn Sch. BL7 65 F1
Crowtrees Gr. BB9 167 F5
Crowtrees Rd. BB7 144 F8
Crowtrees Yd. LA2 233 B8
Croxteth Cl. L31 5 E3
Croxton Wlk. 8 BL6 31 B4
Croyde Cl. PR9 53 B5
Croyde Rd. FY8 89 A5
Croydon Rd. FY3 129 E7
Croydon St. BB2 100 C5
Crummock Pl. 2 FY4 130 C1
Crummock Rd. PR1 118 A1
Crumpax Ave. PR3 139 A8
Crystal Gr. FY8 88 E8
Crystal Rd. Blackpool FY1 129 B1
Crystal Rd. Thornton FY5 173 B5
Cub St. PR5 76 A4
Cuba Mill. BL0 49 C8
Cuba St. 3 BB9 147 D8
Cuckoo Brow. BB1 100 D8
Cuckoo La. Bury BL9 32 C2
Cuckoo La. Bury BL9 32 C3
Cuckoo La. Moss Edge PR3 176 B3
Cuckstool La. BB12 146 E6
Cudworth Rd. FY8 109 F1
Cuerdale La. PR1 & PR5 97 D6
Cuerdale St. BB10 147 E3
Cuerden Ave. PR5 58 D7
Cuerden Cl. PR5 76 E4
Cuerden Rise. PR5 76 C7
Cuerden St. Chorley PR7 42 E7
Cuerden St. Colne BB8 169 B3
Cuerden Valley Pk. PR5 76 F3
Cuerden Way. PR5 76 D7
Culbeck La. PR7 58 F2
Culshaw St. 3 Blackburn BB1 101 A5
Culshaw St. Burnley BB10 127 C5
Culshaw Way. L40 22 F7
Culvert La. WN8 26 A2
Cumberland Ave. Blackpool FY1 129 D4
Cumberland Ave. Burnley BB12 126 A6
Cumberland Ave. Clayton-le-M BB5 124 A3
Cumberland Ave. Cleveleys FY5 172 E4
Cumberland Ave. Leyland PR5 58 E7
Cumberland House. 18 PR4 95 F8
Cumberland Rd. PR8 34 D5
Cumberland St. 12 Blackburn BB1 101 A4
Cumberland St. 5 Colne BB8 169 E5
Cumberland St. Nelson BB9 168 E1
Cumberland View Rd. LA3 212 A3
Cumbrian Ave. FY3 129 E7
Cumbrian Way. BB12 126 B8
Cumeragh La. PR3 138 C6
Cummins Ave. L37 11 E5
Cumpstey St. BB2 100 E3
Cunliffe Ct. BB5 123 F2

Dickinson St. BB2 .... 100 D3
Dickinson St W. BL6 .... 31 B4
Dickson Ave. PR1 .... 117 D2
Dickson Hey. PR4 .... 74 F8
Dickson Rd. FY1 .... 129 B7
Dickson St. Burnley BB12 .... 126 C6
Dickson St. Colne BB8 .... 169 E6
Dickson St. 5 Preston PR1 .... 96 B7
Dickson St W. BL6 .... 31 A4
Didsbury St. BB1 .... 101 C5
Digham Ave. FY5 .... 150 D6
Digmoor Dr. WN8 .... 9 C7
Digmoor Rd. WN8 .... 9 D6
Dill Hall La. BB5 .... 102 F7
Dilworth La. PR3 .... 139 C7
Dimmock St. BB2 .... 100 C2
Dimple Pk. BL7 .... 46 D3
Dimples La. PR3 .... 178 E5
Dinckley Gr. FY1 .... 129 D3
Dinckley Sq. BB2 .... 100 B6
Dinely St. BB5 .... 102 F6
Dingle Ave. Blackpool FY3 .... 129 F8
Dingle Ave. Shevington Vale WN6 19 E8
Dingle Ave. Up Holland WN8 .... 10 C8
Dingle Cl. L39 .... 15 C1
Dingle Rd. WN8 .... 10 B7
Dingle The. PR2 .... 116 D7
Dinmore Ave. FY3 .... 130 A8
Dinmore Pl. FY3 .... 130 A7
Dinorwic Rd. PR8 .... 34 A2
Dirty Leech. OL12 .... 51 F6
Disraeli St. BB10 .... 147 A2
District General Hospl. PR8 .... 34 E4
Ditchfield. L37 .... 12 A2
Division La. FY4 .... 110 C3
Dixey St. BL6 .... 31 A3
Dixon Rd. PR3 .... 139 B7
Dixon St. Barrowford BB9 .... 168 C3
Dixon St. Blackburn BB2 .... 100 C4
Dixon St. Horwich BL6 .... 31 B3
Dixon's Farm Mews. PR4 .... 114 D1
Dob Brow. PR7 .... 41 F4
Dob La. PR4 .... 74 A4
Dobbin Cl. BB4 .... 85 C2
Dobbin La. BB4 .... 85 C2
Dobbs Dr. L37 .... 12 A4
Dobs La. LA2 .... 205 E3
Dobson Ave. FY8 .... 88 E8
Dobson Cl. WN6 .... 27 E2
Dobson St. 2 BB3 .... 80 F2
Dobson's La. FY6 .... 174 E6
Dock Ave. FY7 .... 194 A2
Dock Rd. FY8 .... 90 D4
Dock St. Blackburn BB1 .... 101 A5
Dock St. Fleetwood FY7 .... 194 B4
Docker La. LA6 .... 235 C5
Dockinsall La. PR3 .... 175 D3
Dockray Ct. 2 BB8 .... 169 E5
Dockray St. BB8 .... 169 E5
Dockray Yd. 4 BB8 .... 169 E5
Docky Pool La. FY4 .... 110 A6
Doctor's Hill. LA2 .... 233 B8
Doctor's La. Eccleston PR7 .... 40 B6
Doctor's La. Great Altcar L37 .... 12 E2
Doctor's La. Sollom PR4 .... 55 F3
Doctors Row. PR3 .... 139 A6
Dodd Way. PR5 .... 77 A6
Dodd's La. L31 .... 5 D2
Dodgeons Cl. FY6 .... 151 C2
Dodgson La. BB8 .... 201 F2
Dodgson Pl. PR1 .... 117 C1
Dodgson Rd. PR1 .... 117 C1
Dodney Dr. PR2 .... 115 C1
Dodson Rd. FY3 .... 130 B7
Dodworth Ave. PR8 .... 34 E5
Doe Meadow. WN8 .... 26 A1
Doeholme Rake. LA2 .... 226 F1
Dog Pits La. OL13 .... 87 A6
Dole La. Abbey Village PR7 .... 79 C1
Dole La. Chorley PR7 .... 42 C8
Doles La. PR4 & PR5 .... 57 A7
Dolly's La. PR9 .... 53 E1
Dollywood La. LA7 .... 237 F1
Dolphin House. BB11 .... 126 E5
Dolphinholme CE Sch. LA2 .... 220 A8
Dombey St. Blackburn BB1 .... 101 A3
Dombey St. Blackburn BB1 .... 101 A4
Dominion Rd. BB2 .... 100 C8
Don St. FY8 .... 88 E7
Doncaster Rd. FY3 .... 130 A3
Donnington Lodge. PR8 .... 33 F6
Donnington Rd. Carleton FY6 .... 151 C6
Donnington Rd.
Lytham St Anne's FY8 .... 88 F7
Donshort Mews. 2 BB9 .... 168 C1
Doodstone Ave. PR5 .... 96 B1
Doodstone Cl. PR5 .... 96 B1
Doodstone Dr. PR5 .... 96 B1
Doodstone Nook. PR5 .... 96 B1
Dora St. BL0 .... 49 A4
Dorchester Ave. BB5 .... 102 C4
Dorchester Cl. Blackburn BB1 .... 101 B3
Dorchester Cl. Thornton FY5 .... 151 C8
Dorchester Gdns. LA3 .... 212 F2
Dorchester Rd. Blackpool FY1 .... 129 B8
Dorchester Rd. Garstang PR3 .... 178 B8
Dorchester Rd. Hall Green WN8 .... 10 A7
Doric Gn. WN5 .... 10 D3
Doris Henderson Way. LA3 .... 213 A1
Doris St. Burnley BB11 .... 127 B7
Doris St. Chorley PR6 .... 60 D1
Dorking Rd. PR6 .... 60 F4
Dorman Rd. PR2 .... 117 E3
Dorothy Ave. PR5 .... 76 A1
Dorothy St. Blackburn BB2 .... 80 C8
Dorothy St. 13 Ramsbottom BL0 .... 49 B5
Dorrington Rd. LA1 .... 210 F5
Dorritt Rd. FY4 .... 109 E6
Dorritt St. 19 BB1 .... 101 A4
Dorset Ave. Ainsdale PR8 .... 20 C2
Dorset Ave. Bamber Bridge PR5 .... 96 D3
Dorset Ave. Cleveleys FY5 .... 172 D4
Dorset Ave. Darwen BB3 .... 80 F3
Dorset Ave. Padiham BB12 .... 125 D7
Dorset Dr. Blackburn BB1 .... 101 E4
Dorset Dr. Clitheroe BB7 .... 186 F2
Dorset Dr. Haslingden BB4 .... 67 A8
Dorset Pl. BB5 .... 102 F7
Dorset Rd. Lytham St Anne's FY8 .... 88 F8
Dorset Rd. Preston PR1 .... 117 A1
Dorset Rd. Rishton BB1 .... 123 A1
Dorset Rd. Standish WN1 .... 29 B1
Dorset St. 8 Blackpool FY4 .... 129 D1
Dorset St. Burnley BB12 .... 126 A6
Dotcliffe Rd. BB8 .... 192 A6
Double Row. BB12 .... 125 C8
Doughty St. BB8 .... 169 D4
Douglas Ave. Becconsall PR4 .... 72 F1
Douglas Ave. Blackpool FY3 .... 129 D7
Douglas Ave. Heysham LA3 .... 208 F7
Douglas Ave. Horwich BL6 .... 31 C5
Douglas Ave. Stalmine FY6 .... 174 C7
Douglas Ave. Up Holland WN8 .... 10 B7
Douglas Cl. Bamber Bridge PR5 .... 76 F7
Douglas Cl. Horwich BL6 .... 31 C5
Douglas Cl. Rufford L40 .... 38 C3
Douglas Ct. PR2 .... 116 D3
Douglas Dr. Freckleton PR4 .... 92 B6
Douglas Dr. Heysham LA3 .... 208 F7
Douglas Dr. Maghull L31 .... 5 F2
Douglas Dr. Ormskirk L39 .... 15 D7
Douglas Dr. Orrell WN5 .... 10 F7
Douglas Dr. Shevington WN6 .... 19 F5
Douglas Gr. BB3 .... 80 D4
Douglas Leatham House. 3
FY1 .... 129 D1
Douglas Pl. Blackburn BB1 .... 121 F1
Douglas Pl. Fleetwood FY7 .... 193 D3
Douglas Rd. Bacup OL13 .... 87 A1
Douglas Rd. Brierfield BB10 .... 148 A3
Douglas Rd. Fulwood PR2 .... 116 D3
Douglas Rd.
Shevington Moor WN6 .... 28 B2
Douglas Rd. Southport PR9 .... 53 C4
Douglas Rd N. PR2 .... 116 D3
Douglas Sq. 8 OL10 .... 32 F1
Douglas St. Colne BB8 .... 169 E6
Douglas St. Lytham St Anne's FY8 88 D6
Douglas St. Preston PR1 .... 95 C8
Douglas St. Ramsbottom BL0 .... 49 B6
Douglas Street Back. 4 BL0 .... 49 B6
Douglas Way. BB10 .... 148 A3
Doultons The. PR5 .... 96 C3
Dove Ave. PR1 .... 95 E4
Dove Cl. 6 FY5 .... 172 F1
Dove Dr. BL9 .... 32 B4
Dove La. BB3 .... 80 F2
Dove St. Lytham St Anne's FY8 .... 88 D6
Dove St. Preston PR1 .... 117 B1
Dove Tree Ct. FY4 .... 130 B1
Dovecote. PR5 & PR6 .... 77 A3
Dovedale Ave. Blackpool FY3 .... 130 C2
Dovedale Ave. Fulwood PR2 .... 116 A5
Dovedale Ave. Maghull L31 .... 5 C2
Dovedale Ave. Thornton FY5 .... 173 B3
Dovedale Cl. Brierfield BB10 .... 147 C4
Dovedale Cl. Burnley BB12 .... 126 C8
Dovedale Cl. Fulwood PR2 .... 116 A4
Dovedale Cl. Leyland PR5 .... 59 A6
Dovedale Dr. WN6 .... 28 E2
Dover Cl. Blackburn BB1 .... 101 C4
Dover Cl. Ramsbottom BL8 .... 49 A1
Dover Ct. FY1 .... 129 D2
Dover Gdns. FY6 .... 151 B5
Dover La. PR5 .... 78 C8
Dover Rd. Blackpool FY1 .... 129 E2
Dover Rd. Lytham St Anne's FY8 .... 88 F8
Dover Rd. Southport PR8 .... 33 F2
Dover St. Accrington BB5 .... 103 A4
Dover St. Blackburn BB3 .... 80 F7
Dover St. Nelson BB9 .... 168 E1
Dovetree Cl. PR1 .... 96 A3
Dowbridge. PR4 .... 113 C4
Dowbridge Way. PR4 .... 113 C5
Downes Gr. LA4 .... 212 G4
Downeyfield Rd. LA3 .... 209 C3
Downfield Cl. BL0 .... 49 B6
Downham Ave.
Great Harwood BB6 .... 123 F6
Downham Ave. Rawtenstall BB4 .... 85 A4
Downham Dr. BB5 .... 103 A3
Downham Gr. BB10 .... 127 D5
Downham Pl. Blackpool FY4 .... 109 B4
Downham Pl.
Lytham St Anne's FY8 .... 89 C6
Downham Pl. Preston PR2 .... 115 E2
Downham Rd. Chatburn BB7 .... 187 E5
Downham Rd. Leyland PR5 .... 75 D1
Downham St. BB2 .... 100 C4
Downham Wlk. WN5 .... 10 D1
Downholland Haskayne CE Sch.
L39 .... 13 E3
Downing Ct. PR3 .... 136 C3
Downing St. PR1 .... 96 E8
Downley Cl. OL12 .... 51 B2
Downs The. FY6 .... 151 D4
Dowry St. BB5 .... 103 C6
Dragon St. 5 BB12 .... 125 C8
Drake Cl. Lytham St Anne's FY8 .... 109 E1
Drake Cl. Ormskirk L39 .... 15 C2
Drakelowe Ave. FY4 .... 109 F6
Drakes Hollow. PR5 .... 96 D4
Drammen Ave. BB11 .... 126 B5
Draperfield. PR7 .... 42 A4
Drapers Ave. PR7 .... 40 C6
Draw Well Rd. L33 .... 1 D2
Draycombe Ct. LA3 .... 212 A2
Draycombe Dr. LA3 .... 212 B2
Draycot Ave. FY3 .... 129 F8
Drayton Rd. LA3 .... 209 A7
Drew St. BB11 .... 126 B5
Drewitt Cres. PR9 .... 53 D4
Drewton Ave. LA3 .... 212 A2
Drinkhouse La. PR5 .... 57 A1
Drinkhouse Rd. PR5 .... 57 B1
Driscoll St. 1 PR1 .... 96 B8
Drive The. Bacup OL13 .... 86 F2
Drive The. Carnforth LA5 .... 217 B1
Drive The. Edenfield BL0 .... 67 D3
Drive The. Fulwood PR2 .... 117 B4
Drive The. Hest Bank LA2 .... 215 E1
Drive The. Heysham LA3 .... 208 F7
Drive The. Longton PR4 .... 74 A8
Drive The. Walton-le-D PR5 .... 96 F6
Driver St. 12 BB4 .... 85 A7
Driving Gate. BB4 .... 105 A1
Dronsfield Rd. FY7 .... 193 F4
Druids Cl. BL7 .... 46 D3
Drumacre La E. PR4 .... 74 D6
Drumacre La W. PR4 .... 74 A6
Drummersdale La. L40 .... 23 D7
Drummond Ave. FY3 .... 129 E7
Drybread La. PR3 .... 175 C2
Dryburgh Ave. FY3 .... 129 F3
Dryden Gr. BB6 .... 123 C4
Dryden Rd. FY7 .... 194 A4
Dryden St. 6 Clayton-le-M BB5 123 B5
Dryden St. Padiham BB12 .... 125 E7
Dryfield La. BL6 .... 31 A5
Duchess Ct. FY2 .... 150 B3
Duchess Dr. FY2 .... 150 B3
Duchess St. BB3 .... 80 F7
Duchy Ave. PR2 .... 117 B4
Ducie Pl. PR1 .... 117 F1
Duck St. 2 Clitheroe BB7 .... 164 F8
Duck St. Smallwood Hey PR3 .... 196 A7
Duck St. Wray LA2 .... 232 D6
Duckett St. 3 BB11 .... 126 E6
Duckshaw Rd. BB3 .... 63 F6
Duckworth Cl. PR3 .... 178 D3
Duckworth Dr. PR3 .... 178 D3
Duckworth Hall Brow. BB5 .... 102 A1
Duckworth Hill La. BB1 & BB5 .... 102 B1
Duckworth La. Rawtenstall BB4 .... 67 E8
Duckworth La. Tarleton PR4 .... 55 F8
Duckworth St. Barrowford BB9 .... 168 D2
Duckworth St. Blackburn BB2 .... 100 D3
Duckworth St. 3 Bury BL9 .... 32 A4
Duckworth St. Church BB5 .... 102 E6
Duckworth St. Darwen BB3 .... 80 F2
Duddle La. PR5 .... 96 D2
Duddon Ave. Darwen BB3 .... 80 E3
Duddon Ave. Fleetwood FY7 .... 193 D2
Duddon Ave. Maghull L31 .... 5 F2
Dudley Ave. Blackpool FY2 .... 150 D1
Dudley Ave. Oswaldtwistle BB5 .... 102 C4
Dudley Cl. PR4 .... 94 A1
Dudley St. Brierfield BB9 .... 147 C5
Dudley St. Colne BB8 .... 169 F5
Dudley St. Morecambe LA4 .... 212 F4
Duerden St. BB9 .... 147 D7
Duffins Cl. OL12 .... 51 D3
Dugdale Ct. FY4 .... 109 F5
Dugdale La. BB7 .... 229 F1
Dugdale Rd. BB12 .... 126 C7
Dugdale St. BB11 .... 127 A5
Dugie St. BL0 .... 49 B7
Duke Ave. PR8 .... 34 C4
Duke of Sussex St. BB2 .... 80 B8
Duke St. Bamber Bridge PR5 .... 76 E7
Duke St. Blackburn BB2 .... 100 D5
Duke St. Blackpool FY1 .... 129 B1
Duke St. Brierfield BB10 .... 147 F3
Duke St. Burnley BB11 .... 127 B4
Duke St. Burton in L LA6 .... 236 C3
Duke St. Chorley PR7 .... 42 C6
Duke St. Clayton-le-M BB5 .... 124 A2
Duke St. Colne BB8 .... 169 D4
Duke St. Formby L37 .... 11 F2
Duke St. Great Harwood BB6 .... 123 B5
Duke St. Heysham LA3 .... 208 E7
Duke St. High Bentham LA2 .... 233 D8
Duke St. Lancaster LA1 .... 213 E1
Duke St. Newchurch BB4 .... 68 E8
Duke St. Oswaldtwistle BB5 .... 102 D3
Duke St. Preston PR1 .... 96 B7
Duke St. Ramsbottom BL0 .... 49 A4
Duke St. Rochdale OL12 .... 51 F1
Duke St. Southport PR8 .... 34 B5
Duke St. Trawden BB8 .... 170 B5
Duke St Cty Prim Sch. PR7 .... 42 C6
Duke's Wood La. WN8 .... 9 D3
Dukes Brow. BB2 .... 100 C6
Dukes Ct. BB2 .... 100 B6
Dukes Dr. BB3 .... 81 F1
Dukes Meadow. PR2 .... 116 A5
Dukes Way. L37 .... 11 F2
Dulas Gn. L32 .... 1 A1
Dulas Rd. L32 .... 1 A1
Dumb Tom's La. LA6 .... 236 E1
Dumbarton Rd. LA1 .... 211 A7
Dumfries Cl. FY2 .... 150 F5
Dunald Mill La. LA2 & LA6 .... 231 B6
Dunbar Cl. FY4 .... 110 A6
Dunbar Cres. PR8 .... 20 F8
Dunbar Dr. Fulwood PR2 .... 116 D4
Dunbar Dr. Heysham LA3 .... 208 E7
Dunbar Rd. Fulwood PR2 .... 115 F3
Dunbar Rd. Southport PR8 .... 33 F1
Duncan Ave. FY2 .... 150 C6
Duncan Cl. Brownside BB10 .... 127 F5
Duncan Cl.
Lytham St Anne's FY8 .... 109 D1
Duncan Pl. FY7 .... 193 E4
Duncan St. Burnley BB12 .... 126 A5
Duncan St. Horwich BL6 .... 31 C3
Duncroft Cl. BB7 .... 186 E2
Dundas St. BB8 .... 169 C4
Dundee Cl. OL10 .... 32 F1
Dundee Dr. BB1 .... 101 A4
Dundee La. BL0 .... 49 B6
Dundee St. LA1 .... 211 A7
Dunderdale Ave. BB9 .... 147 C7
Dunderdale St. PR3 .... 139 B7
Dundonald St. PR1 .... 96 D8
Dundonnell Rd. BB9 .... 169 A1
Dunedin Rd. BL8 .... 48 F2
Dunelt Rd. FY1 .... 129 D2
Dunes Ave. FY4 .... 109 B5
Dunes Dr. L37 .... 11 C4
Dungeon La. WN8 .... 18 C7
Dunkeld St. 5 LA1 .... 211 A7
Dunkenhalgh Way. Church BB5 102 E7
Dunkenhalgh Way.
Clayton-le-M BB5 .... 123 E1
Dunkenshaw Cres. LA1 .... 211 B2
Dunkirk Ave. Carnforth LA5 .... 216 E8
Dunkirk Ave. Fulwood PR2 .... 116 C3
Dunkirk La. PR5 .... 75 A1
Dunkirk Rd. PR8 .... 33 F2
Dunlin Cl. FY5 .... 173 A5
Dunlop Ave. PR8 .... 20 C2
Dunmail Ave. FY3 .... 129 F2
Dunmore St. PR1 .... 96 B8
Dunny Shop Ave. BB5 .... 103 A4
Dunoon Cl. PR2 .... 115 F4
Dunoon Dr. BB1 .... 101 D3
Dunoon St. BB11 .... 126 D5
Dunrobin Dr. PR7 .... 59 D1
Dunscar Dr. PR6 .... 60 E1
Dunscar Golf Course. BL7 .... 46 C1
Dunsop Cl. 4
Bamber Bridge PR5 .... 76 F8
Dunsop Cl. 1 Blackpool FY1 .... 129 D1
Dunsop Ct. 2 FY1 .... 129 D1
Dunsop Rd. PR2 .... 117 D4
Dunsop St. BB1 .... 100 F7
Dunster Ave. BB5 .... 102 C5
Dunster Gr. BB7 .... 164 C6
Dunster Rd. PR8 .... 20 E8
Dunvegan Cl. FY4 .... 110 A6
Dunvegan Ct. 2 OL10 .... 32 F1
Durban Gr. BB11 .... 126 E4
Durham Ave. Burnley BB12 .... 126 B7
Durham Ave. Cleveleys FY5 .... 172 E3
Durham Ave. Lancaster LA1 .... 211 A4
Durham Ave.
Lytham St Anne's FY8 .... 88 E7
Durham Cl. Blackburn BB1 .... 100 F4
Durham Cl. Leyland PR5 .... 58 E6
Durham Cl. Morecambe LA3 .... 212 E2
Durham Dr. Oswaldtwistle BB5 .... 102 F3
Durham Dr. Ramsbottom BL0 .... 49 B3
Durham Dr. Wilpshire BB1 .... 121 F6
Durham Gr. PR3 .... 178 B7
Durham House. PR1 .... 96 A6
Durham Rd. Blackpool FY1 .... 129 D5
Durham Rd. Darwen BB3 .... 80 F2
Durham Rd. Wilpshire BB1 .... 121 F7
Durham St. Accrington BB5 .... 103 D7
Durham St. Skelmersdale WN8 .... 17 D2
Durley Rd. FY1 .... 129 D2
Durn St. OL14 .... 108 A1
Dutch Barn Cl. PR7 .... 60 B2
Dutton Ct. FY3 .... 129 D5
Dutton Rd. FY3 .... 129 D5
Dutton St. 16 BB5 .... 103 C6
Duxbury Cl. L31 .... 5 E3
Duxbury Dr. BL9 .... 32 C2
Duxbury Hall Rd. PR7 .... 42 E3
Duxbury Jubilee Pk. PR7 .... 42 D3
Duxbury St. Darwen BB3 .... 64 B6
Duxbury St. Earby BB8 .... 201 C2
Dye House La. 6 LA1 .... 210 F8
Dyer St. PR4 .... 112 F5
Dyers La. L39 .... 15 E4
Dyke Nook. BB7 .... 164 F6
Dykes La. LA5 .... 219 F2
Dymock Rd. PR1 .... 117 D1
Dymock Rd N. PR1 .... 117 D1
Dyneley Ave. BB10 .... 127 F4
Dyneley Rd. BB1 .... 101 C7
Dyson St. BB2 .... 100 E2

Eachill Gdns. BB1 .... 102 B8
Eachill Rd. 2 BB1 .... 123 B1
Eager La. L31 .... 5 B8
Eagle St. Accrington BB5 .... 103 B5
Eagle St. Blackburn BB1 .... 101 C4
Eagle St. Nelson BB9 .... 168 F1
Eagle St. Oswaldtwistle BB5 .... 102 C2
Eagles The. FY6 .... 151 E5
Eagley Bank. OL12 .... 70 E6
Eagley Rd. BB10 .... 147 C4
Ealing Gr. PR6 .... 60 F3
Eamont Ave. PR9 .... 53 B5
Eamont Pl. FY7 .... 193 D2
Eanam. BB1 .... 100 F5
Eanam Old Rd. BB1 .... 100 F5
Earby Cty Prim Sch. BB8 .... 201 C1
Earby Rd. BB8 .... 191 F8
Eardley Rd. LA3 .... 208 E8
Earl Rd. BL0 .... 49 B6
Earl St. Barnoldswick BB8 .... 200 C2
Earl St. Blackburn BB1 .... 100 E6
Earl St. Burnley BB10 .... 127 B8
Earl St. Clayton-le-M BB5 .... 123 F2
Earl St. Colne BB8 .... 169 D4
Earl St. Great Harwood BB6 .... 123 B5
Earl St. Lancaster LA1 .... 213 F1
Earl St. 8 Nelson BB9 .... 168 F1
Earl St. Preston PR0 & PR1 .... 95 F8
Earl St. Ramsbottom BL0 .... 49 D6
Earlesdon Ave. BB8 .... 200 F1
Earlham St. BB8 .... 201 C2
Earls Ave. PR5 .... 76 E8
Earls Dr. BB3 .... 81 E1
Earls Way. PR7 .... 59 D2
Earlsway. FY3 .... 130 D5
Earlswood. WN8 .... 18 E1
Earnsdale Ave. BB3 .... 80 D2
Earnsdale Cl. BB3 .... 80 E2
Earnsdale Rd. BB3 .... 80 E3
Earnshaw Ave. OL12 .... 51 E3
Earnshaw Bridge Cty Infs Sch.
PR5 .... 75 E2
Earnshaw Dr. PR5 .... 75 D1
Earnshaw Rd. OL13 .... 86 F3
Earnshaw Row. 19 OL13 .... 86 F3
Easby Cl. L37 .... 12 A2
Easdale Ave. LA4 .... 213 A5
Easedale Cl. Burnley BB12 .... 126 B8
Easedale Cl. Hest Bank LA5 .... 215 F2
Easedale Dr. PR8 .... 20 B4
Easington. LA1 .... 213 C2
Easington Cres. FY3 .... 130 B8
Easington Wlk. 4 BB1 .... 100 F3
East Ave. BB8 .... 200 B2
East Bank. 2 Barrowford BB9 .... 168 D4
East Bank. Water BB4 .... 106 A1
East Bank Ave. BB4 .... 84 B2
East Bank Rd. FY8 .... 88 E5
East Beach. FY8 .... 90 C3
East Boothroyden. FY1 .... 129 B8
East Cecil St. FY8 .... 90 A3
East Cliff. PR1 .... 95 F6
East Cliff Rd. PR1 .... 95 F6
East Cliffe. FY8 .... 90 C3
East Cres. BB5 .... 103 B8
East Croft. BB9 .... 169 B2
East Ct. FY5 .... 172 D5
East Dene. WN8 .... 26 B2
East End St. BB8 .... 169 C4
East Gate. BB4 .... 84 B3
East Hills St. 16 BB8 .... 200 B2
East Holme. FY8 .... 90 C4
East La. L29 & L38 .... 4 B2
East Lancashire Rd. BB1 .... 121 F3
East Lancashire Rly. BL0 .... 49 C5
East Leigh. WN8 .... 18 D1
East Lodge Pl. BB10 .... 127 E1
East Mead. Blackpool FY3 .... 129 F3
East Mead. Ormskirk L39 .... 15 B2
East Meade. L31 .... 5 C2
East Mount. WN5 .... 10 F6
East Par. 13 Barnoldswick BB8 .... 200 B2
East Par. 17 Rawtenstall BB4 .... 85 A3
East Park Ave. Blackburn BB1 .... 100 D7
East Park Ave. Darwen BB3 .... 63 F8
East Park Dr. FY3 .... 130 A5
East Park Rd. BB1 & BB2 .... 100 D6
East Rd. Fulwood PR2 .... 117 A3
East Rd. Lancaster LA1 .... 211 A8
East Rd. Maghull L31 .... 5 F1
East Sq. PR4 .... 94 A1
East St. Bamber Bridge PR5 .... 76 E7
East St. Blackburn BB2 .... 79 D8
East St. Blackburn BB2 .... 100 C3
East St. Brierfield BB9 .... 147 C5
East St. Chorley PR6 .... 42 D8
East St. Edenfield BL0 .... 67 D4
East St. Hapton BB12 .... 125 C4
East St. Helmshore BB4 .... 67 A7
East St. Leyland PR5 .... 76 B1
East St. Leyland PR5 .... 76 B2
East St. Morecambe LA3 & LA4 .... 212 B4
East St. 10 Nelson BB9 .... 168 D1
East St. Padiham BB12 .... 145 C1
East St. 12 Preston PR1 .... 96 A8
East St. Rawtenstall BB4 .... 84 F5
East St. Southport PR9 .... 34 D7
East Terr. PR7 .... 59 D4
East Topping St. FY1 .... 129 C5
East View. Bacup OL13 .... 86 F2
East View. 9 Barnoldswick BB8 200 B2
East View. Grindleton BB7 .... 187 B7
East View. Haslingden BB5 .... 84 A8
East View. Pendleton BB7 .... 165 B4
East View. Preston PR1 .... 96 A8
East View. Preston PR1 .... 96 C6
East View. Ramsbottom BL0 .... 49 C3
East View. Read BB12 .... 144 D2
East View. Stubbins BL0 .... 67 C1
East View. Trawden BB8 .... 170 C2
East View. Winmarleigh PR3 .... 198 F6
East View Ct. LA1 .... 213 D3
East View Terr. PR6 .... 79 B3
East Ward Cty Prim Sch. BL9 .... 32 B2
East Ward Cty Prim Sch
(Annexe). BL9 .... 32 B3
East Wlk. BL7 .... 46 D2
Eastbank Ave. FY4 .... 110 A7
Eastbank St. PR8 .... 34 B6
Eastbourne Cl. PR2 .... 115 F5
Eastbourne Rd. Blackpool FY4 .... 109 B6
Eastbourne Rd. Southport PR8 .... 34 A3
Eastcliff. LA2 .... 231 F5
Eastcott Cl. BB2 .... 81 A8
Eastern Ave. BB10 .... 147 C1
Eastfield Dr. Longton PR4 .... 94 A1
Eastfield Dr. West Bradford BB7 186 F6
Eastgate. Accrington BB5 .... 103 C6
Eastgate. Fulwood PR2 .... 116 E4
Eastgate. Morecambe LA3 .... 213 A2
Eastgate. Ribchester PR3 .... 140 E4
Eastgate. Wallbank OL12 .... 51 C7
Eastham Pl. BB11 .... 127 B6

Eton Way. WN5 10 F8
Ettington Dr. PR8 20 A5
Ettrick Ave. FY7 193 D3
Euro Trad Est. BB1 100 F7
Europa Way. LA1 210 C8
Euston Rd. LA4 212 E5
Euston St. PR1 95 E7
Euxton CE Sch. PR7 59 C2
Euxton Hall Ct. PR7 59 C2
Euxton Hall Gdns. PR7 59 C1
Euxton Hall Hospl. PR7 59 C1
Euxton Hall Mews. PR7 59 C2
Euxton La. Chorley PR7 60 B3
Euxton La. Euxton PR7 59 E4
Evans St. Burnley BB11 126 F4
Evans St. Horwich BL6 31 D4
Evans St. Preston PR1 116 D1
Evelyn Rd. BB3 80 E5
Evelyn St. BB10 147 A1
Evenwood. WN8 18 D1
Evenwood Ct. WN8 18 C1
Everard Cl. L40 22 F7
Everard Rd. PR8 34 D4
Everest Cl. FY8 110 A1
Everest Ct. PR4 112 F6
Everest Dr. FY2 150 C5
Everest Rd. FY8 110 A2
Evergreen Ave. PR5 59 A7
Evergreens The. Blackburn BB2 . 79 F8
Evergreens The. Fulwood PR4 .. 115 E4
Eversholt Cl. BB12 146 D7
Eversleigh Ave. FY5 173 A3
Eversleigh St. PR1 116 E1
Eversley. WN8 18 D1
Everton. BB2 101 A1
Everton Rd. Blackpool FY4 109 C6
Everton Rd. Southport PR8 34 A4
Everton St. BB3 80 F1
Every St. Brierfield BB9 147 B6
Every St. Burnley BB11 126 E5
Every St. Nelson BB9 147 C8
Every St. Nelson BB9 147 D8
Every St. Ramsbottom BL0 49 D6
Evesham Ave. PR1 95 E2
Evesham Cl. 5 Accrington BB5 103 A7
Evesham Cl. Blackpool FY5 150 E7
Evesham Cl. Hutton PR4 94 C1
Evesham Rd.
Lytham St Anne's FY8 89 A5
Evesham Rd. Normoss FY3 130 B7
Evington. WN8 18 D1
Ewell Cl. PR6 60 F4
Ewood. BB2 100 D1
Ewood Ct. BB2 100 C2
Ewood La. BB4 67 C7
Ewood Park
(Blackburn Rovers FC). BB2 .. 80 D8
Exchange St. Accrington BB5 102 F5
Exchange St. 18 Blackburn BB1 100 E5
Exchange St. Blackpool FY1 129 B6
Exchange St. Colne BB8 169 D4
Exchange St. Darwen BB3 81 A2
Exchange St. Edenfield BL0 67 D3
Exe St. PR1 117 B2
Exeter Ave. LA1 211 B6
Exeter Dr. FY5 173 A2
Exeter Pl. PR2 115 E2
Exeter St. Blackburn BB2 100 D2
Exeter St. Blackpool FY4 129 C1
Exmoor Cl. PR9 53 B6
Exmouth St. BB11 127 A5
Exton St. BB9 147 A5
Extwistle Rd. BB10 128 B7
Extwistle Sq. BB10 127 E5
Extwistle St. Burnley BB10 127 B8
Extwistle St. Nelson BB9 147 D7
Eyes La. Bretherton L40 & PR5 55 E3
Eyes La. Newburgh WN8 26 A3

Factory Brow. Blackrod BL6 30 D3
Factory Brow. Scorton PR3 199 E6
Factory Hill. Horwich BL6 31 D4
Factory Hill. 2 Lancaster LA1 .. 214 A1
Factory La. Adlington PR6 30 B8
Factory La. 15 Padiham BB12 145 C1
Factory La. Penwortham PR1 95 F3
Factory St. BL0 49 C7
Fair Hill. BB4 67 A7
Fair Oak Cl. PR2 117 F3
Fair View. OL13 70 C8
Fair View Cres. OL13 87 B3
Fair View Rd. BB11 127 B5
Fair Way. FY6 174 C7
Fairacres. WN6 28 B1
Fairbairn Ave. BB12 126 C8
Fairbairn St. BL6 31 B3
Fairbank. LA6 238 B2
Fairbank Gr. LA4 212 D3
Fairburn. WN8 18 B3
Fairclough Rd. Accrington BB5 . 103 A3
Fairclough Rd. Thornton FY5 173 A3
Fairfax Ave. FY2 150 E5
Fairfax Cl. PR3 178 D6
Fairfax Pl. PR5 96 D2
Fairfax Rd. PR2 117 E4
Fairfield. PR3 178 C8
Fairfield Ave. Newchurch BB4 85 F2
Fairfield Ave. Normoss FY3 130 B7
Fairfield Ave. Poulton-le-F FY6 . 151 D3
Fairfield Cl. Carnforth LA5 217 E1
Fairfield Cl. Clitheroe BB7 164 C7
Fairfield Cl. Lancaster LA1 210 E8
Fairfield Cl. 2 Ormskirk L39 15 E7
Fairfield Ct. FY7 193 F2
Fairfield Dr. Brierfield BB10 147 C3
Fairfield Dr. Bury BL9 32 D3
Fairfield Dr. Clitheroe BB7 164 C7
Fairfield Dr. 1 Ormskirk L39 15 E7
Fairfield Dr. Preston PR2 116 B2
Fairfield General Hospl. BL9 32 E4
Fairfield Gr. LA3 212 B2
Fairfield Prim Sch. BL9 32 D3
Fairfield Rd. Ainsdale PR8 20 C5
Fairfield Rd. Blackpool FY1 129 C8
Fairfield Rd. Fulwood PR2 117 A4
Fairfield Rd. Lancaster LA1 210 E8
Fairfield Rd. Leyland PR5 58 F8
Fairfield Rd. Morecambe LA3 212 B2
Fairfield Rd. Nelson BB9 148 B8
Fairfield Rd. Poulton-le-F FY6 130 F7
Fairfield St. Accrington BB5 102 F4
Fairfield St. Bamber Bridge PR5 .. 76 B7
Fairfields Dr. BB3 80 F6
Fairgarth Dr. LA6 238 B2
Fairham Ave. PR1 95 D2
Fairhaven. WN8 18 C3
Fairhaven Ave. FY7 172 D7
Fairhaven Cl. FY5 173 D1
Fairhaven Golf Course. FY8 89 E6
Fairhaven La. FY8 88 E5
Fairhaven Rd. Blackburn BB2 100 F1
Fairhaven Rd. Leyland PR5 75 D1
Fairhaven Rd.
Lytham St Anne's FY8 88 F5
Fairhaven Rd. Penwortham PR1 . 95 E5
Fairhaven Rd. Southport PR9 53 B4
Fairhaven Way. LA4 212 G5
Fairheath Rd. LA2 233 B4
Fairhill Terr. BB4 67 A7
Fairholme Rd. BB11 127 B3
Fairholmes Cl. FY5 173 B3
Fairholmes Way. FY5 173 B3
Fairhope Ave. Lancaster LA1 213 E3
Fairhope Ave. Morecambe LA4 . 213 B6
Fairhope Ct. BB2 100 C6
Fairhurst Ave. WN6 28 D3
Fairhurst Ct. FY5 172 D3
Fairhurst St. FY1 129 C6
Fairhurst's Dr. WN8 26 B2
Fairlawn Rd. FY8 89 F3
Fairlea Ave. LA4 213 B6
Fairlie. WN8 18 C3
Fairlie Cty Prim Sch. WN8 18 C3
Fairmont Dr. FY6 174 D2
Fairsnape Ave. PR3 139 B7
Fairsnape Dr. PR3 178 B6
Fairsnape Rd. FY8 90 D4
Fairstead. WN8 18 C3
Fairthorn Wlk. 9 L33 1 A3
Fairview. Kirkby Lonsdale LA6 238 B3
Fairview. Rawtenstall BB4 84 F5
Fairview Ave. FY8 89 A7
Fairview Cl. PR4 73 F5
Fairway. Chorley PR7 60 C2
Fairway. Fleetwood FY7 193 C1
Fairway. Penwortham PR1 95 B6
Fairway. Poulton-le-F FY6 151 A2
Fairway. Southport PR9 52 C2
Fairway. Wallbank OL12 51 C7
Fairway Gdns. FY6 194 D5
Fairway Rd. FY4 109 E8
Fairways. Fulwood PR2 117 A6
Fairways. Horwich BL6 31 C3
Fairways. Lytham St Anne's FY8 .. 89 A6
Fairways Ave. PR3 136 C3
Fairways Ct. Formby L37 11 C5
Fairways Ct. Wilpshire BB1 121 F5
Fairways Dr. BB11 126 E2
Fairways The. WN8 18 C3
Fairweather Ct. BB12 145 D1
Fairwinds Ave. PR4 72 D4
Falcon Ave. BB3 80 E3
Falcon Cl. Blackburn BB1 100 D8
Falcon Cl. Bury BL9 32 B4
Falcon Ct. BB5 123 F2
Falcon Dr. FY6 151 B2
Falcon St. PR1 117 B2
Falinge Fold. OL12 51 D1
Falinge Park High Sch. OL12 ... 51 D1
Falinge Rd. OL12 51 E1
Falkirk Ave. FY2 150 C6
Falkland. WN8 18 C3
Falkland Ave. FY4 129 F2
Falkland Rd. PR8 34 D5
Falkland St. PR1 95 F7
Fall Barn Rd. BB4 85 B2
Fall Birch Hospl. BL6 31 F1
Fall Kirk. LA2 234 F1
Fallbarn Cres. BB4 85 A1
Fallbarn Rd. BB4 85 B2
Fallowfield Cl. PR4 112 E6
Fallowfield Dr. Burnley BB12 ... 126 D8
Fallowfield Dr.
Falinge Fold OL12 51 D2
Fallowfield Rd. FY8 89 C6
Falmouth Ave. Fleetwood FY7 ... 172 C8
Falmouth Ave. Haslingden BB4 ... 84 C2
Falmouth Rd. FY1 129 C2
Falshaw Dr. BL9 49 E1
Falstone Ave. BL0 49 C4
Falstone Rd. L33 1 A4
Far Croft. PR5 96 A1
Far East View. 8 BB8 200 B2
Far Field. PR1 95 D3
Far Moor La. LA1 211 C8
Far Nook. PR6 60 B7
Faraday Ave. BB7 164 D8
Faraday Dr. PR2 117 C7
Faraday St. BB12 126 D7
Farholme La. OL13 69 D8
Faringdon Ave. FY4 109 E5
Farington Ave. PR5 58 D7
Farington Cty Prim Sch. PR5 ... 76 B3
Farington Rd. PR5 76 A6
Farington St Paul's CE
Prim Sch. PR5 75 F7
Farleton Cl. LA5 217 C5
Farleton Ct. LA1 213 F4
Farleton Old Rd. LA2 232 A5
Farley La. WN8 19 A3
Farm Ave. Adlington PR6 30 A8
Farm Ave. Bacup OL13 86 F4
Farm Cl. Southport PR9 35 A8
Farm Cl. Thornton FY5 173 B2
Farm House Cl. BB1 101 C4
Farm Meadow Rd. WN5 10 E5
Farmdale Dr. L31 5 E1
Farmdale Rd. LA1 211 B5
Farmend Cl. PR4 74 B8
Farmer's Row. BB2 80 B7
Farnborough Rd. PR8 20 F8
Farnborough Road
Inf & Jun Sch. PR8 21 A8
Farnell Pl. FY4 109 D6
Farnham Way. FY6 151 C5
Farnlea Dr. LA4 213 A5
Farnworth Rd. FY5 173 D1
Farrer St. BB9 147 C7
Farrier Rd. L33 1 A2
Farringdon Cl. PR1 117 F1
Farringdon Cres. PR1 117 F1
Farringdon La. PR2 117 F3
Farringdon Pl. PR1 117 F1
Farrington Cl. BB11 126 C3
Farrington Ct. BB11 126 C3
Farrington Dr. L39 15 E6
Farrington Pl. BB11 126 C3
Farrington Rd. BB11 126 B3
Farrington St. PR7 42 C8
Farthings The. PR7 59 F1
Faulkner Cl. PR8 20 C6
Faulkner Gdns. PR8 20 C6
Faulkner's La. PR3 204 B1
Faverdale Rd. BB8 170 A5
Fawcett. WN8 18 B3
Fawcett Cl. BB2 100 D3
Fawcett Rd. L31 5 D3
Fayles Gr. FY4 130 A1
Fazackerley St. PR1 116 C1
Fazakerley St. 10 PR6 & PR7 42 C8
Fearnhead Ave. BL6 31 B5
Fearns Cty High Sch. OL13 86 A1
Fearns Moss. BB4 & OL13 86 A1
Fecit La. BL0 & OL12 50 C8
Fecitt Brow. BB1 101 D4
Fecitt Rd. BB2 100 B6
Federation St. BB8 200 A3
Feilden Pl. BB2 79 D8
Feilden St. BB2 100 D5
Felgate Brow. FY3 129 E5
Felix St. BB11 127 B7
Fell Brow. PR3 139 B7
Fell Cl. 2 PR5 76 F8
Fell Rd. High Casterton LA6 238 F3
Fell Rd. Morecambe LA4 213 B4
Fell Rd. Waddington BB7 186 A6
Fell View. Brierfield BB10 147 D3
Fell View. Caton LA2 231 C3
Fell View. Chorley PR7 42 E6
Fell View. Garstang PR3 178 C8
Fell View. Grimsargh PR2 138 C2
Fell View. West Bradford BB7 ... 186 D7
Fell View Cl. PR3 178 C8
Fell Way. FY6 174 D7
Fellborough Lodge. FY8 89 A8
Fellery St. PR6 42 C8
Fellgate. LA3 213 A2
Fellside Cl. BL8 48 F1
Fellside View. LA3 208 F7
Fellstone Vale. PR6 79 A1
Fellstone View. PR6 79 A1
Fellview. PR9 53 D6
Fellway Cl. 4 PR5 76 C8
Felstead. WN8 18 B2
Felstead St. PR1 96 D8
Felton Way. PR4 73 F3
Feltons. WN8 18 B2
Fenber Ave. FY4 109 C7
Fengrove. PR4 74 A8
Feniscliffe Dr. BB2 100 A2
Feniscowles Prim Sch. BB2 79 D8
Fenney Ct. WN8 18 C1
Fennyfold Terr. BB12 125 C6
Fensway. PR4 94 D2
Fenton Ave. BB8 200 D3
Fenton Rd. Blackpool FY1 129 C6
Fenton Rd. Fulwood PR2 117 C4
Fenton St. LA1 210 E8
Fenwick St. BB11 126 D3
Ferguson Rd. FY1 129 E2
Ferguson St. BB2 80 D7
Fermor Rd. Becconsall PR4 72 E1
Fermor Rd. Preston PR1 117 E1
Fern Ave. BB5 102 F3
Fern Bank. Chorley PR6 60 D3
Fern Bank. Lancaster LA1 211 A5
Fern Bank. Maghull L31 5 E1
Fern Bank Ave. BB8 200 A3
Fern Breck Cotts. FY6 195 A2
Fern Cl. Bamber Bridge PR5 76 B8
Fern Cl. Skelmersdale WN8 17 E1
Fern Croft. LA6 238 E4
Fern Ct. FY7 193 C1
Fern Dene. OL12 51 B2
Fern Gore Ave. BB5 103 A3
Fern Gr. FY1 129 C3
Fern Hill La. OL12 51 A3
Fern Isle Cl. OL12 51 B6
Fern Lea St. BB4 68 D8
Fern Meadow. PR6 77 C2
Fern Rd. BB11 126 E4
Fern St. Bacup OL13 86 F3
Fern St. Colne BB8 169 F6
Fern St. Newchurch BB4 85 F1
Fern St. Ramsbottom BL0 49 D7
Fern Terr. BB4 84 A3
Fernbank. BB9 147 E7
Ferncliffe Dr. LA3 212 A2
Ferndale. Blackburn BB1 101 A6
Ferndale. Skelmersdale WN8 18 C2
Ferndale Ave. FY4 109 D7
Ferndale Cl. Freckleton PR4 92 D7
Ferndale Cl. Leyland PR5 59 B7
Ferndale Cl. Thornton FY5 173 C2
Ferndale St. BB10 127 C8
Ferngrove. BL9 32 B5
Fernhill Ave. OL13 69 E8
Fernhill Cl. OL13 69 E8
Fernhill Cres. OL13 86 E1
Fernhill Dr. OL13 69 E8
Fernhill Gr. 1 OL13 69 E8
Fernhill Pk. OL13 69 E8
Fernhill Way. 3 OL13 69 E8
Fernhills. BL7 46 E2
Fernhurst Ave. FY4 129 D1
Fernhurst Gate. L39 15 B1
Fernhurst St. BB2 80 D8
Fernlea Ave. Barnoldswick BB8 . 200 B2
Fernlea Ave. Oswaldtwistle BB5 103 A3
Fernlea Cl. Blackburn BB2 80 B8
Fernlea Cl. Caldershaw OL12 51 B2
Fernlea Dr. BB5 123 F4
Fernleigh. PR5 58 A8
Fernleigh Cl. FY2 150 D4
Fernley Rd. PR8 34 A5
Ferns The. Bacup OL13 87 A1
Ferns The. Bamber Bridge PR5 ... 96 C3
Ferns The. Preston PR1 116 C2
Fernside Way. OL12 51 A1
Fernview Dr. BL0 49 B1
Fernville Terr. 6 OL13 69 D8
Fernwood Ave. FY5 151 B8
Fernwood Cl. FY8 89 E4
Ferny Knoll Rd. WA11 8 F4
Fernyhalgh Ct. PR2 117 D6
Fernyhalgh Gdns. PR2 117 D6
Fernyhalgh La. PR2 117 D7
Fernyhalgh Pl. PR2 117 D6
Ferrier Bank. PR4 91 D5
Ferrier Cl. 1 BB1 101 C5
Ferry Side La. PR9 53 C5
Ffrances Pas. 30 LA1 210 F8
Fiddler's La. Chipping PR3 181 F4
Fiddler's La. Clayton Green PR6 .. 77 B2
Fidler La. PR5 75 F5
Field Rd. LA3 208 D6
Field St. Blackburn BB2 100 B2
Field St. Blackpool FY1 129 C2
Field St. Padiham BB12 125 C7
Field St. Skelmersdale WN8 17 D2
Field Top. OL13 87 A7
Fielden St. Burnley BB11 126 D5
Fielden St. Chorley PR6 42 E8
Fielden St. Leyland PR5 75 D1
Fieldfare Cl. FY5 173 A5
Fieldhouse Ave. FY5 173 D2
Fieldhouse Ind Est. OL12 51 F2
Fieldhouse Rd. OL12 51 F2
Fielding Cres. BB2 100 A1
Fielding La. Great Harwood BB6 123 B5
Fielding La. Oswaldtwistle BB5 . 102 E3
Fielding Pl. PR6 30 B8
Fielding Rd. FY1 129 D8
Fielding St. BB1 123 C1
Fields End. BB6 122 C8
Fields Rd. BB4 84 C1
Fields The. PR7 40 B7
Fieldsend. LA3 209 A7
Fieldside Ave. PR7 59 C1
Fieldside Cl. PR5 96 C3
Fieldway. FY8 109 E2
Fife Cl. PR7 42 E6
Fife St. Accrington BB5 103 A4
Fife St. Barrowford BB9 168 C1
Fifth Ave. Blackpool FY4 109 C7
Fifth Ave. Burnley BB10 147 B3
Fifth Ave. Bury BL9 32 D4
Filberts Cl. PR2 116 C3
Filberts The. PR2 116 C3
File St. PR7 42 C7
Filey Pl. Blackpool FY1 129 B6
Filey Pl. Fulwood PR2 116 A4
Filey Rd. FY8 110 A1
Filton Gr. LA3 213 A3
Finch Cl. BB1 100 E6
Finch La. WN6 27 B1
Finch Mill Ave. WN6 19 D7
Finch St. 5 BB3 80 F2
Finches The. FY6 151 B2
Finchley Rd. FY1 129 B8
Fine Jane's Way. PR9 35 B8
Finnington La. BB2 79 A6
Finsbury Ave. Blackpool FY1 129 D2
Finsbury Ave.
Lytham St Anne's FY8 89 B4
Finsbury Pl. BB2 80 D8
Finsley Gate. BB11 127 A5
Finsley St. BB10 147 E3
Fir Cl. FY7 193 C2
Fir Cotes. L31 5 E1
Fir Ct. BB5 103 E8
Fir Gr. Blackpool FY1 129 E2
Fir Gr. Warton PR4 91 D6
Fir Grove Rd. BB11 127 B4
Fir St. Blackburn BB1 100 F7
Fir St. Burnley BB10 127 B5
Fir St. Bury BL9 32 A2
Fir St. Haslingden BB4 84 B3
Fir St. Nelson BB9 147 F8
Fir St. Ramsbottom BL0 49 D7
Fir St. Southport PR8 34 F6
Fir Tree Ave. PR2 116 B4
Fir Tree Cl. Hest Bank LA5 215 F2
Fir Tree Cl. Much Hoole PR4 73 E3
Fir Tree Cl. Skelmersdale WN8 9 D7
Fir Tree La. L39 14 F3
Fir Tree Pl. FY5 150 F8
Fir Tree Way. 3 BL6 31 E1
Fir Trees Ave.
Bamber Bridge PR5 76 A8
Fir Trees Ave. Fulwood PR2 118 A4
Fir Trees Cres. 1 PR5 76 A8
Fir Trees Gr. BB12 145 E5
Fir Trees La. BB12 145 E5
Fir Trees Pl. PR2 117 F4
Fir Trees Rd. PR5 96 A1
Firbank. PR7 59 C2
Firbank Ave. PR4 56 A7
Firbank Rd. LA1 214 A1
Firbeck. WN8 18 C1
Fircroft. WN6 28 A2
Firfield Cl. PR4 112 E5
Firs Cl. L37 11 D5
Firs Cres. L37 11 D5
Firs La. L39 14 E3
Firs Link. L37 11 D4
Firshill Cl. FY5 151 B8
First Ave. Blackpool FY4 109 C7
First Ave. Church BB5 103 A8
First Ave. Clifton PR4 114 C1
First Ave. Poulton-le-F FY6 151 E3
First Ave. Preston PR2 116 A2
First Ave. Wrea Green PR4 112 B4
First Terr. LA3 205 B5
Firswood Cl. FY8 89 E4
Firswood Rd. L40 & WN8 17 C3
Firtree Cl. Blackburn BB2 79 F8
Firtree Cl. Chorley PR7 42 C3
Firwood. WN8 18 D3
Firwood La. PR5 98 B5
Fish House La. PR3 182 B5
Fish La. L40 37 B2
Fish Rake La. BL0 67 E6
Fisher Dr. Orrell WN5 10 E7
Fisher Dr. Southport PR9 34 F7
Fisher St. FY1 129 C6
Fisher's La. FY4 110 A5
Fishergate. PR0 & PR1 95 F7
Fishergate Ctr. PR1 95 F7
Fishergate Hill. PR1 95 E6
Fishergate Wlk. 7 PR4 95 F7
Fishermans Cl. L37 11 E6
Fishmoor Dr. BB2 & BB3 80 F8
Fishwick Cty Prim Sch. PR1 117 E1
Fishwick Hall Golf Course.
PR1 96 F8
Fishwick La. PR6 78 B1
Fishwick Par. PR1 96 D8
Fishwick Rd. PR1 96 C8
Fishwick View. PR1 96 D8
Fitchfield. PR1 95 F2
Fitzgerald St. PR1 117 C1
Fitzroy Rd. FY2 150 D3
Fitzroy St. PR1 95 E7
Five Acres. PR5 75 E4
Five Lane Ends.
Hampson Green LA2 204 D8
Five Lane Ends. Preesall FY6 195 A2
Five Lane Ends. Singleton FY6 . 152 D4
Flag La. Bamber Bridge PR5 95 F1
Flag La. Bretherton PR5 57 A5
Flag La. Limbrick PR7 42 F5
Flag La.
Runshaw Moor PR5 & PR7 58 D4
Flag St. OL13 69 E8
Flakefleet Ave. FY7 193 E1
Flakefleet Cty Sch. FY7 193 E2
Flamstead. WN8 18 C1
Flare Rd. LA3 208 D6
Flash La. L40 38 B4
Flat La. LA5 219 E3
Flatfield Way. L31 5 E1
Flatman's La. L39 13 E1
Flats Ret Pk The. PR1 & PR5 96 C5
Flats The. PR4 113 B4
Flax Cl. BB4 67 A8
Flax La. L40 24 F2
Flax Moss Cl. BB4 67 A8
Flax St. 8 BL0 49 A4
Flaxfield Rd. L37 12 A3
Flaxfield Way. PR4 113 A5
Flaxton. WN8 18 C1
Fleet La. LA2 232 A8
Fleet St. Blackpool FY1 129 C4
Fleet St. Chorley PR7 42 C7
Fleet St. Horwich BL6 31 D3
Fleet St. Longridge PR3 139 A7
Fleet St. Lytham St Anne's FY8 88 D8
Fleet St. Nelson BB9 168 E1
Fleet St. 3 Preston PR1 95 F7
Fleet Street La. PR3 140 A6
Fleet Wlk. 5 BB11 127 A6
Fleetgreen. LA1 213 E3
Fleetwood Cl. Blackburn BB2 100 F1
Fleetwood Cl. Southport PR9 52 F3
Fleetwood Cres. PR9 54 A6
Fleetwood Dr. PR9 54 A6
Fleetwood High Sch. FY7 193 D2
Fleetwood High Sch
Beach Rd Site. FY7 193 E3
Fleetwood Hospl. FY7 194 B5
Fleetwood Old Rd. PR4 132 E3
Fleetwood Rd. Blackpool FY5 150 D7
Fleetwood Rd. Burnley BB10 147 C2
Fleetwood Rd. Carleton FY6 151 B5
Fleetwood Rd. Esprick PR4 132 D5
Fleetwood Rd. Fleetwood FY7 .. 193 E1

Graver Weir Terr. BB4 ... 106 A1
Graving Dock Rd. FY8 ... 90 D4
Grayrigg Dr. LA4 ... 212 E3
Grays Pl. LA3 ... 212 B2
Great Arley Sch. FY5 ... 173 B3
Great Avenham St. PR1 ... 96 A6
Great Bolton St. BB2 ... 100 E3
Great Close La. BD23 ... 230 D6
Great Eaves Rd. BL0 ... 49 C7
Great Flatt. OL12 ... 51 B1
Great George St. Colne BB8 ... 169 D5
Great George St. Preston PR1 ... 117 A1
Great Gill. PR4 ... 74 A5
Great Greens La. PR5 ... 77 C5
Great Hanover St. PR1 ... 117 A1
Great Harwood Cty Prim Sch. BB6 ... 123 C5
Great Harwood Golf Course. BB6 ... 123 F7
Great Hey. PR4 ... 73 D3
Great John St. 20 LA1 ... 210 F8
Great Lee. OL12 ... 51 D3
Great Lee Wlk. OL12 ... 51 D2
Great Meadow. Bamber Bridge PR5 ... 76 A8
Great Meadow. Chorley PR7 ... 60 A2
Great Shaw St. PR1 ... 95 F8
Great Stone of Fourstones. LA2 ... 233 D5
Great Stones Cl. BL7 ... 46 F2
Great Townley St. PR1 ... 96 D8
Great Tunstead. PR4 ... 74 A7
Great Wood Cty Prim Sch. LA4 ... 213 A5
Greave Cl. BB4 ... 85 A4
Greave Clough Cl. 9 OL13 ... 87 A3
Greave Clough Dr. OL13 ... 87 B3
Greave Cres. 10 OL13 ... 87 A3
Greave Rd. OL13 ... 87 B3
Greave Terr. OL13 ... 87 B3
Greaves Cl. WN6 ... 19 F8
Greaves Dr. LA1 ... 210 F6
Greaves Hall Hosp. PR9 ... 54 B5
Greaves Meadow. PR1 ... 95 E2
Greaves Rd. LA1 ... 210 F6
Greaves St. Great Harwood BB6 123 C4
Greaves St. Haslingden BB4 ... 83 F2
Greaves St. 9 Preston PR1 ... 96 A7
Greaves-Town La. PR2 ... 115 E1
Grebe Cl. FY3 ... 130 B7
Green Acre. PR3 ... 137 D6
Green Acres. PR4 ... 92 C7
Green Ave. FY4 ... 109 C6
Green Bank. Bacup OL13 ... 69 D8
Green Bank. Barnoldswick BB8 200 D4
Green Bank Ind Est. BB1 ... 101 C7
Green Bridge N. BB4 ... 68 E7
Green Bridge S. BB4 ... 68 E7
Green Brook Cl. BL9 ... 32 A4
Green Cl. BB11 ... 126 E2
Green Close Pk. BB2 ... 100 C2
Green Dick's La. PR3 ... 195 E5
Green Dr. Bamber Bridge PR5 ... 96 C1
Green Dr. Barton PR3 ... 136 B8
Green Dr. Cleveleys FY5 ... 172 C5
Green Dr. Clitheroe BB7 ... 187 A2
Green Dr. Fulwood PR2 ... 116 E7
Green Dr. Lytham St Anne's FY8 ... 89 F5
Green Dr. Penwortham PR1 ... 95 B5
Green Dr. Poulton-le-F FY6 ... 130 E8
Green Dr. Saltcotes FY8 ... 90 C5
Green Drive Golf Course. FY8 . 90 B5
Green End. BB2 ... 98 E7
Green End Ave. BB8 ... 201 B2
Green End Cl. 11 OL13 ... 87 A3
Green End Rd. BB8 ... 201 B1
Green Gate. Fulwood PR2 ... 116 C3
Green Gate. Hutton PR4 ... 94 C1
Green Haworth CE Prim Sch. BB5 ... 103 B1
Green Haworth Golf Course. BB5 ... 103 B1
Green Hey. Lytham St Anne's FY8 90 D4
Green Hey. Much Hoole PR4 ... 73 E3
Green Heys Dr. L31 ... 5 F1
Green Hill. OL13 ... 87 A1
Green Hill La. LA2 & LA6 ... 231 B6
Green Hill Rd. OL13 ... 87 A1
Green Howarth View. BB5 ... 103 A3
Green La. Banks PR9 ... 54 C4
Green La. Bilsborrow PR3 ... 157 B2
Green La. Bispham Green L40 ... 26 B7
Green La. Blackburn BB2 ... 100 A1
Green La. Bretherton PR4 & PR5 .. 57 C7
Green La. Chipping PR3 ... 182 F3
Green La. Coppull PR7 ... 29 A8
Green La. Downham BB7 ... 188 B6
Green La. Ellel LA1 & LA2 ... 207 B6
Green La. Farington PR5 ... 75 E7
Green La. Formby L37 ... 11 F5
Green La. Freckleton PR4 ... 92 C6
Green La. Garstang PR3 ... 178 A7
Green La. Grindleton BB7 ... 187 A7
Green La. Halton Green LA2 ... 231 A4
Green La. Holmes PR4 ... 55 C4
Green La. Horton BD23 ... 225 E5
Green La. Horwich BL6 ... 31 B5
Green La. Lancaster LA1 & LA2 .. 214 A6
Green La. Longridge PR3 ... 139 B8
Green La. Maghull L31 ... 5 A2
Green La. Maghull L31 ... 5 C1
Green La. Morecambe LA3 ... 212 E2
Green La. New Gate PR4 ... 95 C1
Green La. Ormskirk L39 ... 15 E6
Green La. Orrell WN5 ... 10 D3
Green La. Padiham BB12 ... 125 C8
Green La. Preesall FY6 ... 195 C2
Green La. Riley Green PR5 ... 78 E8
Green La. Samlesbury Bottoms PR5 ... 98 B7
Green La. Skelmersdale L40 ... 18 A6
Green La. Sollom PR4 ... 55 D1
Green La. Standish WN6 ... 28 D1
Green La. Storth LA7 ... 237 E5
Green La. Woodsfold PR4 ... 134 E6
Green La E. PR3 ... 199 C2
Green La W. Freckleton PR4 ... 92 B5
Green La W. Garstang PR3 ... 199 B1
Green Lane Ave. L39 ... 15 E6
Green Link. L31 ... 5 B2
Green Meadow. BB8 ... 170 B2
Green Meadow La. FY6 ... 174 C1
Green Moor La. PR3 ... 140 B7
Green Mount. BB6 ... 143 D8
Green Nook La. PR3 ... 138 F6
Green Oak Pl. FY5 ... 151 A8
Green Park Dr. L31 ... 5 B1
Green Park Prim Sch. L31 ... 5 B2
Green Pk. BB7 ... 143 C5
Green Pl. PR5 ... 77 A6
Green Rd. BB8 ... 169 D4
Green Row. BB3 ... 80 B6
Green Side. LA6 ... 238 C1
Green Sq. LA6 ... 238 C1
Green St. Adlington PR6 ... 30 B8
Green St. Barnoldswick BB8 ... 200 B2
Green St. Burnley BB10 ... 147 B1
Green St. Chorley PR7 ... 42 A5
Green St. Darwen BB3 ... 81 A1
Green St. Edenfield BL0 ... 67 E3
Green St. Great Harwood BB6 ... 123 B5
Green St. Lancaster LA1 ... 214 A1
Green St. Lytham St Anne's FY8 ... 90 A3
Green St. Morecambe LA4 ... 212 E6
Green St. Oswaldtwistle BB5 ... 102 C2
Green St. Padiham BB12 ... 125 C7
Green St. Rawtenstall BB4 ... 85 A3
Green St E. 16 BB3 ... 81 A1
Green The. Adlington PR6 ... 42 F2
Green The. Bispham Green L40 ... 26 B8
Green The. Churchtown PR3 ... 178 A2
Green The. 5 Darwen BB3 ... 81 A1
Green The. Eccleston PR7 ... 40 C6
Green The. Fulwood PR1 & PR2 . 117 F2
Green The. Hesketh Bank PR4 ... 72 E3
Green The. Nelson BB9 ... 169 B2
Green The. Parbold WN8 ... 26 B2
Green The. Ramsbottom BL8 ... 48 F1
Green The. Silverdale LA5 ... 218 D2
Green The. Weeton PR4 ... 131 F2
Green Way. FY4 ... 109 F7
Green Wlk. Ainsdale PR8 ... 20 D5
Green Wlk. Earby BB8 ... 201 A1
Green's La. Downholland Cross L31 & L39 ... 14 C1
Green's La. Stalmine FY6 ... 174 F7
Greenacre. Blackburn BB3 ... 80 F6
Greenacre. Westhead L40 ... 16 E4
Greenacre Cl. BL0 ... 49 E7
Greenacre Ct. LA1 & LA2 ... 211 B3
Greenacre Pk. LA5 ... 215 E2
Greenacre Rd. LA2 & LA5 ... 215 E2
Greenacre St. BB7 ... 164 E7
Greenacres. Edgworth BL7 ... 47 E6
Greenacres. Fulwood PR2 ... 116 B7
Greenacres. Read BB12 ... 144 D2
Greenacres Ave. PR4 ... 113 A4
Greenacres Dr. PR3 ... 178 D6
Greenacres The. PR4 ... 94 D2
Greenbank. Broadley OL12 ... 51 C5
Greenbank. Horwich BL6 ... 31 D1
Greenbank. Poulton-le-F FY6 ... 151 E3
Greenbank Ave. Maghull L31 ... 5 C3
Greenbank Ave. Orrell WN5 ... 10 D3
Greenbank Ave. Preston PR1 .. 116 D2
Greenbank Ave. Storth LA7 ... 237 E4
Greenbank Dr. Fence BB12 ... 146 E8
Greenbank Dr. Southport PR8 ... 33 E2
Greenbank High Sch. PR8 ... 33 E1
Greenbank Pk. BB4 ... 85 B2
Greenbank Pl. PR1 ... 116 E1
Greenbank Rd. Blackburn BB1 .. 101 B6
Greenbank Rd. Penwortham PR1 95 E4
Greenbank Rd. Rochdale OL12 ... 51 F2
Greenbank Sch. OL12 ... 51 F1
Greenbank St. Preston PR1 ... 116 D2
Greenbank St. Preston PR1 ... 116 E1
Greenbank St. Rawtenstall BB4 .. 85 B2
Greenbank Terr. BB3 ... 80 F6
Greenbanks. FY2 ... 150 F3
Greenbarn Way. BL6 ... 30 D1
Greenber La. LA6 ... 238 F5
Greenberfield La. BB8 ... 200 C4
Greenbrook Cl. BB12 ... 125 F6
Greenbrook Rd. BB12 ... 125 F6
Greenbrook St. 6 BL9 ... 32 A4
Greencliffe La. BB10 ... 128 A1
Greencroft. PR1 ... 95 D3
Greendale Ave. BB4 ... 85 E2
Greendale Cl. Fleetwood FY7 ... 193 C2
Greendale Cl. Over Town BB10 . 107 A7
Greendale Dr. LA5 ... 217 D3
Greendale Mews. PR2 ... 115 E2
Greenfield. PR4 ... 72 D4
Greenfield Ave. Chatburn BB7 . 187 D5
Greenfield Ave. Clitheroe BB7 ... 164 C8
Greenfield Ave. Parbold WN8 ... 26 B2
Greenfield Cl. Fleetwood FY7 ... 193 F2
Greenfield Cl. Southport PR9 ... 53 A3
Greenfield Ct. 2 LA1 ... 211 A7
Greenfield Dr. PR5 ... 76 A8
Greenfield Gdns. 1 BB4 ... 84 B2
Greenfield Rd. Adlington PR6 ... 30 A8
Greenfield Rd. Burnley BB10 ... 127 D4
Greenfield Rd. Chorley PR6 ... 42 E8
Greenfield Rd. Cleveleys FY5 ... 150 E8
Greenfield Rd. Colne BB8 ... 169 B4
Greenfield Rd. Fleetwood FY7 . 193 F2
Greenfield Rd. Nelson BB8 ... 169 A4
Greenfield St. Darwen BB3 ... 64 C6
Greenfield St. Haslingden BB4 ... 84 B3
Greenfield St. 12 Lancaster LA1 ... 211 A8
Greenfield St. Rawtenstall BB4 ... 85 A3
Greenfield Terr. Cornholme OL14 ... 108 A1
Greenfield Terr. Oswaldtwistle BB5 ... 102 A1
Greenfield View. BB3 ... 81 A7
Greenfield Way. PR2 ... 116 B5
Greenfields. LA2 ... 231 C3
Greenfields Cres. PR4 ... 112 E6
Greenfinch Ct. FY3 ... 130 B6
Greenfold Dr. BB4 ... 105 A2
Greenfoot La. LA2 ... 233 B8
Greenford Cl. WN5 ... 10 D6
Greenford Rd. PR8 ... 20 C4
Greengate Cl. BB12 ... 126 D7
Greengate La. LA5 ... 216 C8
Greenhalgh La. Adlington PR6 ... 30 B8
Greenhalgh La. Greenhalgh PR4 ... 132 D4
Greenhall Cl. PR3 ... 178 D6
Greenhaven. WN8 ... 10 B7
Greenhead Ave. BB1 ... 101 B7
Greenhead La. BB12 ... 146 D5
Greenhey Pl. WN8 ... 8 F8
Greenheys Ave. FY6 ... 151 B4
Greenheys Cres. BL8 ... 48 F1
Greenhill. BB6 ... 123 B5
Greenhill Ave. PR4 ... 113 A6
Greenhill Pl. FY1 ... 129 C6
Greenholme Ave. LA4 ... 212 E3
Greenhurst Cl. BB2 ... 100 D4
Greenings La. PR9 ... 36 C3
Greenland Ave. WN6 ... 28 E1
Greenland La. PR6 ... 30 D5
Greenlands Cres. PR2 ... 117 E3
Greenlands Cty Prim Sch. PR2 ... 117 E3
Greenlands High Sch. FY2 ... 150 E2
Greenlea Cl. WN5 ... 10 D5
Greenlea Dr. LA4 ... 212 G5
Greenloon's Dr. L37 ... 11 C3
Greenloon's Wlk. L37 ... 11 C2
Greenmead Cl. PR4 ... 115 E5
Greenmount Ave. Kirkham PR4 113 A5
Greenmount Ave. 1 Thornton FY5 ... 173 A3
Greenmount Cl. BL8 ... 48 F2
Greenmount Dr. BL8 ... 48 F2
Greenmount Golf Course. BL8 ... 48 E1
Greenmount Prim Sch. BL8 ... 48 F2
Greenock Cl. BB11 ... 126 D4
Greenock Dr. OL10 ... 32 F1
Greenock St. BB11 ... 126 D4
Greenpark Cl. BL8 ... 48 F1
Greens Arms Rd. BL7 ... 46 E7
Greens La. Bacup OL13 ... 69 D7
Greens La. Bacup OL13 ... 87 A3
Greens La. Haslingden BB4 ... 67 C7
Greens The. OL12 ... 70 C1
Greenset Cl. LA1 ... 213 E4
Greenside. Euxton PR7 ... 59 C3
Greenside. Fulwood PR4 ... 115 D4
Greenside. Ribchester PR3 ... 140 E3
Greenside Ave. Blackburn BB2 ... 80 A8
Greenside Ave. Preston PR2 ... 115 C1
Greenside Cl. BL8 ... 48 B3
Greenside Dr. BL8 ... 48 F1
Greenside Gdns. PR5 ... 58 B7
Greenslate Ave. WN6 ... 19 E8
Greenslate Ct. WN5 ... 10 E3
Greenslate Rd. WN5 ... 10 E3
Greensnook La. OL13 ... 87 A3
Greensnook Mews. 5 OL13 ... 87 A3
Greensnook Terr. 1 OL13 ... 87 A3
Greenstone Ave. BL6 ... 31 B3
Greensward Cl. WN6 ... 28 B1
Greensway. PR3 ... 136 C3
Greenthorn Cres. PR1 ... 118 A2
Greenthorne Cl. BL7 ... 47 E7
Greenvale. WN6 ... 19 F4
Greenville Dr. L31 ... 5 C1
Greenway. Catterall PR3 ... 178 D3
Greenway. Eccleston PR7 ... 40 B7
Greenway. Fulwood PR2 ... 116 D7
Greenway. Horwich BL6 ... 31 F3
Greenway. Penwortham PR1 ... 95 B4
Greenway Ave. WN8 ... 9 B8
Greenway Cl. WN8 ... 17 E2
Greenway Mews. BL0 ... 49 C4
Greenway St. BB3 ... 80 F3
Greenways. Becconsall PR4 ... 72 F1
Greenways. Lytham St Anne's FY8 89 B6
Greenways. Orrell WN5 ... 10 D3
Greenways. Over Kellet LA6 ... 231 B8
Greenwich Dr. FY8 ... 89 D5
Greenwood. PR5 ... 77 B4
Greenwood Ave. Blackpool FY1 129 E2
Greenwood Ave. Hest Bank LA5 215 F2
Greenwood Ave. Horwich BL6 ... 31 D1
Greenwood Cl. Lytham St Anne's FY8 ... 89 E4
Greenwood Cl. Ormskirk L39 ... 15 C1
Greenwood Cres. LA5 ... 215 F2
Greenwood Dr. LA5 ... 215 F2
Greenwood La. BL6 ... 31 E1
Greenwood Rd. WN6 ... 28 E2
Greenwood St. Bamber Bridge PR5 ... 96 E1
Greenwood St. Preston PR1 ... 96 B7
Greetby Hill. L39 & L40 ... 16 A6
Gregareth Cl. 5 LA1 ... 213 C2
Gregory Ave. FY2 ... 150 C5
Gregory Fold. BB4 ... 67 A7
Gregory La. L39 ... 22 B3
Gregory Meadow. PR3 ... 178 B7
Gregory Pl. FY8 ... 90 A3
Gregory's Ct. LA1 ... 211 A4
Gregson Cl. FY4 ... 109 F7
Gregson Dr. 3 FY7 ... 193 F2
Gregson La. Blackburn BB2 ... 100 D5
Gregson La. Gregson Lane PR5 ... 97 E1
Gregson La. Higher Walton PR5 .. 97 C2
Gregson Rd. LA1 ... 211 A7
Gregson St. Darwen BB3 ... 64 A8
Gregson St. Lytham St Anne's FY8 ... 90 A3
Gregson Way. PR2 ... 117 B5
Gregson's Ave. L37 ... 11 E5
Grenfell Ave. FY3 ... 129 E7
Grenville Ave. Bamber Bridge PR5 ... 96 D2
Grenville Ave. Lytham St Anne's FY8 ... 109 E1
Gresham House. 4 BB11 ... 126 E5
Gresham Rd. FY5 ... 172 D1
Gresham St. BB4 ... 85 F1
Gresley Ct. LA1 ... 210 F6
Gresley Pl. FY2 ... 150 E2
Gressingham Dr. LA1 ... 211 A4
Gressingham House. 3 LA1 .. 211 A3
Greta Heath. LA6 ... 236 C3
Greta Pl. Fleetwood FY7 ... 193 D3
Greta Pl. Lancaster LA1 ... 213 E2
Gretdale Ave. FY8 ... 88 E8
Gretna Cres. FY5 ... 150 D8
Gretna Rd. BB1 ... 121 F1
Grey Heights View. PR6 ... 42 E8
Grey St. Barrowford BB9 ... 168 D3
Grey St. Burnley BB10 ... 127 A8
Greyfriars Ave. PR2 ... 116 D5
Greyfriars Cres. PR2 ... 116 D5
Greyfriars Dr. PR1 ... 95 C5
Greyfriars Rd. PR8 ... 20 B6
Greyhound Bridge Rd. LA1 ... 213 F1
Greymont Rd. BL9 ... 32 A6
Greystock Ave. PR2 ... 116 E6
Greystock Cl. PR5 ... 77 B8
Greystock Pl. PR2 ... 116 E6
Greystoke Ave. BB2 ... 79 E8
Greystoke Pl. FY4 ... 109 B5
Greystokes. L39 ... 15 D2
Greystokes Ct. FY4 ... 109 B5
Greystone Dr. BB12 ... 146 E8
Greystonegill La. LA2 ... 233 F7
Greystones. PR5 ... 75 B1
Greythwaite Ct. LA1 ... 210 D6
Greywood Ave. BL9 ... 32 B2
Griffin Cl. Accrington BB5 ... 124 F1
Griffin Cl. Burnley BB11 ... 126 B5
Griffin Cl. Bury BL9 ... 32 A4
Griffin Ct. BB2 ... 100 C2
Griffin Park Prim Sch. BB2 ... 100 B3
Griffin St. BB2 ... 100 B3
Griffiths Dr. PR9 ... 34 F8
Griffon House. PR9 ... 52 F2
Grime Row. BB5 ... 124 F2
Grime St. Chorley PR7 ... 42 D6
Grime St. Darwen BB3 ... 80 F2
Grime St. 7 Ramsbottom BL0 ... 49 A4
Grimeford La. BL6 & PR6 ... 30 C5
Grimeshaw La. LA2 ... 214 D3
Grimrod Pl. WN8 ... 9 A7
Grimsargh St. 10 PR1 ... 117 D1
Grimsargh St Michaels CE Sch. PR2 ... 138 C1
Grimshaw Green La. WN8 ... 26 C6
Grimshaw La. L39 ... 15 E7
Grimshaw Pk. BB2 ... 100 F3
Grimshaw Rd. WN8 ... 9 D8
Grimshaw St. Accrington BB5 ... 103 A5
Grimshaw St. 6 Barrowford BB9 ... 168 D4
Grimshaw St. Burnley BB11 ... 127 A5
Grimshaw St. 5 Church BB5 ... 102 E6
Grimshaw St. 2 Clayton-le-M BB5 ... 123 F2
Grimshaw St. Darwen BB3 ... 64 B7
Grimshaw St. Great Harwood BB6 ... 123 C5
Grimshaw St. Preston PR1 ... 96 A7
Grindlestone Ct. PR3 ... 137 E6
Grindlestone Hirst. BB8 ... 169 C3
Grindleton Brow. BB7 ... 187 B7
Grindleton CE Prim Sch. BB7 187 C8
Grindleton Cl. FY3 ... 130 B8
Grindleton Gr. BB10 ... 127 D5
Grindleton Hospl Alms Houses. BB7 ... 187 C8
Grindleton Rd. Blackburn BB2 ... 100 C4
Grindleton Rd. Grindleton BB7 . 187 A6
Gringley Rd. LA4 ... 212 F3
Grinstead Cl. PR8 ... 33 F1
Grisedale Ave. BB1 ... 101 C2
Grisedale Cl. L37 ... 11 E3
Grisedale Dr. BB12 ... 126 B8
Grisedale Pl. PR7 ... 42 B5
Grizedale Ave. Garstang PR3 ... 178 B7
Grizedale Ave. Poulton-le-F FY6 151 C3
Grizedale Cl. Clayton-le-M BB5 . 123 E2
Grizedale Cl. Fulwood PR2 ... 117 F2
Grizedale Cres. PR1 & PR2 & PR5 ... 118 A2
Grizedale Ct. FY3 ... 129 E5
Grizedale Pl. Fulwood PR2 ... 117 F2
Grizedale Pl. Morecambe LA3 ... 212 B1
Grizedale Rd. Blackpool FY4 ... 130 C1
Grizedale Rd. Lancaster LA1 ... 214 B2
Grosvenor Cl. PR8 ... 33 E3
Grosvenor Ct. Carnforth LA5 ... 217 C1
Grosvenor Ct. Cleveleys FY5 ... 172 C2
Grosvenor Ct. Lytham St Anne's FY8 ... 89 A8
Grosvenor Gdns. PR8 ... 33 F3
Grosvenor Lodge. BB1 ... 121 F6
Grosvenor Pl. Carnforth LA5 ... 217 C1
Grosvenor Pl. Preston PR1 & PR2 ... 116 B2
Grosvenor Pl. Southport PR8 ... 33 F3
Grosvenor Rd. Carnforth LA5 ... 217 D1
Grosvenor Rd. Chorley PR7 ... 42 B6
Grosvenor Rd. Morecambe LA3 212 A3
Grosvenor Rd. Southport PR8 ... 33 E4
Grosvenor St. Blackpool FY1 ... 129 C5
Grosvenor St. Burnley BB12 ... 126 F7
Grosvenor St. Colne BB8 ... 169 F5
Grosvenor St. Lytham St Anne's FY8 ... 90 C3
Grosvenor St. Preston PR1 ... 96 B7
Grosvenor Way. 4 Blackburn BB1 ... 100 E5
Grosvenor Way. Horwich BL6 ... 31 C3
Grouse St. OL12 ... 51 F1
Grove Ave. Adlington PR6 ... 30 A7
Grove Ave. Longton PR4 ... 73 F8
Grove Cres. PR6 ... 30 A7
Grove Ct. BB5 ... 102 C3
Grove La. BB12 ... 145 E1
Grove Mead. L31 ... 5 F1
Grove Mill Development Ctr. PR7 ... 40 C5
Grove Pk. Ormskirk L39 ... 15 F7
Grove Pk. Southport PR9 ... 34 F8
Grove Rd. Preston PR1 ... 96 C6
Grove Rd. Up Holland WN8 ... 10 C8
Grove St. Accrington BB5 ... 103 A6
Grove St. Bacup OL13 ... 87 A3
Grove St. 12 Bamber Bridge PR5 . 76 F8
Grove St. Barrowford BB9 ... 168 D3
Grove St. Blackburn BB2 ... 100 E2
Grove St. 3 Burnley BB11 ... 126 D5
Grove St. Bury BL9 ... 32 C3
Grove St. Earby BB8 ... 201 B2
Grove St. Leyland PR5 ... 58 D8
Grove St. Lytham St Anne's FY8 ... 88 F7
Grove St. Morecambe LA4 ... 212 C4
Grove St. Nelson BB9 ... 147 E8
Grove St. Oswaldtwistle BB5 ... 102 D3
Grove St. Southport PR8 ... 34 A4
Grove Terr. PR8 ... 34 A5
Grove The. Appley Bridge WN6 ... 27 C2
Grove The. Bilsborrow PR3 ... 157 A5
Grove The. Burnley BB12 ... 126 B6
Grove The. Carnforth LA5 ... 217 B1
Grove The. Chorley PR6 & PR7 ... 60 C2
Grove The. Cleveleys FY5 ... 172 E3
Grove The. Clitheroe BB7 ... 186 F1
Grove The. Lancaster LA1 ... 211 A7
Grove The. Ormskirk L39 ... 6 C7
Grove The. Penwortham PR1 ... 95 B4
Grove The. Preston PR1 ... 116 B1
Grove The. Rufford L40 ... 38 A3
Grove The. Whalley BB7 ... 143 C5
Grovewood. PR8 ... 33 E5
Grovewood Dr. WN6 ... 19 E8
Grundy Cl. PR8 ... 34 E5
Grundy Homes. PR8 ... 34 E5
Grundy Mews. FY4 ... 109 C7
Grundy St. 7 PR5 ... 76 B2
Grundy's La. PR6 & PR7 ... 42 D1
Guard Hill La. LA7 ... 237 E4
Gubberford La. PR3 ... 199 D4
Guide La. BB12 ... 146 A7
Guide Rd. PR4 ... 72 E6
Guide Sq. BB1 ... 81 B8
Guild Hall Arc. 5 PR1 ... 96 A7
Guild Row. 7 PR1 ... 96 A7
Guild Way. PR1 ... 95 D7
Guildford Ave. Blackpool FY2 ... 150 D6
Guildford Ave. Great Knowley PR6 ... 60 E4
Guildford Rd. 30 Preston PR1 ... 96 A7
Guildford Rd. Southport PR8 ... 34 B2
Guildford Way. FY6 ... 151 C6
Guildhall St. PR1 ... 95 F7
Guilford St. BB9 ... 147 B5
Guinea Hall La. PR9 ... 54 A5
Gulf La. LA2 & PR3 ... 197 D7
Gummers Howe Wlk. LA5 ... 216 E8
Gunsmith Pl. 8 BB11 ... 127 A6
Gurney St. BB2 ... 100 B3
Gutter La. BL0 ... 49 B7
Guy St. BB12 ... 145 C1
Guysyke. BB8 ... 169 C4
Gynn Ave. FY1 ... 129 B8
Gynn Sq. FY1 ... 129 B8

Habergham Dr. BB12 ... 125 F8
Habergham High Sch. BB12 ... 126 A7
Habergham High Sch & Sixth Form Ctr. BB12 ... 125 F7
Habergham St. 16 BB12 ... 145 C1
Hackensall Rd. FY6 ... 194 E5
Hacking Cl. BB6 ... 142 C1
Hacking Dr. PR3 ... 138 F5
Hacking St. Bury BL9 ... 32 A2
Hacking St. Darwen BB3 ... 80 F1
Hacking St. 3 Nelson BB9 ... 168 F2
Hacklands Ave. PR2 ... 115 C1
Haddings La. BB12 ... 146 A8
Haddon Pl. PR2 ... 116 D3
Haddon Rd. FY2 ... 150 C5
Hadleigh Rd. FY6 ... 151 C6
Hadstock Ave. L37 ... 11 D1
Hagg La. PR3 ... 154 C8

Hagg St. BB8 169 C4
Haig Ave. Lancaster LA1 210 D8
Haig Ave. Leyland PR5 75 F1
Haig Ave. Preston PR1 116 D2
Haig Ave. Southport PR8 34 E5
Haig Ave. Tarleton PR4 56 A7
Haig Rd. FY1 129 B1
Haigh Cl. PR7 42 A7
Haigh Cres. Chorley PR7 42 B7
Haigh Cres. Maghull L31 5 C4
Haigh Ct. PR8 34 F6
Haigh Hall Cl. BL0 49 B4
Haighton Ct. PR2 117 A7
Haighton Dr. PR2 117 E6
Haighton Green La. PR2 137 E2
Hail St. BL0 49 A4
Hala Cres. LA1 211 A3
Hala Gr. LA1 211 A3
Hala Hill. LA1 & LA2 211 B3
Hala Rd. LA1 211 A3
Hala Sq. LA1 211 A3
Haldane Rd. BB3 80 E4
Haldane St. BB10 147 B2
Halden Rd. LA3 212 B3
Hale Carr Gr. LA3 212 B1
Hale Carr La. LA3 212 B1
Hale St. BB11 127 A4
Hales Rushes Rd. PR3 175 C4
Half Acre. PR5 76 A8
Half Acre La. BL6 30 C2
Halford Pl. FY5 150 E7
Halfpenny La. Andertons Mill PR7 40 B3
Halfpenny La. Longridge PR3 138 F8
Halifax Rd. Ainsdale PR8 20 C5
Halifax Rd. Brierfield BB9 147 C5
Halifax Rd. Lane Bottom BB10 148 D3
Halifax Rd. Nelson BB10 & BB9 147 E5
Halifax Rd. Widdop BB10 149 B1
Halifax St. FY3 129 F3
Hall Ave. FY4 129 C1
Hall Brow Cl. L39 & L40 16 B4
Hall Carr La. PR4 73 D6
Hall Carr Mill Cotts. BB4 85 B2
Hall Carr Rd. BB4 85 A1
Hall Cl. Caton LA2 231 B3
Hall Cl. Rawtenstall BB4 85 A6
Hall Coppice The. BL7 46 E1
Hall Croft. PR4 94 D2
Hall Dr. Caton LA2 231 B3
Hall Dr. Middleton LA3 209 A2
Hall Dr. Morecambe LA4 213 A4
Hall Fold. OL12 51 C8
Hall Garth Gdns. LA6 234 B1
Hall Gate. PR7 60 A2
Hall Gate La. FY6 174 C8
Hall Gdns. OL12 51 C2
Hall Gn. WN8 10 B7
Hall Gr. LA3 209 A2
Hall Green Cl. WN8 10 B7
Hall Green La. PR7 40 A3
Hall Hill. BB7 222 D1
Hall Hill St. 4 BB12 145 C1
Hall La. Appley Bridge WN6 27 D2
Hall La. Bickerstaffe L39 7 E4
Hall La.
Bispham Green L40 & WN8 26 A6
Hall La. Bracewell BD23 225 F3
Hall La. Great Eccleston PR3 154 C4
Hall La. Ince Blundell L38 3 F3
Hall La. Kirkby L33 & L39 1 A8
Hall La. Lathom L40 17 A6
Hall La. Leyland PR5 75 F2
Hall La. Longton PR4 73 E7
Hall La. Maghull L31 5 B7
Hall La. Mawdesley L40 39 D3
Hall La. Orrell WN3 & WN5 10 F4
Hall La. Rivington BL6 44 A2
Hall La. St Michael's on W PR3 155 E6
Hall Meadows. BB8 170 C3
Hall Park Ave. BB10 127 F4
Hall Park Ctr. FY8 89 F4
Hall Park Dr. FY8 89 E6
Hall Park Prim Sch. FY8 89 F3
Hall Pk. LA1 210 F4
Hall Rd. Bescar L40 23 B6
Hall Rd. Fulwood PR2 116 E5
Hall Rd. Penwortham PR1 95 E3
Hall Rd. Trawden BB8 170 B3
Hall St. Bacup OL13 86 F3
Hall St. Blackburn BB2 100 E2
Hall St. Burnley BB11 127 A6
Hall St. Clitheroe BB7 164 E7
Hall St. Colne BB8 169 D4
Hall St. Haslingden BB4 84 B2
Hall St. Morecambe LA4 212 E6
Hall St. Preston PR1 116 C1
Hall St. Ramsbottom BL0 49 C2
Hall St. 12 Rawtenstall BB4 85 A3
Hall St. Southport PR9 34 C7
Hall St. Whitworth OL12 51 B8
Hall St. Whitworth OL12 51 C8
Hall St. Worsthorne BB10 128 A5
Hallam Cres. BB9 148 A8
Hallam La. LA3 209 A2
Hallam Rd. BB9 148 A8
Hallam St. BB5 124 A1
Hallbridge Gdns. WN8 10 B8
Hallcroft. WN8 18 C2
Halley Rd. BB3 80 E3
Hallfield Rd. BB6 123 D6
Hallgate Hill. BB7 223 B4
Halliwell Ct. 6 PR6 42 C7
Halliwell La. PR6 60 C4
Halliwell Pl. 7 PR6 42 C7
Halliwell St. Accrington BB5 103 E2
Halliwell St. Chorley PR6 & PR7 42 C7
Hallmoor Cl. L39 15 E2
Hallows Cl. PR3 155 C6
Hallows Farm Ave. OL12 51 D2
Hallows St. BB10 147 A2
Hallsall Dr. LA4 213 B6
Hallsalls Sq. PR3 154 B5
Hallwell St. BB10 127 A8
Hallwood Cl. BB10 147 B4
Hallwood Rd. PR7 42 A5
Halmot Ct. 2 BB4 85 E1
Halmote Ave. BB12 145 F5
Halsall Ct. L39 15 D6
Halsall Hall Dr. L39 22 B1
Halsall La. Formby L37 11 F3
Halsall La. Halsall L39 14 D6
Halsall La. Ormskirk L39 15 D6
Halsall Rd. Halsall L39 22 C2
Halsall Rd. Southport PR8 21 A8
Halsbury St. PR1 96 B6
Halstead Cl. BB9 168 D4
Halstead La. BB9 168 D4
Halstead Rd. PR2 117 E5
Halstead St. Burnley BB11 126 F5
Halstead St. Bury BL9 32 A4
Halstead St. Worsthorne BB10 128 A6
Halstead Wlk. BL9 32 A5
Halton Ave. Clayton-le-W PR5 76 D1
Halton Ave. Cleveleys FY5 172 E4
Halton Chase. L40 16 E4
Halton Ct. LA4 212 E3
Halton Gdns. Blackpool FY4 109 F8
Halton Gdns. Cleveleys FY5 172 F4
Halton Pl. Fulwood PR2 117 F4
Halton Pl. Longridge PR3 139 B8
Halton Rd. Lancaster LA1 214 A4
Halton Rd. Maghull L31 5 D3
Halton Rd. Nether Kellet LA6 216 E5
Halton St. PR4 131 E6
Hambledon Dr. PR1 95 E2
Hambledon St. BB12 125 D8
Hambledon Terr. Higham BB12 145 F6
Hambledon Terr.
Padiham BB12 125 F7
Hambledon View.
Padiham BB12 125 F7
Hambledon View. Read BB12 144 D1
Hambleton Cl. PR4 93 F1
Hambleton Prim Sch. FY6 174 D2
Hameldon App. BB11 126 D5
Hameldon Ave. BB5 103 E2
Hameldon Cl. BB11 125 C2
Hameldon Rd. Hapton BB11 125 D2
Hameldon Rd. Rawtenstall BB4 105 A2
Hameldon View. BB6 123 D5
Hamer Ave. Blackburn BB1 101 D5
Hamer Ave. Rawtenstall BB4 105 A1
Hamer Rd. PR2 116 D3
Hamer St. Darwen BB3 64 A8
Hamer St. Ramsbottom BL0 49 B2
Hamer St. Rawtenstall BB4 85 A2
Hamerswood Dr. PR3 178 D2
Hamilton Dr. LA1 213 C3
Hamilton Gr. PR2 117 E3
Hamilton House. 6 BB11 126 E5
Hamilton Rd. Barrowford BB9 168 C1
Hamilton Rd. Chorley PR7 42 C7
Hamilton Rd. Fulwood PR2 117 D4
Hamilton Rd.
Morecambe LA2 & LA4 213 C6
Hamilton Rd. Nelson BB8 169 A2
Hamilton St. BB2 100 D2
Hamilton Way. OL10 32 E1
Hamlet Cl. BB2 100 C3
Hamlet Rd. FY7 193 F4
Hamlet The. FY8 109 F2
Hammer Terr. BL0 49 C3
Hammerton Gn. 18 OL13 86 F3
Hammerton Hall Cl. LA1 213 E4
Hammerton Hall La. LA1 213 E4
Hammerton Pl. FY3 130 A8
Hammerton St. Bacup OL13 86 F4
Hammerton St. Burnley BB11 126 F5
Hammond Ave. OL13 69 D8
Hammond Ct. PR1 116 E1
Hammond Dr. BB12 144 C2
Hammond Rd. L33 1 C3
Hammond St. Nelson BB9 147 F7
Hammond St. Preston PR1 116 E1
Hammond St. Preston PR1 116 E2
Hammond St. Preston PR1 116 F2
Hammond's Row. 17 PR1 96 A8
Hampden Ave. BB3 64 B7
Hampden Rd. PR5 76 A2
Hampden St. 7 Burnley BB11 127 B4
Hampden St. Hapton BB12 125 C4
Hampsfell Dr. LA4 212 E3
Hampshire Cl. BB1 122 A7
Hampshire Pl. FY4 109 F6
Hampshire Rd.
Bamber Bridge PR5 96 D3
Hampshire Rd. Rishton BB1 123 A1
Hampson Ave. PR6 76 D1
Hampson Cotts. LA2 207 B1
Hampson Gr. FY6 195 A4
Hampson La. LA2 207 C1
Hampson St. BL6 31 B4
Hampstead Cl. FY8 89 D6
Hampstead Mews. FY1 129 C7
Hampstead Rd.
Fulwood PR1 & PR2 117 D2
Hampstead Rd. Standish WN6 28 D1
Hampton Cl. PR7 42 B8
Hampton Ct. FY8 89 C8
Hampton Pl. FY5 172 E3
Hampton Rd. Blackpool FY4 109 C8
Hampton Rd. Formby L37 11 E1
Hampton Rd. Morecambe LA3 212 B3
Hampton Rd. Southport PR8 34 C5
Hampton St. PR1 116 C2
Hanbury St. PR1 116 C1
Hancock St. BB2 100 C3
Hand La. PR7 39 F5
Handbridge The. PR2 116 E5
Handley Rd. FY1 129 C6
Handsworth Ct. FY1 129 C7
Handsworth Rd. FY1 129 C7
Handsworth Wlk. PR8 34 F3
Hane Row. BB11 106 D7
Hanging Green La. LA2 215 E1
Hanley Cl. FY6 174 C7
Hannah St. Accrington BB5 103 B5
Hannah St. 14 Bacup OL13 87 A3
Hannah St. Darwen BB3 64 B8
Hanover Cres. FY2 150 C5
Hanover St. Colne BB8 169 D5
Hanover St. Morecambe LA4 212 E5
Hanover St. 4 Preston PR1 116 F1
Hanson St. Great Harwood BB6 123 C4
Hanson St. Rishton BB1 123 C1
Hants La. L39 15 E6
Happy Mount Ct. LA4 213 B7
Happy Mount Dr. LA2 & LA4 213 B7
Hapton CE Meth Prim Sch.
BB11 125 C4
Hapton Rd. BB12 125 C7
Hapton St. Padiham BB12 125 D8
Hapton St. Thornton FY5 173 B4
Hapton Sta. BB11 125 C4
Hapton Way. BB4 105 A2
Harbour Ave. PR4 91 E6
Harbour Cl. FY7 193 F2
Harbour La. Brinscall PR6 61 D7
Harbour La. Edgworth BL7 47 D5
Harbour La. Warton PR4 91 E6
Harbury Ave. PR8 20 A4
Harcles Dr. BL0 49 B2
Harcourt Mews. 10 BL6 31 B4
Harcourt Rd. Accrington BB5 103 D3
Harcourt Rd. Blackburn BB2 100 C6
Harcourt Rd. Blackpool FY4 109 D8
Harcourt Rd. Lancaster LA1 213 E3
Harcourt St. 15 Bacup OL13 86 F3
Harcourt St. 1 Burnley BB11 126 D5
Harcourt St. Preston PR1 116 E1
Hard Knott Rise. LA5 216 E8
Hardacre La.
Lucas Green PR6 & PR7 60 C5
Hardacre La. Rimington BB7 225 B2
Hardacre St. L39 15 F6
Hardcastle Rd. PR2 116 E3
Harden Rd. BB8 192 A6
Hardhorn Ct. FY6 151 D3
Hardhorn Rd. FY6 151 D2
Hardhorn Way. FY6 151 D2
Harding Rd. L40 24 D4
Harding St. PR6 30 B8
Hardlands Ave. LA4 213 B4
Hardman Ave. BB4 85 A1
Hardman Cl. Blackburn BB1 101 F4
Hardman Cl. Newchurch BB4 68 F7
Hardman Dr. BB4 68 F7
Hardman St. FY1 129 C6
Hardman Terr. OL13 69 D8
Hardman Way. 23 BB3 81 A1
Hardsough La. BL0 67 D5
Hardwicke St. 4 PR1 96 A8
Hardy Ave. Barnoldswick BB8 200 A3
Hardy Ave. Brierfield BB9 147 B6
Hardy Ct. 10 BB9 147 E8
Hardy Dr. PR7 42 A7
Hardy St. Blackburn BB1 121 F1
Hardy St. Brierfield BB9 147 B6
Hare Clough Cl. BB2 100 F3
Hare Runs House. LA1 213 F3
Harebell Cl. Blackburn BB2 79 D8
Harebell Cl. Formby L37 11 F1
Harebell Cl. Lower Fold OL12 51 D3
Hareden Brook Cl. BB1 100 F3
Hareden Cl. PR5 76 F8
Hareden Rd. PR1 117 F2
Harefield Rise. BB12 126 D7
Hareholme La. BB4 85 D2
Hares La. PR8 35 D1
Harestone Ave. PR7 42 A5
Harewood Ave. Ainsdale PR8 20 C6
Harewood Ave. Blackpool FY3 151 A1
Harewood Ave. Lancaster LA1 211 A3
Harewood Ave. Morecambe LA3 212 B2
Harewood Ave.
Simonstone BB12 144 E2
Harewood Cl. FY6 151 C5
Harewood Rd. PR1 117 C2
Hargate Ave. OL12 51 A2
Hargate Cl. BL9 49 C2
Hargate Rd. FY5 173 C2
Hargher Clough Jun Sch.
BB11 126 D5
Hargher St. BB11 126 D5
Hargreaves Ave. PR5 59 B8
Hargreaves Ct. Clitheroe BB7 164 C7
Hargreaves Ct. Fulwood PR2 115 F4
Hargreaves Ct.
Whitewell Bottom BB4 85 F6
Hargreaves Dr. BB4 84 F2
Hargreaves Fold La. BB4 86 A7
Hargreaves La. 2 BB2 100 E3
Hargreaves Rd. BB5 102 C4
Hargreaves St. 8
Accrington BB5 103 C5
Hargreaves St. Brierfield BB10 147 F3
Hargreaves St. 10
Burnley BB11 126 F6
Hargreaves St. Colne BB8 169 B4
Hargreaves St. Haslingden BB4 84 B3
Hargreaves St. Hoddlesden BB3 81 F1
Hargreaves St. Nelson BB9 147 C7
Hargreaves St. Southport PR8 34 C6
Hargreaves St. Thornton FY5 173 B3
Hargreaves St.
Whitewell Bottom BB4 85 E5
Hargrove Ave. Burnley BB12 126 D7
Hargrove Ave. Padiham BB12 145 C1
Hargrove Rd. BB12 126 D8
Harington Cl. L37 11 D3
Harington Gn. L37 11 D3
Harington Rd. L37 11 D4
Harland St. PR2 116 D3
Harland Way. OL12 51 B2
Harlech Ave. FY1 129 D1
Harlech Cl. BB4 84 B1
Harlech Dr. Leyland PR5 76 C1
Harlech Dr. Oswaldtwistle BB5 102 C4
Harleston Rd. L33 1 A3
Harleston Wlk. 10 L33 1 A3
Harley Cl. LA2 233 C8
Harley Rd. FY3 129 E4
Harley St. BB12 126 C6
Harling Bank. LA6 238 B2
Harling Rd. PR1 117 D1
Harling St. BB12 126 B6
Harold Ave. Blackpool FY4 110 A6
Harold Ave. Burnley BB11 126 C4
Harold St. Burnley BB11 126 D5
Harold St. Colne BB8 169 C4
Harold Terr. PR5 76 A8
Harper St. BB8 200 A3
Harper's La. PR6 60 D1
Harperley. PR7 60 B2
Harpers La. BB12 146 D8
Harridge Ave. OL12 51 C3
Harridge La. L40 23 A1
Harridge St. OL12 51 C3
Harridge The. OL12 51 C3
Harrier Dr. BB1 100 D8
Harriet St. BB11 126 E5
Harrington Ave. FY4 109 B5
Harrington Rd. Chorley PR7 42 B8
Harrington Rd. Morecambe LA3 212 B3
Harrington St. Accrington BB5 124 A1
Harrington St. Preston PR1 116 F1
Harris Ave. FY1 129 D1
Harris Cl. OL10 32 E1
Harris Ct. 2 BB7 164 E8
Harris Ctr. PR2 116 E5
Harris Cty Prim Sch. PR2 116 B7
Harris Rd. WN6 28 B3
Harris St. Fleetwood FY7 194 A4
Harris St. 2 Preston PR1 96 A7
Harrison Ave. FY5 173 B2
Harrison Cres. Blackrod BL6 30 C3
Harrison Cres. Morecambe LA3 212 A1
Harrison Dr. BB8 169 C6
Harrison La. PR4 95 B2
Harrison Rd. Adlington PR7 30 A6
Harrison Rd. Chorley PR7 42 C6
Harrison Rd. Fulwood PR2 116 E6
Harrison St. Bacup OL13 70 A8
Harrison St. Barnoldswick BB8 200 C1
Harrison St. Blackburn BB2 100 D4
Harrison St. Blackpool FY1 129 C3
Harrison St. Brierfield BB10 147 F2
Harrison St. Cornholme OL14 108 B1
Harrison St. Horwich BL6 31 B4
Harrison St. Ramsbottom BL0 49 C7
Harrock La. L40 & WN6 & WN8 26 F6
Harrock Rd. PR6 76 D1
Harrod Dr. PR8 33 E3
Harrogate Cres. BB10 147 D2
Harrogate Rd. FY8 89 C7
Harrogate Way. PR9 53 C6
Harrop Pl. PR2 117 E4
Harrow Ave. Accrington BB5 103 C7
Harrow Ave. Fleetwood FY7 193 F3
Harrow Cl. Orrell WN5 10 F8
Harrow Cl. Padiham BB12 125 E6
Harrow Dr. BB1 101 B3
Harrow Gr. LA4 213 B4
Harrow Pl. Blackpool FY4 109 A5
Harrow Pl. Lytham St Anne's FY8 89 E5
Harrow St. BB5 102 E4
Harrow Stiles La. OL13 106 E1
Harrowdale Pk. LA2 214 F7
Harrowside. FY4 109 B6
Harrowside W. FY4 109 A5
Harry St. Barrowford BB9 168 D3
Harry St. Salterforth BB8 191 D7
Harsnips. WN8 18 C2
Hart St. Blackburn BB1 100 F4
Hart St. Burnley BB11 127 A6
Hart St. Southport PR8 & PR9 34 E6
Hart's Houses. BL6 31 D5
Hart's La. WN8 9 F8
Hartford Ave. FY1 129 D2
Hartington Rd. Brinscall PR7 62 A8
Hartington Rd. Darwen BB3 80 E4
Hartington Rd. Preston PR1 95 D7
Hartington St. Brierfield BB9 147 B5
Hartington St. Colne BB8 170 B5
Hartington St. Lancaster LA1 211 B8
Hartington St. Rishton BB1 123 A1
Hartland. WN8 18 C2
Hartland Ave. PR9 53 B5
Hartlands Cl. BB10 147 D3
Hartlet St. BB6 123 D5
Hartley Ave. BB5 103 A3
Hartley Cres. PR8 33 F2
Hartley Homes The. BB8 170 C6
Hartley Rd. PR8 33 F2
Hartley St. 3 Blackburn BB1 100 E6
Hartley St. Burnley BB11 126 C5
Hartley St. Colne BB8 169 D5
Hartley St. Earby BB8 201 B1
Hartley St. 1 Haslingden BB4 84 B3
Hartley St. Horwich BL6 31 B3
Hartley St. Nelson BB9 147 E7
Hartley St. 2 Oswaldtwistle BB5 102 E4
Hartley St. Passmonds OL12 51 B1
Hartleys Terr. BB8 169 E4
Hartmann St. BB5 103 A6
Hartshead. WN8 18 C2
Hartwood Gn. PR6 60 C3
Hartwood Rd. PR9 34 D7
Harvey St. 14 Nelson BB9 168 E1
Harvey St. Oswaldtwistle BB5 102 D4
Harvington Dr. PR8 20 B5
Harwich Rd. FY8 110 A1
Harwin Cl. OL12 51 D3
Harwood Ave. FY8 88 E8
Harwood Cl. FY6 174 C7
Harwood Gate. BB1 101 B6
Harwood La. BB6 123 E6
Harwood New Rd. BB6 123 E6
Harwood Rd. Rishton BB1 123 A2
Harwood Rd. Wilpshire BB1 122 D4
Harwood St. 12 Blackburn BB1 101 A7
Harwood St. Blackburn BB1 101 B6
Harwood St. Darwen BB3 80 E2
Harwood's La. BB3 81 E1
Haskoll St. BL6 31 D1
Haslam Dr. L39 15 D7
Haslam St. BL9 32 A4
Haslemere Ave. FY3 129 E3
Haslemere Ind Est. PR5 75 F3
Haslingden Cty High Sch. BB4 67 B8
Haslingden Old Rd. BB4 84 E2
Haslingden Prim Sch. BB4 84 B2
Haslingden Rd.
Blackburn BB1 & BB2 101 B2
Haslingden Rd.
Blackburn BB1 & BB5 101 E3
Haslingden Rd.
Oswaldtwistle BB5 82 D7
Haslingden Rd. Rawtenstall BB4 84 E2
Haslingden St James CE
Prim Sch. BB4 84 B3
Haslow Pl. FY3 129 F7
Hassall Dr. PR4 154 A1
Hassett Cl. PR1 95 E6
Hastings Ave. Blackpool FY2 150 E5
Hastings Ave. Warton PR4 91 E7
Hastings Cl. Blackburn BB1 101 C4
Hastings Cl. Thornton FY5 173 C1
Hastings Pl. FY8 90 A3
Hastings Rd. Kirkham PR4 113 B2
Hastings Rd. Lancaster LA1 210 F5
Hastings Rd. Leyland PR5 76 B2
Hastings Rd. Preston PR1 116 B1
Hastings Rd. Southport PR8 33 E1
Hastings Rd. Thornton FY5 173 C1
Hastings The. LA1 210 F5
Haston Lee Ave. BB1 121 F3
Hasty Brow Rd. LA2 213 D6
Hatfield Ave. Fleetwood FY7 193 F3
Hatfield Ave. Morecambe LA4 213 B6
Hatfield Cl. FY5 173 C2
Hatfield Ct. LA4 213 B6
Hatfield Gdns. FY7 193 E2
Hatfield Mews. 2 FY7 193 F2
Hatfield Rd. Accrington BB5 103 D7
Hatfield Rd. Ainsdale PR8 20 C6
Hatfield Rd. Fulwood PR2 117 E3
Hatfield Wlk. FY7 193 E2
Hathaway. FY4 109 E8
Hathaway Fold. 2 BB12 125 D7
Hathaway Rd. Fleetwood FY7 193 E4
Hathaway Rd. Lancaster LA1 213 E3
Hatlex Dr. LA2 215 E2
Hatlex Hill. LA2 215 E2
Hatlex La. LA2 215 E2
Hattersley St. BB11 126 E6
Hatton St. PR7 29 F6
Haugh Ave. BB12 144 E2
Haunders La. PR4 73 B1
Havelock Cl. BB2 100 D3
Havelock Rd. Bamber Bridge PR5 76 E7
Havelock Rd. Penwortham PR1 95 E5
Havelock St. Blackburn BB2 100 C2
Havelock St. Blackpool FY1 129 B4
Havelock St. Burnley BB12 126 B6
Havelock St. Lancaster LA1 211 A6
Havelock St. Oswaldtwistle BB5 102 D3
Havelock St. 9 Padiham BB12 145 C1
Havelock St. Preston PR1 116 D2
Havelock St. Preston PR1 116 E2
Havelock St. Preston PR1 116 F2
Haven Brow. L39 6 C8
Haven Rd. FY8 90 C3
Haven St. BB10 127 C5
Haven Wlk. L31 5 C4
Havenbrook Gr. BL0 49 A3
Haverbreaks Pl. LA1 210 E6
Haverbreaks Rd. LA1 210 E5
Haverholt Cl. BB8 169 C5
Haverholt Rd. BB8 169 C5
Haverthwaite Ave. LA3 208 F7
Havre Pk. BB8 200 C2
Hawarden Ave. LA4 212 F5
Hawarden Rd. 1 PR1 117 E1
Hawarden St. BB9 147 E7
Hawes Dr. BB8 169 F6
Hawes Side La. FY4 109 E8
Hawes Side Prim Sch. FY4 109 E7
Hawes Terr. BB10 147 B2
Hawesside St. PR8 & PR9 34 C7
Haweswater Ave. PR7 42 B6
Haweswater Gr. L31 5 F2
Haweswater Pl. LA4 213 A4
Haweswater Rd. BB5 124 D1
Hawick Gr. OL10 32 E1
Hawk Cl. BL9 32 B4
Hawk St. Burnley BB11 127 A6

High St. Chapeltown BL7 47 C4
High St. Chorley PR6 & PR7 42 C8
High St. Clitheroe BB7 164 B8
High St. Colne BB8 169 E5
High St. Darwen BB3 81 A1
High St. Elswick PR4 153 F1
High St. Fleetwood FY7 194 B4
High St. Garstang PR3 178 C7
High St. Great Eccleston PR3 154 B5
High St. Haslingden BB4 84 B4
High St. Horwich BL6 31 B4
High St. Lancaster LA1 210 F7
High St. Mawdesley L40 39 B1
High St. Nelson BB9 147 D7
High St. Oswaldtwistle BB5 102 F3
High St. Padiham BB12 145 D1
High St. 13 Preston PR1 96 A8
High St. Rishton BB1 123 B1
High St. Skelmersdale WN8 8 E8
High St. Standish WN6 28 E1
Higham CE Prim Sch. BB12 146 A6
Higham Gr. FY3 129 F2
Higham Hall Rd. BB12 145 F5
Higham Rd. BB12 145 C3
Higham Side Rd. PR4 134 C6
Higham St. BB12 145 D1
Highbank. BB1 121 F1
Highbank Ave. FY4 110 A8
Highbury Ave. Blackpool FY3 129 E8
Highbury Ave. Fleetwood FY7 193 F3
Highbury Pl. BB1 100 E6
Highbury Rd. FY8 109 E1
Highbury Rd E. FY8 109 E1
Highbury Rd W. FY8 109 D1
Highcroft Ave. FY2 150 E5
Highcroft Way. OL12 51 F4
Highcross Ave. FY6 130 D8
Highcross Hill. FY6 130 D8
Highcross Rd. FY6 151 D1
Higher Antley St. BB5 103 B5
Higher Audley St. BB1 100 F4
Higher Bank Rd. PR2 116 F3
Higher Bank St. Blackburn BB2 100 B6
Higher Bank St. Withnell PR6 79 A1
Higher Barn. BL6 31 F3
Higher Barn St. 2 BB1 101 A5
Higher Blackthorn. OL13 86 F4
Higher Booths La. BB4 105 A1
Higher Change Villas. OL13 87 B4
Higher Chapel La. BB7 224 A1
Higher Church St. BB3 81 B1
Higher Cockcroft. 13 BB1 100 E5
Higher Commons La. BB2 120 C4
Higher Croft. PR1 95 C2
Higher Croft Rd. BB2 & BB3 80 F8
Higher Cross Row. 9 OL13 86 F3
Higher Cswy. BB9 168 D3
Higher Dunscar. BL7 46 E1
Higher Eanam. BB1 101 A5
Higher Feniscowles La. BB2 79 B8
Higher Field. BB6 122 C8
Higher Fold La. BL0 49 E7
Higher Furlong. PR4 73 F6
Higher Gate. BB5 124 F1
Higher Gate Rd. BB5 124 F1
Higher Gn. FY6 151 E3
Higher Greenfield. PR2 116 B5
Higher Heys. BB5 102 E3
Higher Hill Mus. BB4 66 F8
Higher House Cl. BB2 80 A7
Higher House La. PR6 & PR7 61 B2
Higher La. Barnoldswick BB8 191 B7
Higher La. Dalton WN8 18 C7
Higher La. Haslingden BB4 84 B4
Higher La. Holmes PR4 55 C3
Higher La. Scorton PR3 199 F4
Higher La. Up Holland WN8 10 C7
Higher Lawrence St. 12 BB3 80 F2
Higher London Terr. BB3 81 B2
Higher Meadow. Chorley PR6 59 E8
Higher Meadow. Clayton-le-W PR6 76 E1
Higher Mill St. BB4 85 A3
Higher Moor Cotts. FY2 150 F2
Higher Moor Rd. FY3 151 A2
Higher Moss La. L37 13 A2
Higher Moulding. BL9 32 E5
Higher Park Rd. BB8 191 C8
Higher Peel St. BB5 102 D3
Higher Perry St. BB3 81 B2
Higher Ramsgreave Rd. BB1 & BB2 121 C3
Higher Rd. Longridge PR3 139 C8
Higher Rd. Tosside BD23 230 C5
Higher Reedley Rd. BB10 & BB9 147 D5
Higher Row. BL9 32 B3
Higher Saxifield. BB10 147 E3
Higher South St. BB3 81 A1
Higher Summerseat. BL0 49 B2
Higher Syke. LA2 227 C2
Higher Tentre. BB11 127 B5
Higher Walton CE Prim Sch. PR5 97 B3
Higher Walton Rd. PR5 96 E4
Higher Witton Rd. BB2 100 B4
Highergate Cl. BB5 124 F2
Highfield. Bacup OL13 86 F2
Highfield. Brinscall PR6 61 F8
Highfield. Great Harwood BB6 123 B5
Highfield. Rawtenstall BB4 85 A7
Highfield Ave. Bamber Bridge PR5 96 C1
Highfield Ave. Brierfield BB10 147 B3
Highfield Ave. Foulridge BB8 191 E1
Highfield Ave. Fulwood PR2 117 C4
Highfield Ave. Inskip PR4 134 C8
Highfield Ave. Leyland PR5 76 C3
Highfield Cl. Adlington PR6 30 A7
Highfield Cl. Clifton PR4 114 C1
Highfield Cl. Oswaldtwistle BB5 102 F3
Highfield Cres. 4 Barrowford BB9 168 D3
Highfield Cres. Morecambe LA4 212 C4
Highfield Cres. Nelson BB9 168 E3
Highfield Dr. Fulwood PR2 116 E8
Highfield Dr. Hest Bank LA2 215 D1
Highfield Dr. Longridge PR3 139 B6
Highfield Dr. Longton PR4 73 F6
Highfield Dr. Penwortham PR1 95 D2
Highfield Gdns. BB2 100 E2
Highfield Gr. PR5 96 C2
Highfield High Sch. FY4 109 E6
Highfield Ind Est. PR6 60 D2
Highfield La. L40 23 D7
Highfield Mews. BB3 64 B8
Highfield Pk. L31 5 F1
Highfield Prim Sch. Chorley PR6 42 E8
Highfield Prim Sch. Fulwood PR2 117 F5
Highfield Rd. Adlington PR6 30 A7
Highfield Rd. Blackburn BB2 100 E3
Highfield Rd. Blackpool FY4 109 E6
Highfield Rd. Blackrod BL6 30 E1
Highfield Rd. Carnforth LA5 216 E8
Highfield Rd. Clitheroe BB7 164 F7
Highfield Rd. Croston PR5 57 D2
Highfield Rd. Darwen BB3 81 B1
Highfield Rd. Earby BB8 201 B2
Highfield Rd. Edenfield BL0 67 D3
Highfield Rd. Ormskirk L39 15 E7
Highfield Rd. Rawtenstall BB4 85 D1
Highfield Rd. 5 Rishton BB1 123 A1
Highfield Rd. Southport PR9 53 B3
Highfield Rd N. Adlington PR6 30 A8
Highfield Rd N. Chorley PR7 60 C2
Highfield Rd S. PR7 60 C1
Highfield St. Darwen BB3 64 B8
Highfield St. Haslingden BB4 84 A2
Highfield Terr. LA2 233 C8
Highfurlong Sch. FY3 151 A2
Highgale Gdns. PR5 76 C7
Highgate. Blackpool FY4 109 D5
Highgate. Goosnargh PR3 137 D6
Highgate. Nelson BB9 147 D7
Highgate. Penwortham PR1 95 B5
Highgate Ave. PR2 116 E4
Highgate Cl. Fulwood PR2 116 F4
Highgate Cl. Newton-with-S PR4 113 F3
Highgate Cres. WN6 19 E7
Highgate La. Broadley OL12 51 C5
Highgate La. Warton PR4 91 E6
Highgate Pl. FY8 89 D6
Highgate Rd. Hall Green WN8 10 B7
Highgate Rd. Maghull L31 5 D3
Highgrove Ave. PR7 40 F3
Highgrove Cl. LA4 212 D4
Highgrove Ct. PR5 57 F8
Highland Ave. PR1 95 B4
Highland Brow. LA2 207 A4
Highland Rd. BL6 31 E1
Highmoor. BB9 147 F6
Highmoor Pk. BB7 164 F8
Highrigg Dr. PR3 136 F1
Highsands Ave. L40 38 A3
Hightown. BB4 85 E4
Hightown Rd. BB4 85 F4
Hightown Sta. L38 3 A4
Highways Ave. PR7 59 D1
Higson St. BB2 100 D5
Hilary Ave. FY2 150 C5
Hilary St. BB10 147 A1
Hilbre Cl. PR9 52 F1
Hilbre Dr. PR9 52 F1
Hilderstone La. LA5 & LA6 234 A7
Hildrop Rd. BB9 168 F1
Hill Cl. WN6 19 E8
Hill Cres. PR4 114 A2
Hill Crest. OL13 86 D1
Hill Crest Ave. Burnley BB10 127 F4
Hill Crest Ave. Fulwood PR2 116 E8
Hill Crest Ave. Longridge PR3 139 A7
Hill End La. BB4 85 C1
Hill House Fold La. WN6 27 C5
Hill House La. Jack Green PR5 & PR6 78 A7
Hill House La. Robin Hood WN6 27 C5
Hill La. Blackrod BL6 30 C2
Hill La. Colne BB8 170 C7
Hill La. Nether Kellet LA6 216 F4
Hill Pl. BB9 147 D6
Hill Rd. Lancaster LA1 213 F3
Hill Rd. Leyland PR5 & PR6 76 C1
Hill Rd. Penwortham PR1 95 D4
Hill Rd S. PR1 95 D3
Hill Rise. Haslingden BB4 84 C1
Hill Rise. 1 Ramsbottom BL0 49 A4
Hill Side. LA1 210 E8
Hill St. Accrington BB5 103 C5
Hill St. Barnoldswick BB8 200 C2
Hill St. Blackburn BB1 101 B5
Hill St. Blackpool FY4 129 B1
Hill St. Brierfield BB12 & BB9 146 F6
Hill St. Brierfield BB9 147 B5
Hill St. Carnforth LA5 217 D1
Hill St. Colne BB8 169 D4
Hill St. Enfield BB5 124 A1
Hill St. Oswaldtwistle BB5 102 D5
Hill St. Padiham BB12 125 C8
Hill St. Preston PR1 95 F8
Hill St. Ramsbottom BL9 49 C3
Hill St. Rawtenstall BB4 85 A7
Hill St. Southport PR9 34 B7
Hill Top. Barrowford BB9 168 D4
Hill Top. Colne BB8 170 C4
Hill Top. Foulridge BB8 191 C2
Hill Top. New Longton PR4 75 A6
Hill Top. Trawden BB8 170 B2
Hill Top Cl. PR4 92 D7
Hill Top La. Earby BB8 201 A2
Hill Top La. Whittle-le-W PR6 60 D8
Hill View. Blackburn BB1 121 E1
Hill View. 2 Rawtenstall BB4 84 F1
Hill View Dr. PR7 28 D8
Hill View Rd. PR3 199 C1
Hill Wlk. PR5 76 A2
Hillam La. LA2 203 B7
Hillary Cres. L31 5 D1
Hillbrook Rd. PR5 75 F2
Hillcrest. Maghull L31 5 F1
Hillcrest. Skelmersdale WN8 9 B8
Hillcrest Ave. Bolton-le-S LA5 216 A5
Hillcrest Ave. Fulwood PR2 116 A4
Hillcrest Cl. PR4 56 A8
Hillcrest Dr. Bescar L40 22 F7
Hillcrest Dr. Longridge PR3 139 A7
Hillcrest Dr. Tarleton PR4 56 A8
Hillcrest Rd. Blackburn BB2 99 F2
Hillcrest Rd. Blackpool FY4 109 B4
Hillcrest Rd. Langho BB6 122 C8
Hillcrest Rd. Ormskirk L39 15 E6
Hillcroft. Fulwood PR2 116 C7
Hillcroft. High Bentham LA2 233 D7
Hilldean. WN8 10 C8
Hillingdon Rd. BB10 147 D3
Hillingdon Rd N. BB10 147 D3
Hillmount Ave. LA3 208 F8
Hillock Cl. L40 23 A7
Hillock La. Bescar L40 23 A7
Hillock La. Dalton WN8 18 D7
Hillock La. Warton PR4 91 E7
Hillocks The. PR5 57 B1
Hillpark Ave. Fulwood PR2 116 D4
Hillpark Ave. Gregson Lane PR5 97 D1
Hills Ct. LA1 213 F1
Hillsborough Ave. BB9 147 D5
Hillsea Ave. LA3 208 F8
Hillside. BB11 126 D3
Hillside Autistic Ctr. PR3 139 D7
Hillside Ave. Blackburn BB1 101 C4
Hillside Ave. Blackrod BL6 30 E1
Hillside Ave. Brierfield BB10 147 C5
Hillside Ave. 11 Darwen BB3 64 A8
Hillside Ave. Egerton BL7 47 B1
Hillside Ave. Farington PR5 75 F7
Hillside Ave. Fulwood PR2 116 D4
Hillside Ave. Hill Dale WN8 26 D5
Hillside Ave. Horwich BL6 31 C4
Hillside Ave. Kirkham PR4 113 C5
Hillside Ave. Ormskirk L39 15 D3
Hillside Ave. Preesall FY6 195 B4
Hillside Cl. Blackburn BB1 101 C4
Hillside Cl. Blackpool FY3 129 E6
Hillside Cl. Brierfield BB9 147 C5
Hillside Cl. Burnley BB11 126 D2
Hillside Cl. Clitheroe BB7 164 E6
Hillside Cl. Euxton PR7 59 C1
Hillside Cl. Great Harwood BB6 123 C6
Hillside Cl. Thornton FY5 151 D8
Hillside Cres. Horwich BL6 31 C4
Hillside Cres. Weir OL13 86 F7
Hillside Cres. Whittle-le-W PR6 60 C8
Hillside Cty Prim Sch. WN8 9 D8
Hillside Dr. Newchurch BB4 85 E2
Hillside Dr. Stalmine FY6 174 C7
Hillside Dr. West Bradford BB7 186 F6
Hillside Golf Links. PR8 20 C8
Hillside Rd. Haslingden BB4 84 C3
Hillside Rd. Low Bentham LA2 233 C8
Hillside Rd. Preston PR1 96 C6
Hillside Rd. Ramsbottom BL0 49 A5
Hillside Rd. Southport PR8 33 E1
Hillside Sta. PR8 33 E1
Hillside View. BB9 147 C5
Hillside Way. OL12 70 C1
Hillside Wlk. Blackburn BB1 101 C4
Hillside Wlk. Middle Healey OL12 51 D4
Hillstone Ave. OL12 51 D4
Hillstone Cl. BL8 48 F2
Hillsview Rd. PR8 20 C4
Hilltop. OL12 51 C5
Hilltop Dr. BB4 67 C7
Hilltop Wlk. L39 15 C3
Hillview Rd. PR4 113 A6
Hillylaid Rd. FY5 173 D2
Hilmont Terr. BB1 100 F7
Hilmore Rd. LA4 212 D5
Hilstone La. FY2 150 D1
Hilton Ave. Blackpool FY1 129 B1
Hilton Ave. Horwich BL6 31 A3
Hilton Ave. Lytham St Anne's FY8 89 C6
Hilton Ct. FY8 88 E5
Hilton Rd. BB3 64 B8
Hilton St. Bury BL9 32 A4
Hilton St. Darwen BB3 64 A8
Hilton's Brow. PR6 78 B4
Hinchley Gn. L31 5 B1
Hind St. Burnley BB10 147 B2
Hind St. Preston PR1 95 E6
Hind's Head Ave. WN6 27 F6
Hindburn Ave. L31 5 F2
Hindburn Cl. LA5 217 F2
Hindburn Pl. LA1 213 E2
Hinde St. LA1 214 A1
Hindle Fold La. BB6 123 C6
Hindle St. Accrington BB5 103 B6
Hindle St. Bacup OL13 69 D8
Hindle St. Darwen BB3 80 F2
Hindle St. Haslingden BB4 84 B3
Hindley Beech. L31 5 C2
Hindley Ct. 3 BB9 168 C1
Hindley St. PR7 42 C6
Hinton St. BB10 127 B5
Hippings Meth Prim Sch. BB5 102 E3
Hippings Vale. BB5 102 D4
Hippings Way. BB7 186 E2
Hirst St. Burnley BB11 127 B4
Hirst St. Cornholme OL14 108 B1
Hirst St. Padiham BB12 145 C1
Hoarstones Ave. BB12 146 D7
Hob Gn. BB2 120 F2
Hob La. BL7 47 C7
Hobart Pl. FY5 150 F8
Hobart St. BB10 & BB11 127 B6
Hobbs La. PR3 180 A4
Hobcross La. L40 25 A2
Hobson St. BB4 84 F4
Hobson's La. LA6 234 C2
Hockley Pl. FY3 129 F7
Hodder Ave. Blackpool FY1 129 D1
Hodder Ave. Chorley PR7 42 B5
Hodder Ave. Fleetwood FY7 193 D2
Hodder Ave. Maghull L31 5 F2
Hodder Ave. Morecambe LA1 213 B3
Hodder Brook. PR2 118 A3
Hodder Cl. 3 Bamber Bridge PR5 76 F8
Hodder Cl. Fleetwood FY7 193 C2
Hodder Ct. BB7 163 C4
Hodder Dr. BB7 186 D7
Hodder Gr. Clitheroe BB7 164 C7
Hodder Gr. Darwen BB3 80 E4
Hodder Pl. Blackburn BB1 100 F6
Hodder Pl. Lancaster LA1 211 B5
Hodder Pl. Lytham St Anne's FY8 89 C7
Hodder St. Accrington BB5 103 D6
Hodder St. 1 Blackburn BB1 100 E6
Hodder St. Brierfield BB10 147 C3
Hodder Way. FY6 151 D2
Hoddlesden Fold. BB3 81 F1
Hoddlesden Rd. BB3 81 E1
Hodge Brow. PR7 43 F4
Hodge La. BB8 191 B8
Hodge St. PR8 34 B7
Hodgson Ave. PR4 92 A5
Hodgson High Sch. FY6 151 F3
Hodgson Pl. FY6 151 D2
Hodgson Rd. FY1 129 C8
Hodgson St. Darwen BB3 81 B1
Hodgson St. 3 Oswaldtwistle BB5 102 E4
Hodson St. Bamber Bridge PR5 96 E1
Hodson St. Southport PR8 34 C6
Hogarth Ave. BB11 126 F3
Hogarth Cres. PR4 133 F4
Hogg's La. PR7 42 F5
Hoggs Hill La. L37 11 F1
Hoghton Ave. OL13 70 A8
Hoghton Cl. Lancaster LA1 210 D6
Hoghton Cl. Lytham St Anne's FY8 109 F2
Hoghton Gr. PR9 34 C8
Hoghton La. PR5 97 D3
Hoghton Pl. PR9 34 B7
Hoghton Rd. Leyland PR5 75 D1
Hoghton Rd. Longridge PR3 139 C7
Hoghton St. 6 Bamber Bridge PR5 76 A8
Hoghton St. Southport PR8 & PR9 34 C7
Hoghton Tower. PR5 98 E1
Hoghton View. PR1 96 C6
Holbeck Ave. Blackpool FY4 109 F8
Holbeck Ave. Middle Healey OL12 51 D4
Holbeck Ave. Morecambe LA4 213 B4
Holbeck St. BB10 147 A1
Holborn Dr. L39 15 C3
Holborn Hill. L39 15 C4
Holcombe Brook Prim Sch. BL0 49 A2
Holcombe Ct. BL0 48 F2
Holcombe Dr. BB10 127 B6
Holcombe Gr. PR6 60 E1
Holcombe Lee. BL0 49 A4
Holcombe Mews. BL8 48 F3
Holcombe Old Rd. BL8 & BL0 49 A4
Holcombe Rd. Blackpool FY2 150 E1
Holcombe Rd. Haslingden BB4 66 F8
Holcombe Rd. Ramsbottom BL8 48 F2
Holcombe Village. BL8 49 A6
Holcroft Pl. FY8 89 F4
Holden Ave. Bury BL9 32 E4
Holden Ave. Ramsbottom BL0 49 A5
Holden Cl. BB9 168 C1
Holden Fold. BB3 81 B3
Holden La. BB7 224 B5
Holden Rd. Brierfield BB9 147 A5
Holden Rd. Brierfield BB10 147 B3
Holden St. Accrington BB5 103 B5
Holden St. Adlington PR7 29 F7
Holden St. Belthorn BB1 81 F6
Holden St. Blackburn BB2 100 C4
Holden St. Burnley BB11 126 F5
Holden St. Clitheroe BB7 164 F8
Holden Way. LA1 210 F5
Hole House La. BB7 229 E2
Hole House St. BB1 101 C5
Holgate. FY4 109 F6
Holgate Dr. WN5 10 E6
Holgate St. Brierfield BB10 147 F3
Holgate St. Great Harwood BB6 123 C5
Holhouse La. BL8 48 F2
Holker Cl. Coupe Green PR5 97 E3
Holker Cl. Lancaster LA1 210 D6
Holker La. PR5 58 B4
Holker St. Colne BB8 169 B4
Holker St. Darwen BB3 64 B8
Holland Ave. Bamber Bridge PR5 96 E2
Holland Ave. Rawtenstall BB4 84 F3
Holland Lodge. 4 PR2 117 F4
Holland Moor Prim Sch. WN8 9 E7
Holland Moss. WA11 & WN8 9 A5
Holland Pl. BB9 168 E2
Holland Rd. PR1 116 C1
Holland St. Accrington BB5 102 F6
Holland St. Blackburn BB1 100 D6
Holland St. Padiham BB12 125 B8
Holland's La. WN8 17 A1
Holliers Cl. L31 5 E1
Hollies Cl. Blackburn BB2 79 F8
Hollies Cl. Catterall PR3 178 D2
Hollies Rd. BB1 122 A7
Hollies The. PR8 33 F6
Hollin Bridge St. BB2 100 D2
Hollin Hall. BB8 170 C1
Hollin Hill. BB11 127 B3
Hollin La. Knowley PR7 61 C2
Hollin La. Rawtenstall BB4 85 A4
Hollin Mill St. BB9 147 B6
Hollin St. BB2 100 C2
Hollin Way. Rawtenstall BB4 85 A4
Hollin Way. Rawtenstall BB4 85 A6
Hollingreave Rd. BB11 127 A4
Hollings. PR4 74 F7
Hollington St. BB8 170 B5
Hollinhead Cres. PR2 116 B4
Hollinhurst Ave. PR1 95 C6
Hollinhurst Brow. LA2 233 C2
Hollins Ave. BB10 127 F4
Hollins Cl. Accrington BB5 103 C4
Hollins Cl. Hoghton PR5 98 C3
Hollins Ct. 1 BB8 200 B3
Hollins Gr. PR2 116 B3
Hollins Grove St. BB3 80 F3
Hollins High Sch The. BB5 103 D2
Hollins Hill. PR3 204 C2
Hollins La. Accrington BB5 103 D3
Hollins La. Arnside LA5 237 C1
Hollins La. Edenfield BL0 67 E2
Hollins La. Hollins Lane PR3 204 C2
Hollins La. Runshaw Moor PR5 58 C4
Hollins Rd. Barnoldswick BB8 200 A2
Hollins Rd. Darwen BB3 80 F4
Hollins Rd. Nelson BB9 169 A2
Hollins Rd. Preston PR1 117 B2
Hollinshead St. PR6 42 C8
Hollinshead St Sch. PR6 42 C8
Hollinshead Terr. BB3 63 B7
Hollowell La. BL6 31 D1
Hollowford La. L40 25 D2
Hollowforth La. PR4 135 E5
Hollowhead Ave. BB1 121 F5
Hollowhead Cl. BB1 121 F5
Hollowhead La. BB1 122 A5
Hollowrane. LA6 234 C7
Holly Ave. BB4 84 C1
Holly Bank. Accrington BB5 103 C4
Holly Bank. Entwistle BL7 47 B7
Holly Bank. Fulwood PR2 116 C5
Holly Bank. Warton LA5 217 D5
Holly Cl. Clayton Green PR6 77 B2
Holly Cl. Skelmersdale WN8 17 E1
Holly Cl. Thornton FY5 173 C3
Holly Cl. Westhead L40 16 E4
Holly Cres. PR7 41 E2
Holly Fold La. WA11 8 E3
Holly Gr. Longridge PR3 139 A8
Holly Gr. Tarleton PR4 56 A7
Holly La. Ormskirk L39 15 B4
Holly La. Rainford Junction WA11 & WN8 8 E4
Holly La. Rufford L40 38 C3
Holly Mews. FY8 109 F2
Holly Mount. BB4 67 A7
Holly Mount RC Prim Sch. BL8 48 D1
Holly Pl. PR5 77 B6
Holly Rd. Blackpool FY1 150 C1
Holly Rd. Thornton FY5 173 B3
Holly St. Blackburn BB1 100 F7
Holly St. Burnley BB10 127 B5
Holly St. Bury BL9 32 A2
Holly St. Nelson BB9 147 F8
Holly St. Oswaldtwistle BB5 102 D4
Holly St. Ramsbottom BL0 49 C3
Holly Terr. BB1 100 F8
Holly Tree Cl. BB3 64 A6
Holly Tree Way. BB2 79 F8
Holly Wlk. LA1 210 D8
Hollybank Cl. PR2 115 F5
Hollybrook Rd. PR8 34 A5
Hollywood Ave. Blackpool FY3 129 E5
Hollywood Ave. Penwortham PR1 95 C3
Hollywood Gr. FY7 193 F4
Holman St. 5 PR1 117 C1
Holmbrook Cl. BB2 80 F8
Holmby St. BB10 147 B2
Holmdale Ave. PR9 53 C4
Holme Ave. FY7 172 D8
Holme Bank. BB4 84 F1
Holme CE Prim Sch. BB10 107 B6
Holme Cl. BB8 192 A7
Holme Cres. BB8 170 B3
Holme End. BB12 146 F4
Holme Hill. BB7 186 E2
Holme House Rd. OL14 108 C1
Holme La. Caton LA2 231 C3
Holme La. Haslingden BB4 67 D8
Holme La. Rawtenstall BB4 67 E8
Holme Lea. BB5 123 F4
Holme Mills Ind Est. LA6 234 B8
Holme Pk. LA2 233 D7
Holme Rd. Bamber Bridge PR5 76 E8
Holme Rd. Burnley BB12 126 E7
Holme Rd. Clayton-le-M BB5 123 E4
Holme Rd. Penwortham PR1 & PR4 95 B7
Holme Slack La. PR1 & PR2 117 C3

Lowther Rd. Lancaster LA1 214 B1
Lowther St. Colne BB8 169 E6
Lowther St. Nelson BB9 147 C8
Lowther St. Preston PR1 116 C1
Lowther Terr.
Appley Bridge WN6 19 C8
Lowther Terr.
Lytham St Anne's FY8 90 A3
Lowthian St. 28 PR1 95 F8
Lowthorpe Cres. PR1 117 B2
Lowthorpe Pl. PR1 117 B2
Lowthorpe Rd. PR1 117 B2
Lowthwaite Dr. BB9 147 E6
Lowton Rd. FY8 89 A8
Loxham Gdns. FY4 109 D6
Loxley Pl. FY5 150 E7
Loxley Pl E. FY5 150 F7
Loxley Rd. PR8 34 D4
Loynd St. 9 Great Harwood BB6 123 C5
Loynd St. Ramsbottom BL0 49 D6
Lubbock St. BB12 126 C6
Lucas Ave. PR7 41 D8
Lucas La. PR6 60 C6
Lucas St. BL9 32 A3
Lucerne Cl. PR2 117 C4
Lucerne Rd. PR2 117 C4
Lucy St. 7 Barrowford BB9 168 D3
Lucy St. Lancaster LA1 210 F8
Lucy St. Morecambe LA4 212 E6
Ludlow. WN8 18 C4
Ludlow Dr. L39 15 D7
Ludlow Gr. FY2 150 F2
Ludlow St. WN6 28 D3
Luke St. 17 OL13 69 C8
Lulworth. WN8 18 C4
Lulworth Ave. Blackpool FY3 130 A3
Lulworth Ave.
Preston PR1 & PR2 116 D2
Lulworth Pl. PR5 96 D2
Lulworth Rd. Fulwood PR2 117 A4
Lulworth Rd. Southport PR8 33 F5
Lumb Carr Ave. BL0 & BL8 49 A4
Lumb Carr Rd. BL0 & BL8 49 A4
Lumb Cotts. BL0 67 A4
Lumb Flats. BL0 67 A4
Lumb Holes La. BB4 68 E7
Lumb La. BB4 85 F4
Lumb Scar. 9 OL13 86 F2
Lund St. Blackburn BB2 100 C4
Lund St. 2 Preston PR1 96 A8
Lunds La. PR4 73 D1
Lune Ave. L31 5 E2
Lune Cl. Kirkby Lonsdale LA6 238 C2
Lune Cl. Kirkham PR4 113 C5
Lune Dr. Clayton-le-W PR5 & PR6 76 E2
Lune Dr. Morecambe LA1 213 B3
Lune Gr. FY1 129 C3
Lune House. LA1 210 F7
Lune Ind Est. LA1 210 C8
Lune Rd. Fleetwood FY7 193 F4
Lune Rd. Lancaster LA1 213 D1
Lune St. Colne BB8 169 E4
Lune St. Lancaster LA1 213 F1
Lune St. Longridge PR3 139 B8
Lune St. Padiham BB12 125 D8
Lune St. Preston PR1 95 F7
Lune Terr. LA1 213 F1
Lune View. FY6 194 E6
Lunedale Ave. FY1 129 C1
Lunefield Dr. LA6 238 C1
Lunefield Gdns. LA6 238 C2
Lunesdale Cl. FY8 89 C7
Lunesdale Ct. Butt Yeats LA2 232 B6
Lunesdale Ct. Lancaster LA1 213 D3
Lunesdale Ct. Lancaster LA1 214 B1
Lunesdale Dr. PR3 204 B3
Lunesdale Rd. PR4 113 A5
Lunesdale Terr. LA2 231 E4
Lunesdale View. LA2 214 F7
Luneside. LA1 210 C8
Lunt Rd. L29 4 C1
Lupin Cl. Accrington BB5 103 A7
Lupin Cl. Lucas Green PR7 60 B5
Lupin Rd. BB5 103 B7
Lupton Dr. BB9 168 D4
Lupton Pl. LA1 213 D3
Lupton St. PR7 42 C6
Lutner St. BB11 127 A5
Luton Rd. Cleveleys FY5 172 E1
Luton Rd. Preston PR2 115 F2
Lutwidge Ave. PR1 117 C1
Lyceum Ave. FY3 129 D4
Lychfield. PR5 76 E7
Lychgate. 19 PR1 96 A8
Lydd Gr. PR7 42 A7
Lyddesdale Ave. FY5 150 D8
Lydgate. Brierfield BB10 147 E2
Lydgate. Chorley PR7 42 A5
Lydia St. BB5 103 B4
Lydiate Cty Prim Sch. L31 5 C4
Lydiate La. Bilsborrow PR3 157 C6
Lydiate La. Leyland PR5 76 C4
Lydiate La. Newton PR7 58 B1
Lydiate Lane End. PR7 58 B2
Lydiate Station Rd. L31 4 E5
Lydric Ave. PR5 97 E2
Lyelake La. L40 & L39 16 F2
Lymbridge Dr. BL6 30 D1
Lyme Gr. FY6 194 E5
Lymm Ave. LA1 213 C3
Lyncroft Cres. FY3 129 E7
Lyndale. WN8 18 B4
Lyndale Ave. Bamber Bridge PR5 96 C2
Lyndale Ave. Haslingden BB4 84 B2
Lyndale Ave. Wilpshire BB1 122 A7
Lyndale Cl. Leyland PR5 59 B6
Lyndale Cl. Rawtenstall BB4 85 A7
Lyndale Cl. Wilpshire BB1 122 A7
Lyndale Ct. FY7 194 B5
Lyndale Gr. PR5 96 C2
Lyndale Rd. BB11 125 C3
Lynden Ave. LA4 213 A5
Lyndhurst. Maghull L31 5 D1
Lyndhurst. Skelmersdale WN8 18 B4
Lyndhurst Ave. Blackburn BB1 101 E5
Lyndhurst Ave. Blackpool FY4 129 D1
Lyndhurst Dr. PR2 115 E2
Lyndhurst Gr. BB6 123 E6
Lyndhurst Rd. Blackburn BB2 100 E2
Lyndhurst Rd.
Burnley BB10 & BB11 127 C5
Lyndhurst Rd. Darwen BB3 80 E3
Lyndhurst Rd. Darwen BB3 80 F3
Lyndhurst Rd. Southport PR8 34 B2
Lyndon Ave. BB6 123 E6
Lyndon Ct. BB6 123 E6
Lynfield Rd. BB6 123 E6
Lynn Gr. FY1 129 B7
Lynn Pl. PR1 117 D2
Lynslack Terr. LA5 218 B8
Lynthorpe Rd. Blackburn BB2 100 E2
Lynthorpe Rd. Nelson BB9 169 A1
Lynton Ave. Blackpool FY4 109 D8
Lynton Ave. Leyland PR5 59 C8
Lynton Ct. FY7 172 C8
Lynton Dr. PR8 33 E1
Lynton Rd. Accrington BB5 102 F4
Lynton Rd. Southport PR8 33 E1
Lynwood Ave. Blackpool FY3 129 E8
Lynwood Ave. Clayton-le-M BB5 123 F4
Lynwood Ave. Darwen BB3 80 E4
Lynwood Ave. Grimsargh PR2 138 C2
Lynwood Ave. Ormskirk L39 15 C3
Lynwood Cl. Clayton-le-M BB5 123 F4
Lynwood Cl. Colne BB8 169 D7
Lynwood Cl. Darwen BB3 80 E4
Lynwood Cl. Skelmersdale WN8 9 D7
Lynwood Dr. FY6 174 C7
Lynwood End. L39 15 C3
Lynwood Rd. Blackburn BB2 100 B6
Lynwood Rd. Huncoat BB5 124 E2
Lyons La. PR6 42 D7
Lyons Rd. PR8 34 A5
Lyth Rd. LA1 214 B2
Lythall Ave. FY8 90 D4
Lytham CE Prim Sch. FY8 90 B4
Lytham Cl. PR2 116 D3
Lytham Rd. Blackburn BB2 100 F1
Lytham Rd. Blackpool FY4 109 C6
Lytham Rd. Blackpool FY1 129 B3
Lytham Rd. Brierfield BB10 147 C2
Lytham Rd. Freckleton PR4 92 B6
Lytham Rd. Fulwood PR2 116 D3
Lytham Rd. Moss Side FY8 111 E1
Lytham Rd. Southport PR9 53 A4
Lytham Rd. Warton PR4 91 D5
Lytham St. Chorley PR7 42 E7
Lytham St. Lower Healey OL12 51 E3
Lytham St Anne's High Sch.
FY8 89 C5
Lytham Sta. FY8 90 A3
Lytham Windmill (Mus). FY8 90 C3
Lythcoe Ave. PR2 116 C4
Lythe Fell Ave. LA2 214 F7
Lythe Fell Rd. LA2 228 F8
Lythe La. LA2 233 E2
Lytles Cl. L37 12 A2
Lytton St. BB12 125 F7

Mabel St. Colne BB8 169 F5
Mabel St. Falinge Fold OL12 51 D2
Maberry Cl. WN6 19 D7
Macaulay St. BB11 126 C5
Macauley Ave. FY4 109 F8
Macbeth Rd. FY7 193 E4
Maclaren Cl. FY3 130 D5
Macleod St. BB9 147 D8
Maddy St. PR1 95 D8
Madeley Gdns. OL12 51 C1
Maden Rd. OL13 86 F2
Maden St. BB5 102 E6
Maden Way. OL13 86 F2
Madison Ave. Blackpool FY2 150 E5
Madison Ave. Hest Bank LA5 215 E2
Madryn Ave. L33 1 A2
Mafeking Ave. BL9 32 A5
Mafeking Rd. PR1 116 C2
Magdalen Ave. FY5 172 D1
Maggots Nook Rd. WA11 9 A1
Maghull La. L31 6 B1
Maghull Smallholdings Est.
L31 5 F3
Magnolia Cl. PR2 117 C6
Magnolia Rd. PR1 95 B3
Magpie Cl. BB11 126 C5
Maharishi Sch of the Age of
Enlightenment. L40 18 A5
Maida Vale. FY5 150 D8
Maiden St. BB4 84 B6
Main Ave. LA3 208 F3
Main Cl. LA3 205 D8
Main Dr. FY6 151 E2
Main Rd. Bolton-le-S LA5 216 A4
Main Rd. Bolton-le-S LA5 216 B5
Main Rd. Galgate LA2 207 A3
Main Rd. Hest Bank LA2 215 F1
Main Rd. Nether Kellet LA6 216 F5
Main Sprit Weind. PR1 96 A7
Main St. Bolton-by-B BB7 224 D4
Main St. Burton-in-K LA6 234 B7
Main St. Cockerham LA2 203 D4
Main St. Grindleton BB7 187 B8
Main St. Heysham LA3 208 E8
Main St. High Bentham LA2 233 D8
Main St. Hornby LA2 232 B7
Main St. Kelbrook BB8 192 A6
Main St. Kirkby Lonsdale LA6 238 C2
Main St. Lancaster LA1 213 F2
Main St. Low Bentham LA2 233 B8
Main St. Overton LA3 205 D8
Main St. Rathmell BD23 230 F6
Main St. Warton LA5 217 D5
Main St. Whittington LA6 235 D7
Main St. Wray LA2 232 D6
Mains La. Bispham Green L40 26 A6
Mains La. Poulton-le-F FY6 152 B4
Mainway. LA1 213 F2
Mairscough La. L39 14 B1
Maitland Ave. FY5 172 D1
Maitland Cl. 5 PR1 96 C8
Maitland Pl. BB4 85 A1
Maitland St. 18 Bacup OL13 86 F2
Maitland St. 4 Preston PR1 96 C8
Maitland St. 1 Preston PR5 96 D8
Majestic The. FY8 88 D6
Major St. Accrington BB5 103 B4
Major St. Ramsbottom BL0 49 B6
Major St. Rawtenstall BB4 85 A7
Makinson Ave. BL6 31 E1
Makinson La. BL6 31 F4
Makinsons Row. LA2 207 A4
Malcolm Pl. FY7 193 E4
Malcolm St. PR1 117 D1
Malden St. PR5 76 A1
Maldern Ave. FY6 151 C5
Maldon Pl. PR2 117 D2
Malham Ave. Accrington BB5 102 F4
Malham Ave. Blackpool FY4 109 D8
Malham Cl. Lancaster LA1 213 D3
Malham Cl. Southport PR8 34 E3
Malham Pl. PR2 117 E4
Malham Rd. BB10 147 D3
Malham Wend. BB9 168 C3
Maliff Rd. BB10 149 B2
Malkin Cl. BB9 168 E8
Malkin La. BB7 163 F6
Mall The. Burnley BB11 127 A6
Mall The. Fulwood PR2 117 E2
Mall The. Lytham St Anne's FY8 89 C7
Mallard Cl. Leyland PR5 58 D8
Mallard Cl. Ormskirk L39 15 C2
Mallard Cl. Thornton FY5 173 A4
Mallard Ct. FY3 130 B6
Mallard Dr. BL6 31 A3
Mallard House. L31 5 B4
Mallard Pl. BB5 102 D3
Mallards Wlk. PR5 77 A5
Mallee Ave. PR9 53 A3
Mallee Cres. PR9 53 A3
Malley La. PR4 & PR3 135 C8
Mallom Ave. PR7 59 E1
Mallory Ave. L31 5 B4
Mallow Wlk. LA3 212 E2
Mallowdale Ave. LA3 209 A8
Mallowdale Rd. LA1 213 D2
Malt Kiln Brow. PR3 182 E4
Malt Kiln Gr. PR3 154 A5
Malt St. BB5 103 B7
Maltby Pl. FY4 129 F2
Malthouse Ct. PR1 116 D1
Malthouse The. PR1 116 D1
Malthouse Way. PR1 95 D3
Maltings The. Longton PR4 73 F8
Maltings The. Thornton FY5 173 A4
Maltings The. Whittington LA6 235 D7
Maltkiln La.
Bispham Green L40 & WN8 26 C7
Maltkiln La. Ormskirk L39 6 E8
Malton Dr. PR5 76 A7
Malvern Ave. Blackburn BB2 100 D1
Malvern Ave. Blackpool FY1 129 D2
Malvern Ave. Lancaster LA1 211 A6
Malvern Ave. Oswaldtwistle BB5 102 E3
Malvern Ave. Padiham BB12 125 D6
Malvern Ave. Preston PR1 96 B6
Malvern Ave. Stalmine FY6 174 C7
Malvern Cl. 6 Accrington BB5 103 A7
Malvern Cl. Bamber Bridge PR5 76 C8
Malvern Cl. Horwich BL6 31 C5
Malvern Rd.
Lytham St Anne's FY8 89 D5
Malvern Rd. Nelson BB9 169 A1
Malvern Rd. Preston PR1 96 B6
Malvern St. Preston PR1 96 B5
Malvern St. Standish WN6 28 D3
Malvern Way. BB4 67 A7
Manby Cl. PR5 97 E3
Manchester Rd. Accrington BB5 103 D3
Manchester Rd.
Barnoldswick BB8 200 B1
Manchester Rd. Blackpool FY3 129 D6
Manchester Rd. Blackrod BL6 30 E1
Manchester Rd. Burnley BB11 126 E4
Manchester Rd. Burnley BB11 126 F5
Manchester Rd.
Clow Bridge BB11 & BB4 105 D6
Manchester Rd.
Hapton BB11 & BB12 125 C4
Manchester Rd. Haslingden BB4 67 D7
Manchester Rd. Haslingden BB4 84 B2
Manchester Rd. Nelson BB9 147 D7
Manchester Rd. Preston PR1 96 B7
Manchester Rd.
Ramsbottom BL0 & BL9 49 E4
Manchester Rd. Southport PR9 34 C7
Manchester Road Sta. BB11 126 F5
Mancknols St. BB9 147 F7
Mandella Ct. BB1 100 E6
Mandeville Rd. PR8 20 B5
Mandeville Terr. BL8 48 B2
Manfield. WN8 18 A3
Manghales. BB4 84 B7
Manion Ave. L31 5 B5
Manion Cl. L31 5 B5
Manitoba Cl. BB2 100 B8
Manley Cl. BL9 49 C2
Manner Sutton St. BB1 100 F5
Manning Rd. 4 Preston PR1 117 E1
Manning Rd. Southport PR8 34 E6
Manor Ave. Burscough L40 24 D2
Manor Ave. Fulwood PR2 117 B4
Manor Ave. Hest Bank LA2 213 E8
Manor Ave. Penwortham PR1 95 B4
Manor Ave. Ribchester PR3 140 D3
Manor Beach Cty Prim Sch.
FY5 172 D3
Manor Brook. 1 BB5 103 C6
Manor Cl. Burton in L LA6 236 C3
Manor Cl. Coupe Green PR5 97 F3
Manor Cl. Hest Bank LA2 213 E8
Manor Cres. Burscough L40 24 D2
Manor Cres. Hest Bank LA2 213 F8
Manor Ct. Blackpool FY4 129 E1
Manor Ct. Fulwood PR2 116 B7
Manor Ctyd. LA3 208 E8
Manor Dr. Burscough L40 24 D2
Manor Dr. Cleveleys FY5 172 D3
Manor Dr. Hest Bank LA2 213 E8
Manor Dr. Kirkham PR4 113 C4
Manor Fields. BB7 143 C5
Manor Gdns. L40 24 D2
Manor Gr. Morecambe LA3 212 C2
Manor Gr. Penwortham PR1 95 A4
Manor Gr. Skelmersdale WN8 17 F1
Manor House Cl. Leyland PR5 58 B8
Manor House Cl. Maghull L31 5 C1
Manor House Cres. PR1 117 B3
Manor House Dr. WN8 9 E3
Manor House La. PR1 & PR2 117 C3
Manor House Park Flats. FY5 172 C3
Manor La. Hest Bank LA2 215 F1
Manor La. Penwortham PR1 95 B4
Manor Lodge. L37 11 E4
Manor Pk. PR2 117 C4
Manor Pl. BB5 102 F7
Manor Rd. Blackburn BB2 100 B5
Manor Rd. Blackpool FY1 129 D4
Manor Rd. Burnley BB12 126 B7
Manor Rd. Burscough L40 24 D2
Manor Rd. Clayton Green PR6 77 B3
Manor Rd. Clitheroe BB7 164 D7
Manor Rd. Colne BB8 169 E7
Manor Rd. Darwen BB3 63 F8
Manor Rd. Fleetwood FY7 193 E4
Manor Rd. Garstang PR3 199 C1
Manor Rd. Hest Bank LA2 213 F8
Manor Rd. Horwich BL6 31 D4
Manor Rd. Inskip PR4 134 C8
Manor Rd. Shevington WN6 19 F6
Manor Rd. Southport PR9 53 A2
Manor Rd. Whalley BB7 143 C5
Manor Rd. Wrea Green PR4 112 B4
Manor Road Cty Prim Sch.
PR6 77 B2
Manor St. Accrington BB5 103 D7
Manor St. Bacup OL13 86 F1
Manor St. Bury BL9 32 A2
Manor St. Nelson BB9 147 F8
Manor St. Ramsbottom BL0 49 B7
Manor Steet. BB9 147 F8
Manor Way. PR4 112 B3
Manor Wood. Fleetwood FY7 193 E4
Manor Wood. Kirkham PR4 113 B7
Manorcroft. PR4 73 F8
Manse Ave. WN6 27 F5
Mansergh St. BB10 147 C2
Mansfield Ave. BL0 49 B2
Mansfield Cres. BB9 147 C6
Mansfield Dr. PR5 97 E3
Mansfield Gr. BB9 147 C6
Mansfield Rd. FY3 129 D8
Mansion House Bldgs. 2 BB4 85 A7
Mansion St S. BB5 103 D6
Manston Gr. PR7 42 A7
Manx Jane's La. PR9 53 A4
Manxman Rd. BB2 100 F1
Maple Ave. Blackpool FY3 129 D5
Maple Ave. Brinscall PR6 61 F7
Maple Ave. Burscough L40 24 E4
Maple Ave. 7 Bury BL9 32 B2
Maple Ave. Fleetwood FY7 172 F8
Maple Ave. Haslingden BB4 84 C3
Maple Ave. Horwich BL6 31 E1
Maple Ave. Morecambe LA3 212 B2
Maple Ave. Thornton FY5 151 C8
Maple Cl. Formby L37 11 C1
Maple Cl. Newton-with-S PR4 113 F2
Maple Cl. Whalley BB7 143 D6
Maple Cl. Wilpshire BB1 121 E6
Maple Cres. BB1 102 B8
Maple Ct. PR3 199 C1
Maple Dr. Bamber Bridge PR5 96 F1
Maple Dr. Oswaldtwistle BB5 102 F3
Maple Dr. Poulton-le-F FY6 151 E2
Maple Gr. Chorley PR6 60 D3
Maple Gr. Fulwood PR2 118 A4
Maple Gr. Grimsargh PR2 138 D1
Maple Gr. Penwortham PR1 95 B4
Maple Gr. Ramsbottom BL0 49 D6
Maple Gr. Warton PR4 91 D6
Maple Rd. PR3 199 C1
Maple St. Blackburn BB1 101 A7
Maple St. Clayton-le-M BB5 123 F1
Maple St. Great Harwood BB6 123 D6
Maple St. 1 Rishton BB1 123 B1
Maple St. Southport PR8 34 E6
Maplebank. PR2 115 C1
Maples The. PR5 57 F6
Maplewood. Skelmersdale WN8 18 A4
Maplewood. Southport PR9 52 F2
Maplewood Ave. FY6 195 A5
Maplewood Cl. Leyland PR5 58 E8
Maplewood Cl.
Lytham St Anne's FY8 89 F4
Maplewood Dr. FY5 150 C8
Maplewood Gdns. LA1 211 A2
Mapsden Dr. BB9 147 D6
Marabou Dr. BB3 80 E3
Marathon Pl. PR5 75 C3
Marble Pl. PR8 34 B7
Marble St. BB5 102 E4
March St. BB12 126 F8
Marchbank Rd. WN8 17 D1
Marchwood Rd. FY3 130 B8
Marcroft Ave. FY4 109 E7
Mardale Ave. Blackpool FY4 130 C1
Mardale Ave. Morecambe LA4 212 G5
Mardale Cl. PR8 20 B4
Mardale Cres. PR5 59 B7
Mardale Rd. Fulwood PR1 118 A1
Mardale Rd. Lancaster LA1 214 A1
Mardale Rd. Longridge PR3 138 F5
Maresfield Rd. PR1 95 E5
Marewood. PR7 60 B2
Margaret Rd. PR1 95 E4
Margaret St. Blackburn BB1 101 D4
Margaret St. Burnley BB10 127 A8
Margaret St. Oswaldtwistle BB5 102 C2
Margaret St. 1 Preston PR1 96 A8
Margaret St. Rawtenstall BB4 84 F4
Margate Ave. FY4 109 E6
Margate Rd. Fulwood PR2 116 A4
Margate Rd.
Lytham St Anne's FY8 88 F8
Maria Ct. 10 BB11 127 B4
Maria Sq. BL7 45 D4
Maria St. BB3 64 B6
Marians Dr. L39 15 E7
Maricourt Ave. BB1 101 D5
Marilyn Ave. 2 PR5 76 B8
Marina Ave. Blackpool FY1 129 D2
Marina Ave. Poulton-le-F FY3 130 D8
Marina Cl. PR5 96 A1
Marina Dr. Bamber Bridge PR5 96 A1
Marina Dr. Fulwood PR2 116 E7
Marina Gr. PR5 96 A1
Marina Rd. L37 11 F1
Marine Ave. BB11 126 C4
Marine Dr. Hest Bank LA2 215 D1
Marine Dr. Lytham St Anne's FY8 89 D3
Marine Dr. Southport PR8 & PR9 52 D4
Marine Ind Ctr. FY8 90 D4
Marine Par. Fleetwood FY7 193 C1
Marine Par. Southport PR8 34 A8
Marine Rd E. LA4 212 F6
Marine Rd W. LA3 & LA4 212 C4
Marine Road Central. LA4 212 D5
Mariners Cl. FY7 193 E1
Mariners Way. PR1 & PR2 95 B8
Marino Cl. FY5 151 D8
Maritime St. FY7 193 F2
Mark Cl. PR5 95 F1
Mark Rd. L38 2 F4
Mark Sq. PR4 56 A6
Mark St. Bacup OL13 69 C8
Mark St. Burnley BB10 147 B1
Mark's Ave. PR5 75 E5
Market Ave. 2 BB1 100 E5
Market Cross. L39 15 E5
Market Gate. 27 LA1 210 F8
Market Pl. Adlington PR6 30 A7
Market Pl. 12 Chorley PR7 42 C8
Market Pl. 8 Clitheroe BB7 164 E8
Market Pl. 10 Colne BB8 169 E5
Market Pl. Edenfield BL0 67 D3
Market Pl. Garstang PR3 178 C7
Market Pl. 1 Leyland PR5 59 A8
Market Pl. Longridge PR3 139 B7
Market Pl. 3 Poulton-le-F FY6 151 D3
Market Pl. Ramsbottom BL0 49 C7
Market Pl. Standish WN6 28 E1
Market Sq. Burnley BB11 127 A6
Market Sq. Kirkby Lonsdale LA6 238 C2
Market Sq. Kirkham PR4 113 B5
Market Sq. 10 Lancaster LA1 210 F8
Market Sq. Lytham St Anne's FY8 90 A3
Market Sq. Nelson BB9 147 D8
Market St. Adlington PR6 30 A6
Market St. Bacup OL13 86 F2
Market St. 3 Barnoldswick BB8 200 B2
Market St. Blackpool FY1 129 B5
Market St. Carnforth LA5 217 D2
Market St. Chorley PR6 & PR7 42 C7
Market St. Church BB5 102 E5
Market St. Colne BB8 169 E5
Market St. Darwen BB3 81 A1
Market St. Edenfield BL0 67 D4
Market St. Hambleton FY6 174 C2
Market St. Kirkby Lonsdale LA6 238 C2
Market St. Kirkham PR4 112 F6
Market St. Lancaster LA1 210 F8
Market St. Morecambe LA4 212 D5
Market St. 9 Nelson BB9 147 D8
Market St. 5 Newchurch BB4 68 F8
Market St. Preston PR1 95 F8
Market St. Southport PR8 34 B7
Market St. Standish WN6 28 E1
Market St.
Whitworth OL12 & OL13 70 D4
Market St W. PR1 95 F8
Market Street La. BB2 100 E4
Market Way. 7 Blackburn BB1 100 E5
Market Way. Ormskirk L39 15 E5
Market Wlk. PR6 42 C8
Markham Dr. PR8 34 E2
Markham Rd. BB2 100 B3
Markham St. PR1 116 C1

New Way. Whitworth OL12 ... 70 C1
New Wellington Cl. BB2 ... 100 C1
New Wellington Gdns. BB2 ... 100 C1
New Wellington St. BB2 ... 100 C1
Newark Pl. Fulwood PR2 ... 116 D8
Newark Pl. Preston PR2 ... 115 E2
Newark Rd. OL12 ... 51 F3
Newark Sq. OL12 ... 51 F3
Newark St. BB5 ... 102 F5
Newarth La. PR4 ... 72 E3
Newbigging Ave. BB4 ... 85 F2
Newburgh CE Prim Sch. WN8 . 26 A1
Newbury Ave. FY4 ... 109 D8
Newbury Cl. PR2 ... 116 C8
Newbury Gn. PR2 ... 116 C8
Newbury Rd. FY8 ... 89 A4
Newby Ave. Fleetwood FY7 ... 193 D1
Newby Ave. Poulton-le-F FY6 ... 151 D1
Newby Back La. BB7 ... 225 A1
Newby Cl. Ainsdale PR8 ... 20 B3
Newby Cl. Burnley BB11 ... 126 E2
Newby Dr.
Clayton-le-W PR5 & PR6 ... 76 E2
Newby Dr. Lancaster LA1 ... 213 F3
Newby La. BB7 ... 189 B8
Newby Pl. Blackpool FY4 ... 130 B1
Newby Pl. Fulwood PR2 ... 117 D4
Newcastle Ave. Blackpool FY3 .. 129 D4
Newcastle Ave. Cleveleys FY5 .. 172 F4
Newcastle St. BB2 ... 100 C3
Newchurch CE Prim Sch. BB4 . 85 E1
Newchurch Cl. BB2 ... 100 F2
Newchurch Old Rd. BB4 ... 86 E1
Newchurch Rd. Bacup OL13 ... 69 C8
Newchurch Rd. Rawtenstall BB4 85 C2
Newcombe Rd. BL0 ... 49 B2
Newcroft. LA5 ... 217 E6
Newfield Dr.
Blackburn BB1 & BB2 ... 81 A8
Newfield Dr. Nelson BB9 ... 147 E8
Newfield Rd. PR5 ... 77 A7
Newgate. PR2 ... 116 E4
Newgate Ave. WN6 ... 19 E8
Newgate La. PR4 ... 75 C8
Newgate Rd. WN8 ... 9 F7
Newhaven Dr. PR3 ... 178 D2
Newhouse Rd. Accrington BB5 . 124 D1
Newhouse Rd. Blackpool FY4 ... 129 F2
Newington Ave. BB1 ... 121 F3
Newlands. PR7 ... 40 C6
Newlands Ave. Blackpool FY3 ... 129 F2
Newlands Ave. Burscough L40 ... 24 F4
Newlands Ave. Clitheroe BB7 ... 164 C7
Newlands Ave. Lancaster LA1 ... 211 B5
Newlands Ave.
Lower Healey OL12 ... 51 F3
Newlands Ave. Penwortham PR1 95 B5
Newlands Cl. Blackburn BB2 ... 79 E8
Newlands Cl. Lower Healey OL12 51 F3
Newlands Rd. Lancaster LA1 ... 211 C5
Newlands Rd.
Lancaster LA1 & LA2 ... 211 E6
Newlands Rd.
Lytham St Anne's FY8 ... 89 C5
Newlands Rd. Morecambe LA4 .. 212 F4
Newlands Way. FY6 ... 151 C1
Newlyn Ave. Blackpool FY4 ... 109 E5
Newlyn Ave. Maghull L31 ... 5 E1
Newlyn Ct. FY4 ... 109 E5
Newlyn Dr. WN8 ... 9 D7
Newlyn Pl. PR2 ... 115 F5
Newman Rd. FY1 ... 129 D8
Newman St. BB10 ... 147 A2
Newmarket Ave. LA1 ... 211 B3
Newmarket St. LA4 ... 213 A7
Newport St. BB9 ... 168 E1
News La. WA11 ... 8 F2
Newsham Hall La. PR4 & PR3 .. 135 F3
Newsham Pl. LA1 ... 211 A5
Newsham Rd. LA1 ... 211 A5
Newsham St. PR1 ... 116 D1
Newsham St Mary's &
St Andrews RC Sch. PR4 ... 136 A5
Newsome St. PR5 ... 76 A1
Newstet Rd. L33 ... 1 C2
Newthorn. BB5 ... 103 A1
Newton Ave. Poulton-le-F FY6 ... 151 C2
Newton Ave. Preston PR1 ... 97 A8
Newton Bluecoat CE Prim Sch.
PR4 ... 114 A2
Newton Cl. Freckleton PR4 ... 92 C7
Newton Cl. Leyland PR5 ... 58 B8
Newton Dr. Accrington BB5 ... 103 D3
Newton Dr. Blackpool FY3 ... 129 E5
Newton Dr. Over Town BB10 ... 107 A7
Newton Dr. Ramsbottom BL8 ... 49 A1
Newton Dr E. FY3 ... 130 B7
Newton Gr. FY5 ... 151 D7
Newton Pl. FY3 ... 130 A7
Newton Rd.
Lytham St Anne's FY8 ... 89 A7
Newton Rd. Preston PR1 & PR2 . 116 B2
Newton St. Blackburn BB1 ... 101 B5
Newton St. Burnley BB12 ... 126 C7
Newton St. Clitheroe BB7 ... 164 D7
Newton St. Darwen BB3 ... 81 B2
Newton St. Oswaldtwistle BB5 ... 102 C5
Newton St. 2 Preston PR1 ... 96 B8
Newton St. Southport PR9 ... 35 A7
Newton Terr. LA1 ... 214 A3
Newtown. BB8 ... 169 E5
Newtown St. BB8 ... 169 E5
Nib La. PR5 ... 75 E8
Nichol St. PR6 & PR7 ... 60 C1
Nicholas St. Brierfield BB10 ... 147 E3
Nicholas St. Burnley BB11 ... 127 A5
Nicholas St. Colne BB8 ... 169 C4
Nicholas St. Darwen BB3 ... 80 F1
Nicholl St. 1 BB10 ... 127 A8
Nicholson Cres. LA4 ... 212 G5
Nick Hilton's La. PR6 ... 43 D3
Nickey La. BB2 ... 120 F2
Nickleton Brow. PR6 ... 43 C2
Nicksons La. FY6 ... 195 B4
Nightfield La. BB2 ... 119 F6
Nightingale Cres. BB11 ... 126 C4
Nightingale Dr. FY6 ... 151 B2
Nightingale Rd. BL6 ... 30 C3
Nightingale St. PR6 ... 30 A8
Nile St. 5 Lancaster LA1 ... 210 F8
Nile St. 12 Nelson BB9 ... 168 D1
Nile St. Preston PR1 ... 96 A7
Nimes St. PR1 ... 96 D8
Nine Elms. PR2 ... 116 C6
Nineteen Acre La. LA5 ... 219 F4
Nineveh St. 12 BB8 ... 169 E5
Nipe La. WA11 & WN8 ... 9 B5
Nithside. FY4 ... 130 C1
Niton Cl. BB4 ... 84 C1
Nixon La. PR5 ... 58 A8
Nixon's La. PR8 ... 20 E7
Nixons Cl. PR5 ... 57 F8
Nixons La. WN8 ... 9 D7
Noble St. Darwen BB3 ... 64 A8
Noble St. Great Harwood BB6 ... 123 C4
Noble St. Rishton BB1 ... 123 B1
Noblett Ct. 9 FY7 ... 193 F2
Noblett St. BB1 ... 100 F5
Noel Gate. L39 ... 15 B1
Noel Jones Ct. FY8 ... 88 E7
Noel Rd. LA1 ... 213 E3
Noel Sq. PR2 ... 117 E1
Nolan St. PR8 ... 34 C5
Nook Cres. PR2 ... 138 C1
Nook Farm Ave. OL12 ... 51 F3
Nook Field. PR3 ... 137 D6
Nook Glade. PR2 ... 138 C1
Nook La. Bamber Bridge PR5 ... 76 D6
Nook La. Blackburn BB2 ... 99 F1
Nook La. Churchtown PR3 ... 178 A3
Nook La. Mawdesley PR7 ... 39 E5
Nook La. Oswaldtwistle BB5 ... 102 B2
Nook Terr. Blackburn BB2 ... 100 A1
Nook Terr. Lower Healey OL12 ... 51 F3
Nook The. Bolton-le-S LA5 ... 216 A4
Nook The. Shevington Vale WN6 .. 19 E7
Nook The. Staining FY3 ... 130 D5
Nookfield. PR5 ... 75 A1
Nookfield Cl. FY8 ... 90 A4
Nooklands. PR2 ... 116 E4
Noon Sun St. OL12 ... 51 F1
Noor St. PR1 ... 117 A1
Nora St. BB9 ... 168 D3
Norbreck Cl. BB2 ... 80 F8
Norbreck Dr. PR2 ... 115 E1
Norbreck Rd. FY5 ... 150 C7
Norbreck Sch (Prim). FY5 ... 150 C8
Norburn Cres. L37 ... 11 F2
Norbury Cl. PR9 ... 53 C5
Norcliffe Rd. FY2 ... 150 C5
Norcross Brow. PR7 ... 62 B8
Norcross La. FY5 ... 151 A7
Norcross Pl. PR2 ... 115 F1
Norden Cty High Sch. BB1 ... 123 A2
Norfield. L39 ... 15 F5
Norfolk Ave. Blackpool FY2 ... 150 B3
Norfolk Ave. Burnley BB12 ... 126 B7
Norfolk Ave. Cleveleys FY5 ... 172 E3
Norfolk Ave. Morecambe LA3 ... 212 B2
Norfolk Ave. Padiham BB12 ... 125 D6
Norfolk Cl. 7 Clayton-le-M BB5 123 F3
Norfolk Cl. Leyland PR5 ... 58 E7
Norfolk Gr. Church BB5 ... 103 A7
Norfolk Gr. Southport PR8 ... 33 F1
Norfolk Rd. Bamber Bridge PR5 .. 96 D4
Norfolk Rd. Blackpool FY3 ... 130 A2
Norfolk Rd. Longshaw WN5 ... 10 E1
Norfolk Rd. Lytham St Anne's FY8 90 C5
Norfolk Rd. Preston PR1 ... 117 A1
Norfolk Rd. Southport PR8 ... 33 F1
Norfolk St. Accrington BB5 ... 103 D7
Norfolk St. Blackburn BB2 ... 100 C2
Norfolk St. Colne BB8 ... 169 E5
Norfolk St. Darwen BB3 ... 81 B1
Norfolk St. Lancaster LA1 ... 213 F2
Norfolk St. Nelson BB9 ... 168 D1
Norfolk St. Rishton BB1 ... 123 A1
Norkeed Rd. FY5 ... 150 C7
Norland Dr. LA3 ... 208 F8
Norman Cl. FY5 ... 172 F1
Norman Rd. BB5 ... 102 C5
Norman St. Blackburn BB2 ... 100 C3
Norman St. Burnley BB10 ... 127 A7
Norman St. Bury BL9 ... 32 B4
Normandie Ave. FY2 ... 150 D3
Normandy Rd. PR3 ... 136 B3
Normanhurst. L39 ... 16 A4
Normington Cl. L31 ... 5 C4
Normoss Ave. FY3 ... 130 A7
Normoss Rd. FY3 ... 130 C7
Norris House Dr. L39 ... 6 C8
Norris St. Chorley PR7 ... 42 C6
Norris St. Darwen BB3 ... 81 B1
Norris St. Fulwood PR2 ... 116 D3
Norris St. Preston PR1 & PR2 ... 116 E2
Norris Way. L37 ... 12 B3
North Albert St. FY7 ... 194 B5
North Albion St. FY7 ... 194 A4
North Arthur St. FY7 ... 194 B5
North Ave. Barnoldswick BB8 ... 200 B2
North Ave. Blackpool FY3 ... 129 D7
North Ave. Ramsbottom BL8 ... 48 F1
North Bank Ave. BB1 ... 121 E1
North Church St. FY7 ... 194 B5
North Cliff St. PR1 ... 95 E6
North Cliffe Sch. BB6 ... 123 B6
North Clifton St. FY8 ... 90 B3
North Cres. FY8 ... 88 E6
North Ct. FY5 ... 172 D5
North Dr. Appley Bridge WN6 ... 27 C2
North Dr. Blackpool FY5 ... 150 D6
North Dr. Cleveleys FY5 ... 172 E2
North Dr. Inskip PR4 ... 155 C1
North Dr. Kirkham PR4 ... 112 F6
North Dr. Whalley BB7 ... 143 B7
North End Football Gd (Preston
North End FC). PR1 ... 117 B2
North End La. L38 ... 3 A6
North Gr. 1 PR5 ... 76 C8
North Highfield. PR2 ... 117 E6
North Houses La. FY8 ... 110 D1
North Leach Dr. PR8 ... 20 A5
North Meade. L31 ... 5 C2
North Meadowside. PR4 ... 74 A6
North Mersey Bsns Ctr. L33 ... 1 D4
North Moor La. L39 ... 22 E2
North Moss La. L37 & L39 ... 12 D7
North Par. BB8 ... 200 B3
North Park Ave. BB9 ... 168 C1
North Park Dr. FY3 ... 129 F5
North Perimeter Rd. L33 ... 1 D4
North Prom. FY8 ... 88 D7
North Rd. Blackburn BB1 ... 101 C3
North Rd. Bretherton PR5 & PR4 .. 57 B7
North Rd. Carnforth LA5 ... 217 E2
North Rd. Lancaster LA1 ... 210 F8
North Rd. Preston PR0 & PR1 ... 116 F1
North Rd. Rawtenstall BB4 ... 85 C2
North Rd. Southport PR9 ... 53 C4
North Ribble St. PR1 ... 96 C6
North Road Sch. LA5 ... 217 D1
North Shore Golf Course. FY2 150 C3
North Sq. Blackpool FY3 ... 129 D6
North Sq. Cleveleys FY5 ... 172 D5
North St. Barnoldswick BB8 ... 200 B1
North St. Brierfield BB10 ... 147 F3
North St. Burnley BB10 ... 147 A1
North St. Chorley PR6 ... 60 D2
North St. Clitheroe BB7 ... 186 F1
North St. Colne BB8 ... 169 E6
North St. Fleetwood FY7 ... 194 B5
North St. Hapton BB12 ... 125 C5
North St. Haslingden BB4 ... 84 C1
North St. Morecambe LA4 ... 212 E5
North St. 14 Nelson BB9 ... 168 D1
North St. Newchurch BB4 ... 85 E1
North St. Padiham BB12 ... 145 C1
North St. Preston PR1 ... 95 F8
North St. Ramsbottom BL0 ... 67 C2
North St. Rawtenstall BB4 ... 85 A2
North St. Southport PR9 ... 34 C8
North St. Water BB4 ... 86 A8
North St. Whitworth OL12 ... 70 C1
North Syke Ave. PR2 ... 115 C1
North Terr. PR7 ... 59 D4
North Vale. PR6 ... 42 F1
North Valley Rd. Colne BB8 ... 169 C5
North Valley Rd. Colne BB8 ... 169 D5
North View. Kirkham PR4 ... 112 F5
North View. Leyland PR5 ... 58 F8
North View. Ramsbottom BL0 ... 49 B2
North View. Rawtenstall BB4 ... 85 A8
North View. Strongstry BL0 ... 67 C2
North View Cl. PR3 ... 154 C5
North Warton St. FY8 ... 90 C3
Northall. PR4 ... 73 E2
Northam Cl. PR9 ... 53 A5
Northbrook Gdns. PR5 ... 75 E1
Northbrook Rd. PR5 ... 75 F1
Northcliffe. BB6 ... 123 B6
Northcote Rd. Langho BB6 ... 142 C3
Northcote Rd. Preston PR1 ... 95 D7
Northcote St. Darwen BB3 ... 64 B6
Northcote St. 4 Haslingden BB4 84 B2
Northcote St. 8 Leyland PR5 ... 76 A1
Northdene. WN8 ... 26 B2
Northdunes. L38 ... 2 F4
Northenden Rd. PR7 ... 41 E1
Northern Ave. PR4 ... 73 E2
Northern Cty Prim Sch. OL13 ... 86 F6
Northfield. WN8 ... 18 B4
Northfield Ave. FY1 ... 129 B8
Northfield Rd. Blackburn BB1 ... 100 E7
Northfield Rd. Haslingden BB5 ... 84 A8
Northfleet Ave. FY7 ... 193 E2
Northfold Cty Prim Sch. FY5 .. 172 E4
Northgate. 14 Blackburn BB2 ... 100 E5
Northgate. Blackpool FY2 ... 150 C4
Northgate. Goosnargh PR3 ... 137 D6
Northgate. Leyland PR5 ... 76 B2
Northgate. Lytham St Anne's FY8 . 88 D6
Northgate.
Morecambe LA1 & LA3 & LA4 ... 213 A2
Northgate. Wallbank OL12 ... 51 C7
Northgate Dr. PR6 ... 60 E2
Northlands. Fulwood PR2 ... 116 E6
Northlands. Leyland PR5 ... 58 C7
Northleach Ave. PR1 ... 95 F2
Northside. PR7 ... 59 C3
Northumberland Ave.
Blackpool FY2 ... 150 B1
Northumberland Ave.
Cleveleys FY5 ... 172 F5
Northumberland House. 14
PR4 ... 95 F8
Northumberland St. 2
Chorley PR6 ... 42 D7
Northumberland St.
Morecambe LA4 ... 212 D5
Northway. Broughton PR3 ... 136 C3
Northway. Fleetwood FY7 ... 193 D1
Northway. Fulwood PR2 ... 116 D7
Northway. Maghull L31 & L39 ... 5 E4
Northway. Ormskirk L39 ... 15 A1
Northway. Skelmersdale WN8 ... 18 B2
Northway Prim Sch. L31 ... 5 E3
Northways. WN6 ... 28 D2
Northwood Cl. Burnley BB12 ... 126 D7
Northwood Cl.
Lytham St Anne's FY8 ... 89 E4
Northwood Way. FY6 ... 151 D2
Norton Ave. LA3 ... 212 A3
Norton Dr. LA3 ... 212 B2
Norton Gr. LA3 ... 212 A2
Norton Pl. LA3 ... 212 A2
Norton Rd. LA3 ... 212 A2
Norton Rd. Garstang PR3 ... 199 C2
Norton Rd. Lower Healey OL12 ... 51 F3
Norton St. BB12 ... 125 C4
Norwich Pl. Blackpool FY2 ... 150 D5
Norwich Pl. 35 Preston PR1 ... 96 A7
Norwich St. BB1 ... 100 F7
Norwood Ave. Becconsall PR4 ... 72 F2
Norwood Ave. Blackburn BB2 ... 100 E2
Norwood Ave. Blackpool FY3 ... 129 E8
Norwood Ave. Nelson BB9 ... 168 F2
Norwood Ave. Southport PR9 ... 34 E7
Norwood Cl. PR6 ... 30 A8
Norwood Cres. PR9 ... 34 E7
Norwood Dr. LA4 ... 213 B3
Norwood Gdns. PR9 ... 34 F7
Norwood Prim Sch. PR9 ... 34 E7
Norwood Rd.
Lytham St Anne's FY8 ... 88 C8
Norwood Rd.
Southport PR8 & PR9 ... 34 F6
Notre Dame Gdns. BB1 ... 101 A6
Nottingham Rd. PR1 ... 117 A1
Nottingham St. BB1 ... 101 A4
Novak Pl. LA4 ... 213 B4
Nowell Gr. BB12 ... 144 D2
Nowell St. 13 BB6 ... 123 C5
Noyna Ave. BB8 ... 191 E1
Noyna St. BB8 ... 169 E6
Noyna View. BB8 ... 169 E7
Nun's St. LA1 ... 211 A8
Nuns Ave. LA7 ... 237 E3
Nurseries The. L37 ... 12 A2
Nursery Ave. L39 ... 16 A6
Nursery Cl. Coppull PR7 ... 41 E4
Nursery Cl. Leyland PR5 ... 58 F8
Nursery Dr. Becconsall PR4 ... 72 F1
Nursery Dr. Formby L37 ... 11 F2
Nursery La. PR4 ... 74 E8
Nursery Nook. BB3 ... 81 D5
Nursery Rd. L31 ... 5 C4
Nuthall Rd. PR8 ... 34 F3
Nuttall Ave. Great Harwood BB6 123 C4
Nuttall Ave. Horwich BL6 ... 31 A3
Nuttall Cl. BL0 ... 49 C5
Nuttall Hall Cotts. BL0 ... 49 D5
Nuttall Hall Rd. BL0 ... 49 D5
Nuttall La. BL0 ... 49 C4
Nuttall Rd. Blackpool FY1 ... 129 D2
Nuttall Rd. Ramsbottom BL0 ... 49 D4
Nuttall St. Accrington BB5 ... 103 C5
Nuttall St. Bacup OL13 ... 87 B3
Nuttall St. Blackburn BB2 ... 80 D8
Nuttall St. Blackburn BB2 ... 100 D1
Nuttall St. 8 Burnley BB11 ... 127 B4
Nuttall St. Bury BL9 ... 32 A1
Nuttall St. Rawtenstall BB4 ... 85 B3
Nuttall St Mews. 3 BB5 ... 103 C5
Nutter Cres. BB12 ... 145 F5
Nutter Rd. Accrington BB5 ... 103 C7
Nutter Rd. Cleveleys FY5 ... 172 D3
Nutter Rd. Preston PR1 ... 95 E7

O'Hagan Ct. BB9 ... 147 B6
Oak Ave. Blackpool FY4 ... 109 D8
Oak Ave. Euxton PR7 ... 59 D3
Oak Ave. Galgate LA2 ... 206 F4
Oak Ave. Haslingden BB5 ... 84 A8
Oak Ave. 9 Horwich BL6 ... 31 E1
Oak Ave. Kirkham PR4 ... 113 B4
Oak Ave. Longridge PR3 ... 139 A7
Oak Ave. Morecambe LA4 ... 213 B6
Oak Ave. Ormskirk L39 ... 15 D4
Oak Ave. Penwortham PR1 ... 95 B3
Oak Ave. Ramsbottom BL0 ... 49 A2
Oak Ave. Thornton FY5 ... 151 C8
Oak Bank. Accrington BB5 ... 124 D2
Oak Bank. Gregson Lane PR5 ... 97 E1
Oak Cl. Barrow BB7 ... 164 D1
Oak Cl. Rishton BB1 ... 102 B8
Oak Cl. Whitworth OL12 ... 70 D4
Oak Cres. WN8 ... 17 D1
Oak Croft. PR6 ... 77 B2
Oak Dr. Chorley PR6 ... 60 C3
Oak Dr. Freckleton PR4 ... 92 A5
Oak Dr. Halton LA2 ... 214 F7
Oak Gates. BL7 ... 46 E1
Oak Gn. L39 ... 15 F5
Oak Gr. Darwen BB3 ... 81 B2
Oak Gr. New Longton PR4 ... 75 A6
Oak Hill Cl. BB5 ... 103 C4
Oak La. Accrington BB5 ... 103 D5
Oak La. Newton-with-S PR4 ... 113 F2
Oak Rd. PR3 ... 178 B8
Oak Ridge. BB7 ... 186 D7
Oak St. Accrington BB5 ... 103 C5
Oak St. Blackburn BB1 ... 100 F7
Oak St. Brierfield BB9 ... 147 B6
Oak St. Burnley BB12 ... 126 C6
Oak St. Clayton-le-M BB5 ... 123 F1
Oak St. Colne BB8 ... 169 F6
Oak St. Fleetwood FY7 ... 194 A4
Oak St. Great Harwood BB6 ... 123 C6
Oak St. 2 Nelson BB9 ... 168 E1
Oak St. Oswaldtwistle BB5 ... 102 D3
Oak St. Preston PR1 ... 96 A7
Oak St. Ramsbottom BL0 ... 49 B5
Oak St. Rawtenstall BB11 ... 105 B4
Oak St. Southport PR8 ... 34 E6
Oak St. Whitworth OL12 ... 70 D5
Oak Terr. BB8 ... 200 C3
Oak Tree Ct. WN8 ... 18 D3
Oak View. Leyland PR5 ... 75 E2
Oak View. Whitworth OL12 ... 70 D4
Oakdene Ave. BB5 ... 124 E1
Oaken Bank. BB10 ... 147 E3
Oaken Cl. OL13 ... 87 B3
Oakenclough Cotts. PR3 ... 220 C2
Oakenclough Rd. OL13 ... 87 B3
Oakeneaves Ave. BB11 ... 126 D2
Oakengate. PR2 ... 117 C7
Oakengates. WN6 ... 28 F1
Oakenhead St. PR1 ... 117 E1
Oakenhead Wood Old Rd. BB4 84 E3
Oakenhurst Rd. BB2 ... 100 D4
Oakenshaw Ave. OL12 ... 51 C6
Oakenshaw View. OL12 ... 51 C6
Oakfield. Fulwood PR2 ... 116 F7
Oakfield. Preston PR1 ... 116 B1
Oakfield Ave. Accrington BB5 ... 124 E1
Oakfield Ave. Barnoldswick BB8 200 A3
Oakfield Ave. Clayton-le-M BB5 . 123 E3
Oakfield Cl. BL6 ... 31 F2
Oakfield Cres. BB5 ... 102 F4
Oakfield Dr. Formby L37 ... 11 D4
Oakfield Dr. Leyland PR5 ... 58 B8
Oakfield Rd. Blackburn BB2 ... 80 D7
Oakfield Rd. Hightown L38 ... 2 F2
Oakgate Cl. PR4 ... 55 F5
Oakgrove. FY4 ... 109 D6
Oakham Ct. 13 PR1 ... 96 A7
Oakhill Cl. L31 ... 5 D2
Oakhill Coll. BB7 ... 143 D6
Oakhill Cottage La. L31 ... 5 D4
Oakhill Dr. L31 ... 5 D4
Oakhill Rd. L31 ... 5 D3
Oakhurst Ave. BB5 ... 124 E1
Oakland Ave. FY5 ... 150 D6
Oakland Glen. PR1 ... 96 A3
Oakland St. 3
Bamber Bridge PR5 ... 96 E1
Oakland St. Nelson BB9 ... 147 E8
Oaklands Ave. Barrowford BB9 168 D3
Oaklands Ave. Tarleton PR4 ... 56 A7
Oaklands Ct. LA1 ... 210 C5
Oaklands Dr. Penwortham PR1 ... 95 A4
Oaklands Dr. Rawtenstall BB4 ... 84 E2
Oaklands Gr. PR2 ... 115 F1
Oaklands Rd. BL0 ... 67 D2
Oaklea. WN6 ... 28 A2
Oakleaf Cl. PR3 ... 137 C6
Oakleaf Ct. FY5 ... 172 D4
Oakleaf Way. FY4 ... 130 D1
Oaklee Gr. L33 ... 1 A4
Oakleigh. WN8 ... 9 D2
Oakleigh Terr. OL14 ... 108 B1
Oakley Rd. Morecambe LA3 ... 212 A2
Oakley Rd. Rawtenstall BB4 ... 84 F2
Oakley St. BB4 ... 84 E2
Oakmere. PR6 ... 77 C3
Oakmere Ave. PR6 ... 78 D2
Oakmoor Ave. FY2 ... 150 E4
Oakridge Cl. PR2 ... 116 F7
Oakroyd Cl. LA5 ... 237 B2
Oaks Bar. BB1 ... 121 C8
Oaks Brow. BB1 ... 121 C7
Oaks The. Bamber Bridge PR1 ... 96 B3
Oaks The. Chorley PR7 ... 42 B4
Oaks The. Leyland PR5 ... 58 A7
Oaks The. Poulton-le-F FY6 ... 151 D4
Oaks The.
St Michael's on W PR3 ... 155 C7
Oaksfield. BB3 ... 80 E5
Oakshaw Dr. OL12 ... 51 A1
Oakshott Pl. PR5 ... 77 B7
Oaktree Ave. Clayton-le-W PR5 ... 76 D4
Oaktree Ave. Fulwood PR2 ... 116 A4
Oaktree Cl. PR2 ... 116 A4
Oakville Rd. LA3 ... 208 E5
Oakwood. WN8 ... 18 D3
Oakwood Ave. Ainsdale PR8 ... 20 D6
Oakwood Ave.
Bamber Bridge PR5 ... 96 C4
Oakwood Ave. Blackburn BB1 ... 122 B1
Oakwood Ave.
Lytham St Anne's FY8 ... 89 E4
Oakwood Ave. Shevington WN6 .. 19 F5
Oakwood Cl. Blackpool FY4 ... 109 F4
Oakwood Cl. Brierfield BB10 ... 147 D3
Oakwood Cl. Thornton FY5 ... 173 D2
Oakwood Dr. Ainsdale PR8 ... 20 E5
Oakwood Dr. Fulwood PR2 ... 116 D8
Oakwood Gdns. LA1 ... 211 A2
Oakwood Gr. LA5 ... 215 F2
Oakwood Rd. Accrington BB5 ... 103 D3
Oakwood Rd. Chorley PR7 ... 42 B6
Oakwood Rd. Coppull PR7 ... 41 F2
Oakwood View. PR7 ... 42 B4
Oakworth Ave. PR2 ... 117 F5
Oasis Cl. L40 ... 38 B3
Oat St. BB12 ... 125 D7
Oban Cres. PR2 ... 117 D3
Oban Ct. PR2 ... 138 D1
Oban Dr. BB1 ... 101 C3
Oban Pl. FY2 ... 150 E6
Oban St. BB10 ... 127 C8
Observatory Rd. BB2 ... 101 A2
Ocean Bvd. FY4 ... 109 A7
Ocean Ct. FY6 ... 194 C5
Ocean Way. FY5 ... 172 C3
Oddfellows Terr. BB4 ... 85 F3
Off Botanic Rd. PR9 ... 53 A1

Off Mount Pleasant St. 7 BB5 102 E4
Offerton St. BL6 31 A3
Old Acre. L38 2 F3
Old Back La. BB7 143 F7
Old Bank La. Blackburn BB2 101 A2
Old Bank La. Blackburn BB1 & BB2 101 B2
Old Bank St. BB2 100 E4
Old Boundary Way. L39 15 F6
Old Bridge La. FY6 152 B7
Old Bridge Way. PR6 60 D1
Old Buckley La. PR3 140 D7
Old Clitheroe Rd. PR3 161 C3
Old Cock Yd. PR1 96 A7
Old Croft. PR2 116 D8
Old Dawber's La. PR7 59 B1
Old Engine La. Ramsbottom BL0 49 D6
Old Engine La. Skelmersdale WN8 17 C2
Old Gates Dr. BB2 79 F8
Old Green. BL8 48 F1
Old Greenwood La. BL6 31 D1
Old Ground St. 8 BL0 49 C6
Old Hall Cl. Bamber Bridge PR5 76 E8
Old Hall Cl. Morecambe LA4 213 B4
Old Hall Cl. Roughlee BB9 168 B5
Old Hall Dr. Accrington BB5 124 F1
Old Hall Dr. Bamber Bridge PR5 76 E8
Old Hall La. Charnock Green PR7 41 B6
Old Hall La. Pleasington BB2 99 C2
Old Hall Sq. BB10 128 A5
Old Hall St. BB10 127 A8
Old Hey Croft. PR1 95 D2
Old Hive. PR3 182 D4
Old House La. FY4 110 D7
Old Kiln. OL13 69 D8
Old La. Barnoldswick BB8 191 A8
Old La. Bispham Green L40 26 D8
Old La. Earby BB8 201 B2
Old La. Formby L37 11 F6
Old La. Haskayne L39 13 E3
Old La. Horwich BL6 31 F2
Old La. Kelbrook BB8 191 F4
Old La. Maghull L31 5 E4
Old La. Salterforth BB8 191 B5
Old La. Shawforth OL12 & OL13 70 E6
Old La. Thornton-in-C BD23 201 C6
Old Lancaster La. PR1 116 D1
Old Lancaster Rd. PR3 178 B2
Old Langho Rd. BB6 & BB7 142 C5
Old Laund St. BB12 146 E8
Old Links Cl. PR9 35 B8
Old Lord's Cres. BL6 31 B5
Old Lostock La. PR5 76 E7
Old Mains La. FY6 151 F6
Old Meadow Ct. FY3 129 E3
Old Meadow La. FY3 129 E3
Old Meadows Rd. OL13 87 A5
Old Mill Ct. PR4 73 F5
Old Mill Dr. BB8 169 F4
Old Mill Hill. L39 15 D3
Old Mill La. Formby L37 11 F4
Old Mill La. Hill Dale L40 26 F6
Old Mill St. BB1 100 F6
Old Mill Terr. PR6 60 E1
Old Mill The. PR5 96 F2
Old Millstones. PR1 95 D7
Old Moss La. L39 13 B5
Old Nab Rd. BB6 122 E8
Old Oak Gdns. PR1 96 A2
Old Oliver La. BD23 230 C6
Old Park La. PR9 35 A8
Old Parsonage La. BB12 125 B8
Old Pepper La. WN6 28 B2
Old Prescot Cl. L31 6 C2
Old Quarry La. BL7 46 F1
Old Raike. BD23 230 C4
Old Rake. BL6 31 E5
Old Rectory Gn. L39 6 A7
Old Roman Rd. BB12 & BB7 144 A3
Old Rough La. L33 1 A2
Old Row. Barrow BB7 164 D2
Old Row. Kirkham PR4 113 B4
Old Row. 4 Rawtenstall BB4 84 E2
Old School Cl. PR5 58 A8
Old School La. Adlington PR7 29 E5
Old School La. Bamber Bridge PR5 76 C6
Old School La. Euxton PR7 59 D3
Old School La. Tockholes BB3 79 F2
Old School Mews. 12 OL13 69 C8
Old School Row. BB12 126 B6
Old St. BB4 85 F1
Old Station Cl. PR2 138 D1
Old Station Ct. Clitheroe BB7 164 E8
Old Station Ct. 4 Clitheroe BB7 164 E8
Old Stone Brow. BB8 192 A4
Old Stone Trough La. BB8 192 A5
Old Swan Cl. BL7 46 E2
Old Swan Cotts. BL7 46 E2
Old Tom's La. FY6 & PR 174 E8
Old Town La. L37 11 E4
Old Tram Rd. Bamber Bridge PR5 76 F7
Old Tram Rd. Preston PR1 96 A4
Old Vicarage. PR1 96 A8
Old Vicarage Rd. BL6 31 F3
Old Will's La. BL6 31 B6
Oldbury Pl. FY5 150 F8
Oldfield. Much Hoole PR4 73 F4
Oldfield. Penwortham PR1 95 D2
Oldfield Ave. Blackpool FY2 150 C4
Oldfield Ave. Darwen BB3 80 E3
Oldfield Carr La. FY6 151 E1
Oldfield Cl. FY6 151 E1
Oldfield Cres. FY6 151 E3
Oldfield Rd. PR5 77 A7
Oldham St. Burnley BB11 126 F4
Oldham St. Morecambe LA4 212 E6
Olivant St. BB12 126 C7
Olive Cl. PR6 60 C5
Olive Gr. Blackpool FY3 129 E5
Olive Gr. Skelmersdale WN8 17 E1
Olive Gr. Southport PR8 & PR9 34 E7
Olive Gr. Warton PR4 91 D6
Olive La. BB3 81 B2
Olive Rd. LA1 213 F2
Olive St. OL13 69 E8
Olive Terr. BB4 84 F5
Oliver St. 10 OL13 69 C8
Oliver's Pl. PR2 117 B8
Olivers Pl. PR2 117 A8
Oliverson's Ce Prim Sch. PR3 137 D6
Ollerton La. PR6 78 E4
Ollerton Rd. FY8 89 D5
Ollerton St. PR6 43 A1
Ollerton Terr. PR6 78 E3
Olympia St. BB10 127 C5
Onchan Dr. OL13 87 B1
Onchan Rd. BB2 100 E1
One Ash Cl. OL12 51 F2
Onslow Cres. PR8 34 A2
Onslow Rd. FY3 129 F7
Ontario Cl. BB2 100 A8
Oozebooth Terr. BB1 100 E7
Oozehead La. BB2 100 B5
Opal St. BB1 121 F2
Openshaw Dr. BB1 100 E8
Openshaw St. BL9 32 A1
Oram Rd. PR5 77 F8
Oram St. BL9 32 A4
Orange St. BB5 103 B8
Orchard Ave. Blackpool FY4 109 C6
Orchard Ave. Bolton-le-S LA5 216 A6
Orchard Ave. New Longton PR4 75 A7
Orchard Ave. Poulton-le-F FY6 151 E1
Orchard Bridge. 3 BB11 126 F6
Orchard Cl. Becconsall PR4 72 F3
Orchard Cl. Freckleton PR4 92 A6
Orchard Cl. Fulwood PR2 116 A5
Orchard Cl. Hest Bank LA2 213 F8
Orchard Cl. Silverdale LA5 218 B2
Orchard Cl. Thornton FY5 173 B4
Orchard Cl. Wrea Green PR4 112 B3
Orchard Croft. 2 PR5 76 A8
Orchard Ct. L31 5 F1
Orchard Dr. Fleetwood FY7 193 E1
Orchard Dr. Lucas Green PR6 60 C5
Orchard End. PR3 154 C5
Orchard La. Ainsdale PR8 20 D4
Orchard La. Lancaster LA1 210 D7
Orchard La. Longton PR4 73 F8
Orchard Lodge. L39 15 F6
Orchard Rd. Arnside LA5 237 B2
Orchard Rd. Lytham St Anne's FY8 88 E6
Orchard St. 1 Barnoldswick BB8 200 B2
Orchard St. Great Harwood BB6 123 C4
Orchard St. 1 Leyland PR5 76 B1
Orchard St. 29 Preston PR1 95 F8
Orchard The. Burnley BB11 126 C4
Orchard The. Croston PR5 57 C3
Orchard The. Ormskirk L39 15 D5
Orchard The. Warton PR4 91 E6
Orchard The. Woodplumpton PR4 135 E1
Orchard View. L39 15 D1
Orchards The. Barnoldswick BB8 200 C3
Orchards The. Carleton FY6 151 B5
Orchid Way. OL12 51 D3
Ord Ave. FY4 129 F1
Ord Rd. PR2 116 C2
Orders La. PR4 113 A4
Ordnance St. BB1 101 A5
Oregon Ave. FY3 129 E8
Oriole Cl. 9 BB1 100 F6
Orkney Cl. BB1 101 D3
Orkney Rd. FY1 129 C2
Orme St. FY1 129 C3
Ormerod Rd. BB10 & BB11 127 B7
Ormerod St. Accrington BB5 103 B5
Ormerod St. Burnley BB11 127 A5
Ormerod St. Colne BB8 169 C4
Ormerod St. Haslingden BB4 & BB5 84 B7
Ormerod St. 5 Nelson BB9 147 F8
Ormerod St. Rawtenstall BB4 85 A2
Ormerod St. Thornton FY5 173 B4
Ormerod St. Worsthorne BB10 128 A5
Ormerod Terr. BB6 143 D8
Ormond Ave. Blackpool FY1 129 B8
Ormond Ave. Westhead L40 16 E4
Ormond St. BL9 32 A3
Ormonde Cres. L33 1 A2
Ormont Ave. FY5 172 E2
Ormrod St. BL9 32 A2
Ormrods The. BL9 32 F5
Orms Way. L37 11 E3
Ormsby Cl. WN6 28 E2
Ormskirk Bsns Pk. L39 15 F6
Ormskirk CE Prim Sch. L39 16 A6
Ormskirk & District General Hospl. L39 16 A4
Ormskirk Gram Sch. L39 15 F4
Ormskirk Old Rd. L39 7 F7
Ormskirk Rd. Hall Green WN8 10 A7
Ormskirk Rd. Preston PR1 96 A8
Ormskirk Rd. Rainford Junction WA11 8 D1
Ormskirk Rd. Skelmersdale WN8 9 D7
Ormskirk Rd. Skelmersdale WN8 9 F7
Ormskirk Rd. Skelmersdale WN8 17 C1
Ormskirk Rd. Stanley Gate L39 7 E7
Ormskirk Sta. L39 15 F5
Ormskirk West End Cty Prim Sch. L39 15 E7
Ormston Ave. BL6 31 C5
Orpen Ave. BB11 126 F3
Orpington Sq. BB10 147 D3
Orrell Cl. PR5 75 D1
Orrell Gdns. WN5 10 F6
Orrell Hill La. L38 3 C4
Orrell Holgate Prim Sch. WN5 10 E5
Orrell La. L40 24 D5
Orrell Rd. WN5 10 E7
Orrell St James' Road Cty Jun & Inf Sch. WN5 10 D4
Orrell Sta. WN5 10 E4
Orrell Water Pk. WN5 10 E4
Orrest Rd. PR1 118 A1
Orton Ct. BB9 168 D4
Orwell Cl. L37 11 D1
Osbaldeston La. BB2 120 D5
Osbert Croft. PR4 94 A1
Osborne Cres. LA3 212 C3
Osborne Gr. Cleveleys FY5 172 D5
Osborne Gr. Morecambe LA4 212 D3
Osborne Rd. Ainsdale PR8 20 B6
Osborne Rd. Bamber Bridge PR5 96 D3
Osborne Rd. Blackburn BB2 100 B6
Osborne Rd. Cleveleys FY5 172 D5
Osborne Rd. Formby L37 11 E1
Osborne Rd. Lytham St Anne's FY8 88 F5
Osborne Rd. Morecambe LA3 & LA4 212 C3
Osborne St. PR1 95 E7
Osborne Terr. Bacup OL13 86 D1
Osborne Terr. Darwen BB3 80 E2
Osborne Terr. 1 Rawtenstall BB4 84 E2
Osborne Terr. Spen Brook BB12 167 D2
Osborne Terr. Whitewell Bottom BB4 85 F4
Osborne Way. BB4 84 A1
Osbourne Ave. FY5 172 F1
Osbourne Rd. FY4 109 B8
Oscar St. FY4 129 F2
Oslo Rd. BB11 126 B5
Osprey Cl. BB1 100 D8
Oswald Rd. Lytham St Anne's FY8 90 D4
Oswald Rd. Preston PR1 116 C1
Oswald St. Accrington BB5 103 D6
Oswald St. Blackburn BB1 100 E6
Oswald St. Burnley BB12 126 F8
Oswald St. Oswaldtwistle BB5 102 D3
Oswald St. Rishton BB1 123 C2
Otley Rd. FY8 89 B7
Ottawa Cl. BB2 100 A8
Otterburn Cl. FY6 151 B1
Otterburn Gr. BB10 127 D6
Otterburn Rd. BB2 80 C7
Otters Cl. PR1 117 F2
Ottershaw Gdns. BB1 100 E8
Ottery Cl. PR9 53 A5
Otway St. PR1 116 E2
Oulton Cl. L31 5 B4
Our Lady of Compassion Hospl. BB2 100 A6
Our Lady Of Compassion RC Prim Sch. L37 12 A3
Our Lady of Lourdes RC Prim Sch. Carnforth LA5 217 E1
Our Lady of Lourdes RC Prim Sch. Southport PR8 34 A1
Our Lady of Perpetual Succour RC Prim Sch. BB2 80 E8
Our Lady of the Assumption RC Prim Sch. FY4 109 F5
Our Lady Queen of Peace RC High Sch. WN8 17 F4
Our Lady & St Edward's RC Prim Sch. PR2 116 D8
Our Lady & St Gerard's RC Prim Sch. PR5 76 A8
Our Lady & St John RC High Sch. BB1 101 C3
Our Lady & St Paul's RC Prim Sch. OL10 32 F1
Our Lady Star of the Sea RC Prim Sch. FY8 88 F6
Our Lady's RC High Sch. Fulwood PR2 116 C4
Our Lady's RC High Sch. Lancaster LA1 213 F1
Ousby Ave. LA3 212 E2
Ousby Rd. LA3 212 E2
Ouseburn Rd. BB2 80 C8
Out La. PR5 57 C2
Out Moss La. LA4 212 E4
Out Rawcliffe CE Prim Sch. PR3 175 F2
Outer Prom. FY7 193 E5
Outlet La. L31 & L39 6 F1
Outram La. BB1 121 E1
Outram Way. PR5 76 E8
Outterside St. PR7 30 A6
Outwood Rd. BB11 127 B4
Oval The. WN6 19 F5
Ovangle Rd. LA1 & LA3 213 B2
Over Houses. BL7 47 B6
Overdale Gr. FY3 130 A8
Overdell Dr. OL12 51 C4
Overfield Way. OL12 51 F2
Overshores Rd. BL7 47 B8
Overton Rd. PR2 94 E8
Ovington Dr. PR8 34 E3
Owen Ave. L39 15 F6
Owen Rd. LA1 213 F2
Owen St. Accrington BB5 103 C7
Owen St. Burnley BB12 126 A5
Owen St. Darwen BB3 81 A3
Owen St. Preston PR1 96 B8
Owen's La. L39 13 E2
Owen's Row. BL6 31 C3
Owens St. PR7 42 E7
Owlet Hall Rd. BB3 80 E2
Owtram St. 2 PR1 96 C8
Ox Hey. BB5 123 F4
Ox Hey Ave. PR2 115 C1
Ox St. 15 BL0 49 B5
Oxcliffe Ave. LA3 212 A2
Oxcliffe Gr. LA3 212 A1
Oxcliffe Rd. LA3 212 C2
Oxendale Rd. FY5 173 D2
Oxenholme Ave. FY5 172 D4
Oxenhurst Rd. FY3 130 A8
Oxford Ave. BB5 124 A3
Oxford Cl. Blackburn BB1 100 F4
Oxford Cl. Padiham BB12 125 D6
Oxford Ct. Lytham St Anne's FY8 89 D4
Oxford Ct. Southport PR8 33 F4
Oxford Dr. Blackburn BB1 101 E4
Oxford Dr. Kirkham PR4 113 C4
Oxford Gdns. PR8 33 E4
Oxford Pl. Burnley BB10 127 B5
Oxford Pl. Lancaster LA1 213 E3
Oxford Rd. Bamber Bridge PR5 76 F8
Oxford Rd. Blackpool FY1 129 D5
Oxford Rd. Burnley BB11 127 B5
Oxford Rd. Cleveleys FY5 172 D3
Oxford Rd. Fleetwood FY7 193 E3
Oxford Rd. Fulwood PR2 116 D4
Oxford Rd. Lytham St Anne's FY8 88 E8
Oxford Rd. Lytham St Anne's FY8 89 D4
Oxford Rd. Nelson BB9 169 A2
Oxford Rd. Orrell WN5 10 F8
Oxford Rd. Skelmersdale WN8 17 E1
Oxford Rd. Southport PR8 33 E4
Oxford St. Accrington BB5 103 B6
Oxford St. Adlington PR7 30 A6
Oxford St. Brierfield BB9 147 B5
Oxford St. Bury BL9 32 A1
Oxford St. Carnforth LA5 217 D1
Oxford St. 8 Chorley PR6 42 C7
Oxford St. Colne BB8 169 E5
Oxford St. Darwen BB3 80 F4
Oxford St. Lancaster LA1 213 F3
Oxford St. Morecambe LA4 212 E6
Oxford St. Preston PR1 96 A6
Oxhey Cl. BB10 127 F6
Oxheys Ind Est. PR1 116 D2
Oxheys St. PR1 116 D2
Oxhill Pl. FY5 150 F7
Oxhouse Rd. WN5 10 D4
Oxley Rd. PR1 117 D1
Oxley Rd N. PR1 117 D1
Paa La. BB7 225 C7
Packet La. LA5 216 A4
Paddington Ave. PR3 155 C7
Paddock Dr. FY3 130 C2
Paddock Rd. WN8 9 C5
Paddock St. 9 BB5 102 E4
Paddock The. Ainsdale PR8 20 C4
Paddock The. Blackburn BB2 100 A8
Paddock The. Carleton FY6 151 C5
Paddock The. Formby L37 12 A5
Paddock The. Fulwood PR2 117 A6
Paddock The. Ormskirk L39 15 C3
Paddock The. Penwortham PR1 95 E2
Paddock The. Ramsbottom BL0 49 B7
Paddock The. Rufford L40 38 C4
Paddock The. Sawley BB7 224 C1
Paddock The. Thornton FY5 151 B8
Paddock Way. LA7 237 F4
Padgate Pl. BB11 126 B4
Padiham Cty Prim Sch. BB12 125 D8
Padiham Green CE Sch. BB12 125 C8
Padiham Rd. Burnley BB12 126 C7
Padiham Rd. Burnley BB11 & BB12 126 E6
Padiham Rd. Padiham BB12 125 F7
Padiham Rd. Sabden BB12 & BB7 145 A7
Padstow Cl. PR9 53 A5
Padway. PR1 95 D2
Page Ct. L37 11 F3
Pagefield Cres. BB7 165 A7
Pages Ct. PR5 76 B7
Paignton Rd. BB1 100 D7
Painley Cl. FY8 90 A4
Paisley St. BB11 126 D5
Palace Ct. LA3 212 B4
Palace Gdns. BB12 126 B7
Palace Rd. PR8 33 E5
Palace St. Burnley BB12 126 C7
Palace St. Bury BL9 32 A2
Palais Bldgs. L40 24 E5
Palatine Ave. LA1 211 A5
Palatine Cl. FY3 130 C6
Palatine High Sch. FY4 109 C8
Palatine Rd. Blackburn BB2 100 C5
Palatine Rd. Blackpool FY1 129 C4
Palatine Rd. Cleveleys FY5 172 D4
Palatine Rd. Southport PR8 33 F5
Palatine Sq. BB11 126 E5
Palatine St. 10 BL0 49 C6
Paley Rd. PR1 95 D7
Pall Mall. Blackburn BB2 99 E5
Pall Mall. Chorley PR7 42 C6
Palm Ct. WN8 17 E2
Palm Gr. PR8 & PR9 34 E6
Palm St. Blackburn BB1 101 A7
Palm St. 4 Burnley BB11 126 D5
Palma St. OL14 108 B1
Palmaston Cl. LA1 210 E6
Palmer Ave. FY1 129 C2
Palmer Gr. LA4 213 A6
Palmer St. BB1 100 D6
Palmerston Cl. BL0 49 C4
Palmerston Rd. PR9 34 F6
Palmerston St. BB12 125 D7
Pansy St N. BB5 103 B7
Pansy St S. BB5 103 B7
Panton St. BL6 31 D1
Parade The. LA5 217 B1
Paradise La. Blackburn BB2 100 E4
Paradise La. Formby L37 12 A6
Paradise La. Leyland PR5 75 B1
Paradise St. Accrington BB5 103 B5
Paradise St. Barrowford BB9 168 E5
Paradise St. Blackburn BB2 100 D4
Paradise St. 9 Burnley BB11 126 F6
Paradise St. Little Knowley PR6 60 F3
Paradise St. Newchurch BB4 85 F2
Paradise St. Ramsbottom BL0 49 C7
Paragon Way. LA1 210 C8
Parbold Cl. L40 24 E3
Parbold Douglas CE Prim Sch. WN8 26 D3
Parbold Hill. WN8 26 E2
Parbold Our Lady & All Saints RC Prim Sch. WN8 26 C2
Parbold Sta. WN8 26 C2
Pardoe Cl. PR4 72 E3
Pardoe Ct. L40 24 F3
Paris. BB1 121 E4
Parish St. 1 BB12 125 C8
Park Ave. Barnoldswick BB8 200 B1
Park Ave. Barrowford BB9 168 C1
Park Ave. Blackburn BB1 100 D6
Park Ave. Burnley BB11 126 E4
Park Ave. Chatburn BB7 187 D5
Park Ave. Clitheroe BB7 186 E1
Park Ave. Euxton PR7 59 D2
Park Ave. Fleetwood FY7 193 F3
Park Ave. Formby L37 11 F1
Park Ave. Great Harwood BB6 123 D6
Park Ave. Haslingden BB4 84 B1
Park Ave. Lancaster LA1 211 B7
Park Ave. Longshaw WN5 10 E1
Park Ave. Lytham St Anne's FY8 89 E3
Park Ave. Maghull L31 5 D3
Park Ave. Much Hoole PR4 73 E2
Park Ave. New Longton PR4 74 F8
Park Ave. Ormskirk L39 15 E5
Park Ave. Preston PR1 117 B2
Park Ave. Ramsbottom BL0 49 D6
Park Ave. Salterforth BB8 191 E8
Park Ave. Southport PR9 34 E8
Park Bridge Rd. BB10 & BB11 127 D3
Park Brow Dr. L32 1 A1
Park Cl. Formby L37 2 E8
Park Cl. Parbold WN8 26 D3
Park Cl. Penwortham PR1 95 D4
Park Cotts. BB8 149 D7
Park Cres. Accrington BB5 103 A4
Park Cres. Bacup OL13 69 F8
Park Cres. Blackburn BB2 100 C6
Park Cres. Haskayne L39 13 F4
Park Cres. Haslingden BB4 84 C1
Park Cres. Morecambe LA4 213 A7
Park Cres. Southport PR9 52 D1
Park Ct. LA1 210 F3
Park Cty Prim Sch. BB8 169 F5
Park Dr. Brierfield BB9 147 C5
Park Dr. Nelson BB9 147 F7
Park Dr. Preston PR2 115 D1
Park Farm Rd. BB2 79 D8
Park Gate Rd. BB1 141 D1
Park Hall L Ctr. PR7 41 A4
Park Hall Rd. PR7 40 F3
Park Hey Dr. WN6 19 E7
Park High Sch. BB8 169 F6
Park Hill. Barnoldswick BB8 200 C1
Park Hill. 21 Rochdale OL12 51 F1
Park Hill Convent Prep Sch. BB12 126 A8
Park Hill Rd. PR3 178 C7
Park House La. LA2 233 A5
Park La. Brierfield BB10 & BB9 147 C5
Park La. Caton LA2 231 B5
Park La. Garstang PR3 199 A4
Park La. Great Harwood BB6 123 D6
Park La. Holmes PR4 55 B2
Park La. Horwich BL6 31 D3
Park La. Kirkham PR4 113 A7
Park La. Maghull L31 5 F3
Park La. Moss Side L31 6 A2
Park La. Oswaldtwistle BB5 102 E3
Park La. Penwortham PR1 95 E3
Park La. Preesall FY6 195 B3
Park La. Wennington LA2 232 E8
Park Lane Dr. L31 6 B2
Park Lane End. LA2 232 E8
Park Lee Hospl. BB2 100 E2
Park Lee Rd. BB2 100 E2
Park Link. L39 15 B1
Park Mill Pl. PR1 117 A1
Park Pl. Blackburn BB2 79 D7
Park Pl. Blackburn BB2 100 B3
Park Pl. 25 Preston PR1 96 A7
Park Pl. Walton-le-D PR5 96 E4
Park Prim Sch. WN8 17 E1
Park Rd. Accrington BB5 103 A6
Park Rd. Adlington PR7 29 F6
Park Rd. Bacup OL13 86 F1
Park Rd. Barnoldswick BB8 200 B1
Park Rd. Blackburn BB1 & BB2 100 E3
Park Rd. Blackpool FY1 129 D3
Park Rd. Burnley BB10 127 E1
Park Rd. Chorley PR6 & PR7 42 C8

Silver Birch Way. L31 5 B5
Silver St. Clifton PR4 114 D1
Silver St. Ramsbottom BL0 49 C6
Silverburn. FY8 89 A8
Silverdale. Becconsall PR4 72 F3
Silverdale. Blackpool FY2 150 E6
Silverdale. Southport PR8 33 E4
Silverdale Ave. Fleetwood FY7 193 D1
Silverdale Ave. Heysham LA3 208 F7
Silverdale CE Prim Sch. LA5 218 C3
Silverdale Cl. Blackburn BB2 80 F8
Silverdale Cl. Brierfield BB10 147 B3
Silverdale Cl. Clayton-le-M BB5 123 E2
Silverdale Cl. Coupe Green PR5 97 E4
Silverdale Cl. Leyland PR5 59 B6
Silverdale Dr. PR2 117 E5
Silverdale Golf Course. LA5 218 E3
Silverdale Moss Rd. LA5 218 D7
Silverdale Rd. Arnside LA5 237 B1
Silverdale Rd. Chorley PR7 42 E7
Silverdale Rd. Lytham St Anne's FY8 89 C7
Silverdale Rd. Yealand Redmayne LA5 219 E4
Silverdale Sta. LA5 218 F3
Silverstone Gr. L31 5 B4
Silverthorne Dr. PR9 52 F1
Silverwell St. BL6 31 B4
Silverwood Ave. FY4 109 D8
Silverwood Cl. FY8 89 E4
Silvester Rd. PR7 42 C6
Silvester St. BL6 30 D2
Silvia Way. FY7 193 E4
Simmonds Way. BB9 147 B7
Simmons Ave. PR1 96 B3
Simmons' St. BB2 100 D5
Simonstone CE Prim Sch. BB12 144 F1
Simonstone La. BB12 124 E8
Simonstone Rd. BB12 & BB7 144 F6
Simonswood Ind Pk. L33 1 B6
Simonswood La. Kirkby L32 & L33 1 A2
Simonswood La. Royal Oak L39 7 A2
Simonswood Prim Sch. L33 1 A2
Simonswood Wlk. L33 1 A2
Simpson Cl. BB8 200 D3
Simpson St. Blackpool FY4 109 B8
Simpson St. Hapton BB12 125 C4
Simpson St. Oswaldtwistle BB5 102 D3
Simpson St. 10 Preston PR1 95 F8
Sinclair Ct. FY8 89 B7
Sineacre La. L33 & L39 1 E8
Singleton. PR2 116 F7
Singleton Ave. Horwich BL6 31 C5
Singleton Ave. Lytham St Anne's FY8 89 B8
Singleton Ave. Read BB12 144 D2
Singleton CE Prim Sch. FY6 152 E1
Singleton Cl. PR2 116 F7
Singleton Rd. Weeton PR4 131 F4
Singleton Rd. Weeton Camp PR4 131 E6
Singleton Row. 18 PR1 95 F8
Singleton St. FY1 129 B3
Sion Cl. PR2 117 F4
Sion Hill. PR2 117 F4
Sir Simon's Arc. 26 LA1 210 F8
Six Acre La. PR4 74 C6
Sixpenny La. PR8 20 D1
Sixth Ave. Blackpool FY4 109 C7
Sixth Ave. Bury BL9 32 D4
Size House Village. 5 BB4 84 B2
Size St. OL12 70 D1
Sizehouse St. 25 PR1 95 F8
Sizer St. PR1 116 F1
Sizergh Ct. LA1 210 D7
Sizergh Rd. LA4 213 A5
Skaithe The. BB7 223 C7
Skeffington Rd. PR0 & PR1 117 C1
Skeleron La. BB7 189 B6
Skelmersdale Coll. Skelmersdale WN8 18 B1
Skelmersdale Coll. Skelmersdale WN8 18 B4
Skelmersdale Coll (Westbrook Ctr). WN8 9 B8
Skelmersdale Rd. L39 & WN8 8 B7
Skelmersdale Sports Ctr. WN8 9 C7
Skelshaw Cl. BB1 101 A3
Skelton St. BB8 169 E5
Skelwith Rd. FY3 130 B2
Skerton. LA1 213 F2
Skerton Ct. LA1 213 F2
Skerton High Sch. LA1 213 F2
Skerton House. LA1 213 F2
Skerton Prim Sch. LA1 213 F2
Skiddaw Cl. BB12 146 C1
Skiddaw Rd. Blackpool FY4 109 F8
Skiddaw Rd. Lancaster LA1 214 A2
Skiddaw St. BB1 101 A5
Skip La. PR4 94 B3
Skippool Ave. FY6 151 E5
Skippool Rd. FY5 151 F7
Skipton Ave. Carleton FY6 151 C5
Skipton Ave. Southport PR9 53 C6
Skipton Cl. FY4 129 F1
Skipton Cres. PR2 117 E5
Skipton Gate. LA6 236 C2
Skipton New Rd. BB8 191 E2
Skipton Old Rd. Colne BB8 170 B6
Skipton Old Rd. Foulridge BB8 191 D3
Skipton Rd. Barnoldswick BB8 200 B2
Skipton Rd. Barnoldswick BB8 200 D4
Skipton Rd. Colne BB8 169 E6
Skipton Rd. Earby BB8 201 B3
Skipton Rd. Lytham St Anne's FY8 89 B6
Skipton Rd. Trawden BB8 170 B3
Skipton St. Morecambe LA4 212 D5
Skipton St. Nappa BB7 225 E7
Skitham La. PR3 176 D4
Skull House La. WN6 19 D8
Skye Cl. OL10 32 F1
Skye Cres. BB1 101 C3
Slack. BB12 145 F6
Slack Booth. BB8 170 C1
Slack Gate. OL12 51 F8
Slack House Cotts. L39 16 A3
Slack La. LA2 205 C1
Slack's La. PR6 43 B2
Slackwood La. LA5 218 E2
Slade La. Padiham BB12 145 C1
Slade La. Padiham BB12 145 C2
Slade St. PR1 95 E7
Sladen St. OL12 51 F1
Slaidburn Ave. Burnley BB10 127 D5
Slaidburn Ave. Rawtenstall BB4 85 A4
Slaidburn Cres. PR9 53 B5
Slaidburn Dr. Accrington BB5 103 A4
Slaidburn Dr. Lancaster LA1 211 A3
Slaidburn Pl. PR2 118 A2
Slaidburn Rd. Fulwood PR2 118 A2
Slaidburn Rd. Lowgill LA2 233 E4
Slaidburn Wlk. 5 FY3 130 A8
Slape La. LA6 234 C8
Slate La. WN8 17 C2
Slater Ave. Colne BB8 169 D6
Slater Ave. Horwich BL6 31 C4
Slater La. Leyland PR5 58 C8
Slater La. Leyland PR5 58 D8
Slater Rd. FY5 172 C2
Slater St. BB2 100 C1
Slinger Rd. FY5 172 C3
Slip Inn La. 28 LA1 210 F8
Sliven Clod Rd. BB4 104 E2
Sluice La. L40 38 B3
Slyne Hall Hts. LA2 216 A1
Slyne Rd. Bolton-le-S LA2 & LA5 216 A2
Slyne Rd. Lancaster LA1 & LA2 213 F6
Slyne Rd. Morecambe LA2 & LA4 213 C4
Smalden La. BB7 224 A3
Small La. Clieves Hills L39 15 A3
Small La. Drummersdale L40 23 E8
Small La. Ormskirk L39 15 F4
Small La N. L39 22 E2
Small La S. L39 14 D6
Smalley Croft. PR1 95 F3
Smalley St. Burnley BB11 127 B4
Smalley St. Standish WN6 28 E1
Smalley Thorn Brow. BB6 122 F6
Smalley Way. BB2 100 E2
Smallshaw Ind Est. BB11 126 C4
Smallshaw La. Burnley BB11 126 B5
Smallshaw La. Burnley BB12 126 B6
Smallshaw Rd. OL12 51 A4
Smallwood Hey Rd. PR3 196 C5
Smeaton St. BL6 31 C2
Smethurst Hall Pk. WN5 10 C2
Smethurst Hall Rd. BL9 33 A4
Smethurst Rd. WN5 10 C2
Smirthwaite St. BB11 126 D5
Smith Ave. PR4 72 F1
Smith Brow. BL6 30 C3
Smith Croft. PR5 58 B8
Smith La. BL7 46 F1
Smith Rd. FY5 172 D2
Smith St. Adlington PR7 29 F6
Smith St. 13 Bamber Bridge PR5 76 F8
Smith St. Barnoldswick BB8 200 A1
Smith St. Burnley BB12 126 E6
Smith St. Bury BL9 32 A3
Smith St. Chorley PR7 42 D6
Smith St. Colne BB8 169 C4
Smith St. Kirkham PR4 112 F5
Smith St. Nelson BB9 147 F8
Smith St. Ramsbottom BL0 49 B5
Smith St. Skelmersdale WN8 17 D1
Smith St. Whittle-le-W PR6 60 C8
Smith St. Worsthorne BB10 128 B5
Smith's La. PR4 56 A1
Smithills Cl. PR6 61 E5
Smithills Hall Cl. BL0 49 C5
Smithy Bridge St. BB5 102 D3
Smithy Brow. Abbeystead LA2 226 F1
Smithy Brow. Haslingden BB4 84 B4
Smithy Brow. Newburgh WN8 26 A1
Smithy Brow. Wrightington Bar WN6 27 C8
Smithy Cl. Brindle PR6 77 F5
Smithy Cl. Formby L37 12 B4
Smithy Cl. Garstang PR3 178 C8
Smithy Cl. Stalmine FY6 174 C7
Smithy Croft. FY8 89 C6
Smithy Fold. Spotland Fold OL12 51 C1
Smithy Fold. Wrea Green PR4 112 B4
Smithy Gn. L37 12 B4
Smithy How. LA6 238 E3
Smithy La. Barton L39 14 A6
Smithy La. Brindle PR6 77 F5
Smithy La. Claughton PR3 179 B2
Smithy La. Colne BB8 169 B8
Smithy La. Heysham LA3 208 E6
Smithy La. Holmeswood PR4 37 C6
Smithy La. Holt Green L39 6 A6
Smithy La. Hurlston Green L40 23 B3
Smithy La. Lytham St Anne's FY8 89 C6
Smithy La. Mawdesley L40 39 C2
Smithy La. Much Hoole PR4 73 E2
Smithy La. Preesall FY6 195 B3
Smithy La. Staining FY3 130 E6
Smithy La. Stalmine FY6 174 C7
Smithy La. Westhouse LA6 236 E4
Smithy Lane Ends. L40 23 D6
Smithy Mews. FY1 129 C7
Smithy Row. BB7 162 E1
Smithy St. 2 Bamber Bridge PR5 76 E8
Smithy St. 8 Haslingden BB4 84 B3
Smithy St. 7 Ramsbottom BL0 49 C6
Smithy Wlk. L40 24 E5
Smithyfield Ave. BB10 127 F6
Snaefell Rd. BB2 100 E1
Snape Gn. PR8 22 D8
Snape La. LA5 219 F1
Snape Rake La. PR3 180 D4
Snape St. BB3 80 F3
Snapewood La. PR3 199 B3
Snell Cres. BB8 169 F6
Snell Gr. BB8 169 F6
Sniddle Hill La. BB3 63 E8
Snipe Cl. Blackpool FY3 130 B6
Snipe Cl. Thornton FY5 172 F5
Snipewood. PR7 40 B6
Snodworth Rd. BB6 122 D7
Snow Hill. PR1 95 F8
Snow St. BB1 100 F6
Snowden Ave. Blackburn BB1 100 E7
Snowden Ave. Morecambe LA3 212 A3
Snowden St. BB12 126 B6
Snowdon Cl. FY1 129 D3
Snowdon Dr. BL6 31 C5
Snowdon Rd. FY8 110 A2
Snowdrop Cl. BB4 66 F8
Snowhill La. PR3 199 F6
Snowshill Cres. FY5 150 F7
Sod Hall La. PR4 & PR5 75 A5
Sollam's Cl. PR5 96 F2
Sollom La. L40 56 B2
Solway Cl. Blackpool FY2 150 C6
Solway Cl. Penwortham PR1 95 E3
Somerby Rd. LA4 212 F4
Somerford Cl. BB12 126 D7
Somerset Ave. Blackpool FY1 129 D3
Somerset Ave. Chorley PR7 60 C1
Somerset Ave. Clitheroe BB7 186 F2
Somerset Ave. Darwen BB3 80 F3
Somerset Ave. Lancaster LA1 211 A6
Somerset Ave. Wilpshire BB1 121 F6
Somerset Cl. BB5 102 F3
Somerset Ct. FY1 129 D3
Somerset Dr. PR8 20 C3
Somerset Gr. Church BB5 102 F7
Somerset Gr. 6 Passmonds OL12 51 A1
Somerset Pk. PR2 116 B7
Somerset Pl. BB9 169 A1
Somerset Rd. Leyland PR5 76 B2
Somerset Rd. Preston PR1 117 A1
Somerset Rd. Rishton BB1 123 A1
Somerset St. BB11 127 A4
Somerset Wlk. BB4 67 B8
Sorrel Cl. FY5 172 F5
Sorrel Ct. PR1 95 C2
Soudan St. BB10 147 B2
Sough La. Belthorn BB1 82 A7
Sough La. Blackburn BB1 & BB5 101 F2
Sough La. Sough BB8 192 A7
Sough Rd. BB3 64 B7
South Ave. Barnoldswick BB8 200 B3
South Ave. Chorley PR7 42 D6
South Ave. Cleveleys FY5 172 C4
South Ave. Morecambe LA4 212 F5
South Ave. New Longton PR4 74 F8
South Cliff St. PR1 95 E6
South Clifton St. FY8 90 B3
South Cross St. BL9 32 A1
South Dr. Appley Bridge WN6 27 C2
South Dr. Fulwood PR2 116 E7
South Dr. Inskip PR4 134 C8
South Dr. Padiham BB12 125 E8
South End. PR1 95 E5
South Gr. Barton PR3 136 B8
South Gr. Fulwood PR2 116 E8
South Gr. Morecambe LA4 212 F5
South Hey. FY8 89 C6
South Holme. FY8 90 B4
South King St. FY1 129 C5
South Lawn. FY1 129 E2
South Meade. L31 5 B1
South Meadow La. PR1 95 E6
South Meadow St. PR1 96 A8
South Moss Rd. FY8 89 C7
South Par. 5 Barnoldswick BB8 200 B3
South Par. Cleveleys FY5 172 E1
South Park Dr. FY3 129 F2
South Pier. FY4 109 A8
South Pine St. BL9 32 B2
South Pk. FY8 90 A4
South Prom. FY8 88 E5
South Rd. Bretherton PR5 56 F5
South Rd. Coppull PR7 41 E1
South Rd. Lancaster LA1 210 F7
South Rd. Morecambe LA4 212 G5
South Shore Hospl. FY4 109 C5
South Shore St. Church BB5 102 E5
South Shore St. Haslingden BB4 84 A3
South Sq. Blackpool FY3 129 D6
South Sq. Cleveleys FY5 172 D5
South St. Accrington BB5 103 C5
South St. Accrington BB5 103 E8
South St. Bacup OL13 87 A2
South St. Burnley BB11 127 A6
South St. 15 Darwen BB3 81 A1
South St. Great Eccleston PR3 154 B5
South St. Haslingden BB4 84 C1
South St. Lytham St Anne's FY8 90 D4
South St. Newchurch BB4 85 E1
South St. Ramsbottom BL0 49 D6
South St. 16 Rawtenstall BB4 85 A3
South Strand. FY7 172 E7
South Terr. Euxton PR7 59 D4
South Terr. Ormskirk L39 15 E4
South Terr. Ramsbottom BL0 67 C2
South View. Bamber Bridge PR5 76 B7
South View. Belmont BL7 45 C5
South View. 3 Great Harwood BB6 123 C5
South View. 17 Haslingden BB4 84 B3
South View. Kirkham PR4 113 A4
South View. Moss Side FY8 111 D1
South View. Nelson BB9 147 D7
South View. Simonstone BB12 144 E3
South View St. OL14 108 C1
South View Terr. 2 PR5 59 A8
South Warton St. FY8 90 C3
South Westby St. FY8 90 B3
Southbank Ave. FY4 110 A7
Southbank Rd. PR8 34 C5
Southbourne Ave. FY6 151 C2
Southbourne Rd. FY3 130 A2
Southbrook Rd. PR5 75 F1
Southcliffe. BB6 123 B6
Southcliffe Ave. BB12 126 C7
Southdene. WN8 26 B2
Southdown Dr. FY5 151 D8
Southdowns Rd. PR7 42 D6
Southern Ave. Burnley BB12 126 C7
Southern Ave. Preston PR1 96 C6
Southern Cl. PR3 139 A6
Southern Par. PR1 96 B6
Southern Rd. PR8 34 A6
Southey Cl. PR2 116 F7
Southey St. 2 BB11 126 E6
Southfield. PR4 73 E3
Southfield Dr. New Longton PR4 74 F7
Southfield Dr. Poulton-le-F FY3 130 C8
Southfield Dr. West Bradford BB7 186 F5
Southfield Gdns. PR4 73 E3
Southfield La. BB10 & BB8 148 C7
Southfield Rd. BL0 49 A2
Southfield Sq. BB9 147 F8
Southfield St. BB9 147 F7
Southfield Terr. BB8 170 E6
Southfleet Ave. FY7 193 E1
Southfleet Pl. FY7 193 E1
Southfold Pl. FY8 90 A4
Southgate. Fleetwood FY7 172 D8
Southgate. Fulwood PR2 116 D5
Southgate. Morecambe LA3 213 A2
Southgate. Preston PR1 116 F1
Southgate. Wallbank OL12 51 C7
Southgates. PR7 41 D3
Southlands. PR4 113 A4
Southlands Ave. PR5 96 C1
Southlands Dr. PR5 58 C8
Southlands High Sch. PR7 42 A5
Southport & Ainsdale Golf Links. PR8 20 D7
Southport Coll. PR9 34 C7
Southport General Hospl. PR8 34 D5
Southport New Rd. Banks PR4 & PR9 54 D3
Southport New Rd. Holmes PR4 55 D3
Southport Old Links (Golf Course). PR9 35 B8
Southport Old Rd. L37 & PR8 12 B7
Southport Rd. Barton L39 14 A6
Southport Rd. Brown Edge PR8 35 B2
Southport Rd. Chorley PR7 42 A8
Southport Rd. Formby L37 12 A5
Southport Rd. Hurlston L40 23 A2
Southport Rd. Maghull L31 & L39 5 B5
Southport Rd. Newton PR5 & PR7 58 B2
Southport Rd. Scarisbrick L40 & PR8 22 E7
Southport Terr. PR6 & PR7 42 E7
Southport Zoo. PR8 33 F7
Southside. PR7 59 C3
Southwark. BB12 126 C6
Southway. Fleetwood FY7 193 D1
Southway. Skelmersdale WN8 18 B1
Southwood Ave. FY7 193 F3
Southwood Cl. FY8 89 E4
Southwood Dr. BB5 103 E3
Southworth Ave. FY4 109 E7
Southworth St. BB2 100 D2
Sow Clough Rd. OL13 86 D1
Sower Carr La. FY6 174 D4
Sowerby Ave. FY4 109 D8
Sowerby Rd. PR3 155 E3
Sowerby St. BB12 125 C8
Spa Garth. BB7 164 F8
Spa La. L40 & WN8 17 C4
Spa Rd. PR1 95 D7
Spa St. Burnley BB12 126 E7
Spa St. Padiham BB12 125 D8
Spa St. Preston PR1 95 D8
Spark La. L40 38 B6
Sparrow Hill. WN6 & WN8 27 A2
Sparth Ave. BB5 123 F3
Sparth Rd. BB5 123 F3
Speakmans Dr. WN6 19 C6
Speedwell Cl. FY5 172 F5
Speedwell St. BB2 100 B2
Speke St. BB2 100 B2
Spen Brook Houses. BB12 167 C2
Spen Brow. LA2 233 B6
Spen Cnr. FY4 129 D1
Spen Farm. FY4 110 C8
Spen La. PR4 113 E6
Spen Pl. FY4 109 F8
Spenbrook Rd. BB12 167 C3
Spencer Ct. FY1 129 C7
Spencer Gr. BB6 123 B5
Spencer St. Accrington BB5 103 D6
Spencer St. Burnley BB10 147 A1
Spencer St. Ramsbottom BL0 49 B5
Spencer St. 10 Rawtenstall BB4 85 A7
Spencer's La. Ainsdale L39 21 B3
Spencer's La. Orrell WN5 10 D7
Spencers. BB12 167 F1
Spencers Dr. PR4 56 A8
Spencers La. WN8 9 B7
Spendmore La. PR7 41 E1
Spenleach La. BL8 48 D3
Spenser Cl. BB10 128 C4
Spenser St. BB12 125 D7
Spey Cl. Leyland PR5 58 E8
Spey Cl. Standish WN6 28 D1
Speyside. FY4 109 D7
Spinners Gn. OL12 51 F2
Spinners Sq. PR5 76 E7
Spinney Brow. PR2 117 D4
Spinney Cl. Lucas Green PR7 60 B6
Spinney Cl. New Longton PR4 74 F8
Spinney Cl. Ormskirk L39 15 D3
Spinney La. LA5 218 C8
Spinney The. Arnside LA5 218 C8
Spinney The. Blackburn BB2 100 A8
Spinney The. Chapeltown BL7 47 C2
Spinney The. Chorley PR6 & PR7 60 C3
Spinney The. Cleveleys FY5 150 F7
Spinney The. Formby L37 12 A5
Spinney The. Lancaster LA1 211 B5
Spinney The. Penwortham PR1 94 F3
Spinney The. Poulton-le-F FY6 151 E4
Spinney The. Tarleton PR4 56 A7
Spinnings The. BL0 49 C3
Spiredale Dr. WN6 28 F2
Spires Gr. PR4 115 E5
Spod Rd. OL12 51 D1
Spodden Cotts. OL12 70 D2
Spodden Fold. OL12 51 C8
Spotland Tops. OL12 51 B1
Spout La. LA2 235 F1
Spouthouse La. BB5 124 F1
Spread Eagle St. BB5 102 C5
Spring Ave. BB6 123 C6
Spring Bank. Appley Bridge WN6 19 C8
Spring Bank. Middle Healey OL12 51 D4
Spring Bank. Preston PR1 95 E7
Spring Bank. Silverdale LA5 218 C3
Spring Bank Terr. BB2 100 C2
Spring Brook House. BB5 123 F2
Spring Cl. Ramsbottom BL0 49 B6
Spring Cl. Southport PR8 34 A5
Spring Cres. PR6 60 E5
Spring Field. WA11 8 E2
Spring Gardens Rd. BB8 169 D4
Spring Gardens St. 4 BB4 68 F8
Spring Gardens Terr. 3 BB12 145 C1
Spring Gdn St. 33 LA1 210 F8
Spring Gdns. 7 Accrington BB5 103 C5
Spring Gdns. 2 Bacup OL13 87 A3
Spring Gdns. Darwen BB3 64 A8
Spring Gdns. Freckleton PR4 92 B8
Spring Gdns. 12 Horwich BL6 31 B4
Spring Gdns. Leyland PR5 58 F8
Spring Gdns. Lytham St Anne's FY8 109 F1
Spring Gdns. Newchurch BB4 68 F6
Spring Gdns. Penwortham PR1 95 F2
Spring Gr. BB8 170 C6
Spring Hall. BB5 123 F5
Spring Hill. 5 Blackburn BB1 100 E5
Spring Hill. Freckleton PR4 92 D7
Spring Hill Cty Prim Sch. BB5 103 B5
Spring Hill Rd. Accrington BB5 102 F4
Spring Hill Rd. Burnley BB11 126 F4
Spring La. Blackburn BB2 100 B3
Spring La. Colne BB8 169 D5
Spring La. Haslingden BB4 84 B4
Spring La. Nab's Head BB2 & PR5 98 C8
Spring Meadow. PR6 76 E1
Spring Meadows. BB3 64 D7
Spring Mews. PR6 60 E6
Spring Pl. Colne BB8 169 D5
Spring Pl. Whitworth OL12 70 D3
Spring Rd. Gathurst WN5 19 F1
Spring Rd. Orrell WN5 10 F8
Spring Side. Newchurch BB4 68 F6
Spring Side. Whitworth OL12 70 D4
Spring Side Cotts. BL7 46 A2
Spring St. Accrington BB5 102 F4
Spring St. Bacup OL13 86 F1
Spring St. Bank Lane BL0 49 D7
Spring St. Cornholme OL14 108 C1
Spring St. Horwich BL6 31 B4
Spring St. Leyland PR5 76 B1
Spring St. Nelson BB9 147 C7
Spring St. 5 Oswaldtwistle BB5 102 E4
Spring St. Ramsbottom BL0 49 B6
Spring St. Rawtenstall BB4 85 A8
Spring St. Rishton BB1 123 B2
Spring Terr. 4 Bacup OL13 69 D8
Spring Terr. Langho BB6 142 D1
Spring Terr. Oswaldtwistle BB5 102 D4
Spring Terr. Passmonds OL12 51 A1
Spring Terr S. 5 BB4 84 E2
Spring Vale. PR3 204 B3
Spring Vale Garden Village. BB3 64 C6
Spring Vale Rd. BB3 64 B7
Spring View. BB2 100 C5
Spring Villas. OL14 108 B1
Spring Wood St. BL0 49 B7
Spring Yd. 3 BB8 169 D5
Springbank Ave. FY5 173 C2
Springbank Gdns. BB4 104 F2
Springbrook Ave. FY5 150 F8
Springcroft. PR5 76 C3
Springdale Rd. BB6 122 C8
Springfield. Arnside LA5 237 B2
Springfield. Blacko BB9 168 D8
Springfield. High Bentham LA2 233 E8
Springfield Ave. Accrington BB5 102 F4

Stubbins Vale Rd. BL0 67 C1
Stubbins Vale Terr. BL0 67 B1
Stubbylee La. OL13 69 F8
Stubley Holme. OL14 108 A1
Stubley La. OL14 108 B1
Studfold. PR7 60 B2
Studholme Ave. PR1 95 E2
Studholme Cl. PR1 95 E2
Studholme Cres. PR1 95 E2
Stump Cross La. BB7 224 F5
Stump La. PR6 42 D8
Stunstead. BB8 170 C2
Sturgess Cl. L39 15 F7
Sturminster Cl. PR1 95 E2
Styan St. FY7 194 A4
Stydd La. PR3 140 E4
Sudell Ave. L31 5 F2
Sudell Cl. BB3 81 C1
Sudell Cross. 20 BB1 100 E5
Sudell La. L31 & L39 5 E6
Sudell Prim Sch. BB3 81 B1
Sudell Rd. BB3 81 B1
Sudellside St. BB3 81 B1
Suffolk Ave. BB12 126 A6
Suffolk Cl. PR5 58 E6
Suffolk Rd. Blackpool FY3 130 A2
Suffolk Rd. Preston PR1 117 A1
Suffolk Rd. Southport PR8 21 A8
Suffolk St. BB2 100 C2
Sugar Stubbs La. PR9 54 C4
Sugham La. LA3 208 F8
Sulby Cl. PR8 33 F3
Sulby Dr. Fulwood PR2 117 F5
Sulby Dr. Lancaster LA1 210 F6
Sulby Gr. Fulwood PR2 118 A5
Sulby Gr. Morecambe LA4 213 A6
Sulby Rd. BB2 100 E1
Sullivan Dr. BB2 101 A1
Sullom Side La. PR3 179 C5
Sullom View. PR3 178 C6
Sultan St. BB5 103 D7
Sulyard St. LA1 210 F8
Summer St. Horwich BL6 31 B4
Summer St. Nelson BB9 147 C7
Summer St. Skelmersdale WN8 18 A4
Summer Trees Ave. PR4 115 D3
Summerdale Dr. BL0 49 B2
Summerer Rd. PR4 131 F6
Summerfield. PR5 75 F3
Summerfield Dr. LA2 213 E7
Summerfields. FY8 88 C8
Summerhill. LA2 233 D7
Summerseat La. BL0 49 A2
Summerseat Meth Prim Sch. BL9 49 D2
Summerseat Special Sch. BL0 49 B2
Summerseat Sta. BL9 49 C2
Summersgill Rd. LA1 213 D2
Summerton Wlk. BB3 81 A2
Summerville. FY4 109 C6
Summerville Ave. FY3 130 E5
Summerville Wlk. BB2 100 D5
Summerwood Cl. FY2 150 D1
Summerwood La. L39 22 C1
Summit Cl. BL9 32 F4
Summit Dr. PR4 92 C6
Summit St. OL10 32 F3
Summit Works. BB11 126 E2
Sumner Ave. L39 13 F4
Sumner Rd. L37 11 F3
Sumner St. Blackburn BB2 100 E3
Sumner St. Leyland PR5 76 A1
Sumner's La. PR7 39 A7
Sumpter Croft. PR1 95 E2
Sumpter Ct. PR1 95 F2
Sun St. Clitheroe BB7 164 E7
Sun St. Colne BB8 169 E5
Sun St. Lancaster LA1 210 F8
Sun St. Nelson BB9 147 C8
Sun St. Ramsbottom BL0 49 B7
Sun Terr. OL14 108 B1
Sunacre Ct. LA3 212 B3
Sunbank Cl. OL12 51 D2
Sunbury Ave. PR1 95 D3
Sunbury Dr. PR8 20 B4
Suncliffe Rd. BB9 147 D4
Sunderland Ave. Cleveleys FY5 172 F4
Sunderland Ave. Hambleton FY6 174 D2
Sunderland Dr. LA3 212 D2
Sunderland St. BB12 126 B6
Sunfield Cl. FY4 110 A7
Sunnindale Ave. BB4 86 A1
Sunningdale. PR3 136 B3
Sunningdale Ave. Blackpool FY4 130 A2
Sunningdale Ave. Fleetwood FY7 172 D7
Sunningdale Ave. Hest Bank LA2 215 D1
Sunningdale Cl. PR4 113 A4
Sunningdale Cres. LA2 215 D1
Sunningdale Dr. FY5 151 D8
Sunningdale Gdns. BB10 147 D3
Sunningdale Pl. PR4 134 C8
Sunny Bank. PR4 112 F5
Sunny Bank Ave. Blackpool FY2 150 C4
Sunny Bank Ave. Newton-with-S PR4 114 A2
Sunny Bank Cl. BB4 67 A6
Sunny Bank Cotts. BB4 66 F5
Sunny Bank Mill. PR4 112 F5
Sunny Bank Rd. Blackburn BB2 100 E1
Sunny Bank Rd. Helmshore BB4 66 F6
Sunny Bank Terr. OL14 108 B1
Sunny Bower Cl. BB1 122 B1
Sunny Bower Rd. BB1 122 B1
Sunny Brow. PR7 42 A2
Sunny Dr. WN5 10 F6
Sunny Lea St. BB4 84 F5
Sunny Rd. PR9 53 A2
Sunny View. BB2 79 C2
Sunnybank Dr. BB5 102 C2
Sunnybank Rd. LA5 216 A5
Sunnybank St. Darwen BB3 81 A1
Sunnybank St. 6 Haslingden BB4 84 A3
Sunnycliff Ret Pk. LA3 212 G1
Sunnyfield Ave. Morecambe LA4 213 A6
Sunnyfield Ave. Over Town BB10 107 A8
Sunnyfield La. BB3 65 A8
Sunnyfield Sch. LA3 213 B3
Sunnyfields. L39 16 A5
Sunnyhill Cl. BB3 80 D2
Sunnyhurst Ave. FY4 109 D6
Sunnyhurst Cl. BB3 80 D2
Sunnyhurst La. BB3 80 D2
Sunnyhurst Rd. Blackburn BB2 100 C5
Sunnyhurst Rd. Blackburn BB2 100 D4
Sunnymede Dr. L31 5 D3
Sunnymede Sch. PR8 33 F6
Sunnymede Vale. BL0 49 A3
Sunnymere Dr. BB3 80 E2
Sunnyside. Ormskirk L39 6 C7
Sunnyside. Southport PR8 33 F3
Sunnyside Ave. Billington BB7 143 B4
Sunnyside Ave. Blackburn BB2 79 E8
Sunnyside Ave. Ribchester PR3 140 D3
Sunnyside Ave. Warton PR4 91 E6
Sunnyside Ave. Wilpshire BB1 122 A7
Sunnyside Cl. Freckleton PR4 92 B7
Sunnyside Cl. Lancaster LA1 210 E7
Sunnyside Cl. Rawtenstall BB4 85 A6
Sunnyside La. LA1 210 E7
Sunnyside Terr. FY6 195 C3
Suoth Ribble St. PR1 96 C6
Super St. BB5 123 E4
Surgeon's Ct. PR1 95 F7
Surrey Ave. Burnley BB12 126 B7
Surrey Ave. Darwen BB3 80 F3
Surrey Cl. PR9 53 C5
Surrey Rd. Barrowford BB9 168 D2
Surrey Rd. Blackburn BB1 101 D5
Surrey St. Accrington BB5 103 D6
Surrey St. Preston PR1 96 C8
Sussex Ave. OL10 32 E1
Sussex Cl. Church BB5 102 F7
Sussex Cl. Standish WN1 29 B1
Sussex Dr. Blackburn BB1 101 A4
Sussex Dr. Garstang PR3 178 B7
Sussex Dr. Haslingden BB4 67 B8
Sussex Rd. Blackpool FY3 129 E6
Sussex Rd. Rishton BB1 101 F8
Sussex Rd. Southport PR8 & PR9 34 D6
Sussex St. 18 Barnoldswick BB8 200 B2
Sussex St. Burnley BB11 127 B4
Sussex St. 1 Nelson BB9 168 E1
Sussex St. Preston PR1 117 A1
Sussex Wlk. 10 BB1 101 A4
Sutch La. L40 25 B5
Sutcliffe St. Bacup OL13 70 C8
Sutcliffe St. Brierfield BB10 147 F3
Sutcliffe St. Burnley BB11 126 F6
Sutcliffe St. Chorley PR6 42 D7
Sutcliffe Terr. BB1 81 F6
Sutherland Cl. BB1 122 A7
Sutherland Rd. Blackpool FY1 129 C8
Sutherland Rd. Heywood OL10 32 F1
Sutherland St. BB8 169 C4
Sutherland View. FY1 129 C7
Sutton Ave. Brierfield BB10 147 D2
Sutton Ave. Tarleton PR4 56 A8
Sutton Cres. BB5 124 F1
Sutton Dr. PR2 94 D8
Sutton Gr. PR6 60 F4
Sutton La. Adlington PR6 43 A1
Sutton La. Tarleton PR4 55 F5
Sutton Pl. FY1 129 C4
Sutton Rd. L37 11 E1
Sutton St. Blackburn BB2 79 D8
Sutton St. Weeton Camp PR4 131 E6
Sutton's La. L37 12 E3
Sutton's Yd. FY6 151 E4
Swain St. OL12 51 E1
Swainbank St. BB11 127 B5
Swaine St. BB9 147 C8
Swainson St. Blackpool FY1 129 C6
Swainson St. Lytham St Anne's FY8 89 F3
Swainstead Raike. BD23 230 E8
Swaledale Ave. BB10 147 B4
Swalegate. L31 5 C2
Swallow Ave. PR1 95 E4
Swallow Cl. FY5 173 A4
Swallow Ct. PR6 77 C1
Swallow Dr. Blackburn BB1 100 E6
Swallow Dr. Bury BL9 32 B4
Swallow Field. PR4 73 E3
Swallow Pk. BB11 126 C5
Swallowfields. BB1 100 E8
Swan Alley. L39 15 E5
Swan Delph. L39 15 C2
Swan Dr. FY5 172 F1
Swan Farm Cl. BB3 80 F7
Swan La. L39 5 F6
Swan Rd. BL8 48 F2
Swan St. Blackburn BB2 100 E3
Swan St. Darwen BB3 64 B6
Swan St. Preston PR1 96 C8
Swan Yd. 1 LA1 211 A7
Swanage Ave. FY4 109 B6
Swanage Rd. BB10 147 C1
Swanfield Ct. BB8 170 A5
Swanpool La. L39 15 C2
Swansea St. PR1 95 C8
Swansey La. PR6 77 C1
Swarbrick Cl. FY1 129 D7
Swarbrick Ct. PR3 139 B7
Swarbrick St. PR4 113 A4
Sweet Briar Cl. OL12 51 E2
Sweet Briar La. OL12 51 E2
Swift Cl. BB1 100 F5
Swilkin La. FY6 174 E6
Swill Brook La. PR1 96 C6
Swinate Rd. LA5 237 C1
Swinburn Gr. WN5 10 D1
Swinburne Cl. BB5 103 E2
Swinden Hall Rd. BB9 168 E2
Swinden La. BB8 169 A2
Swindon Ave. FY4 109 D8
Swindon St. BB11 126 D5
Swinless St. BB10 127 B8
Swinshaw Cl. BB4 105 A2
Swiss St. BB5 102 F6
Swithemby St. BL6 31 A4
Swollowfold. PR2 138 D1
Sword Meanygate. PR4 55 C6
Sycamore Ave. Blackpool FY4 109 F5
Sycamore Ave. Burnley BB12 126 B7
Sycamore Ave. Euxton PR7 59 D3
Sycamore Ave. Garstang PR3 178 B8
Sycamore Bglws. BB7 225 C3
Sycamore Cl. Blackburn BB1 100 F8
Sycamore Cl. Burnley BB12 126 C6
Sycamore Cl. Fulwood PR2 117 C6
Sycamore Cl. Mawdesley L40 39 C2
Sycamore Cl. Rishton BB1 102 B8
Sycamore Cres. Caton LA2 231 C3
Sycamore Cres. Clayton-le-M BB5 124 A5
Sycamore Cres. 1 Rawtenstall BB4 84 F1
Sycamore Ct. PR7 42 B5
Sycamore Dr. Penwortham PR1 95 E3
Sycamore Dr. Skelmersdale WN8 17 E2
Sycamore Gdns. Foulridge BB8 191 D1
Sycamore Gdns. Heysham LA3 208 E6
Sycamore Gr. Accrington BB5 103 E3
Sycamore Gr. Darwen BB3 81 B2
Sycamore Gr. Formby L37 11 C1
Sycamore Gr. Lancaster LA1 210 D8
Sycamore Rd. Bilsborrow PR3 157 A5
Sycamore Rd. Blackburn BB1 100 F8
Sycamore Rd. Caton LA2 231 C3
Sycamore Rd. Chorley PR6 60 D2
Sycamore Rd. Fulwood PR2 117 E2
Sycamore Rise. BB8 191 D1
Sycamore Trading Est. FY4 109 F5
Sycamore Way. BB8 200 A1
Sycamore Wlk. 1 BL6 31 E1
Syd Brook La. PR5 & PR7 39 E7
Sydenham Terr. OL12 51 D3
Sydney Ave. BB7 143 D5
Sydney St. Accrington BB5 103 C6
Sydney St. 1 Burnley BB11 & BB12 126 F6
Sydney St. Darwen BB3 64 B7
Sydney St. Enfield BB5 124 A1
Sydney St. Hoddlesden BB3 81 F1
Sydney St. Lytham St Anne's FY8 88 F6
Sydney Terr. BB8 170 C3
Syke Hill. 14 PR1 96 A7
Syke House La. PR3 158 E4
Syke La. OL12 51 F4
Syke Rd. OL12 51 F4
Syke Side Dr. BB5 124 E6
Syke St. Haslingden BB4 84 C1
Syke St. Preston PR1 96 A7
Sykelands Ave. LA2 214 F7
Sykelands Gr. LA2 214 F7
Sykes St. BL9 32 A3
Sylvan Gr. PR5 97 A2
Sylvan Pl. LA3 208 E6
Sylvancroft. PR2 116 A5
Sylvester St. LA1 210 E7
Symonds Rd. PR2 116 E3

Tabby Nook. PR4 54 F2
Tabby's Nook. WN8 26 A1
Taberner Cl. WN6 28 F1
Tabley La. PR2 & PR4 115 E7
Tabor St. BB12 126 D6
Tadema Gr. BB11 126 F2
Tadlow Cl. L37 11 C1
Tag Croft. PR2 115 F5
Tag Farm Ct. PR2 115 F5
Tag La. PR2 116 A4
Talaton Cl. PR9 53 A5
Talbot Ave. 3 BB5 123 F2
Talbot Cl. Clitheroe BB7 164 F7
Talbot Cl. Rawtenstall BB4 67 E8
Talbot Ct. FY8 89 A8
Talbot Dr. Brierfield BB10 147 F2
Talbot Dr. Euxton PR7 59 D2
Talbot Dr. Southport PR8 34 B6
Talbot Gr. BL9 32 A6
Talbot House. PR6 60 C2
Talbot Liby. PR1 95 D8
Talbot Mkt. FY1 129 B1
Talbot Rd. Accrington BB5 103 A8
Talbot Rd. Blackpool FY1 & FY3 129 C6
Talbot Rd. Leyland PR5 75 E2
Talbot Rd. Lytham St Anne's FY8 90 C4
Talbot Rd. Penwortham PR1 95 E5
Talbot Rd. Preston PR1 95 D7
Talbot Row. PR7 59 D1
Talbot Sq. FY1 129 B5
Talbot St. Brierfield BB10 147 F2
Talbot St. Burnley BB11 127 B6
Talbot St. Chipping PR3 182 E3
Talbot St. Chorley PR6 60 E1
Talbot St. Colne BB8 169 D6
Talbot St. Fulwood PR2 116 D4
Talbot St. Rishton BB1 123 C1
Talbot St. Southport PR8 34 A6
Talbot Terr. FY8 90 B3
Tamar Cl. PR5 59 B7
Tamar St. PR1 96 E8
Tamneys The. WN8 17 F1
Tan Hill Dr. LA1 213 F3
Tan House Cl. WN8 26 C3
Tan House La. WN8 26 C2
Tan Pit Cotts. WN8 19 C4
Tanfield Nook. WN8 26 C2
Tanfields. WN8 17 F1
Tanglewood. PR2 117 B5
Tanhouse La. PR6 60 F6
Tanhouse Rd. Skelmersdale WN8 9 C8
Tanhouse Rd. Skelmersdale WN8 9 E7
Tanner Barn. BB5 84 B7
Tanner St. 8 BB11 126 F6
Tanners Croft. 5 BL0 49 B6
Tanners St. BL0 49 B6
Tannersmith La. PR7 39 F5
Tanpits La. LA6 234 B7
Tanpits Rd. BB5 102 F6
Tansley Ave. PR7 41 D1
Tansy La. PR 203 F4
Tanterton Hall Rd. PR2 116 A6
Tanyard Cl. PR7 41 D1
Tape St. 2 BL0 49 B6
Taper St. BL0 49 B6
Tapestry St. BB2 100 D1
Tarbert Cres. BB1 101 D4
Tarbet St. LA1 211 A7
Tardy Gate Trad Ctr. PR5 76 A8
Tarleswood. WN8 17 F1
Tarleton Ave. BB11 127 B4
Tarleton CE Prim Sch. PR4 56 A5
Tarleton Cty High Sch. PR4 56 A7
Tarleton Cty Prim Sch. PR4 55 F8
Tarleton Mere Brow CE Prim Sch. PR9 54 F2
Tarleton Rd. PR9 35 A8
Tarleton St. BB11 127 B4
Tarlscough La. L40 37 D1
Tarn Ave. BB5 123 F4
Tarn Brook Cl. BB5 124 A5
Tarn Brow. L39 15 C3
Tarn Cl. Penwortham PR1 94 F4
Tarn Cl. Storth LA7 237 F5
Tarn Ct. FY7 193 D1
Tarn Hows Cl. PR7 42 B5
Tarn La. LA5 & LA6 234 B6
Tarn Rd. Formby L37 11 D3
Tarn Rd. Thornton FY5 151 D7
Tarnacre La. PR3 177 E2
Tarnacre View. PR3 178 C6
Tarnbeck Dr. L40 39 D2
Tarnbrick Ave. PR4 92 C7
Tarnbrook Cl. Carnforth LA5 217 C1
Tarnbrook Cl. Hest Bank LA5 215 F2
Tarnbrook Cotts. PR3 196 E5
Tarnbrook Dr. FY3 130 A7
Tarnbrook Rd. Heysham LA3 208 F8
Tarnbrook Rd. 2 Lancaster LA1 213 D2
Tarnside. FY4 130 B1
Tarnside Rd. WN5 10 E6
Tarnsyke Rd. LA1 213 D2
Tarnway Ave. FY5 151 D8
Tarradale. PR4 93 F1
Tarry Barn La. BB7 165 A3
Tarvin Cl. Brierfield BB10 147 F3
Tarvin Cl. Southport PR9 53 D5
Tasker St. 14 BB5 103 C6
Taskers Croft. BB7 143 F8
Tatham Ct. FY7 193 C1
Tatham Fells CE (VC) Prim Sch. LA2 233 C4
Tattersall St. Blackburn BB2 100 E4
Tattersall St. Haslingden BB4 84 B6
Tattersall St. Oswaldtwistle BB5 102 D4
Tattersall St. 1 Padiham BB12 125 D8
Tattershall Sq. BB4 85 F3
Tatton St. BB8 169 B3
Tauheedul Islam Girls High Sch. BB1 100 E6
Taunton Rd. BB2 100 B5
Taunton St. 6 Blackpool FY4 129 D1
Taunton St. Preston PR1 117 D1
Tavistock Dr. PR8 20 B6
Tavistock St. BB9 168 F1
Tawd Rd. WN8 9 C8
Tay St. Burnley BB11 126 D5
Tay St. Preston PR1 95 D6
Taybank Ave. FY4 109 D7
Taylor Ave. Newchurch BB4 85 F2
Taylor Ave. Ormskirk L39 16 A5
Taylor Cl. BB2 100 C3
Taylor Gr. LA4 213 B6
Taylor Holme Ind Est. OL13 69 B8
Taylor St. Barnoldswick BB8 200 A2
Taylor St. Blackburn BB2 100 D3
Taylor St. Brierfield BB9 147 B6
Taylor St. Burnley BB10 127 A8
Taylor St. Bury BL9 32 A3
Taylor St. Chorley PR7 42 B5
Taylor St. Clitheroe BB7 164 F8
Taylor St. Darwen BB3 64 A8
Taylor St. Haslingden BB4 84 B6
Taylor St. Horwich BL6 31 B3
Taylor St. Preston PR1 95 D6
Taylor St. 6 Rawtenstall BB4 85 A3
Taylor St. Rochdale OL12 51 F1
Taylor St. Skelmersdale WN8 17 C1
Taylor St. Whitworth OL12 51 D8
Taylor St W. BB5 103 B6
Taylor's Bldgs. BB6 142 D1
Taylor's La. Fisher's Row PR3 196 D6
Taylor's La. Holmes PR4 55 D3
Taylor's Meanygate. PR4 55 A7
Taylors Cl. FY6 151 C5
Taylors Pl. 18 OL12 51 F1
Taywood Cl. FY6 151 F4
Taywood Rd. FY5 173 A4
Teak St. BL9 32 B2
Teal Cl. Blackburn BB1 100 D8
Teal Cl. Ormskirk L39 15 C2
Teal Pl. PR5 58 D7
Teanlowe Ctr. FY6 151 D3
Tears La. WN8 17 F8
Teasel Wlk. LA3 212 E2
Tebay Ave. Cleveleys FY5 172 D4
Tebay Ave. Kirkham PR4 113 C5
Tebay Cl. L31 5 F2
Tebay Ct. LA1 213 E4
Tedder Ave. Burnley BB12 126 B6
Tedder Ave. Southport PR9 35 A7
Teenadore Ave. FY4 109 E7
Tees Ct. FY7 193 D2
Tees St. PR1 117 C2
Teesdale Ave. FY3 129 D8
Teil Gn. PR2 117 E6
Telford St. Burnley BB12 126 C7
Telford St. Horwich BL6 31 D2
Temperance St. 3 PR6 42 E8
Temple Cl. 2 BB1 101 B4
Temple Ct. PR1 95 F7
Temple Dr. BB1 101 B4
Temple St. Blackpool FY1 129 B5
Temple St. Burnley BB11 127 B5
Temple St. Colne BB8 169 E6
Temple St. Nelson BB9 147 F8
Templegate Cl. WN6 28 F2
Templemartin. WN8 17 F2
Templeton Cl. BB3 81 A2
Ten Row. LA2 205 E5
Tenby. WN8 17 E2
Tenby Cl. BB1 100 E7
Tenby Gr. 6 OL12 51 C1
Tenby Rd. PR1 96 A6
Tenby St. OL12 51 C1
Tennis St. BB10 127 A8
Tennyson Ave. Chorley PR7 42 C6
Tennyson Ave. Lytham St Anne's FY8 90 D4
Tennyson Ave. Oswaldtwistle BB5 102 C4
Tennyson Ave. Padiham BB12 125 E7
Tennyson Ave. Read BB12 144 D2
Tennyson Ave. Thornton FY5 173 A3
Tennyson Ave. Warton PR4 91 E6
Tennyson Cl. LA5 216 A5
Tennyson Dr. Longshaw WN5 10 D1
Tennyson Dr. Ormskirk L39 15 D6
Tennyson Pl. Bamber Bridge PR5 96 D2
Tennyson Pl. Great Harwood BB6 123 B4
Tennyson Rd. Blackpool FY3 129 F7
Tennyson Rd. Colne BB8 169 D5
Tennyson Rd. Fleetwood FY7 194 A4
Tennyson Rd. Preston PR1 117 D1
Tennyson St. Brierfield BB10 147 F3
Tennyson St. Burnley BB11 126 D5
Tennyson St. Hapton BB12 125 C4
Tensing Ave. FY2 150 D5
Tensing Rd. L31 5 D1
Tenterfield St. 6 Newchurch BB4 68 F8
Tenterfield St. 26 Preston PR0 & PR1 95 F8
Tenterheads. BB4 68 F7
Terance Rd. FY4 109 E8
Terra Cotta Bldgs. BB4 106 A1
Terrace Row. BB7 143 C4
Terrace St. PR1 117 C1
Terry St. BB9 169 A2
Tetbury Cl. BB2 79 E8
Teven St. 4 PR5 96 E1
Teversham. WN8 17 F2
Teviot Ave. FY7 193 D3
Tevlot. WN8 17 E2
Tewkesbury. WN8 17 E2
Tewkesbury Ave. FY4 109 D5
Tewkesbury Cl. BB5 103 E3
Tewkesbury Dr. FY8 90 D5
Tewksbury St. BB2 100 B1
Thames Ave. BB10 147 C3
Thames Dr. WN5 10 F7
Thames House. 5 PR1 96 D8
Thames Prim Sch. FY4 109 B7
Thames Rd. FY4 109 B7
Thames St. PR4 113 F2
Thanet. WN8 17 F2
Thanet Lee Cl. BB10 127 E1
Thealby Cl. WN8 17 E2
Theatre St. PR1 95 F7
Thelma St. BL0 49 B6
Thermdale Cl. PR3 178 B7
Thetis Rd. LA1 210 C8
Thickrash Brow. LA2 233 D7
Third Ave. Blackpool FY4 109 C7
Third Ave. Bury BL9 32 D4
Thirlemere Ave. FY7 193 C1
Thirlemere Ct. LA1 214 B1
Thirlmere Ave. Burnley BB10 147 A2
Thirlmere Ave. Carleton FY6 151 C4
Thirlmere Ave. Colne BB8 169 F6
Thirlmere Ave. Formby L37 12 A2
Thirlmere Ave. Haslingden BB4 67 C8
Thirlmere Ave. Horwich BL6 31 C2
Thirlmere Ave. Orrell WN5 10 F7
Thirlmere Ave. Padiham BB12 145 C2

Thirlmere Ave. Up Holland WN8 10 B7
Thirlmere Cl. Accrington BB5 124 D1
Thirlmere Cl. Adlington PR6 30 B8
Thirlmere Cl. 6 Blackburn BB1 100 F6
Thirlmere Cl. Knott End-on-S FY6 194 F6
Thirlmere Cl. Longton PR4 74 B8
Thirlmere Cl. Maghull L31 5 E2
Thirlmere Dr. Ainsdale PR8 20 B3
Thirlmere Dr. Darwen BB3 81 C2
Thirlmere Dr. Longridge PR3 138 F5
Thirlmere Dr. Morecambe LA4 212 D4
Thirlmere Dr. Withnell Fold PR6 78 D2
Thirlmere Gdns. LA4 212 E4
Thirlmere Rd. Blackpool FY4 109 C7
Thirlmere Rd. Blackrod BL6 30 C3
Thirlmere Rd. Burnley BB10 127 E5
Thirlmere Rd. Chorley PR7 42 B6
Thirlmere Rd. Hightown L38 3 A4
Thirlmere Rd. Lancaster LA1 214 B2
Thirlmere Rd. Preston PR1 117 F1
Thirlmere Way. BB4 105 A1
Thirnby Ct. LA6 238 C2
Thirsk. WN8 17 E2
Thirsk Ave. FY8 89 B7
Thirsk Gr. FY1 129 D2
Thirsk Rd. LA1 211 B4
Thistle Cl. FY5 172 F5
Thistle St. 15 OL13 86 F2
Thistlecroft. PR2 116 A5
Thistlemount Ave. BB4 85 F1
Thistleton Rd. Preston PR2 94 E8
Thistleton Rd. Thistleton PR4 &FY6 153 C1
Thomas Gr. LA4 212 E5
Thomas St. Blackburn BB2 100 D4
Thomas St. Brierfield BB9 147 A5
Thomas St. Burnley BB11 127 A5
Thomas St. Colne BB8 169 C4
Thomas St. Cornholme OL14 108 C1
Thomas St. 4 Haslingden BB4 84 A3
Thomas St. Nelson BB9 147 E7
Thomas St. Oswaldtwistle BB5 102 D3
Thomas St. 3 Preston PR1 96 B7
Thomas St. Whitworth OL12 70 D2
Thomason Fold. BL7 47 D6
Thompson Ave. L39 16 B5
Thompson Dr. BL9 32 C3
Thompson St. Blackburn BB2 100 C4
Thompson St. Darwen BB3 64 B7
Thompson St. Horwich BL6 31 A3
Thompson St. Kirkham PR4 112 F6
Thompson St. Padiham BB12 125 D7
Thompson St. Preston PR1 117 D1
Thonock Rd. LA4 212 G3
Thorburn Dr. OL12 51 B7
Thorn Bank. OL13 87 A2
Thorn Cl. OL13 87 A2
Thorn Cres. OL13 87 A2
Thorn Cty Prim Sch. OL13 86 F3
Thorn Dr. OL13 87 A2
Thorn Gdns. OL13 87 A2
Thorn Gr. Blackpool FY1 129 E2
Thorn Gr. Colne BB8 169 F6
Thorn Hill Cl. BB1 101 A5
Thorn La. PR3 139 B2
Thorn St. Bacup OL13 87 A2
Thorn St. Burnley BB10 127 A8
Thorn St. Clitheroe BB7 164 D8
Thorn St. Great Harwood BB6 123 D6
Thorn St. Preston PR1 117 C1
Thorn St. Ramsbottom BL0 49 C3
Thorn St. Rawtenstall BB4 84 F5
Thorn St. Sabden BB7 145 A7
Thorn View. BL9 32 C3
Thornbank. FY3 130 B7
Thornbank Dr. PR3 178 D2
Thornbeck Ave. L38 2 F3
Thornber. WN8 17 F2
Thornber Gr. FY1 129 D3
Thornber St. BB2 100 C3
Thornbridge Ave. L40 24 E3
Thornbury. WN8 17 F2
Thornby. WN8 17 F2
Thorncliffe Dr. BB3 64 D8
Thorndale. WN8 17 F2
Thorne St. BB9 169 A2
Thorney Bank St. 4 BB11 126 F5
Thorneybank Ind Est. BB11 125 C2
Thorneycroft Cl. FY6 151 B5
Thorneyholme Rd. BB5 103 C8
Thorneyholme Sq. BB9 167 E5
Thorneylea. OL12 70 D1
Thornfield. Lancaster LA1 210 F5
Thornfield. Much Hoole PR4 73 E4
Thornfield Ave. Fulwood PR2 117 F3
Thornfield Ave. Longridge PR3 139 A8
Thornfield Ave. Newchurch BB4 85 E1
Thornfield Ave. Thornton FY5 151 D8
Thorngate. PR1 95 B4
Thorngate Cl. PR1 95 B4
Thornham Ct. FY3 129 E5
Thornhill. L39 6 B8
Thornhill Ave. Knott End-on-S FY6 195 A5
Thornhill Ave. Rishton BB1 102 A8
Thornhill Cl. Blackpool FY4 109 F5
Thornhill Cl. Ormskirk L39 6 B8
Thornhill Rd. Chorley PR6 60 E2
Thornhill Rd. Leyland PR5 58 D8
Thornhill Rd. Ramsbottom BL0 49 A1
Thornhill St. BB12 126 A6
Thornlea Dr. OL12 51 B2
Thornleigh Cl. FY5 173 A2
Thornleigh Dr. LA6 234 C7
Thornley Ave. BB1 101 C6
Thornley Pl. PR2 118 A3
Thornley Rd. PR2 & PR5 118 A3
Thornpark Dr. PR2 115 D1
Thorns Ave. LA2 215 D1
Thorns The. L31 5 B2
Thornton. WN8 17 F2
Thornton Ave. Fulwood PR2 116 B4
Thornton Ave. Lytham St Anne's FY8 89 B8
Thornton Ave. Morecambe LA4 212 F6
Thornton Cl. Accrington BB5 103 A8
Thornton Cl. Blackburn BB2 80 F8
Thornton Cl. Rufford L40 38 C4
Thornton Cres. Burnley BB10 127 E5
Thornton Cres. Morecambe LA4 212 F5
Thornton Ctr. FY5 173 C1
Thornton Dr. Gregson Lane PR5 97 D4
Thornton Dr. Leyland PR5 75 E4
Thornton Gate. FY5 172 D4
Thornton Gr. LA4 212 F5
Thornton La. Morecambe LA4 212 F6
Thornton La. Thornton in L LA6 236 F5
Thornton Manor Ct. BD23 201 A5
Thornton Rd. Burnley BB10 127 E5
Thornton Rd. Morecambe LA4 212 F6
Thornton Rd. Southport PR9 34 F7
Thornton-in-Craven Cty Prim Sch. BD23 201 B6
Thorntrees Ave. Newsham PR3 136 B5
Thorntrees Ave. Preston PR2 115 D1
Thornway Ave. FY5 151 D8
Thornwood. WN8 17 F2
Thornwood Cl. Blackburn BB1 121 E1
Thornwood Cl. Lytham St Anne's FY8 89 E4
Thorough Way. PR3 198 E7
Thoroughfare The. LA5 217 D5
Thoroughgood Cl. L40 24 D2
Thorpe. WN8 17 F2
Thorpe Ave. LA4 213 B4
Thorpe Cl. PR1 116 F1
Thorpe St. BL0 49 B5
Thrang Brow La. LA5 219 C6
Threagill La. LA5 & LA6 217 F5
Three Lane Ends. PR6 61 C4
Three Nooks. PR5 77 C5
Three Oaks Cl. L40 25 B2
Three Pools. PR9 53 C3
Three Tuns La. L37 11 F3
Three Turns. PR3 141 A8
Threefields. PR2 116 A5
Threlfall. PR7 59 F2
Threlfall Rd. FY1 129 D1
Threlfall St. 1 PR1 116 C1
Threlfall's La. PR9 52 F2
Threlfalls Cl. PR9 52 F3
Threshers Ct. PR3 204 C2
Threshfield Ave. LA3 208 F8
Thrimby Ct. LA4 212 E4
Thrimby Pl. LA4 212 E4
Thropps La. PR4 74 D6
Throstle Cl. BB12 127 A7
Throstle Gr. LA2 213 F8
Throstle Nest La. PR3 198 C4
Throstle St. Blackburn BB2 100 C4
Throstle St. 7 Nelson BB9 168 E1
Throstle Way. 1 FY5 172 F1
Throstle Wlk. LA2 213 F8
Throughs La. LA7 237 F5
Throup Pl. BB9 168 E2
Thrum Fold. OL12 51 D3
Thrum Hall La. Lower Fold OL12 51 D3
Thrum Hall La. Lower Healey OL12 51 E3
Thrush Dr. BL9 32 B4
Thrush St. OL12 51 C1
Thrushgill Dr. LA2 214 F7
Thurcroft Dr. WN8 17 E2
Thurland Ct. LA4 212 D3
Thurnham Rd. PR2 94 E8
Thurnham St. LA1 210 F7
Thursby Ave. FY4 109 D6
Thursby Cl. PR8 20 B3
Thursby Pl. 11 BB9 168 F2
Thursby Rd. Burnley BB10 147 C1
Thursby Rd. Nelson BB9 168 F2
Thursby Sq. BB10 127 A8
Thursden Ave. BB10 147 F3
Thursden Pl. BB9 169 B1
Thursfield Ave. FY4 109 E8
Thursfield Rd. BB10 127 B5
Thursford Gr. BL6 30 D1
Thursgill Ave. LA4 212 F3
Thurston. WN8 17 E2
Thurston Rd. PR5 76 A1
Thurston St. BB10 & BB11 127 B6
Thwaite Brow La. LA5 216 B6
Thwaite La. LA2 233 C5
Thwaites Ave. BB2 120 E2
Thwaites Rd. BB5 102 C4
Thwaites St. BB5 102 C3
Tib St. 18 BL0 49 B5
Tiber Ave. BB11 126 C4
Tiber St. PR1 96 B7
Tibicar Dr E. LA3 212 A1
Tibicar Dr W. LA3 212 A1
Tilbury Gr. WN6 19 D7
Tilcroft. WN8 17 E2
Timber Brook. PR7 60 A2
Timber St. Accrington BB5 103 C5
Timber St. Bacup OL13 86 F1
Timber St. Brierfield BB9 147 B6
Timberhurst. BL9 32 D2
Timbrills Ave. BB7 144 F8
Timms Cl. L37 11 F5
Timms La. L37 11 F5
Tincklers La. PR7 40 A6
Tinedale View. BB12 145 D1
Tinker's La. LA2 220 B7
Tinkerfield. PR2 116 E7
Tinklers La. BB7 223 E7
Tinline St. BL9 32 A2
Tinniswood. PR1 116 B1
Tinsley Ave. PR8 34 E3
Tinsley's La. Brown Edge PR8 35 A1
Tinsley's La. Out Rawcliffe PR3 175 D4
Tintagel. WN8 17 E2
Tintagell Cl. BB2 79 C7
Tintern Ave. Chorley PR7 42 D5
Tintern Ave. Falinge Fold OL12 51 E2
Tintern Cl. Accrington BB5 103 E2
Tintern Cl. Read BB12 144 D1
Tintern Cres. BB1 101 B8
Tintern Dr. L37 12 B2
Titan Way. PR5 75 B2
Tithe Barn La. Knowley PR6 61 A4
Tithe Barn La. Runshaw Moor PR5 & PR7 58 F5
Tithe Barn La. Scorton PR3 199 E5
Tithebarn Gate. FY6 151 D4
Tithebarn Hill. LA2 205 E5
Tithebarn Pl. FY6 151 D4
Tithebarn Rd. PR8 & PR9 34 E6
Tithebarn St. 6 Preston PR1 96 A7
Tithebarn St. Preston PR1 96 A8
Tithebarn St. Thornton FY6 151 D4
Tithebarn St. Up Holland WN8 10 B7
Tittrington Brow. BB7 223 C2
Tiverton Ave. WN8 17 E2
Tiverton Cl. PR2 116 F8
Tiverton Dr. Blackburn BB2 80 C8
Tiverton Dr. Brierfield BB10 147 F3
Tockholes CE Prim Sch. BB3 80 A3
Tockholes Rd. Darwen BB3 & PR7 80 A3
Tockholes Rd. Darwen BB3 80 F2
Tod Holes La. BD23 230 E4
Todd Carr Rd. BB4 85 F1
Todd Hall Rd. BB4 83 F4
Todd La N. PR5 96 C2
Todd La S. PR5 76 C8
Todd's La. PR9 54 A6
Todmorden Old Rd. OL13 87 B5
Todmorden Rd. Bacup OL13 & OL14 87 B4
Todmorden Rd. Burnley BB11 127 B3
Todmorden Rd. Cockden BB10 148 B1
Todmorden Rd. Lytham St Anne's FY8 88 C8
Todmorden Road Prim Sch. BB11 127 B5
Toll Bar Bsns Pk. OL13 69 C8
Toll Bar Cres. LA1 210 F3
Tollgate. PR1 95 E4
Tollgate Rd. L40 24 B3
Tolsey Dr. PR4 94 D2
Tom Benson Way. PR2 & PR1 115 F4
Tom La. BB4 85 F2
Tomlinson Rd. Heysham LA3 208 F6
Tomlinson Rd. Leyland PR5 75 F2
Tomlinson Rd. Preston PR1 116 C2
Tomlinson St. BL6 31 B3
Tonacliffe Cty Prim Sch. OL12 51 C6
Tonacliffe Rd. OL12 51 C6
Tonacliffe Terr. OL12 51 C7
Tonacliffe Way. OL12 51 C6
Tong End. OL12 70 C2
Tong La. Bacup OL13 87 B2
Tong La. Whitworth OL12 70 D1
Tongbarn. WN8 17 E2
Tongues La. PR3 195 C6
Tontine. WN5 10 C5
Tontine Rd. WN5 & WN8 10 C6
Tontine St. BB1 100 E5
Toogood La. WN6 27 D6
Tootell St. PR7 42 B6
Tootle La. L40 38 A3
Tootle Rd. PR3 139 B8
Top o' th' Croft. BB2 80 D8
Top Acre. PR4 94 C1
Top Barn La. BB4 85 E1
Top Locks. L40 25 A4
Top of Fawna Rd. PR3 161 D1
Top of Heap. OL10 32 F2
Top of Wallsuches. BL6 31 F4
Top Row. BB7 144 F8
Topaz St. BB1 121 F2
Topham St. BL9 32 A1
Topping Fold Rd. BL9 32 C3
Topping St. Blackpool FY1 129 B5
Topping St. Bury BL9 32 A3
Tor Ave. BL8 48 F2
Tor End Rd. BB4 66 F6
Tor Scar Rd. LA6 236 F7
Tor View. Haslingden BB4 84 C1
Tor View. Rawtenstall BB4 85 A1
Tor View Rd. BB4 84 C1
Tor View Sch Valley Site. BB4 67 D8
Torcross Cl. PR9 53 A5
Torn Cotts. LA5 216 C6
Toronto Ave. Blackpool FY2 150 E3
Toronto Ave. Fleetwood FY7 193 E2
Toronto Rd. BB2 100 C8
Torquay Ave. Blackpool FY3 130 A2
Torquay Ave. Brierfield BB10 147 D2
Torra Barn Cl. BL7 46 E3
Torrentum Ct. FY5 173 C1
Torrisholme Cty Prim Sch. LA4 213 B5
Torrisholme Rd. LA1 213 D3
Torrisholme Sq. LA4 213 B4
Torsway Ave. FY3 129 F6
Torver Cl. BB12 126 B8
Totnes Cl. FY6 151 C5
Totnes Dr. PR9 53 A5
Tottenham Rd. BB3 80 F6
Tottington Rd. BL7 & BL8 47 F2
Tottleworth. BB6 123 D3
Tottleworth Rd. BB1 123 C2
Toulmin Cl. PR3 178 D2
Tower Ave. BL0 49 A5
Tower Ct. Chapeltown BL7 47 C4
Tower Ct. Lancaster LA1 210 F7
Tower End. L37 11 C5
Tower Gn. PR2 116 F7
Tower Hill. Clitheroe BB7 186 F1
Tower Hill. Ormskirk L39 16 A5
Tower Hill Rd. WN8 10 B6
Tower La. PR2 & PR3 116 F7
Tower Nook. WN8 10 A5
Tower Rd. Blackburn BB2 99 E2
Tower Rd. Darwen BB3 64 B8
Tower St. 13 Bacup OL13 86 F2
Tower St. Blackpool FY1 129 B5
Tower St. Chapeltown BL7 47 C4
Tower St. Cornholme OL14 108 A1
Tower St. Oswaldtwistle BB5 102 C5
Tower The. FY1 129 B5
Tower View. Belthorn BB1 82 A5
Tower View. Blackrod BL6 30 C3
Tower View. Darwen BB3 81 C1
Tower View. Penwortham PR1 95 C7
Towers Ave. L31 5 C2
Town Brook House. 4 PR1 116 E1
Town Brow. PR6 76 F2
Town End. Bolton-le-S LA5 216 A3
Town End. Kirkham PR4 113 A5
Town End. Slaidburn BB7 223 C7
Town End. Thornton FY5 173 A2
Town Green & Aughton Sta. L39 6 C8
Town Green Ct. L39 6 C8
Town Green La. L39 6 C8
Town Hall Sq. 6 BB6 123 C5
Town Hall St. 16 Blackburn BB1 & BB2 100 E5
Town Hall St. 7 Great Harwood BB6 123 C5
Town Hill Bank. BB12 145 D1
Town House Rd. BB9 148 B8
Town La. Coppull PR7 41 C1
Town La. Heskin Green PR7 40 C2
Town La. Much Hoole PR4 73 D1
Town La. Southport PR8 34 E3
Town La. Whittle-le-W PR6 60 D6
Town Lane (Kew). PR8 34 E3
Town Rd. PR5 57 B2
Towneley High Sch. BB11 127 C4
Towneley Rd. PR3 139 A7
Towneley Rd W. PR3 139 A7
Towneley St. BB10 147 B1
Townely Ave. BB5 124 F2
Townfield Ave. BB10 127 F6
Townfield Cl. PR4 73 F7
Townfield La. LA2 213 E7
Towngate. Eccleston PR7 40 B7
Towngate. Foulridge BB8 191 D1
Towngate. Leyland PR5 58 F7
Towngate. Leyland PR5 59 A8
Townhouse Sch. BB9 169 C1
Townley Ave. FY4 109 E8
Townley Cl. LA1 210 D7
Townley La. PR1 94 D4
Townley St. Brierfield BB9 147 B5
Townley St. Brierfield BB10 147 F3
Townley St. Chorley PR6 & PR7 42 D7
Townley St. Colne BB8 169 E6
Townley St. Morecambe LA4 212 E6
Townsend St. Haslingden BB4 84 A3
Townsend St. Newchurch BB4 68 F8
Townsfield. LA5 218 C4
Townshill Wlk. PR4 113 A6
Townsley St. BB9 147 E6
Townsway. PR5 76 C8
Towpath Wlk. LA5 217 D1
Toxhead Cl. BL6 31 A3
Tracks La. WN5 10 D3
Trafalgar Cl. PR2 116 D3
Trafalgar Rd. Blackpool FY1 129 B2
Trafalgar Rd. Lancaster LA1 211 A6
Trafalgar Rd. Southport PR8 33 E3
Trafalgar St. Burnley BB11 126 F5
Trafalgar St. Chorley PR6 60 D1
Trafalgar St. Lytham St Anne's FY8 88 F7
Trafford St. PR1 116 E2
Tram La. LA6 238 C2
Tramway La. PR5 77 B6
Tranmere Ave. LA3 212 A1
Tranmere Cres. LA3 212 A1
Tranmere Rd. FY4 129 E1
Tranmoor. PR4 73 F6
Trans Brittania Enterprise Ctr. BB11 126 A3
Trap Hill. L37 11 C2
Trapp La. Sabden BB12 144 F4
Trapp La. Simonstone BB12 144 F2
Trash La. Darwen BB3 80 B2
Trash La. Rimington BB7 225 B1
Travers Pl. PR1 95 C8
Travers St. BL6 31 D1
Travis St. BB10 127 A8
Trawden Cl. BB5 103 C4
Trawden Cres. PR2 117 E4
Trawden Cty Prim Sch. BB8 170 C2
Trawden Rd. BB8 170 B5
Traylen Way. OL12 51 A1
Treales CE Prim Sch. PR4 133 E2
Treales Rd. PR4 114 B6
Trecastle Rd. L33 1 A4
Tredgold St. BL6 31 C2
Treen Cl. PR9 53 B6
Treesdale Cl. PR8 33 F4
Treetops Ave. BL0 49 A3
Trefoil Cl. FY5 173 A5
Tremellen St. BB5 103 A6
Trengrove St. 7 OL12 51 C1
Trent Ave. Maghull L31 5 F2
Trent Ave. Moss Side L31 6 A2
Trent Cl. Burscough Bridge L40 24 F5
Trent Cl. Lancaster LA1 213 B2
Trent Rd. Blackpool FY4 109 B7
Trent Rd. Nelson BB9 148 A8
Trent St. Longridge PR3 138 F7
Trent St. Lytham St Anne's FY8 90 D3
Tresco Cl. BB2 100 B1
Trevarrick Ct. BL6 31 E2
Trevelyan Dr. WN5 10 D1
Trevor Cl. BB1 100 F7
Trevor Rd. Ainsdale PR8 20 C4
Trevor Rd. Burscough L40 24 E4
Triangle The. PR2 116 E4
Trigg La. PR6 & PR7 61 D5
Trigge House. PR6 60 C2
Trinity Cl. BB12 125 D6
Trinity Ct. 3 BB1 100 F6
Trinity Fold. 23 PR4 95 F8
Trinity Gdns. Southport PR8 34 A6
Trinity Gdns. Thornton FY5 173 A3
Trinity Gn. BL0 49 B2
Trinity Mews. PR9 34 C7
Trinity Pl. 27 PR1 95 F8
Trinity Prim Sch. WN8 17 F1
Trinity Rd. PR7 42 B7
Trinity St. 15 Bacup OL13 69 C8
Trinity St. Blackburn BB1 100 F6
Trinity St. Oswaldtwistle BB5 102 D3
Trinity Towers. 6 BB11 126 E6
Trinket La. LA2 232 E6
Tristan Ave. PR4 74 A5
Triumph House. BB11 126 E5
Troon Ave. Blackburn BB1 101 C3
Troon Ave. Thornton FY5 151 D8
Troon Ct. PR1 95 A6
Trough Rd. BB7 222 B5
Troughton Cres. FY4 109 E8
Trout Beck. BB5 123 F4
Trout St. 8 Burnley BB10 127 A8
Trout St. Preston PR1 96 C7
Troutbeck Ave. Fleetwood FY7 193 D2
Troutbeck Ave. Forton PR3 204 B3
Troutbeck Ave. Maghull L31 5 E2
Troutbeck Cl. Burnley BB12 126 B8
Troutbeck Cl. Hawkshaw BL8 48 B2
Troutbeck Cres. FY4 110 D8
Troutbeck Dr. BL0 49 C7
Troutbeck Pl. PR2 117 E5
Troutbeck Rd. Chorley PR7 42 B5
Troutbeck Rd. Lancaster LA1 214 A1
Troutbeck Rd. Lytham St Anne's FY8 109 D1
Trowbarrow Cotts. LA5 218 F5
Trower St. PR1 96 B6
Troy St. BB1 100 F7
Trumacar Cty Prim Sch. LA3 208 E5
Trumacar La. LA3 208 E5
Truman Ave. LA1 210 C7
Trumley Ct. LA3 212 D2
Trunnah Gdns. FY5 173 B3
Trunnah Rd. FY5 173 B3
Truro Ave. PR9 53 B5
Truro Pl. 8 PR1 117 D1
Truro St. 5 FY4 129 D1
Truscott Rd. L40 24 D4
Tucker Hill. BB7 186 E1
Tucker's Hill Brow. WN2 30 B1
Tudor Ave. Preston PR2 115 D1
Tudor Ave. Preston PR1 117 F1
Tudor Cl. Blackpool FY6 151 A4
Tudor Cl. 1 Cleveleys FY5 172 F1
Tudor Cl. Darwen BB3 81 A2
Tudor Cl. Langho BB6 142 D1
Tudor Cl. Preston PR2 115 D1
Tudor Croft. PR5 76 C7
Tudor Ct. L39 15 F6
Tudor Dr. PR4 113 B2
Tudor Gr. LA4 213 A6
Tudor Mansions. PR8 33 F6
Tudor Pl. FY4 109 B6
Tudor Rd. Ainsdale PR8 20 B6
Tudor Rd. Lytham St Anne's FY8 88 D8
Tuer St. PR5 75 F2
Tulip Gr. OL12 51 E3
Tulketh Ave. PR1 116 B1
Tulketh Brow. PR1 116 C1
Tulketh Cres. PR1 116 C1
Tulketh High Sch. PR2 116 B4
Tulketh Rd. PR1 & PR2 116 B1
Tulketh St. PR8 34 B7
Tullyallen Sch. BB3 80 E3
Tunbridge Pl. 7 PR1 117 D1
Tunbridge St. 4 PR0 & PR1 117 D1
Tunbrook Ave. PR2 138 E1
Tunley Holme. PR5 77 C5
Tunley La. WN6 27 E5
Tunley Moss. WN6 27 E4
Tunnel St. Burnley BB12 126 D6
Tunnel St. Darwen BB3 64 C7
Tunstall Mill Terr. 4 OL13 69 B8
Tunstall St. LA4 212 D5
Tunstead Ave. BB12 124 F8
Tunstead Cres. OL13 86 C1
Tunstead La. OL13 86 B1
Tunstead Rd. OL13 86 C1
Tunstill Fold. BB12 167 F1
Tunstill St. BB10 147 B1
Turbary Rd. LA6 236 E7
Turbary The. PR2 116 C3
Turf Moor Football Gd (Burnley AFC). BB10 127 B6
Turf St. BB11 127 B6

Westbrook Cres. PR2 116 A3
Westbury Cl. Blackpool FY5 150 C7
Westbury Cl. Brierfield BB10 147 E2
Westbury Gdns. BB1 101 C4
Westby Ave. FY4 109 E5
Westby Gr. FY7 194 B5
Westby Pl. PR2 115 F1
Westby Rd. Lytham St Anne's FY8 88 E8
Westby Rd. Westby PR4 111 E5
Westby St. FY8 90 B3
Westby Way. FY6 151 D2
Westcliff Inf Sch. FY5 150 C5
Westcliffe. BB6 123 B6
Westcliffe Dr. Blackpool FY3 129 E8
Westcliffe Dr. Morecambe LA3 212 D2
Westcliffe Rd. PR8 33 F5
Westcliffe Wlk. BB9 147 D7
Westcote St. BB3 64 B6
Westcroft. PR4 73 E3
Westend Ave. PR7 41 D1
Westerlong. PR2 115 D1
Western Ave. BB11 126 E4
Western Ct. OL13 69 B8
Western Dr. PR5 75 D2
Western Rd. OL13 69 C8
Westfield. Bamber Bridge PR5 76 A8
Westfield. Nelson BB9 168 D1
Westfield Ave. Blackpool FY3 151 A1
Westfield Ave. Fleetwood FY7 193 E2
Westfield Ave. Normoss FY3 130 B7
Westfield Ave. Read BB12 144 D1
Westfield Dr. Bolton-le-S LA5 216 A6
Westfield Dr. Fulwood PR2 117 E4
Westfield Dr. Gregson Lane PR5 97 D1
Westfield Dr. Leyland PR5 75 E1
Westfield Dr. Warton PR4 91 F5
Westfield Dr. West Bradford BB7 186 E6
Westfield Gr. LA4 212 D4
Westfield Rd. FY1 129 D1
Westfields. PR5 57 A2
Westgate. Barnoldswick BB8 200 A1
Westgate. Burnley BB11 126 E6
Westgate. Fulwood PR2 116 D5
Westgate. Leyland PR5 58 F8
Westgate. Morecambe LA3 & LA4 212 F3
Westgate. Read BB12 144 C1
Westgate. Skelmersdale WN8 8 D8
Westgate. Wallbank OL12 51 B7
Westgate Ave. Morecambe LA3 & LA4 212 E2
Westgate Ave. Ramsbottom BL0 49 A2
Westgate Cl. OL12 51 B7
Westgate Cty Prim Sch. LA4 212 E3
Westgate Dr. WN5 10 D5
Westgate La. LA6 236 E5
Westgate Park Rd. LA4 212 F3
Westgate Rd. FY8 109 C4
Westgate Trad Ctr. 2 BB11 126 F6
Westham St. LA1 211 A7
Westhaven Cres. L39 15 C1
Westhead Ave. L33 1 A1
Westhead Cl. L32 & L33 1 A1
Westhead Rd. PR5 57 B2
Westhead Wlk. 1 Fleetwood FY7 193 F2
Westhead Wlk. Kirkby L32 & L33 1 A1
Westholme Lower Sch. BB2 100 B6
Westholme Sch. Blackburn BB2 99 E6
Westholme Sch. Blackburn BB2 100 A6
Westhoughton Rd. PR6 42 F1
Westland Ave. BB3 63 F8
Westlands. PR5 58 C7
Westlands Ct. FY5 151 B8
Westleigh Rd. PR2 115 F1
Westminster Ave. LA4 212 C4
Westminster Cl. Accrington BB5 103 E3
Westminster Cl. Morecambe LA3 212 E2
Westminster Cl. Read BB12 144 D1
Westminster Dr. PR8 20 A4
Westminster Pl. Eccleston PR7 40 A8
Westminster Pl. Hutton PR4 94 D1
Westminster Rd. Blackpool FY1 129 C8
Westminster Rd. Chorley PR7 42 C7
Westminster Rd. Darwen BB3 80 E3
Westminster Rd. Morecambe LA3 & LA4 212 B3
Westmoor Gr. LA3 208 E5
Westmoreland Rd. PR8 34 D5
Westmoreland St. BB9 147 C8
Westmorland Ave. Blackpool FY1 129 D3
Westmorland Ave. Cleveleys FY5 172 D4
Westmorland Cl. Leyland PR5 58 E7
Westmorland Cl. Penwortham PR1 95 B4
Westmorland House. 15 PR4 95 F8
Westmorland St. BB11 126 D5
Weston La Heads. PR4 131 F1
Weston Pl. FY1 129 D1
Weston St. PR1 95 D8
Westover Ave. LA5 217 E5
Westover Cl. L31 5 C1
Westover Gr. LA5 217 E5
Westover Rd. Maghull L31 5 C1
Westover Rd. Warton LA5 217 E5
Westover St. LA4 212 E5
Westside. FY4 109 F8
Westway. Burnley BB11 126 D6
Westway. Freckleton PR4 92 A6
Westway. Fulwood PR2 117 A4
Westway. Hightown L38 2 F4
Westway. Maghull L31 5 C2
Westway Ct. PR2 117 B4
Westway Sch. BB12 126 F8
Westwell Gr. FY1 129 C4
Westwell Rd. PR6 60 D1
Westwell St. Darwen BB3 80 E4
Westwell St. 11 Great Harwood BB6 123 C5
Westwood Ave. Blackpool FY3 129 E4
Westwood Ave. Fleetwood FY7 193 E3
Westwood Ave. Poulton-le-F FY6 151 E3
Westwood Ave. Rishton BB1 123 A1
Westwood Cl. PR8 34 E3
Westwood Ct. BB1 101 A6
Westwood Mews. FY8 90 A3
Westwood Rd. Blackburn BB1 101 B4
Westwood Rd. Burnley BB12 126 C8
Westwood Rd. Clayton Brook PR5 & PR6 77 C4
Westwood Rd. Leyland PR5 76 B2
Westwood Rd. Lytham St Anne's FY8 90 A3
Westwood St. BB5 103 B7
Wetherall St. PR1 116 D1
Wetherby Ave. FY4 109 B5
Wetherfield Cl. LA1 214 A4
Weymouth Rd. FY3 129 F3
Weythorne Dr. BL9 32 F4
Whalley Banks. BB2 100 D4
Whalley CE Prim Sch. BB7 143 C5
Whalley Cres. Darwen BB3 81 B1
Whalley Cres. Staining FY3 130 E5
Whalley Dr. Formby L37 12 A2
Whalley Dr. Ormskirk L39 6 D8
Whalley Dr. Rawtenstall BB4 85 A4
Whalley Gdns. OL12 51 B1
Whalley Ind Pk. BB7 143 D8
Whalley La. FY4 110 A8
Whalley New Rd. Billington BB6 & BB7 142 F3
Whalley New Rd. Blackburn BB1 121 F1
Whalley New Rd. Langho BB6 & BB1 142 D1
Whalley Old Rd. Billington BB6 & BB7 143 B3
Whalley Old Rd. Blackburn BB1 101 A7
Whalley Old Rd. Sunny Bower BB1 122 B1
Whalley Pl. FY8 89 B6
Whalley Range. BB1 100 F6
Whalley Rd. Accrington BB5 103 B7
Whalley Rd. Bank Lane BL0 49 E7
Whalley Rd. Barrow BB7 164 D2
Whalley Rd. Clayton-le-M BB5 & BB6 123 F5
Whalley Rd. Clitheroe BB7 164 D5
Whalley Rd. Heskin Green PR7 40 D4
Whalley Rd. Hurst Green BB7 163 B1
Whalley Rd. Lancaster LA1 213 F4
Whalley Rd. Langho BB6 142 D2
Whalley Rd. Mellor Brook BB2 120 C3
Whalley Rd. Padiham BB12 125 B8
Whalley Rd. Passmonds OL12 51 B1
Whalley Rd. Read BB12 & BB7 144 C1
Whalley Rd. Sabden BB7 144 D6
Whalley Rd. Turner Green BB2 & PR5 119 C2
Whalley Rd. Wilpshire BB1 122 B7
Whalley St. Bamber Bridge PR5 96 F2
Whalley St. Blackburn BB1 100 E6
Whalley St. Burnley BB10 147 A1
Whalley St. 4 Chorley PR7 42 C7
Whalley St. Clitheroe BB7 164 D8
Whalley Sta. BB7 143 B6
Whalley Terr. BB3 80 B6
Whalleys Rd. WN8 18 B5
Wham Bottom La. OL12 51 D4
Wham Brook Cl. BB5 102 B5
Wham Hey. PR4 75 A7
Wham La. New Longton PR4 75 A7
Wham La. Walmer Bridge PR4 74 D4
Whams La. LA2 204 D7
Wharf St. Blackburn BB1 100 F5
Wharf St. Lytham St Anne's FY8 90 C3
Wharf St. Rishton BB1 123 C1
Wharfdale Ave. BB10 147 B4
Wharfdale Ct. FY6 151 C3
Wharfe Ct. LA1 213 B3
Wharfedale. FY4 109 F7
Wharfedale Ave. Fulwood PR2 117 E5
Wharfedale Ave. Thornton FY5 173 B3
Wharfedale Cl. Blackburn BB2 79 D7
Wharfedale Cl. Leyland PR5 59 A7
Wharfedale Rd. LA1 210 D8
Wharton Ave. FY5 173 D1
Whave's La. PR6 78 D4
Wheat La. L40 25 A4
Wheat St. Accrington BB5 103 A6
Wheat St. Padiham BB12 125 D7
Wheatacre. WN8 8 E8
Wheatcroft Ave. BB12 146 D8
Wheatfield. PR5 58 A8
Wheatfield Ct. 5 LA1 210 E8
Wheatfield St. Lancaster LA1 210 E8
Wheatfield St. Rishton BB1 123 B2
Wheathead La. BB9 168 B8
Wheatholme St. BB4 85 B2
Wheatlands Cres. FY3 130 C2
Wheatley Cl. Burnley BB12 126 D7
Wheatley Cl. Fence BB12 146 D7
Wheatley Dr. PR3 139 B8
Wheatley Gr. BB9 168 C3
Wheatley Lane Prim Sch. BB12 146 E8
Wheatley Lane Rd. Barrowford BB12 & BB9 168 B2
Wheatley Lane Rd. Fence BB12 146 E8
Wheatsheaf Ave. PR3 139 A7
Wheatsheaf Wlk. L39 15 E5
Wheel La. PR3 196 A6
Wheelton La. PR5 76 A3
Wheelwrights Cl. BB7 225 C3
Wheelwrights Wharf. L40 22 F4
Whernside. FY4 109 F7
Whernside Cl. BB8 200 A2
Whernside Cres. PR2 117 D5
Whernside Gr. LA5 217 F2
Whernside Rd. LA1 213 D3
Whernside Way. PR5 76 C1
Whimberry Cl. 1 PR6 42 E8
Whimbrel Dr. FY5 173 A4
Whin Ave. LA5 216 B6
Whin Dr. LA5 216 B6
Whin Gr. LA5 216 B6
Whin La. PR3 153 B8
Whinberry Ave. BB4 85 A1
Whinfell Dr. LA1 211 A3
Whinfield Ave. Chorley PR6 60 D1
Whinfield Ave. Fleetwood FY7 193 E2
Whinfield La. PR1 & PR2 95 A8
Whinfield Pl. Blackburn BB2 100 A6
Whinfield Pl. Preston PR2 95 A8
Whinfield St. BB5 124 A1
Whinney Brow. PR3 204 C3
Whinney Heys Rd. FY3 130 A6
Whinney Hill Rd. BB5 124 C1
Whinney La. Blackburn BB1 & BB2 100 C8
Whinney La. Langho BB6 142 D1
Whinney La. Mellor BB2 121 B2
Whinny La. Euxton PR7 59 E3
Whinny La. Knott End-on-S FY6 194 E4
Whinny La. Waddington BB7 185 E6
Whinnyfield La. PR4 135 D2
Whinnysty La. LA3 212 A1
Whinpark Ave. FY3 130 A6
Whins Ave. BB7 144 E7
Whins La. Read BB12 144 E3
Whins La. Wheelton PR6 61 A8
Whinsands Cl. PR2 117 D5
Whinsfell View. LA4 212 E5
Whipp Ave. BB7 164 D7
Whitaker St. BB5 103 B7
Whitbarrow Sq. 8 LA1 211 A8
Whitburn. WN8 17 D1
Whitburn Rd. L33 1 A4
Whitby Ave. Fulwood PR2 115 F5
Whitby Ave. Southport PR9 53 D6
Whitby Dr. BB2 101 A1
Whitby Pl. PR2 115 F5
Whitby Rd. Lytham St Anne's FY8 110 A1
Whitby Rd. Morecambe LA4 212 F5
White Acre Rd. BB5 103 E2
White Ash Est. BB5 102 D4
White Ash La. BB5 102 D3
White Birk Cl. BL8 48 F2
White Bull St. BB12 126 C6
White Carr La. Baldingstone BL9 50 A1
White Carr La. Cleveleys FY5 151 A8
White Carr La. Hollins Lane PR3 204 E4
White Carr La. Moor Side PR4 133 C2
White Cross St. LA1 210 F7
White Gate Fold. PR7 41 E3
White Gr. BB8 169 C6
White Hill Cl. OL12 51 D4
White Horse Cl. BL6 31 C5
White Horse La. PR3 156 E1
White House La. Drummersdale L40 36 C1
White House La. Lane Heads PR3 154 E4
White Lea. PR3 199 C1
White Lee Ave. BB8 170 C2
White Lee La. PR3 180 C2
White Lund Ave. LA3 212 F2
White Lund Rd. LA3 212 F2
White Lund Trad Est. LA3 212 G2
White Meadow. PR4 115 E3
White Moss La. FY6 174 E4
White Moss Rd. WN8 8 C7
White Moss Rd S. WN8 8 D7
White Rd. BB2 100 B6
White St. Burnley BB12 126 B6
White St. Colne BB8 169 B4
White Walls Cl. BB8 169 A3
Whiteacre. WN6 28 A2
Whiteacre La. BB6 143 E8
Whitebeam Cl. Penwortham PR1 95 B3
Whitebeam Cl. Thornton FY5 172 F5
Whitebeck La. LA6 234 B4
Whitebirk Dr. Blackburn BB1 101 C8
Whitebirk Dr. Blackburn BB1 101 D6
Whitebirk Ind Est. BB1 122 C1
Whitebirk Rd. BB1 101 D5
Whitechapel Prim Sch. PR3 158 D7
Whitecotes Dr. FY8 90 D4
Whitecrest Ave. 3 FY5 172 F4
Whitecroft Ave. 7 BB4 84 B2
Whitecroft Cl. BB4 84 B2
Whitecroft La. BB2 120 E2
Whitecroft Meadows. BB4 84 B2
Whitecroft View. BB5 103 E2
Whitefield Cl. L38 2 F2
Whitefield Cty Prim Sch. BB9 147 C8
Whitefield La. L40 38 C3
Whitefield Meadow. PR5 96 F2
Whitefield Pl. LA3 212 F2
Whitefield Prim Sch. PR1 95 A4
Whitefield Rd. PR1 95 A4
Whitefield Rd E. PR1 95 B4
Whitefield Rd W. PR1 95 A4
Whitefield St. BB12 125 C4
Whitefriar Cl. PR2 116 A5
Whitegate. LA3 212 G3
Whitegate Cl. BB12 125 E7
Whitegate Dr. FY3 129 E3
Whitegate Gdns. BB12 125 E7
Whitehalgh La. BB6 142 C1
Whitehall Ave. WN6 19 E8
Whitehall La. Blackrod BL6 30 D3
Whitehall La. Grindleton BB7 224 A1
Whitehall Rd. Blackburn BB2 100 B7
Whitehall Rd. Darwen BB3 64 A5
Whitehall St. Darwen BB3 64 B5
Whitehall St. Nelson BB9 168 F1
Whitehall St. Rochdale OL12 51 F1
Whitehaven Cl. Ainsdale PR8 20 B3
Whitehaven Cl. Blackburn BB2 101 A1
Whitehaven St. 11 BB11 126 E5
Whitehead Cl. FY3 130 D5
Whitehead St. Blackburn BB2 100 C5
Whitehead St. 10 Rawtenstall BB4 85 A3
Whitehey. WN9 8 E8
Whitehey Rd. WN8 8 E8
Whitehill Rd. FY4 110 E6
Whiteholme Dr. FY6 151 B6
Whiteholme Pl. PR2 115 E1
Whiteholme Rd. FY5 150 E7
Whitehough Pl. BB9 169 B1
Whitehouse Ave. L37 12 A3
Whitehouse La. L37 12 A3
Whiteledge Rd. WN8 9 B6
Whitelees Way. FY6 151 D3
Whiteley Ave. BB2 100 A1
Whiteley St. BB4 84 C1
Whiteleys La. L40 16 D2
Whitelow Rd. BL0 49 E5
Whitemoor Rd. BB8 191 C2
Whitemoss. OL12 51 B2
Whitemoss Ave. FY3 130 B7
Whitendale. 8 LA1 213 C2
Whitendale Cres. BB1 101 A3
Whitendale Dr. Bamber Bridge PR5 76 F8
Whitendale Dr. Hest Bank LA5 215 F2
Whitendale Hall. PR1 116 F1
Whitepits La. LA2 233 D5
Whiterails Dr. L39 15 D6
Whiterails Mews. L39 15 D6
Whiteray Rd. 9 LA1 213 D2
Whiteside Fold. OL12 51 A1
Whiteside St. FY1 129 C6
Whiteside Way. FY5 172 E3
Whitestock. WN8 8 E8
Whitethorn Cl. PR6 77 A2
Whitethorn Mews. FY8 110 A2
Whitethorn Sq. PR2 115 D1
Whitethorne Mews. FY5 151 C8
Whitewalls Dr. BB8 169 A4
Whitewalls Ind Est. BB8 169 A3
Whitewell Cl. PR3 178 D3
Whitewell Dr. BB7 164 C7
Whitewell Pl. 11 BB1 100 F6
Whitewell Rd. BB5 103 D8
Whitewood Cl. FY8 89 E4
Whitley Ave. Blackpool FY3 129 D5
Whitley Ave. Cleveleys FY5 172 E5
Whitley Rd. WN8 19 D3
Whitmore Dr. PR1 & PR2 118 A2
Whitmore Gr. PR1 118 A2
Whitmore Pl. PR1 & PR2 118 A2
Whitstone Dr. WN8 9 D7
Whittaker Ave. FY3 129 E7
Whittaker Cl. BB12 126 B8
Whittaker St. BB2 100 C5
Whittakers La. BB7 186 F8
Whittam Ave. FY4 129 E1
Whittam Cres. BB7 143 B6
Whittam Rd. Chorley PR7 42 B5
Whittam Rd. Whalley BB7 143 B6
Whittam St. BB11 126 F5
Whitters La. PR3 198 D2
Whittingham Dr. BL0 49 C3
Whittingham Hosp. PR3 137 F4
Whittingham La. Goosnargh PR3 137 C5
Whittingham La. Grimsargh PR2 138 B2
Whittingham Rd. PR3 138 F7
Whittle Brow. PR7 41 C1
Whittle Cl. BB7 186 F1
Whittle Dr. L39 15 E7
Whittle Gn. PR4 135 E3
Whittle Hill. BB7 46 E3
Whittle La. WN6 & WN8 26 F4
Whittle St. Haslingden BB4 84 A2
Whittle St. Rawtenstall BB4 85 A3
Whittle-le-Woods CE Sch. PR6 60 B8
Whittlefield Cty Prim Sch. BB12 126 D7
Whittles St. OL13 70 B8
Whitton Mews. 5 BL6 31 B4
Whittycroft Ave. BB9 168 C6
Whittycroft Dr. BB9 168 E6
Whitwell Ave. 4 FY4 109 C5
Whitwell Cl. WN6 28 D2
Whitwell Gdns. BL6 31 B5
Whitworth Ct. PR4 113 B4
Whitworth Dr. PR7 42 A7
Whitworth High Sch. OL12 51 C8
Whitworth Rake. OL12 51 D8
Whitworth Rd. OL12 51 F2
Whitworth Sq. OL12 51 D8
Whitworth St. Horwich BL6 31 C2
Whitworth St. Kirkham PR4 112 F6
Whitworth Way. BB8 200 C4
Wholesome La. Drummersdale PR9 36 E3
Wholesome La. New Longton PR4 74 E5
Whytha Rd. BB7 & BB9 189 D6
Wicken Tree Row. BB12 144 F3
Wickentree Holt. OL12 51 A1
Wickliffe St. 7 BB9 168 F1
Wicks Cres. L37 11 C4
Wicks Gdns. L37 11 D3
Wicks Gn. L37 11 C3
Wicks Green Cl. L37 11 C3
Wicks La. L37 11 D3
Wickworth St. BB9 148 A7
Widford Wlk. BL6 30 E1
Widgeon Cl. 5 FY5 172 F4
Widow Hill Rd. BB10 147 D1
Wigan Golf Course. PR7 29 D2
Wigan La. PR6 & PR7 42 E2
Wigan Rd. Bamber Bridge PR5 76 E7
Wigan Rd. Euxton PR6 & PR7 & PR5 59 C5
Wigan Rd. Ormskirk L39 & L40 16 A5
Wigan Rd. Skelmersdale WN8 8 F8
Wigan Rd. Westhead L40 16 E4
Wiggins La. L40 & PR4 37 B6
Wignall St. 8 PR1 117 C1
Wignalls Meadow. L38 2 F3
Wigston Cl. PR8 20 B4
Wigton Ave. PR5 58 D7
Wilbraham St. PR0 & PR1 117 C1
Wilcove. WN8 17 F1
Wild La. FY4 110 D4
Wilderswood Ave. BL6 31 C4
Wilderswood Cl. PR6 77 C2
Wilderswood Ct. BL6 31 D4
Wilding's La. FY8 89 B8
Wildman St. Blackpool FY3 129 D7
Wildman St. Preston PR1 & PR2 116 E2
Wildoaks Dr. FY5 151 D8
Wildwood Cl. BL0 49 A4
Wilfield St. BB11 126 E6
Wilford St. FY3 129 E7
Wilfred Dr. BL9 32 B4
Wilfred St. BB5 103 C4
Wilfrid's Pl. WN6 28 F1
Wilkie Ave. BB11 126 E2
Wilkin Sq. 6 BB7 164 E8
Wilkinson Ave. FY3 129 E4
Wilkinson Mount. BB8 201 B2
Wilkinson St. Bamber Bridge PR5 76 B8
Wilkinson St. Barrowford BB9 168 C2
Wilkinson St. Haslingden BB4 84 B4
Wilkinson St. Higham BB12 145 F5
Wilkinson St. Rawtenstall BB11 105 B4
Wilkinson Way. FY6 194 F5
Willacy La. PR4 134 E3
Willacy Par. LA3 212 B2
Willard Ave. WN5 10 D3
Willaston Ave. BB9 168 E8
William Henry St. 6 PR1 96 C8
William Herbert St. 13 BB1 100 F6
William Hopwood St. 8 BB1 101 A4
William St. Accrington BB5 103 C7
William St. Bacup OL13 70 C8
William St. Blackburn BB2 100 E2
William St. Blackpool FY3 129 E7
William St. Brierfield BB9 147 B6
William St. Carnforth LA5 217 D3
William St. Colne BB8 169 E4
William St. 11 Darwen BB3 81 A1
William St. Earby BB8 201 B1
William St. Enfield BB5 124 A1
William St. Horwich BL6 31 A3
William St. 17 Nelson BB9 168 E1
William St. Ramsbottom BL0 67 C1
William St. Whitworth OL12 70 C1
William Thompson Rec Ctr. BB11 127 A5
Williams Ave. LA2 & LA4 213 C6
Williams La. PR2 117 C7
Williams Pl. 2 BB9 147 F8
Williams Rd. BB10 127 B8
Williamson Rd. LA1 211 A8
Willis Rd. BB2 100 A2
Willis St. BB11 126 E5
Willoughby Ave. FY5 172 D2
Willoughby St. 6 BB1 100 E6
Willow Ave. BB4 85 A4
Willow Bank. BB3 64 A6
Willow Brook. BB5 103 B6
Willow Cl. Adlington PR6 30 B8
Willow Cl. Bamber Bridge PR5 76 A8
Willow Cl. Barrowford BB9 168 B1
Willow Cl. Clayton-le-M BB5 123 E3
Willow Cl. Forton PR3 204 B3
Willow Cl. Freckleton PR4 92 A5
Willow Cl. Gregson Lane PR5 97 E1
Willow Cl. Penwortham PR1 95 A4
Willow Cl. Thornton FY5 173 D1
Willow Coppice. PR4 115 E3
Willow Cres. Burscough Bridge L40 24 F6
Willow Cres. Clayton-le-W PR5 76 D3
Willow Cres. Fulwood PR1 & PR2 117 E2
Willow Dr. Barrow BB6 143 D8
Willow Dr. Charnock Richard PR7 41 D3
Willow Dr. Freckleton PR4 92 A5
Willow Dr. Garstang PR3 199 C1
Willow Dr. Poulton-le-F FY6 130 D8
Willow Dr. Skelmersdale WN8 17 E1
Willow Dr. Wrea Green PR4 112 C4
Willow Field. PR6 77 C3
Willow Field Chase. PR5 98 B2
Willow Gn. Ormskirk L39 15 F5
Willow Gn. Preston PR1 95 A8
Willow Gr. Blackpool FY3 151 A1
Willow Gr. Formby L37 11 F4
Willow Gr. Goosnargh PR3 137 D6
Willow Gr. Hambleton FY6 174 B2
Willow Gr. Morecambe LA4 213 B6
Willow Gr. Rufford L40 38 A3
Willow Gr. Southport PR9 34 E7
Willow Gr. West Bradford BB7 186 D7

288 Wil – Woo

Willow Hey. Skelmersdale WN8 17 F1
Willow Hey. Tarleton PR4 56 A7
Willow La. LA1 210 C7
Willow Lodge. FY8 89 C7
Willow Mill. LA2 231 C3
Willow Mount. BB1 121 F3
Willow Pk. BB5 102 C2
Willow Pl. PR4 153 F1
Willow Rd. Chorley PR6 60 E2
Willow Rd. Wymott PR5 57 F6
Willow St. Accrington BB5 103 B6
Willow St. Blackburn BB1 101 A7
Willow St. Burnley BB12 126 E6
Willow St. Bury BL9 32 B3
Willow St. Clayton-le-M BB5 123 E3
Willow St. Darwen BB3 80 F1
Willow St. Fleetwood FY7 194 A4
Willow St. Great Harwood BB6 123 C4
Willow St. Haslingden BB4 84 B3
Willow St. Newchurch BB4 68 E8
Willow Tree Ave. Broughton PR3 136 D3
Willow Tree Ave. Rawtenstall BB4 84 E2
Willow Tree Cres. PR5 75 D1
Willow Tree Gdns. FY5 173 D1
Willow Trees Dr. BB1 121 C1
Willow Way. PR4 74 F7
Willow Wlk. WN8 18 B4
Willow-Dale. FY5 173 D1
Willowbank Ave. FY4 109 E6
Willowcroft Dr. FY6 174 B1
Willowdene. FY5 172 E1
Willowfield Rd. LA3 209 A7
Willowhey. PR9 52 F4
Willowmead Way. OL12 51 A2
Willows Ave. Cleveleys FY5 172 E1
Willows Ave. Lytham St Anne's FY8 89 E3
Willows La. Accrington BB5 103 A3
Willows La. Kirkham PR4 112 F5
Willows Park La. PR3 139 B8
Willows RC Prim Sch The. PR4 112 F5
Willows The. Broadley OL12 51 C5
Willows The. Coppull PR7 28 E8
Willows The. Lytham St Anne's FY8 89 E3
Willows The. Mawdesley L40 39 C2
Willows The. Southport PR8 33 F6
Wills Ave. L31 5 C2
Willshaw Rd. FY2 150 B1
Willy La. LA2 203 D6
Wilmar Rd. PR5 76 C2
Wilmcote Gr. PR8 20 B4
Wilmore Cl. BB8 169 C5
Wilmot Rd. PR2 117 E3
Wilpshire Banks. BB1 121 F4
Wilpshire Golf Course. BB1 122 A6
Wilpshire Rd. BB1 122 E4
Wilson Cl. PR4 56 A7
Wilson Dr. PR4 153 F1
Wilson Fold Ave. BL6 31 F1
Wilson Gr. LA3 208 E8
Wilson Sq. FY5 150 D7
Wilson St. Blackburn BB2 100 D2
Wilson St. Bury BL9 32 A1
Wilson St. Clitheroe BB7 164 E7
Wilson St. Foulridge BB8 191 D1
Wilson St. Horwich BL6 31 A4
Wilson's Endowed CE Prim Sch. LA6 231 B8
Wilton Cl. LA1 214 A4
Wilton Gr. PR1 95 A4
Wilton Par. FY1 129 B7
Wilton Pl. PR5 76 B1
Wilton St. Barrowford BB9 168 D3
Wilton St. Brierfield BB9 147 B5
Wilton St. Burnley BB10 147 B1
Wiltshire Ave. BB12 126 B7
Wiltshire Dr. BB4 67 B8
Wilvere Dr. FY5 150 C8
Wilworth Cres. BB1 121 E2
Wimberley Banks. BB1 100 F7
Wimberley Gdns. 7 BB1 100 E6
Wimberley Pl. 8 BB1 100 E6
Wimberley St. BB1 100 E7
Wimbledon Ave. FY5 150 D7
Wimbledon Ct. FY5 150 D6
Wimborne Cl. BL6 31 F1
Wimbourne Pl. FY4 109 B6
Wimbrick Cres. L39 15 D3
Winchcombe Rd. FY5 150 E7
Winchester Ave. Accrington BB5 103 C7
Winchester Ave. 4 Blackpool FY4 129 D1
Winchester Ave. Chorley PR7 42 E4
Winchester Ave. Lancaster LA1 211 B5
Winchester Ave. Morecambe LA4 212 G6
Winchester Cl. Morecambe LA3 212 E2
Winchester Cl. Orrell WN5 10 F7
Winchester Dr. FY6 151 B6
Winchester Rd. Longshaw WN5 10 D1
Winchester Rd. Padiham BB12 125 D6
Winchester St. BB1 101 A3
Winckley Ct. 10 PR4 95 F7
Winckley Rd. Clayton-le-M BB5 123 F2
Winckley Rd. Preston PR1 95 E6
Winckley Sq. PR1 95 F7
Winckley St. 9 PR4 95 F7
Winder Garth. LA6 234 B1
Winder La. PR3 204 B2
Windermere Ave. Accrington BB5 124 D1
Windermere Ave. Burnley BB10 147 A2
Windermere Ave. Clitheroe BB7 164 C7
Windermere Ave. Colne BB8 169 F6
Windermere Ave. Fleetwood FY7 172 D8
Windermere Ave. Leyland PR5 76 A3
Windermere Ave. Morecambe LA4 212 G4
Windermere Cl. 4 BB1 100 F6
Windermere Cres. PR8 20 C3
Windermere Ct. 4 LA4 212 G4
Windermere Dr. Adlington PR6 43 B1
Windermere Dr. Darwen BB3 81 C3
Windermere Dr. Maghull L31 5 E2
Windermere Dr. Rainford Junction WA11 8 F2
Windermere Dr. Ramsbottom BL0 49 C7
Windermere Dr. Rishton BB1 123 A1
Windermere Rd. Bacup OL13 87 A3
Windermere Rd. Blackpool FY4 109 C8
Windermere Rd. Bolton-le-S LA5 216 A4
Windermere Rd. Carnforth LA5 216 E8
Windermere Rd. 5 Chorley PR7 42 E7
Windermere Rd. Fulwood PR2 117 C4
Windermere Rd. Hightown L38 3 A4
Windermere Rd. Lancaster LA1 211 B8
Windermere Rd. Orrell WN5 10 F8
Windermere Rd. Padiham BB12 145 C2
Windermere Rd. Preston PR1 118 A1
Windermere Sq. FY8 109 F2
Windgate. Much Hoole PR4 73 E2
Windgate. Skelmersdale WN8 17 F1
Windgate. Tarleton PR4 56 A5
Windham Pl. LA1 213 C3
Windholme. 6 LA1 213 C2
Windle Ash. L31 5 C2
Windmill Ave. Kirkham PR4 113 C4
Windmill Ave. Ormskirk L39 15 F5
Windmill Cl. Blackpool FY4 109 F6
Windmill Cl. Staining FY3 130 E5
Windmill Ct. 9 LA1 211 A3
Windmill Hts. WN8 10 A8
Windmill La. PR5 & PR6 78 B7
Windmill Rd. WN8 9 F7
Windmill St. LA1 210 D8
Windmill View. PR4 113 A6
Windrows. WN8 17 F1
Windrush Ave. BL0 49 A2
Windrush The. OL12 51 C4
Windsor Ave. Adlington PR7 29 F6
Windsor Ave. Blackpool FY4 109 B8
Windsor Ave. Church BB5 103 A8
Windsor Ave. Clitheroe BB7 164 C7
Windsor Ave. Fulwood PR2 116 B2
Windsor Ave. Haslingden BB4 84 A1
Windsor Ave. Lancaster LA1 211 B5
Windsor Ave. Longridge PR3 138 F7
Windsor Ave. Morecambe LA4 212 D3
Windsor Ave. New Longton PR4 95 A1
Windsor Ave. Newchurch BB4 85 E1
Windsor Ave. Penwortham PR1 95 C3
Windsor Ave. Thornton FY5 173 B2
Windsor Cl. Blackburn BB1 101 B3
Windsor Cl. Burscough L40 24 E3
Windsor Cl. Chorley PR7 42 B7
Windsor Cl. Ramsbottom BL8 49 A1
Windsor Cl. Read BB12 144 D2
Windsor Ct. Poulton-le-F FY6 151 E3
Windsor Ct. Southport PR8 33 E4
Windsor Dr. Brinscall PR6 61 E8
Windsor Dr. Fulwood PR2 116 D6
Windsor Dr. Horwich BL6 31 E2
Windsor Gdns. PR3 178 B7
Windsor Gr. LA4 212 D4
Windsor Lodge. FY8 89 D4
Windsor Pl. Barnoldswick BB8 200 D3
Windsor Pl. Fleetwood FY7 194 B5
Windsor Rd. Bamber Bridge PR5 96 D3
Windsor Rd. Blackburn BB2 100 B6
Windsor Rd. Blackburn BB1 101 E4
Windsor Rd. Chorley PR7 42 B7
Windsor Rd. Darwen BB3 80 F3
Windsor Rd. Eccleston PR7 40 C7
Windsor Rd. Formby L37 11 F1
Windsor Rd. Garstang PR3 178 B7
Windsor Rd. Great Harwood BB6 123 D5
Windsor Rd. Hall Green WN8 10 A8
Windsor Rd. Lytham St Anne's FY8 89 A5
Windsor Rd. Lytham St Anne's FY8 89 D4
Windsor Rd. Maghull L31 5 C1
Windsor Rd. Morecambe LA3 & LA4 212 C3
Windsor Rd. Normoss FY3 130 B7
Windsor Rd. Southport PR9 34 D7
Windsor St. Accrington BB5 103 C6
Windsor St. Burnley BB12 126 C6
Windsor St. Colne BB8 169 E5
Windsor St. Nelson BB9 148 A7
Windsor Terr. FY7 194 B5
Windy Bank. BB8 169 E5
Windy Harbour Rd. Singleton FY6 153 A4
Windy Harbour Rd. Southport PR8 20 E7
Windy Hill. LA2 233 E8
Windy St. PR3 182 E3
Windyhill. 35 LA1 210 F8
Winery La. PR1 & PR5 96 C5
Winewall La. BB8 170 C5
Winewall Rd. BB8 170 B5
Wingate Ave. Cleveleys FY5 150 D7
Wingate Ave. Morecambe LA4 212 F4
Wingate Pl. FY5 150 D8
Wingate Rd. 1 L33 1 A3
Wingate Wlk. 3 L33 1 A3
Wingate-Saul Rd. LA1 210 E7
Wingates. PR1 95 C3
Wingrove Rd. FY7 193 F2
Winifred Ave. BL9 32 F4
Winifred La. L39 6 B8
Winifred St. Blackpool FY1 129 B4
Winifred St. Passmonds OL12 51 B1
Winifred St. Ramsbottom BL0 49 B5
Winmarleigh Rd. Lancaster LA1 211 A2
Winmarleigh Rd. Preston PR1 116 B1
Winmarleigh St. 3 BB1 101 C5
Winmarleigh Wlk. BB1 101 C4
Winmorleigh CE Prim Sch. PR3 198 E5
Winnipeg Cl. BB2 100 B8
Winnipeg Pl. FY2 150 E3
Winsford Cres. FY5 150 C8
Winsford Wlk. BB11 126 B5
Winslow Ave. FY6 151 B5
Winslow Cl. PR1 95 E2
Winsor Ave. PR5 59 B8
Winstanley Coll. WN5 10 F3
Winstanley Gr. FY1 129 C5
Winstanley Rd. Orrell WN5 10 F3
Winstanley Rd. Skelmersdale WN8 8 F8
Winster Cl. PR5 97 E4
Winster Ct. BB5 123 E2
Winster Pk. LA1 213 C2
Winster Pl. FY4 130 D1
Winster Wlk. LA1 213 C2
Winsters The. WN8 17 F1
Winston Ave. Cleveleys FY5 172 F2
Winston Ave. Lytham St Anne's FY8 89 B6
Winston Cres. PR8 34 E2
Winston Rd. BB1 100 D7
Winter Gdns. FY1 129 B5
Winter Hey La. BL6 31 B3
Winterburn Rd. BB2 80 C7
Winterley Dr. BB5 124 E1
Winterton Rd. BB3 81 A2
Winthorpe Ave. LA4 212 G3
Winton Ave. Blackpool FY4 130 A1
Winton Ave. Fulwood PR2 116 F6
Winton Gn. BL6 31 F1
Winton Rd. FY4 130 A2
Wiseman St. BB11 126 F6
Wisp Hill Gr. LA2 214 F6
Wiswell Cl. Brierfield BB10 147 E2
Wiswell Cl. Rawtenstall BB4 85 A4
Wiswell La. BB7 143 D6
Wiswell Shay. BB7 143 E7
Witham Cl. WN6 28 D1
Witham Rd. WN8 17 D1
Withens Rd. L31 5 D3
Withers St. BB1 100 F4
Witherslack Cl. LA4 212 E3
Within Gr. BB5 103 D8
Withington La. PR7 40 E2
Withins Field. L38 2 F3
Withins La. L38 4 A7
Withnell Fold Old Rd. PR6 78 E1
Withnell Fold Prim Sch. PR6 78 C3
Withnell Gr. PR6 60 E1
Withnell Rd. FY4 109 B8
Withy Ct. PR2 116 E3
Withy Grove Cl. PR5 96 F1
Withy Grove Cres. PR5 96 F1
Withy Grove Rd. PR5 96 F1
Withy Par. PR2 116 E4
Withy Trees Ave. PR5 96 F1
Withy Trees Cl. PR5 96 F1
Witney Ave. BB2 79 E8
Witton Ave. FY7 193 E1
Witton Ctry Pk. BB2 99 F4
Witton Gr. FY7 193 E1
Witton Par. BB2 100 C3
Witton Park High Sch. BB2 100 A4
Witton St. PR1 96 B8
Woborrow Rd. LA3 208 E8
Woburn Cl. BB5 103 E3
Woburn Gn. PR5 76 B2
Woburn Rd. FY1 129 C7
Wolfenden Gn. BB4 68 F8
Wollaton Dr. PR8 34 F3
Wolseley Cl. PR5 59 A8
Wolseley Pl. 21 PR1 96 A7
Wolseley Rd. PR1 95 E5
Wolseley St. Blackburn BB2 100 D1
Wolseley St. Lancaster LA1 211 A8
Wolsey Cl. FY5 172 E3
Wolsley Rd. Blackpool FY1 129 B1
Wolsley Rd. Fleetwood FY7 193 F4
Wolverton. WN8 8 F8
Wolverton Ave. FY2 150 B2
Wood Bank. PR1 95 C3
Wood Cl. BB9 168 A5
Wood End. BB12 146 F3
Wood End Rd. PR6 77 B2
Wood Gn. Kirkham PR4 113 B7
Wood Gn. Leyland PR5 75 E2
Wood Green Dr. FY5 150 F8
Wood Hey Gr. OL12 51 F4
Wood House La. BB7 223 A8
Wood La. Great Altcar L37 & L39 13 D1
Wood La. Heskin Green PR7 40 E3
Wood La. Hoscar L40 25 E5
Wood La. Mawdesley PR7 39 D5
Wood La. Parbold WN8 26 D2
Wood Lea Bank. 8 BB4 68 F8
Wood Lea Rd. BB4 68 F8
Wood Nook. 1 BB4 85 A7
Wood Park Rd. FY1 129 E1
Wood Road La. BL8 & BL9 49 C1
Wood St. Blackpool FY1 129 B5
Wood St. Brierfield BB9 147 B5
Wood St. Burnley BB10 127 A8
Wood St. Church BB5 102 E5
Wood St. Colne BB8 169 E4
Wood St. Darwen BB3 80 F1
Wood St. Fleetwood FY7 172 E8
Wood St. Great Harwood BB6 123 C5
Wood St. Hapton BB12 125 C4
Wood St. Horwich BL6 31 C3
Wood St. 1 Lancaster LA1 210 F8
Wood St. Lytham St Anne's FY8 88 E6
Wood St. Poulton-le-F FY6 152 A3
Wood St. Ramsbottom BL0 49 B5
Wood Street Livesey Fold. 9 BB3 80 F2
Wood View. Blackburn BB2 99 F1
Wood View. Burton in L LA6 236 C3
Wood's Brow. PR3 140 B6
Wood's La. PR3 177 A6
Woodacre Rd. PR1 & PR2 118 A2
Woodale Laithe. BB9 168 C3
Woodale Rd. PR5 & PR6 77 B3
Woodbank Ave. BB3 80 E2
Woodbine Gdns. BB12 126 C7
Woodbine Rd. Blackburn BB2 100 B6
Woodbine Rd. Burnley BB12 126 C6
Woodbine Terr. OL14 108 B1
Woodbridge Gdns. OL12 51 C2
Woodburn Cl. BB2 100 A8
Woodbury Ave. Blackburn BB2 100 D2
Woodbury Ave. Fence BB12 146 D7
Woodcock Cl. FY5 173 A5
Woodcock Est. PR5 76 B6
Woodcock Fold. PR7 40 C7
Woodcourt Ave. BB11 126 D3
Woodcrest. BB1 121 F5
Woodcroft. Appley Bridge WN6 19 E6
Woodcroft. Skelmersdale WN8 8 F8
Woodcroft Ave. BB4 84 F5
Woodcroft Cl. PR1 95 C2
Woodcroft St. BB4 84 F5
Woodfall. PR7 60 B2
Woodfield. PR5 77 C6
Woodfield Ave. Accrington BB5 103 D3
Woodfield Ave. Blackpool FY1 129 B2
Woodfield Ave. Falinge Fold OL12 51 E2
Woodfield Rd. Blackpool FY1 129 B2
Woodfield Rd. Chorley PR7 60 C1
Woodfield Rd. Ormskirk L39 15 D3
Woodfield Rd. Thornton FY5 173 D1
Woodfield Terr. BB9 147 C5
Woodfield View. BB7 143 C5
Woodfields. BB7 163 B3
Woodfold Cl. BB2 120 C3
Woodfold La. PR3 199 C5
Woodfold Pl. BB2 100 B5
Woodford Copse. PR7 42 A7
Woodgate. LA3 213 B2
Woodgate Ave. BL9 32 D4
Woodgate Hill Rd. Bury BL9 32 C4
Woodgate Hill Rd. Bury BL9 32 D4
Woodgates Rd. BB2 99 F5
Woodgrove Rd. BB11 127 B4
Woodhall Cres. PR5 97 E4
Woodhall Gdns. FY6 174 C2
Woodhart La. PR7 40 C5
Woodhead Cl. Ramsbottom BL0 49 C4
Woodhead Cl. Rawtenstall BB4 86 A2
Woodhead Rd. BB12 144 D2
Woodhey High Sch. BL0 49 A3
Woodhey Rd. BL0 49 A3
Woodhill Ave. LA4 212 D3
Woodhill Cl. LA4 212 D3
Woodhill La. LA4 212 D4
Woodhouse Rd. FY5 151 E8
Woodhouse St. 1 BB11 127 B4
Woodhurst Dr. WN6 28 D1
Woodland Ave. Bacup OL13 86 F5
Woodland Ave. Bescar L40 22 F7
Woodland Ave. Thornton FY5 173 B2
Woodland Cl. Hambleton FY6 174 D1
Woodland Cl. Wrea Green PR4 112 B3
Woodland Cres. FY6 195 A6
Woodland Dr. Clayton-le-M BB5 123 F5
Woodland Dr. Poulton-le-F FY6 151 E1
Woodland Dr. Standish WN6 28 E2
Woodland Gr. Blackpool FY3 129 E4
Woodland Gr. Egerton BL7 46 D2
Woodland Gr. Penwortham PR1 95 B5
Woodland Pk. BB7 143 C5
Woodland Pl. BB3 80 F7
Woodland Rd. OL12 51 C2
Woodland Terr. OL13 86 F4
Woodland View. Bacup OL13 86 F4
Woodland View. Brinscall PR7 61 F7
Woodland View. Great Harwood BB6 123 C6
Woodlands Ave. Bamber Bridge PR5 97 A2
Woodlands Ave. Blackburn BB2 99 E1
Woodlands Ave. Fulwood PR2 117 E2
Woodlands Ave. Kirkham PR4 112 F5
Woodlands Ave. Penwortham PR1 95 E2
Woodlands Cl. Formby L37 11 D2
Woodlands Cl. Newton-with-S PR4 113 F3
Woodlands Cl. Ormskirk L39 16 A4
Woodlands Cl. Storth LA7 237 F4
Woodlands Cl. West Bradford BB7 186 D7
Woodlands Cl. Whalley BB7 143 B7
Woodlands Cres. PR3 136 B5
Woodlands Ct. FY8 89 D4
Woodlands Dr. Fulwood PR2 116 E8
Woodlands Dr. Kirkham PR4 113 B7
Woodlands Dr. Leyland PR5 75 F1
Woodlands Dr. Morecambe LA3 212 B2
Woodlands Dr. Shevington WN6 19 F4
Woodlands Dr. Silverdale LA5 218 C4
Woodlands Dr. Warton PR4 91 C5
Woodlands Dr. West Bradford BB7 186 D7
Woodlands Dr. Whalley BB7 143 C5
Woodlands Gr. Darwen BB3 80 D2
Woodlands Gr. Grimsargh PR2 138 E1
Woodlands Gr. Morecambe LA3 212 B2
Woodlands Gr. Padiham BB12 145 B1
Woodlands Meadow. PR7 42 C3
Woodlands Prim Sch. L37 11 D3
Woodlands Rd. Edenfield BL0 67 D2
Woodlands Rd. Formby L37 11 D3
Woodlands Rd. Lancaster LA1 214 A4
Woodlands Rd. Lytham St Anne's FY8 89 D4
Woodlands Rd. Nelson BB9 147 F8
Woodlands Sch. PR2 117 E2
Woodlands Special Sch. FY3 129 E4
Woodlands The. Ainsdale PR8 20 C5
Woodlands The. Garstang PR3 178 B8
Woodlands The. Preston PR2 115 E1
Woodlands View. Over Kellet LA6 231 B8
Woodlands View. 12 Ramsbottom BL0 49 C6
Woodlands Way. Longton PR4 73 F8
Woodlands Way. Newsham PR3 136 B5
Woodlea Chase. BB3 64 C3
Woodlea Cl. PR9 53 D5
Woodlea Gdns. BB9 147 D5
Woodlea Jun Sch. PR5 58 F8
Woodlea Rd. Blackburn BB1 101 B4
Woodlea Rd. Leyland PR5 58 F8
Woodlee Rd. PR4 72 F2
Woodleigh Cl. L31 5 B5
Woodley Ave. Accrington BB5 103 C4
Woodley Ave. Thornton FY5 173 D1
Woodley Park Rd. WN8 18 B4
Woodman La. LA6 235 F6
Woodmancote. PR7 60 B2
Woodmoss La. PR9 & L40 35 E2
Woodnook Cty Prim Sch. BB5 103 C4
Woodnook Rd. WN6 19 E8
Woodpecker Hill. BB11 126 C5
Woodplumpton La. PR3 136 C2
Woodplumpton Rd. Burnley BB11 126 F1
Woodplumpton Rd. Fulwood PR2 116 C3
Woodplumpton Rd. Moor Side PR4 135 D4
Woodplumpton Rd. Preston PR1 & PR2 116 C2
Woodplumpton Rd. Woodplumpton PR4 135 E2
Woodridge Ave. FY5 150 C8
Woodrow. WN8 8 E8
Woodrow Dr. WN8 26 A1
Woodroyd Dr. BL9 32 C3
Woodruff Cl. FY5 172 F5
Woodrush. LA4 213 B6
Woods Brow. BB2 119 D5
Woods Cl. L39 14 A4
Woods Gn. PR1 95 E6
Woods La. PR4 & PR3 134 E8
Woodsend Cl. BB2 81 A8
Woodside. Chorley PR7 42 E4
Woodside. Euxton PR7 59 C3
Woodside. Haslingden BB4 84 C1
Woodside. Leyland PR5 76 C4
Woodside Ave. Ainsdale PR8 20 B3
Woodside Ave. Clayton Green PR6 77 B1
Woodside Ave. Fulwood PR2 116 E4
Woodside Ave. New Longton PR4 74 F7
Woodside Ave. Ribbleton PR2 117 E3
Woodside Ave. Rishton BB1 101 F8
Woodside Cl. Accrington BB5 124 F1
Woodside Cl. Up Holland WN8 10 C8
Woodside Cres. BB4 85 D1
Woodside Dr. Blackpool FY3 130 A5
Woodside Dr. Ramsbottom BL0 49 A5
Woodside Gr. BB2 80 A8
Woodside Rd. Accrington BB5 124 F1
Woodside Rd. Huncoat BB5 103 E8
Woodside Rd. Simonstone BB12 144 E2
Woodside Terr. BB9 147 C8
Woodsley St. BB11 126 B5
Woodstock Ave. FY5 151 C8
Woodstock Cl. 3 PR5 76 C8
Woodstock Cres. BB2 79 E8
Woodstock Dr. PR8 20 F8
Woodstock Gdns. FY4 109 B7
Woodstock St. 12 OL12 51 C1
Woodtop CE Inf Sch. BB11 126 D5
Woodvale. Darwen BB3 80 F1
Woodvale. Leyland PR5 58 A8
Woodvale Airfield. PR8 20 A2
Woodvale Prim Sch. PR8 20 D3
Woodvale Rd. PR8 20 E2
Woodville Rd. Adlington PR6 42 F1
Woodville Rd. Blackburn BB1 101 A7
Woodville Rd. Brierfield BB9 147 C6
Woodville Rd. 2 Chorley PR7 42 C8
Woodville Rd. Penwortham PR1 95 D2
Woodville Rd W. PR1 95 C2
Woodville St. Lancaster LA1 211 A8
Woodville St. Leyland PR5 76 B2
Woodville Terr. Darwen BB3 64 B6
Woodville Terr. Lytham St Anne's FY8 89 F3
Woodward Rd. L33 1 D4
Woodway. PR2 116 C4
Woodwell La. LA5 218 C1
Wookey Cl. PR2 117 D6

Ordnance Survey

STREET ATLASES
ORDER FORM

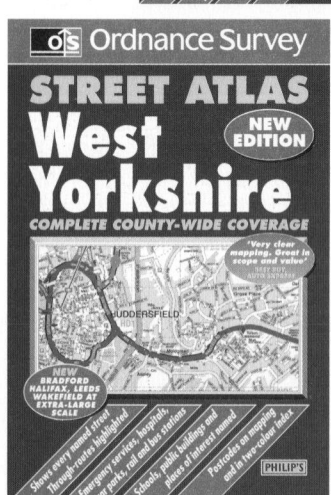

PHILIP'S

The Street Atlases are available from all good bookshops or by mail order direct from the publisher. Orders can be made in the following ways. **By phone** Ring our special Credit Card Hotline on **01933 443863** during office hours (9am to 5pm) or leave a message on the answering machine, quoting your full credit card number plus expiry date and your full name and address. **By post or fax** Fill out the order form below (you may photocopy it) and post it to: **Philip's Direct, 27 Sanders Road, Wellingborough, Northants NN8 4NL** or fax it to: **01933 443849.** Before placing an order by post, by fax or on the answering machine, please telephone to check availability and prices.

COLOUR LOCAL ATLASES	PAPERBACK	Quantity @ £3.50 each	£ Total
CANNOCK, LICHFIELD, RUGELEY		☐ 0 540 07625 2 ➤	
DERBY AND BELPER		☐ 0 540 07608 2 ➤	
NORTHWICH, WINSFORD, MIDDLEWICH		☐ 0 540 07589 2 ➤	
PEAK DISTRICT TOWNS		☐ 0 540 07609 0 ➤	
STAFFORD, STONE, UTTOXETER		☐ 0 540 07626 0 ➤	
WARRINGTON, WIDNES, RUNCORN		☐ 0 540 07588 4 ➤	

COLOUR REGIONAL ATLASES	HARDBACK	SPIRAL	POCKET	£ Total
	Quantity @ £10.99 each	Quantity @ £8.99 each	Quantity @ £4.99 each	£ Total
MERSEYSIDE	☐ 0 540 06480 7	☐ 0 540 06481 5	☐ 0 540 06482 3 ➤	
	Quantity @ £12.99 each	Quantity @ £8.99 each	Quantity @ £5.99 each	£ Total
BERKSHIRE	☐ 0 540 06170 0	☐ 0 540 06172 7	☐ 0 540 06173 5 ➤	
	Quantity @ £12.99 each	Quantity @ £9.99 each	Quantity @ £4.99 each	£ Total
DURHAM	☐ 0 540 06365 7	☐ 0 540 06366 5	☐ 0 540 06367 3 ➤	
	Quantity @ £12.99 each	Quantity @ £9.99 each	Quantity @ £5.50 each	£ Total
GREATER MANCHESTER	☐ 0 540 06485 8	☐ 0 540 06486 6	☐ 0 540 06487 4 ➤	
TYNE AND WEAR	☐ 0 540 06370 3	☐ 0 540 06371 1	☐ 0 540 06372 X ➤	
	Quantity @ £12.99 each	Quantity @ £9.99 each	Quantity @ £5.99 each	£ Total
BEDFORDSHIRE	☐ 0 540 07801 8	☐ 0 540 07802 6	☐ 0 540 07803 4 ➤	
BIRMINGHAM & WEST MIDLANDS	☐ 0 540 07603 1	☐ 0 540 07604 X	☐ 0 540 07605 8 ➤	
BUCKINGHAMSHIRE	☐ 0 540 07466 7	☐ 0 540 07467 5	☐ 0 540 07468 3 ➤	
CHESHIRE	☐ 0 540 07507 8	☐ 0 540 07508 6	☐ 0 540 07509 4 ➤	
DERBYSHIRE	☐ 0 540 07531 0	☐ 0 540 07532 9	☐ 0 540 07533 7 ➤	
EDINBURGH & East Central Scotland	☐ 0 540 07653 8	☐ 0 540 07654 6	☐ 0 540 07656 2 ➤	
NORTH ESSEX	☐ 0 540 07289 3	☐ 0 540 07290 7	☐ 0 540 07292 3 ➤	
SOUTH ESSEX	☐ 0 540 07294 X	☐ 0 540 07295 8	☐ 0 540 07297 4 ➤	
GLASGOW & West Central Scotland	☐ 0 540 07648 1	☐ 0 540 07649 X	☐ 0 540 07651 1 ➤	
NORTH HAMPSHIRE	☐ 0 540 07471 3	☐ 0 540 07472 1	☐ 0 540 07473 X ➤	

STREET ATLASES ORDER FORM

COLOUR REGIONAL ATLASES

	HARDBACK Quantity @ £12.99 each	SPIRAL Quantity @ £9.99 each	POCKET Quantity @ £5.99 each	£ Total
SOUTH HAMPSHIRE	☐ 0 540 07476 4	☐ 0 540 07477 2	☐ 0 540 07478 0	➢ ☐
HERTFORDSHIRE	☐ 0 540 06174 3	☐ 0 540 06175 1	☐ 0 540 06176 X	➢ ☐
EAST KENT	☐ 0 540 07483 7	☐ 0 540 07276 1	☐ 0 540 07287 7	➢ ☐
WEST KENT	☐ 0 540 07366 0	☐ 0 540 07367 9	☐ 0 540 07369 5	➢ ☐
NORTHAMPTONSHIRE	☐ 0 540 07745 3	☐ 0 540 07746 1	☐ 0 540 07748 8	➢ ☐
OXFORDSHIRE	☐ 0 540 07512 4	☐ 0 540 07513 2	☐ 0 540 07514 0	➢ ☐
SURREY	☐ 0 540 07794 1	☐ 0 540 07795 X	☐ 0 540 07796 8	➢ ☐
EAST SUSSEX	☐ 0 540 07306 7	☐ 0 540 07307 5	☐ 0 540 07312 1	➢ ☐
WEST SUSSEX	☐ 0 540 07319 9	☐ 0 540 07323 7	☐ 0 540 07327 X	➢ ☐
WARWICKSHIRE	☐ 0 540 07560 4	☐ 0 540 07561 2	☐ 0 540 07562 0	➢ ☐
SOUTH YORKSHIRE	☐ 0 540 06330 4	☐ 0 540 07667 8	☐ 0 540 07669 4	➢ ☐
WEST YORKSHIRE	☐ 0 540 07671 6	☐ 0 540 07672 4	☐ 0 540 07674 0	➢ ☐

	Quantity @ £14.99 each	Quantity @ £9.99 each	Quantity @ £5.99 each	£ Total
LANCASHIRE	☐ 0 540 06440 8	☐ 0 540 06441 6	☐ 0 540 06443 2	➢ ☐
NOTTINGHAMSHIRE	☐ 0 540 07541 8	☐ 0 540 07542 6	☐ 0 540 07543 4	➢ ☐

	Quantity @ £14.99 each	Quantity @ £10.99 each	Quantity @ £5.99 each	£ Total
STAFFORDSHIRE	☐ 0 540 07549 3	☐ 0 540 07550 7	☐ 0 540 07551 5	➢ ☐

BLACK AND WHITE REGIONAL ATLASES

	HARDBACK Quantity @ £11.99 each	SOFTBACK Quantity @ £8.99 each	POCKET Quantity @ £3.99 each	£ Total
BRISTOL & AVON	☐ 0 540 06140 9	☐ 0 540 06141 7	☐ 0 540 06142 5	➢ ☐

	Quantity @ £12.99 each	Quantity @ £9.99 each	Quantity @ £4.99 each	£ Total
CARDIFF, SWANSEA & GLAMORGAN	☐ 0 540 06186 7	☐ 0 540 06187 5	☐ 0 540 06207 3	➢ ☐

Name...
Address...
....
....
....
..............................Postcode......................

◆ Add £2 postage and packing per order

◆ All available titles will normally be dispatched within 5 working days of receipt of order but please allow up to 28 days for delivery

☐ Please tick this box if you do not wish your name to be used by other carefully selected organisations that may wish to send you information about other products and services

Registered Office: 2-4 Heron Quays, London E14 4JP
Registered in England number: 3597451

Total price of order £ ☐
(including postage and packing at £2 per order)

I enclose a cheque/postal order, for £ ☐
made payable to *Octopus Publishing Group Ltd,*
or please debit my ☐ Mastercard ☐ American Express
☐ Visa account by £ ☐

Account no
☐☐☐☐ ☐☐☐☐ ☐☐☐☐ ☐☐☐☐
Expiry date ☐☐ ☐☐

Signature...

Post to: Philip's Direct, 27 Sanders Road, Wellingborough, Northants NN8 4NL

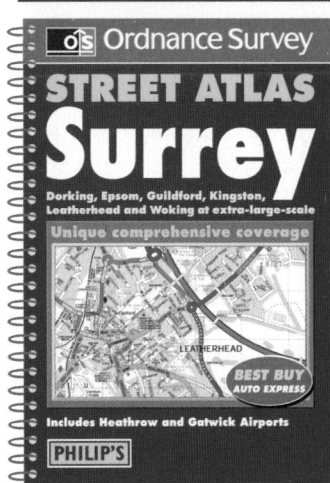

The best-selling *OS Motoring Atlas Britain* uses unrivalled and up-to-date mapping from the Ordnance Survey digital database. The exceptionally clear mapping is at a large scale of 3 miles to 1 inch (Orkney/Shetland Islands at 5 miles to 1 inch).

A special feature of the atlas is its wealth of tourist and leisure information. It contains comprehensive directories, including descriptions and location details, of the properties of the National Trust in England and Wales, the National Trust for Scotland, English Heritage and Historic Scotland. There is also a useful diary of British Tourist Authority Events listing more than 300 days out around Britain during the year.

Available from all good bookshops or direct from the publisher:
Tel: 01933 443863

The atlas includes:

- ◆ 112 pages of fully updated mapping
- ◆ 45 city and town plans
- ◆ 8 extra-detailed city approach maps
- ◆ route-planning maps
- ◆ restricted motorway junctions
- ◆ local radio information
- ◆ distances chart
- ◆ county boundaries map
- ◆ multi-language legend